Bigger than Blockbusters

Bigger than Blockbusters

Movies That Defined America

James Roman

GREENWOOD PRESS
Westport, Connecticut • London

Thanks to Jarah Moesh and Sha Sha Feng for their valuable editorial assistance.

Library of Congress Cataloging-in-Publication Data

Roman, James W.
  Bigger than blockbusters : movies that defined America / James Roman.
    p. cm.
  Includes bibliographical references and index.
  ISBN 978-0-313-33995-0 (alk. paper)
  1. Motion pictures—United States—History. 2. Motion pictures—Social aspects—
United States. I. Title. II. Title: One hundred films that changed the twentieth century.
  PN1993.5.U6R64   2009
  791.430973—dc22   2008033457

British Library Cataloguing in Publication Data is available.

Library of Congress Catalog Card Number: 2008033457
ISBN: 978-0-313-33995-0

First published in 2009

Greenwood Press, 88 Post Road West, Westport, CT 06881
An imprint of Greenwood Publishing Group, Inc.
www.greenwood.com

Printed in the United States of America

∞™

The paper used in this book complies with the
Permanent Paper Standard issued by the National
Information Standards Organization (Z39.48-1984).

10 9 8 7 6 5 4 3 2 1

For Mardee, Heather Gail, and Benjamin Ziggy
And in loving memory of Savannah (tootie), who huddled at my feet
during the writing of this book

Contents

Preface

The purpose of writing and editing a book entitled *Bigger than Blockbusters: Movies that Defined America* is not simply to add to the clutter of edited texts that purport to articulate what the reader should consider as important films, but rather to offer the reader a compelling rationale to consider why any of the films listed deserve to be cultural icons that changed twentieth and twenty-first century America. To accomplish this, one must make determinations that may not always be agreeable to a larger audience of critics but indeed will accommodate the rationale for choosing films as they are defined as prominent cultural forces in America. Because America's population is so diverse, part of the objective is to identify films that reach beyond the discrete interests of audiences and touch a vibrant chord in everyone's psyche. That doesn't necessarily presume a film must be a blockbuster or have been awarded a gaggle of Academy Awards. It does mean that such a film should have had some influence on the literary, cinematic, and behavioral culture of our time, reflecting not only our virtues but also our hypocrisy. Such a film is expressive of defining our foibles and measuring the capacities of behavior within a dynamic of a film's canvas that goes beyond nurturing the public's taste.

Some films also make dramatic and prominent statements about historical events that have affected America and the world, thus becoming part of the narrative associated with a time and place ritualizing events that took place. Films do not have to be dramatically compelling to be culturally impressive; they may have a lighter side that offers humor and pathos in an endearing theme. They may also be provocative and revealing, creating a resonating disturbance of truth and fact.

We speak of revolutions and identify various chronological epochs as revolutionary, such as the Industrial Revolution, or with political inference like the American or Russian Revolutions. The term has also entered the vernacular within the context of society as the Cultural Revolution. What is a cultural revolution, and can we define it when it's happening? Or is it the case, as Supreme Court Justice Potter Stewart noted about the definition of hardcore pornography, "I know it when I see it."

The world of film, narrative, and nonfiction has been a defining force for American and global culture since the first publicly screened short films. In 1895, when the brothers Lumière projected their first films of everyday life at a theater in Paris, one of those films, *The Arrival of the Train at the Station*, shocked some of the audience as it appeared that the projected image of the train was heading straight for them. Thomas Edison, inventor of the phonograph and the peephole kinetoscope, exhibited the first films in the United States. Two notable ones were *Fred Ott's Sneeze* (January 1894) and

The Kiss, which was a reenactment of what was considered to be a "risqué" scene from the Broadway show *The Widow Jones*. When the film made its debut at Koster & Bial's Music Hall, it became Edison's hit film of 1896.

The phenomenon of theatrical feature films has created a cultural imperative that influences every aspect of American life. Films have been catalysts in creating a consumer culture and influencing behavior, fashion, and style. Some films have had profound political implications pertaining to issues of race and sexuality. Others have defined new industry trends, reflecting rapidly changing technologies that stretch the canvas of traditional cinematic storytelling. Then there are those films that provide an intimate experience for the American public, delighting or shocking them into a euphoric state. Therefore, developing criteria that identifies these films must provide a rather subjective measure based upon the impact a film has had and how it has become contextualized within the American cultural milieu.

The larger issue of this book is to articulate how a film has changed the twentieth and twenty-first centuries. Once again, determining factors are behavioral attitudes and the assimilation of an ideology of narrative entertainment within the dynamic of American culture. There is little doubt that film is a catalyst for change and action and has an enduring legacy in the past and present.

Placing the films into a historical perspective assists the reader in defining the theme and story within the time and place of a particular decade. The documentary *Nanook of the North* (1922), directed by Robert Flaherty, was an influential film that explored the lives and culture of the Inuit people of Alaska. It was the first film to record their lives and culture as well as their struggle to survive against the harsh conditions of the frozen north.

A narrative film like D. W. Griffith's *The Birth of a Nation* (1915) demonstrated how a controversial film could move an audience to either embrace, reject, or actively protest against its theme and its portrayal of history.

Each of these films, one a documentary, the other a narrative theatrical feature film, had a profound effect on the technical and thematic rudiments of the motion picture industry. Therefore, this book addresses the value of these film genres and their influence on American culture.

Among high school and college students, there is a profound interest in movies as entertainment and forms of personal expression. In the classroom, directors and their films are studied for their style, structure, technical innovations, and content, and how their technique influenced later films and directors.

This book offers students of film a resource of information about movies; narrative and documentary, foreign and American, providing worthy discussion about their cultural relevance and influence upon American society. The noted psychologist and philosopher Rudolph Arnheim wrote:

> The arts, as a reflection of human existence at its highest, have always and spontaneously lived up to this demand of plenitude. No mature style of art in any culture has ever been simple.

Film as an art form can be a reflection of the human existence and a mirror of the desire, hope, and will of humanity. As Arnheim notes, the art of film is a cultural form of expression and in its mature expressive form is complex and demanding.

In addition to providing a discussion of films and their relevance as cultural idioms, this book also provides readers with a valuable resource tool. Special features include an alphabetical filmography of cited films, excerpts from film reviews, production credits for each film, and a comprehensive bibliography of print and electronic resources.

One of the most distinctive features of this book is its arrangement by decade providing the reader with the historical and cultural context of the films discussed during that period. For example, chapter 3 "Boom and Bust: The Films of Post-War America, 1946–1947," features the film *The Best Years of Our Lives*, which is about returning World War II veterans while providing the reader with historical and cultural information about America transitioning from a war footing to a peacetime economy. It provides a time line to thought and further discussion about a movie's ability to capture the mood and sense of history.

1

Through a Glass...
Darkly, 1915–1938

It was the turn of the century, and the global political realities of the day were making an impact upon a United States hoping to remain aloof to foreign involvement. But, events in Europe would forever change the balance of world power and the stature of the United States. On June 28, 1914, Archduke Francis Ferdinand of Austria and his wife Sophie were traveling in a motorcade visiting Bosnia to observe military maneuvers and to preside over the opening of the state museum in Sarajevo. A group of Serbian nationalists known as The Black Hand assassinated the archduke and his wife, causing Austria to seek assurances from Germany that it would support them in any means of retaliation they chose. On July 28, 1914, Austria-Hungary declared war on Serbia, beginning World War I. Although President Woodrow Wilson attempted to shield America from being involved and declared the country's neutrality, it was the threat to America's commercial shipping by German submarine warfare that forced America's entry on April 6, 1917. America had a taste of the lethal German submarine fleet when a German U-boat sank the *Lusitania*, a British passenger ship sailing from New York to Liverpool, killing most of the passengers onboard, including 123 Americans.

THE BIRTH OF A NATION (1915)

PRODUCER/DIRECTOR: D. W. Griffith, H. E. Aitken (executive producer, uncredited)
WRITER(S): Thomas F. Dixon Jr.
CAST: Lillian Gish (Elsie Stoneman), Mae Marsh (Flora Cameron), Henry B. Walthall (Col. Ben Cameron), Miriam Cooper (Margaret Cameron), Mary Alden (Lydia Brown), Ralph Lewis (Austin Stoneman), George Siegmann (Silas Lynch), Walter Long (Gus), Robert Harron (Tod Stoneman), Wallace Reid (Jeff the blacksmith)
CINEMATOGRAPHY: G. W. Bitzer
MUSIC: Joseph Carl Breil, D. W. Griffith
LENGTH AND RATING: 125 min; NR

Although the French and Italians were the first to introduce feature-length films, it was the controversial and visionary director D. W. Griffith who brought the epic film to the screen. Under his authorship, *The Birth of a Nation* and *Intolerance* became spectacular

1

Walter Long (as Gus) surrounded by Ku Klux Klan members. [Photofest]

statements of revisionist history told on a grandiose scale and richly portrayed on film. An experienced director with about four hundred shorter films to his credit, Griffith had been employed by the Biograph Company but left shortly after completing his longest film (it required four reels) in 1913: *Judith of Bethulia*. He joined the small film company Mutual, hoping to be free to pursue his artistic vision of creating longer film projects. While at Mutual, Griffith began researching and planning *Birth of a Nation* based upon Thomas Dixon's novel *The Clansman* (1905), which was part of his Klan Trilogy that also included *The Leopard's Spots* (1902) and *The Traitor* (1907). Born in 1864, Dixon was a lawyer, state legislator, novelist (22 novels), preacher, screenwriter, actor, movie producer, lecturer, and real estate speculator. Although he renounced slavery when the period of Reconstruction ended, Dixon remained a confirmed segregationist, warning that African Americans must be denied equality and integration because those actions would lead to miscegenation and the disintegration of American values, family, and civilized society. In 1915, when the film opened in Los Angeles, it made its debut under the title *The Clansman* but opened in New York as *The Birth of a Nation*. The change in title was made at Dixon's urging; he felt it more accurately reflected the film's ambitious tableau.

With a running time of three hours and a budget of $110,000, *The Birth of a Nation* achieved what we now term "blockbuster" status while charging the unheard of admission price of $2 in some venues. The financial, logistical, and post-production commitment was staggering. After exhausting the money of his backers, Griffith sought other sources, including his own. He spent three weeks in rehearsals, shot the film from July to October, then took three months to edit the film. Although there are no accurate figures concerning the film's earnings, there are estimates it could have grossed as much as $50 million. Because of the manner in which blacks were portrayed in the film, there were riots, protests, and demonstrations across the country. Although Griffith asserted that he was not racist, the film was a condemnation of African Americans visualized in stereotypical roles during and after the Civil War and the era of Reconstruction. It articulated their inferiority and accused those of mixed blood as being the worst of the lot led by unscrupulous greedy white people. Griffith was sustained by the romantic vision of the South in all its gossamer finery, where the "coloreds" were childlike and subservient. Those African Americans who were loyal to the South and its values were considered the "good" blacks. The film also endorsed the concept of slavery and glorified the Ku Klux Klan, referred to in a March 4 *New York Times* review as, "...the night riding of the men of the Ku Klux Klan, who look like a company of avenging spectral crusaders sweeping along the moonlit roads" (http://www.africanamericans. com/BirthofaNation.htm). It was criticized by the National Association for the Advancement of Colored People (NAACP) for its virulent depiction of blacks, causing riots to break out in major cities and distribution denials in eight states.

Although critics of Griffith and *The Birth of a Nation* may disagree with the manner in which he contextualized the content of the work within a framework of bigotry and stereotypes of blacks, they nevertheless agree that he mastered the cinematic technique with a unique sense of empowerment. His talent for presenting scenes from various perspectives in an animated fashion added tension and drama. The actors mastered their characters with a sublime sense of purpose, avoiding the exaggerated stylized pantomime that so often was a hallmark of silent film. Instead, they relied upon the nuances of subtlety in their facial expressions and actions.

Griffith's attention to the historically accurate details of the period brings the audience into the time and place of the film. Its costumes and rich reproduction of interior sets, as well as the visual interpretation of battle, provides a texture of authenticity that sustains a vivid tableaux of the time.

INTOLERANCE (1916)

PRODUCER/DIRECTOR: D. W. Griffith
WRITER(S): D. W. Griffith (scenario), Anita Loos (titles)
CAST: Mae Marsh (The Dear One), Robert Harron (The Boy), F. A. Turner (The Girl's Father), Sam De Grasse (Arthur Jenkins), Vera Lewis (Mary T. Jenkins), Mary Alden (Self-Styled Uplifter), Eleanor Washington (Self-Styled Uplifter), Pearl Elmore (Self-Styled Uplifter), Lucille Browne (Self-Styled Uplifter), Mrs. Arthur Mackley (Self-Styled Uplifter)
CINEMATOGRAPHY: G. W. Bitzer
MUSIC: Carl Davis
LENGTH AND RATING: 163 min; NR

The world was in a chaotic state when D. W. Griffith released *Intolerance* in 1916. As implied by the title, Griffith envisioned *Intolerance* as a response to his critics who condemned his earlier *The Birth of a Nation* as blatantly racist. The timing of the film's release and its theme of pacifism and tolerance was the antithesis of the American mood, which embraced the fear and anxiety of America's entry into the war in Europe. The film's theme traces the tragedy of bigotry, hatred, persecution, and hypocrisy through the ages by telling four stories that highlight the dreadful and heartbreaking results. Griffith began this effort as a more modest film entitled *The Mother and the Law*, but soon realized that his need to preach the sermon of tolerance and respond to charges of racism required a more monumental work. The four stories not only are thematically associated but are also linked by the virtues of "The Woman Who Rocks the Cradle," played by actress Lillian Gish, who is "the uniter of here and hereafter," representing eternal motherhood. She is Griffith's metaphor for the human race from birth to death. In a cameo shot, Gish rocks the cradle that bridges the stories while showing the title of Walt Whitman's controversial volume of poems, *Leaves of Grass*. At the time Whitman's first volume was published in 1855, it was considered controversial and indecent because it exulted in the body and sexual love. Perhaps in Whitman Griffith shared the same feeling of being an artistic agent provocateur condemned by his critics.

The amber-tinted "Modern Story" (1914) is about the beleaguered factory worker during a time of labor unrest in California heightened by strikes in a push to organize. A young Irish Catholic boy working under harsh conditions is wrongly accused of murder and sentenced to hang. His wife, whose baby was taken by "righteous" women deeming her an unfit mother, relentlessly pursues his innocence. He is saved at the last moment as she arrives with the governor's pardon. In the blue-tint "Judean Story," the shortest of the four, Griffith presents a passion play about Christ and his confrontation with the Pharisees, who rejected his teachings, and his later betrayal and crucifixion. "The French Story" (sepia tint) takes place during the sixteenth-century Renaissance and portrays the savage organized persecution and murder of the French Huguenots during the reign of King Charles the IX of France and his diabolical Catholic mother, Catherine de Medici. Catherine was the widow of Henry II and mother to three successive kings: Francis II, Charles IX, and Henry III. The film describes the horrific events of the St. Bartholomew's Day Massacre, in which thousands of Protestants in Paris and outside the city were killed, and its effect on the upcoming wedding of a young and pure Huguenot couple, Brown Eyes and Prosper Latour, also victims of the slaughter. "The Babylonian Story" (gray/green tint) takes place in 539 BC. It tells the story of the peaceful prince Belshazzar, who promotes tolerance and religious freedom, and the attack and eventual capitulation of Babylon under the siege by King Cyrus the Persian. The film focuses on the poignant story of the Mountain Girl, who is devoted to the prince and attempts to prevent the tragedy. A rival sect plans to aid the Persians and overthrow Babylon, but the Babylonians successfully repel them. As the Babylonians celebrate, the Mountain Girl learns of another plot to invade the city. She rushes to warn the prince but it is too late; both are killed as the city is conquered.

Griffith's *Intolerance* distinguishes itself as an epic film that articulates an innovative narrative structure that defines a parallel nonlinear visual composition for the cinema. At a cost of $2 million, the film was the most expensive ever produced and a monument to Griffith's vision, as revealed in the film's grandiose production values. The magnificent sets for "The Babylonian Story" employed innovative cinematography techniques (crane and elevator tower tracking shot) while also creating extravagant crowd scenes that even included live elephants; indeed, Griffith spared no expense in portraying his stories on the screen. The director's attention to detail and the mise-en-scène is a tribute to his ability to visualize the tone, tenor, and fabric of the story. Griffith captures the drama and creates a stunning portrait painted in the chiaroscuro of color tinting and light that gives texture to the film. His use of montage and cross-cutting between the four stories, although difficult at times to follow, is a brilliant tool to allow the stories to unfold in a thematic manner. Described by a historian as the only film fugue, *Intolerance* has a rhythm and melody that created a dissonance among viewers who found the parallel action and intercutting difficult to follow. The film, however, did not succeed with the public because of its innovative structure and the expense of providing full orchestration. Nonetheless, Griffith's technique and style were emulated by later directors, including Sergei Eisenstein, Cecil B. DeMille, Alfred Hitchcock, and Akira Kurosawa. Griffith's *Intolerance* had a tremendous influence on global cinema as a primer for future directors and as a means for indoctrinating movie audiences into modern visual storytelling.

NANOOK OF THE NORTH (1922)

PRODUCER/DIRECTOR: Robert J. Flaherty (producer), John Révillon (executive producer)
WRITER(S): Frances H. Flaherty (idea), Robert J. Flaherty (writer)
CAST: Allakariallak (Nanook), Nyla (Nanook's wife, the smiling one), Cunayou (Nanook's wife), Allee (Nanook's son), Allegoo (Nanook's son), Berry Kroeger (Narrator for 1939 re-release; uncredited)
CINEMATOGRAPHY: Robert J. Flaherty
MUSIC: Rudolph Schramur (1947), Stanley Silverman (1976)
LENGTH AND RATING: 79 mins; NR

The world was only recently recovering from the Great War as it greeted with trepidation the news of Mussolini's march on Rome and the formation of a Fascist government. It was a defining moment in world politics that would have wide repercussions on the global community. In the United States, there was labor unrest as the United Mine Workers of America struck for six months, demanding higher wages and crippling the coal mining industry. One of the English language's greatest writers, James Joyce, published *Ulysses* in 1922, although it was banned in the United States until 1933 because of its perceived use of obscenities. America was still a very puritanical society and once again faced challenges from within and without. Perhaps, then, it was time for a film about a peaceful race of people who consistently battled only one formidable enemy while struggling to survive in the harsh climate and environment of the North. As America faced new national and international challenges, Robert J. Flaherty produced one of the most compelling films ever made. It was a majestic effort to record the daily lives of Eskimos, and Flaherty, an explorer by profession with no filmmaking experience, was the least likely candidate to accomplish this effort. He lived in Canada among the Eskimos for many years doing trade, observing their lifestyle, and informally photographing them in their daily routine. In 1913, Flaherty set forth on an exploring ship fitted with lumber and material with enough food for eight men over a span of two years. Working as a prospector for a railroad

5

[Pathe/Photofest]

company, Flaherty was embarking on his third expedition to the Hudson Bay area and his boss, Sir William Mackenzie, suggested he take a motion picture camera along to record the people and wildlife he encountered. It was also hoped that the photography might help to defray some of the costs associated with exploration. His only training was the two weeks he spent prior to the trip with a motion picture camera demonstrator. Flaherty wintered on the Belcher Islands and shot film of Eskimos, but while completing the editing in Toronto, Canada, a fire destroyed 30,000 feet of film. Fortunately, the negative print was saved. After looking at his original material, Flaherty realized that the film was far too episodic and lacked cohesiveness. He decided to embark on another journey north, this time with the explicit purpose of making a motion picture about Eskimos.

Flaherty had a particular interest in one Inuit family and its leader, Nanook, and lived with them for some time before filming. Funding for this second, more ambitious project came from Revillon Frères, a French fur trading company that had outposts on the Hudson Bay. In the newer version of the film, Flaherty was not simply an observer of the challenges Nanook and his family faced in the harsh climate of the Arctic; he also became a director of the drama, staging and manipulating the action for the camera. He forbade the Eskimos to use their rifles to hunt, instead preferring the tension and conflict that harpoon hunting provided. In addition, Flaherty staged the ending of the film as Nanook and his family appeared to be near death due to their inability to find shelter even though an igloo had been built beforehand.

After completing the film, Flaherty faced the challenge of distributing it and was rejected by most distribution companies. They told him people would not want to see a movie about Eskimos. Finally, he arranged an agreement with Pathé and the film was exhibited at Samuel "Roxy" Rothafel's Capitol Theatre in New York. Rothafel was an impresario of the great silent movie palaces of that era, having built the Capitol, the Strand, and the Roxy movie theater in New York City. He didn't expect much in the way of box office revenue and was stunned when in the first week *Nanook of the North* earned $43,000. It was a critical and artistic success.

A review in the June 12, 1922, *New York Times* heralded Flaherty's film as a "real life-and-death struggle." The reviewer went on to describe Nanook, the main protagonist in the film, this way:

> He is emphatically a leader, a man who does things, a man who wins, but who at any moment, may lose. He is a genuine hero then, one who is watched with alert interest and suspense and far-reaching imagination.

The *New York Times* review also comments on Flaherty's ability to create the mise-en-scène of the movie:

> It took more than just a man with a camera to make *Nanook of the North*. Mr. Flaherty had to wait for his light, he had to select his shots, he had to compose his scenes, he had to direct his people, in order that Nanook's story might develop its full force of realism and drama on the screen (*New York Times*, "The Screen," June 12, 1922).

Nanook of the North was the first commercially successful silent film theatrical documentary, and this gave Flaherty a great deal of recognition. In his pursuit of making films in collaboration with local communities, Robert J. Flaherty became known as the father of documentary film. He used his success to create other compelling documentaries that explored the cultural and natural challenges people face. They are *Moana* (1926), *Man of Aran* (1934), *Elephant Boy* (1937), and *Louisiana Story* (1948). (Sherwood, http//cinemaweb.com/silentfilm/bookshelf.)

CINEMATIC TRIPTYCH (1927)

Metropolis (1927)
The General (1927)
The Jazz Singer (1927)

The year was 1927 and it was remarkable not only because it was distinguished by so many "firsts" in technology and engineering and the unfortunate tragedy of a great national disaster, but also because of three unique and compelling films that could be considered masterpieces and landmarks in content, style, form, and function. Those films are *Metropolis, The General,* and *The Jazz Singer.* Each expresses a distinctive cinematic voice that articulates sensibilities and virtues while challenging convention.

METROPOLIS (1927)

PRODUCER/DIRECTOR: Fritz Lang (director), Giorgio Moroder (producer for 1984 restoration), Erich Pommer (producer)

WRITER(S): Thea von Harbou (screenplay and novel), Fritz Lang (screenplay; uncredited)

CAST: Alfred Abel (Joh Fredersen), Gustav Fröhlich (Freder, Joh Fredersen's son), Rudolf Klein-Rogge (C. A. Rotwang, the inventor), Fritz Rasp (The Thin Man), Theodor Loos (Josaphat), Erwin Biswanger (11811), Heinrich George (Grot, the guardian of the Heart Machine), Brigitte Helm (Maria)

CINEMATOGRAPHY: Karl Freund, Günther Rittau, Walter Ruttmann

MUSIC: Gottfried Huppertz, Abel Korzeniowski (2004), Giorgio Moroder (1984), Peter Osborne (1998), Bernd Schultheis (2001), Wetfish (1999)

LENGTH AND RATING: 153 mins; NR

In 1927, the Great Mississippi Flood affected 700,000 people and at the time was considered America's greatest national tragedy. In Great Britain, an influenza epidemic claimed the lives of one thousand people a week. There were compelling technological innovations such as the first transmission of electronic television pictures, the first Pan American Airways flight from Key West, Florida, to Havana, Cuba; the opening of the Holland Tunnel in New York City; and the first transatlantic telephone call from New York City to London. It appears that *Metropolis*, directed by Fritz Lang, was released at a fortuitous time in the history of global technology. It tells a story set in the year 2026 about a city-state dominated by a bourgeois class: the leaders and thinkers who live in plush luxury on the surface of the Earth. They have subjugated the working class, who live underground and toil endlessly in harsh conditions to support the leaders.

The film portrays a technological culture in which Lang anticipates future inventions such as the television, automatic doors, monorails, and the "Maschinenmensch Hel," a robot or Machine Man oriented toward a consumer culture. The set design, with its symbolism and modernistic texture, is a testimony to German Expressionism, and the special effects create an abstract impressionistic design enhanced by creative lighting.

Fritz Lang was intrigued with how people behave when challenged by powerful large bureaucracies, such as corporations, businesses, and criminal gangs. To Lang, people are pawns in a game of power and can be engineered to behave a certain way. And, even when these people have truth and justice on their side, their individualism is destroyed by the dynamic of force and control. Lang was a consummate and autocratic filmmaker with a versatile ability to adapt to many different genres and themes. Even though he treated his actors poorly, major stars appeared in his films, among them Henry Fonda, Spencer Tracy, Marlene Dietrich, Joan Bennett, Barbara Stanwyck, Tyrone Power, and Edward G. Robinson. Lang preferred leading ladies with strong character, and for that trait he turned to Joan Bennett, who starred in four of his film classics: *Woman in the Window* (1944), *Scarlet Street* (1945), *Secret Beyond the Door (1947), and Man Hunt* (1941).

As an epic science fiction drama, *Metropolis* established newly defined techniques in cinematography and narrative storytelling and set the tone for many subsequent films that dealt with similar technological themes. Lang also uses the film to demonstrate his knowledge of art and architecture. *Metropolis* was produced by the giant

German studio, Universun – Film – Aktiengesellschaft (UFA), and featured thousands of extras and the latest cinematic technological innovations. It was a box office disaster and was quickly withdrawn from distribution, then re-edited and re-released. Eventually it was restored and scenes that hadn't been viewed in decades were reintegrated into the print. *Metropolis* sustains the legacy of Lang and the pursuit of epic filmmaking, which in turn allows directors to embrace the language and objective of the auteur.

THE GENERAL (1927)

PRODUCER/DIRECTOR: Clyde Bruckman (director), Buster Keaton (director and producer), Joseph M. Schenck (executive producer and producer)
WRITER(S): Al Boasberg (adaptation), Clyde Bruckman (writer)
CAST: Marion Mack (Annabelle Lee), Glen Cavender (Union Capt. Anderson, chief spy), Jim Farley (Gen. Thatcher, US Army), Frederick Vroom (Confederate general), Charles Henry Smith (Mr. Lee, Annabelle's father), Frank Barnes (Annabelle's brother), Joe Keaton (Union general), Mike Donlin (Union general), Tom Nawn (Union general), Buster Keaton (Johnny Gray)
CINEMATOGRAPHY: Bert Haines, Devereaux Jennings
MUSIC: Carl Davis (1987), Joe Hisaishi (2004), Robert Israel (1995)
LENGTH AND RATING: 75 mins; NR

As an actor, comedian, and director, Buster Keaton used the classic traits of drama and plot development to create films that were true to the integrity and character of a film's period. He was a dedicated artist, and each frame in *The General* adheres to his meticulous sense of detail and his compelling need for historic relevance. Indeed, some critics have compared the visual traits of this film to the black-and-white photographs taken by Matthew Brady during the Civil War. The movie is a resounding comedic tour de force with a physicality and uniqueness provided by the sophisticated technique employed by the creative use of design, form, and function. Although great comedians, both Chaplin and Keaton could light up the silent screen with humor, compassion, and pathos but it was Keaton who became a great storyteller and a masterful director.

The General was one of the most expensive films ($400,000) (http://www.imdb.com/title/tt0017925) of that era. Based on a true story, it told of daring Union officers who posed as confederate soldiers to capture a confederate train near Atlanta and return it to the Union. Most of those soldiers were eventually caught and hanged as spies. A book describing this event, *Daring and Suffering: a History of the Great Railway Adventure*, by William Pittenger, provided the story line for Keaton's fictional interpretation.

Keaton portrays the lovelorn Johnny Gray, who pines for his girl, Annabelle Lee (perhaps a reference to Edgar Allan Poe's poem "Annabelle Lee"), and the *General*, the locomotive that is his other true love. With the outbreak of the Civil War, Annabelle Lee anticipates that Johnny, like her brother and all the other young men, will join the army. Poor Johnny tries to enlist but the Confederacy values his experience as a locomotive engineer more than his potential as a soldier. Because his true love spurns him (after her father and brother are both wounded), Johnny is forlorn but rises to the occasion, chasing the spies who also chase him and pursuing his beloved *General* and his girlfriend Annabelle Lee, who has been taken prisoner on the train by the spies.

For Buster Keaton, *The General* was a triumph for his vision, art, and talent. It was, of course, a silent film made on the dawn of the "talkies." Unfortunately, the critics were not enthusiastic. In his February 8, 1927, review in the *New York Times*, Mordaunt Hall notes,

> This is by no means so good as Mr. Keaton's previous efforts. Here he is more the acrobat than the clown and his vehicle might be described as a mixture of cast iron and jelly (http://movies.nytimes.com/movie).

Other reviewers also diminished its worth, referring to Keaton's "woefully bad judgment and gruesomely bad taste," and pointing out it was the "least funny thing Buster Keaton has done."

Although the film's critical and box office failure ($500,000) disturbed Keaton, he did not publicly articulate his disappointment but continued to refer to *The General* as "my pet." In 1928, he was forced to sell his film unit to MGM, a decision he later regretted due to the restrictive nature of the agreement. As a result he was forced into the studio system giving up the autonomy that he had previously enjoyed. He became despondent and lapsed into an alcoholic stupor, spending most of the 1930s in obscurity. During that time he became a joke writer for a number of MGM Marx Brothers films and some movies featuring Red Skelton. His influence on American culture as a comedian and film director had a profound effect on comedy, filmmaking, and the art of cinema.

THE JAZZ SINGER (1927)

PRODUCER/DIRECTOR: Alan Crosland
WRITER(S): Samson Raphaelson (play), Alfred A. Cohn (adaptation)
CAST: Al Jolson (Jakie Rabinowitz), May McAvoy (Mary Dale), Warner Oland (Cantor Rabinowitz), Eugenie Besserer (Sara Rabinowitz), Otto Lederer (Moisha Yudelson), Robert Gordon (Jakie Rabinowitz, age 13), Richard Tucker (Harry Lee), Cantor Joseff Rosenblatt (Himself, concert recital)
CINEMATOGRAPHY: Hal Mohr (photography)
MUSIC: Louis Silvers
LENGTH AND RATING: 88 mins; NR

They danced the Charleston, and women defied convention as "flappers," wearing short hair and short dresses with powdered knees. Prohibition was ignored, with Americans consuming more alcohol than ever before. When the term "jazz" entered the American lexicon, it took on various meanings that were contextualized by different groups. Some found it to be vulgar and lacking any aesthetic to be considered art, while others embraced the rhythm and blues and became devoted fans of Fats Waller, Bessie Smith, George Gershwin, and Paul Whiteman. As the music scene changed to the cadence and beat of the blues, film embraced a new technology: the technique of sound recording.

The first sound on disc process was developed by Bell Telephone's research lab, Western Electric, and was named the Vitaphone. After repeated rejections from the major studios, including Paramount, Warner Brothers, a smaller studio embarking on

Al Jolson as Jakie Rabinowitz. [Warner Bros. Pictures/Photofest]

an ambitious program of expansion, bought the Vitaphone system. The larger studios were ambivalent about sound because of the expense of equipping motion picture theaters (about $20,000 per theater) and competing sound systems (optical and disc). Also, the major studios were, for the most part, lulled into a false sense of security by stability and profits.

On August 6, 1926, Warner Brothers presented a program of short sound films and also screened a feature film, *Don Juan*, with synchronized musical accompaniment. It should be noted that *The Jazz Singer* was not the first film to synchronize image with speech and it was not the first sound film. However, it was the first full-length feature to utilize synchronized sound to tell a story. The narrative was adapted by Alfred A. Cohn from a 1921 short story by Samson Raphaelson titled *The Day of Atonement*. Most of the film was shot silent using intertitles but included at least five scenes with synchronized speech. In one scene, Jakie Rabinowitz, after forsaking his heritage as a Jewish cantor, visits his parents and performs *Blue Skies* for his mother, Sara. When his father arrives home he commands that the blasphemous music stop and the movie reverts to silence. This served as a visual and aural metaphor for the sound film as being modern and the silent film a thing of the past.

Although *The Jazz Singer* had both sound and silent sequences, Al Jolson's voice in dialogue and song imbued his character with a rich, colorful, and compelling presence. During the silent sequences, his large rolling banjo eyes and over-pronounced gestures are a portrait of a film aesthetic on the verge of extinction. However, the fluid camera technique during the silent sequences is not matched during those with sound, where the camera by necessity (because of microphones) was more static. Those moments with sound created a dramatic context that could not be matched by the silent film. Jolson then utters that famous line

> You ain't heard nothin' yet! Wait a minute. I tell ya, you ain't heard nothin'. You want to hear "Toot Toot Tootsie"? All right, hold on...

The audience's enthusiasm embraced the line and was overwhelmed by the moment.

As a result of *The Jazz Singer*, which was a huge hit, the American motion picture industry was revitalized. Jolson's second movie for Warner Brothers, *The Singing Fool* (1928), was an even bigger success. Better than *The Jazz Singer*, the film became a huge moneymaker for the studio and held the record as the top grossing sound film until Disney's *Snow White and the Seven Dwarfs* was released in 1937.

At the first Academy Awards ceremony in May 1929, *The Jazz Singer* was excluded from the "Best Picture" category because it was thought unfair to have it compete with silent films. However, producer Darryl F. Zanuck was presented with a special Oscar for pioneering the production of talking films and revolutionizing the industry. Indeed, sound changed the entire dynamic of the motion picture industry, and by 1929 the silent film was no longer a marketable form of entertainment.

Although not a masterpiece, and by today's sophisticated standards rather cumbersome, *The Jazz Singer* left its legacy on American culture and film. It had an effect on every nuance of the American psyche, demonstrating the compelling sensuality of adding sound to image and creating a new aesthetic that challenged the senses. The film was not an epic (it had no grandiose ambitions), but it was the story of a cantor's son who rejects his heritage and becomes a music hall entertainer. What distinguishes *The Jazz Singer* is that it could take this theme and build a cohesive dramatic narrative that embodies the essence of character through picture and sound. It touched the depth of emotions with tools and techniques that would become part of the lingua franca of cinema.

ALL QUIET ON THE WESTERN FRONT (1930)

PRODUCER/DIRECTOR: Lewis Milestone (director), Carl Laemmle Jr. (producer)

WRITER(S): Erich Maria Remarque (novel), Maxwell Anderson (adaptation)

CAST: Louis Wolheim (Kat Katczinsky), Lew Ayres (Paul Bäumer), John Wray (Himmelstoss), Arnold Lucy (Professor Kantorek), Ben Alexander (Franz Kemmerich), Scott Kolk (Leer), Owen Davis Jr. (Peter), Walter Rogers (Behn), William Bakewell (Albert Kropp), Russell Gleason (Mueller)

CINEMATOGRAPHY: Arthur Edeson, Karl Freund (uncredited)

MUSIC: Sam Perry (silent version, uncredited), Heinz Roemheld (silent version, uncredited)

LENGTH AND RATING: 138 mins (copyright length) | USA: 133 mins (restored version: Library of Congress); NR

The "Blue Plate Special" is a square meal for two bits. It was a symbol of the 1930s and the unease that America faced during and after the Depression. The 1930s were filled with the incongruous images of Americans lining up for food, families crowding into small apartments and homes, children and adults suffering from lack of medical care and malnutrition, and people trying to survive by selling pencils and apples in the city. A popular song, "Brother Can You Spare a Dime," lamented the decline of a fellow they once called Al, who served his country, built railroads and towers, and now was reduced to standing in line waiting for bread. Hundreds of thousands of people left their homes and traveled the country looking for food and work, as depicted in the novel and film, *The Grapes Of Wrath*, and articulated in the song.

By 1932 one out of every four Americans was unemployed. Between 1929 and 1932, the average American family's income was reduced by 40 percent, from $2,300 to $1,500. In 1933, President Franklin Roosevelt adopted his "New Deal", which introduced many social and economic reforms already available to Europeans. For example, his administration created the Civilian Conservation Corps (CCC), which provided jobs for young men between the ages of 18 and 25 at thirty dollars a month.

One of the most effective means of escapism during these turbulent times was radio. Radio programming provided audiences with relief from their daily challenges as they listened to comedies and dramas such as *Amos 'n' Andy, Jack Benny, Burns and Allen*, and *Dick Tracy*. And films offered distraction for so many weary people. There were gangster movies like *Little Caesar, Public Enemy*, and *Scarface*, which depicted the ruthless efforts of criminals to beat the system, and there were movies like *Mr. Deeds Goes To Town* and *Mr. Smith Goes to Washington* that exemplified the American hero and his fight with the establishment. There were also comedies with Mae West and W. C. Fields that featured sexual innuendos and double entendres that poked fun at the rigid sexual mores of American society and managed to offend more than a few Americans.

During the depths of the Depression, 60 to 80 million people bought a movie ticket each week. But, the movies were susceptible to the economic variables of the Depression, and theater attendance and revenue fell 40 percent in 1933. Theaters were closed, budgets slashed, the price of admission was cut, more double bills and premiums were offered, and Bank Nights were created, with winners receiving a cash prize.

The mood of America was solemn in 1930, when perhaps one of the greatest anti-war films ever produced, *All Quiet on the Western Front*, based on Erich Maria Remarque's autobiographical novel, was released. It was a compelling indictment of the horrors and tragedy of war. The author was a young German soldier who had served in World War I and then written about his experiences. For many, memories of this Great War were still lingering as this film was released, twelve years later. Produced under the auspices of Universal Studios head of production Carl Laemmle, Jr., at a cost of $1.25 million, the film used two thousand extras along with sprawling California ranch land to film the epic battle scenes. Director Lewis Milestone won the Academy Award for best director (it was his first sound film) and the movie also won an Academy Award for best picture. In his *New York Times* review of the film dated April 30, 1930, Mordaunt Hall praises the vivid portrayal of battle and the frightening sounds of war.

Often the scenes are of such excellence that if they were not audible one might believe that they were actual motion pictures of activities behind the lines, in the trenches and in No Man's Land. It is an expansive production with views that never appear to be cramped. In looking at a dugout one readily imagines a long line of such earthly abodes. When shells demolish these underground quarters, the shrieks of fear, coupled with the rat-tat-tat of machine guns, the bangs of the trench mortars and the whining of shells, it tells the story of the terrors of fighting better than anything so far has done in animated photography coupled with a microphone (http://movies.nytimes.com/movie).

The film begins with a prologue which is adapted almost verbatim from Remarque's novel. It articulates the theme of the movie, contextualizing it within the horrors of war and how even those who survive are burdened with its tragic legacy.

"This story is neither an accusation nor a confession, and least of all an adventure, for death is not an adventure to those who stand face to face with it. It will try simply to tell of a generation of men who, even though they may have escaped its shells, were destroyed by the war."

This movie made a profound statement about the impact of war on the men who fought, died, and survived. It addressed the themes of brutality, comradeship, and the compelling sense of futility. This film had a major influence on other war films that told the story from a soldier's perspective, including the more recent movies *Platoon* (1986), *Full Metal Jacket* (1987), and *Saving Private Ryan* (1998).

LITTLE CAESAR (1930) AND *THE PUBLIC ENEMY* (1931)

The public's fascination with crime and the characteristics of gangsters has held a timeless infatuation with audiences. The exploits of outlaws, whether glorified in westerns like *Billy the Kid, Jesse James,* and *Butch Cassidy and the Sundance Kid* or their modern-day counter parts in theatrical films such as *The Untouchables, Bonnie and Clyde, The Godfather,* and *Goodfellas,* or featured in the popular HBO television series *The Sopranos,* have become cultural icons in the fabric of American film and television. Early sound films set the tone of the gangster genre, characterizing it with the harsh reality of overcoming poverty and social disillusionment within the unending hardships of the Depression era. *Little Caesar* and *The Public Enemy* provided the fundamentals for later interpretations of the genre by contextualizing the character of the gangster within the social milieu of the times.

The 1930s was also the time of the Production Code and the rise of the Catholic Church as a means of oversight for film content. Censorship was nothing new to the American motion picture industry. National scandals involving Hollywood celebrities in the 1920s shocked fans and tested the faith of audiences. There was the "quicky" Nevada divorce of "America's Sweetheart" Mary Pickford from husband Owen Moore so that she could marry Douglas Fairbanks, as well as the scandals involving Fatty Roscoe Arbuckle and his notorious parties, including one in 1917 that ended with a Massachusetts district attorney receiving a $100,000 gift, leaving people to wonder what he had kept quiet about to earn that sum. At another, held at the St. Francis Hotel in San Francisco in 1921, one of his guests, Virginia Rappe, was found dead in her hotel room. Although eventually acquitted after three trials, Arbuckle's career was over.

Reeling from these high-voltage indiscretions, the Hollywood studios decided it would be best if they engaged in self-censorship rather than have Congress assert their own form of it. The Motion Picture Producers and Distributors of America (MPPDA) was created and Will H. Hays, President Harding's campaign manager, the United States

Postmaster General, a Republican and church-going Presbyterian elder, was named its first commissioner and he served for twenty-three years. In 1945, the name of the organization was changed to the Motion Picture Association of America (MPAA).

In addition to the economic challenges facing the motion picture industry during the Depression in the 1930s, there was an aggressive initiative to "clean up" motion pictures and make them morally pure. To this end, two Catholic laymen, Martin Quigley and, later, Joseph I. Breen, helped create and enforce the Hollywood Production Code as part of the Production Code Administration (PCA). At the MPPDA, also known as the Hays Office, Breen went to work administering the PCA, issuing a seal of approval only to the films that met the rigid content standards of the Code. Any producer or distributor who released a film without obtaining the seal would be fined $25,000. The Code clearly articulated the do's and don'ts of story content and expected the industry to respect the sacrament of marriage and avoid the more deviant forms of promiscuous sex, including "unwedded," "extramarital," and "unnatural." There was a list of forbidden words, including "sex," "God," "hell," and "damn." Some words that appeared rather innocuous and part of America's lingua franca, such as "guts," "nuts," and "louse" were also on the list. Then there was the screen innovation of the "Hollywood beds": married couples sleeping separately in twin beds. This legacy remained with some of the early television sitcoms, including *The Dick Van Dyke Show*, which had the Petrys sleeping in separate beds about five feet apart.

As human sexuality was being scrubbed and neutered by the Code administrators, stipulations began to control how violence was portrayed. Brutality was to be avoided by gangsters, and especially by the police. Also, any immoral or illegal lifestyle was to be depicted in a way that would be considered distasteful to audiences, echoing the theme that "crime doesn't pay." While the Code attempted to sanitize film content and was an unrealistic representation of American mores and culture, the motion picture industry had little choice but to comply. Throughout the Depression, even though audiences scraped their nickels and dimes to see a movie, audience attendance had fallen. In addition, the banks that supported the motion picture industry were eager to sustain the conservative values and economic empowerment they enjoyed. The industry faced the challenges of the early 1930s by creating the double feature (two movies for the price of one) and adding trailers, cartoons, shorts, and newsreels. They also featured games like Keno, Bingo, and Screeno, giving away cash prizes and dishes.

LITTLE CAESAR (1930)

PRODUCER/DIRECTOR: Mervyn LeRoy (director), Hal B. Wallis (producer, uncredited), Darryl F. Zanuck (producer, uncredited)
WRITER(S): W. R. Burnett (novel), Robert N. Lee (continuity)
CAST: Edward G. Robinson (Little Caesar, aka "Rico"), Douglas Fairbanks, Jr. (Joe Massara), Glenda Farrell (Olga Stassoff), William Collier, Jr. (Tony Passa), Sidney Blackmer (Big Boy), Ralph Ince (Pete Montana), Thomas E. Jackson (Sargeant Flaherty), Stanley Fields (Sam Vettori), Maurice Black (Little Arnie Lorch), George E. Stone (Otero)
CINEMATOGRAPHY: Tony Gaudio
MUSIC: David Mendoza (uncredited)
LENGTH AND RATING: 79 mins; NR

The historical context of these developments is related to the evolution of the gangster genre in film, as *Little Caesar* and *The Public Enemy* were two of the last films of this type to be produced prior to the enforcement of the Code. Indeed, after the Codes implementation, both films were withdrawn from distribution and were not re-released until 1953. The actor Edward G. Robinson, who had portrayed "tough guys" in earlier films, was superb in the role of Caesar "Rico" Bandello, a character modeled after the ruthless mobster Al Capone, with a tribute to the Brooklyn underworld figure Bugsy Goldstein. Facing the chaotic tensions of a country challenged by a Depression, Little Caesar, at first a small-time hoodlum in an unnamed burg, finds opportunity on the streets of Chicago and with ruthless determination ascends to the top of the criminal heap. After tasting success and earning the fearful respect of his cohorts, he embarks on an often psychotic adventure of crime, striving for society's acceptance and thwarting his ambition by terrorizing the innocents who repulse at his behavior.

The film begins with this prescient quote from St. Matthew:

...for all they that take the sword shall perish with the sword. (Matthew:26-52)

Caesar, flush with ambition, confides in his sidekick Joe that he's aiming for bigger and better things in life. Once in Chicago, he cajoles his way into Sam Vetorri's gang. In scenes that established the image and dialogue that foreshadowed other gangster films to follow, including *The Godfather* and *Goodfellas*, Sam introduces Rico to "the boys," giving him the nom de guerre "Little Caesar." During the introduction, the rough-hewn faces of the gang members are prominently shown and introductions (including nicknames) are made, praising their unique talents as such:

Tony Passa who can drive better than anyone; Otero, he's little but got the goods; and others like Killer Peppie and Kid Bean.

Rico makes a name for himself and soon wins the loyalty of Sam Vetorri's crew, assuming the position as gang leader and telling Sam that he's through. His ruthless, unbridled ambition portends a precipitous fall, and once Rico is betrayed by his best friend Joe and in a face off cannot shoot him, he flees from the police and goes into hiding. While Rico is living on the lam, the police plant stories in the newspapers, calling him a coward and luring him to a confrontation. Allowing his ego to get the better of him, Rico confronts his law enforcement nemesis, Flaherty, who guns him down in a hail of machine gun bullets. Facing death and still in denial about his fate, Rico says:

Mother of Mercy! Is this the end of Rico?

Because of the thematic elements introduced and sustained in this film, *Little Caesar* is a classic that had a profound impact on its audience and the culture of the twentieth century. In his January 10, 1931, review, *New York Times* critic Mordaunt Hall noted there were unusual crowds gathered at the Strand Theater in New York for the opening of the film. The character of Little Caesar no doubt appealed to Depression-era audiences because of his bravado, contempt for the rule of law, and initial success in overcoming overwhelming odds. The themes of ambition, greed, arrogance, betrayal, and retribution became the hallmark of later incarnations of the mobster film. In his review, Hall writes about Edward G. Robinson's portrayal of Little Caesar:

> Little Caesar becomes at Mr. Robinson's hands a figure out of Greek epic tragedy, a cold, ignorant, merciless killer, driven on and on by an insatiable lust for power, the plaything of a force that is greater than himself.

THE PUBLIC ENEMY (1931)

PRODUCER/DIRECTOR: William A. Wellman (director), Darryl F. Zanuck (producer, uncredited)
WRITER(S): Kubec Glasmon, John Bright
CAST: James Cagney (Tom Powers), Jean Harlow (Gwen Allen), Edward Woods (Matt Doyle), Joan Blondell (Mamie), Donald Cook (Mike Powers), Leslie Fenton (Nails Nathan), Beryl Mercer (Ma Powers), Robert Emmett O'Connor (Paddy Ryan), Murray Kinnell (Putty Nose)
CINEMATOGRAPHY: Devereaux Jennings
LENGTH AND RATING: 83 mins; NR

In *The Public Enemy*, the hoodlum Tommy Powers, played by James Cagney, is modeled after two real-life mobsters from the notorious Valley Gang of Chicago: Terry Druggan and Frankie Lake, enterprising bootleggers who were the first large-scale beer distributors in Chicago after Prohibition. Other locals who influenced the creation of the Tommy Powers character were Dion O'Banion and Hymie Weiss, both members of the Chicago North Siders gang that challenged the supremacy of Al Capone. The story was adapted from the novel *Beer and Blood* by John Bright and Kubec Glasmon, who also wrote the screenplay. It was directed by William Wellman and completed in less than a month at a cost of about $151,000 (http://www.filmsite.org/publ.html). In an effort to accommodate concerns about glorifying ruthless criminals, Warner Brothers displayed the text of an opening preface that read:

> It is the ambition of the authors of *The Public Enemy* to honestly depict an environment that exists today in a certain strata of American life, rather than glorify the hoodlum or the criminal. While the story of *The Public Enemy* is essentially a true story, all names and characters appearing herein are purely fictional.

Interestingly, Darryl F. Zanuck, the head of Warner Brothers production and producer of *The Public Enemy*, attempted to placate the members of the Production Code by stating that the means toward curbing law-breaking was through the betterment of environment and education. Another rationale that the studio hoped would satisfy potential critics of the film was to present it as a sociological study attempting to reconcile the road to criminality with poverty, deprivation, and a lack of education. However, those arguments in favor of the film's merits did not deter the New York censor board from cutting six scenes before allowing its release. Although *The Public Enemy* was not subject to the provisions of the Production Code, it did create more oversight toward the treatment of crime and gangsters by the MPPDA.

The film was a tremendous hit at the box office and established James Cagney as a movie star. Indeed, James Cagney became a favorite of the urban male audience.

DRACULA (1931)

PRODUCER/DIRECTOR: Tod Browning (director), Tod Browning (producer), Carl Laemmle, Jr. (producer)
WRITER(S): Bram Stoker (novel), Hamilton Deane (play), John L. Balderston (play)
CAST: Bela Lugosi (Count Dracula), Helen Chandler (Mina Harker), David Manners (John Harker), Dwight Frye (Renfield), Edward Van Sloan (Prof. Abraham Van Helsing), Herbert Bunston (Dr. Jack Seward), Frances Dade (Lucy Weston), Joan Standing (Briggs), Charles K. Gerrard (Martin)
CINEMATOGRAPHY: Karl Freund
MUSIC: Philip Glass (1999)
LENGTH AND RATING: 75 mins; NR

In *Dracula*, Carl Laemmle's Universal Pictures fostered an enduring genre of the horror film versed in the nuances of image and language that would serve generations of screen writers, authors, and directors. At Universal, the horror film led to a lingua franca of imagery as a descendent of classics such as *The Golem* and *Nosferatu*. One essential ingredient of the horror film was a knowledge of the creative lighting techniques that originated in Germany; those techniques were implicit to creating a chiaroscuro effect for mood and impending terror.

After performing on Broadway as the bloodthirsty Count Dracula, Hungarian actor Bela Lugosi starred in Tod Browning's movie adaptation of the story. ("The man of a thousand faces," Lon Chaney, Sr., was originally cast in the lead but died of throat cancer.) The first unauthorized film adaptation of Bram Stoker's 1897 novel *Dracula* was the silent film *Nosferatu: A Symphony in Terror* (1922), directed by F. W. Murnau and starring Max Schreck. The 1931 film was closer to the stage play, written by John Balderston and Hamilton Deane, than to Stoker's novel. Although the 1931 production was described by some reviewers as "stage-like," Lugosi's portrayal of the count was a chilling evocation of bloodcurdling terror. His accent and lilting voice made his articulation of the lines a memorable verse of literary fright. Four lines evoked the nuances of language and made them lasting pronouncements of impending doom:

I am...Drac-u-la... I bid you welcome.
Listen to them. Children of the night. What m-u-u-sic they make.
I never drink... wi-i-i-ne.
For one who has not lived even a single life time, you are a wise man, Van Helsing.

A *New York Times* review by Hal Erickson notes that it is a classic horror film and Bela Lugosi "...gives the performance of a life time."

Karl Freund, a German immigrant and talented cameraman, brought his aesthetic to the brooding imagery of *Dracula*. Many talented German filmmakers, including Freund, pioneered the visual elements of classic horror, and Freund worked with the

Helen Chandler and Bela Lugosi. [Photofest]

most creative directors of that time, including Robert Wiene (*The Cabinet of Dr. Caligari*), F. W. Murnau *(Nosferatu),* and Fritz Lang *(Metropolis).* Freund directed his first feature for Universal, *The Mummy,* in 1932.

For many, this classic set the tone and tenor for later horror films and served as a benchmark for others to follow. It became a twentieth-century icon, lingering in a timeless vault of terror without the vivid portrayal of "blood and guts" but instead the subdued deadly sense of lust dominated by a powerful force rendered on the screen.

FRANKENSTEIN (1931)

PRODUCER/DIRECTOR: James Whale (director), Carl Laemmle, Jr. (producer)
WRITER(S): Mary Shelley (novel), Peggy Webling (play)
CAST: Colin Clive (Dr. Henry Frankenstein), Mae Clarke (Elizabeth), John Boles (Victor Moritz), Boris Karloff (The Monster), Edward Van Sloan (Dr. Waldman), Frederick Kerr (Baron Frankenstein), Dwight Frye (Fritz), Lionel Belmore (Herr Vogel), Marilyn Harris (Little Maria)
CINEMATOGRAPHY: Arthur Edeson, Paul Ivano (uncredited)
MUSIC: Bernhard Kaun (uncredited)
LENGTH AND RATING: 71 mins; NR

This film, directed by James Whale, was also a product of Carl Laemmle's Universal Pictures and its success, along with that of *Dracula*, helped to make the studio financially solvent. Nonetheless, this was not the first film adaptation of Mary Shelley's classic (1818) tale of horror. The first, entitled *Frankenstein*, was a sixteen-minute silent film released by the Edison Company and directed by J. Searle Dawley; the second was the first *Frankenstein* silent feature-length film *Life Without a Soul* (1915), directed by Joseph W. Smiley and produced by the Ocean Film Corporation. The 1931 film starred Boris Karloff (who was born in England to a privileged family and whose real name was William Henry Pratt) as the Frankenstein monster. The role was a turning point in the actor's career, although he was not credited at the opening of the film. In addition, at the beginning of the film a man in a tuxedo, Edward van Sloan, who plays the part of Dr. Waldman, appears from behind a curtain and admonishes the audience with a "friendly warning." He tells them that the film deals with, "...the two great mysteries of creation—life and death." He goes on to say, "I think it will thrill you. It may shock you. It might even horrify you." Indeed, *Frankenstein* accommodated all of those emotions and became a classic in the genre of horror films. When we first see the monster, he gradually appears as a scarred and grotesque hulking figure, a flawed copy of a human without a soul. There are chilling low-angle shots of a cemetery and its weathered tombstones, an archetypal image that became fundamental to the horror film genre and other directors who used it to create foreboding and fear. The monster is a tragic figure rejected by his creator, and in one of the most poignant scenes in the film he befriends the young girl Maria and they play together by a pond, tossing daisies onto the water. A child lost in her innocence, Maria has not learned to be frightened of the unknown. The two play together, touching hands, until the monster, seeing the petals float on the water, throws Maria in, believing she will float, and she subsequently drowns. The monster is childlike but deadly in his actions. In the original release of the film, the drowning scene was cut, as it was considered too gruesome and not restored until the 1980s.

In his *New York Times Review* of December 5, 1931, Mordaunt Hall revels in how much excitement the movie created among audiences in New York's Mayfair Theatre. He writes:

It is naturally a morbid, gruesome affair, but is something to keep the spectator awake, for during its most spine-chilling periods it exacts attention. No matter what one may say about the melodramatic ideas here, there is no denying that it is far and away the most effective thing of its kind.

At Universal Studios, Jack Pierce, who became a master makeup artist, was responsible for the design and look of the Frankenstein monster. Although he did not work on Bela Lugosi's makeup for the Dracula character, his work on the other characters in the film earned him the coveted spot as the makeup designer and artist for Frankenstein. Pierce conceived the scar and the seal, along with the now famous neck bolts (which make sense as conductors of electricity). Frankenstein also had scarred, elongated hands and heavy eyelids. Under the talented hand of Pierce, Boris Karloff endured four hours of makeup each day, including the building up of his head with cotton collodion and gum, and toxic green paint on his face and hands to make him look pale on black-and-white film. After *Frankenstein*, Pierce went on to do the makeup for *The Mummy* (1932) and various Frankenstein sequels. This film helped to define and nurture the horror genre in films, as there have been many iterations of *Frankenstein*, some referred to by that name or other incarnations such as *Jason* and *Freddy*. Its influence on generations of audiences cannot be diminished.

I AM A FUGITIVE FROM A CHAIN GANG (1932)

PRODUCER/DIRECTOR: Mervyn LeRoy, Hal B. Wallis (producer, uncredited)
WRITER(S): Robert E. Burns, Howard J. Green (screenplay), Brown Holmes (screenplay), Sheridan Gibney (uncredited)
CAST: Paul Muni (James Allen), Glenda Farrell (Marie), Helen Vinson (Helen), Noel Francis (Linda), Preston Foster (Pete), Allen Jenkins (Barney Sykes), Berton Churchill (The Judge), Edward Ellis (Bomber Wells), David Landau (The Warden), Hale Hamilton (Rev. Allen)
CINEMATOGRAPHY: Sol Polito
MUSIC: Bernhard Kaun (uncredited)
LENGTH AND RATING: 93 mins; NR

Perhaps one of the most socially conscious films ever made about the prison system and the brutality of incarceration in the United States, *I Am a Fugitive from a Chain Gang*, starring Paul Muni and directed by Mervyn LeRoy, is a stark story about the harsh gulag-like conditions of a southern chain gang, where human beings are treated like chattel, guards are abusive, and life has no worth. It is an important film because of the true story it is based on and the prison reforms it helped to initiate. The film portrays the life and misfortune of Robert Elliott Burns, a World War I veteran who avoids returning to a factory job in New Jersey, leads a transient life traveling across the country looking for work during the Depression, and unknowingly becomes involved in a grocery store robbery with two other destitute men. The robbery nets only $5.80, and Burns is sentenced to six to ten years of hard labor. The movie is based upon his book, *I Am a Fugitive from a Georgia Chain Gang*. The Georgia reference was deliberately omitted so as not to identify the location of his brutish incarceration.

In the movie, Paul Muni portrays James Allen based upon the Robert Burns character. After being sent to the chain gang and suffering its violent indignations, he escapes after several months by having a fellow inmate strike a blow to his leg shackles with a sledgehammer the prisoners use for crushing rock. While taking a bathroom break, he slips his feet out of the shackles and runs into the brush. As the guards and dogs chase him, Allen eludes them by submerging in a stream, breathing air through a hollow reed.

He relocates to Chicago, finds a job at an engineering firm, and works his way up the corporate ladder. He also marries a woman who later turns him in when he asks her for a divorce so that he can be with another woman. Although the people and law enforcement officials of Chicago support him, Allen decides to return to the chain gang in a deal that would require him to do "easy time" as a trustee for several months, and then be released. Upon his return, Georgia officials renege on their promise and Allen is forced to serve the remainder of his term. He escapes again and now is desperately on the lam. In one of the most famous scenes in film history, the end of the movie shows Allen in stark shadow, surreptitiously visiting his girlfriend Helen. She is upset that he hasn't contacted her in the year since his escape. She pleads with him, but he must go. Finally she asks,

"How do you live?"
He replies from the darkness of the shadows:
"I steal."

And then vanishes.

Robert Burns did escape a second time and was found in Newark, New Jersey, whose governor refused to extradite him. Eventually he was pardoned.

This movie, along with the book, created a national scandal over the corrupt and abusive Georgia chain gangs, and served as a catalyst for their eventual demise. It also served as a reference for later films with similar themes, including *The Defiant Ones* (1958), *Cool Hand Luke* (1967), and *O Brother, Where Art Thou* (2000), and for the ABC network series *The Fugitive*.

KING KONG (1933)

PRODUCER/DIRECTOR: Merian C. Cooper, Ernest B. Schoedsack
WRITER(S): Merian C. Cooper (story, uncredited), Edgar Wallace (story, uncredited), James Ashmore Creelman (screenplay), Ruth Rose (screenplay)
CAST: Fay Wray (Ann Darrow), Robert Armstrong (Carl Denham), Bruce Cabot (John "Jack" Driscoll), Frank Reicher (Capt. Englehorn), Sam Hardy (Charles Weston), Noble Johnson (Skull Island nation leader), Steve Clemente (Witch King), James Flavin (Second Mate Briggs)
CINEMATOGRAPHY: Edward Linden, J. O. Taylor, Vernon L. Walker, Kenneth Peach (uncredited)
MUSIC: Max Steiner
LENGTH AND RATING: 100 mins; NR

As both the narrative and featured cinematography attest, *King Kong* is one of the greatest American movies of all time. It is a spectacular story with a literary foundation, as in *Beauty and the Beast*; the hulking giant ape and the beautiful actress Fay Wray, with visual predatory sexual innuendo. She at first invades his habitat on Skull Island, and he then rescues her from sacrifice by an indigenous tribe; he also protects her from being a victim of repeated assaults by other animal predators. Eventually Kong is captured and returned to New York City, where he is relegated to "freak show" status as *KING KONG EIGHTH WONDER OF THE WORLD*. On his opening night, Kong, unnerved by the flash photography and thinking the "explosions" are harming his beloved Ann (Fay Wray), breaks loose from his hardened chrome shackles, finds Ann, and wreaks havoc on New York City. In one of the most enduring apoplectic scenes in movie history, Kong, who has placed Ann on a ledge at the top of the Empire State Building, is attacked by airborne biplane machine gunners (played by co-producers and directors Merian C. Cooper and Ernest B. Schoedsack). Acknowledging his mortal wounds, Kong lifts Ann one last time, gazes at her beauty and gently strokes her, then returns her to the building's ledge. He collapses and falls to the street below. While gazing at the giant ape, a police officer says, "Well, Denham, the airplanes got him." And Denham, played by actor Bruce Cabot, replies, "Oh, no. It wasn't the airplanes. It was beauty killed the beast." The film was an enormous success, breaking box office records and providing greatly needed revenue to the ailing RKO Studios. It was also a technically groundbreaking film notable for its advances in rear screen projection, miniature models, and stop-motion animation sequences, supervised by chief technician Willis O'Brien. The screenplay was written by James Ashmore Creelman and Ruth Rose based on a story by Merian C. Cooper and Edgar Wallace. When the film was first released, some sequences had to be cut due to the 1934 Production Code. These included scaling down from five to three victims of the brontosaurus killing, a giant spider scene, a scene where Kong begins to remove Fay Wray's clothing, and Kong chewing one victim and dropping another from the Empire State Building.

In the heading of his March 3, 1933, *New York Times* review, Mordaunt Hall describes *King Kong* as, "A Fantastic Film in Which a Monstrous Ape Uses Automobiles for Missiles and Climbs a Skyscraper."

There have been many incarnations of *King Kong*, most recently Peter Jackson's 2005 three-hour remake starring Jack Black, Adrian Brody, and Naomi Watts as the Fay Wray character.

IT HAPPENED ONE NIGHT (1934)

PRODUCER/DIRECTOR: Frank Capra (director and producer), Harry Cohn (producer)
WRITER(S): Samuel Hopkins Adams (story, "Night Bus"), Robert Riskin (screenplay)
CAST: Clark Gable (Peter Warne), Claudette Colbert (Ellie Andrews), Walter Connolly (Alexander Andrews), Roscoe Karns (Oscar Shapeley), Jameson Thomas (King Westley), Alan Hale (Danker), Arthur Hoyt (Zeke), Blanche Friderici (Zeke's wife), Charles C. Wilson (Joe Gordon)
CINEMATOGRAPHY: Joseph Walker
MUSIC: Howard Jackson (uncredited), Louis Silvers (uncredited)
LENGTH AND RATING: 105 mins; NR

Frank Capra was a master at capturing the innocence, virtues, and mores of small-town America, celebrating the character of the "little guy" going up against the wealthy. His films were didactic but spoke to the audience, declaring their worth and essence as people when compared to the arrogance of the more affluent. *It Happened One Night* possesses all of the rudiments of classic "screwball" comedy: a brash, spoiled, rich heiress

(Claudette Colbert); a brazen, bold, down-on-his-luck newspaperman (Clark Gable); and a sundry of interesting and peculiar characters. It is indeed a road movie; she is running away from her father to consummate her marriage to a playboy husband whom her dad detests, and he has just been fired from his newspaper for drinking. They both wind up on the same Greyhound bus from Miami to New York. She takes his seat, the last one on the bus, and they are forced to share on the ride. Their chemistry is initially repellant, each with a strong personality, dogmatic and independent.

There are several classic scenes in this film that richly describe the evolving relationship between Peter (Clark Gable) and Ellie (Claudette Colbert). He has taken on the role as her protector, but solely as a mercenary gesture to sell a story about her flight. After they leave the bus, Peter registers them as Mr. and Mrs. in a motel, and as night falls, he strings a clothesline between the twin beds and hangs over it with a blanket, naming the partition the "walls of Jericho," thus protecting Ellie's chastity. In another scene, once Peter has finished arranging Ellie's bed of hay in a deserted barn, she realizes that she is falling in love with him and he tries to hide similar feelings for her. In a very famous hitchhiking scene, Peter eloquently provides Ellie with a treatise on hitchhiking, and when he fails to stop a car she saunters to the side of the road, raises her dress to above her knee, and the next passing car screeches to a halt. The next evening, in another motel, Ellie breaches the walls of Jericho and submissively declares her love and devotion to Peter. After some misdirection and suspenseful distraction, Peter appears on Ellie's wedding day to collect a debt from her father for expenses incurred on their trip, eventually admitting that he loves Ellie. As Ellie's father walks her down the aisle to enter into a loveless marriage with her playboy "husband," he whispers that Peter loves her and has an escape plan ready. When the minister begins reciting the marriage vows she shakes her head "no" and runs away, a "run away bride." Ellie and Peter leave for Michigan, her first marriage is annulled, and the "walls of Jericho" come tumbling down.

The film's romantic theme and "battle of the sexes" one-upmanship gave audiences an escape from the drudgery of life during the Depression. Capra enables his audience to identify with ordinary people as Peter and Ellie encounter characters and situations viewers could ostensibly experience themselves. For example, Peter teaches Ellie how to properly dunk a doughnut. The film was a sleeper hit in 1934 and won Academy Awards in the five categories in which it was nominated: Best Picture, Best Actor (Clark Gable), Best Actress (Claudette Colbert), Best Director (Frank Capra), and Best Adaptation (Robert Riskin). The screenplay was adapted from a *Cosmopolitan* magazine story entitled *Night Bus*, by Samuel Hopkins Adams.

MODERN TIMES (1936)

PRODUCER/DIRECTOR: Charles Chaplin

WRITER(S): Charles Chaplin

CAST: Charles Chaplin (A factory worker), Paulette Goddard (A gamin), Henry Bergman (Cafe proprietor), Tiny Sandford (Big Bill), Chester Conklin (Mechanic), Hank Mann (Burglar), Stanley Blystone (Gamin's father), Al Ernest Garcia (President of the Electro Steel Corp.), Richard Alexander (Cellmate), Cecil Reynolds (Minister)

CINEMATOGRAPHY: Ira H. Morgan, Roland Totheroh

MUSIC: Charles Chaplin

LENGTH AND RATING: 87 mins; NR

Charles Chaplin (as a factory worker). [United Artists/Photofest]

Charlie Chaplin is a revered figure in cinematic history because of his ability to find humor in the pathos of the difficult circumstances that effect ordinary people. He became a global icon as the first actor to attract an international audience. His attire was symbolic of the down-and-out character of "the Tramp," his signature role model. The Tramp was immediately recognizable, with his baggy pants, cut away coat and vest, frayed derby hat, and worn-out shoes. His success as an artist and entertainer provided him with the resources needed to exact complete control over his work, allowing him to produce, direct, write, and score his own movies. In addition, he was a founding member of the United Artists studio along with Douglas Fairbanks, Mary Pickford, and director D. W. Griffith.

During an eighteen-month world tour from 1931 to 1932, chaplin became acutely aware of the poverty, inequality, and suffering in the world. He was also concerned about the advance of technology and its impact upon the working class as a means toward unemployment. He publicly expressed his concern that machinery should benefit humanity and not result in massive layoffs. Another issue that touched Chaplin was the use of addictive drugs.

In *Modern Times*, the Tramp symbolizes the working class thrown into a world gone berserk with technology and efficiency. We see him as a mechanic armed with a wrench in each hand, tightening the giant gears in a factory assembly line. Even when he takes a break, his body gyrates with the lasting effects of the rhythm of his job. As the president of the company monitors the workplace on a movie screen, the Tramp attempts to try a newfangled invention that would eliminate the lunch break and feed workers on the job. Of course, the Tramp is selected as the subject, and in a hilarious sequence Chaplin becomes a victim of the machine as it force-feeds him everything but his lunch. In another sequence, he is consumed by the machine and run through its gears, only to be released when the gears are placed in reverse. Eventually, the Tramp is driven crazy by the machine and he runs around the factory trying to tighten the buttons on the rear end of a woman and on the bosom of another female factory worker.

After being released from a sanitarium and declared "cured," the Tramp inadvertently picks up a red warning flag that has fallen from a construction vehicle. He is then mistakenly identified as the leader of a communist party demonstration and is hauled off to jail. In jail, an inmate, in an effort to avoid detection of his cocaine, stores the white powder in a saltshaker. Of course, the Tramp uses it liberally on his food and as a result cannot walk in step back to his cell.

The film also addresses the social issues of poverty, unemployment, and the harshness of life in post-Depression America. In a parallel story line, which eventually coincides with the Tramp, a young woman, played by Paulette Goddard, must steal bread to feed her younger sisters and unemployed father. When her father is tragically shot in a riot, the child welfare authorities take her sisters away but she manages to escape. After release from prison on a letter of recommendation from the warden, the Tramp is unsuccessful at finding work and longs to return to a life of carefree incarceration. He meets the young woman as she is pursued by police for stealing a loaf of bread and pretends that he is the thief. In the end, though, the police arrest the girl. The Tramp then goes into a restaurant and orders a fine meal, but refuses to pay. He is subsequently arrested and winds up in the same paddy wagon as the young lady. The wagon swerves, they fall out, and he joins her in an escape.

As the two sit on a curb in a suburban community, they see a typical family and dream about how it would be if they shared that same good fortune. Throughout *Modern Times* there are symbolic metaphors that speak to the misfortune of others, the turbulence of the times with its strikes and riots, and the frantic pursuit to achieve the American dream. This film demonstrates Chaplin's commitment to articulating his concern over the ills of society. He couches those concerns on a canvas of humor while displaying a satirical view of the circumstances. The film remains a timely reminder in the modern age of economic turmoil, with surging energy prices, failing banks, rampant outsourcing, and drained pension funds. *Modern Times* offers a satirical view of society's ills, and while we laugh at the Tramp's misadventures, we pull aside the veil of humor to see that those substantive societal issues of 1936 are still with us today.

SNOW WHITE AND THE SEVEN DWARFS (1937)

PRODUCER/DIRECTOR: David Hand (director), Walt Disney (producer, uncredited)

WRITER(S): Brothers Grimm (fairy tale), Ted Sears (story adaptation), Richard Creedon (story adaptation), Otto Englander (story adaptation), Dick Rickard (story adaptation), Earl Hurd (story adaptation), Merrill De Maris (story adaptation), Dorothy Ann Blank (story adaptation), Webb Smith (story adaptation)

CAST: Roy Atwell (Doc, voice, uncredited), Stuart Buchanan (Huntsman, voice, uncredited), Adriana Caselotti (Snow White, voice, uncredited), Eddie Collins (Dopey, voice, uncredited), Pinto Colvig (Sleepy/Grumpy, voice, uncredited), Marion Darlington (Bird Sounds and Warbling, voice, uncredited), Billy Gilbert (Sneezy, voice, uncredited), Otis Harlan (Happy, voice, uncredited), Lucille La Verne (Queen/Witch, voice, uncredited), James MacDonald (Yodeling Man, voice, uncredited)

CINEMATOGRAPHY: Maxwell Morgan

MUSIC: Frank Churchill, Leigh Harline, Paul J. Smith

LENGTH AND RATING: 83 mins; NR

Theatrical film animation holds a unique place in cinematic history and has been sustained as part of entertainment culture in the movies, on television, and across the Internet. One of the earliest pioneers was Max Fleischer of the Fleischer Studio, who used his creativity and technical virtuosity to do hybrid animation, integrating live action with animation. One of the most enduring of Fleischer's cartoon characters was Betty Boop.

Walt Disney learned from Fleischer about the branding of a particular animated character, which Fleischer had done so successfully with Betty Boop, and he also was taught a harsh lesson about protecting his intellectual property when one of his earliest cartoon characters, Oswald the Rabbit, was stolen from him. Oswald may have been the precursor to Mickey Mouse (Mickey has round ears). The rabbit also proved to be the first in the juggernaut of merchandised Disney characters. In an ironic twist of fate, Walt Disney reacquired the rights to Oswald in 2006. Disney, along with his brother Roy, started their studio in 1923, and in 1928, with the release of *Steamboat Willie*, the first talking animated movie, the Mickey Mouse character was introduced. It was a

The Seven Dwarfs and Snow White. [Walt Disney/Photofest]

timely introduction, as down-on-their-luck Depression-era audiences immediately embraced the cute mouse.

Because Disney spent almost four years producing *Snow White*, his efforts to create the first animated color feature film were mocked by the industry. The film cost $1.7 million to produce and was distributed by RKO Studios. The story was an adaptation of the classic fairy tale by the Brothers Grimm, and Disney took liberties to make it less frightening for children. Although there are moments in the film when Snow White is deeply afraid of her surroundings and feels threatened by the creatures in the forest, Disney brilliantly turns that fear into sheer enjoyment. The positive pro-social message is enhanced by the deft composition of the musical score and Snow White singing, "Whistle While You Work" while the Dwarfs march to "Heigh-ho, heigh-ho, it's off to work we go." In an innovative stylistic departure, Disney gives each of the dwarfs his own personality that is cultivated through movement, voice, and dialogue. Indeed, this animated feature integrates human characters into the substance of the story, setting the tone and the image of subsequent animated feature-length films.

Although some critics argue that because of Disney's resounding commercial success, along with his modernist sentimentality, his films have little cultural significance. However, Walt Disney's films do promote American idealism and the ethics of discipline and resourcefulness to overcome difficult odds. He created a world of fantasy, allowing animals to talk and inanimate objects to be personified with human qualities, thus creating a canvas of virtues nurtured by things, animals and people that offer pragmatic lessons for life. His films, especially *Snow White*, offered Depression-era audiences a respite via themes that imbued them with hope and resilience. His art was woven into the fabric of popular culture, and audiences had ready access to it within the mainstream of entertainment. Disney was a populist artist, and his audience continues to be sustained by the virtues he espoused.

2 A Rumble to War, 1939–1942

By 1939, the world had felt the iron fist of Hitler, and the Jews of Germany were being persecuted and turned away from safe haven. The Molotov-Ribbentrop Pact, signed by Germany and Russia, articulated how the two countries would divide Eastern Europe among themselves. September 1939 was a busy month, with the Nazis attacking Poland and subsequently France, Austria, and the United Kingdom, which declared war on Germany while the United States remained neutral. Indeed, Great Britain, under the leadership of Prime Minister Neville Chamberlain, attempted to appease Hitler with the Munich Agreement, which he broke by invading Czechoslovakia.

But 1939 also contained a rich treasure of American films. These include *Gone with the Wind, Stagecoach*, and *The Wizard of Oz*. While these films were conceived and began production prior to the upheaval of World War II, they were nevertheless viewed by American audiences within the context of troubling times.

GONE WITH THE WIND (1939)

PRODUCER/DIRECTOR: Victor Fleming (director), David O. Selznick (producer)

WRITER(S): Margaret Mitchell (novel), Sidney Howard (screenplay)

CAST: Clark Gable (Rhett Butler), Vivien Leigh (Scarlett O'Hara), Leslie Howard (Ashley Wilkes), Olivia de Havilland (Melanie Hamilton), Thomas Mitchell (Gerald O'Hara), Barbara O'Neil (Ellen O'Hara), Evelyn Keyes (Suellen O'Hara), Ann Rutherford (Carreen O'Hara), George Reeves (Brent Tarleton), Fred Crane (Stuart Tarleton), Hattie McDaniel (Mammy), Oscar Polk (Pork), Butterfly McQueen (Prissy), Victor Jory (Jonas Wilkerson), Everett Brown (Big Sam)

CINEMATOGRAPHY: Ernest Haller, Lee Garmes (uncredited)

MUSIC: Max Steiner

LENGTH AND RATING: 226 mins (copyright length) | USA: 238 mins (restored DVD version); NR

Margaret Mitchell, who wrote the novel *Gone with the Wind*, was somewhat like her character Scarlett O'Hara—independent and free-spirited. Growing up in Atlanta, Mitchell heard stories of wizened Confederate veterans and their exploits during the Civil War. She left college in 1920, after her mother died, to take care of her family, and scandalized Atlanta society by dancing provocatively with a young man at her debutante ball. She was also pursued by a number of men, marrying one and later divorcing to marry another. After her book was published and became a best seller, she wrote about upheaval, specifically how some people survive while others don't, and the qualities and characteristics of those who manage to triumph, a quality she described as "gumption."

> So I wrote about the people who had gumption and the people who didn't (www.gwtw.org/margaretmitchell.html).

In his December 20, 1939, *New York Times* review of *Gone with the Wind* the movie, Frank Nugent described the sheer spectacle of the film as pure narrative rather than great drama. He praised the film as an unstinting version of the 1,037-page novel; indeed, the movie matched the book almost scene by scene. Nugent noted that all of the actors appeared to be embodiments of the characters in the novel, as though Mitchell had written their parts with them in mind.

As a film, *Gone with the Wind* demonstrates the value of popular epic cinema based on a beloved novel. Like D. W. Griffith's *Birth of a Nation*, it addresses the distinctive culture of the South, with its polite customs and social milieu that resonate in the fiery ashes of tragic defeat and a harsh resurrection. The film has all the qualities of a blockbuster: a great cast, beautiful costumes, realistic sets, and the majesty of a bygone era beautifully filmed in Technicolor and accompanied by a resounding Max Steiner score.

In 1936, the film's producer, David O. Selznick, paid Mitchell fifty thousand dollars for the film rights to her book—a very generous sum for a first time author with a single publication. The movie cost $4 million and is estimated to have earned nearly $200 million. Five directors were associated with the film: Sam Wood, George Cukor, William Cameron Menzies, B. Reeves (Breezy) Eason, and Victor Fleming, although Fleming received the only credit (he directed forty-five percent of the film). About five percent of the final version was directed by Cukor, but he left because he wasn't pleased with the screenplay by Sidney Howard. After Fleming left the set due to exhaustion, Wood assumed the role of director for a short time. Both Menzies and Wood were credited with directing fifteen percent of the film, while Eason directed about two percent.

Every frame of *Gone with the Wind* evokes a timeless vision of the Old South, colored by its vivid depiction of ladies and gentlemen dressed in the best silk and lace while mingling in the lavish surroundings of their plantations. It's also about a love for the land and its vast stores of nature that provide a treasure of memories for the fantasy world of Tara. The scenes of devastation, such as the burning of Atlanta, were unfortunate harbingers of the terror to come, with cities like London burned by Nazi bombs.

The movie addresses the enduring themes of struggle and survival during the Civil War, which became paramount in Europe during World War II. It is also a love story between people and with a way of life that had to end, including the deep connection to the land they cherished. But even more than a testimony to overcoming the hardships of civil war and the romantic interludes of the privileged, *Gone with the Wind* is an American film about America, its past, its people, its history, and its culture. It is a timeless story of jealously, love, greed, and survival that unfolds during a period of American history that was romanticized in Mitchell's novel. The film, as historical

From Dorothy's ruby red shoes, worn by the deceased Wicked Witch of the East and visualized in full three-strip Technicolor, to the soulful, floppy, comedic melody of the Scarecrow's (Ray Bolger) "If I Only Had a Brain"...

I could wile away the hours, Conferrin' with the flowers
Consultin' with the rain, And my head I'd be scratchin'
While my thoughts were busy hatchin', If I only had a brain...

this film is an artistic representation of a great American story, a fantasy with themes children and adults understand, loveable characters, and a clear delineation between good and evil. The film was adapted from L. Frank Baum's 1900 book *The Wonderful Wizard of Oz*. It sold millions of copies and was followed by thirteen subsequent *Oz* books (similar to the success of *Harry Potter*). It also was a musical, opening at the Grand Opera House in 1902 and in 1903 on New York City's Broadway at the Majestic Theatre. The first full-length silent feature of *The Wizard of Oz* was released in 1925 by Chadwick Pictures and featured comedian Oliver Hardy (of the famous comedy duo Laurel and Hardy) as the Tin Woodsman. Through the years there have been other references in films and Broadway adaptations: *The Wiz* (1978) and the stage play *Wicked* (2003), which is based on Gregory Maguire's 1995 novel *Wicked: The Life and Times of the Wicked Witch of the West*.

The story is about a lonely orphan girl, Dorothy Gale (Judy Garland), who lives with her loving Auntie Em (Clara Blandick) and Uncle Henry (Charley Grapewin) on a farm in a desolate part of Kansas. Her most prized possession and best friend is her little dog, Toto. But that relationship is threatened when the neighborhood bully and the town's richest resident, Miss Almira Gulch (Margaret Hamilton), who claims to have

Ray Bolger (as the Scarecrow), Jack Haley (as the Tin Man), Judy Garland (as Dorothy), Bert Lahr (as the Cowardly Lion). [Photofest]

been bitten by Toto, appears with a court order to remove Toto to the sheriff and have him destroyed. This event, which would pull at the heartstrings of any child or adult, is the narrative arc of the film and the catalyst for all of the subsequent action.

Acquiescing to Gulch's demands, Auntie Em and Uncle Henry reluctantly hand over Toto while Dorothy runs to her room and cries. However, as Miss Gulch rides away on her bicycle, Toto escapes from the basket mounted in the rear and returns to Dorothy. As Toto jumps into her room through an open window, Dorothy makes the decision to pack her suitcase and run away. After being on the road only a short time, Dorothy decides to return home, but as she turns back a powerful tornado rips through the area. She reaches the house and shouts for the underground cellar door to be opened but her calls go unheeded.

From the drab black-and-white landscape in Kansas, the scene shifts to the vibrant Technicolor images of Oz, where Dorothy is seen in her blue-and-white dress, surrounded by richly colored flowers and a spiraling yellow brick walkway. Realizing that she has been transported to a strange yet beautiful fairy-tale land, she utters one of the most famous lines in film:

Toto, I've a feeling we're not in Kansas anymore. We must be over the rainbow.

Of course, most of the "imaginary" characters she meets are transposed from the adults she has known in Kansas. The ranch's hired hands, Hunk, Hickory, and Zeke, respectively morph into Scarecrow (Ray Bolger), Tin Man (Jack Haley), and the Cowardly Lion (Bert Lahr). Miss Almira Gulch becomes the Wicked Witch of the West, and Professor Marvel (Frank Morgan) turns into the Wizard and is the charlatan Dorothy meets on the road who convinces her to return home.

While there is the conflict between the good and bad witches, MGM's *The Wizard of Oz* also provides a leitmotif in the beloved lyrics to songs like "Somewhere Over the Rainbow," written by E. Y. "Yip" Harburg. He was an avowed socialist who may have integrated some of his political doctrine into the narrative of the film, as he did in his Depression-era hit song, "Brother Can You Spare a Dime?" Harburg was an ardent supporter of President Roosevelt's New Deal, and said the Emerald City represented the New Deal: Just as the Wizard restored faith in Dorothy's companions, Roosevelt's New Deal restored America's faith in the country. Although Harburg received credit as the lyricist for the film and along with songwriter Harold Arlen won an Academy Award for best original song, his contribution to the film was far greater. As the final script editor, Yip Harburg wrote a great deal of the dialogue, the prologue to the songs, and even visualized some of the routines, although he never received a screenwriting credit.

There has been a great deal of speculation about the symbolism in the film. Some scholars have noted that the theme of returning home reflects America's turn toward isolationism in lieu of facing the rise of totalitarianism and the turbulence in Europe. To that end, democracy is represented by the Good Witch of the North and the Wizard of Oz while totalitarianism is symbolized by the Wicked Witch of the East and the Wicked Witch of the West.

Speculation about the film's symbolism abounds, but the single constant of truth is that *The Wizard of Oz* was an artistic and cultural tour de force that transported its audience to a fantasy world and provided both distraction and comfort while making Judy Garland a star. It is an icon in America's cultural milieu, as Frank Nugent confirmed in his August 18, 1939, *New York Times* review:

> Not since Disney's *Snow White* has anything quite so fantastic succeeded half so well. A fairybook tale has been told in a fairybook style with witches, goblins, pixies, and other wondrous things drawn in the brightest colors and set cavorting to a merry little score.

THE GRAPES OF WRATH (1940)

PRODUCER/DIRECTOR: John Ford (director), (producer)
WRITER(S): Nunnally Johnson (screenplay), John Steinbeck (novel)
CAST: Henry Fonda (Tom Joad), Jane Darwell (Ma Joad), John Carradine (Casy), Charley Grapewin (Grandpa), Dorris Bowdon (Rosasharn), Russell Simpson (Pa Joad), O. Z. Whitehead (Al), John Qualen (Muley), Eddie Quillan (Connie), Zeffie Tilbury (Grandma)
CINEMATOGRAPHY: Gregg Toland
MUSIC: Alfred Newman (musical director)
LENGTH AND RATING: 128 min; NR

Adapted for film from the novel by John Steinbeck, *The Grapes of Wrath* is a classic that captures the essence of the struggle between the harsh reality of living off a hostile land and losing one's livelihood due to the greed of big business and the giant farming interests. Placed within the time frame of the Depression and the eight-year drought of the 1930s known as the Dust Bowl, the film juxtaposes a number of compelling themes. The characters offer rich portrayals that personify the essence of the narrative, illustrating the virtues and hardships of a migratory life. The Joads were tenant farmers working the hardscrabble land in the Oklahoma Dust Bowl. Condemned to be on the road searching for work as itinerant farm laborers, they are thrust into the maelstrom of the downtrodden, competing for the crumbs thousands of other unemployed migrants scrambled for. Amidst hardship and suffering and shattered hope for the American dream, they are united by the bonds of family and the resolute leadership and tenacity of their matriarch, Ma Joad, played by Jane Darwell. She reigns with dignity and fortitude, creating a cultural icon of an enduring woman undeterred by the niceties of her sex but determined to keep her family alive. Her son, Tom Joad (Henry Fonda), has been recently released from a four-year prison sentence for murder, and has an edge that matches the rubble of their lives. Although he is a cynic and feels persecuted by the harshness of his life, Tom sustains his pride and dignity in the face of overwhelming adversity and pledges his life's work toward social reform.

This film has a cultural legacy sustained by a reversal of roles that defines a woman as the personification of courage and leadership. As she contemplates leaving her home forever, Ma Joad must release herself from the feminine ritual of storing keepsakes for a secret rendezvous. Wistfully holding up a pair of earrings, she's lost for a moment in the reverie of another time and place. Moments later, however, she returns to reality, dismissing those longings and announcing she's ready to leave. As Ma Joad, she transforms the heritage of family leadership from patriarchy to matriarchy, shattering the myths of feminine guile and weakness. At the close of the film, she articulates her enduring strength and fortitude by uttering words that are both profound and relics of masculinity: "Scared, ha! I ain't never gonna be scared no more. A woman can change better 'n a man. A man lives, sorta, well, in jerks. With a woman, it's all in one flow, like a stream." She speaks of the courage and determination of the "people" and how they can never be wiped out. With those words, Ma Joad becomes a majestic figure, a woman of courage who spurns the ideals of the rich and remains undeterred by fear.

When the movie was released, in 1940, the world was on the fringe of another global war. Great Britain had run out of cash to buy arms, and under Franklin Roosevelt the Lend & Lease Act was passed, allowing the president the freedom to ostensibly give away arms to any country, even though the legislation was designed to aid Britain. It was a time of anxiety for America, as the tensions between Germany, the United States, and Japan escalated. *The Grapes of Wrath* and its theme of endurance in the face of adversity was indeed an inspiration to American audiences. Ma Joad foreshadowed the role women would play in the war effort by working factory jobs formerly held by men. She became "Rosie the Riveter," leaving behind those cherished earrings for the oil and grime of industry.

The film was nominated for seven Academy Awards and won two: Best Supporting Actress for Jane Darwell (Ma Joad) and Best Director for John Ford. It was popular with pre-World War II Hollywood for its left-leaning ideology that promoted a theme of social reform. Cinematographer Gregg Toland used vivid black-and-white photography to create monochrome textures, painting on a canvas of realism recorded in a newsreel fashion. Toland later gained substantial credits, including *Wuthering Heights* (1939) and *Citizen Kane* (1941).

Alfred Newman, who did the musical score, used haunting variations of "Red River Valley" to foster a harmonic of musical poignancy that added to the emotional tenor of the film. Prior to scoring *The Grapes of Wrath*, Newman's film credits included *Prisoner of Zenda, Beau Geste, Gunga Din*, and *The Hunchback of Notre Dame* (1939).

Frank S. Nugent's review of the film in the January 25, 1940, *New York Times* referred to it as a "screen classic," one of "cinema's masterworks," and a film that would be remembered not just at the end of the year it was released "...but whenever great motion pictures are mentioned." Nugent praises Ford's direction as having the images "...burned indelible into memory by a director, a camera, and a cast." Nugent goes on to say that "...Direction, when it is as brilliant as Mr. Ford's has been, is easy to recognize, but impossible to describe." He speaks of the "fidelity to a book's spirit" and screenwriter Nunnally Johnson's (*The Three Faces of Eve*, 1957) use of Steinbeck's dialogue in the movie. As for the actors, Nugent states, "...still stranger has been the almost incredible rightness of the film's casting." He notes that Henry Fonda (Tom Joad) and Jane Darwell (Ma Joad) are exactly the way readers of the novel pictured them, and he refers to many of the actors as "...Hollywood's most typical people in untypical roles." He concludes his review with "What we've been trying to say is that *The Grapes of Wrath* is just about as good as any picture has a right to be" (http://www.movies.nytimes.com).

🎥 *CITIZEN KANE* (1941)

PRODUCER/DIRECTOR: Orson Welles

WRITER(S): Herman J. Mankiewicz (screenplay) and Orson Welles (screenplay)

CAST: Joseph Cotten (Jedediah Leland), Dorothy Comingore (Susan Alexander Kane), Agnes Moorehead (Mary Kane), Orson Welles (Charles Foster Kane), Ruth Warrick (Emily Monroe Norton Kane), Ray Collins (James W. Gettys), Erskine Sanford (Herbert Carter), Everett Sloane (Mr. Bernstein), William Alland (Jerry Thompson), Paul Stewart (Raymond), George Coulouris (Walter Parks Thatcher)

CINEMATOGRAPHY: Gregg Toland

MUSIC: Bernard Herrmann

LENGTH AND RATING: 119 min; NR

Recognized as one of the greatest films ever produced, Orson Welles' *Citizen Kane* is a monument to the art of film and its use as a tool in developing an unfolding narrative. Orson Welles demonstrated his genius with the October 30, 1938, Mercury Theatre on the Air radio broadcast of an adaptation of the H. G. Wells novel *War of the Worlds*, and panic ensued as some listeners believed there indeed was an invasion from Mars. Many of the radio performers from Welles' ensemble group of actors at the Mercury Theatre made their screen acting debuts in *Citizen Kane*, including Joseph Cotton, Agnes Moorehead, Everett Sloane, and Paul Stewart.

In the summer of 1939, Welles signed a two-picture contract with RKO. His intention was to make a screen version of Joseph Conrad's *Heart of Darkness*, but the picture was deemed too costly to produce. When Welles visited his friend Herman Mankiewicz, former drama critic at *The New Yorker*, notorious alcoholic, and noted screenwriter of *Gentlemen Prefer Blondes* and *The Pride of the Yankees*, he mentioned doing a film about a larger-than-life American figure. Soon, they both agreed to use a prominent public figure known by Mankiewicz and known to Welles by reputation, William Randolph Hearst, and Welles commissioned Mankiewicz to write the script. When the script was delivered in April 1940, it was far too biographical and potentially libelous, and as a result Welles removed much of that focused detail. Although there were many similarities between Charles Foster Kane and William Randolph Hearst, one of the most glaring was the extravagance of their shared architectural vision: Kane's fictional Xanadu and Hearst's palatial San Simeon.

In their defense, Welles and Mankiewicz noted that there was very little resemblance between Kane's mistress, the untalented fictional Susan Alexander, and Hearst's real-life mistress, screen star and comedienne Marion Davies. But, like Kane, Hearst made every effort to advance Davies's career, including founding Cosmopolitan Pictures to promote film projects for her. And there were other similarities between the two: they were blonde, enjoyed doing jigsaw puzzles, and liked to drink.

In playing the role of Charles Foster Kane, Welles chose not to mimic the behavioral characterizations of Hearst, but he does fill the screen just as Hearst dominated newspaper publishing. Indeed, at the beginning of the film, as a newsreel tells the tale of Kane's life, the announcer's voice-over says that he was not only, "the greatest newspaper tycoon of this or any other generation,…more newsworthy than the names in his own headlines."

In an effort to ameliorate any negative reaction from the critics, Welles arranged screenings for the two most widely read gossip columnists in the nation, Hedda Hopper

Orson Welles (as Charles Foster Kane). [RKO Radio Pictures Inc./Photofest]

and Louella Parsons. Hopper called the film "an impudent, murderous trick," and Louella Parsons mounted an insidious campaign to discredit Welles and limit the distribution of the film. Many prominent and influential people were susceptible to siding with Hearst including Nelson Rockefeller, whose family had a significant investment in RKO and controlled Radio City Music Hall, where *Citizen Kane* was to be premiered. Other Hollywood moguls, including L. B. Mayer and Jack Warner, feared retribution if they were to book the film. After *Variety* reported that RKO's latest theatrical release, *Kitty Foyle*, had been eliminated from all Hearst newspapers, the odds that *Citizen Kane* would not be released were quoted at two to one. Efforts were made to implicate Welles in different sorts of illicit activities, sexual liaisons with a minor. As he was lecturing in Pittsburgh, a detective cautioned him about returning to his hotel room because a fourteen-year-old girl had been planted in his closet and two photographers were waiting for him to enter.

After the film opened to unanimous rave reviews with critics using language like "best picture," "most cinematically exciting motion picture," and "greatest creation," the Hearst papers did not take any overt action. Instead they remained silent without any coverage of the film. Although there has been a great deal of speculation about how William Randolph Hearst may have used his influence to hurt the film at the box office, others, including critics and biographers, note that *Citizen Kane*'s narrative style and unique production techniques made it difficult for traditional audiences to follow the story.

Welles was brilliant as the director, star, and producer, all at the age of twenty-five. As a student of film, Welles adapted the cinematic techniques he saw in other films, such as *Rebecca* (1940), *Stagecoach*, and *His Girl Friday (1940)*. He was fortunate to have Gregg Toland as his cinematographer, who was on loan to RKO for *Citizen Kane* from Samuel Goldwyn Productions. His experience with some of the most creative and demanding directors of the time (Karl Freund, William Wyler, Howard Hawks, John Ford) made Gregg Toland a master of technique of the deep focus and the mise-en-scene. Welles was an eager student who soaked up all the knowledge but demanded that Toland go beyond the limits he had set before. His stylistic use of the subjective camera, unconventional lighting, deep focus, low angle shot, depth of field, flashbacks, and overlapping sound were integrated as visual and aural metaphors in the film. It received nine Oscar nominations and won only one for best original screenplay, which went to Welles and Herman J. Mankiewicz. *Citizen Kane* is a remarkable portrait of power and indulgence told on a revealing cinematic canvas that enables the audience to be sustained not only by the strength of the word but also by the command of the picture. It is indeed an iconic film of the twentieth century.

CASABLANCA (1942)

PRODUCER/DIRECTOR: Michael Curtiz (director), Hal B. Wallis (producer), Jack L. Warner (executive producer)

WRITER(S): Murray Burnett and Joan Alison (play); Julius J. Epstein, Philip G. Epstein, and Howard Koch (screenplay)

CAST: Humphrey Bogart (Rick Blaine), Ingrid Bergman (Ilsa Lund), Paul Henreid (Victor Laszlo), Claude Rains (Captain Renault), Conrad Veidt (Major Strasser), Sydney Greenstreet (Signor Ferrari), Peter Lorre (Ugarte), S. Z. Sakall (Carl), Madeleine LeBeau (Yvonne), Dooley Wilson (Sam)

CINEMATOGRAPHY: Arthur Edeson
MUSIC: Max Steiner
LENGTH AND RATING: 102 min; NR

Casablanca has defied age to become a timeless epic that appeals to later generations of fans. It's a story of political intrigue, sacrifice, love, and the squalor of life. It features enduring characters who are able to maintain and at time compromise their values in a time of war. Much of the mythology of the film can be attributed to the classic writing of twin brothers Julius and Philip Epstein and Howard Koch, who shared an Oscar for their screenplay. Another element is the studio production nature of the film (it was shot entirely in a studio except for a sequence filmed at the Van Nuys airport) and the absence of a completed script. There are also the memorable characterizations of Humphrey Bogart as Rick, Ingrid Bergman as Ilsa, Claude Rains as the corrupt Vichy official Captain Renault, and Peter Lorre as the sleazy petty crook Guillermo Ugarte, who in an effort to strike it big arranges to have two German couriers killed in order to obtain two priceless letters of transit that would allow the bearers to travel freely throughout Nazi-occupied Europe. During a manhunt by the police, under the leadership of Captain Renault, Ugarte is killed and the letters of transit happen to not be in his possession. He had entrusted the precious letters to Rick, explaining that although Rick despised him, he was the only person in Casablanca he could trust.

Humphrey Bogart, Claude Rains, Paul Henreid, and Ingrid Bergman. [Warner Bros. Pictures/ Photofest]

Casablanca is also a modern love story about the interrupted romance between Rick and Ilsa. They meet in Paris and fall in love; Ilsa believes that her husband, Victor Laszlo (Paul Henreid), a wanted resistance fighter, has been killed by the Nazis. When her husband returns alive, Ilsa abruptly forsakes Rick and returns to Victor, leaving Rick to nurse his lovelorn wounds. They meet again in Casablanca, with Ilsa desperate to obtain the letters of transit for Victor's safe passage. It is a story of conflict, resurging emotion, pride, nationalism, and virtue.

The movie is based on Murray Burnett and Joan Alison's un-produced play *Everybody Comes to Rick's*. Warner Brothers paid $20,000 for the rights, changed the name to *Casablanca*, and shot it in a studio in two-and-a-half months at a cost of $950,000.

All of the writing for *Casablanca* was the collaboration of the unique talents of Julius and Philip Epstein and Howard Koch. Reminiscing about his work on *Casablanca*, Julius Epstein remarked that the screenplay contained, "more corn than in the states of Kansas and Iowa combined. But when corn works there's nothing better."

One of the most famous lines in the movie, "here's looking at you," was not written in any screenplay drafts but is attributed to the poker lessons Bogart gave to Bergman in between takes. Also, the last line was written by the creative force behind the film, producer Hal Wallis. After shooting ended, Bogart returned to utter this famous line: "Louis, I think this is the beginning of a beautiful friendship." Other lines from the film that have become integrated into the vernacular are: "Round up the usual suspects," "we'll always have Paris," and the often misquoted line, "play it again Sam," which in fact was never uttered in the film. Instead the lines read:

Rick: You played it for her, you can play it for me. Play it!
Ilsa: Play it Sam. Play "As Time Goes By."

The line, "play it again Sam," appears in the Marx Brothers film, *A Night in Casablanca* (1946). The song "As Time Goes By" was written by Herman Hupfeld and made its debut in the 1931 show *Everybody's Welcome*. Interestingly, Dooley Wilson, who played Sam, was a professional drummer and could not play the piano and thus had to fake it.

The director of *Casablanca*, Michael Curtiz, was a Hungarian native who moved to the United States in 1926 and joined Warner Brothers. He was nominated and received an Academy Award for Best Director in 1943. The film was rushed to release on November 26, 1942, in New York to coincide with the Allied invasion of Casablanca on November 8, but the official release date was 1943 because it did not play in Los Angeles until January of that year. Therefore, it was placed in competition for an Academy Award in 1943. In addition to Oscars for Best Director and Best Screenplay, *Casablanca* won Best Picture for producer Hal B. Wallis.

Casablanca has become one of the most beloved films of all time thanks to its timeless themes of love, manhood, romance, and courage. The lead characters are steeped in the morass of sinister personalities, but their love remains eternal in the frenzy of war. And while they yearn for the past and its idyllic fantasy ("we'll always have Paris") they must yield to the realities of war and the challenges and responsibilities they face. By its very nature, true love can be fraught with disappointment, yet even as they exit to go their separate ways, the audience knows that Rick and Ilsa's love will endure...forever.

3 Boom and Bust: The Films of Post-War America, 1946–1947

For the United States, transitioning from a war footing to a peace-time economy was a harsh reality. In addition to the nearly twelve million soldiers returning from war and seeking employment, there were some ten million people who had staffed the factories, churning out the materiels needed for fighting, and who now had to be assimilated into America's postwar economy. During the war, California saw enormous growth as people migrated there for employment in the burgeoning shipbuilding yards. In 1936, Moore's Drydock in Oakland, California, had 600 employees; that number grew to 35,000 by 1944. A company that didn't even exist in 1940, Kaiser Shipyards of Richmond, California, employed 100,000 people by 1943 and produced 747 ships in the four shipyards. And there was a huge influx of African Americans moving to California for these jobs because President Roosevelt had outlawed racial discrimination in wartime factory plants. In addition, there was labor unrest, strikes, and demonstrations for more housing.

But, with the end of the war came an abundance of manufacturing which led to a rise in the consumer culture. Some products, such as the suntan lotion produced for the soldiers, were made available to the public, along with Tide laundry detergent, which could be used to wash the bikini bathing suit, which was introduced after the war. And when Americans wanted to be entertained, they could turn to the new comedy team of Dean Martin and Jerry Lewis.

Fear also gripped the nation as the cold war and communism created a frenzy called the Red Scare. In 1945, the Special Committee on Un-American Activites became a permanent investigating committee and the name was changed to the House Un-American Activities Committee (HUAC). In 1947, the committee focused its attention on the communist infiltration of the Hollywood film industry and ten writers and directors were subpoenaed to testify. These individuals were later known as the "Hollywood Ten" and included some of the prominent names in the industry, including Dalton Trumbo, Albert Maltz, Edward Dmytryk, John Howard Lawson, Ring Lardner Jr., Elia Kazan, and Adrian Scott. Those who refused to testify and implicate their friends and colleagues as communists were held in contempt and sentenced to between six- and twelve-month prison terms and blackballed by the Hollywood studio community. Interestingly, two principals responsible for bringing the movie *Crossfire* (1947), a film about anti-Semitism, to the screen, director Edward Dmytryk and producer Adrian Scott, were implicated. For Dmytryk, who testified shortly after being released from a six-month prison term, revealing the names of communists was a moral obligation and he was never forgiven by many of his friends. In fact, Adrian Scott was named by Dmytryk and blacklisted. Another cooperative witness, director Elia Kazan, who directed *Gentleman's Agreement*, was condemned by many in the industry. Indeed, in 1999, when the Academy of Motion Picture Arts and Sciences honored Kazan with the distinction of a lifetime achievement award, his prior actions were still controversial enough that many in the audience refused to stand or applaud his acknowledgement.

Both *Crossfire* and *Gentleman's Agreement* were seminal films addressing racial bigotry in the form of anti-Semitism. They were controversial and met with resistance at their respective studios, RKO Radio Pictures and Twentieth Century Fox, and within the Hollywood Jewish community. The three other films discussed in this chapter, *The Best Years of Our Lives*, *It's A Wonderful Life*, and *My Darling Clementine*, all released in 1946, resonate with the themes of alienation, fear, greed, loss of innocence, and preserving civilization. From three returning World War II veterans trying to fit in to the once familiar routine of their hometown, to the greed of a ruthless banker that nearly drives a faithful soul to suicide, to the heroism of a man attempting to tame the wild frontier, these films portrayed the human spirit and endurance required to overcome the most difficult of life's challenges.

THE BEST YEARS OF OUR LIVES (1946)

PRODUCER/DIRECTOR: William Wyler (director), Samuel Goldwyn (producer)
WRITER(S): MacKinlay Kantor (novel), Robert E. Sherwood (writer)
CAST: Myrna Loy (Milly Stephenson), Fredric March (Al Stephenson), Dana Andrews (Fred Derry), Teresa Wright (Peggy Stephenson), Virginia Mayo (Marie Derry), Cathy O'Donnell (Wilma Cameron), Hoagy Carmichael (Butch Engle), Harold Russell (Homer Parrish), Gladys George (Hortense Derry), Roman Bohnen (Pat Derry)
CINEMATOGRAPHY: Gregg Toland
MUSIC: Hugo Friedhofer
LENGTH AND RATING: 172 min; NR

This film was released in 1946, juxtaposing the difficulty of World War II veterans returning home and the new postwar political and economic realities in the United States. The film is based on Mackinlay Kantor's narrative poem "Glory for Me." He was a Pulitzer Prize-winning author who wrote over forty books and several screenplays. The screenplay was written by Robert E. Sherwood, who won an Academy Award for best adapted screenplay.

The narrative focuses on three returning veterans. Al Stephenson (Fredric March) is an army sergeant in the Pacific returning to a family and a job as a loan officer in a local bank. He's the oldest, most established veteran in the group and appears to have a problem with alcohol. The highest-ranking member of the group is Air Force Captain Fred Derry, a former bombardier in Europe who was a soda jerk before the war and is anxious about returning to this occupation after serving as an officer. Another aspect of Fred's anxiety is returning to his wife Marie, whom he met shortly after completing basic training; she worked as a nightclub waitress while he was overseas. The third person in the group is also the youngest, Homer Parish (Harold Russell), a returning Navy seaman who lost both hands when his ship was hit, and who demonstrates the use of his prosthesis with great facility. Having been drafted right from high school, Homer's biggest fear is how his girlfriend Wilma (Cathy O'Donnell) will react to his status as a handicapped amputee. "Wilma's only a kid, she's never seen anything like these hooks," he says. The portrayal of Russell's character was quite an achievement, as he, too, had lost his hands while handling faulty explosives for an Army training film. He received two Academy Awards for his performance.

In peace time, these three men from the same midwestern town, Boone City, probably never would have made each other's acquaintance because they are from distinctively different backgrounds and socioeconomic status. They meet while hitching a ride on an old Air Force bomber and share their intimate thoughts about returning to a life whose memories comforted them during war. As they approach the inevitable reality of homecoming, they are fearful of what they might find. This anxiety is eloquently stated in the visual landscape of the town when the three men share a taxi that takes them past the sights and sounds of what was the home they knew but is no longer a place of cherished memories. Their three faces are seen in the rear-view mirror, and it is a portrait of insecurity looking backward while moving toward a new reality.

The homecoming scenes are some of the most poignant moments in the film. The first to be dropped off is Homer, but he proposes that the three new friends go to his Uncle Butch's bar for a few drinks, hoping to delay his meeting with Wilma. But Al and Fred decline his offer and Homer exits the taxi. His younger sister, Luella (Marlene Ames), shrieks with excitement as she greets him and immediately races away to find Wilma while Homer's parents rush out of the house to greet him. Wilma joins in the group hug as Homer's mother (Minna Gombell) notices his prosthesis, muffles a gasp, and then says, "It's nothing." After enduring an excruciatingly long conversation with his future father-in-law about his employment prospects, Homer suddenly leaves for his uncle's bar, "Butch's Place."

The issue of employment and its thematic elements serve as a critical subtext in the narrative of the film. For Al it's the return to the Cornbelt Trust Company with a promotion to vice president and a salary of twelve thousand dollars a year. Still, he is disdainful about returning to the bank—a reflection of his discomfort over being home. His children have grown: His son, Rob, is an obnoxious adolescent, and his daughter, Peggy, who works at a local hospital, has taken on the household chores usually done by a maid.

The respect of Fred's rank and the valor of his ribbons serve as a harsh juxtaposition to where he is dropped off by the taxi: in front of a rundown rickety shack greeted by his tipsy father, Pat (Roman Bohen), and his disheveled stepmother, Hortense (Gladys George). He is told that his wife, Marie (Virginia Mayo), has moved to the Grandview Arms and he leaves to find her.

The three friends convene that evening at Butch's (Hoagy Carmichael) and get drunk. At one point, Fred winds up at Al's place asleep in Peggy's bedroom. Hearing Fred crying out in his sleep, Peggy leaves the couch in the living room to sooth his nightmares. The next morning, she makes his breakfast, and a romantic bond forms between them. When Fred returns to the drugstore where he worked as a soda jerk, he learns that it has been sold to a national chain, Midway Drugs, and he has none of the requisite skills for employment. Indeed, the store manager, Mr. Thorpe, informs him that they are under no obligation to hire him but he offers Fred an assistant-to-the-floor-manager job, with part-time duties as a soda jerk, for thirty-two dollars and fifty cents a week. Fred is dumbfounded and replies that he used to earn over four hundred dollars a month in the service, but the war is now over and other employees fear that returning soldiers like Fred will take their jobs. Fred realizes that his time in the service may have been the best years of his life.

The film progresses toward its climax in a sensitive scene between Wilma and Homer, in Homer's bedroom. She watches as he removes his prosthesis to reveal the stumps that remain, and ensures him their love can endure Homer's disability. For Fred, the challenge is to find employment after squandering all his savings wining and dining Marie. He returns to the drugstore but must endure the withering contempt of his wife, who berates him for being a failure and confronts him with the reality that she has been seeing other men. And, as a gesture to Al (Peggy's father), Fred agrees to stop seeing her. Of course, all of the protagonists (except Marie) meet together at the wedding of Wilma and Homer, where, after the ceremony, Fred and Peggy are reunited and mutually declare their love.

The Best Years of Our Lives is a testament to the skillful art of building a literary and visual narrative around substantial characters who have a profound effect on each other's lives. Perhaps it's the simplicity of the plot, with its nuances of the actors, that makes the story so compelling. Three World War II veterans returning home to the same city, strangers before and during the war, by the end of the movie bond and become friends. The film provides a visual canvas that paints each of their portraits in a pose of insecurity that exposes feelings that all who see can feel. They are very human characters who have been displaced from the normal routines of life only to be thrust back without the requisite time to prepare for new surroundings. For Al, Fred, and Homer, their experience in the service gave them a new "family" with devotion, loyalty, courage, and friendship, providing the necessary bond for their survival. Returning home, they no longer are sustained by the trust that enabled them to survive the war, and instead face threats and challenges that military service denied them preparation for. The film won seven Oscars: Best Picture (Samuel Goldwyn), Best Actor (Fredric March), Best Supporting Actor (Harold Russell), Best Director (William Wyler), Best Screenplay (Robert E. Sherwood), Best Editing, and Best Musical Score. Harold Russell received an additional Special Honorary Oscar "for bringing hope and courage to fellow veterans."

In his November 22, 1946, *New York Times* review, Bosley Crowther writes about the superlative excellence of the film and its humanizing experience:

But this (film) plainly is a labor of not only understanding but of love from three men who put their hearts into it—and from several others who gave it their best work. William Wyler, who directed, was surely drawing upon the wells of his richest talent and experience with men of the Air Force during the war. And Robert E. Sherwood, who wrote the screenplay from a story by MacKinlay Kantor, called "Glory for Me," was certainly giving genuine reflection in his observations as a public pulse-feeler these past six years. Likewise, Mr. Goldwyn, who produced, must have seen this film to be the fulfillment of a high responsibility. All their efforts are rewarded eminently.

🎥 *IT'S A WONDERFUL LIFE* (1946)

PRODUCER/DIRECTOR: Frank Capra (director), Frank Capra (producer)
WRITER(S): Philip Van Doren Stern (story), Frances Goodrich (writer)
CAST: James Stewart (George Bailey), Donna Reed (Mary Hatch Bailey), Lionel Barrymore (Henry F. Potter), Thomas Mitchell (Uncle Billy Bailey), Henry Travers (Clarence), Beulah Bondi (Ma Bailey), Frank Faylen (Ernie Bishop), Ward Bond (Officer Bert), Gloria Grahame (Violet Bick), H. B. Warner (Mr. Emil Gower)
CINEMATOGRAPHY: Joseph F. Biroc, Joseph Walker
MUSIC: Dimitri Tiomkin
LENGTH AND RATING: 130 min; NR

It's a Wonderful Life is a good example of a film that was a box office flop that has become an American holiday cultural icon. Although it was nominated for five Academy Awards, it lost to the poignant *The Best Years of Our Lives*, about returning World War II veterans and the challenges and adjustments they faced. But *It's a Wonderful Life* was elevated to becoming a classic holiday film when it was thought to have lost copyright protection in the early 1970s and considered by many to be in the public domain so that television stations could schedule it for broadcast without paying any royalty fees. A clerical error at National Telefilm Associates resulted in the non-renewal of the copyright in 1974, but the film was still protected as a derivative work due to the copyrighted material used to produce the film (script, music). The irony, of course, is that each year the film is broadcast to a new generation of viewers, who are touched by George Bailey (James Stewart), his "fallen" angel Clarence Oddbody (Henry Travers), "Angel Second Class," and George's family, friends, and business associates in Bedford Falls. It is a true piece of Americana as it reflects on the insecurities that Americans faced, but it demonstrates the unbridled faith, determinism, and ethic that resonate as an eternal theme of Americans.

The movie has an element of fantasy that establishes the narrative as a backstory of George's life on Earth. It begins with the whimsical introduction of apprentice angel Clarence Oddbody, who must help George Bailey in order to earn his "wings." The senior angel, Joseph, provides Clarence with the story of George's life from the time he rescued his younger brother, Harry, from falling through the ice to the incident while working in Mr. Gower's drugstore and his ability to prevent a disoriented Gower from sending tainted, poisonous capsules to a child. These events immediately establish George's character as a selfless person who eagerly embraces the needs of others while sacrificing his own ambition.

Like so many young people in small-town America, George Bailey yearns to escape its provinciality and study architecture abroad, but a confluence of events continually frustrates his ambitions, including the death of his father, which places him in a leadership position at Bailey Building and Loan. So, instead of attending college, he uses the money to pay for younger brother Harry's tuition at an out-of-town college, hoping that when his brother returns he will take over the family business. Once again, George's plans are thwarted when Harry returns to Bedford Falls with a new wife and announces that he will be moving to Buffalo, New York, to work for his father-in-law.

After Mary Hatch (Donna Reed), George's childhood sweetheart, returns to Bedford Falls, having graduated from college, he reluctantly pays a visit and although he loves her realizes that admitting his feelings and getting married would forever shatter his dreams of travel. Neither of them can hide their passion for each other, and after an initial fierce embrace, they lovingly kiss and later marry. As they plan to leave on their honeymoon, their plans are interrupted during a run by depositors on the Building and Loan, created by the Scrooge-like Mr. Potter (Lionel Barrymore), the wealthiest person in town who has managed to get a controlling interest in City Bank. In a shrewdly diabolical scheme to lure George's depositors to his bank, Potter offers them a refund of fifty cents on the dollar for their accounts. Once again, George convinces his customers to give him a week and withdraw only what they need from the bank while he and his new bride Mary use the two thousand dollars saved for their honeymoon to pay off the depositors.

The crisis that drives George to attempted suicide is the loss of an eight thousand dollar deposit that his uncle Billy (Thomas Mitchell) mistakenly folds into Mr. Potter's newspaper as he attempts to make a deposit. Potter discovers the money and keeps it, knowing it will place the Bailey Building and Loan in default, and threatens to take out a warrant for George's arrest. It is Christmas Eve and George, who is despondent, crashes his car into a tree near the frigid river and is about to jump in when he sees a figure (Clarence the Angel) jump, and he follows in an attempted rescue. Saved by the bridge keeper, Clarence shows George what Bedford Falls would be without him. It has become Pottersville, a strip of gaudy bars, clubs, and burlesque houses. The housing that George built for the people of Bedford Falls does not exist, and all the good George has done never happened. Realizing that life is worth living, George comes to his senses and returns to the Bedford Falls he loves, his family, and his friends. And, all the people George has helped come to his aid, donating money, and his high school friend Sam Wainright, who made a fortune in plastics, wires a line of credit for twenty-five thousand dollars. His brother Harry, in Washington to receive the Congressional Medal of Honor, returns home in George's time of need and toasts his brother "... George is the richest man in town."

In *It's a Wonderful Life*, director Frank Capra once again returns to the simplicity of his theme of the unassuming small-town guy who must rise to the challenge of facing the corruption, greed, and ambition of those who would conspire to cheat the public good. It's a classic morality tale, a struggle between good and evil, nuanced by divine intrusion as a plot device to further the narrative by creating another story within the context of the film. The film heralds the respect for the traditional values of family, honesty, and morality.

In his December 23, 1946, *New York Times* review, Bosley Crowther writes that "... Mr. Capra has gone all out to show that it is really a family, friends and honest toil that makes 'the wonderful life'." Indeed, as this film was released shortly after World War II and the knowledge of the Nazi death camps, its embrace of homespun values was a welcome one to audiences.

The story for *It's a Wonderful Life* had an interesting evolution, having first appeared in the 1940s on a private Christmas card with the title *The Greatest Gift*, by writer Philip Van Doren Stern, a noted Civil War historian. Later, RKO Pictures bought the story and sold it to Capra, who wrote the screenplay with Frances Goodrich, Albert Hackett, and Jo Swerling, with uncredited participation by Dorothy Parker, Dalton Trumbo, and Clifford Odets. The film cost $3.7 million, expensive for an independent production. It received mixed reviews from critics and only earned $3.3 million during its initial box office run.

🎥 *MY DARLING CLEMENTINE* (1946)

PRODUCER/DIRECTOR: John Ford (director), Samuel G. Engel (producer)

WRITER(S): Samuel G. Engel (screenplay), Winston Miller (screenplay)

CAST: Henry Fonda (Wyatt Earp), Linda Darnell (Chihuahua), Victor Mature (Dr. John "Doc" Holliday), Cathy Downs (Clementine Carter), Walter Brennan (Old Man Clanton), Tim Holt (Virgil Earp), Ward Bond (Morgan Earp), Alan Mowbray (Granville Thorndyke), John Ireland (Billy Clanton), Roy Roberts (Mayor)

CINEMATOGRAPHY: Joseph MacDonald

MUSIC: Cyril J. Mockridge

LENGTH AND RATING: 97 min; NR

Director John Ford's westerns are rich in the allegorical metaphors of American expansion, the settling of the frontier, and the move toward civilizing the west and beyond. His imagery captured both the desolate loneliness of the prairie yet to be tamed, and the lawlessness of what appeared to be civilized society. In *My Darling Clementine*, Ford has taken the legend of Wyatt Earp and built a narrative to demonstrate the symbolic return to law and order that Earp and his brothers left in Dodge City to become private citizens.

Upon entering Tombstone with his brothers, Wyatt Earp (Henry Fonda) marks himself as a civilized individual in his effort to get a haircut and a shave. Interrupted by gun shots, he realizes that Tombstone is a lawless city but, when offered to be its marshal, he declines. This may be an allusion to World War II and director Ford's experience in the Pacific Theater. During that time he filmed two documentaries for the Navy: *The Battle of Midway* (1942), and *December 7th* (1943). World War II was viewed as a battle for civilization, with the Allies defending society against the Axis. In their book, *A Short History of the Movies*, Gerald Mast and Bruce F. Kawin suggest that when the Clantons attack and kill Wyatt's younger brother James, who is left guarding their herd of cattle, it is an allegorical expression of Japan's sneak attack on the American naval base at Pearl Harbor. Although the authors may be speculating about director John Ford's intentions, there are many visual metaphors in the film that imply the theme of civilization versus the chaos of the untamed frontier.

Before the arrival of Clementine Carter (Cathy Downs), Doc (Victor Mature) Holliday's girlfriend from the civilized city of Boston, Thorndyke (Alan Mowbray), a Shakespearean actor, recites "To be or not to be," the soliloquy from *Hamlet*. The Clantons, who represent the coarse, vulgar, rough-hewn part of Tombstone mock the actor, while Doc Holliday, who has been a member of polite society, respects Thorndyke's attempts and completes the soliloquy when he is unable to.

When Clementine Carter arrives in Tombstone, she is clearly a symbol of culture and propriety, seeking her love Doc Holliday, who has abandoned those principles in his degeneration into the depths of alcoholic and tubercular despair. Although Holliday orders her to leave town, Marshal Wyatt Earp, identifying more with culture and breeding, has taken an interest in her and escorts her to a dance celebrating the construction of Tombstone's first church. The building of a church is symbolic of the virtues of faith and worship, articulating a move from anarchy to order. For Doc Holliday, his preference for the saloon slut Chihuahua is an accommodation to his denial of his education and affiliation to science. His ill treatment of Clementine is an expression of this sense of rejection, as well as his need to protect Clementine from Tombstone's seen and unforeseen dangers.

John Ford's westerns always involve the majesty of the marshal or sheriff representing law and order, taming the unruly, and keeping the peace. That is the theme of the final moments of the film, when Wyatt and his brother, Morgan, along with Doc Holliday, representing civilization, confront the Clantons, who are symbolic of ruthless, primal herd mentality. Although Doc Holliday is mortally wounded, they succeed in killing the remaining sons of the Clanton family except the father, and they allow him to live so that he may experience the same anguish and pain that Wyatt's father must endure with the loss of James and Virgil.

There are many didactic lessons articulated by *My Darling Clementine* that are indicative of the era and political climate of the time. They are a reflection of traditional values that include worship, honesty, morality, and courage; all of these are ritualized in this film. Of course there is so much more to *My Darling Clementine* than sheer allegory. As Bosley Crowther notes in his December 4, 1946, *New York Times* review, the film is the story of Marshal Earp's pursuit "of a gang of rustlers and a maiden's heart." He adds that Ford has a keen eye for comprehending rugged people in a rugged world where violence is an expression "of the rawness and meanness of the frontier to set his vital human beings in relief."

CROSSFIRE (1947)

PRODUCER/DIRECTOR: Edward Dmytryk (director), Dore Schary, Adrian Scott (producers)
WRITER(S): Richard Brooks (novel), John Paxton (writer)
CAST: Robert Young (Finlay), Robert Mitchum (Keeley), Robert Ryan (Montgomery), Gloria Grahame (Ginny), Sam Levene (Samuels), William Phipps (Leroy)
CINEMATOGRAPHY: J. Roy Hunt
MUSIC: Roy Webb
LENGTH AND RATING: 86 min; NR

Indeed, after it became known that RKO was making a film based on the novel *The Brick Foxhole*, about the murder of a homosexual, but had changed the victim to a Jew, influential members of the Jewish community lobbied to kill the project. This attempt was initially led by Mendel Silberberg, head of the Los Angeles-based Community Committee (later called the Community Relations Council), a Jewish watchdog group. At this time, many of the Hollywood studios were controlled by Jews, who were not only sensitive about such portrayals but also very concerned about the box office and their bottom line. However, the head of production at RKO was former screenwriter Dore Schary, who was Jewish and had lectured about anti-Semitism to the troops during WWII. He was committed to the film and received the green light to produce it after he assured studio executives that the movie could be shot on a low budget ($500,000, with a twenty-day shooting shedule) and thus couldn't lose money. It was a modest commercial success. Indeed, in an effort to promote the film, Dore Schary was featured in a trailer shown to movie audiences that highlighted the theme, some of the resistance to having it made, and favorable audience reaction.

The film features some great actors, including Robert Young as police detective Captain Finlay, who investigates the murder of Joseph Samuels (Sam Levene), a Jewish WWII veteran. The investigation slowly leads to a group of soldiers who had met Sam at a bar and invited themselves to his apartment for drinks after he and his girlfriend befriended one of the group. After the body is found, the search slowly proceeds and the prime suspect is a virulent anti-Semite named Montgomery (Robert Ryan). Another noted actor is Robert Mitchum, who portrays their military sergeant, Peter Keeley.

The film is a sleek, low-budget black-and-white film noir and an engaging detective story that reveals some of the ignorance associated with anti-Semitism. At one point, it engages in preaching as Finlay tries to persuade Leroy (William Phipps), a young soldier from a rural area, to help entrap the murderer, Montgomery, who is shot and killed while trying to flee.

Reviews for the film were positive, and Bosley Crowther, in his July 23, 1947, *New York Times* review expressed his admiration for the courage of Dore Schary and others for bringing the subject of anti-Semitism to the screen:

> An unqualified A for effort in bringing to the screen a frank and immediate demonstration of the brutality of religious bigotry as it festers and fires ferocity in certain seemingly normal American minds is due to producers Schary, Adrian Scott, and everyone else at RKO who had a hand in the making of *Crossfire*, which came to the Rivoli yesterday. For here, without hints or subterfuges, they have come right out and shown that such malice—in this case, anti-Jewish—is a dark and explosive sort of hate which, bred of ignorance and intolerance, can lead to extreme violence.

 ## *GENTLEMAN'S AGREEMENT* (1947)

PRODUCER/DIRECTOR: Elia Kazan (director), Darryl F. Zanuck (producer)
WRITER(S): Laura Z. Hobson (novel), Moss Hart (screenplay)
CAST: Gregory Peck (Philip Schuyler Green), Dorothy McGuire (Kathy Lacy), John Garfield (Dave Goldman), Celeste Holm (Anne Dettrey), Anne Revere (Mrs. Green), June Havoc (Elaine Wales), Albert Dekker (John Minify), Jane Wyatt (Jane), Dean Stockwell (Tommy Green), Nicholas Joy (Dr. Craigie)
CINEMATOGRAPHY: Arthur C. Miller
MUSIC: Alfred Newman
LENGTH AND RATING: 118 min; NR

Arriving in movie theaters shortly after *Crossfire* and based on the Laura Z. Hobson novel, *Gentleman's Agreement* also involved an investigation surrounding anit-Semitism, but this time a journalistic one. The film was produced by Darryl F. Zanuck, one of the founders and the head of 20th Century Fox, and at the time he was the only studio head who wasn't Jewish. He was also committed to the film's theme, and told a story about how it once took him two hours to convince the manager of a resort hotel that he wasn't Jewish. His closest friend was Jewish talent agent and producer Charles K. Feldman (*A Streetcar Named Desire*, 1951).

In the Hollywood community, Zanuck had a reputation for producing socially conscious films, including *The Grapes of Wrath* (1940), *How Green Was My Valley* (1941), and *The Ox-Bow Incident* (1943). He was convinced his film would be a box office success and to that end committed a budget of two million doallars and an A-list of talent, including director Elia Kazan, screenwriter Moss Hart, and actors Gregory Peck,

Dorothy McGuire, and John Garfield. He was correct: The movie won Academy Awards for Best Picture, Best Director (Elia Kazan), and Best Supporting Actress (Celeste Holm).

The film is about a recently widowed journalist, Philip Schuyler Green, who relocates to New York City from California with his mother and young son Tommy (Dean Stockwell). He is hired by a magazine to write an article about anti-Semitism; there, he meets and falls in love with Kathy Lacey (Dorothy McGuire), a socially prominent divorcee and niece of the magazine publisher. He struggles with an angle on the story and finally decides to claim he's Jewish to experience anti-Semitism firsthand.

His deception causes tension in his relationship with Kathy, who perceives herself as a liberal but is part of the social mileu that is exclusionary toward Jews. A number of anti-Semitic incidents in the movie portray the ugliness of hate, from the essentially benign building superintendent warning Schuyler when he changes the name on his mailbox to Phil Green to a fight in a restaurant after Dave Goldberg (John Garfield), Schuyler's best friend, is berated for being a Jew. Tommy, too, is bullied and taunted by other children for being Jewish.

Although at times the film is contrived, as in a scene at a resort where Schuyler challenges the management on their policy toward members of the "Hebrew faith," it is nevertheless a powerful portrait of the dangers and tactics of bigotry and racism. The movie was received well by critics, and Bosley Crowther, in his November 12, 1947, *New York Times* review called it a "sizzling film" with a fine cast. He also wrote:

Shaped by Moss Hart into a screen play of notable nimbleness and drive, the bewilderments of Miss Hobson's hero become absorbing and vital issues on the screen and the eventual outcome of his romance becomes a matter of serious concern. For such aspects of anti-Semitism as professional bias against Jews, discrimination by swanky hotels and even the calling of ugly names have been frankly and clearly demonstrated for the inhuman failings that they are and the peril of a normal and happy union being wrecked on the ragged edges of prejudice is affectingly raised.

4 The Hop, Bop, and Stroll, 1950–1959

The era of the 1950s is rich in redefining American culture with the new voice of rock and roll. It was a defining moment for American teenagers, who embraced the gyrating sounds of Elvis Presley, Buddy Holly, and legendary disc jockey Alan Freed, who brought black rhythm and blues artists to prominence and coined the term rock and roll. Television became a part of the entertainment fabric of America, creating cultural icons such as Milton Berle (*Texaco Star Theater*), Lucille Ball and Desi Arnaz (*I Love Lucy*), and Steve Allen and Jack Paar (*Tonight*). Television also featured legendary journalist, Edward R. Murrow, whose move from radio to television was marked by the pursuit of excellence in investigative journalism and his confrontation with Senator Joseph McCarthy on his television program *See It Now*.

In 1953, the five most popular television shows were: *I Love Lucy* (CBS), *Dragnet* (NBC), *Arthur Godfrey Talent Scouts* (CBS), *You Bet Your Life* (NBC), and *The Milton Berle Show* (NBC). Hollywood had to respond to television's overbearing influence on American entertainment and culture. In doing so, they were able to address more adult themes with greater promiscuity and sexuality, such as the lovemaking beach scene between Deborah Kerr and Burt Lancaster in *From Here to Eternity* (1953).

Another way to combat the popularity of television in the 1950s was to lure its viewers to movie theaters by giving a new look and sound to the theatrical film image. As a result, in the 1950s, the number of Hollywood films produced in color rose from twenty to fifty percent. Color was a feature that television at the time could not match, and the rich tones of Technicolor (a three-strip dye transfer process) were a striking example of its lush color palette. Soon, Eastman developed a single-strip, mono-pack color film that was easier to handle and process and which resulted in a greater number of color Hollywood films.

Wide Screen Formats

Given that the size of most television screens in the fifties were small, the Hollywood film industry made an effort to adjust the proportions of the theatrical movie screen. In 1952, *This is Cinerama*, the first Cinerama movie (three-projector system), was released. It required interlocking semi-curved screens measured at an angle of 146 degrees and four-track stereophonic sound. The film, a travelogue, debuted at New York's Broadway

Theater on September 30, 1952, and played for three years, grossing about $5 million. The last Cinerama film to be released was *How the West Was Won* (1962), which was budgeted at $15 million and grossed $45 million in its initial release. As of this writing, only two movie theaters in the United States are permanently equipped to exhibit Cinerama format films: the Seattle Cinerama and the Arclight Hollywood Cinerama Dome.

Another process that was more functional and less costly was CinemaScope, introduced by 20th Century Fox, which used 35 millimeter film and a simple anamorphic lens to create a wide-screen effect. The first movie to be released in this format was the biblical epic *The Robe* (1953), which opened at New York's Roxy Theater in September 1953.

Movie Gimmicks

In the early fifties, 3-D movies were another marketing tool to bring television audiences into motion picture theaters. Viewers were equipped with cardboard-framed "stereoscopic" glasses to view the three-dimensional images; unfortunately, the glasses were often blurry and cumbersome to wear. The first full-length 3-D presentation was Universal Artists' *Bwana Devil* (1952), starring Robert Stack. Horror films were especially notable in the 3-D format and included such bloodcurling classics as *House of Wax* (1953), featuring Vincent Price, *It Came from Outer Space* (1953), and *The Creature from the Black Lagoon* (1954). Notable director Alfred Hitchcock made a 3-D version of his classic film, *Dial M for Murder* (1954).

Other formats to increase screen size and provide film audiences with alternatives to small-screen television included Vista Vision (*White Christmas*, 1954), SuperScope (*Invasion of the Body Snatchers*, 1956), Warner Scope (*The Naked and the Dead*, 1958), Todd-AO (*Oklahoma*, 1955), Panavision (*The Apartment*, 1960), Super Panavision 70 (*West Side Story*, 1961), Super Technirama (*Sleeping Beauty*, 1959), Ultra Panavision 70 (*Mutiny on the Bounty*, 1962), and Techniscope (*A Fistful of Dollars*, 1964). These wide-screen 65 mm and 70 mm film formats were prohibitively expensive for Hollywood to produce, and eventually the studios reverted back to 35 mm film, utilizing special lenses to project the image.

Some of the more bizarre attempts to capture the television audience with a movie gimmick were Aroma-Rama and Smell-O-Vision. The first, developed by Charles Weiss, operated by piping Oriental fragrances through the air-conditioning system of a movie theater and was featured in the Italian documentary *Behind the Great Wall* (1959). As for Smell-O-Vision, developed by Swiss-born osmologist Hans Laube, it was featured in just one movie, *Scent of Mystery* (1960). To achieve the effect, thirty different smells were released into theater seats at strategic points in the film. In 1981, in the B-movie melodrama *Polyester*, director John Waters paid tribute to the 1950s gimmickry of associating smells with film scenes through a process he dubbed Odorama. Using scratch and sniff cards, audiences responded to on-screen number cues.

Another short-lived technique was called Emergo 3-D, used in William Castle's *House on Haunted Hill* (1959, remade in 1999), starring Vincent Price. At a point where a skeleton rises from a vat of acid, a luminescent plastic skeleton on a wire was released from a black box near the screen, traveling over the audience on the wire. Its return to the box corresponded with Price reeling in the skeleton. In *The Tingler* (1959), another Castle film, a technique called Percepto used buzzers hidden in the seats to provide a jolt to viewers whenever there was a bloodcurdling scream.

As television continued to erode, movie audiences Hollywood turned to demographically themed films for adults, children, and teenagers. The Disney studio was one of the most successful, as it developed live-action features adapted from the classics (*Treasure Island*, 1950, *Old Yeller*, 1957). The teenage market was also cultivated by Hollywood, and included clean teen comedies and romances and rock-and-roll musicals along with the science fiction and horror genres.

Art Houses

Two economical tools that affected small theater survival in the 1950s included importing foreign films, which were less costly to exhibit, and the evolution of the art theater. In 1950, there were only 100 such theaters, but by the mid-sixties, there were in excess of 600. A few of these foreign films were popular, and some earned high grosses in the United States. They include Vittorio De Sica's *The Bicycle Thief* (*Ladridi biciclette*, 1948) and Roger Vadim's *And God Created Woman* (1957), starring Brigitte Bardot.

Drive-Ins

The drive-in theater was invented by Richard Hollingshead, who worked for his father's Whiz Auto Products Company and experimented with the concept on the driveway of his home in Camden, New Jersey. After experimenting with sound, projection, and parking techniques, the first patent for a drive-in theater was issued on May 16, 1933. With an initial investment of $30,000, Hollingshead opened the first drive-in on June 6, 1933, on Crescent Boulevard in Camden, New Jersey. Sound was provided by three RCA Victor speakers mounted next to the screen, and the price of admission was twenty-five cents per person and car. The number of "ozoners" grew slowly, and in 1945 there were two dozen, but by 1956 the number grew to 4,000. During the 1950s, approximately one-quarter of box office revenue was generated from drive-ins.

As box office receipts diminished, drive-ins offered another revenue stream by featuring movies long past their original run. They did not require a substantial investment, families could attend without hiring a babysitter, and ease of moving about brought higher profits at the concession stand.

Political Intrigue

The war in Korea, the testing of the nuclear bomb, and the rise of the Soviet Union to global significance brought about the phrase *the cold war*. Fear and paranoia were associated with the perceived communist menace and the threat to civil liberties engendered by American demagogue Joseph McCarthy, who used intimidation to browbeat his victims. As a function of the paranoia of the time, the House Un-American Activities Committee investigated artists, including actors, writers, and directors, asking them to testify about their communist affiliations and divulge the names of those they suspected. Another organization, American Business Consultants, published *Red Channels*, which named artists in television who were communists. As a result, many performers, writers, and other creative talent working in motion pictures and television were blacklisted and thus prevented from working and earning a living.

The fifties was also a time of economic resurgence, the rise of a consumer culture. and American prosperity. The empowerment of the middle class helped drive the American economy through sales of new homes and automobiles. After the Depression and World War II, there was a renewed faith in the American dream and a sense of individual worth and achievement. And so the films of the 1950s reflected these values and included westerns (*High Noon*), World War II movies (*Stalag 17*), and elaborate period costume dramas (*Ben-Hur*).

▓▓ THE AFRICAN QUEEN (1951)

PRODUCER/DIRECTOR: John Huston (director), Sam Spiegel (producer)
WRITER(S): C. S. Forester (novel), James Agee (adaptation)
CAST: Humphrey Bogart (Charlie Allnut), Katharine Hepburn (Rose Sayer), Robert Morley (Rev. Samuel Sayer), Peter Bull (Captain of *Louisa*), Theodore Bikel (First Officer), Walter Gotell (Second Officer), Peter Swanwick (First Officer of *Shona*), Richard Marner (Second Officer of *Shona*)
CINEMATOGRAPHY: Jack Cardiff
MUSIC: Allan Gray
LENGTH AND RATING: 105 min; NR

In this film, an unlikely couple, Charlie Allnut (Humphrey Bogart), and Rose Sayer (Katharine Hepburn), fall in love. However, *The African Queen* is far from a traditional love story. It articulates the themes that John Huston personified in so many of his films: how to deal with the irony of vanity, avarice, and unfulfilled quests. Many of his characters are nonconformists, others are misfits who don't fit the norm. These values are beautifully expressed in the relationship between Charlie and Rose. He's a crude boat operator who delivers the mail to Rose and her brother, Samuel, both of whom are missionaries in Africa. Even by Samuel's admission during a bout with the delirium of a fever, Rose is a spinster who's only worth is supporting him in God's work. And, her brother is also wanting, having been passed over for "promotion" by a younger classmate.

The contrast between Charlie Allnut and Rose in the early scenes creates a visual portrait of two people who are in clear opposition to one another. He is an unkempt boatman with a weakness for gin who has little use for polite society, and she is a prim, prudish, and passionless high-buttoned woman. They share the beauty, awe, and danger of the jungle, with Rose encouraging Charlie to fashion and arm the *African Queen* with torpedoes so that they can sink the German gunboat *Louisa*. Although Charlie protests that the river is too treacherous to navigate, he yields to Rose's plan. When the rudder on the *African Queen* is damaged, it is Rose who gently persuades Charlie that he can remove and repair it onshore by engineering a makeshift bellows for welding.

For Rose, being with Charlie on the *African Queen* has liberated her from a rigorous life of sacrifice and solitude. She relishes the adventure and challenge of facing the jungle and taming Charlie Allnut. All his life, Charlie has been a drifter devoid of ambition and avoiding responsibilities and personal entanglements. In each other they see a spark of life that has a compelling attraction which drives them to overcome their differences and build a relationship of mutual respect and love.

The movie was based on the 1935 novel entitled *The African Queen* by C. S. Forester, and is set in the year 1914 in Central Africa during World War I. Despite the time and setting, there is a subtle reference to the emerging dominance of the United States as a world power, given that the influence of the colonial powers has waned. The film was shot almost entirely on location in Uganda and on the Lualaba River, except for scenes in which Bogart and Hepburn are immersed in the river. Those were shot in a tank on a London soundstage to protect the actors from the possibility of infection from malaria and other diseases that infested the river waters.

Although *The African Queen* takes place during World War I and weaves a political tone into the narrative, it is more than anything an adult love story. Rose and Charlie are caught in the dynamic of a world war and challenged not only by political circumstances but also by the natural laws of the jungle. It is indeed a story of faith for Rose, who has now embarked on an even greater adventure with Charlie than with her brother. And for Charlie, who has always avoided confrontation, preferring to take solace in the bottle, his journey with Rose invigorates his manhood. This is a timeless story of love and adventure and a great film classic.

AN AMERICAN IN PARIS (1951)

PRODUCER/DIRECTOR: Vincente Minnelli (director); Arthur Freed (producer)
WRITER: Alan Jay Lerner
CAST: Gene Kelly (Jerry Mulligan), Leslie Caron (Lise Bolivier), Oscar Levant (Adam Cook), Georges Guetary (Hank Baurel), Nina Foch (Milo Roberts)
CINEMATOGRAPHY: John Alton (ballet, photography), Alfred Gills (director of photography)
ORIGINAL MUSIC: Saul Chapin
LENGTH AND RATING: 113 min; NR

An American in Paris director Vincente Minnelli used the traditions of musical theater to stage the dance and vocal numbers for this film. Some scenes are elaborately costumed and reminiscent of filmed musicals from the 1940s. For example, the George Gershwin song, "I Got Rhythm," was first performed in the 1943 movie *Girl Crazy*, starring Judy Garland and Mickey Rooney. That was an elaborate production, featuring dancers and musicians dressed in cowboy costumes, and the Tommy Dorsey orchestra conducted by Dorsey. The same song adapted for *An American in Paris* features Gene Kelly tap dancing for a group of Parisian children as he shows them the different steps and they repeat a fragment of the lyrics in English, "I got..." The staging ranges from the more sedate, as when Gene Kelly sings "Our Love is Here to Stay" to Leslie Caron by the river Seine, to the elaborate, "I'll Build A Stairway to Paradise," with its beautifully dressed show girls descending a steep staircase with accent lights adding embellishment and drama.

An American in Paris uses the classic love triangle as a plot device. In the film, Jerry, the American, falls in love with Lise, a French girl. However, she has a relationship with singer/performer Henri "Hank" Baurel (Georges Guetary) and feels an obligation to marry him because he rescued her from the Nazis and their love blossomed. Complicating the triangle with another angle is Milo Roberts (Nina Foch), a wealthy American heiress and woman of influence who helps support Jerry by buying his paintings but also has amorous intentions toward him, which he snubs. When she invites him to a party for two in her home, he confronts her and attempts to return her money. Jerry has close friends, especially Adam Cook (Oscar Levant), the concert pianist who lives in the same building and is friends with Henri. In a café, Henri shows Adam a picture of Lise and as Adam asks, "What's she like?" Lise appears in a charming montage wearing different costumes in five portraits that reveal her varying personalities while dancing to Gershwin's "Embraceable You." Eventually, Adam introduces Jerry to his friend, Henri Baurel, and Jerry by chance meets Lise in a nightclub while he's with Milo, thus beginning the competition for Lise's love. Jerry enrages Milo with his obvious and incessant flirting with Lise. Eventually, Lise leaves and Jerry daydreams about her and the great painters he admires— Monet, Renoir, and Toulouse-Lautrec, are stylistically interpreted in each of six sequences he and Lise dance in. The fantasy scenes are set around Paris in various locales that are referenced to the artists. At the end of the movie, Jerry awakes from his dream and sees Lise, who has returned in Henri's car and was released from their engagement when he saw that she was in love with Jerry. The two lovers then have their final embrace.

For *An American in Paris*, director Vicente Minnelli and Gene Kelly collaborated on an epic masterpiece of modern musical cinematic ballet. The film lingers on the visual rhapsody between Leslie Caron and Gene Kelly as they dance with a graceful fluidity that provides the audience with its reason for watching. In one epic moment of the ballet, the dancers are bathed in a golden steamy shot as they approach each other, and Gene Kelly gently embraces Leslie Caron, picking her up in his arms and swaying back and forth to George Gershwin's music. They are enveloped in the steam (or smoke), and the color changes to a blue hue as they dance on a huge fountain that, instead of spouting water from its heads, is flowing with steam.

In his October 5, 1951, *New York Times* review, Bosley Crowther wrote that the romance seemed stale and the story wrinkled:

> Alongside this crisp and elfin youngster who plays the Parisian girl with whom the ebullient American of Mr. Kelly falls in love, the other extravagant characters of the romance seem standard and stale, and even the story seems wrinkled in the light of her freshness and charm. (http://movies.nytimes.com/movie)

An *American in Paris* is more than a movie; it's a portrait that provides a richness of art, music, and dance rarely seen on the screen today. It is defined not by its story but by the poetry of two dancers who, through the creative use of their talent, live in a timeless Parisian ballet.

SINGIN' IN THE RAIN (1952)

PRODUCER/DIRECTOR: Gene Kelly and Stanley Donen (directors); Arthur Freed (producer)
WRITER(S): Adolph Green and Betty Comden
CAST: Gene Kelly (Don Lockwood), Donald O'Connor (Cosmo Brown), Debbie Reynolds (Kathy Selden), Jean Hagen (Lina Lamont), Millard Mitchell (R. F. Simpson), Cyd Charisse (Guest Artist)
CINEMATOGRAPHY: Harold Rosson
MUSIC: Jeff Alexander, Stanley Doren, Arthur Freed, Lennie Hayton
LENGTH AND RATING: 103 min; NR

In the 1950s, MGM released some of the most enduring movie musicals, including *An American in Paris* (1951), *Singin' in the Rain* (1952), *The Band Wagon* (1953), and *Seven Brides for Seven Brothers* (1957). It was the Freed Unit at MGM, shepherded by producer Arthur Freed, who used the top Hollywood stars of the era, including Judy Garland, Fred Astaire, Vera-Ellen, and Gene Kelly.

Today, *Singin' in the Rain* is recognized as one of the most iconic film musicals of all time. It was directed by Gene Kelly and Stanley Donen and written by Betty Comden and Adolph Green. It's a musical comedy that is set at the time when Hollywood was making a transition from silent to sound movies. The story features the silent screen star Don Lockwood (Gene Kelly) and his leading lady Lina Lamont (Jean Hagen), whom the studio has publicized as lovers on-screen and off. Escaping from a crowd of admiring fans, Don manages to jump into a convertible driven by young aspiring actress Kathy Selden (Debbie Reynolds). They meet again at a studio party: Kathy is one of the chorus girls who jump out of a cake. Seeing Don's interest in Kathy angers Lina, and she becomes furious when Kathy aims a cream pie at Don but hits Lina in the face instead. At the same party, R. F. Simpson (Millard Mitchell), the head of the studio, screens a demonstration clip of a talking picture and his guests express their disdain for its commercial success. In the interim, a romantic relationship blossoms between Don and Kathy.

After the success of *The Jazz Singer*, a talking picture starring Al Jolson, Simpson decided to shoot "The Dueling Cavalier" in sound; however the attempt is a dismal failure, as Lina Lamont's voice is pitched too high and her speech pattern and language are too urban and colloquial. There are several hilarious scenes that depict Lina taking diction lessons, the microphone hidden in several locations, including her bosom, but only picking up sections of her dialogue, and Don using his stylistic silent screen persona over acting for the film. At the film's debut for a test audience, the patrons leave the theater either laughing at how funny it is or condemning it for being just awful.

Embarrassed and thinking his career is over, Don laments his fate but is buoyed by the support of Kathy and his good friend and sidekick Cosmo Brown (Donald O'Connor). They concoct the idea of turning "The Dueling Cavalier" into a musical called *The Dancing Cavalier*. To avoid using Lina's terrible voice, they arrange for Kathy to secretly read her lines during filming, but when Lina finds out she threatens to sue the studio and demands that Kathy never star in a film and that her only role will be as Lina's voice stand-in. After the premiere of the film and the audience's overwhelming reaction to her singing, they demand that Lina sing live on stage. Quickly arranging a backstage microphone for Kathy, Don and Cosmo watch the charade and then decide to raise the curtain, revealing the ruse. As Kathy runs from the theater, Don takes the stage, announces her name, and says that she is the true star of the film.

The film is notable for Gene Kelly's classic "Singin' in the Rain" dance routine in which he uses an umbrella as a creative prop, splashing and sloshing on a street during an evening in the pouring rain while singing the title song. It's a masterpiece of clever choreography and perfect timing as his reverie is stopped by a policeman dressed in a rubber raincoat, eerily watching him. Other notable song and dance numbers include "Moses Supposes" with Kelly and O'Connor, "Make 'Em Laugh," performed by Donald O'Connor, "Beautiful Girl," and Kelly's legendary dance number with the sultry and sexy Cyd Charisse.

In his March 28, 1952, *New York Times* review, critic Bosley Crowther describes the color and spectacle of the movie:

> Compounded generously of music, dance, color, spectacle and a riotous abundance of Gene Kelly, Jean Hagen and Donald O'Connor on the screen, all elements in this rainbow program are carefully contrived and guaranteed to lift the dolors of winter and put you in a buttercup mood. (http://movies.nytimes.com/movie)

HIGH NOON (1952)

PRODUCER/DIRECTOR: Fred Zinnemann
WRITER(S): John W. Cunningham (story), Carl Foreman (screenplay)
CAST: Gary Cooper (Marshal Will Kane), Thomas Mitchell (Mayor Jonas Henderson), Lloyd Bridges (Deputy Marshal Harvey Pell), Katy Jurado (Helen Ramírez), Grace Kelly (Amy Fowler Kane), Otto Kruger (Judge Percy Mettrick), Lon Chaney, Jr. (Martin Howe), Harry Morgan (Sam Fuller), Ian MacDonald (Frank Miller), Eve McVeagh (Mildred Fuller)
CINEMATOGRAPHY: Floyd Crosby
MUSIC: Dimitri Tiomkin
LENGTH AND RATING: 85 min; NR

One of the most compelling films to address issues of justice, morality, and loyalty ever made, *High Noon* reflects the troubling political climate in America at the time it was released. Recent movies, such as *Good Night, and Good Luck* (2005) have exposed a new generation to the fear, retribution, and persecution that so many faced during the McCarthy era. The screenplay was taken from *The Tin Star*, a short story written by John W. Cunningham and adapted by screenwriter Carl Foreman. During the filming, Foreman was summoned before the House Committee on Un-American Activities (HUAC), where he admitted that as a student he had been a member of the American Communist Party, even though he later became disillusioned and quit. When asked to identify his fellow communist party members, he refused, was labeled an uncooperative witness, and blacklisted by the Hollywood studios: Denied employment in America, Foreman and other blacklisted writers left the United States for England, where they used pseudonyms to write scripts that were then sent to Hollywood. Woody Allen featured this in his 1976 film, *The Front*. Sadly, Foreman's creative effort was not acknowledged when *High Noon* was released. It was only near the end of his life, while ill with a brain tumor, that he returned to the United States, in 1984.

High Noon is an allegory on the events during the McCarthy era when some, like Foreman, chose to stand alone, shunned by their communities and losing their livelihoods for standing up for their beliefs while others capitulated (for example, director Elia Kazan), fearing retribution and isolation. The movie, directed by Fred Zinnemann, is a taut drama that creates tension through the real-time unfolding of events. For Will Kane (Gary Cooper), the marshal of Hadleyville, the day is both a blessing and a curse. He is retiring from his position as the town's law enforcement officer and marrying his beautiful Quaker fiancée, Amy Fowler (Grace Kelly). His day turns into a nightmare when an old nemesis, Frank Miller (Ian MacDonald), whom Kane apprehended for

Gary Cooper as Marshal Will Kane. [United Artists/Photofest]

murder and who was later sentenced to hang, is paroled and due to arrive on the noon train to meet up with his brother and two other associates to seek revenge on the marshal.

Although Kane and his new bride are quickly spirited out of town on a horse and buggy to begin new lives as a couple running a small store, he is torn by his need to serve the town in the absence of the new marshal, who is scheduled to arrive the next day. His conscience will not allow him to "cut and run," but Amy cannot understand his decision and threatens to leave on the same train that Miller will be arriving on. Although Will attempts to assuage Amy's fears by telling her he will swear in a number of deputies, she is convinced that he faces imminent death and is betraying her Quaker stand against violence. In the end Amy is correct when the citizens of Hadleyville demur from assisting their marshal.

The code of honor that Marshal Kane fosters is not shared by the citizens of Hadleyville. Indeed, Kane's deputy, the young and arrogant Harvey Pell (Lloyd Bridges), resigns because of his anger toward the marshal for not recommending him for the marshal's position. He also has been having a relationship with Helen Ramirez (Katy Jurado), who was alternately the mistress of Miller and Kane.

Pell isn't the only one who denies Kane his support. The local denizens of the saloon mock his request for special deputies, as do his "dear" friends Sam and Mildred Fuller. When the marshal enters the church seeking the deputies, he is admonished by the minister for not getting married there. His request for special deputies sets off a debate among the parishioners, who for the most part want nothing to do with Kane or his confrontation with Miller. Indeed, one of them suggests that such murder and mayhem would be detrimental to Hadleyville's economic future because of northern interest in building factories in the town. Another worshiper places blame on the northern politicians for releasing Frank Miller. These events, along with various shots of clocks showing the time remaining until noon, create tension and demonstrate the conflict between the marshal and the town. Marshal Will Kane is a monument to the self-sacrificing lone defender of law and order who upholds traditional values as others turn a blind eye to his courage. This portrayal is a reference to the McCarthy era and its condemnation of the freedoms guaranteed by the Constitution denying the virtues that Kane represents.

The attributes personified by Kane have made *High Noon* the most requested film to be screened by American presidents, including Eisenhower, who wasn't a movie buff but saw it at least three times, and Clinton, who is reported to have screened it at least twenty times. It is also a favorite of Junichiro Koizumi, the former Japanese prime minister (2001–2006). The same year that *High Noon* was released, Arthur Miller published *The Crucible*, a play about the Salem witch trials, which he also envisioned as a parable on the McCarthy "witch hunt." Although Miller was not indicted by HUAC, his dear friend and collaborator Elia Kazan testified and revealed the names of former communist party members. It was this action, and the climate of fear that prevailed, that motivated Miller to write the play.

In his essay "*High Noon*: Liberal Classic? Conservative Screed?" Professor Manfred Weidhorn of Yeshiva University in New York City writes about the interpretation of the movie as a testimony of liberal thought which also addresses conservative values. His example is the lamentation by characters in the movie of northerners and their narrow-minded view of justice; for example, paroling a convicted murderer to return and place their town in harm's way. In rationalizing this argument, Weidhorn articulates the sensibilities of present-day right-wing conservatives who rebuke the Eastern liberal establishment for its "soft take" on law and order. Indeed, even Kane's new Quaker bride Amy, who vehemently opposes violence, embraces the formidable task of vigilance by defending her beloved and shooting one of his attackers in the back. It is a measure of her forbearance in grasping the reality of the moment that she would abandon her liberal principles for the law-and-order conservative morality of her husband. However, as Weidhorn correctly states, the movie hasn't changed, it is how the film is contextualized in the time frame of today that has altered the viewing experience.

A work of art is like a mirror in which each age sees its own face, its own set of priorities and anxieties. Another way to put it is to say that selectivity is unavoidable in the art of life, but in propaganda the selectivity is determined by ideology, while in art it is determined by verisimilitude. Being true to all the messiness and contradictions of life results in a movie in which liberal and conservative considerations stumble over each other. (Weidhorn, 2005, http://www.brightlightsfilm.com/47/highnoon)

🎥 *SHANE* (1953)

PRODUCER/DIRECTOR: George Stevens (director)

WRITER(S): Jack Schaefer (novel), A. B. Guthrie Jr. (screenplay)

CAST: Alan Ladd (Shane), Jean Arthur (Marian Starrett), Van Heflin (Joe Starrett), Brandon De Wilde (Joey Starrett), Jack Palance (Jack Wilson), Ben Johnson (Chris Calloway), Edgar Buchanan (Fred Lewis), Emile Meyer (Rufus Ryker), Elisha Cook, Jr. (Frank "Stonewall" Torrey), Douglas Spencer (Axel "Swede" Shipstead)

CINEMATOGRAPHY: Loyal Griggs

MUSIC: Victor Young

LENGTH AND RATING: 118 min; NR

Like *High Noon*, *Shane* is an allegory that presents the western as a canvas to show the stark distinctions against good and evil and demonstrate the spread of civilization and progress. It's a story about homesteaders, pejoratively referred to as sodbusters and pig farmers, the end of free-range grazing by ranchers, and the demise of the gunfighter. The movie also addresses traditional values of courage, perseverance, sacrifice, and family as a means toward achieving success.

The Starrett family—Joe (Van Heflin), his wife Marion (Jean Arthur), and their son Joey (Brandon DeWilde)—is struggling to raise crops, graze a few head of cattle, and defend their land against Rufus Ryker (Emile Meyer), the cattle baron who is attempting to force all of the homesteaders off their land in order to grow his own herd and fulfill a large beef contract. Entering the scene is a lone rider dressed in white buckskin and armed with a white pearl handled revolver: the gunfighter and drifter Shane (Alan Ladd). After a brief misunderstanding and to the delight of Joey, Shane is invited to dinner and decides to stay and work for the Starrett family. For the gunfighter who knows that his days are numbered, this is an opportunity for him to experience the virtues of family life and the sweat of honest labor. There is also a subtle attraction between Marion and Shane, and for Joey the gunfighter represents a mythic hero reflecting the awe that a young boy places in the masculine pursuits of shooting and fighting.

As tensions rise and each side proves intractable, Ryker hires a gunfighter from Cheyenne named Wilson (Jack Palance), who epitomizes the essence of evil and is dressed entirely in black. Soon Joe, Joey, and Shane bond as they share work and play and facing off Ryker's threats.

In a pivotal scene that articulates the position of men with divergent points of view who are entrenched in their beliefs, Ryker rides to Starrett's homestead and offers to buy him out, at a fair price, pay him good wages for his work, and run his cattle with his own herd. Each of the men presents his own rationale based upon need, with Ryker arguing that he and men like him settled the area by taking all of the risks, making the sacrifice, and sustaining myriad deprivations. Confronting Ryker, Starrett reminds him that all of the land is not his, and the homesteaders have rights to settle there. Neither man is willing to yield, and Ryker leaves, but not before handing a veiled threat to Starrett.

While staying with the Starrett's, Shane has bonded with the family and built a strong and trusting relationship with Joey, who idolizes the aging gunfighter and admits that he loves him as much as he loves his father. Even as Shane attempts to resist involvement in the homesteaders' confrontation with Ryker, he is reluctantly drawn into it because of the ties he has built with his adopted family. For Shane, this is a battle between the old and new world of the west, and he is profoundly aware of the personal impact it will have on him. His thoughts are reinforced by two confrontations: one with Marion and the other with Ryker. In a scene in which Shane is teaching Joey how to shoot with a wooden gun, Marion interrupts and chastises Shane for teaching him the lessons of manhood and urging little Joey to adopt his values. "Guns aren't going to be my boy's life," she says angrily. Shane responds by reminding Marion that a gun is like any other tool, such as an axe or a shovel, and that it is as good or as bad as the man using it. Marion's response is indicative of the future when she says that everyone would be better off if there were no guns left in the valley, including Shane's. Once again the implication is that civilized people will not accept the ruthlessness of frontier justice.

After Ryker and his henchmen succeed in intimidating many of the settlers by murdering one of their own, Starrett decides to put on his gun belt and confront the rancher on his own terms. Shocked by what she perceives to be a suicide mission, Marion pleads with her husband to put his gun away and then begs Shane to intercede. In a very moving scene, Joe tells his wife that although he may be slow at times, he has noticed things between Marion and Shane, and that if he was killed there was someone who could probably take better care of her than he could.

There is a confrontation between Shane and Joe, and they fight as the gunfighter attempts to prevent Joe from facing Wilson. Finally, Shane uses the butt of his gun to subdue Joe and mounts his horse to face Ryker and Wilson. Marion knows she will be seeing Shane for the last time and tells him that she thought he had given up gun fighting, and then asks if he is doing it just for her. He tells her that it's for her husband, for her, and her son. There is a knowing look of desire between Shane and Marion as she moves to kiss him but is interrupted by her son.

As Shane enters the saloon, he confronts Ryker, telling him he has lived too long and his kind of days are over. Ryker responds by asking Shane whether his gunfighter days are over. In a revealing moment, Shane says that the difference between him and Ryker is that he *knows* his days as a gunfighter are over.

With little Joey and his dog watching from below the saloon doors, Shane subdues Ryker and his gang and then hears Joey warn him of a rear ambush from the balcony, which causes an injury. His work now done in defending the Starrett family and the rest of the homesteaders, Shane knows it is time for him to leave since he doesn't fit in with the ways of civilized society. He articulates these thoughts to Joey after the boy pleads with him to return home with him. He explains to Joey that a man must be what he is, that you cannot break the mold, and that you cannot live with killing, it is a brand that sticks. He tells Joey to run home and tell his mother that there are no longer any guns in the valley, and to grow up strong and straight and take care of his parents. In essence, he is admonishing Joey not to be like him but to respect the traditions and values of the family. As Shane rides off, little Joey, in one of the most poignant scenes in the movie, calls out,

> Pa's got things for you to do, and Mother wants you. I know she does. Shane. Shane! Come back! Bye, Shane.

Shane was the first flat widescreen (soft matted 1.66:1) color western to be produced. It was shot in the standard 1.37:1 Academy ratio, which is the format for 35mm film, with music recorded in stereophonic sound. It was cropped in the film projector because of the studio's desire for it to compete with the CinemaScope version, which was to be released. *Shane* won a single Academy Award for best color cinematography.

This is a movie that eloquently describes the passions, conflicts, and tensions among homesteaders and cattlemen to secure their territory on the open range. It demonstrates how these passions can drive ordinary men to take extraordinary action by hiring gunfighters to commit unjustified but legal murder. But most astonishingly, it shows the innocence of a young boy caught up in the battle for frontier justice and his worship of an aging gunfighter whom he grows to love and idolize.

FROM HERE TO ETERNITY (1953)

PRODUCER/DIRECTOR: Fred Zinnemann (director), Buddy Adler (producer)
WRITER(S): James Jones (novel), Daniel Taradash (screenplay)
CAST: Burt Lancaster (1st Sgt. Milton Warden), Montgomery Clift (Pvt. Robert E. Lee "Prew" Prewitt), Deborah Kerr (Karen Holmes), Donna Reed (Alma "Lorene" Burke), Frank Sinatra (Pvt. Angelo Maggio), Philip Ober (Capt. Dana "Dynamite" Holmes), Mickey Shaughnessy (Cpl. Leva), Harry Bellaver (Pvt. Mazzioli), Ernest Borgnine (Sgt. James R. "Fatso" Judson), Jack Warden (Cpl. Buckley)
CINEMATOGRAPHY: Burnett Guffey
MUSIC: George Duning
LENGTH AND RATING: 118 min; NR

While *Shane* captured the wholesome characteristics of humankind and clearly delineated good from evil and right from wrong, *From Here to Eternity* displaced frontier justice to a peacetime pre-Pearl Harbor army base and used the culture of the military as a means to articulate the dysfunction of that community. While Marion Starrett resisted her attraction to Shane, Karen Holmes (Deborah Kerr), the wife of Captain Dana Holmes (Phillip Ober), easily succumbs to First Sergeant Milton Warden (Burt Lancaster). Both *Shane* and *From Here to Eternity* express the theme of individualism within the context of a larger community. However, in the latter film, when bugler/ boxer Robert E. Lee Prewitt (Montgomery Clift), a top middleweight contender, is urged by Captain Holmes to join the regimental boxing team, he refuses because of an incident in which he blinded his opponent while sparring in the ring. Holmes chastises Prewitt, letting him know that his "lone wolf" mentality is disobedient, and that in the army there is no place for individualism. In films like *High Noon* and *Shane*, individualism is prized as a heroic quality that is an enduring expression of courage and fortitude. Contrary to what Captain Holmes says to Prewitt, the main characters in *From Here to Eternity* are individualists, including Private Angelo Maggio (Frank Sinatra), who rebel against abusive authority rather than succumb to the indignity of submission. After his confrontation with the captain, Sergeant Warden lets Prewitt know that he runs the Army base and likes to keep the captain happy so that he doesn't interfere in the sergeant's routine. He also advises Prewitt that in the days of the pioneers, one could demonstrate individualism, but that these times required a man to "...play ball."

As the narrative unfolds, each of the main protagonists embarks on what could be construed as self-destructive behavior. For Prewitt's steadfast refusal to box, he becomes the victim of abusive treatment by others in the company. He also begins a romance with Alma (Donna Reed), whose real name is Lorna and who is a hostess at the New Congress Club. For Sergeant Warden and Private Maggio, the risks they take are dangerous and fraught with personal sacrifice. The sergeant, who is recognized by his men as honorable and fair, risks twenty years in the stockade for fraternizing with the captain's wife. At the New Congress Club, Maggio, who defends Prewitt, confronts the sadistic sergeant of the stockade, "Fatso" Judson (Ernest Borgnine), after Judson calls him a "Wop" and denigrates a photograph of Maggio's sister. A tense face-off between the two men is defused when Warden steps in, following up on Fatso's threat to cut Maggio's heart out.

Relationships peak and ebb in the tense parallel action of the main characters. Tired of sneaking around, Warden asks Karen to divorce her husband so they can marry. She in turn asks him to become a commissioned officer, something Warden refuses to do. When Prewitt asks Alma to marry him she turns him down, saying that what they have together is better than marriage and that her long-term goal is to elevate her stature by finding a husband of position and status.

A turning point in the film occurs when Maggio goes AWOL from guard duty and is court-martialed and confined to the stockade, where he is brutally beaten by Fatso Judson. One calm night, as Warden and Prewitt get drunk and commiserate with each other over their troubled love affairs, a mortally injured Maggio, who has escaped from the stockade, tells of the torture by Judson and dies in Prewitt's arms. That night the base grieves Maggio's passing with a mournful rendition of taps, played by Prewitt on his bugle.

Seeking revenge for his friend, Prewitt stalks Fatso and they have a knife fight and Fatso dies. Badly wounded, Prewitt hides at Alma's apartment while the police search for Fatso's killer. As for Captain Holmes, he is found guilty of abusing Prewitt and must resign to avoid a court-martial. Hoping to avoid returning to the United States with her husband, Karen asks Warden if he has filed to be a commissioned officer and he admits that he will always be an enlisted man. They agree to part ways, knowing that Warden loves the army more than he does her. On December 7, 1941, the base is attacked by the Japanese and Prewitt decides to join his squad to fight them. Alma begs him not to go because his wounds haven't healed and she promises to marry him if he returns to the mainland with her. Prewitt is a career soldier and he chooses to leave Alma, but in the darkness of a chaotic evening he is tragically shot and killed by nervous American guards.

The movie's heroes internalize the pride of American forbearance and sacrifice, yielding only for the greater good of those they serve. They are indeed romantics, chastened by tough military standards but still sensitive to the scent of a woman. These men represent the heroes that America celebrates: They are ready to fight and die to protect those cherished ideals. This film celebrates the culture of the military, no matter how flawed or corrupt it might be, as well as the devotion of soldiers to serve. The story, characters, and fine performances pay tribute to the legacy of those men and women who choose to serve their country, and reveal the personal sacrifices they make.

The screenplay was written by Daniel Taradash, adapted from the 1951 novel by James Jones. Its adult themes, powerful narrative, and outstanding performances made it a box office success, and it took audiences away from their television sets and into the movie theater. It was directed by Fred Zinnemann, who in 1952 also directed *High Noon*, produced by Buddy Adler, and distributed by Columbia Pictures. *From Here to Eternity* received eight Academy Awards: Best Picture, Best Supporting Actor (Frank

Sinatra), Best Supporting Actress (Donna Reed), Best Black-and-White Cinematography (Burnett Guffey), and Best Director (Fred Zinnemann). The movie also won for film editing, sound recording, and screenplay.

ON THE WATERFRONT (1954)

PRODUCER/DIRECTOR: Elia Kazan (director), Sam Spiegel (producer)
WRITER(S): Malcolm Johnson (suggested by articles), Budd Schulberg (story, screenplay)
CAST: Marlon Brando (Terry Malloy), Karl Malden (Father Barry), Lee J. Cobb (Johnny Friendly), Rod Steiger (Charley "the Gent" Malloy), Pat Henning (Timothy J. "Kayo" Dugan), Leif Erickson (Glover), James Westerfield (Big Mac), Tony Galento (Truck), Tami Mauriello (Tullio), John F. Hamilton ("Pop" Doyle)
CINEMATOGRAPHY: Boris Kauffman
MUSIC: Leonard Bernstein
LENGTH AND RATING: 108 min; NR

This film is an epic, gritty drama about corruption, greed, and redemption. It is filled with both political and religious metaphors and is based on a 1948 twenty-four part series entitled "Crime on the Waterfront," written for the old *New York Sun* by Malcolm M. Johnson, who won a 1949 Pulitzer Prize for local reporting. It's about Terry Malloy, a self-described waterfront bum spectacularly portrayed by Marlon Brando in a defining role of his career. Forced by his brother Charley "the Gent" (Rod Steiger) to take "dives" as a prizefighter for union boss Johnny Friendly (Lee J. Cobb), he has become a flunky for the corrupt union and indirectly implicated in a murder. Terry's knowledge of Friendly's questionable criminal activities makes him a prime subject for the crime commission, which is investigating dishonest union tactics on the docks. He is subpoenaed to appear. Hoping to vindicate her brother's death, Edie (Eva Marie Saint) befriends Terry, whom she first met in Catholic school, urging him to testify. He is torn between his allegiance to his brother, the union, and his love for Edie. Frustrated by Terry's inability to commit to truthful testimony, Edie calls him a bum. Finally, Terry is swayed, but his brother cautions him that he could be making a deadly mistake. In one of the most famous and heart-rendering scenes in movie history, the two brothers are sitting bathed in shadows in the rear seat of a New York City taxicab, struggling with the life-and-death emotions consuming them. Charley, the older brother, admonishes Terry, warning him that death could be imminent if he doesn't make up his mind to become "D and D" (deaf and dumb). Making his point, Charley draws a revolver and aims it at Terry. Terry moves the gun muzzle down and away, trusting his older brother to not harm him. In a rare and moving exchange of dialogue, the brothers briefly reminisce about the past as Charley brings up Terry's abbreviated boxing career. This angers Terry because he took the falls for the short-end money. He tells his brother that all he got out of it was "a one-way ticket to Palookaville." Then, in one of the most emotional and tender scenes between two men on the screen, Terry says:

> You don't understand! I coulda had class. I coulda been a contender. I coulda been somebody instead of a bum, which is what I am. Let's face it (pause)… it was you Charley.

Marlon Brando and Eva Marie Saint. [Columbia Pictures/Photofest]

The taxicab stops and Terry quickly gets out; later, he is confronted with the murdered remains of his brother. After his testimony, Terry returns to the docks and is initially ostracized by the workers. He and Johnny Friendly have a brutal fight and the union thugs nearly kill Terry. After his beating, the men refuse to return to work unless Terry leads them. Father Barry (Karl Malden) urges Terry to lead the men, and he helps him to his feet. Terry, brutally beaten and somewhat disoriented, is then followed triumphantly by the men.

The film was shot on location on the Hoboken, New Jersey, docks over a period of thirty-six days. This added to the realism and natural texture of the film. The first attempt at a screenplay was *The Hook*, by playwright Arthur Miller. In 1950, Kazan hired Miller to do research on the longshoremen working in Brooklyn's Red Hook section and to investigate the corruption that manifested on the docks, but personal and political reasons prevented Miller from completing the project. Over at Columbia Pictures, studio head Harry Cohn told Miller to change the evil characters from corrupt waterfront union officials to communists, thus complying with the anti-communist mood of the time. Miller would neither compromise his principles nor his art and resigned from the project. After Miller left the project, Kazan hired writer Bud Schulberg, who had been a friendly witness and had implicated other Hollywood artists as communist sympathizers, naming them before the House Un-American Activities Committee (HUAC).

During the investigation by the HUAC in the 1950s, Miller, unlike his friend and colleague Kazan, had refused to testify and was blacklisted, although his plays continued to be produced. Since Kazan was at the pinnacle of his career and would not risk the consequences of blacklisting, and because he had been a member of the communist party in his youth, he became friendly to the HUAC, offering names of other communist supporters. Indeed, of the Hollywood Ten who were blacklisted by the HUAC, Kazan named eight of them.

As a director, Kazan had managed to conquer New York's Broadway theatrical community and Hollywood. As a graduate of the Group Theatre and an avid proponent of Method acting, Kazan was one of the founders of the Actors Studio, which teaches the principles of Method acting within the context of an actor's personal experience. In the 1950s, Kazan was directing plays such as *Death of a Salesman*, *A Streetcar Named Desire*, and *Cat on a Hot Tin Roof*, along with movies based on screen adaptations of these plays.

For Kazan, *On the Waterfront* was a metaphor for his testimony before the HUAC and his attempt to redeem his virtue among the Hollywood community. Through the character of Terry Malloy, who eventually breaks the code of silence pledged to the corrupt union boss Johnny Friendly by agreeing to testify against the union, Kazan attempts to rationalize his actions before the HUAC. He provides an explanation for his actions and tries to vindicate himself by declaring that there are times when one may be forced to make a judgment and testify against colleagues and friends for a "greater good." In 1999, Kazan was given a lifetime achievement award by the Academy of Motion Picture Arts and Sciences. The award was presented by Robert de Niro and Martin Scorsese, but more than fifty years after his HUAC testimony there were still those who would not stand and applaud his achievements.

To this day, *On the Waterfront* offers a powerful narrative about corruption and greed and its impact on society. In the wake of scandals in corporate America, such as the Enron and Tyco fiascos, the greed of Wall Street causing the demise of Bear Stearns and Lehman Brothers, as well as political malfeasance, this film has an enduring legacy about self-sacrifice and the courage it takes to be a whistle-blower. It is indeed a cinematic masterpiece, with outstanding direction, acting, and music along with an enduring theme integrated in the dynamic of labor and love challenged by greed and power and sustained by faith.

LA STRADA (THE ROAD) (1954)

PRODUCER/DIRECTOR: Federico Fellini (director), Dino De Laurentiis (producer), Carlo Ponti (producer)

WRITER(S): Federico Fellini (story), Tullio Pinelli (story)

CAST: Anthony Quinn (Zampanò), Giulietta Masina (Gelsomina), Richard Basehart (Il Matto), Aldo Silvani (Signor Giraffa), Marcella Rovere (La Vedova), Livia Venturini (La Suorina)

CINEMATOGRAPHY: Otello Martelli

MUSIC: Nino Rota

LENGTH AND RATING: 108 min; NR

In 1954, while Americans were busy ogling the contestants on the first-televised Miss America Pageant and staring at the newly released twelve-inch screen color television sets manufactured by RCA, a unique presence in Italian cinema emerged, with its expressive sensibility stylized by the influences of neo-realism. The director, Federico Fellini, used film as a canvas to portray the essence of relationships driven by raw emotions that are evocative of both the fantasy and reality of life. Fellini was a master of neo-realism. He was able to capture the frustration, despair, and poverty of the lower classes, and was sensitive of the need to display their plight on the screen.

La Strada earned Fellini his first international recognition and the attention of American audiences. For post-World War II American audiences, *La Strada* was a significant departure from the movies they were accustomed to. There was, however, the familiarity of two American actors playing leads in the movie: Richard Basehart as the circus high-wire performer and clown known as The Fool, and Anthony Quinn as Zampano, a brutish two-bit carnival strongman who breaks chains on his chest and evokes the harshness of poverty, ignorance, and emptiness.

The story centers on Zampano and the young simpleminded woman, Gelsomina (Giulietta Masina), whom he buys from an impoverished mother to serve as his maid and concubine. He had also bought Gelsomina's older sister from the same woman, but she had died. Zampano trains Gelsomina to accompany his cheap strongman act as a clown while also learning simple tunes on the cornet, and they eventually join the small but established Giraffa's circus. There they meet The Fool, who develops an affection for Gelsomina and attempts to instill in her a sense of self-worth while taunting, insulting, and belittling Zampano. Frustrated by the taunts of The Fool, Zampano is jailed for threatening him with a knife, and The Fool asks Gelsomina to join him on the road but recognizes that she is devoted to Zampano. After they are reunited, Gelsomina and Zampano meet The Fool and Zampano murders him. Haunted by her whimpering and his conscience, Zampano abandons Gelsomina in the snow, where she dies, and when he hears the soft, sad, gentle tune she used to play on her cornet, he breaks down and cries, knowing that he is truly alone.

Innocence, virtue, rage, and boorishness are captured within a chronicle of people who appear to lead lives with no destiny but in the end become martyrs to those values that are cherished by most. For American audiences, these characters represented archetypes that revealed a culture of poverty that reflected not only a lack of means but a struggle for emotional values within a context of denial and hostility. *La Strada* brought a new vision to film and provided American audiences with an opportunity to experience a unique cinematic voice and a masterful sense of symbolic storytelling. The 1999 Woody Allen film *Sweet and Lowdown* was loosely based on *La Strada*. Fellini said of his film:

> If I were even more shameless than I am, I could point out other reasons, perhaps deeper roots, that certainly gave life to the characters and the narration of their story in my fantasy: remorseful feelings, nostalgia, regrets, the fairy tale of a betrayed innocence, the melancholy hope for a pure world made up of trustworthy relationships and the impossibility and the betrayal of all this; in short, all the confused, obscure sense of guilt that has been nourished, increased and administered with tireless care by Catholic blackmail. (*New York Times*, "Classics of 20th-Century Film," Sept. 29, 2006, E10)

In his July 17, 1956, *New York Times* Review, A. H. Weiller wrote:

We have no idea why *La Strada*, which won a prize at the 1954 Venice Film Festival, has not been exposed to American audiences until now. Perhaps it is because Signor Fellini's theme offers neither a happy ending so dear to the hearts of escapists nor a clear-cut and shiningly hopeful plot. Suffice it to say that his study of his principals is honest and unadorned, strikingly realistic and yet tender and compassionate. *La Strada* is a road well worth traveling. (http://movies.nytimes.com/movie/review)

SEVEN SAMURAI (1954)

PRODUCER/DIRECTOR: Akira Kurosawa (director), Sojiro Motoki (producer)
WRITER(S): Akira Kurosawa (screenplay), Shinobu Hashimoto (screenplay)
CAST: Takashi Shimura (Kambei Shimada), Toshirô Mifune (Kikuchiyo), Yoshio Inaba (Gorobei Katayama), Seiji Miyaguchi (Kyuzo), Minoru Chiaki (Heihachi Hayashida), Daisuke Katô (Shichiroji), Isao Kimura (Katsushiro Okamoto), Keiko Tsushima (Shino), Yukiko Shimazaki (Rikichi's Wife), Kamatari Fujiwara (Manzo, father of Shino)
CINEMATOGRAPHY: Asakazu Nakai
MUSIC: Fumio Hayasaka
LENGTH AND RATING: USA: 207 min (restored version); NR

A number of themes shaped the work of Japanese director Akira Kurosawa, who was a master of camera movement and action. Classical Japanese influences include the Noh plays, which are beautifully choreographed musical drama, and Kabuki Theater, known for its stylized dramatic structure and the elaborate makeup worn by the performers. There is a great deal of western characteristic in Kurosawa's work, and he acknowledges that the films of American directors John Ford, Abel Gance, Frank Capra, and William Wyler had inspired him. Indeed, just as director John Ford was morally outraged by the exploitation of others, Kurosawa was equally disturbed and he expressed this in *Seven Samurai*. He had a compassionate interest in individuals who sacrificed themselves for the needs of others, and he had a passion for American westerns.

Kurosawa's early training as a painter afforded him a unique sense of vision that allowed him to portray the events in this film in an authentic way. This is also a reason for the intimacy and wordless action that prevails in some of the scenes. When a kidnapped wife who was forced to serve as a concubine is reunited with her husband after a samurai raid on the bandit fort that is set aflame, they look at each other with an extended pause, and without a word she turns around and runs into the flames. In another scene, the camera focuses on a close-up of the frozen face of one of the villagers and then pulls back to reveal that he is holding a long pole with one of the bandits impaled on it. Dialogue is not necessary to convey the action and emotion of the moment.

The story is set in the sixteenth century at a time when the celebrity of samurai warriors was waning, and many of them were unemployed and impoverished. It's about a poor Japanese farming village that endures the attacks of bandits who raid their rice crops and steal their women. They approach a master samurai named Kanbei (Takashi Shimura), who poses as a monk to rescue a farmer's child. Because the rescue effort is successful, the farmers ask Kanbei to assist them in defending themselves against the bandits. He agrees and recruits five others, including a young samurai named Katsushiro (Isao Kimura), who earns a place as Kanbei's disciple, and master swordsman Kyuzo (Seiji Miyaguchi). The seventh member is Kikuchiyo (Toshiro Mifune), a samurai poseur who is the son of a farmer and who eventually wins the respect of the others. In the first half of the film, the samurai bond with each other and become acquainted with the villagers, while the second half focuses on confrontation with the bandits and the raging battles that are fought.

Kurosawa was a director who was challenged by innovation, never fearing it. In the movie, battle scenes were filmed with multiple cameras and he also used a telephoto lens, panning the camera to follow the action. Using multiple cameras allowed Kurosawa to film uninterrupted, thus allowing the actors to perform without being conscious of the presence of the camera. His use of dynamic framing, editing, and camera movements influenced many directors, including George Lucas, whose *Star Wars* is indebted to Kurosawa's *The Hidden Fortress,* and the technical mastery of his editing had a great impact on *The Empire Strikes Back.* Other notable directors influenced by Kurosawa's artistry are Francis Ford Coppola and Martin Scorsese.

In his *New York Times* review of November 20, 1956, Bosley Crowther compares *Seven Samurai* to *High Noon:*

> wherein the qualities of human strength and weakness are discovered in a crisis taut with peril. And although the occurrence of this crisis is set in the sixteenth century in a village in Japan, it could be transposed without surrendering a basic element to the nineteenth century and a town on our own frontier.

The review also compares the film in style and excellence to the work of Fred Zinnemann and John Ford, praising its use of close-ups and sudden mood changes within scenes.

In addressing the value of a good script, Kurosawa was somewhat pragmatic about a director's ability to create a film:

> With a good script, a good director can produce a masterpiece. With the same script, a mediocre director can produce a passable film. But with a bad script even a good director can't possibly make a good film. For truly cinematic expression, the camera and the microphone must be able to cross both fire and water. The script must be something that has the power to do this. (Kurosawa, 2006, ThinkExist. com/quotes/Akira_Kurosawa)

As a director, Akira Kurosawa was a masterful storyteller who was able to communicate a kinetic sense of action in *Seven Samurai* while portraying his heroes as caring warriors sacrificing themselves for the good of humanity. His values are articulated in the breadth of the film, and although his heroes are not invincible they do leave an enduring legacy of honor sustained by their heroic deeds. In speaking about *Seven Samurai* Kurosawa said:

I think we ought to have richer foods, richer films. And so I thought I would make this kind of film, entertaining enough to eat as it were.

In response to a critical remark about *Seven Samurai*, Kurosawa said:

You try to give a film a little pictorial scope, and the journalists jump on you for spending too much money.

Kurosawa started his career as an illustrator for popular magazines and he continued his art after becoming a director by using his talent to make full-scale storyboard paintings for his films. His artistic vision and attention to character development made him a great director, and his *Seven Samurai* became an icon of excellence that had an enormous impact on generations of filmmakers. In 1960, *The Magnificent Seven*, a western directed by John Sturges, was adapted from Kurosawa's masterpiece *Seven Samurai*.

REBEL WITHOUT A CAUSE (1955)

PRODUCER/DIRECTOR: Nicholas Ray (director), David Weisbart (producer)
WRITER(S): Stewart Stern (screenplay), Irving Shulman (adaptation)
CAST: James Dean (Jim Stark), Natalie Wood (Judy), Sal Mineo (John "Plato" Crawford), Jim Backus (Frank Stark), Ann Doran (Mrs. Carol Stark), Corey Allen (Buzz Gunderson), William Hopper (Judy's Father), Rochelle Hudson (Judy's Mother), Dennis Hopper (Goon), Edward Platt (Ray Fremick)
CINEMATOGRAPHY: Ernest Haller
MUSIC: Leonard Rosenman
LENGTH AND RATING: 111 min; NR

The 1950s were marked by an era of affluence, with many American families caught up in the quest for materialistic values. There was also a confluence of events that would create a vast sea change in American youth culture. From 1946 to 1960, America's teenage population increased from 5.6 to 11.8 million (Frascella and Weisel, 2005, p. 8). Also, from 1948 to 1953, so-called "juvenile delinquents" charged with a crime went up forty-five percent (http://www.jsteri.org/pss/3348604). This caused a Boston judge to remark:

We have the spectacle of an entire city terrorized by one-half of one percent of its residents. And the terrorists are children.

As many social critics have noted, it was a time when the baby boom generation came of age. And, as historian William Manchester writes, a teenage subculture developed "with its own customs, status symbols, stigmata, rites, and fads." Indeed, the film's title is the same as psychoanalyst Robert Lindner's book, *Rebel Without a Cause: The Hypnoanalysis of a Criminal Psychopath* (New York: Grove Press, 1944), a case study of a troubled teenager that brought these concerns to national consciousness.

The Hollywood studios understood the value of teenagers, as they were the target audience of the moment, spending money to go to the movies, and the studios accommodated them. Select film genres appealed to this teenage audience, including horror films such as *The Giant Gila Monster* (1959), *The Blob* (1958), *I Was a Teenage Werewolf* (1957), and *Monster on the Campus* (1958). Also, the fears many Americans had about wild and unruly teenage behavior, as expressed by noted authors such as Benjamin Fine in his 1955 book, *1,000,000 Delinquents* (Cleveland: The World Publishing Company, 1955), were a perfect foil for the portrayal of the teenage criminal in the movie *The Wild One* (1953), starring Marlon Brando.

Director Nicholas Ray, the driving force behind *Rebel Without a Cause*, was destined to direct this film. He was an iconoclastic artist who studied architecture under Frank Lloyd Wright's Taliesin fellowship, where he learned an appreciation of the horizontal line and then applied his aesthetic to CinemaScope. Ray worked in radio and learned the rudiments of film production by watching Elia Kazan direct his first feature film, *A Tree Grows in Brooklyn* (1944); he then directed his first film *They Live By Night* in 1947. He was a student of film noir, and was very interested in young people on the periphery of society. He created the "love on the run" subgenre, which was popularized by later movies such as *Gun Crazy* (1949), *Bonnie and Clyde* (1967), and *Thieves Like Us* (1974), a remake of *They Live By Night*.

His personal and professional life was one of complex relationships and seductions. He was bisexual and a heavy drinker and drug user who seduced the sixteen-year-old actress Natalie Wood, a costar in *Rebel*. In describing his experience making *Johnny Guitar*, featuring Joan Crawford, Ray called it "an appalling experience" and referred to Crawford as "one of the worst human beings ever encountered" (Frascella and Weisel 2005).

The many hostile encounters between alienated youth and dysfunctional adults in *Rebel Without a Cause* defined the film's theme as a testament to disaffected American teenagers. Ray was an astute observer of the dynamics involved in heterosexual and homosexual relationships, both important threads in the film.

The three principal characters, Jim "Jimbo" Stark (James Dean), Judy (Natalie Wood), and Plato (Sal Mineo), are troubled adolescents from what outwardly appear to be decent families who are cornered into a frustrated sense of alienation and fear. As the new kid in town, Jim is confronted and tested by the neighborhood gang, headed by its leader Buzz. Jim also carries a lot of baggage: His family has been moving from town to town because of his behavioral difficulties and his lack of respect for his father (Jim Backus), who is dominated by his wife and Jim's mother (Ann Doran). As a son, Jim views his father as a helpless pawn manipulated by his mother and unwilling to assert himself. For Judy, the difficulties are with her father (William Hopper), who no longer shows her the affection she yearns for and received as a child. At sixteen, Judy is realizing a sexual awakening that she attempts to reconcile with her father, who rejects her aggressive desire toward him. His reaction to his daughter's use of red lipstick is one of disdain and contempt, because to him she looks and behaves like a harlot. While Jim and Judy deal with the dynamics of their families, Plato has no parents to relate to. Instead, he lives in a large house with a nanny who cares for him. His father has left and his mother travels extensively, neither remembering his birthday. As such, he is the most troubled of the three youths.

While all three have repressed desire, Plato's sexual orientation is homosexual, and as such he takes a keen interest in Jim. Indeed, during the production of the movie, it was known that James Dean manifested this relationship offscreen between himself and Sal Mineo (although it appears never to have been consummated), encouraging it as an onscreen connection between the characters Jim and Plato.

In a tragic turn of events, Jim survives a "chickie run" and gang leader Buzz is killed when his coat sleeve gets caught on a door handle of the car he's driving as it goes over the cliff. His gang decides to assert retribution and hunts Jim down in a deserted mansion, where he is staying with Judy and Plato. To protect Jim and his new "family," Plato has taken his father's gun and he shoots one of Jim's pursuers and then flees to a planetarium. The police surround the building and order Plato to surrender, and then Jim enters, convincing Plato to leave with him. He unloads the gun, keeping the bullets, and to bond the trust of their friendship, Jim gives Plato his red wind-breaker and returns the empty gun to him. Leaving the empty building, the police turn the flood lights on and, seeing the gun, shoot and kill Plato.

Alienation, rebellion, and the struggle with personal identity and feelings of belonging are all themes in *Rebel Without a Cause*. The film made James Dean in death an icon for youth, and defined a manifesto for the voices of young people searching for the meaning in their lives. The film also influenced other directors, actors, and performers such as Bob Dylan, Al Pacino, Michael Parks, and the late Jim Morrison, lead singer of The Doors. It had a profound influence on American culture and cinema and has had a sustaining legacy on the structure, characters, and aesthetics of film.

In his October 27, 1955, *New York Times* review, Bosley Crowther compared the movie to *Blackboard Jungle*:

> It is a violent, brutal, and disturbing picture of modern teen-agers that Warner Brothers presents in its new melodrama at the Astor, *Rebel Without A Cause*. Young people neglected by their parents or given no understanding and moral support by fathers and mothers who are themselves unable to achieve balance and security in their homes are the bristling heroes and heroines of this excessively graphic exercise. Like *Blackboard Jungle* before it, it is a picture to make the hair stand on end. (http://www.nytimes.com/movie/review)

THE SEARCHERS (1956)

PRODUCER/DIRECTOR: John Ford (director), Merian C. Cooper (executive producer), Patrick Ford (associate producer), C. V. Whitney (producer)

WRITER(S): Alan Le May (novel), Frank S. Nugent (screenplay)

CAST: John Wayne (Ethan Edwards), Jeffrey Hunter (Martin Pawley), Vera Miles (Laurie Jorgensen), Ward Bond (Rev. Capt. Samuel Johnston Clayton), Natalie Wood (Debbie Edwards), John Qualen (Lars Jorgensen), Olive Carey (Mrs. Jorgensen), Henry Brandon (Chief Cicatrice), Ken Curtis (Charlie McCorry), Harry Carey, Jr. (Brad Jorgensen)

CINEMATOGRAPHY: Winton C. Hoch

MUSIC: Max Steiner

LENGTH AND RATING: 119 min; NR

For John Wayne, who plays Ethan Edwards, this role was probably one of the defining moments of his career. He is a returning Confederate army sergeant who kept his uniform and saber, refusing to capitulate to the Yankees. Although the war has been over for three years, Ethan has wandered, and the implication is that he has been an outlaw filling his pockets with Yankee gold. He is also a hardened man with a hatred toward the Indians and little compassion for them or civilization. When he returns to his brother Aaron's home, set on the lonely Texas frontier, he is greeted by his nieces and nephew, along with Aaron's wife Martha (Dorothy Jordan). There is a subtle attraction and longing that Martha and Ethan have toward each other, but it appears they reconciled those passions long ago. When he is introduced to his brother's adopted son Martin Pawley (Jeffrey Hunter), who is part Cherokee Indian, Ethan shows nothing but contempt toward him and demonstratively denies that Martin is any blood relation to him.

The Searchers was John Ford's 115th feature film and was one of his most complex narratives. As in so many of his other movies, Ford pursued the contradiction between civilization, the wild frontier, and the men and women who attempted to settle in these hostile environments. The character of Ethan Edwards has been consumed by hatred and sexual repression since the woman he so longed for was raped and murdered, along with her husband and son, as he and a posse were lured away by a Comanche ruse used to attack his brother's home. They kidnap Ethan's two nieces Debbie portrayed as a youth (Lana Wood), and her sister as a teenager (Natalie Wood) and Lucy (Pippa Scott). Nomadic by nature and with few differences between himself and the Comanches he is hunting, Ethan, along with Martin, embarks on a five-year odyssey to find Debbie, who has become a squaw to her abductor, Chief Scar. Early in the search they find the mutilated remains of Lucy, who has been brutally raped.

As a bigoted example of the Old West, Ethan's character is juxtaposed against Martin's, who represents the more modern example of tolerance and forbearance. For Ethan, there is no such thing as a good Indian, only a dead one. He rebukes the sentimentality and etiquette of civilization, preferring the harsh and unforgiving reality of the open plains and frontier. Indeed, only a man with this level of endurance, discipline, and unrelenting focus could undertake such an epic quest. In this he can be compared to the Greek warrior Odysseus, who led the siege of Troy for nine years and took ten years to return home, facing off with Cyclops and Circe.

A driving compulsion for Ethan is the knowledge that Chief Scar raped Martha before killing her. Although Ethan had repressed his feelings for her, he secretly embraced the same desire but would never consciously admit it. Thus, the retribution he must pursue against Scar and all Indians is a testament to his need to release his sexual tension and frustration. In doing so, he determines that his niece, Debbie, has become a squaw to Scar. In Ethan's view of humanity, she is no longer white, and to satisfy his unrequited lust he must kill her.

The film, as were so many other John Ford westerns, was shot in the majestic Monument Valley on the Arizona-Utah border. Nature serves as a principal character with its stark, natural beauty and towering bluffs. The setting distinguishes the dominance of nature over man and his need to tame or reconcile his existence in that habitat.

The Searchers is a remarkable tribute to John Ford and his ability to treat the themes of bigotry within the context of a character out of reach with the society he covets but cannot accept. It resonates with the strong characters and symbolism that reflect the nature of the American experience confronting a hostile land and indigenous population.

In his May 31, 1956, *New York Times* review, Bosley Crowther wrote of *The Searchers*, "it bristles and howls with Indian fighting, goes into tense, nerve-rasping brawls between the Texan and his hunting companion, explodes with fiery comedy, and lays into some frontier heroics that make the welkin ring" (http://www.movies.nytimes.com/movie/review).

INVASION OF THE BODY SNATCHERS (1956)

PRODUCER/DIRECTOR: Don Siegel (director), Walter Wanger (producer)
WRITER(S): Jack Finney (*Collier's* magazine serial), Daniel Mainwaring (screenplay)
CAST: Kevin McCarthy (Dr. Miles J. Bennell), Dana Wynter (Becky Driscoll), Larry Gates (Dr. Dan "Danny" Kauffman), King Donovan (Jack Belicec), Carolyn Jones (Theodora "Teddy" Belicec), Jean Willes (Nurse Sally Withers), Ralph Dumke (Police Chief Nick Grivett), Virginia Christine (Wilma Lentz), Tom Fadden (Uncle Ira Lentz), Kenneth Patterson (Stanley Driscoll)
CINEMATOGRAPHY: Ellsworth Fredericks
MUSIC: Carmen Dragon
LENGTH AND RATING: 80 min; NR

In my practice, I've seen how people have allowed their humanity to drain away. Only when we have to fight to stay human do we realize how precious it is to us, how dear. (Dr. Miles Bennell [Kevin McCarthy] *Invasion of the Body Snatchers*)

Invasion of the Body Snatchers unfolds in Santa Mira, California, a "normal" place in small-town America. Strange things have been happening to its inhabitants, and there is a sense of collective alienation experienced by the residents, who are suddenly aware that the people they are most intimate with are not who they are supposed to be. The grocer's son, a small boy named Jimmy Grimaldi, is brought to Bennell by his grandmother in a state of hysteria, claiming his mother is not really his mother. The doctor sends Jimmy back to his mother, Wilma, and later the two appear reconciled and comfortable with each other. But the sudden change of demeanor between son and mother raises Dr. Bennell's suspicions:

Sick people who couldn't wait to see me, then suddenly were perfectly all right. A boy who said his mother wasn't his mother. A woman who said her uncle wasn't her uncle.

Resident psychiatrist Dr. Kauffman attributes the strange behavior to a contagious epidemic of mass hysteria. When asked what caused it Kauffman replies, "Worry about what's going on in the world, probably." For many, the timing of the film and its story about pod-like aliens replicating themselves as identical twins of their chosen hosts is a parable of the cold war era and Senator Joseph McCarthy's pursuit of communist infiltrators. Those called to testify at the House Un-American Activities Committee (HUAC) hearings were asked to prove their loyalty by naming communists, and if they refused they were banished to the blacklist.

The citizens of Santa Mira are consumed by the pods, which strip them of their individualism and will to resist. Once their bodies are appropriated they became conformists, bowing as devoted supplicants to their masters. In the shadow of the HUAC and the enforced blacklist, Hollywood imposed a culture of uniformity where resistance was met with a pod-like consensus. In the book *Cult Movies* by Danny Peary, the notion of regimentation and the loss of individuality are explored:

> The pod people represent a completely regimented society. Metaphorically, they are all alike as "two peas in a pod" because they have been sapped of their emotional individuality. The vegetarian metaphor literalizes Red-scare rhetoric of the "growth" of communism as well as the idea that revolutions are made by planting seeds. There is a scene in which the pod people are assembled in the town square, where a loud speaker reads out the day's orders; it is the quintessential fifties image of socialism. And, of course, the simile that without freedom of thought people are... vegetables is a central theme of the narrative. (http://www.gadflyonline.com/11-26-01/film-snatchers.html)

For the film's director Don Siegel, *Invasion of the Body Snatchers* is a metaphor on the loss of individualism in daily life:

> Many of my associates are certainly pods. They have no feelings. They exist, breathe, sleep. To be a pod means that you have no passion, no anger, the spark has left you...Of course, there's a very strong case for being a pod. These pods, who get rid of pain, ill health and mental disturbances, are, in a sense, doing good. It happens to leave you in a very dull world but that, by the way, is the world that most of us live in. It's the same as people who welcome going into the army or prison. There's regimentation, a lack of having to make up your mind, face decisions... People are becoming vegetables. I don't know what the answer is except an awareness of it. That's what makes a picture like *Invasion of the Body Snatchers* important.

As the townspeople are taken over by the pods, Miles and his girlfriend Becky (Dana Wynter) watch the replicants load the seeds into trucks and cars to be distributed to nearby towns and communities. They are confronted by Miles' friend, Jack, and Dr. Kauffman, who inform them they cannot let them leave because they are a threat. Indeed, Kauffman explains to Miles why he and Becky should allow themselves to be consumed by the pods and become part of the new life order:

> Your new bodies are growing in there. They're taking you over cell for cell, atom for atom. There is no pain.... Tomorrow you'll be one of us... There's no need for love... Love. Desire. Ambition. Faith. Without them, life is so simple, believe me.

Becky tells Miles she does not want to live in a world without love, grief, or beauty, and that she would rather die. To escape, Miles injects Dr. Kauffman and Jack with drugs and they attempt to integrate themselves into the life of the town by acting like replicants. Their plan is foiled when Becky screams as a dog is nearly run over by a truck, and the townspeople take chase after them. They hide in a cave and Miles leaves Becky for a few minutes. When he returns he finds her slumped over with exhaustion. He picks her up, gently kissing her on the lips and realizes from her blank look that she is now one of them. Becky alerts her pod people that Miles is in the cave with her and that they should get him.

Miles escapes but realizes that he is utterly alone. Running on the highway, he shouts like a madman to drivers asking for their help, pleading that the people chasing him are not human. Finally, looking straight into the camera, he says:

> Look, you fools. You're in danger. Can't you see? They're after you. They're after all of us. Our wives, our children, everyone. YOU'RE NEXT!

The ending of the film is a classic cliff-hanger, with a raving Dr. Miles Bennell attempting to warn people that his pursuers are not human and shouting that they are next. However, Allied Artists Pictures, the studio that released the film, felt that the ending expressed little hope for the world's redemption from the evils it faced, and that the tone of mass paranoia could make audiences uncomfortable. The studio added a prologue and epilogue which were not part of the original film. In that scene, Miles is confined to a hospital and considered a lunatic by attending physicians. Eventually his story is confirmed and the FBI and other law enforcement agencies move to control the pod epidemic.

The narrative, by Jack Finney, originally appeared in 1954 as a three-part serial in *Collier's* magazine and was expanded into a novel, *Body Snatchers*, in 1955. Many directors were inspired by the movie, which served as a foundation for the large body of future science fiction movies. It was so popular there were three remakes: *Invasion of the Body Snatchers* (1978), directed by Philip Kauffman; *Body Snatchers* (1993), directed by Abel Ferrara; and *Invasion* (2007), directed by Oliver Hirschbiegel. In her review of the 1956 *Invasion of the Body Snatchers*, Pauline Kael wrote that the film "has an idea that confirms everyone's suspicions. A B-picture classic. This plain and inexpensive piece of science fiction employs few of the resources of the cinema (to put it mildly), but it has an idea that confirms everyone's suspicions. People are being turned into vegetables— and who can tell the difference? Kevin McCarthy and Dana Wynter, who try to cling to their animality and individuality, seem inexplicably backward to the rest of the townspeople. Some of the best lines of dialogue are voice-overs—the voice chatter of the dehumanized" (http://www.geocities.com/paulinekaelreviews/i3).

THE TEN COMMANDMENTS (1956)

PRODUCER/DIRECTOR: Cecil B. DeMille (director), Cecil B. DeMille (producer)
WRITER(S): J. H. Ingraham (novel), A. E. Southon (novel)
CAST: Charlton Heston (Moses), Yul Brynner (Rameses), Anne Baxter (Nefretiri), Edward G. Robinson (Dathan), Yvonne De Carlo (Sephora), Debra Paget (Lilia), John Derek (Joshua), Cedric Hardwicke (Sethi), Nina Foch (Bithiah), Martha Scott (Yochabel)
CINEMATOGRAPHY: Loyal Griggs
MUSIC: Elmer Bernstein
LENGTH AND RATING: 220 min; NR

In the 1920s and 1930s, the biblical spectacle on film proved to be a popular genre among audiences, which translated into box office success. A director who appeared to be particularly adept at translating the epic of the Bible into popular culture was

Cecil B. DeMille. He began his career as a theatrical actor but by 1913 had joined with Jesse L. Lasky and Lasky's brother-in-law Sam Goldfish (Sam Goldwyn), creating the Jesse L. Lasky Feature Play Company. He directed the company's first feature film, *The Squaw Man* (1914). The company eventually assumed control of Paramount, and in 1916 DeMille fulfilled his desire for producing grand film spectacles with the movie *Joan the Woman* (1916). Although a critical success, the film did poorly at the box office and DeMille had to delay additional cinematic spectacles. His next opportunity came in 1923, with the silent screen version of *The Ten Commandments*, and although it was one of the most popular films of the time, it went significantly over budget.

In 1927, DeMille made his favorite film, *The King of Kings*, about the life of Jesus Christ. Before the age of video it held the record as the most screened film on Earth, having been seen by about one billion people. It was seen all over the world and made available for free viewing in what we now call third world countries. In addition, DeMille donated his share of the earnings to charity.

He went on to produce other biblical epics, but Cecil B. DeMille's crowning achievement was his 1956 sound remake Technicolor Vista Vision version of his 70th film, *The Ten Commandments*. Everything about the film was done on a grand scale, including the research, which included consulting 1,900 books, 3,000 photographs, and thirty libraries; that research was then adapted into a 308-page script. One of the largest movie sets ever built was constructed in Egypt and included the Gates of Per Rameses: some 107 feet high and nearly a quarter of a mile long, with the Avenue of the Sphinxes. To film the Exodus scene, DeMille used 15,000 people, 12,000 animals, and 100,000 props. The Hollywood sets for the film were huge, including the gigantic water trip tanks, which the film's special effects coordinator, John Fulton, used to create the parting of the Red Sea. At a cost of just over $13 million, *The Ten Commandments* was the most expensive movie made at that time.

Politically, Cecil B. DeMille was a fervent anti-communist but he never testified against anyone before the House Un-American Activities Committee. Indeed, he hired Elmer Bernstein, a "gray-listed" writer, to write the music for the film, and actor Edward G. Robinson, who had been blacklisted, to play the role of Dathan.

To help promote the film, DeMille entered into a partnership with the Fraternal Order of Eagles, a nationwide group of civic-minded clubs founded by theater owners. Through them he was able to distribute several thousand Ten Commandment monuments, or decalogues, which were unveiled across the country to popularize and promote the film.

In his November 9, 1956, *New York Times* review of *The Ten Commandments*, Bosley Crowther writes about the rich telling of a biblical story in "the colloquial idiom of the screen." He also notes that it is a moving story of man's freedom under the divine inspiration of his maker and is relevant to the current day (1956) and mentioned "in its remarkable settings and décor, including an overwhelming façade of the Egyptian city from which the Exodus begins, and in the glowing Technicolor in which the picture is filmed—Mr. DeMille has worked photographic wonders" (http://www.movies/nytimes.com/movie/review).

Being relevant and articulating the importance of faith makes *The Ten Commandments* an enduring film narrative. It has been seen by generations of television and video audiences, and while some reviewers criticized its staging and horizontal blocking, its epic scale and technical excellence make it one of the most popular films of all time. It also helped to establish the grandiose historical film as a legitimate genre for the movies. The film won eleven Oscars and held that record for several decades until 1997, when *Titanic,* another epic historical film with production values pioneered by *The Ten Commandments,* matched that number. It also held the record as the fifth-highest grossing movie, with adjusted-for-inflation earnings of $838.4 million. It was the top earner for a religious film until the release of *The Passion of the Christ* in 2004.

THE BRIDGE ON THE RIVER KWAI (1957)

PRODUCER/DIRECTOR: David Lean (director), Sam Spiegel (producer)

WRITER(S): Pierre Boulle (novel)

CAST: William Holden (Cmdr. Shears), Jack Hawkins (Maj. Warden), Alec Guinness (Col. Nicholson), Sessue Hayakawa (Col. Saito), James Donald (Maj. Clipton), Geoffrey Horne (Lt. Joyce), André Morell (Col. Green), Peter Williams (Capt. Reeves), John Boxer (Maj. Hughes), Percy Herbert (Pvt. Grogan)

CINEMATOGRAPHY: Jack Hildyard

MUSIC: Malcolm Arnold

LENGTH AND RATING: 161 min; NR

This film was released during the time of the cold war and the Russian launch of the first orbital satellite, Sputnik. It was also the year the civil rights movement grew, mafia chiefs were assassinated while vying for leadership, and Senator Joseph McCarthy died. *The Bridge on the River Kwai,* while appearing to be a tribute to the traditional values of heroism, fortitude, and perseverance, in reality questions those constructs within the context of defining bravery and militarism during a time of war.

It is a story of will and defiance between two commanding officers, Japanese Colonel Saito (Sessue Hayakawa), commandant of the Burmese prison camp, and British Colonel Nicholson (Alec Guinness), who arrives with a contingent of British prisoners of war displaying the rigid virtues and arrogance of colonial England.

The film is a character study of these two men, who match wills over their determination to be the dominant leader. Citing the Geneva Convention, Nicholson refuses to allow his officers to work alongside the enlisted men to build Saito's bridge. Colonel Saito scoffs at such rules, belittling their influence in a time of war, and demonstrates his power by placing all of the officers in "sweat boxes."

At the camp is a lone American sailor, "Commander" Shears (William Holden), who along with an Australian corporal are the only survivors remaining from the prisoners of war who built the camp. He is a foil for Colonel Nicholson, opposite in character from the by-the-book discipline so conspicuously displayed by the British officer. Instead, Shears uses his ingenuity, wit, and charm to survive and mocks the straitlaced virtues of Nicholson, who views war as the ultimate means for heroic destiny. For Shears, the war's death and destruction make little sense and he is determined to use any means to survive.

The battle of wills is won by Nicholson, who then seizes upon the bridge building project as a means for his own heroic redemption. He assumes total command of the effort, rationalizing that his men need to be occupied and therefore should work on a project they can be proud of. Nicholson becomes consumed with the idea of building a monument to himself, and he couches that desire within the context of creating an enduring legacy for the British soldiers. His obsessive need to prove he can complete the bridge on time provides the rationale to order his men to work longer hours and ask his officers to "volunteer" to do manual labor. He also approaches the doctor, Major Clipton (James Donald), about releasing some of the men in the hospital, who may be malingerers, to work on the bridge. Although Nicholson endured the punishments Colonel Saito inflicted on him, he abandons those principles for his own quest for heroic self-fulfillment. When Major Clipton suggests that by building such a superb bridge they may be collaborating with the Japanese, Nicholson dismisses the thought.

Although Shears escapes, nearly dying in the process, he recovers at Mount Lavinia Hospital, where he frolics with a pretty nurse on the beach, drinking a martini. He is approached by Major Warden (Jack Hawkins) and asked to return to the prison camp and destroy the bridge with Warden's commando unit. The notion of such heroics is nonsense to Shears, but he is forced to volunteer when he admits he has been impersonating an officer to receive better treatment in the camp and at the hospital.

Once the bridge is wired with explosives, the commandos get into position, ready to blow it up as a train loaded with Japanese dignitaries approaches. In the morning the tide had moved out, exposing the demolition wire, which Nicholson notices while walking on the bridge. He and Colonel Saito walk into the water as Nicholson grabs the wire, following it to the young Canadian commando, Lieutenant Joyce (Geoffrey Horne), who is hiding behind a rock with the detonator. Realizing the threat, Joyce lunges at Saito, stabbing him to death and yells at Nicholson, who wrestles him to the ground, that he is a British commando ordered to blow up the bridge. The stunned Nicholson cannot accept the destruction of his creation, and Shears dives into the water in an attempt to reach Nicholson and kill him. Both Joyce and Shears are eventually shot by Warden to save them from being captured by the Japanese, and Nicholson, stunned and injured from Warden's mortars, utters these final words: "What have I done?" He then falls onto the plunger, destroying the bridge as the train passes. Viewing the destruction and carnage from a distant vantage point, Major Clipton says the final words of the film: "Madness! Madness! Madness!"

Although Nicholson and Saito view themselves as opposites and enemies, they have a great deal in common: Each is devoted to the rituals of command and their respect for the military code of honor. While Saito is abusive toward the prisoners and publicly belittles his own men, Nicholson is equally callous toward his men by forcing them to work longer hours, having officers work, and requesting sick men to do arduous labor. The two characters who appear to be more rational are Shears and Major Clipton. While Shears selfishly pursues a means for his survival, he belittles the game-playing antics of men like Warden and Nicholson, whose actions bring death and destruction. To Clipton, the arrogance and stubbornness embodied by Nicholson and Saito are counterproductive to the survival and welfare of British prisoners of war.

The Bridge on the River Kwai portrays people in a harsh environment where they must face the daily hardships of survival. Its theme of defining the virtues of heroism and sacrifice in a time of war have been revisited in many films, but *The Bridge on the River Kwai* maintains a legacy as a film that captures the romance of war and the bonds it creates among those who fight. It reflects on the costs to individuals, who are defined by the rituals of leadership and command and who rationalize their effort as self-sacrifice but are driven by an innate sense of how they define heroism.

In his December 19, 1957, *New York Times* review, Bosley Crowther wrote that the film is "loaded with mortal tension that holds the viewer in sweating suspense," and called the movie "brilliant. Brilliant is the word, and no other, to describe the quality of skills that have gone into the making of this picture, from the writing of the script out of a novel by the Frenchman Pierre Boulle, to direction, performance, photographing, editing, and application of a musical score" (http://www.movies.nytimes.com/movie/review).

THE FILMS OF ALFRED HITCHCOCK

The films of Alfred Hitchcock expose the depths of the human psyche and explore sexual tensions as the camera's presence acts as a voyeuristic bystander. His films take the audience into dimensions they may enter only in their dreams, creating an expressive canvas of suspense as their fears are realized in the taut narrative of his stories. The audience, like the main character, is restrained from knowing all of the facts until Hitchcock determines that such information is necessary. He had an abiding respect for his audience and a keen instinct as to their needs and desires: "Newspaper headlines tell too many outlandish stories from real life that drive the spinner of suspense fiction to further extremes. I always regard the fact that we've got to outwit the audience to keep them with us. They're highly trained detectives looking at us out there right now."

Hitchcock was very realistic in how audiences related to certain material and he acknowledged there had to be some familiarity with the situation and the characters:

> I've never dealt with whodunits. They're simply clever puzzles, aren't they? They're intellectual rather than emotional, and emotion is the only thing that keeps my audience interested. I prefer suspense rather than surprise—something the average man can identify with. The audience can't identify with detectives; they're not part of his everyday life.

As a director, Hitchcock chose his leading men and women for their suave, cool, and debonair sexuality. Surprisingly, he had a love-hate relationship with actors and once publicly described them as cattle but later denied the statement and elaborated on it by saying that what he had meant was that actors should be *treated* like cattle. Although he had a reputation for pampering his stars, he also expressed misgivings about the limitations of using them in a film: "The minute you put a star into a role you've already compromised because it may not be perfect casting.... In television we have a greater chance to cast more freely than in pictures. Star names don't mean all that much in television, at least in dramatic terms" (Rebello, 1998).

Hitchcock was particularly drawn to one actor: Cary Grant. Hitchcock said of Grant that he was the only actor he ever loved. Another of his favorite leading men was James Stewart. As for women, he preferred the passionate allure of blondes such as Kim Novak, Tippi Hedren, Grace Kelly, Eva Marie Saint, and Janet Leigh.

Hitchcock's recurring themes include mistaken identity, ordinary people thrust into extraordinary situations, authority figures such as the police portrayed as bunglers, and grown men attempting to free themselves from their mother's influence. He was also a master of technique who demonstrated a disciplined control of the audiences' point of view while utilizing framing, editing, tracking shots, and zooms to convey the tension and sexuality of the scene.

Although at the time of its release *Vertigo* was not received well by the critics, it is now revered as Hitchcock's greatest movie and one of the best films ever made. It is filled with psychological drama experienced within the context of human sexuality, fear, and longing. This dynamic is a challenge for the audience, who become immersed in a tale of murder, deception, reincarnation, and emotional greed. In many ways it's a ghost story, with James Stewart playing retired detective Scottie Ferguson, who is searching for the spirit of the woman he loves only to be betrayed by his fears and desires.

Interestingly, some parallels exist between the plot of the film and Hitchcock's ambitions for it. The director had chosen Vera Miles, his new protégé, whom he hoped to remake in the image of actress Grace Kelly, for the female lead of the character Madeleine just as Scottie tries to remake Judy in the image of his lost love, Madeleine. Indeed, Hitchcock had such high hopes for Vera Miles he signed her to a five-year contract. However, she got married and soon after was pregnant, deeply disappointing the director. He was so committed to Miles that she had costume fittings, and the portrait of the ghostly Carlotta Valdes, an important plot element, was painted to resemble her. She had previously starred opposite Henry Fonda in Hitchcock's *The Wrong Man* (1957). In a 1956 *Look* magazine article, Hitchcock mused about Miles, saying, "She's an attractive, intelligent and sexy woman." He was deeply disappointed that Miles was unable to star in *Vertigo* and some say he never forgave her.

Commenting on his displeasure with Miles, Hitchcock is quoted in François Truffaut's book *Hitchcock/Truffaut*: "She became pregnant just before the part that was going to turn her into a star. After that, I lost interest. I couldn't get the rhythm going with her again."

So instead he cast Kim Novak in the role; according to *Box Office* magazine, she was the most popular star of 1957. Novak was not the supple, subjective talent Hitchcock was hoping for, and when he dictated specific hairstyles and costume requirements she openly resisted. She refused to wear a tailored gray suit that Hitchcock insisted upon. He asked the notable Edith Head, costume designer for Paramount, to intercede and she was able to provide a more "collaborative" environment for the actress.

Hitchcock had a unique relationship with his female leads, making them objects of simmering sexuality. He had an obsessive personality, which he translated into a fixation with the details of his leading ladies' lives. Although labeled a misogynist, Hitchcock was particularly adept at portraying how women are treated by cold, calculating men, and how their selfless devotion to the leading man makes them vulnerable to danger and rejection. Perhaps, more than any other director, Hitchcock understood how important the female dynamic was to the narrative of his film; thus he obsessed over every nuance of their character and appearance. His reputation for being condescending to actors and especially cruel to his actresses comes, of course, from some of the comments he made during his career, including this one "I always believe in following the advice of the playwright Sardou, Torture the women ... the trouble today is that we don't torture women enough'" (Fawell, 2000).

It was his obsession and need to be in command that made him take control of Vera Miles' costumes and her everyday wardrobe because when she was off the set, Hitchcock wanted to cultivate a certain look, and not one of a Van Nuys housewife. Speaking about Grace Kelly, he was proud he had made her bloom in *Rear Window* because in his estimation she looked mousy in *High Noon*. As for Eva Marie Saint, he gave her sexual allure through hairstyle, makeup, and costuming, and was not amused when she was cast in the film *Exodus*, in which he said she looked "dissipated." He was adamant in defining her look in *North by Northwest* with a basic black suit and a heavy black silk cocktail dress with an imprint of wine-red flowers when she deceives Cary Grant, and then a charcoal-brown, full-skirted jersey dress, along with a burnt or-ange burlap outfit, for the action sequences. For Grace Kelly, by far his favorite actress, Hitchcock plotted the style and color for every costume in the completed script, sending it to revered designer, Edith Head. She notes "There was a reason for every color, every style, and he was absolutely certain about everything he settled on. For one scene he saw her in pale green, for another in white chiffon, for another in gold. He was really putting a dream together in the studio" (Fawell, 2000).

Hitchcock was extremely aware of the emotional suggestiveness of colors. His phi-losophy in selecting leading ladies was to create them in a way that they would be more pleasing to women than to men, and he respected the role women played in his films. Although he obsessed on using the most glamorous movie star actresses, he attempted to de-glamorize them and avoided using them as sex symbols. In expressing this notion he said: "The very beautiful woman who just walks around avoiding the furniture, wearing fluffy negligees and looking very seductive, may be an attractive ornament, but she doesn't help the film any."

Some actresses, like Joan Fontaine, were uncomfortable with Hitchcock's singular need to dominate their look and behavior. She commented that he was a Svengali who wanted to control her. Although he was the dominant force in the relationship with his leading ladies, he was also a victim of their seduction. His actresses, for the most part, had a deep affection and respect for him. But Hitchcock, in his dream world, created a mythology of a psycho-sexual dynamic with them. This could explain how he felt when Vera Miles became pregnant and could not play the lead in *Vertigo*, and also his feeling like a jilted lover when Grace Kelly retired from her acting career. Like Scotty in *Vertigo*, Hitchcock was on an epic journey, trying to cast his leading ladies in the image of Grace Kelly, and one of his most resounding failures was Tippi Hedren who, like Kelly, began her career as a model. He had hoped to turn Hedren into a major star by casting her in the female lead in *Marnie* (1964) and prior to that in his successful film *The Birds* (1963). After just a few weeks of filming *The Birds*, he was flush with excitement over Hedren's debut as an actress, saying, "Tippi Hedren is really remarkable. She's already reaching the lows and highs of terror" (www.shambala.org/tippi.htm).

He also described her as a dormant volcano about to erupt. In a cover story in the December 4, 1962, issue of *Look* magazine, Hitchcock compared Hedren to Grace Kelly, who for him was the ultimate icy blonde but also was "the one who got away."

"Tippi has a faster tempo, city glibness, more humor (than Grace Kelly). She dis-played jaunty assuredness, pertness, an attractive throw of the head. And she memo-rized and read lines extraordinarily well and is sharper in expression" (http://www.shambala.org/tippi).

Speaking of her experiences making *The Birds*, Hedren spoke about Hitchcock's need to take a woman and destroy her character and fortitude: "Well, that's what Hitchcock loves to do with his women. Take a woman who is in control of herself, very sure of herself, and beat her up and see how much she can take."

During the filming of *Marnie*, her second and final film with Hitchcock, Hedren noticed that he had developed a predatory sexual fascination toward her. He lavished her with gifts and extraordinary accommodations on the set. She said that she was the object of his obsession and "was not interested in being the object."

She says that one evening in February 1964 he made an overt sexual proposition in the luxurious trailer he had outfitted for her. Afterward, Hedren wanted to get out of her contract, but Hitchcock refused, saying he would destroy her career. He continued to pay her for two years when, finally, he sold her contract to Universal. To her delight, she was eventually fired.

At the start of producing *Marnie*, Hitchcock dedicated himself to the film and to the needs of its star, Hedren. After the tensions between them became unbearable, Hitchcock lost interest toward the end of the film's production and during post-production. Hoping to make Hedren a star in the tradition of Hollywood's glamour idols, Hitchcock was supremely disappointed by the failure of the film.

For Hedren, she was placed in the untenable position as Hithcock's heir-apparent to Grace Kelly, whom he originally wanted for the part. She represented Hitchcock's idealized notion of femininity: a throwback to the 1950s and its representational values of studio glamour.

> Hedren consequently finds herself much more uncomfortably poised between two kinds of cinemas—in looks, personality and physical bearing evoking a certain kind of glamorous Hollywood star of the past while at the same time she is called on to embody a new direction in Hitchcock's work.

For Eva Marie Saint, a Method actress, working with Alfred Hitchcock was very different from acting in the film *On the Waterfront*, directed by Elia Kazan. She recalled that Hitchcock gave her three directions: "lower your voice, don't use your hands and look directly into Cary Grant's eyes at all times."

Just as with the other icy blondes he coveted, Hitchcock had plans to create a new direction for Saint's career. According to Saint, he didn't want her to continue taking on the more drab pedestrian roles. "I don't want you to do a sink-to-sink movie again, ever. You've done these black-and-white movies like *On the Waterfront*. It's drab in that tenement house. Women go to the movies, and they've just left the sink at home. They don't want to see you at the sink" (Garrett, 1999).

REAR WINDOW (1954)

PRODUCER/DIRECTOR: Alfred Hitchcock (director), James C. Katz (producer)
WRITER(S): Cornell Woolrich (short story "It Had to be Murder"), John Michael Hayes (screenplay)
CAST: James Stewart (L. B. Jefferies), Grace Kelly (Lisa Carol Fremont), Wendell Corey (Det. Lt. Thomas J. Doyle), Thelma Ritter (Stella), Raymond Burr (Lars Thorwald), Judith Evelyn (Miss Lonelyheart), Ross Bagdasarian (Songwriter), Georgine Darcy (Miss Torso), Sara Berner (Wife living above Thorwalds), Frank Cady (Husband living above Thorwalds)
CINEMATOGRAPHY: Robert Burks
MUSIC: Franz Waxman
LENGTH AND RATING: 112 min; NR

This film features James Stewart, once again disabled but this time with a broken leg that contrives to affect his emotional stability. As a master of technique, Hitchcock controls the point of view of the audience, fulfilling his adage to, "always make the audience suffer as much as possible."

Hitchcock was at the height of his creative genius when filming *Rear Window* and has said he felt very creative at the time and that his batteries were well-charged. As the reviewer Vincent Canby notes, "*Rear Window* is as much of a romance as it is a brilliant exercise in suspense."

His fascination with the screen image is sustained by the measured shots of Stewart's character, L. B. Jeffries (Jeff), that focus on his point of view as he gazes through his apartment's rear window at his neighbors' open windows off the courtyard. In his unfolding of the narrative, Hitchcock tells the story almost exclusively from Jeff's point of view until he finds it necessary to provide the audience with information his character does not have. As a director, Hitchcock once again demonstrates his unique technical skills in editing, structure, and composition, such as the dizzying tracking shots in *Vertigo*, and, in *Rear Window*, the cinematic window-framing of shots that emphasize the detached theatrical experience of watching a movie until the characters intrude on Jeff's reality. Like *Vertigo*, this film is a study in obsession with the added dimension of voyeurism.

A roving photojournalist, Jeff's testosterone-filled lifestyle is upset when he breaks his leg and must convalesce in his Greenwich Village apartment during a hot summer, with nothing more to do than spy on his neighbors. An experienced photographer, he is accustomed to closely observing people and events and has a trained eye for snooping. In this, he is admirably assisted by a pair of binoculars and a telephoto lens. Here Hitchcock provides the audience with an opportunity to be voyeurs just like Jeff and fulfill their prurient interest in seeing the personal and private actions of others. And when he gets bored, Jeff can simply "turn the channel" and look through another window.

As Hitchcock noted in an interview, he could have simply told the audience what L. B. Jeffries does for a living but instead uses his skill as a director to create a montage of images to begin the exposition of the story and reveal Jeff's occupation and his physical condition. Over a rendition of jazz music and introductory credits, the screen shows shades slowly rising over several windows. Then the camera moves to show buildings, a courtyard, and a garden. It takes the audience into an apartment where a man is sleeping and sweating heavily, and another scene, in which a couple escapes the heat by sleeping on a fire escape, establishes the weather pattern of a heat wave. The camera moves on to reveal a blonde woman, who hasn't much clothing on, doing her chores while moving like a dancer, and then it sweeps into a long pan of Jeff's apartment, settling on a man in a wheelchair with a cast on his leg and various photographs hanging on the wall of a racing car accident, war scenes, and an explosion, along with some smashed camera equipment. The audience learns from a telephone conversation with his editor that Jeff is laid up in a cast for six weeks, will miss a photo shoot in Kashmir, is reluctant to get married, and is terribly bored convalescing in the apartment. His reflections on marriage are confirmed by watching the behavioral dynamics of Lars Thorwald (Raymond Burr), his neighbor across the courtyard, as he returns home from work and argues with his sick wife, who is confined to bed.

At the time we meet Jeff, two women are in his life: his nurse and therapist Stella (Thelma Ritter), who has an acerbic tongue, and love interest Lisa Carol Fremont (Grace Kelly), a beautiful model and affluent high society Park Avenue girl who wants to marry him. As Stella observes Jeff and his obsession with being a Peeping Tom, she sarcastically tells him that the New York State penalty for spying on neighbors is six months in the workhouse. In the old days, the penalty was having your eyes burned out with a red hot poker. As Stella takes Jeff's temperature, she comments on his sexual impotence by alluding to how his indiscreet viewing of scantily clad women hasn't raised his temperature.

In his intrusive escapades, Jeff has categorized the couples and individuals he spies on, giving them appropriate names like the "Newlyweds," who after they enter their apartment are the only ones to keep their shades down. There is also "Miss Lonelyhearts" (Judith Evelyn), whom Jeff watches setting a dinner table for two while fantasizing about the entrance of her gentleman caller. A young woman dubbed "Miss Torso" (Georgine Darcy), who has the athletic build of a ballet dancer, is watched as she entertains three men in her apartment. Lisa comments to Jeff that Miss Torso doesn't love any of them. Jeff "changes the channel" and watches the hulking jewelry salesman carry a dinner tray adorned with a rose to the bed of his sickly wife, which she flings away with disdain. There is also a middle-aged bachelor, a composer, and an alcoholic who has difficulty playing the piano in his tiny studio apartment.

As he watches the subjects in his docudrama, Jeff and Lisa have a tense argument about his need for freedom and her desire for commitment. At the end, she puts on her gloves and says goodbye. Fearing the worst, Jeff replies with a good night and Lisa reaffirms what she meant. Jeff would like to maintain the status quo, and she indicates there is no future for her, but when pressed she relents and admits she will return the next evening.

For Hitchcock, suspenseful narrative has an implicit sense of rising action and tension. He avoids using the element of surprise, preferring to sustain the anxiety of the audience by letting them know that something may happen, but not when. Using the example of a bomb under a table, the surprise would be the bomb exploding. However, if the audience sees and hears a ticking bomb, not knowing when it will explode, the result is suspense and tension. And so in *Rear Window*, Jeff is a prisoner in his apartment. His freedom has been compromised and threatened by a broken leg and by the matrimonial intentions of the lovely Lisa Fremont. The suspense begins to build after Jeff hears a scream and the sound of breaking glass. This is followed by the strange nocturnal exploits of Thorwald and his sample case, which provides Jeff with the seeds for his vivid imagination and causes him to suspect that some nefarious deed has taken place involving the salesman's nagging wife. The story becomes even more suspenseful when Thorwald suddenly meets Jeff's gaze as he and Stella watch him. Now Jeff has become the victim of someone watching him, and that realization frightens him. He suspects Thorwald of murdering his wife and sets out to find the evidence.

Before Stella leaves, she hands Jeff his camera with the telephoto lens. The lens may be symbolic of Jeff's repressed sexuality and a reaction to the impotence he is experiencing because of his broken leg. He has seen Thorwald in his kitchen, wrapping a knife and a saw in newspaper. Lisa, realizing that the way to Jeff's heart is to accept his theory about the murder, agrees with him, and the next night she arrives with a small tote bag, announcing that she will spend the night. This is followed by delicate, sexually laced dialogue.

In a second visit, Jeff's friend, detective Tom Doyle (Wendell Corey), presents solid evidence that Mrs. Anna Thorwald is alive and well after receiving a suspicious trunk in a place called Mertisville, confirming its delivery with her signature. He rejects Jeff and Lisa's notion of a murder and leaves them to plot other absurd scenarios. After some bantering, Lisa returns from another room elegantly dressed in a white silk nightgown, capturing Jeff's attention with her striking sexuality. But the sexual tension of the moment is interrupted by a bloodcurdling scream as one of the neighbors discovers her little pet dog strangled in the courtyard. The dog had been shooed away by Thorwald as it aggressively dug in his flower bed, and this gave rise to Jeff's suspicion that parts of Mrs. Thorwald, or the saw and knife, might be buried there.

In a gesture of bravery and determination to prove to Jeff that she has the mettle to face danger, Lisa volunteers to slide a note ("What Have You Done With Her?"), written by Jeff, under Thorwald's door nearly confronting him in the effort. The two women decide to dig up the garden while Jeff distracts Thorwald by calling him on the telephone and asking to meet at a nearby hotel. After digging in vain, Lisa decides, against Jeff's objections, to climb into Throwald's apartment to look for evidence. Once there she is confronted by a returning Thorwald, who grabs Lisa and violently throws her to the floor. This action runs parallel to Miss Lonelyhearts and her preparation for suicide as she places pills on a table. The tension builds as Jeff watches helplessly as Lisa is attacked, but finally ebbs with the arrival of the police. During the scene, Lisa poses with her back toward Jeff, revealing Mrs. Thorwald's wedding band, which she has slipped on her finger. The police lead Lisa away, and Stella leaves Jeff behind in the apartment to go bail Lisa out at the police station. Anxious, Jeff calls Tom, explaining what has happened, and he promises to follow up and arrange Lisa's release.

As the finale unfolds, Hitchcock's mastery of suspenseful action shows Jeff alone, hearing the sound of footsteps approaching his door. Suddenly, he is confronted by the object of his obsession and may become Thorwald's next victim. Using the camera as a weapon, Jeff loads flashbulbs and fires them at his attacker, disorienting him. But he cannot escape Thorwald's aggressive embrace as he hauls Jeff to the open window and throws him out. Finally, he is restrained by the arriving police, but Jeff, hanging from the window, lets go and falls, his descent broken by a group of police in the courtyard. Now Jeff has become the subject of all the neighbors he's been spying on as they watch him. As he lies on the ground, he is comforted by his "girl Friday," Lisa.

In the final scene, we see Jeff in his wheelchair, each leg in a cast and his back to the window. Lisa is with him and the impression is that she is now there to stay. She has proven herself to be a courageous foil to Jeff's "fearless" globe-trotting adventures, and has shrewdly manipulated the events to satisfy her own matrimonial agenda. The audience also has closure on the actions of the neighbors, with Miss Lonelyhearts visiting the composer, the couple who lost their precious pet with a new dog, and Miss Torso welcoming back her true love, a young man in a soldier's uniform. The arc has been completed and Lisa has transformed herself into a compelling object of Jeff's affection, making her the obsession for his attention. Before the screen fades to black, the shade comes down and the audience ceases to be the voyeurs who enjoyed the anonymous satisfaction of spying on the intimate details of others, and the dangers that such action present.

VERTIGO (1958)

PRODUCER/DIRECTOR: Alfred Hitchcock (director/producer uncredited), Herbert Coleman (associate producer)

WRITERS: Pierre Boileau and Thomas Narcejac (novel); Alec Coppel and Samuel Taylor (screenplay)

CAST: James Stewart (Detective John "Scottie" Ferguson), Kim Novak (Madeleine Elsler/Judy Barton); Barbara Bel Geddes (Marjorie "Midge" Wood), Tom Helmore (Gavin Elster)

CINEMATOGRAPHY: Robert Barks
MUSIC: Bernard Hermann
LENGTH AND RATING: 128 min; NR

The story for *Vertigo* was adapted from the book *D'Entre Les Morts* (*From Among the Dead*), by Pierre Boileau and Thomas Navcejac. It also alludes to Greek mythology and the tale of Orpheus and his wife, Eurydice, whom he fails to rescue from Hades when he violates Pluto's command and turns to look back at her in their journey to the upper world of the living. Other literary and film references of a man's attempt to remake a woman include George Bernard Shaw's *Pygmalion* and the film *My Fair Lady* (1964). The authors had previously written *Les Diaboliques* and *The Wages of Fear*, which were both adapted into French films. Their stories were set in the cities of Paris and Marseilles during World War II, but the setting was changed to San Francisco, which made the city and the mission church characters in the film. The screenplay was written by Alec Coppel, who also wrote *Moment to Moment* (1966), *The Bliss of Mrs. Blossom* (1968), and *The Statue* (1971), and Samuel A. Taylor, who penned the screenplays *Sabrina* (1954), *The Eddie Duchin Story* (1956), and *Topaz* (1969). He also did an un-credited rewrite for the *Psycho* screenplay.

In the first frames of the film, the audience learns about Scottie's fear of heights and the dizzying sensation known as vertigo that he experiences looking down while hanging from the loose gutter of a San Francisco building. He is a police detective chasing a criminal along with a uniformed officer across a flat rooftop, and as the officer and fugitive jump over the gap to the next roof, Scottie doesn't make it and is left dangling high in the air. His friend, the uniformed officer, reaches out to him but as he does he loses his balance and falls to the pavement below. This event serves as a narrative catalyst in the film and creates the context for Scottie's relationship with Madeleine/Judy played, by Kim Novak.

Recuperating from the tragic incident, Scottie, now retired, is summoned by a college friend, shipping tycoon Gavin Elster (Tom Helmore), who asks him to follow his wife Madeline because he fears that she is possessed by a woman of the past named Carlotta, and may commit suicide. As Madeleine travels to historic sites around San Francisco, Scottie journeys with her and falls in love as he experiences her and the city's mystique. They visit the Palace of the Legion of Honor Museum, the Portals of the Past, the ancient Redwood forest, and the graveyard of the Mission Dolores. Soon, Scottie becomes consumed by Madeleine's behavior and is taken in by her trance and reincarnation as Carlotta Valdes. In a key scene, Scottie finally meets Madeleine when she falls into San Francisco Bay, right below the Golden Gate Bridge. He takes her to his apartment, removing her wet clothes and putting her in his bed. When she wakes, they become acquainted with each other, developing a rapport with an undercurrent of desire.

When Madeleine abruptly disappears from his apartment, Scottie continues to follow her the next day, and they both wind up in front of his building. She is there to drop off a formal note of apology, and Scottie asks if he can join her on her journeys. Their new friendship evolves into a close relationship, and they embrace and passionately kiss on a Monterey Bay cliff as waves crash around them, and Scottie vows to protect her.

After Madeleine appears at his apartment one morning, relating a dream about a bell tower at an old Spanish mission, he realizes that she is describing the historic San

Juan Bautista's Spanish Mission and they travel there so that Madeleine can find closure to her dreams. Outside the mission, Madeleine tells Scottie she must go into the church alone but he begs her to stay with him. She breaks away from his grasp and runs up the steps to the bell tower as Scottie attempts to go after her, but is confronted by his fear of heights and the dizzying complications of vertigo. He hears a scream and then a body falls, landing on an adjacent rooftop. Madeleine's death is ruled a suicide, but Scottie is blamed for indirectly causing the accident because his fear of heights rendered him powerless to act.

After suffering a nervous breakdown and being released from an institution, Scottie returns to the places he visited with or while following Madeleine and is haunted by her memory. He meets and confronts a woman named Judy Barton, who has an uncanny resemblance to Madeleine. Although she initially resists, he convinces her to have dinner with him. In a flashback, the audience learns that Judy is also Madeleine, Gavin Elster's mistress, who had a remarkable resemblance to his wife. After murdering her, Elster threw her dead body from the bell tower. When Scottie leaves Judy, she writes him a confessional letter declaring her love and explaining the plot, but she destroys the letter in the hope of making him love her as Judy. Scottie obsessively pursues a makeover of Judy into his image of Madeleine, from the clothing he buys for her to the color and style of her hair. Before going out to dinner, Judy coyly asks Scottie to clasp the latch of the locket around her neck. Obliging, Scottie notices that it is the red ruby necklace pictured in the portrait of Carlotta, and he then realizes he has been the victim of Elster's murderous plot.

In an effort to sustain a closure to his dreams and overcome his acrophobia and vertigo, Scottie drives to the mission and confronts Judy. She resists him as he drags her up to the tower and tells her how she revealed the truth by keeping the necklace as a memento. Judy confesses but tearfully pleads her love for him, but Scottie is consumed by rage and passion. They embrace and then she breaks away, seeing a shrouded figure (a nun) in the shadows, which startles and causes her to step back. She falls through an opening to her death. In the end, Scottie overcomes his fears but has once again lost the woman he loves.

Hitchcock was influenced by the work of Russian filmmaker Val Lewton, the Spanish surrealist Luis Bunuel, and the German expressionist Fritz Lang. He in turn influenced generations of filmmakers including: Spielberg, Mann, the Coen brothers, Lynch, Tarantino, and De Palma.

In his May 29, 1958, *New York Times* review, Bosley Crowther wrote that the film "is a fascinating mystery...based upon a tale written by the same fellows, Pierre Boileau and Thomas Navcejac, who wrote the story from which was taken that excellent French mystery, *Diabolique*. That film, if you remember, told of a terribly devious plot to simulate a murder that didn't happen" (http://movies.nytimes.com/movie/review).

NORTH BY NORTHWEST (1959)

PRODUCER/DIRECTOR: Alfred Hitchcock (director, producer, uncredited), Herbert Coleman (associate producer)

WRITER(S): Ernest Lehman

CAST: Cary Grant (Roger O. Thornhill), Eva Marie Saint (Eve Kendall), James Mason (Phillip Vandamm), Jessie Royce Landis (Clara Thornhill), Leo G. Carroll (The Professor), Josephine Hutchinson (Mrs. Townsend), Philip Ober (Lester Townsend), Martin Landau (Leonard), Adam Williams (Valerian), Edward Platt (Victor Larrabee)

CINEMATOGRAPHY: Robert Burks

MUSIC: Bernard Herrmann

LENGTH AND RATING: 136 min; NR

For Americans, 1959 ended one of the most tumultuous decades in history. There was still the cold war to be reckoned with, and reminders of the growth of communism. In Cuba, Fidel Castro had become triumphant in assuming leadership of the country, and the little-known Lee Harvey Oswald defected to the USSR, asserting he would never return to the United States. The first astronauts were selected and named the Mercury Seven, and the Barbie Doll was introduced. America flexed its muscles as the defender of the free world and launched the USS *George Washington*, the first submarine to carry ballistic missiles. And Karl Fuchs, the physicist and British subject involved in the Manhattan Project, who was imprisoned for sharing atomic bomb secrets with the Soviets, was released from prison and immigrated to East Germany.

In many ways, Hitchcock's *North by Northwest* is a tale filled with the intrigue of the cold war and romanticized with stunning images of the United Nations, the Plaza Hotel, and Mount Rushmore. Screenwriter Ernest Lehman wanted to make the Hitchcock picture to end all Hitchcock pictures. He had been working with Hitchcock on the nautical thriller *The Wreck of the Mary Deare* and, unable to succeed with that story, the two created the plot for *North by Northwest*. He later told French director François Truffaut, "In this picture nothing was left to chance." The film also made ample use of the MacGuffin, a Hitchcock device that keeps the story moving but by itself is meaningless. In *North by Northwest*, it is the secret information wanted by the spy Vandamm, played by James Mason. Discussing possible scenarios, Lehman recalled reading a newspaper article about French intelligence agents who created a fictional spy to mislead other foreign agents. Incorporating this theme of mistaken identity, Hitchcock and Lehman were able to produce one of the most suspenseful and elegantly crafted spy capers ever made. Building on the beauty and magnificence of Mount Rushmore, Hitchcock uses other place settings to develop a striking vibrancy of compelling imagery. Like the child's game, *Where in the World is Carmen Santiago?*, Hitchcock takes Roger O. Thornhill to unfamiliar locales while the audience tries to figure out where he is and why he's there. And there is always the incongruity of the images, since they question the logic of the action within the context of the environment.

As Roger O. Thornhill, Cary Grant exhibits a suave and cool demeanor as the man in the gray flannel suit who, even under the most stressful circumstances, remains calm and collected. He is matched by Eve Kendall, portrayed by Eva Marie Saint, as a beautiful spy whose sexuality is defined by her intelligence and cunning. The 1955 novel, *The Man in the Gray Flannel Suit*, by Sloan Wilson, addresses the career trajectory men take, sacrificing their personal lives and families. (In 1956, the novel was made into a film starring Gregory Peck.) There is a hint of that in Roger O. Thornhill, as the audience learns that he is divorced from his wife.

Through Hitchcock's scene structure and dialogue, the audience is introduced to a charming, debonair, and self-confident Madison Avenue advertising executive, always in a hurry and exuding an aura of self-control. Late for a business meeting at the Plaza, he

Cary Grant (as Roger O. Thornhill). [MGM/Photofest]

rushes, along with his secretary, Maggie (Doreen Land), and commandeers a taxi already spoken for by someone else using Maggie's "condition" as an excuse. When Maggie scolds him for being dishonest to satisfy his selfish need, he responds that there are no lies in advertising, only what he refers to as "expedient exaggeration." In many respects, the adventure Roger Thornhill is about to embark on is a monumental exaggeration that will transform his life of privilege and make him the subject of deceit and betrayal.

Once again, Hitchcock's protagonist, Roger Thornhill, is a man who is the victim of mistaken identity. Wanting to confirm a dinner/theater reservation with his mother, he raises his hand from the hotel bar to send a wire at the same time that a page calls for a Mr. George Kaplan. This confluence of circumstance identifies him to two surreptitious men hiding in an effort to identify George Kaplan, a fictitious individual created by a team of American spies to trap foreign agents attempting to leave the United States with valuable microfilm.

George Kaplan, Thornhill is hustled away by the two men to a waiting car, where he is wedged like a sardine between them. The car speeds off to a country estate where Thornhill meets Phillip Vandamm (James Mason), a head foreign operative posing as Lester Townsend. Refusing to admit that he is George Kaplan, he frustrates Vandamm's effort at interrogation and it is decided to get rid of him by getting him drunk and having him drive down a treacherous road. He is put into a convertible roadster but manages to push his "escort" out. In a suspenseful and comical scene, Thornhill drives the car with abandon, avoiding several near-crashes until he is pursued, rear-ended, and stopped by a police officer. Thornhill calling his mother from the police station creates a dynamic of confusing conversation, where once again someone isn't listening to him and this time it's his mother. He is bailed out the next day and takes his mother and the police to visit the estate where a Mrs. Townsend (an imposter) greets him as Mr. Kaplan and verifies that he was there the night before and had too much to drink. She also announces that her husband will address the General Assembly at the United Nations that afternoon.

Determined to find George Kaplan, Thornhill and his reluctant mother, Clara (Jessie Royce Landis), go back to the Plaza Hotel and search Kaplan's room. Before going in, a maid greets him as Mr. Kaplan, but upon further investigation they learn that none of the staff have ever seen this room's guest. While in the room, Thornhill answers the phone and is greeted as Mr. Kaplan by the spy on the other end. Realizing the danger, he and Clara enter a crowded elevator among the spies, and Clara jokingly asks them if they want to kill her son. Using the passengers as a barrier, he eludes them and rushes to the United Nations.

Once at the United Nations, Thornhill, using the George Kaplan identity, has Townsend paged, although trying to vindicate himself and prove that he is not George Kaplan, he slips into his guise. When the two men meet, Thornhill is surprised that this person is not the one he was expecting. Townsend then tells him that he has been living in Manhattan while the General Assembly is in session, and that his wife has been deceased for many years. As Thornhill shows Townsend the picture of Vandamm that he found in the room at the Plaza, the real Lester Townsend is fatally stabbed in the back, falling into Thornhill's arms. Not thinking, Thornhill instinctively removes the knife and is believed by everyone to be the murderer. To validate his guilt, a photograph is taken of him holding the knife in the air. Once again, Thornhill is mistaken for someone else, this time a murderer, and his picture is plastered on the front page of newspapers across the country.

At this strategic point in the film, the audience is introduced to a team of secret American CIA agents led by "the Professor" (Leo G. Carroll). In typical Hitchcock fashion, the audience discovers that George Kaplan is a fictional figure contrived by the Americans to throw Vandamm and his foreign agents off the trail of their own spy, who has become part of Vandamm's team. The Professor realizes the fortuitous new dynamic in the events and how beneficial it is to their objective. He decides that Thornhill's accidental assumption of George Kaplan's identity must continue, and that his vulnerability as a victim is worth the risk to protect their agent and operation.

Having learned that Kaplan has checked out of the Plaza Hotel and is on his way to Chicago, Thornhill heads to New York's Grand Central Station to board the Twentieth Century Limited. The police are there watching for him, and his picture is prominently displayed on the front page of newspapers. Recognized while attempting to buy a ticket, he manages to board the train, where he meets a gorgeous blonde, Eve Kendall (Eva Marie Saint), an American double agent who helps him evade the police. Tipping the steward five dollars to seat him at her table for dinner, Eve and Thornhill engage in sexually charged dialogue and innuendo, creating one of the most riveting "courtship" scenes in film. Indeed, during their conversation she says, "I never discuss love on an empty stomach." To please the censors, for its initial theatrical release that line was changed from the original: "I never make love on an empty stomach."

Sequestered in her room with only a single bed, they engage in verbal and physical foreplay. Expecting to "score," Thornhill is disappointed when Eve indicates that he'll be sleeping on the floor. In the second piece of information the audience is made aware of but not Thornhill, we learn that Eve sends a written message to Vandamm and his henchman, who are in another sleeping car.

The next day, Eve tells Thornhill to change into a redcap porter's uniform so that he can evade the police, and when the real porter steps off the train without his clothes, the police frantically stop every redcap in the station, checking their faces, as the now defrocked porter blissfully counts his money. Eve says she'll call Kaplan to arrange a rendezvous which, she informs him, will be at a desolate bus stop on a remote highway. She has set him up to be Vandamm's victim in one of the most memorable scenes ever to be filmed: the crop dusting sequence.

In the next scene, Thornhill, dressed in a suit, is waiting on a country dirt road in a wide open expanse of land, anticipating a meeting with George Kaplan. A car arrives and drops off a man at the bus stop who is obviously not George Kaplan. In a vivid premonition of the action about to unfold, the other man waiting makes a succinct observation: "That's funny ... That plane's dustin' crops where there ain't no crops."

The bus arrives to pick up the other passenger, and the plane heads for Thornhill, who is exposed and can only duck to avoid it. On the second pass it banks low, firing a machine gun, and he vainly tries to wave down a passing car. The plane again flies low, knocking him down, and he runs for cover in a cornfield.

These scenes of lone confrontation with the enemy contrast sharply from many other sequences, such as the United Nations, Grand Central Station, the auction house, and the finale at the Mount Rushmore visitor's center, where Thornhill is embedded in the crowds for protection. Here, in the middle of nowhere, he is utterly alone. As the plane flies over the cornfield it releases a dusting bomb, which causes Thornhill to have a coughing spasm, forcing him out in the open.

Running from the cornfield and standing on the road, he waves down a gasoline truck, holding his hands in front of him, and it stops, with him dropping underneath. The two truck drivers and Thornhill run from the truck as the plane hits it, creating an explosive fireball. Stealing another truck, he drives to Chicago, his destination the Ambassador hotel, and learns that Kaplan checked out that morning before Eve could have talked to him. At that point he sees her walk across the lobby. He realizes she set him up, and after some awkward dialogue during which she pleads with him to leave and forget about her, Eve agrees to have dinner with him and he pretends to take a shower while his suit is being cleaned. Taking a call, Eve writes down an address on a notepad and leaves the room. Using a pencil, Thornhill darkens the impression left by her note on the new top page and heads for the address, which is an art auction gallery.

Once again, amidst a crowd of spectators, Thornhill confronts Vandamm and Eve, clearly implicating her in a tense exchange and challenging the spy. As he attempts to leave the gallery, Thornhill finds all of the exits blocked by Vandamm's henchmen and he creates a diversion by acting irrationally, upsetting the auction process by shouting out ridiculous bids. The police arrive but instead of taking him to the local precinct as Thornhill insists, they drive him to Chicago's Midway Airport, where the professor is waiting. At this point Thornhill is told the truth about the fictional George Kaplan, and after learning that Eve Kendall is their agent whose life is in danger, he consents to fly to Rapid City, South Dakota, pretending to be George Kaplan.

In a plan to eliminate any suspicion by Vandamm of Eve's loyalty, a meeting is arranged in the cafeteria at the base of Mount Rushmore. Here, Vandamm appears with Leonard, his trusted lieutenant (Martin Landau), and Thornhill offers him a free pass out of the country if he turns Eve over to him. Refusing his offer, Vandamm starts to leave with Eve; Thornhill grabs her arm as she resists, drawing a gun filled with blanks from her bag. Urged by Leonard not to intercede, a shocked Vandamm retreats to follow Eve, who has run out of the cafeteria. Meanwhile, Thornhill lies critically wounded on the floor until he is taken to a vehicle by the professor's park rangers.

Meeting in the chill of the woods, Thornhill and Eve are reunited and after some playful dialogue, they kiss. Then Thornhill learns that Eve must leave with Vandamm on a plane flying out of the country to continue her work. He is upset with the professor for not telling him of this plan, and Eve insists she must complete her assignment. Confined to a hospital room to prevent him from being seen by Vandamm and interfering in Eve's departure, Thornhill is given a clean set of clothes and a pair of shoes. He asks the professor to go out and buy some bourbon and the professor consents, hoping to join Thornhill in the libation. Once alone, Thornhill tries to escape. First he triesthe door, but it is locked. He then decides to exit from the window. In the next scene, we see him climbing the beams of Vandamm's modern house, where he overhears Vandamm and Leonard plotting to kill Eve. Warning Eve by throwing a matchbook with a message on the inside cover and displaying his initials R.O.T. on the front, the two briefly meet in her room. She leaves with Vandamm, and Thornhill is discovered by the, housemaid, who holds him hostage with a gun.

As Eve is about to board the plane, shots are fired and she breaks away from Vandamm and Leonard and is rescued by a speeding car driven by Thornhill, who has discovered that the housekeeper's gun was the one filled with blanks. They cannot get beyond the locked gate so they reach the top of Mount Rushmore and must start to descend. In a scene filled with tension and apprehension, Roger is jumped by one of Vandamm's henchman, whom he manages to throw off Mount Rushmore. This is followed by Eve struggling with Leonard, who seizes the statue holding the microfilm and pushes her down a wall. In a scene reminiscent of so many Hitchcock films (*Saboteur, Vertigo*), Eve ends up hanging from a ledge, clinging to life. As Thornhill tries to pull her up he pleads to Leonard for help and he responds by stepping on and crushing his hand. A shot rings out and Leonard falls and drops the statue, which breaks into pieces. In the last scene, the action cuts from Thornhill's outstretched arm on Mount Rushmore to his extended arm in a Pullman railroad car, pulling Eve up to the fold-out bed in their private train car. They are now married, and in the last scene, clearly phallic symbolism, the train enters a tunnel.

For Hitchcock, *North by Northwest* was one of his most glamorous and stylish films. In his August 7, 1959, *New York Times* review, A. H. Weiler notes:

> Although they are involved in a lightning-fast romance and some loose intrigue, it is all done in brisk, genuinely witty and sophisticated style. With Mr. Hitchcock at the helm, moving *North by Northwest* is a colorful and exciting route for spies, counterspies and lovers.

This was Cary Grant's fourth and final film with the director whom he had collaborated with on *Suspicion* (1941), *Notorious* (1946), and *To Catch a Thief* (1955). Although there has been a great deal of speculation about the title's origin, it was most likely from the direction Thornhill was traveling and his Northwest Airlines flight to South Dakota and Mount Rushmore. The titles that were first suggested for the film were *Breathless, In a Northwesterly Direction*, and *The Man on Lincoln's Nose*.

PSYCHO (1960)

PRODUCER/DIRECTOR: Alfred Hitchcock

WRITER(S): Robert Bloch (novel), Joseph Stefano (screenplay)

CAST: Anthony Perkins (Norman Bates), Janet Leigh (Marion Crane), Vera Miles (Lila Crane), John Gavin (Sam Loomis), Martin Balsam (Milton Arbogast), John McIntire (Sheriff Al Chambers), Simon Oakland (Dr. Fred Richmond), Vaughn Taylor (George Lowery), Frank Albertson (Tom Cassidy), Lurene Tuttle (Eliza Chambers)

CINEMATOGRAPHY: John L. Russell

MUSIC: Bernard Herrmann

LENGTH AND RATING: 109 min; NR

Perhaps the most unsettling developments of 1960 were the cold war confrontations between the Soviet Union and the United States. In May, a Soviet missile shot down an American Lockheed U-2 spy plane piloted by Francis Gary Powers. This was followed by a Russian MiG's downing of an American subsonic RB-47 bomber jet with a six-man crew over the Barents Sea, with two officers surviving. For many Americans, these events, along with the appearance of Soviet leader Nikita Khrushchev pounding his shoe on the podium at the United Nations General Assembly in New York City, created a foreboding atmosphere with frightening implications. It was also the year that four Israeli Mossad agents abducted the notorious Nazi, Adolph Eichmann, from Buenos Aires, Argentina, to stand trial in Israel for crimes against humanity.

The cold war appeared threatening to many Americans and the fear that was sustained by the politics of brinkmanship caused many to feel off-balance and afraid. Therefore, the timing of Hitchcock's *Psycho* and the dimension of evil portrayed in the film hit a raw nerve in the psyche of many Americans.

Although film directors Orson Welles and Alfred Hitchcock had different voices and visions, there is some evidence that Welles' *Touch of Evil* (1958) influenced the look of *Psycho*. Perhaps one of the most dominant of the similarities is the casting of Janet Leigh as the female lead in both films. In *Touch of Evil*, she is the newly married American wife of Mexican narcotics detective Miguel "Mike" Vargas, played by Charlton Heston. The film exudes her sexuality as she lounges in her lingerie and is the victim of leering miscreants who want to harm her. The sexuality in the film reaches a crescendo when her character, Susan Vargas, is assaulted by a group from Grandi's drug mob in a seedy motel run by a leering, dysfunctional, and mentally challenged night manager played by Dennis Weaver. His strange behavior may have been a model for the Norman Bates (Anthony Perkins) motel manager character in *Psycho*. In another scene, she lies kidnapped and drugged, dressed only in her lingerie. As the Marion Crane character in *Psycho*, Janet Leigh is seen in a hotel room dressed in a stark white bra and slip after a lunchtime liaison with her boyfriend Sam (John Gavin). This scene demonstrates her sexuality, which is very reminiscent of *Touch of Evil*.

Another similarity is the three-minute uninterrupted crane-tracking shot that opens *Touch of Evil*. In *Psycho*, Hitchcock begins with an aerial shot of the Phoenix, Arizona, skyline, with the camera eventually finding a window to enter. The technique of overlapping dialogue that Welles used in *Touch of Evil* was also used in *Psycho*. A number of artists worked on both films, including art director Robert Clatworthy and Welles' camera operator, John Russell, who became the director of photography for *Psycho*.

Janet Leigh (as Marion Crane) and Anthony Perkins (as Norman Bates). [Paramount Pictures/ Photofest]

Disturbed that the heroine is killed forty-seven minutes into the film and concerned about a horror film's success at the box office and the failure of *Vertigo*, a Paramount film, Hitchcock was forced to finance *Psycho* himself. Working with a budget of $800,000, he shot the film at Revue Studios, the television production facility for Universal Pictures where his weekly *Alfred Hitchcock Presents* show was produced. As a result of his television work he had a good understanding of how to use limited financial resources in a creative way.

The screenplay, by Joseph Stefano, was adapted from the novel *Psycho*, written by Robert Bloch and based on a gruesome event that occurred in 1957 in Plainfield, Wisconsin. When police investigated Ed Gein's dilapidated farmhouse they found a decapitated woman strung upside down and gutted like a deer, along with various decorative embellishments, including skulls for soup bowls, and human skin used to make an entire wardrobe of clothes as well as lampshades, belts, and cushions. Gein had exhumed the bodies of middle-aged women who resembled his mother and tanned their skin to tailor his macabre artifacts.

For the movie, Hitchcock meticulously planned every scene and daringly pushed the envelope on censorship. In a rather innocuous salute to reality, *Psycho* was the first American movie to feature a flushing toilet. Also, there are ample shots of Janet Leigh wearing only her undergarments, and in the famous shower scene there appears to be a number of shots of a woman's naked body (all very suggestive), with Marli Renfro serving as the naked body double. At the end of the film, psychiatrist Dr. Richmond (Simon Oakland) provides an analysis of Norman's behavior and uses the word *transvestite*. The line of dialogue that included that word required an aggressive campaign by screenwriter Joseph Stefano to be spared censorship.

The film earned mixed reviews when it was released in 1960, probably because Hitchcock would not allow any preview performances in an effort to preserve the shockingly surprise nature of the narrative. Writing in the *New York Times* on June 17, 1960, Bosley Crowther called the film a bloodcurdler that "comes at you with a club." He also described the film as being slowly paced, with great attention to detail. Audiences ignored any negative criticism and the film was a blockbuster, with long lines waiting for admission and three-mile back-ups at drive-ins. A master showman, Hitchcock raised anticipation by creating a buzz about forbidding anyone from entering the theater after the film had started, a rule enforced by uniformed Pinkerton guards. In a poster for the film, there is a red-outlined image of Alfred Hitchcock with his right index finger pointing to the wristwatch on his left hand and the following text:

NO ONE...BUT NO ONE...WILL BE ADMITTED TO THE THEATRE AFTER THE START OF EACH PERFORMANCE OF ALFRED HITCHCOCK's *PSYCHO*.

On another poster there is a full-length picture of Hitchcock in the identical pose, pointing to his watch, and with the text:

IT IS REQUIRED THAT YOU SEE *PSYCHO* FROM THE VERY BEGINNING.

Under the text was a white box and adjacent, the next scheduled screening time:

The next screening of *PSYCHO* BEGINS AT

The basic plot structure of the story is rather mundane but its visual execution by Alfred Hitchcock is brilliant. In a 1962 interview with French director François Truffaut, Hitchcock spoke of the shower scene and his comments illustrate how he approached the imagery for the entire film: "It wasn't a message that stirred the audience. Nor was it a great performance. They were aroused by pure film" (http://film.guardian.co.uk/features/apicturestory).

The movie begins with a sweeping aerial view of the Phoenix skyline and a title that reads, FRIDAY, DECEMBER THE ELEVENTH TWO FORTY–THREE P.M. The camera has entered a seedy hourly rate hotel room where a couple, Marion Crane (Janet Leigh) and Sam Loomis (John Gavin), have just completed a lunchtime tryst. The backstory of the characters reveals that Marion wants to marry Sam and is frustrated by the circumstances of their clandestine meetings and also by the ten years she's spent at her job in a realtor's office. For Sam, his reluctance toward marriage is because he enjoys the excitement of these secret meetings, and he uses the excuse of being burdened by the debt of alimony payments to his ex-wife and settling his dead father's financial obligations. For Marion, these weekly rendezvous are a tawdry realization of her situation, and she longs to legitimize the relationship by marriage. She threatens to end the furtive meetings if Sam doesn't commit himself to a more permanent bond.

Upon returning to the office, Marion is asked by her boss, Mr. Lowry (Vaughn Taylor) to make a $40,000 cash deposit in the bank's safe deposit box. This is the money turned over by Mr. Tom Cassidy (Frank Albertson) for a house he has purchased as a wedding present for his eighteen-year-old daughter. Cassidy is arrogant and vulgar, leering at Marion and asking her if she is unhappy, and he tries to tempt her by offering a weekend in Las Vegas. Cassidy's talk about the impending marriage of his daughter is preceded by a conversation Marion has with her newlywed colleague, Caroline (Patricia Hitchcock), about her nagging mother and a doctor's prescription for tranquilizers on her wedding night. Having just returned from her "illicit" encounter with Sam, the conversation about marriage unnerves her such that when she returns to her apartment we see her suitcase packed and then watch as she thrusts the envelope with the money in it into her purse.

Marion has decided to drive to Fairvale, California, where Sam lives and works, imagining that the money might provide the catalyst for him to consider marrying her. Driving out of town in her car, she stops at a light as Lowry and Cassidy cross. Her boss acknowledges her by smiling at first and then furrows his brow because she had told him she had a headache and would immediately return home after making the bank deposit.

In *Psycho*, Hitchcock treats his audience to sudden, jarring images that serve as harbingers of impending action. This happens in the scene where Marion has spent the night sleeping on the front seat of her car and is abruptly woken by a knock on her side window and confronted by the ominous face of a uniformed California highway patrolman (Mort Mills) wearing oversized reflecting sun glasses. There is a tense conversation as the police officer admonishes her for sleeping in the car when there are many motels available along the highway. Suspicious of Marion's nervous behavior, he asks to see her license and registration, then reluctantly allows her to drive away but slowly follows behind.

She turns off the highway and into a town and finds a used car lot. There, she nervously negotiates with a salesman over the sale of her car and the purchase of a new used car. The salesman grows suspicious as she rushes to close the deal, cautioning her about the need to test-drive the car and take more time to consider the purchase. In addition, the California highway patrolman has followed her, parked across the street from the lot, and is observing her behavior. When Marion finally gets behind the wheel of her new car and attempts to drive off, she is startled by the mechanic's voice calling her back because she had left her luggage in the back seat of the old car.

After driving thirty hours, Marion, hungry and tired, allows her mind to wander and she imagines a number of scenarios about her crime, ranging from the shock of Mr. Lowry, her employer, and the anger of Mr. Cassidy, who deposited the cash, to a conversation between the highway patrolman and the car salesman. In the darkness and a driving rain, she meanders off the main road and sees a neon sign that reads, BATES MOTEL VACANCY.

The action that follows consists of carefully plotted and blocked scenes that are revealing by lighting, camera angle, mise-en-scène, and dialogue. As Marion leaves her car she notices the ominous presence of the large Victorian house on the hill and sees the passing image of an elderly woman in a window. After she honks her horn, Norman Bates (Anthony Perkins) rushes down the steps of the house and escorts Marion into his office. He nervously tells her that since the highway no one stops at the motel unless they take a wrong turn. There are twelve rooms, all vacant, and at first he offers Room 3 and then changes his mind to Room 1, near the office. He awkwardly shows her the room and opens the window because it's stuffy inside. Then, he asks Marion if she would join him for a simple dinner of sandwiches in the main house, which she consents to. When he leaves, she wraps the $40,000 she has stolen in a *Los Angeles Tribune* newspaper and places it in a drawer while overhearing a punishing argument between Norman and his "mother" about his intended dinner plans. Abandoning dinner in the main house, Norman delivers a tray of milk and sandwiches and invites Marion into his parlor behind the motel office.

The parlor scene is one of the most telling in the film. Its richness in visual detail expresses a psychological dynamic between the two characters that moves the narrative and serves as a harbinger of future events. It's a small room decorated with birds stuffed by Norman Bates, an "amateur" taxidermist. The lighting is evocative of the characters' moods and is a telling counterpoint of the upcoming action. For Marion, there are soft tones enhanced by props, including a round picture frame on the wall behind her, a Tiffany lamp with its shade exuding warmth, and a full pitcher of milk, its white color and the soft lines of the pitcher expressive of her inner good. For Norman, given a low camera angle and harsh lighting, which together produce angular, dark shadows, the portrait is of a troubled psyche. Indeed, one of the large stuffed birds with a long wingspan in harsh shadow appears as if it will swoop down any moment and attack.

Their parlor conversation punctuates the visual mood created by Hitchcock. Although Marion has committed a crime, we learn from her dialogue that she is a compassionate and sensitive person. She talks to Norman about his mother's harsh treatment of him and suggests that perhaps he should leave her or place her somewhere. The thought upsets him and he becomes unsettled, mocking her advice in an irrational way before regaining control of himself. During their conversation, Norman nervously stutters, contradicting himself, and then recovers with a more normal speech pattern.

After talking with Norman, Marion realizes she has trapped herself by committing the theft and is ensnared, just as he is by circumstance. Feeling somewhat of a bond and forgetting that she signed the register with an assumed name, she tells Norman that her name is Crane, revealing her true identity, and admits that she stepped into a private trap and must return to Phoenix to extricate herself. After Marion returns to her room, Norman checks the motel register and grins as he confirms that she has lied about her identity. He returns to the parlor, removes a picture of a female nude from the wall, and peers through a peephole, leering at Marion as she undresses and prepares to shower. The audience sees a close-up of his unflinching eye as he enjoys the voyeuristic sexual arousal of seeing Marion nude. After she puts on a robe and enters the bathroom, Norman rushes to the main house and sits in the kitchen, betraying his nervous impulses.

The scene of Marion's murder is perhaps the most famous in cinema history and one that has been analyzed, studied, and written about more than any other in the annals of film. For Hitchcock, the murder of Marion was compelling because of its timing and suddenness: "I think the thing that appealed to me was the suddenness of the murder in the shower, coming, as it were, out of the blue. That was about all."

Janet Leigh said that after she saw the shower scene she was afraid to take a shower or bath in a hotel unless she was facing out, with her back against the faucets. She also spoke of the censorship oversight by the Hays office and the difficulties

Hitchcock encountered with the scenes in which she appeared in a bra and half-slip. In the shower scene, which took seven days to shoot, they could not use a nude model but through a brilliant editing process, which required 50 cuts, 78 pieces of film, 70 camera setups, and 71 to 78 angles, the result is an exercise in suggestion and imagination. As Janet Leigh said in an interview:

> The brilliance of *Psycho* was that your imagination was allowed to flourish... And you never see anything in the shower scene. That was the genius of Hitchcock. People swear they saw the knife go in, but they never showed that—it was not allowed. You saw a belly button, and even that was something that was very difficult and was almost not allowed. But that was all you saw—you thought you saw more, but you didn't. (http://www.bmonster.com/horror19)

Although Janet Leigh denies that the knife penetrates the skin, a frame-by-frame analysis of the shower scene reveals that in three almost subliminal frames there is a penetration of a fraction of an inch. However, for those viewing the film, seeing this on the screen and consciously noting it would be impossible.

The shower scene is shot almost exclusively in close-up, with sudden jarring thrusts of the knife as the horrifying action is accompanied by the screeching violin music composed by Bernard Herrmann. At first Hitchcock wanted the scene to appear without music, but Herrmann prevailed upon him to test it and the result was even greater than Hitchcock anticipated. Also a perfectionist, Herrmann recalled his confrontation with Hitchcock over the music in a conversation with director Brian De Palma:

> I remember sitting in a screening room after seeing the rough cut of *Psycho*. Hitch was nervously pacing back and forth, saying it was awful and that he was going to cut it down for his television show. He was crazy. He didn't know what he had. "Wait a minute," I said, "I have some ideas. How about a score completely for strings? I used to be a violin player you know..." Hitch was crazy then. You know, he made *Psycho* with his own money and he was afraid it was going to be a flop. He didn't even want any music in the shower scene. Can you imagine that? ("Sound in Psycho" http://filmsound.org/articles/hitchcock/makingpsycho)

As a composer, Hermann respected Hitchcock's devotion to music as a tool to amplify and help move the narrative in his films.

> Bernard Herrmann, for example, who created the scores for *Psycho*, *North by Northwest* and some of Hitchcock's other masterpieces, said there were only "a handful of directors like Hitchcock who really know the score and fully realize the importance of its relationship to a film." (Rothstein, 2007)

His talent as a director gave Hitchcock the unique ability to understand the power of music.

> Hitchcock, without ever drawing a line between the popular and high arts, explored his chosen genre with a firm belief about the powers of music. Music can provide an archetype for Hitchcockian suspense. Music can hint at more than it

says; it can unfold with both rigorous logic and heightened drama; and despite all expectations it can shock with its revelations. (Rothstein, January 8, 2007)

The pulsating terror of the shower scene is enhanced by the routine innocence of a woman taking a shower only to be savagely attacked and brutalized. She is naked, trapped, and vulnerable, with no means to defend herself. The audience is just as surprised as she, hearing her piercing screams above the undulating violins. It is a visual symphony of horror as the victim attempts to ward off her attacker with her left hand but cannot stop the vicious onslaught. Through the deft editing technique it appears as if Marion is being attacked from all angles. She turns but has no place to hide as the vicious assault continues. We see the attacker leave and Marion's left hand is pressed hard against the tile, the tips of her fingernails scraping down the flat, wet, tiled surface. Then she turns, and with her head and back against the wall, she slowly slides down to the floor of the shower. As she descends, she thrusts out her right hand, grabbing the shower curtain, and with her last ounce of strength pulls it from the hooks above. She frontally falls over the curtain with her body partially outside the shower as water mixed with her blood swirls down the drain. The "blood" was chocolate syrup and the sound effect used to simulate flesh being stabbed was that of a knife piercing a Casaba melon.

According to Janet Leigh, she and Hitchcock had discussed the meaning of the shower scene and its intended metaphor. It had a religious connotation associated with the ecumenical ritual of cleansing:

> Marion had decided to go back to Phoenix, come clean, and take the consequence, so when she stepped into the tub it was as if she were stepping into the baptismal waters. The spray beating down on her was purifying the corruption from her mind, purging the evil from her soul. She was like a virgin again, tranquil, at peace. (Leigh, 69–70)

As Hitchcock had anticipated, the shower scene caused a great deal of controversy even before the film was released. Some members of the Hays office (government censors and precursor to the MPAA) contended they saw one of Janet Leigh's breasts. In Hitchcock's defiant but shrewd manner, he attempted to appease them by holding on to the film for several days without making any changes to the print. When he resubmitted it to the panel, the members who complained no longer saw the breast while those who did not initially see it said they witnessed it. After removing a buttock shot of Leigh's stand-in, the censors approved the shower scene. As noted earlier, the censors were also concerned about the opening scene of a post-coital sexual encounter between Marion, dressed only in a bra and half-slip, and Sam. Hitchcock bartered the shower scene for a reshoot of the opening, inviting the censors to the studio for the reshoot. They never showed up so he kept the opening scene.

A persistent rumor was that graphic designer Saul Bass, who designed the titles for many of Hitchcock's films and also storyboarded some of his scenes, claimed credit for directing the shower scene. That claim has been disputed by Janet Leigh and Hitchcock's assistant director and cameraman, Hilton A. Green. For Leigh, there was no doubt it was Hitchcock because he was present for the seven days required for the shoot:

> I was in the shower for seven days, and, believe you me, Alfred Hitchcock was right next to his camera for every one of those seventy-odd shots. (Leigh, 67–68)

Hilton Green shared the same sentiment as he recalled his experience shooting *Psycho*:

> There is not a shot in that movie that I didn't roll the camera for. And I can tell you I never rolled the camera for Mr. Bass.

Noted film critic Roger Ebert echoed similar feelings when he surmised that a perfectionist director with a giant ego like Alfred Hitchcock would hardly allow someone else to direct the most important scene in his film.

After the murder, the story moves to act three as Marion's sister Lila (Vera Miles) visits Sam at the hardware store in Fairvale and inquires about her sister. Joining them is private investigator Milton Arbogast (Martin Balsam), hired by the real estate office to find Marion and recover the money. He suspects that Sam may be involved and that a girl with $40,000 cannot stay anonymous for long. Following his intuition, Arbogast canvasses a number of hotels and motels, finally coming upon the Bates Motel. After meeting Norman, who initially denies that Marion spent the night, he recants when Arbogast matches the Marie Samuels signature in the register with Marion Crane's. Throughout Arbogast's questioning, Norman nervously attempts to allay his suspicions but fails to convince the dogmatic detective. Seeing an image in the window of the main house, Norman admits it is his invalid mother, and Arbogast asks to question her but Norman demands that he leave. Acquiescing, he leaves, then calls Lila to inform her he has a lead on Marion and no longer suspects Sam's implication. He says he will get back to her in an hour, after doing some additional investigating. Insistent on pursuing his suspicions about Norman, Arbogast enters the house and starts climbing the stairs.

Once again the audience is unsuspecting about the action about to unfold. As Arbogast climbs the stairs, the camera follows him but then quickly changes perspective, moving ahead and above him. The audience sees a sliver of light, which gradually gets wider, emanating from Mother's room as Arbogast continues up the stairs. The camera angle moves again to an overhead shot as he reaches the top. Announcing another horrific murder, the sound of strings anticipates the next sequence as "Mother" lunges at Arbogast with a carving knife and the audience sees the stunned and shocked expression on his bloodied face. He stumbles and falls backward down the stairs and collapses as "Mother" jumps on top of him and continues her attack, stabbing him with the knife.

The shot was filmed with the camera gliding down the staircase while Martin Balsam sat in a chair wildly waving his arms as the image of the staircase was projected behind him. The action culminates with a visit by Sam and Lila to Fairvale's deputy sheriff Al Chambers (John McIntire) and his wife Eliza (Lurene Tuttle), who were surprised when Sam said he had seen Mother and that Arbogast mentioned he was going to question her. According to Chambers and his wife, Mother had died ten years earlier in a murder-suicide after killing her lover, and Norman had discovered their bodies in bed together.

At the Fairvale church the next morning, Sam and Lila meet Chambers and his wife, and Chambers insists that he searched the Bates Motel and found nothing urging them to file a missing person's report for Marion Crane. Rejecting Chambers's request, Lila and Sam visit the Bates Motel, registering as husband and wife and determined to do an exhaustive search. Assigned to Room 10 by Norman, Lila insists on Room 1, the room Marion had stayed in. Inside the room, Sam comments about the missing shower curtain and Lila notices a scrap of paper in Marion's handwriting containing numbers stuck to the toilet. They agree to split up, with Sam keeping Norman busy at the motel while Lila explores the main house. She enters Mother's and Norman's room and then sees Norman running toward the house; she descends into the cellar to hide. There, she confronts a mummified Mother, turning her around and seeing her hollow eyes and toothy grin, which frightens Lila, causing her to scream. Then, in another sudden and frightening moment Norman, dressed as Mother, lunges toward Lila holding the familiar knife but is subdued by Sam.

In the final epilogue, police psychiatrist Dr. Richmond (Simon Oakland) explains how the personality of Norman's mother has completely taken over his mind and that his behavior is related to his guilt for murdering his mother and her lover in a jealous rage. The final scene of the movie shows Norman in a cell and his musings as Mother blaming her son for the murders and advocating her own innocence.

In 1959, Alfred Hitchcock wanted to redefine his career and make a film that was not typical of those he had previously produced. He commented to the press that he had been somewhat typecast as a director: "If I made Cinderella, the audience would be looking for a corpse to turn up in the coach." "Style is self-plagiarism" (Rebello).

In 1955, Hitchcock had been bested by French director Henri-Georges Clouzot in acquiring the English translation rights of the novel *Celle Qui N'Etait Plus* (*The Woman Who Was No More*), by Pierre Boileau and Thomas Narcejac. The film became *Les Diaboliques* and was very successful in Europe and the United States. In some of the American reviews, Clouzot was heralded as the new master of suspense and referred to as the "French Hitchcock." Making matters worse, Hitchcock purchased the rights to *D'Entre Les Morts* (roughly, *From Amongst the Dead*), another book by the same authors, and turned it into *Vertigo*, today considered a masterpiece but when released in 1958 received poorly by audiences and critics.

Hitchcock was a shrewd observer, noting that when *Les Diaboliques* played in Europe, audiences were urged to see the film from the beginning and theater doors were locked after the movie started. When the film was distributed in the United States, the same public relations technique was used. Recognizing the additional suspense, word of mouth, and excitement this campaign created, Hitchcock adopted it for *Psycho*, which was a resounding audience and financial success.

THE FRENCH NEW WAVE (NOUVELLE VAGUE)

Post-war France was a reservoir for youthful talent and intellectualism while embracing a culture of consumerism and relaxation. There was a compelling interest in cinema, nurtured by clubs and serious film criticism profiled in magazines such as *Cahiers du Cinema*. In an effort to support a declining film industry after the failure of several major films, the French government created the *Centre National du Cinema*, establishing the *prime de la qualité*, or subsidy for quality. This provided an opportunity for new directors to produce short films. Then, in 1959, the French government formed the *avance sur recettes*, an advance on receipts program which provided financing for first feature films based on a script. This was a chance for young filmmakers to produce their first feature films, and from 1958 to 1961 many did.

New-wave cinema had several characteristics associated with it that defied various long-held conventions. Some were autobiographical, selfishly embracing the auteur philosophy and reflecting a reverence for particular directors like Alfred Hitchcock. Many of the directors had been film critics, such as François Truffaut, and had an enduring respect for the art of cinema. They believed their films should reflect their experiences and personal vision of the world. These films were a testimony to the frugality of independent filmmaking, which necessitated utilizing portable equipment, shooting on location, using small crews, and casting either unknown actors or amateurs. The directors had a very practical approach to filmmaking, as was summed up by Claude Chabrol: "You become a director, when you find the money to make your first film."

Three films define the New Wave and demonstrate the philosophy of the filmmakers. They are: *The 400 Blows* (Les Quatre Cent Coups) and *Jules and Jim* (Jules et Jim) by François Truffaut and *Breathless* (A Bout de Soufflé) by Jean-Luc Godard. They were made in 1960, 1962, and 1960, respectively.

THE 400 BLOWS (LES QUATRE CENT COUPS) (1959)

PRODUCER/DIRECTOR: François Truffaut

WRITER(S): François Truffaut (scenario), Marcel Moussy (adaptation), Marcel Moussy (dialogue)

CAST: Jean-Pierre Léaud (Antoine Doinel), Claire Maurier (Gilberte Doinel), Albert Rémy (Julien Doinel), Guy Decomble ("Petite Feuille"), Georges Flamant (Mr. Bigey), Patrick Auffay (René), Daniel Couturier (Les enfants), François Nocher (Les enfants), Richard Kanayan (Les enfants), Renaud Fontanarosa (Les enfants)

CINEMATOGRAPHY: Henri Decaë

MUSIC: Jean Constantin

LENGTH AND RATING: 99 min; NR

As a young director, Truffaut established a gritty, honest, and somewhat damning portrayal of the rituals of family, school, and authority. He once said, "I demand that a film express either the joy of making cinema or the agony of making cinema. I am not at all interested in anything in between" (http://rogerebert.suntimes.com, 1999).

Throughout this autobiographical film there is a thread of betrayal, institutional failure, and adult malaise. These themes pertaining to neglected children are very much a part of modern social dynamics, which makes the film a timeless portrait of a troubled system. It's the poignant story of Antoine Doinel (Jean Pierre-Léaud), a twelve-year-old boy born out of wedlock and raised by a scheming mother (Claire Maurier) and a stepfather (Albert Remy), who has provided him with a modest home and his name. His mother, who envisions herself a sexy blonde in form-fitting sweaters, is having a liaison with a male colleague from work. He has been shuttled back and forth from his home to his grandmother's house, enduring the internal pain of rejection and humiliation. He finds a life on the street and begins a downward spiral into lying, stealing, and truancy. His school, his family, and the social safety net have failed him and he feels alone but remains rebellious and defiant.

It seems that even when Antoine attempts to accommodate his parents and teachers, he is mistakenly accused of cheating and lying. He is an avid admirer of Balzac (considered the founding father of realism), even building a shrine to his favorite author. But, when he writes a term paper on one of Balzac's readings, he is accused by his teacher of plagiarism. To honor Balzac, he lights a candle in his shrine, but when it starts a fire his father at first slaps him as punishment. Then there is a sense of forgiveness and they go to the movies as a family and on the way home frolic and laugh together. In class, the boys pass a "girlie" calendar around, and when the teacher discovers it circulating, it has passed to Antoine's hand and he is punished. His problems in school escalate when he feigns sickness for missing class, and for another absence he lies that his mother has died. This, of course, brings on the wrath of his parents and school administrators. His circumstances are also complicated when he is caught returning a stolen typewriter to his father's office because he couldn't sell it to finance a plan to run away. Learning of this, Antoine's father accompanies him to the police station, where he is booked and locked in a cell. His mother grasps at the opportunity to be rid of her troublesome son, and while speaking to a police magistrate consents to have him sent to an observation center, preferably by the sea. The magistrate scoffs at this request, reminding her that Antoine is not going to a summer camp.

In writing and casting the film, Truffaut's allegiance to cinema in the first-person singular and loyalty to its autobiographical nature changed with the casting of Jean Pierre-Léaud in the lead because the novice actor was more confident and demonstrative then Truffaut had been at that age. Eventually, Truffaut departed from the script and allowed Léaud's dialogue and demeanor to become more dominant on-screen.

There is an especially revealing scene when Antoine is being interviewed by a psychologist, who asks him about his behavior and to explain various things he has done. He explains that he returned the typewriter because he couldn't sell it, and that he stole ten thousand francs from his grandmother because she was old, didn't eat much, would soon die, and so didn't need the money. Then he accuses his mother of going through his pockets, taking the money, and selling a book his grandmother gave him. Antoine responds to the accusation of lying by saying that he is not a persistent liar, and that when he tells the truth he is not believed, so he prefers to lie. When asked why he doesn't like his mother, Antoine answers that he was sent to live with a wet-nurse and when money became an issue he was sent to live with his grandmother. When she became too old to care for him, he returned home, at the age of eight. He could tell his mother didn't like him because she yelled at him for no reason. Finally, toward the end of the interview, there is a substantive revelation when Antoine responds that he was born out of wedlock and that if it wasn't for his grandmother's intervention, his mother would have aborted him. The interview ends on a lighter note when Antoine is asked if he has ever slept with a girl. In a rather circuitous tale and with a sheepish grin, Antoine tells of a North African man who took him to a hotel to meet with a woman "who liked guys my age." After waiting, she didn't show up and he left.

The exchange between Antoine and the unseen psychologist presents a compelling portrait of a child caught in a conflicting web of survival, dependence, and perseverance within a flawed social system that advocates punishment while failing to recognize the behavioral dynamics of the child's situation. During the interview, he is both defensive and bold in responding to the questioning. The audience acknowledges that he is a shrewd subject adept at parrying the questions and showing only a hint of emotion. Perhaps he is too confident and brazen, or it is the protection of a hardened exterior, a shell, that is a defense against having to endure additional emotional violations.

In the final scene of the film, Antoine is running though the countryside, moving away from the confused reality that confronts him and toward a lyrical freedom of his own design. He is out in the open, engaged in an exhilarating exercise of thought and action, when he reaches the ocean. He runs down the steps leading to the beach, glances right and left, steps into the water, looks down, and then turns toward the camera, which zooms in and freezes on a full shot of his face from the neck up. This final shot is a stunning portrait of a child whose life the audience has come to know but whose future is in doubt. There is no resolution or formulaic happy ending. Instead, the audience is left to make their own conclusions and also be burdened with some of the blame.

Only 27 years old when he made this film with a budget of $110,000, François Truffaut made an auspicious debut, winning the Cannes Film Festival award for best direction. There was a continued collaboration with Jean Pierre-Léaud (Antoine Doinel) in three other films: *Antoine and Colette* (1962), *Stolen Kisses* (1968), and *Bed and Board* (1970).

BREATHLESS (À BOUT DE SOUFFLE) (1960)

PRODUCER/DIRECTOR: Jean-Luc Godard (director), Georges de Beauregard (producer)
WRITER(S): Jean-Luc Godard (writer), François Truffaut (story)
CAST: Jean-Paul Belmondo (Michel Poiccard), Jean Seberg (Patricia Franchini), Daniel Boulanger (Police Inspector Vital), Jean-Pierre Melville (Parvulesco), Henri-Jacques Huet (Antonio Berrutti), Van Doude (Himself), Claude Mansard (Claudius Mansard), Jean-Luc Godard (An Informer), Richard Balducci (Tolmatchoff), Roger Hanin (Cal Zombach)
CINEMATOGRAPHY: Raoul Coutard
MUSIC: Martial Solal
LENGTH AND RATING: 90 min; NR

As one of the new-wave filmmakers, Jean Luc Godard had a prominent role in defining the direction and substance of the genre. Like Truffaut, he was at first a critic, writing for the influential film journal *Cahiers du Cinema*. After becoming a director he developed an interesting perspective on film criticism, which he articulated during a 1964 interview. He said then that he thought highly of reviewers, probably because he was one, and that he didn't take bad reviews personally. As a reviewer, he admitted to saying a lot of bad things and being cruel and mean to a lot of people, and as a filmmaker he found most reviews to be personal:

> I find that in general critics are always personal. When they say something bad they're trying to hurt the person. (http://www.youtube.com/watch?v=Y_zCPiYhVBQ)

He also noted that the occupation of a critic was transitory by design:

> Seventy-five percent of critics are only in that line of work temporarily. That's why critics are always bitter and sad toward those they praise and those they disparage. (http://www.youtube.com/watch?v=Y_zCPiYhVBQ)

When Godard was asked about recognizing honesty in a critic, he answered that he felt all critics are sincere, and that whether right or wrong, they had to be sincere because they cannot be dishonest.

In *Breathless*, Godard pays homage to the B movies made by American studios like Monogram Pictures in the 1940s (opening credits dedicate *Breathless* to Monogram), which produced low-budget Charlie Chan and Bela Lugosi movies. The anti-hero of the film, Michel Poiccard, alias Laslo Kovaks (Jean-Paul Belmondo), is a wannabe gangster, swaggering, posturing, and mimicking the mannerisms of the actor Humphrey Bogart, whom he admires. Throughout the film, he pauses to brush his thumb across his lips, mirroring Bogart's defining gesture. In reality, Michel is no more than a petty thief who steals cars and mugs unsuspecting victims in the men's room.

After stealing a car in Marseilles, Michel rides through the countryside, shooting and killing a motorcycle policeman who pulls him over. As a result of this brazen, defiant act, Michel is on the run and heads toward Paris to be with his former American girlfriend, Patricia (Jean Seberg), a student at the Sorbonne who peddles the *Herald Tribune* on the street. She is also an aspiring journalist who flirts with one of the newspaper's editors to get ahead. Her character embodies a spirit of emotional contradictions as she struggles to reconcile her feelings about love and her attraction to Michel.

In *Breathless*, the movies themselves become a plot device to help define the characters and tell the story. They are a reference to American culture and the influence of American cinema and its heroes on the young New Wave directors. As he walks the streets of Paris, Michel pauses in front of theaters displaying movie posters of Humphrey Bogart in the film noir *The Harder They Fall* (1956), co-starring Rod Steiger, and another poster for the film *Ten Seconds to Hell* (1959), featuring Jeff Chandler and Jack Palance. After the police visit Patricia at the *Herald Tribune*, they tail her and she ducks into a movie theater, escaping through a window in the ladies' room and then meeting Michel and hiding with him in another theater. They kiss in the theater, which is showing the 1958 western *Westbound*, directed by Bud Boetticher and featuring western star Randolph Scott, who plays John Hayes. He is a Civil War veteran and manager of Overland Stage Lines, shipping a vast quantity of gold to the North, but Clay Putnam (Andrew Duggan) wants to steal the gold to revive the fortunes of the Confederacy. Of course, there is a plot complication by a woman played by Virginia Mayo, Putnam's wife and Hayes' ex-girlfriend. Similarly, Patricia, the object of Michel's passion, becomes a complication by the end of *Breathless*. The dialogue unfolding on the screen in *Westbound* has relevance to Michel and Patricia, whose short time together is indicative of being nobly tragic with shattered memories:

Have a care, Jessica; in the crossways of kisses the years pass too quickly. Beware, beware, beware of shattered memories! You're wrong, Sheriff, our story is as nobly tragic as a tyrant's face. No heroic drama, no slightest detail but confirms our love in grace. (Alemdar, http://www.geociites.com/melisalemdar/breathless)

As a filmmaker, Godard had a reverence for American films, especially film noir. He also made many literary references in *Breathless* to the writers William Faulkner, Dylan Thomas, and Rainer Maria Rilke. In *Breathless*, there is a reference to Faulkner's

Wild Palms, in which a prominent character is based on another American literary master, Ernest Hemingway. Patricia quotes a reference from *Wild Palms* to Michel that implies the existentialist and nihilistic philosophy that was a fundamental aspect of the New Wave.

She says: "Between grief and nothing I will take grief." She then asks Michel which he would choose, and he answers, "I'd choose nothingness...grief is a compromise." Godard also uses the works of the renowned artists whose posters adorn the walls of Patricia's bedroom. These include Paul Klee, Picasso, and Renoir. Patricia poses in front of a Renoir poster of a young girl and asks Michel, "Who is prettier?"

It's not surprising that New Wave directors such as Godard would embrace writers like Faulkner, who in many ways expressed the same dogmatic philosophy about their art. For example, Faulkner wrote:

> The writer's only responsibility is to his art. He will be completely ruthless if he is a good one. He has a dream. It anguishes him so much he must get rid of it. He has no peace until then. Everything goes by the board: honor, pride, decency, security, happiness, all, to get the book written. If a writer has to rob his mother, he will not hesitate; the "Ode on a Grecian Urn" is worth any number of old ladies. (from *Writers at Work: The Paris Review Interviews*, 1959)

Technically, *Breathless* is a significant departure from traditional filmmaking. In it, Godard uses jump cuts and quick cuts to move from scene to scene. He also uses an iris shot, just as American director D. W. Griffith did in his films. These innovations came about more as necessity than aesthetic principles. The finished film was ninety minutes too long, and Godard chose to edit within the scene instead of cutting out entire scenes, creating a new style for narrative film. He shot without a script, although the story outline was written by François Truffaut and he modeled *Breathless* after American gangster films.

In his book *Jean-Luc Goddard*, John Francis Kreidl writes that the three elements that make *Breathless* unique are its generationalism, storytelling innovations, and editing. He credits Godard for pursuing a form of cinema that is neither formalistic violation of narrative nor recapitulation of conventional narrative structure. As Godard noted, *Breathless* is about con games, and Americans are the biggest con artists because they like Lafayette and Maurice Chevalier, whom he describes as the biggest French con artists.

The end of the movie is unconventional in the sense that while hiding from the police in a friend's studio, Patricia telephones the police inspector to inform on Michel. Upon returning to the studio, she tells Michel what she has done and her explanation is that she is proving to herself that she no longer loves him. Nonetheless, she urges him to flee but he says he is tired. The final scenes are conventional as one of his friends driving by offers Michel a gun, which he tosses back in the convertible, and while running from the police he is shot, eventually staggers, falls, and dies.

In his February 8, 1961, *New York Times* review of *Breathless*, Bosley Crowther refers to the film as "raw drama" and describes the editing as "pictorial cacophony." He describes the story: "Sordid is really a mild word for its pile-up of gross indecencies—it is withal a fascinating communication of the savage ways and moods of some of the rootless young people of Europe (and America) today." Crowther goes on to say that the movie is vicious, erotic, and lacks any semblance of morality: "It is emphatically, unrestrainedly vicious, completely devoid of moral tone, concerned mainly with eroticism and the restless drives of a cruel young punk to get along. Although it does not appear intended deliberately to shock, the very vigor of its reportorial candor compels that it must do so."

At the end of his review, Crowther acknowledges the artistic merit of the film, saying it is not a cliché and that it graphically and artfully shows "the tough underbelly of modern metropolitan life."

JULES AND JIM (1962)

PRODUCER/DIRECTOR: François Truffaut
WRITER(S): Henri-Pierre Roché (novel), François Truffaut (adaptation)
CAST: Jeanne Moreau (Catherine), Oskar Werner (Jules), Henri Serre (Jim)
CINEMATOGRAPHY: Raoul Coutard
MUSIC: Georges Delerue
LENGTH AND RATING: 105 min; NR

The story is that as François Truffaut was browsing at secondhand bookstalls in Paris, he came upon the semiautobiographical novel *Jules et Jim*, by Henri-Pierre Roche. Roche was a well-respected journalist, art dealer, and collector who was friendly with some of the prominent artists of the time, including Pablo Picasso. Married twice, Roche was quite the ladies' man and he had a number of affairs, although his relationship with German-Jewish writer Franz Hessel and his wife, journalist Helen Grund, formed the basis for his novel.

The story is about Jules (Oskar Werner), a shy Austrian writer, and his friend Jim (Henri Serre), who is more gregarious, and the woman they both love, Catherine (Jeanne Moreau). The men meet in Paris in 1912 and immediately become inseparable. They teach each other their native languages, German for Jules and French for Jim. Bonding together in a tightly knit relationship, Jules and Jim even share women, demonstrating their trust and honesty toward each other. Jules, however, appears to have more difficulties finding the right woman and resorts to "professionals" but finds them equally unfulfilling. He settles on Theresa (Marie Dubois), but becomes frustrated with her, finally declaring, "She was both mother and daughter to me."

While attending a slide show, the men see a breathtakingly beautiful image of a goddess, which inspires them to travel to the Adriatic Ionian Basin (the area of Greece and Italy) to find this woman. They are indeed naive romantics, embarking on a journey to realize their fantasy and fulfill their inspiration. The goddess appears to them upon their return to Paris in the form of Catherine, who is beautiful and free-spirited and joins them, bonding in friendship and love. However, Jules admonishes Jim that his interest in Catherine precludes their usual arrangement of sharing women. Although Jim is also in love with Catherine, he agrees to Jules' demand. Shortly before World War I is declared, Jules moves to Austria with Catherine and they get married. Each man serves in his respective army during the war, and each fears he may have killed the other.

After the war, the three reunite at a cottage on the Reine, where Jules and Catherine live with their daughter (Sabine Haudepin). The marriage is an unhappy one, and

Jules confides to Jim that Catherine has had numerous affairs. Hoping to sustain a relationship with Catherine and preserve his friendship with Jim, Jules offers to divorce Catherine so she can marry Jim. The four live together, enjoying their relationship, until Jim leaves, in part because of Catherine's frustration over her inability to conceive a child. Meeting by chance in Paris after Jules, Catherine, and Sabine return to France, Catherine tries to entice Jim to return to her, but he rebuffs her attempt.

For Catherine, the need to fulfill her desire to be with Jim is consummated by her final act of possession, when she has him join her in a car and admonishes Jules to watch as she drives off a bridge. It is a tragic end to a youthful story of indulgence, fantasy, and joie de vivre as the transition to adulthood shatters the dreams and hopes of youth.

François Truffaut had a unique style and pursued innovation and creative cinematic visual structure. In *Jules and Jim*, he uses a combination of newsreel footage, photographic stills, freeze-frames, panning, and dolly shots and wipes, in addition to voice-over narration. This results in a fluid and poetic camera style.

5 The Space Race, Civil Rights, and a Nation Torn, 1960–1969

The minimum wage was one dollar an hour in the 1960s, and seventy million children from the postwar baby boom became teenagers and transitioned into young adulthood. It was also a time of civil and racial unrest. The cold war was raging and the Cuban Missile Crisis of 1962 tested the resolve of a young president, John F. Kennedy, and generated fear of a nuclear war. Respect for authority declined and the youth of America embraced the alternative lifestyles offered by the mystical religion of Zen Buddhism and the teachings of the Maharishi Mahesh Yogi. The women's liberation movement was growing and their rights were being asserted professionally and in the reproductive process. The birth control pill became available, and by 1967 abortion and artificial insemination were legalized in some states. Under the leadership of Martin Luther King, the civil rights movement evolved into a chorus of protest advocating equality for blacks and other people of color.

There were assassinations (John and Robert Kennedy, Martin Luther King, Malcolm X), and there were riots. The war in Vietnam dragged on and became a symbol of misguided American foreign policy. There were antiwar demonstrations and civil rights marches. And, 400,000 young Americans came together in the spirit of love and outreach at the Woodstock Festival. It was a time when America trembled, and many of the films of the decade reflected a feeling of detachment, misdirection, and longing.

LA DOLCE VITA (1960)

PRODUCER/DIRECTOR: Federico Fellini (director), Giuseppe Amato (producer), Angelo Rizzoli (producer), Franco Magli (executive producer)

WRITER(S): Federico Fellini, Ennio Flaiano, Tullio Pinelli

CAST: Marcello Mastroianni (Marcello Rubini), Anita Ekberg (Sylvia), Anouk Aimée (Maddalena), Yvonne Furneaux (Emma), Magali Noël (Fanny), Alain Cuny (Steiner), Annibale Ninchi (Marcello's father), Walter Santesso (Paparazzo), Valeria Ciangottini (Paola), Riccardo Garrone (Riccardo)

CINEMATOGRAPHY: Otello Martelli

MUSIC: Nino Rota

LENGTH AND RATING: 174 min; NR

112

Marcello Mastroianni and Anita Ekberg. [Astor Pictures/Photofest]

Contemplating *The Graduate* and Benjamin Braddock's lack of motivation, loss of focus, and disdain for authority figures, director Mike Nichols demonstrates similar themes that have served as a foundation for the work of Italian director Federico Fellini. His film, *La Strada*, was discussed earlier in this book, and in the 1960s his expressive voice evolved into a social commentary on the meaning of life and the search, no matter how disdainful, for purpose.

La Dolce Vita is a visual masterpiece that treats its audience to a banquet of images that richly portray the empty lives of its characters. It is an allegory for those who may aspire to lives of worth but are consumed with the insecurity of their efforts or distracted by the pulse of life that shows contempt for substance but worships the glitter of empty pursuit and ennui.

The characters in *La Dolce Vita* are, for the most part, like the cardboard facades of celebrities whom tourists pose with for pictures as a means of associating and cavorting with the rich and famous. Indeed, the main character in the film, Marcello Rubino (Marcello Mastroianni), is a journalist and photographer earning his living as a tabloid hack who spends his nights pursuing the vanity of others, chronicling their vapid pursuits of hedonistic pleasures. Although he aspires to write a novel, he is spirited away by the vanities and superfluity of others and imprisoned by their soulless pursuit of joie de vivre.

As a social critic, Fellini exposes the excess of Italian society as it experiences a postwar economic boom. He is also a harsh critic of the Catholic Church, demeaning its symbols of faith and empty rituals. The film opens with a helicopter carrying a statue of Christ over Rome as Marcello and his photographer, Paparazzo (Walter Santesso), follow in a second helicopter to document the event. They pass over the rooftops of slums, new apartment buildings and, finally, over a roof where several pretty bikini-clad women are sunbathing. He motions to them, trying to get their telephone numbers. This interaction, with the women serving as a distraction, helps to articulate the midway carnival-like impression of the event.

In his pursuit of the sweet life, Marcello spends nine days and eight nights experiencing an epic of debauchery punctuated by episodic bouts of desire and regret. He meets Maddalena (Anouk Aimee), a woman from a wealthy family who becomes his lover on the first night. Together they pick up a prostitute, Fanny (Megali Noel), and give her a lift to her flooded flat. While she is making coffee for them, Maddalena and Marcello have sex on her bed. Perhaps Maddalena evokes an image of Paris Hilton, as sex becomes a game of chance pursued on the run. In another scene, Marcello meets Maddalena during a castle romp and she leaves the room they are in and walks to another, using an old ventilation chamber to carry her voice to Marcello with an uncanny presence, causing him to try to locate her. She declares her love for him, saying they should marry, and he responds as she denies her worth, referring to herself as a whore. The scene is arranged like a confessional and as Marcello continues to share his feelings with Maddalena, she is joined by another man whom she has sex with while Marcello continues to confess. This is a reference to the act of confession that is besmirched by Maddalena's sexuality and Marcello's desire.

In his role as a paparazzo, Marcello meets the famous movie star Sylvia (the beautiful and bosomy Anita Ekberg), and pursues her throughout Rome, from the heights of Saint Peters to the depths of the cavernous underground nightclubs. In the Fiesta en Caracella scene, Sylvia, as the pied piper of hedonism, leads the partygoers in a spectacle of celebration as they circle the room, dancing and delighting in their carefree spirit and pursuing their ritual of pleasure. This is followed by the sudden outburst of a group of youths shouting "Rock 'n' Roll," which culminates in a hyper-performance by the group. The scene reinforces Fellini's portrait of decadence as perceived by the privileged class of Rome. They are moved by the rhythm and beat of the moment and its instant gratification. But while Marcello participates in the sacrament, he remains uncomfortable with the trappings of this endless indulgence.

After Sylvia's argument with her drunken American boyfriend, Robert (Lex Barker of *Tarzan* fame), Marcello tries in vain to secure a friend's apartment to take her to. He cannot take her to his flat because his possessive girlfriend, Emma (Yvonne Furneaus), is there. In one of the most famous scenes in cinema, Marcello and Sylvia are roaming the narrow streets of Rome early in the morning when she finds a kitten and asks Marcello to find some milk. Alone with the kitten, Sylvia stumbles on one of Rome's most magnificent sights, the Trevi Fountain. When Marcello returns with a glass of milk, Sylvia has waded into the fountain and is allowing the water to shower her ample frame. He reluctantly joins her and at one point, Sylvia scoops water into her hand and anoints Marcello's head in an allusion to ceremonial baptism. As Marcello caresses Sylvia's face and moves closer for a kiss, the fountain suddenly stops flowing and silence consumes the screen. The reverie has ended with a sudden return to reality.

In a character-revealing scene, Marcello returns to the Via Veneto, the street where the nightlife is sustained, and is told that his father, Mr. Rubini (Annibale Ninchi), is waiting for him. They meet at his table and Marcello, accompanied by paparazzo, decides to show his father a good time by taking him to a nightclub. Several bottles of champagne are ordered and while Mr. Rubini is dancing with a beautiful, leggy French nightclub performer, Marcello confides that he barely knows his father because he was away for weeks at a time as a traveling liquor salesman. The audience never learns why Mr. Rubini has come to Rome, but the essence of his visit is that, like everyone else in the movie, he is searching for something: perhaps his youth, or amissed opportunity, or even regret for not spending enough time with his son. He becomes ill after arriving at the woman's apartment, and Marcello, who arrives later, shows real concern for his father's well-being, an emotion rarely displayed. It is revealed in two other scenes: Emma's attempted suicide and Steiner's murder of his two children and subsequent suicide.

The relationship Marcello has with the intellectual Steiner (Alain Cuny) is an interesting dynamic because their friendship is based on an assumed understanding of each other. However, while Steiner knows everything about Marcello, there is much that Marcello does not know about Steiner. As Marcello perceives it, Steiner's world consists of literary substance, intellectual rigor, and expressive dialogue. He has a beautiful wife and two adorable children but his world is fraught with insecurity and doubt. He is conflicted and reveals his feelings when he says, "I'm too serious to be an amateur, and not serious enough to be a professional." So, when Marcello learns of the murder-suicide, he rushes to the scene with the other paparazzi and is shocked by this revelation: A man who encouraged him to write a novel and appeared well-grounded was perhaps even more disillusioned than Marcello.

Fellini's childhood ties to the Catholic Church left a profound impression on him. His attendance at various Catholic schools instilled him with both fear and faith. Although he ridiculed the church in his films and abandoned its rituals, he always identified himself as Catholic. Placing religious ideology in perspective, Fellini observed that he would only enter a church to shoot a scene or for an aesthetic or nostalgic reason. Regarding issues of faith, he suggested that it is probably more religious to go to a woman. He described *La Dolce Vita* as a deeply Christian film, if indeed Christianity means love toward one's neighbor. In a scene invoking a vision of the Virgin Mary, the Madonna, Fellini captures the cultural kitsch of spirituality practiced in a world begging to be connected to faith yet lacking any devotion to it. Instead, the people attempt to witness the spectacle like an audience at the circus, pushing and shoving each other to get a glimpse of the children who saw the Madonna by a tree. The brother and sister have been held in protective custody by the police and in preparation for their return, a television director is choreographing the scene, readying it for a live shoot. Paparazzi interview the mother and grandfather, who are posed for pictures with religious symbolism but would like a gratuity for their effort. When the children are finally released, it starts to rain and the huge arc lights begin to explode and must be turned off. The two children run in the mud helter–skelter, shouting that they see the Madonna, and the crowd follows with feverish passion. They are fabricating the visions and feeding on the frenzy of the moment, finally announcing that the Madonna will not return to the spot unless a church is built. Marcello's girlfriend Emma is with him. She prays for the sustenance of their relationship and joins the others in a herd as they descend on the lone tree, tearing it to shreds, savoring their mementoes. In the end, enduring the rain, Marcello does not bear witness to the spirit but only to the trampled remains of a sickly old man. Fellini has symbolically used one of the most revered icons in the Catholic Church as a tool to demonstrate the fraud and manipulation perpetrated by some on the faithful. Can these visions be reality or are they merely a fantasy provoked by insecurity and doubt?

Ironically, thirty-two years after the release of *La Dolce Vita*, in 1992, a man named Joseph Januszkiewycz of New Jersey, who had a statue of the Virgin Mary at the end of his patio, announced that the Virgin appeared next to the statue on the first Sunday of each month. As word of the "miracle" spread, thousands of people came to the small town of Marlboro, in Monmouth County, followed by the paparazzi. As the faithful overran the town in Felliniesque fashion, the mayor implored them not to come and the Bishop of the Diocese of Trenton, New Jersey, asked that they reserve judgment until the miracle could be verified. People trekked from near and far to witness the vision and voiced their belief saying, "We can believe without proof. That's what faith is." "It feels joyous when you're with all these people who believe. They're like family." "A lot of people are responding to a feeling of emptiness and bewilderment." "You can't stop the power of God no matter what you do." "Just because it's 1992 it doesn't mean miracles can't be happening."

Perhaps New Jersey is ripe for fantasy, as other sightings of the Virgin have been claimed on a smudgy window in Perth Amboy and in the form of a tree stump in Passaic. But as in the movie, the visions are more about fantasy and perhaps a need to believe as a response to a feeling of emptiness and disorientation (*New York Times*, "Undeterred by Pleas, the Faithful Again Seek Out a Vision of the Virgin," Robert Hanley, September 7, 1992).

At the end of the film, Marcello and his friends locate the home of a film producer for a party celebrating Nadia's (Nadia Gray) annulment. He throws a rock through a glass door and they all enter, ready to celebrate. Marcello, dressed in a white suit, is now a publicist who has relinquished his self-respect and is the master of ceremonies for the disoriented and misdirected people at the party. At the encouragement of the revelers, Nadia does a striptease and the party is interrupted by the producer, who works and must leave for Rome early in the morning. Anyone who works appears to be an incongruous interruption. The group leaves and proceeds to the beach, where they observe fishermen hauling in a huge fish (another religious symbol) with an open, glaring eye. On the beach, an attractive young woman waves and motions to Marcello, but they are separated by the surf and the crushing sound of the waves. She is Paola (Valeria Ciangottini), the young girl who served him at the café where he was writing his novel. He doesn't remember her and in the end turns away, symbolically leaving that part of his life behind (http://www.culturecourt.com/F/Fellini/LaDV.htm) (http://rogerebert. suntimes.com).

As the director of *La Dolce Vita*, Fellini revealed that the characters in the film only talk about love but are unable to find fulfillment. This is tragically seen in Steiner's murder-suicide. In adulthood, Fellini embraced the occult, believing in omens, astrology, and séances. During the Sixties, he became interested in Carl Jung's theories of psychoanalysis and the importance and meanings of dreams, which became a prominent theme in *Otto e mezzo* (8 1/2). In discussing his films, Fellini was particularly taken with the world of fantasy and preferred it to reality:

Everyone lives in his own fantasy world, but most people don't understand that. No one perceives the *real* world. Each person simply calls his private, personal fantasies the Truth. The difference is that I *know* I live in a fantasy world. I prefer it that way and resent anything that disturbs my vision. (http://www.adherents.com/people/pf/Federico_Fellini.html)

THE HUSTLER (1961)

PRODUCER/DIRECTOR: Robert Rossen (producer, director)
WRITER(S): Sidney Carroll, Robert Rossen, Walter Tevix (novel)
CAST: Paul Newman ("Fast" Eddie Felson), Jackie Gleason (Minnesota Fats), Piper Laurie (Sarah Packard), George C. Scott (Bert Gordon), Myron McCormick (Charlie Burns)
CINEMATOGRAPHY: Eugene Shuftan
MUSIC: Kenyon Hopkins
LENGTH AND RATING: 134 min; NR

Some films can create atmosphere with a depth of tone, texture, and feeling an audience can almost touch. It creates a tactile sense within a context of emotion that vividly displays every nuance of sentiment and passion. The characters and setting of Robert Rossen's *The Hustler* do this and more.

Although the action takes place in the netherworld of the pool hall, the themes are arrogance, greed, insecurity, and loneliness. Each of the characters depicts their virtues within the dynamic of the game—not pool, but the contest of life. The tone is set in the first scene, when Fast Eddie Felson (Paul Newman) and his manager Charlie Burns (Myron McCormick), posing as traveling salesmen to the drugstore trade, enter the Homestead Bar and Grill outside Pittsburgh, Pennsylvania. They are foils of the grift, enticing their "marks" to wager on Fast Eddie's implausible shot, betting that the bourbon-filled young pool shark could never repeat the feat. In this context, director Rossen moves the scene slowly to its denouement as they cultivate their marks by playing off each other, with Eddie "losing" to Charlie. As their script progresses, Charlie urges Eddie to leave, and when the bartender offers to take a piece of the action, he calls Eddie a "chump," provoking even more interest among other poolroom patrons. This scene is prescient of what will take place next, and the misfortune that will haunt Fast Eddie Felson. Of course, the unwitting marks succumb to the greed of a "sure thing" and are swindled by the pair. But for Fast Eddie, hoping to leave the two-bit road of nickel-and-dime hustling, the match of a lifetime with the legendary king of pool, Minnesota Fats (Jackie Gleason), can be his ticket out of oblivion.

Pivotal to the film is the first confrontation between Fats and Fast Eddie at the Ames Billiard Hall in New York City. As they enter this pantheon of "shooters," Eddie becomes reverential and compares the atmosphere to a church: the "Church of the Good Hustler." Charlie makes a more cogent, morbid, and prophetic observation, saying that it looks more like a morgue and that the pool tables are slabs to lay the stiffs on.

In their first meeting, Eddie comes across as a brash player while Fats exudes an aura of sophistication, confidence, and even elegance. When Fats walks in at 8:00 P.M., his daily arrival time, he is treated royally, with the attendant taking his overcoat. The camera tracks Fats as he lights a cigarette, takes a drag, and walks to Eddie's table, watching from the side. He stands out in this seedy environment, dressed in a stylish suit with a carnation on his left lapel, and he calmly watches as Eddie pockets a couple of balls and says, "You shoot a good stick." Then the conversation moves to a coy question from Eddie inquiring if Fats shoots straight pool, and Fats' reply is equally evasive: "Now and then." The two men are sizing each other up, each knowing the other's identity. After acknowledging the extent of Fats' reputation (Eddie is from Oakland, California, where they say Fats "…shoots the eyes right off them balls"), Fats asks what he already knows: "Is your name Felson, Eddie Felson? I hear you've been looking for me." After Eddie's affirmative response, Fats turns slightly and says, "Big John, you think this boy is a hustler?" He chuckles and the two men make a match, but when Fats suggests one hundred dollars a game, Eddie, with a large grin, reminds him that he shoots big-time pool and they agree to two hundred dollars a game. Before the match begins, Fats washes his hands in a sink and sprinkles talcum powder on them in a cool and calm fashion, signaling that he is the ultimate professional. They begin the match and initially Eddie is behind but as the early morning hours arrive, he moves ahead, demonstrating his naiveté and inexperience by boasting that he dreamed so much about the game every night on the road that he can't miss, and owns the table. His bravado gets the best of him when he raises the stakes to a thousand dollars a game. After twenty-five hours, he is $18,000 ahead but will not quit and insists on goading Fats into admitting defeat. Mimicking the more seasoned Fats, Eddie orders his favorite bourbon but is no match in sustaining play and holding his liquor. Before deciding to return to the table, Fats turns to Bert Gordon (George C. Scott), his benefactor and the coldhearted gambler bankrolling his game. He assesses the situation accurately when he says to Fats, "Stay with this kid. He's a loser." As Fats prepares for the final round, he combs his hair, washes and powders his hands, and puts on and straightens his suit jacket in a fluid, aristocratic manner when compared to the rumpled, disheveled appearance of Eddie, and then he says: "Fast Eddie let's play some pool." He is a seasoned veteran of all-night pool games and is just as fresh as when he started. As Eddie attempts to break, he is seized by an uncontrollable laughing fit that signals the end of his winning streak. By the next morning, Fats has beaten and humiliated Eddie, who has succumbed to the bourbon and is sloppy drunk, begging Fats to continue the game before he collapses.

The *Hustler* is a film about how people use and prey on other people, destroying their will and their dreams. After abandoning his partner, Charlie, Eddie finds Sarah Packard (Piper Laurie), a part-time college student and would-be author who is also an alcoholic and has a lame foot, a physical defect. She has been abandoned and lives like a hermit in her small apartment, drinking herself into a daily stupor, until Eddie comes along. He gives her hope by showing an interest in her. When Charlie tracks them down, he urges Eddie to return to the hustling life with him and offers to have Sarah join them. When Eddie learns that Charlie has held out on him, secretly collecting his twenty-five percent ($1,500), he blames him for his loss to Fats and disparages Charlie for using him for his own financial security. He adamantly rejects Charlie's pleas and tells him to, "…lay down and die by yourself." From this scene on, Eddie demonstrates his selfish pursuit of success and his willingness to sacrifice anyone in his way.

The relationship between Sarah and Eddie is self-centered, each of them using the other to satisfy his or her own compelling needs. It is mutually destructive and empty, crudely emphasizing sex and drinking. In a moment of confrontation, Eddie tells Sarah to buy herself another rich old lover and angrily slaps her, and Sarah responds calling him a "pool room bum." Soon, Eddie is approached by Bert Gordon, who offers to stake him to a 25/75 split in Gordon's favor to play Minnesota Fats. He admits Eddie has talent but says he lacks character and goads him by calling him a "born loser." An astute judge of character, Gordon understands how to push the right buttons, and although Eddie rejects his offer Gordon knows how to insure that Fast Eddie will be his hustler. He accomplishes this by having his thugs beat up Eddie and break his thumbs on the pretext that they have been hustled by a professional.

His hands bound up by a cast, Eddie is dependent on Sarah to nurse him back to health, and she is pleased to have this responsibility. It brings them closer together but also binds her to him, generating a feeling of love, which Eddie rejects. She wants him to articulate the same love toward her but he cannot and when, after a fancy dinner, Sarah learns that Eddie has accepted Gordon's offer of management and is leaving to play pool in Louisville, Kentucky, with the millionaire James Findlay (Murray Hamilton), she senses that he will abandon her and angrily protests, declaring her love for him.

The three go to Louisville, and in the railroad dining car Gordon lectures them about winning and losing. After inquiring about Eddie's hand and being reassured that he's fine, Gordon remarks that he is pleased, because he wouldn't want to gamble on a cripple. Coming to Sarah's defense, Eddie asks why he would say something so hurtful but she dismisses it as a simple figure of speech, wisely defusing a potentially tense situation.

At Findlay's, both men express surprise when he uncovers a billiard table, not a pool table, and Gordon wants to leave but Eddie convinces him to stay. After the stakes are raised, Eddie loses a considerable amount of money, and when Gordon refuses to stake him, he goes to an upstairs bedroom where Sarah is sleeping off her inebriation and takes his savings, losing it all to Findlay. When Sarah joins them she witnesses Eddie pleading with Gordon for his support, and she tells him not to beg and describes all of the "players" as perverted, twisted, and crippled. Ordering Sarah to return to the hotel, Gordon accedes to staking Eddie who eventually beats Findlay and decides to walk back to the hotel, refusing a ride from Gordon. Arriving before Eddie, Gordon lies to Sarah that Eddie had asked him to pay her off to get rid of her. Emotionally distraught, Sarah enters Gordon's suite, they sleep together, and she wakes up, scrawls the words "perverted, twisted, crippled" with lipstick on a mirror, and then kills herself. Upon arriving at the hotel, Eddie angrily attacks Gordon, blaming him for Sarah's death, and then is restrained by the police.

In the final scene, Fast Eddie is at the Ames Billiard Hall, playing Minnesota Fats and telling Gordon that he's not going to play it safe because now he has the character he acquired in a Louisville hotel room. He wins the entire stake and Minnesota Fats admits defeat. Eddie now realizes how much he loved Sarah, and that he traded her in on a pool game. When Gordon demands his cut of the winnings and threatens him if he doesn't pay up, Eddie tells Gordon that they better kill him, otherwise when he heals he'll return and kill him. Acknowledging that he has lost Eddie as a hustler, Gordon calls off his thugs but warns Eddie to never again set foot in a big-time pool hall. The last dialogue exchange is between Eddie and Fats, who mutually admire each other's talent:

Eddie: Fat Man, you shoot a great game of pool.
Fats: So do you, Fast Eddie.

In *The Hustler*, there is a richness of characterization that evokes a sense of morbid fascination within the audience. These are people who tread upon life's edge and cannot be assimilated into the righteousness of civility and Sunday sermons. They preach the psalms from their own bible of greed and manipulation, never pondering more than the virtues of the mighty buck. And for those like Sarah, who are vulnerable to the fantasy of a better life, their virtue is destroyed by the depth of malevolence and shame.

OTTO E MEZZO (8 1/2) (1963)

PRODUCER/DIRECTOR: Federico Fellini (director), Angelo Rizzoli (producer)
WRITER(S): Federico Fellini, Ennio Flaiano, Tullio Pinelli, Brunello Rondi
CAST: Marcello Mastroianni (Guido Anselmi), Claudia Cardinale (Claudia), Anouk Aimée (Luisa Anselmi), Sandra Milo (Carla), Rossella Falk (Rossella), Barbara Steele (Gloria Morin), Madeleine LeBeau (Madeleine, l'attrice francese), Caterina Boratto (La signora misteriosa), Eddra Gale (La Saraghina), Guido Alberti (Pace, il produttore)
CINEMATOGRAPHY: Gianni Di Venanzo
MUSIC: Nino Rota
LENGTH AND RATING: 138 min; NR

For Federico Fellini, *Otto e Mezzo* is his most autobiographical work and one that once again addresses his world of fantasy defined within the constructs of the psychological dynamic of Jung and Freud. On one level, it's about the frustrations of a film director who has a creative mental block and has grown bored with the science fiction theme of his film. However, the film's theme of alienation and desperation, fraught by personal and professional demands, has relevance in today's world.

Although Marcello Mastroianni portrays Guido, the central character in the film, he is indeed Federico Fellini, who at this time in his life was suffering a midlife crisis. He searched for a movie to make and actors to perform in it, but he had a great deal of self-doubt. This is a complex film filled with symbolism, fantasy, and dreams, and at times it is difficult for the audience to understand where the reality ends and the dreams begin. Sometimes the transition is clear, as in the opening scene of a traffic jam in a tunnel where cars sit, stuck in silence. Smoke then begins to escape from a dashboard as a man, Guido, struggles to get out of the car. He sees the odd-looking inhabitants of the other automobiles and buses, Fellini's cast of freaks and zombies, looking on. They ignore his crisis as he flails against the windows and doors of the car, desperately trying to kick himself free. The other occupants passively ignore him, with one of them ogling and fondling the breasts of his passenger. Unable to breathe, Guido is drowning in the fumes and finally gets his window open, floats out of the tunnel toward the sky, and is now spiritually free. There is more symbolic imagery, including a mounted horse galloping down a beach, followed by a kite-like string attached to Guido's ankle that pulls him back to Earth. Finally, Guido, taking the cure in a health spa, wakes up in a startle from his dream and is quickly attended to by physicians who prescribe various quantities of mineral water and mud baths.

Facing the reality of pressure from his producer, agent, screenwriter, and actors, along with his wife and mistress, Guido finds greater comfort in a world of fantasy where he believes he is able to assert control; but that is not always the case, even in his dreams.

Although he loves his wife, Louisa (Anouk Aimee), he is passionately attracted to his mistress, Carla (Sandra Milo). At one point, both women appear at the spa at his invitation, which causes Louisa to become unhinged and accuse Guido of lying when he tells her that his relationship with Carla has ended. As the tension with Louisa increases, Guido retreats into a world of fantasy where he envisions Louisa and Carla as best friends strolling together and enjoying each other's company at the spa. Guido's writer verbosely questions his creative genius as a director and criticizes him as having little substance and inspiration, with themes of loneliness and despair fifty years behind the avant-garde and unable to write a love story. He offers his critical advice throughout the film, and in one fantasy scene, while Guido and others view audition film, he motions for his assistant to hang the writer.

In a frenzied scene at the spa, a ringmaster shouts out numbers for various treatments, including "showers and mud," "massages," and "inhalations" as the client-residents, many of them elderly and wrapped in sheets, parade down the steps toward tables where a sort of triage takes place. As Guido, wearing a sheet, proceeds with the others, his producer, also in a sheet, tells him he knows what Guido's story is about: "It's about the confusion a man feels inside himself. But you must be clear. You must make yourself understood or what's the use. If it's interesting you must make everyone interested. Why shouldn't you care whether people understand? It's pride then presumption." There is some credence to this advice as Guido grapples with the meaning of his film, which is a metaphor for his struggle to find the purpose of his existence. The man is taken away in a fog of steam and told to breathe deeply, then he is informed by the attendant that a seat has been reserved for him by the blowhole—perhaps a reference to the "hot air" of his remarks. During the entire time the producer is talking, Guido has been walking behind him in silence, and as he turns away he is escorted to his destination. As Guido sits on a steamy bench, someone else mentions that he has checked out the spaceship and it's 150 feet high. This is a reference to the science fiction movie Guido is supposed to direct but has lost interest in. Seated on the bench, Guido recognizes the man sitting next to him. Everyone sitting in the steam is breathing deeply and appears detached, almost comatose, except for Guido. There is an announcement on the loudspeaker for Guido telling him that his Eminence, the Cardinal, is waiting for him. A suited attendant then tells Guido to quickly dress because the Cardinal is waiting. He advises Guido to tell the Cardinal everything and to hold nothing back, and, while he is at it, to put in a good word for him, adding that it's a lucky, golden opportunity to see the Cardinal. Another toweled spa resident walks by, gesticulating and saying that the Cardinal can issue all of the necessary permits, even for his Mexican divorce. Then he turns toward Guido, pleading for his divorce and saying that the Cardinal cannot refuse Guido. Even in his fantasy world, Guido must deal with those who demand favors of him, much like the actors who wish to be in his film. He is met by another suited attendant carrying his clothes who tells Guido to act devoutly, kneel before the Cardinal, kiss his ring, and cry. He is told to say he has repented their goodwill and that it can get you everything you need in life. Guido is also cautioned to mind what he does because all of their fates are in his hands. This is a parable of the burden he feels for all of those relying on him to produce a successful film. As if on a movie set, a priest holds up a hand to indicate that Guido has five minutes. Then there is a rush of air and the audience is taken through a low window that opens to an area filled with steam; the legs of people dressed in white are visible. When he finally meets the Cardinal, Guido tells him he is not happy. He makes this statement on the other

121

side of a sheet because the Cardinal's attendants are readying to wrap him as he is removed from a mud bath. As the Cardinal speaks, the audience sees him in shadow, raising the scrawny forefinger of his right hand to make a point. He responds to Guido by asking why he should be happy and explaining that it's not his task. Indeed, he poses a rhetorical question, asking Guido who told him we come into the world to be happy. The Cardinal continues by referencing Origen of Alexandria, an early Christian scholar, telling Guido that outside the church there is no salvation and no one will be saved. Then, in Latin and behind a wall of steam, which may symbolize the depths of hell, the Cardinal says that those who are not in the Civitas Dei (city of God) are in the Civitas Diaboli (city of the Devil), and the window seen earlier slowly closes. Seeking the advice of the Church in his fantasy, Guido is rebuked for his desire to be "happy" and is deemed by the Cardinal to be out of touch with his faith.

The description of the above scene is an example of the complexity in understanding Fellini's narrative. Some critics have disdained the film's disjointed narrative structure, not knowing where fantasy ends and reality begins. This is a deliberate act of misdirection by Fellini, who preferred fantasy over reality. He said, "I make my films because I like to tell lies, to imagine fairy tales.... I mostly like to tell about myself." To Pauline Kael, the well-known film critic, Fellini was pretentious, narcissistic, and self-indulgent in expecting the audience to make sense of his ideas. Still, most critics found *Otto e Mezzo* to be an intellectually stimulating masterpiece with Fellini providing a psychological analysis of himself as a frustrated film director. In his June 26, 1963, *New York Times* review, Bosley Crowther expressed his fascination with the film, writing that it would make viewers sit up and think. He described it as a "fascinating intellectual game, having no more plot than a horse race, no more order than a pin ball machine." He continues his review by writing that, "the film harbors some elegant treasures of wit and satire along the way." Crowther also mentions Fellini's facility with drollery and wit, his satire of social aberrations, and his sardonic comments about sex.

Perhaps one of the most expressive scenes in the film is when Guido imagines he is the leader of a harem and the object of all the women's affection. They jealously compete for his attention in an effort to cater to his whims. Even in this pleasure dome, Guido faces a revolt by the women due to his egotism and inability to return love to others.

As the scene begins, Guido enters from the snowy outdoors, carrying packages (gifts) and remarks that even his sister-in-law likes him now. It's time for a bath and as the women fuss over him he meets a mystery woman and a black girl, who does a suggestive dance. He is greeted as the Emir and his harem is compared to that of King Solomon. After his bath, the women dry and powder him and carry him on a sheet. One of the women, Jacqueline, who claims she is twenty-six but looks older, is ordered upstairs because she is too old. She begs Guido for a reprieve but he is resolved to adhere to the rules. Other women in the harem take her side and begin a revolt, saying they deserved to be loved even when they reach the age of seventy. In response, Gudio wields his whip to bring them into submission and when they are subdued, Jacqueline performs an awkward song and dance to an unenthusiastic audience before moving upstairs. Although he has succeeded in taming his "shrews," Guido is more the victim of his fantasy than are the women.

The substance of Guido's character is fraught with conflict and insecurity and is contextualized within the domains of the Church, marriage, and his art. He is a prisoner of his own deficiencies, attempting to compensate for them by creating a fantasy world of dreams and memories that cloud reality while comforting his soul.

MUSICALS OF THE 1960s

West Side Story (1960)
My Fair Lady (1964)
The Sound of Music (1965)

🎥 *WEST SIDE STORY* (1960)

PRODUCER/DIRECTOR: Jerome Robbins (director), Robert Wise (director), Robert Wise (producer)
WRITER(S): Jerome Robbins (conception), Arthur Laurents (play), Ernest Lehman (screenplay)
CAST: Natalie Wood (Maria), Richard Beymer (Tony), Russ Tamblyn (Riff), Rita Moreno (Anita), George Chakiris (Bernardo), Simon Oakland (Lieutenant Schrank), Ned Glass (Doc), William Bramley (Officer Krupke), Tucker Smith (Ice), Tony Mordente (Action)
CINEMATOGRAPHY: Daniel L. Fapp
MUSIC: Leonard Bernstein
LENGTH AND RATING: 152 min; NR

The American movie musical has a rich tradition that evolved from the infancy of the first sound films to the modern interpretation of musicality in films such as *Flashdance* (1983) and *Footloose* (1984). A number of different genres defined their evolution, including revue musicals, which featured a string of songs performed within a show-case of talent. One of the first films to embrace this concept was *The Hollywood Revue of 1929*, also one of the first talking pictures. This was MGM's second musical directed by Charles Riesner, and it was a lavish two-hour extravaganza. Promoted as an all-star musical gala, it featured performances by budding stars, including Joan Crawford, and was hosted by comedian Jack Benny and Conrad Nagel.

Another genre is the backstage musical exemplified by MGM's *Broadway Melody of 1933*, considered a high-concept film for the time and featuring glossy sets and a stable of stars including Eleanor Powell, Robert Taylor, Judy Garland, and Sophie Tucker. For Garland, her rendition of the song, "Dear Mr. Gable," also known as "You Made Me Love You," made her an overnight star. This genre is defined by backstory narratives of young performers seeking stardom. Most recently, the backstage musical was vividly portrayed in the 2006 movie *Dreamgirls*, which treats the difficult road to stardom with poignant sensitivity.

The operetta musical is another category that was exemplified by two films, each starring Maurice Chevalier and Jeanette MacDonald. The first was *Love Parade* (1929), directed by Ernst Lubitsch, a musical comedy about the plight of a queen and her new husband. In the second film, *Love Me Tonight* (1932), directed by Rouben Mamoulian with music by Richard Rodgers and Lorenz Hart, Chevalier is a poor tailor posing as a baron to eventually win the heart of Princess Jeanette (Jeanette MacDonald.) For Mamoulian, the aesthetic was an integration of action and camera movement. For Hart it was "rhythmic dialogue," as explained:

> I decided to make it lyrical, thoroughly stylised: a film in which the whole action of actors, as well as the movement of camera and cutting was rhythmic. Then I got Rodgers and Hart to write the music. We finished the whole score before I began to work on the script. We did the whole thing to a metronome, because we couldn't carry an orchestra round with us.

I'm a great believer in conversational rhythm. I think in terms of rhythmic dialogue. It's so easy, you can talk naturally. It's like peas rolling off a knife. Take the great screen actors and actresses, Bette Davis, Eddie Robinson, Jimmy Cagney, Spencer Tracy. They all talk in rhythm. And rhythm and movement are the life of the screen. ("Love Me Tonight," by Peter Kemp, www.sensesofcinema.com)

Yet another iteration of the musical format is the integrated musical, which combines song, dance, and story into a coherent literary narrative. The performer/dancer/ entertainer Fred Astaire pioneered the integration of dance numbers into both Broadway and Hollywood musicals. With Astaire's glamorous dance partner, Ginger Rogers, they personified the various musical genres in films such as *Swing Time* (1936) and *Follow the Fleet* (1936).

The film adaptation of the play *West Side Story* is a salute to the integrated musical that combined opera, drama, and ballet into a modern interpretation of the movie musical. It retells William Shakespeare's classical romantic tale of Romeo and Juliet but this time is set on the mean streets of New York City, within a cultural milieu of established second-generation Caucasian teens and newly arrived young Puerto Rican immigrants. In many ways the play and, later, the movie was a harbinger of a major transition in American culture of disaffected youth, juvenile delinquency, and the rise of gangs. Instead of the ancient rivalry between the Capulets and Montagues, the modern incarnation focuses on the territorial and status-conscious jealousy between the established Jets and the people of color, the Sharks.

As in Shakespeare's *Romeo and Juliet*, the two lovers, Maria and Tony, must endure the suspicions of their friends as they attempt to sustain a relationship. As for Maria, she is subjected to the limits her older brother, Bernardo, leader of the Sharks, has set for her. Tony, once leader of the Jets, is reluctantly lured back to gang culture by Riff, the current leader, to assist in mediating terms for a "rumble" between the Jets and Sharks. Tony had left the gang to work in a candy store, earning a legitimate livelihood and forsaking the violence and rituals of his previous lifestyle. When Tony enters the candy store, where terms for the rumble are being negotiated, he persuades the two sides to abandon the use of weapons and instead choose their best fighters to represent them in a one-on-one battle.

After being urged by Maria to stop the fight, Tony steps in, but his interference ends in tragedy when Bernardo stabs Riff to death and Tony retaliates by killing Bernardo. Although Maria is distraught over Bernardo's death, she forgives Tony and they declare their love for each other. While being questioned by the police, Maria sends Anita to the candy store with a coded message warning Tony that he is a suspect. When Anita arrives she is taunted by the Jets, and her fear and annoyance lead her to tell them that Chino has killed Maria. After learning that Maria is "dead," Tony madly pursues Chino, and in the playground he sees Maria but as they move toward each other, Chino shoots Tony and Maria tearfully comforts him as he dies.

In many ways, the film adaptation of *West Side Story* offers a unique visual narrative and presents an iconic American showcase of imagery that reflects the virtues and hostilities of America as a vast melting pot. As a musical, it helped to define a rich tradition of music and dance that was distinctive to American culture and resounded with exuberance and excitement. From the rhythmic finger snapping of *Cool* to the delightful *Officer Krupke* and the edgy, clever, and stylistic *I Like to Be in America*, the film is an expressive canvas of American ingenuity, talent, and design.

MY FAIR LADY (1964)

PRODUCER/DIRECTOR: George Cukor (director), James C. Katz (producer), Jack L. Warner (producer)

WRITER(S): Alan Jay Lerner (book), George Bernard Shaw (play), Alan Jay Lerner (screenplay)

CAST: Audrey Hepburn (Eliza Doolittle), Rex Harrison (Professor Henry Higgins), Stanley Hollo-
way (Alfred P. Doolittle), Wilfrid Hyde-White (Colonel Hugh Pickering), Gladys Cooper
(Mrs. Higgins), Jeremy Brett (Freddy Eynsford-Hill), Theodore Bikel (Zoltan Karpathy),
Mona Washbourne (Mrs. Pearce), Isobel Elsom (Mrs. Eynsford-Hill), John Holland (Butler)

CINEMATOGRAPHY: Harry Stradling Sr.

MUSIC: Frederick Loewe

LENGTH AND RATING: 170 min; NR

This is a classic story told in many variations, originating with Ovid's poetic tribute to
unrequited desire and beauty in the myth of *Pygmalion*, who blamed women for so
many ills that he pledged never to take a wife. As a talented sculptor, he carved an
ivory statue of a beautiful woman and subsequently fell in love with this lifeless
beauty. He became so entranced by her beauty that he dressed her in exquisite fabrics,
exacerbating the fantasy by lovingly caressing her and calling her "wife." While partici-
pating in a festival to Venus, Pygmalion prayed for a wife resembling the virtue and
beauty of his ivory virgin. Hearing his plea, Venus granted his wish, and when Pygmalion returned home he kissed the ivory statue and this time her lips were warm and as
he caressed her soft skin, he realized his prayer had been answered.

In his adaptation of Ovid's poem, George Bernard Shaw's play *Pygmalion* created quite a
stir when it premiered in London in 1914. It was a clever, witty play that used sharp amusing
dialogue to comment on the British class system and its mores and customs. It was an essay
on social class, interpersonal relationships, and male/female affairs. In Shaw's hands, the linguist Henry Higgins is Pygmalion, who is challenged into making the cockney flower girl,
Eliza Doolittle (Audrey Hepburn), into a proper-speaking lady.

A movie based on the play, also entitled *Pygmalion*, premiered in 1939 and starred
Leslie Howard as Henry Higgins and Wendy Hiller as Eliza Doolittle, and was directed
by Leslie Howard and Anthony Asquith and produced by Gabriel Pascal. The Broadway
musical, with book and lyrics by Alan Jay Lerner and music by Frederick Loewe,
opened March 15, 1956, and ran for 2,717 performances. It was directed by Moss Hart,
choreographed by Hanya Holm, and starred Rex Harrison and Julie Andrews.

The movie adaptation made its debut in 1964, starring Rex Harrison as Henry Higgins
and Audrey Hepburn as Eliza Doolittle. Although Julie Andrews became famous for her role
as Eliza Doolittle, prior to her starring role in the Broadway and London versions of the play,
she was relatively unknown to movie-going audiences. Jack Warner, the head of Warner
Brothers, which paid $5.5 million for the movie rights and would make *My Fair Lady* its most
expensive production to date, wanted a star with a great deal of name recognition to perform
the role of Eliza Doolittle, and so he chose Audrey Hepburn. In his autobiography, Warner
rationalized his decision with the following explanation:

Why did I choose Audrey Hepburn instead of Julie Andrews, the original Eliza (for
My Fair Lady)? There was nothing mysterious or complicated about that decision.
With all her charm and ability, Julie Andrews was just a Broadway name known
primarily to those who saw the play. But in Clinton, Iowa, and Anchorage, Alaska,

and thousands of other cities and towns in our 50 states and abroad you can say Audrey Hepburn, and people instantly know you're talking about a beautiful and talented star. In my business I have to know who brings people and their money to a movie theatre box office. I knew Audrey Hepburn had never made a financial flop.

And so the hit Broadway play was lovingly transformed to the screen in a sumptuous production with lavish sets, handsome costumes, and rhythmically choreographed dance numbers. Soon, Eliza Doolittle became a vision of persistence and gender independence for American audiences. Although the film addressed the long-held and biased class traditions of English culture, where speech could be an obstacle to social and professional advancement, many Americans understood the implications of how it related to them. This was a different kind of love story, one set within a context of class distinctions and the obstacles to social mobility. And, of course, the songs were especially delightful and moved the story along at a constant pace. It should be noted that Marnie Nixon's singing voice was dubbed in for Audrey Hepburn's.

From the beginning, and her rendition of the song, "Wouldn't It Be Loverly," the audience learns that Eliza is a dreamer, singing about a better life and someone who will love her. Professor Higgins is lurking around, transcribing the cockney English uttered by Eliza, and he sings, "Why Can't the English Teach Their Children How to Speak." After a chance meeting with Colonel Pickering (Wilfred Hyde-White), Higgins wagers that he can rid Eliza of her cockney accent in six months and pass her off as a duchess at the Embassy Ball. The next day, Eliza appears at Higgins' house, determined to learn proper English, and announces that she is willing to pay for the lessons. At first he resists, but when Colonel Pickering reminds Higgins of his boast the previous night, about making Eliza a lady by teaching her proper pronunciation, he consents to the experiment and has his housekeeper burn her clothing and give her a bath. Then, he brazenly predicts that Eliza will become the most popular woman in London.

Concerned about the living arrangements, Colonel Pickering asks Higgins, the bachelor, if he is a virtuous man who will not take advantage of Eliza. In response, Higgins sings "An Ordinary Man" and declares that he enjoys living his life unencumbered by the meddling interference of a woman.

In juxtaposition to Higgins' pronouncement of not needing a woman in his life is Alfred Doolittle (Stanley Holloway), Eliza's lazy, boozing, dustman father, who sings "With a Little Bit 'O Luck," his anthem to avoiding work and declaring that women were made to marry and be domesticated but with some luck the man won't get hooked. Then he learns from a lady friend that Eliza has sent for her things, minus clothing, to be sent to Professor Higgins' home, and he adds a lyric to his song that while it's a father's responsibility to support his children, it's better when the child supports dear Dad. Following up on his attempt to extort money from Higgins, Doolittle arrives at his house and winds up with a five-pound note instead of the fifty pounds he was hoping for. Upon leaving, he urges Higgins to use the strap on Eliza if she misbehaves.

After many long days of frustrated lessons, both Higgins and Pickering are exasperated and wondering if Eliza can ever achieve the success they had hoped for. Suddenly, she utters a perfect pronunciation of the phrase, "The rain in Spain stays mainly in the plain." They all rejoice at her perfect enunciation, dancing and singing with delightful glee. Then, Higgins grasps Eliza and they dance together as she begins to fall in love with him. As Eliza is led to bed by the housemaids, she sings "I Could Have Danced All Night," an exultation of her growing love for Henry Higgins.

The next day, Higgins and Pickering escort an exquisitely dressed Eliza to opening day at the high-society Ascot Racecourse. As Eliza is introduced to Henry's mother and young Freddie Eynsford-Hill (Jeremy Brett) and his mother, Mrs. Eynsford-Hill (Isobel Elsom), she sticks to her script, discussing health and weather until she gets more familiar and lapses into her street talk. Although Freddie is infatuated with Eliza, Mrs. Higgins warns her son to give up the effort and accuses him and Pickering of using her as their play doll.

Prior to the ball, Pickering voices his concerns about the rigorous and harsh training that Higgins has put Eliza through, and expresses some doubts of her ability to succeed in portraying a lady at the event. Then, Eliza appears at the top of the stairs and is an angelic vision dressed in a white evening gown. Watching her descend, Higgins takes a carnation and pins it to his lapel and moves toward the door, pausing for the butler to drape him in his cape. He walks to the door and suddenly pauses, then turns, walks back to Eliza, and holds out his arm as her escort. This action constitutes the validation of Eliza as a "proper" woman and Higgins' acknowledgement of her in that role.

The Embassy Ball is an elegant affair, with guests who include the Queen of Transylvania. Providing some tension to the event is the risk of exposure by one of Higgins' former students, Hungarian linguist Zoltan Karpathy (Theodore Bikel), who speaks many languages and considers himself an expert at detecting imposters. As the Queen passes and a stunning Eliza dutifully bows, the Queen gently strokes her chin in a gesture contemplating her radiance and beauty. She is escorted to a table filled with dignitaries and the Queen's son, the Prince of Transylvania, requests the first dance. Unaware of Eliza's true identity, Karpathy, wanting to share in the glory of her "coming out," rumors that she is a Hungarian princess.

At home, Higgins and Pickering congratulate each other on their success, ignoring Eliza. She is angered by them taking all of the credit and debasing her as the mere subject of a bet. When Higgins asks for his slippers, she throws them at him. Higgins responds by calling Eliza a presumptuous insect and she answers that he is a selfish brute. She feels used and contemplates what is to become of her now that she is a lady, and she reluctantly acknowledges that the differences between herself and Higgins are so profound there cannot be any feelings between them.

Once again, Freddie appears, announcing his desire for Eliza, but she is now more worldly and declares her independence, singing, "Show me...if you're in love, show me." Upon returning to Covent Garden, she learns that her father has inherited a great deal of money from an American man creating moral reform societies, and that Higgins wrote, recommending Alfred Doolittle as the most original moralist in England. Now Alfred must reluctantly enter middle-class morality by marrying Eliza's stepmother, and he sings, "Get Me to the Church on Time."

At home, Higgins contemplates the reasons for Eliza's sudden departure and attempts to rationalize the reasons for her leaving. He sings, "Why Can't a Woman be More Like a Man" and concludes that women are irrational and have heads filled with cotton. In the interim, Eliza has retreated to Mrs. Higgins' home, where Henry's mother provides solace and understanding for the rude and harsh treatment Eliza has received from her son. When Higgins arrives, his mother chastises him for his ill-mannered and unappreciative behavior toward Eliza, but he rejects her condemnation of his actions.

Asserting her independence, Eliza confronts Higgins with the "truth" about their relationship, and says that although she has become a lady he will always treat her as the guttersnipe flower girl fetching and carrying his slippers. She admits she cares for him but then announces that she is going to marry Freddie. Higgins acknowledges his sadness by singing "I've Grown Accustomed to Her Face." At home alone, Higgins listens to a recording of his first lessons with Eliza, reminiscing about their relationship. Unseen, Eliza walks behind him, turns off the recording machine, and says in her cockney accent:

"I washed my face and hands before I come, I did." Although Higgins is delighted that Eliza has returned, he characteristically responds "Eliza? Where the devil are my slippers?"

The theme of transforming someone from a lower strata of society has been a popular one portrayed in many successful movies, including *Trading Places* and *Educating Rita*, both 1983, *Pretty Woman* (1990), *She's All That* (1999), and *The Princess Diaries* (2001).

THE SOUND OF MUSIC (1965)

PRODUCER/DIRECTOR: Robert Wise
WRITER(S): Howard Lindsay (book), Russel Crouse (book)
CAST: Julie Andrews (Maria), Christopher Plummer (Captain Von Trapp), Eleanor Parker (The Baroness), Richard Haydn (Max Detweiler), Peggy Wood (Mother Abbess), Charmian Carr (Liesl), Heather Menzies (Louisa), Nicholas Hammond (Friedrich), Duane Chase (Kurt), Angela Cartwright (Brigitta)
CINEMATOGRAPHY: Ted D. McCord
MUSIC: Richard Rodgers, Oscar Hammerstein
LENGTH AND RATING: 174 min; NR

Some critics viewed *The Sound of Music* as overly sentimental and saccharine-coated entertainment. In Bosley Crowther's *New York Times* review dated March 3, 1965, he referrs to the "...cheerful abundance of kirche-küche-kinder sentiment." He compliments Richard Rodgers and Oscar Hammerstein II on their "generally melodic felicity." The review describes Julie Andrews as having an "air of radiant vigor" but is far less accommodating to the young actors, whom he refers to as, "The septet of blond and beaming youngsters who have to act like so many Shirley Temples and Freddie Bartholomews when they were young." His most vigorous denigration is reserved for Christopher Plummer, who portrays Captain von Trapp and whom Crowther describes as "...handsome and phony as a store-window Alpine guide, Mr. Plummer acts the hard-jawed, stiff-backed fellow with equal artificiality and isn't at all complementary toward the other adult actors except of course Julie Andrews."

Another respected reviewer, Pauline Kael, writing for *McCall's* magazine, gave the film a negative review in a piece entitled "The Sound of Money." In it she berates the film, calling it "mechanically engineered" and "shrewdly calculated." She writes:

> Set in Austria in 1938, this is a tribute to freshness that is so mechanically engineered and so shrewdly calculated that the background music rises, the already soft focus blurs and melts, and, upon the instant, you can hear all those noses blowing in the theatre. Wasn't there perhaps one little Von Trapp who didn't want to sing his head off, or who screamed that he wouldn't act out little glockenspiel routines for Papa's party guests, or who got nervous and threw up if he had to get on a

stage? The only thing the director, Robert Wise, couldn't smooth out was the sinister, archly decadent performance by Christopher Plummer—he of the thin, twisted smile; he seems to be in a different movie altogether. (http://www.geocities.com/paulinekaelreviews)

It is said that Kael's editor at *McCall's* fired her for her caustic comments about the film. Despite these reviews, when it was released in 1965 it became the highest-grossing film of all time, exceeding *Gone with the Wind*. It was surpassed in 1972 by *The Godfather*, and in 1978 by the musical *Grease*.

How did this movie about a family struggling under a stern father, who embraces a novice postulant as their nanny while she teaches them about music, life, and love, become such a favorite with the American public? Although some critics may have scorned the wholesome family values and the "love conquers all theme," *The Sound of Music* provides a rich narrative of two people struggling with their own identities while providing a glimpse of how they are viewed by others.

For Maria, it's a question of her commitment to a cloistered religious life while for widower Captain Von Trapp, the challenge is his rigid military style governance of his household and children, the suit of armor he wears to shield him from the pain of his loss. The film quickly establishes Maria as a free-spirited woman not easily categorized as a supplicant novice. This virtue is recognized by the nuns of the abbey and the Mother Abbess (Peggy Wood), who sing, "How do you solve a problem like Maria?" Wisely, the Mother Abbess decides that Maria should spend time in the secular world as a governess to the seven motherless Von Trapp children.

Although Maria is somewhat daunted by the size of the Von Trapp mansion, she quickly expresses her independence by telling the stern captain that neither she nor the children will respond to the pitch of a whistle. Eventually, Maria wins the children over and continues to defy the captain's strict behavioral orders. When bolts of fabric arrive for Maria's new dresses, she inquires about play clothes for the children but is told that since they are not allowed to play, there is no need for such clothing. In a resourceful move, Maria uses the fabric of soon-to-be replaced drapes to create clothes for the children. Although ordered by the captain to maintain a strict regimen with the children during his time with the Baroness Elsa (Eleanor Parker) in Vienna, Maria instead decides to take them on trips. She is indeed a liberated woman.

Upon his return to the estate with the Baroness Elsa, the captain is incensed to learn that his children have been playing and enjoying themselves, and in a fit of anger he orders Maria to leave. As Maria leaves to pack, he hears and sees his children singing and is so taken with their voices he realizes that Maria was right when she urged him to reacquaint himself with his family and love his children. Acknowledging his fault, he urges Maria to reconsider and stay on as governess, and she consents.

Several subplots integrate into the story, including the efforts of Max Detweiler (Richard Haydn) to find a performing singing troupe, which turns out to be the Von Trapp Family Singers; the Baroness Elsa and her jealous attempts to rid the family of Maria so that she can marry the Captain; and the despicable Herr Zeller (Ben Wright), the Nazi sympathizer. The baroness is partially successful, as Maria returns to the Abbey fearing the reality of her love toward the captain, but she is counseled by the wise Mother Abbess, who asks her to return to the Von Trapp family, acknowledging that the love between a man and a woman is also holy.

When she returns, the children announce that their father and the Baroness are to be married, but the captain finally realizes his true affection for Maria, breaks off his engagement to the baroness, and, in a moving scene, he and Maria acknowledge their love for each other and marry at the abbey.

Political intrigue intrudes when the captain is ordered to command a ship for the Third Reich and a plan is hatched to immediately leave Austria. That plan is interrupted by Herr Zeller, and the family uses the excuse of performing at the Salzburg music festival to cover their escape. After their performance and prior to the award announcement, the Von Trapps retreat to the abbey and are pursued by the Nazis. Hidden by the nuns, they use the abbey's car to escape and when the Nazis attempt to follow, their cars won't start. Later the nuns admit to the Mother Abbess that they have sinned and reveal the missing parts from the Nazis' cars under their robes.

In addition to the entertaining musical score by Rodgers and Hammerstein, who wrote songs that would become an enduring legacy of musical culture, the story offered inspiration at a time when America was experiencing racial unrest and challenges abroad. In 1965, the first American troops were sent to Vietnam, and 190,000 soldiers were stationed there by the end of the year. The civil rights movement was very prominent, with 2,600 people, along with Dr. Martin Luther King Jr., arrested during a march on Selma, Alabama. Black Nationalist leader Malcolm X. was assassinated in Harlem, and there was a six-day riot in the Watts section of Los Angeles.

The Sound of Music was a testimony to the resilience of the human spirit and the power of faith in a world that appears to have abandoned its virtues. As a movie, it was a jewel in the crown of entertainment.

LAWRENCE OF ARABIA (1962)

PRODUCER/DIRECTOR: David Lean (director), Robert A. Harris (producer), Sam Spiegel (producer)
WRITER(S): T. E. Lawrence (writings), Robert Bolt (screenplay)
CAST: Peter O'Toole (T. E. Lawrence), Alec Guinness (Prince Feisal), Anthony Quinn (Auda abu Tayi), Jack Hawkins (General Lord Edmund Allenby), Omar Sharif (Sherif Ali), José Ferrer (Turkish Bey), Anthony Quayle (Colonel Brighton), Claude Rains (Mr. Dryden), Arthur Kennedy (Jackson Bentley), Donald Wolfit (General Sir Archibald Murray)
CINEMATOGRAPHY: Freddie Young
MUSIC: Maurice Jarre
LENGTH AND RATING: 216 min; NR

Some films offer audiences glamour, sex, and stars in settings both luxuriously exotic and romantic. Then there are the biblical epics that portray the words of the Bible in an expansive setting, replete with deadly chariot races and the parting of raging seas. But *Lawrence of Arabia*, directed by David Lean and starring Peter O'Toole, offers a very different image, one that is foreign to most Americans even in a time of America's conflict in Iraq. It is a story about one man, T. E. Lawrence, and a tribal culture harshly imbued with traditions from the past and his consuming mission to unite them into a legitimate military and political force while serving the needs of Great Britain as a British officer during World War I.

Although the film can be viewed as a grandiose adventure epic, it addresses many more substantive themes. Noted anthropologist Steven C. Caton studied the re-released and digitally restored 1989 version of *Lawrence of Arabia* and addressed its three "readings" as an allegory of anthropology, as anti-imperialist deployment of orientalism, and as a treatise on homosexuality and feminism. He also discusses post-colonial discourse and its critique of orientalism, imperialism, and neo-colonialism.

The film is based on the British archeological scholar and adventurer Thomas Edward Lawrence. He rose to the rank of lieutenant colonel, and his exploits were extensively profiled by journalist Lowell Thomas, whose character is Jackson Bentley, portrayed by actor Arthur Kennedy. He was the illegitimate son of Sir Thomas Robert Tighe Chapman, attended Jesus College, Oxford, and showed early signs as an adventurer by serving as a boy soldier with the Royal Garrison Artillery, backpacking through Syria and covering one thousand miles on foot, eventually becoming an archeologist in the Middle East and learning fluent Arabic. At the outbreak of World War I, Lawrence was engaged by the British military to map the Negev Desert for strategic wartime purposes and eventually enlisted, fighting with the Arab irregulars and acting as a liaison between British and Arab armies.

The film portrays Lawrence (Peter O'Toole) as a rampant exhibitionist and latent homosexual consumed by delusions of grandeur. It begins with Lawrence on a speeding motorcycle and swerving to avoid two bicyclists on a country road, followed by a memorial service for him with those in attendance offering personal testaments to his character and achievements. After joining the British army, he becomes bored with his assignment in Cairo and is dispatched to Arabia to survey the effectiveness of the Arab revolt against Turkey and to locate Prince Feisal (Alec Guinness) and gain his support. This effort is to prevent Turkey, which is allied with Germany, from controlling the Suez Canal.

In a scene where Lawrence first confronts the ancient Arabian tribal hostilities, he and his guide, Tafas, are drinking water from a desert well when a figure appears in the distance, shrouded by the glimmering heat of the desert as he slowly rides in to the foreground. Their first impression is that it is the Turks and as the camel rider comes closer, Tafas panics, rushing to his camel to retrieve his revolver, and is shot in the head by the rider, Sheik Sherif Ali (Omar Sharif). He is killed because members of his tribe are forbidden from drinking at the Bedouin wells. Angered, Lawrence condemns Sherif's actions and tells him that as long as the Arab tribes fight against each other they will always be cruel and barbaric.

After meeting his local superior, Colonel Harry Brighton (Anthony Quale), Lawrence is told to keep his mouth shut during their meeting with Prince Feisal. The Prince's encampment is under air attack from the Turks, and the Bedouins have few modern weapons to defend themselves. In their meeting, Colonel Brighton urges Prince Feisal to retreat to Yenbo, where the Bedouins can be trained and protected under the command of European officers. Not heeding the colonel's admonition to stay quiet, Lawrence speaks against this recommendation and later, in a private discussion with Prince Feisal, he says that the Arabs were once great and that it is time to be great again.

In a defining moment of the film and a precursor to Lawrence's achievement of being accepted into the tribal community, he proposes to Sherif that they cross the unforgiving Nefud Desert, also known as An-Nafud, which is 180 miles long and 140 miles wide, encompassing an area of 140,000 square miles. He advocates that a group of fifty men cross the desert and once they've crossed, enlist the aid of the Howeitat tribe and take the port of Aqaba, which is occupied by the Turks. Not anticipating an

131

attack from the landward side, the Turks' huge guns are facing the sea. Telling Lawrence he is mad, they nevertheless undertake the crossing.

In one melodramatic scene, as they reach the end of the desert, a rider-less camel appears and Lawrence decides to return to the desert and find its rider, Gasim. He is urged not to, but characteristically defies the others and returns with Gasim, who is alive. This dramatic gesture makes him a hero to the men, as Lawrence sacrificed his life for an Arab when the others would not attempt a rescue. As a tribute, Sherif gives him an Arabic name, El Aurens, and that evening burns his British uniform and in the morning gives him a flowing, shimmering white Arab robe, marking his ascendancy as an Arab.

Many dramatic highlights portray Lawrence as a hero who unites the Arab tribes, although he also displays an arrogance and defiance that alienate his superiors. He successfully invades Aqaba, crosses the Sinai, and arrives in Cairo to be greeted by General Allenby (Jack Hawkins), and is promoted to the rank of major. The narrative continues with Lawrence leading an attack on a Turkish train; being profiled and having his photograph taken by journalist Bentley; being captured, beaten, and sodomized in a Turkish stronghold; and then rescued by Sherif Ali. He returns to Cairo and learns that he has been a pawn in the imperialistic plans of England and France to divide Arabia among themselves after the war, and then is convinced by General Allenby to lead one last campaign on Damascus. He arrives in Damascus but the disparate Arab tribes quickly argue and their cohesiveness disintegrates, frustrating Lawrence's dream of Arab unity. Promoted to the rank of colonel, he is sent home while Prince Feisal and the British negotiate terms and the wise king notes that young men make wars and old men make peace.

There are many reasons why *Lawrence of Arabia* was popular with audiences in 1962. It is a heroic story of a man against the natural elements of the hostile desert challenged by an insular culture at war with itself. But it also is a story of adventure, about a man zealously devoted to a mission and his ultimate achievement of being accepted by the people he loved. Furthermore, the film portrays the deception of political leaders and how they used Lawrence as a pawn to achieve their own ends.

The film, directed by David Lean with a screenplay by Robert Bolt, is based on the writings of T. E. Lawrence, originally published as *Revolt in the Desert* and later appearing under the title *The Seven Pillars of Wisdom*. With a musical score written by Maurice Jarre, *Lawrence of Arabia* is an epic painted on a majestic canvas of color, showing the desolate beauty of the desert beckoning its splendor to those who seek its poetic rhythm and uninitiated in the harsh reality of its design.

The film was originally 222 minutes long but was later cut by 35 minutes, to 187 minutes, to accommodate multiple showings in movie theaters. (The movie was restored to 222 minutes in 1989.) The budget was $12 million, and it generated a box office of over $20 million. It won seven Academy Awards, including Best Director, Best Picture, and Best Musical Score.

TO KILL A MOCKINGBIRD (1962)

PRODUCER/DIRECTOR: Robert Mulligan (director), Alan J. Pakula (producer)
WRITER(S): Harper Lee (novel), Horton Foote (screenplay)
CAST: Gregory Peck (Atticus Finch), John Megna (Charles Baker "Dill" Harris), Frank Overton (Sheriff Heck Tate), Rosemary Murphy (Maudie Atkinson), Ruth White (Mrs. Dubose),

Brock Peters (Tom Robinson), Estelle Evans (Calpurnia), Paul Fix (Judge Taylor), Collin
Wilcox Paxton (Mayella Violet Ewell), James Anderson (Robert E. Lee "Bob" Ewell)
CINEMATOGRAPHY: Russell Harlan
MUSIC: Elmer Bernstein
LENGTH AND RATING: 129 min; NR

It was a moment of reckoning in 1962, when James Meredith, a black student, entered
the all-white bastion of the University of Mississippi, becoming its first African American student. Meredith had attended Jackson State College and was twice denied admission by the University of Mississippi. His admission to the school was opposed by
Governor Ross Barnett, and it generated campus riots. After denying him entry to the
university on September 20, 1962, Meredith was escorted by federal troops and U.S.
marshals, ordered by President John F. Kennedy to protect him as he entered the campus on October 1, 1962. As a result of the hostilities, two people were killed and 48 soldiers and 30 marshals were wounded. It was a defining moment for the civil rights
movement, and Meredith graduated on August 18, 1963, and then earned a law degree
from Columbia University in 1968.

In 1931, when Harper Lee, the author of the novel *To Kill a Mockingbird*, was five
years old, two white women from Scottsboro, Alabama, accused nine black men of
rape. The hostility surrounding the trial nearly resulted in the defendants being
lynched, and they were not afforded legal representation until the first day of the trial.
Although medical evidence confirmed that the women had not been raped, an all-
white jury convicted the men to a sentence of death, except for one defendant, who
was twelve years old. After six years of trials, all of the sentences were repealed and all
but one of the defendants were either freed or paroled.

Growing up in the small southern town of Monroeville, Alabama, Harper Lee
befriended the young Truman Capote and the friendship endured for Capote's lifetime.
While Capote worked on the literary journalistic novel *In Cold Blood*, Harper Lee was
his research assistant. For her novel, *To Kill a Mockingbird*, Lee drew upon her own
experience growing up in a small Alabama town, where her father was a lawyer who
had worked as a newspaper editor and served in the state legislature. It was her only
novel and in 1961 it won a Pulitzer Prize.

The movie is set in the fictional southern town of Maycomb, Alabama, at the
height of the Depression, in the early 1930s. The audience is introduced to the Finch
family, led by the widowed father, Atticus, a principled attorney whose children are
Jean Louise Finch (Mary Badham), known as "Scout," a six-year-old tomboy, and her
ten-year-old brother Jem (Phillip Alford). It is a quiet, poor town but the Finch children are innocently happy, playing and fearing the local bogeyman, Arthur "Boo"
Radley (Robert Duvall), and befriending a precocious visiting boy, John Baker Harris
(John Megna), known as "Dill" and based on a young Truman Capote.

The exposition is quickly established as Walter Cunningham (Crahan Denton), a
poor farmer, rides up in his horse and buggy, dropping off a sack of hickory nuts to
work off a legal debt owed to Atticus. When Jem complains to their neighbor, Miss
Maudie Atkinson (Rosemary Murphy), that his father is "too old for anything," Maudie
fiercely defends Atticus by telling Jem what a great lawyer his father is. Atticus' virtues
are confirmed when the local judge, Taylor (Paul Fix), stops by the house and informs
him that a grand jury will charge Tom Robinson (Brock Peters), a black resident

133

accused of raping a white woman. After deliberating a short time, Atticus agrees to take the case and act as Robinson's defense attorney.

For Scout, Jem, and Dill, the adult world of Maycomb is filled with people who are both friendly and to be feared and, in some cases, as with Boo Radley, that fear is the imaginary conjuring of a child based upon the rumor of adults. Both Jem and Scout quickly establish themselves as strong-willed characters who emulate their father's fearless, resolute character. In their game of "chicken," Jem "rescues" his sister Scout as she accidentally rolls in a tire to the front steps of the Radley house. He drags her away and then returns to touch the front door, fulfilling a challenge by Dill that he wasn't afraid to "confront" Boo Radley. In another instance, Jem, Scout, and Dill sneak up to the Radley house to peer through a window and get a glimpse of Boo, only to be discovered by a man lurking in the shadows who does not confront them but scares the three into fleeing. In his haste, Jem gets stuck on a wire fence and wriggles out of his pants as he runs away. He later returns to retrieve his overalls when Radley takes a shot at him, thinking he's a prowler.

Although Scout is shy about appearing in a dress on her first day of school, it doesn't prevent her from getting into a schoolyard fight with Walter Cunningham, Jr. She tries to explain to the teacher that Walter doesn't have his lunch money because he is poor and too proud to accept the twenty-five cents the teacher offers. Instead, she is reprimanded and takes out her frustrations on Walter, beating him up until Jem can separate them. Attempting to assuage the hard feelings caused by Scout, Jem invites Walter to dinner that evening. As the conversation around the table turns to guns, Atticus tells Jem, who pines for his own gun, that his father told him that when he got a gun he could shoot all the blue jays he wanted, if he could hit them, but that it was a sin to kill a mockingbird because all they do is make beautiful music and sing their hearts out for people to enjoy.

The tension over Atticus' defense of Tom Robinson manifests itself when he takes Jem and Scout on a drive to visit Robinson's wife, Helen (Kim Hamilton), to discuss the case. A drunken bigot, Bob Ewell, confronts the children and Atticus, calling their father a nigger lover. Although Atticus tries to deflect Ewell's harsh talk as "bluff," both Scout and Jem are frightened.

A counterpoint to the fear generated by Atticus' defense of Robinson is the revelation of a "connection" between Jem and Boo. Using a knothole in a tree, Jem has found objects inside placed there for Scout and him by Boo Radley. They include soap carvings of Jem and Scout, along with crayons, marbles, a spelling medal, a whistle, an old pocket watch, and a pocketknife.

The racially charged atmosphere has engulfed the school, and Scout gets into a fight with Cecil Jacobs (Kim Hector). Later she asks Atticus why he defends "niggers" and explains that that's the reason she had to fight Cecil. Although Atticus is annoyed that Scout had a fight, he explains that if he didn't defend Tom Robinson, he could never hold his head high again, implying that he would lose his self-respect.

In one of the most compelling scenes in the film, Atticus is unarmed, sitting on a chair in front of the jail and reading a book. He's there because he fears for the safety of Tom Robinson, and those fears are realized when a lynch mob drives up and threatens to take him. Watching from the bushes are Jem, Scout, and Dill, and when the cars appear and the men get out, Scout, followed by Jem and Dill, wade through the crowd.

The men are set on their objective to lynch Tom Robinson, and Walter Cunningham is among them. Angry that Scout, Jem, and Dill are present, Atticus asks them to leave but the children refuse, with Jem and Scout stubbornly holding their ground. When Scout sees Walter Cunningham, Sr., in the crowd, she greets him and innocently engages him in conversation about entailments and about his son, Walter, with whom she attends school. She ends the conversation with Walter, Sr., by asking him to say "hey" from her to his son. The innocence of this exchange between Scout and Walter, Sr., defuses the tension of the confrontation, and when Walter leaves the other men follow.

In his final summation before the jury, Atticus reviews the evidence against Tom Robinson, noting that the defendant is right-handed and has a useless left hand, the result of an accident as a young boy. Earlier, he had established that the alleged victim, Mayella Ewell, had been assaulted by a left-handed perpetrator and revealed that her father, Bob Ewell, is left-handed. He tells the jury how Mayella attempted to seduce Tom by holding and kissing him, then tried to cover up the events and the shame she would endure in the community by accusing an innocent man of rape. He pleads with the jury, in the name of God, to do the right thing, but the twelve men convict him and as Atticus leaves the courtroom, the black spectators in the gallery stand to show their respect. Observing the trial with them are Scout and Jem and as Atticus passes below, the Reverend Sykes tells her to stand out of respect for her father. A sad reality intercedes when Tom Robinson is transferred to another jail and killed while trying to escape.

Later in the year, as Scout and Jem, are returning from a Halloween party late in the evening, they are viciously accosted by a drunken Bob Ewell. As Jem tries to defend them, he is brutally attacked and knocked unconscious. A shadowy figure comes to their defense, subduing Ewell and rescuing Jem and carrying him to the Finch home. After Sheriff Tate is notified and Ewell is found stabbed to death, Tate decides there has been enough injustice and that Boo Radley could never endure the scrutiny and notoriety of a trial, so he and Atticus agree that the inebriated Ewell fell on his own knife and killed himself.

The film is a harsh reminder of the prejudice that was an enduring characteristic of America. Its approach to that troubling time, as seen through the innocence of children, made it more compelling and provided a context for understanding how hate can be taught and resisted. This is what distinguishes *To Kill a Mockingbird* as an essay on tolerance and inclusion.

RIDE THE HIGH COUNTRY (1962)

PRODUCER/DIRECTOR: Sam Peckinpah (director), Richard E. Lyons (producer)
WRITER(S): N. B. Stone, Jr.
CAST: Randolph Scott (Gil Westrum), Joel McCrea (Steve Judd), Mariette Hartley (Elsa Knudsen), Ron Starr (Heck Longtree), Edgar Buchanan (Judge Tolliver), R. G. Armstrong (Joshua Knudsen), Jenie Jackson (Kate), James Drury (Billy Hammond), L. Q. Jones (Sylvus Hammond), John Anderson (Elder Hammond)
CINEMATOGRAPHY: Lucien Ballard
MUSIC: George Bassman
LENGTH AND RATING: 94 min; NR

The legacy of America's West has a rich tradition in American film, thanks to director John Ford's majestic treatment of its beauty, violence, morality, and heroism. A director who followed in Ford's footsteps, Sam Peckinpah also had great respect for the traditions and values of the Old West, and in his later westerns he took a harsh view of the violence he depicted as the reality of the time.

His film, *Ride the High Country*, is a tribute to that time and the men of honor who helped to tame the Old West. It's also a story about change, growing old, and becoming a relic as time moves on and forgets the pioneers. There are also allusions to religion, faith, and honor, which Steven Judd (Joel McCrea), a former U.S. marshal, and his old friend and former deputy, Gil Westrum (Randolph Scott), who has strayed from the straight and narrow, vigorously defend.

Although McCrea and Scott were friends and icons of the western film genre, this was the first film in which they co-starred. At the time the film was made they were both older men who brought the knowledge and wisdom of age to their roles as fading heroes. It was Randolph Scott's last film and Joel McCrea made several independent films after *Ride the High Country*. An interesting footnote to the film is that initially McCrea was to play the role of Gil Westrum, and Scott that of Steven Judd. The two actors provided a convincing argument to reverse the roles and film history was made.

At the opening of the film, Steven Judd, too old to be a marshal, is searching for a job in a town when he is almost run down by a "motor car" and is warned by a local policeman to "Watch out, old timer." His life has been diminished by degrading jobs such as brothel bouncer, far removed from the glory of his law enforcement days. He has applied for a job guarding $250,000 in gold deposits, in reality $20,000, from the unruly mining town of Coarsegold in the High Sierras to the bank, and he faces his potential bank employers in a shirt with worn cuffs. Presented with a contract, Judd, too embarrassed to pull out his reading spectacles, feigns needing to use the bathroom and surreptitiously reads the contract there. For Steve Judd, his greatest achievement will be to reclaim his self-respect as a proud, God-fearing man with simple tastes buttressed by a devotion to faith, honor, and morality.

Judd needs additional help for the four-day ride and meets his old friend and former deputy, Gil Westrum, who, billing himself as the "Omaha Kid," is fleecing the locals in a rigged carnival game. He and his young, inexperienced sidekick, Heck Longtree (Ron Starr), join Judd on the journey while Gil hopes to enlist Steve into a scheme to steal the gold. As they depart, Gil seizes the moment to convince Steve that their service as lawmen was met by indifference and a lack of gratitude by the public they served. He is attempting to rationalize the theft of the gold as a deserved tribute for their sacrifice and forbearance. As they discuss the virtues of character and will, Gil asks Steve, "The clothes of pride—is that all you want?"

Steve turns to Gil and says, "All I want is to enter my house justified."

When they reach the Knudsen homestead they meet Elsa Knudsen (Mariette Hartley), the sprightly daughter of the Bible-spouting patriarch whose repressive doctrinaire behavior toward Elsa prompts her to join the four men on their trip to Coarsegold so that she can marry her fiancé, Billy Hammond (James Drury). Struck by her beauty and resourcefulness, Heck is infatuated with her but Elsa is determined to marry Billy Hammond.

The mining town of Coarsegold is inhabited by an unruly, unwashed band of miners, drunks, and prostitutes. At the top of the dysfunctional hierarchy is the Hammond clan, with the brutish brothers who have less than pure thoughts about Billy's future bride.

Doing business from a tent, Steve and Gil accept the gold deposits from the miners and later attend the wedding of Billy and Elsa at the local whorehouse. Eager to consummate the relationship, Billy tries to have sex with Elsa in the tent at his mining camp. She rejects him, admonishing that they must wait until they are married. The marriage ceremony is a raucous affair, and the local besotted Judge Tolliver (Edgar Buchanan) sobers himself up enough to speak about the miracle of marriage as the prostitute bridesmaids look on. Following the vows, there's a drunken explosion of reverie as a Hammond brother dances with Elsa, trying to invade her virtue. Finally, the couple retreats to a back room, where drunken Billy violently attempts to deflower his bride. He passes out and Elsa, in her torn bridal gown, attempts to flee but is blocked by the Hammond brothers. Hearing a shot, Heck enters and confronts the now-conscious Billy, and as they fight, Steve and Heck come in with guns drawn to save the damsel, Elsa. Demanding his bride, Billy cites his legal right since the marriage was performed by a sitting judge. The parties agree to a miner's court and Gil takes matters into his own hands by visiting the drunken judge, tearing up his license, and telling him to testify that he performed an illegal ceremony.

On the trail they are met by the Hammonds, who have discovered Gil's heavy-handed yet persuasive technique with the judge, and vow to get Elsa back. Making camp for the evening, Gil and Heck attempt to steal the gold but are met by Steve, who angrily calls Gil a tinhorn and challenges him to draw. He ties them up and as night falls, Gil stretches out his bound wrists and asks Steve to cut them free because, "I don't sleep so good anymore," a reference to the creeping passing of time both men face.

As they ride on, the group is ambushed by the Hammond brothers, killing one of them as the others ride away in fear. Learning that Steve plans to bring him and Heck before a judge, Gil walks out of the camp, locates the Hammond brother who was killed, and takes his horse and rifle.

As the three riders, Elsa, Heck, and Steve, approach the Knudsen homestead they are ambushed by the Hammonds, who have killed Elsa's father, posing him upright to lure them into the trap. Riding in with guns blazing to aid in their rescue, Gil joins in their defense. Realizing they are outgunned and sitting ducks, Steve and Gil taunt the Hammond brothers into coming out from hiding to fight like men. They are the righteous men protecting the innocent youths, Elsa and Heck. In the final-shoot out, Steve is mortally wounded but the Hammonds have been killed.

In the poignant last scene of the film, Steve laments that all of the bullets seemed to have landed at the same place in his abdomen. Always proud, he does not want Elsa and Heck to see him die. Seeing his old friend near death, Gil assures him he will take care of everything, and Steve says he never doubted it.

Although it is a fairly standard story, the acting by all of the principals, especially the stars Randolph Scott and Joel McCrea, provide an added dimension to their roles because of their age; they are no longer matinee idols. The film also demonstrates the worth of a man based on his commitment to honesty, fairness, respect, and faith. It showcases the presumptions of youth and the steady course of wisdom earned with age. There is also the possibility of redemption for a man like Gil, who may have strayed because of temptation but in the end returned to traditional values.

📽 DR. STRANGELOVE OR: HOW I LEARNED TO STOP WORRYING AND LOVE THE BOMB (1964)

PRODUCER/DIRECTOR: Stanley Kubrick

WRITER(S): Peter George, Stanley Kubrick, Terry Southern

CAST: Peter Sellers (Group Captain Lionel Mandrake/President Merkin Muffley/ Dr. Strangelove), George C. Scott (Gen. "Buck" Turgidson), Sterling Hayden (Brig. Gen. Jack D. Ripper), Keenan Wynn (Col. "Bat" Guano), Slim Pickens (Maj. T. J. "King" Kong), Peter Bull (Russian Ambassador Alexi de Sadesky), James Earl Jones (Lt. Lothar Zogg), Tracy Reed (Miss Scott), Jack Creley (Mr. Staines), Frank Berry (Lt. H. R. Dietrich)

CINEMATOGRAPHY: Gilbert Taylor

MUSIC: Laurie Johnson

LENGTH AND RATING: 93 min; NR

Dr. Strangelove was released during a presidential election year, with incumbent Lyndon Johnson of Texas going against Senator Barry Goldwater of Arizona. One of the most controversial political advertisements ever produced was created by Tony Schwartz, of the advertising firm Doyle, Dane, Bernbach, for the Johnson campaign. It featured a young girl in an idyllic meadow setting with the sound of chirping birds in the background; she counts as she pulls the petals off a daisy. Adding to the aura of innocence is her childish stumbling over the numbers, missing some and saying others out of sequence. When she reaches the number nine, a male voice is heard counting down a missile launch. As she turns toward the sky, the pupil of her eye fills the screen, and when the countdown reaches zero, the screen fills with a flash and the mushroom cloud of a nuclear explosion. A voice-over by President Johnson emphasizes the visual message:

> These are the stakes! To make a world in which all of God's children can live, or to go into the dark. We must either love each other, or we must die.

Another voiceover then says:

> Vote for President Johnson on November 3. The stakes are too high for you to stay home.

The commercial was seen once during the September 7, 1964, broadcast of the NBC Monday Night Movie, *David and Bathsheba*. After its broadcast, there was an outpouring of negative criticism accusing the Johnson campaign of fearmongering and casting Senator Goldwater as a hawkish warrior. Soon after, the advertisement was taken off the air, but the effect had achieved its purpose and Johnson won the election by a landslide.

This was the climate in America when *Dr. Strangelove* was released, but the satirical parody was a brilliant portrayal of the political and cultural dynamic of the time. The film features Peter Sellers in three roles: Group Captain Mandrake, the crisp British Group Leader; the serious yet ineffectual President Merkin Muffley; and, of course, Dr. Strangelove, a wheelchair-confined presidential advisor and German scientist who may have been modeled after Henry Kissinger; who later became Secretary of State. He is equipped with an uncontrollable robotic hand that makes impromptu Nazi salutes accompanied by shouts of "Mein Fuhrer." The names of all the characters in the movie have sexual, political, cultural, or historical connotations, including Strategic Air Command General Jack D. Ripper (Sterling Hayden), Major T. J. "King" Kong (Slim Pickens), and General "Buck" Turgidson (George C. Scott).

The film begins with a panoramic shot of a vast mountainous area shrouded in clouds and devoid of human life. A voice-over sets the tone and pretense of the narrative by informing the audience that rumors have reached western leaders about an ultimate weapon, a Doomsday Machine, being built by the Soviet Union near the frozen Arctic, and although no one can confirm the rumor there is a great deal of speculation about such a project. Interestingly, Columbia Pictures inserted a disclaimer that denied any similarities to real people, living or dead, and reassured viewers that the United States Air Force has the requisite means to prevent the events seen in the film:

> It is the stated position of the United States Air Force that their safeguards would prevent the occurrence of such events as are depicted in this film. Furthermore, it should be noted that none of the characters portrayed in this film are meant to represent any real persons living or dead.

An expectation of the film's sexual innuendos and manifestations is presented in the opening title sequence, when a large phallic fueling rod fills the screen and two giant B-52 nuclear bombers engage in a refueling exercise that is visually demonstrative of fornication.

The movie is a damning satire of cold war politics, presenting caricatures of inept civilian and military leaders and the folly of nuclear deterrent brinkmanship. The catalyst of the story arc is the order given by paranoid Strategic Air Command General Jack D. Ripper (Sterling Hayden) to Group Captain Mandrake (Peter Sellers), a proper upper-crust British exchange officer, that he put the base on "condition red," order it sealed tight and confiscate all radios, fearing they may be used by saboteurs to communicate with the enemy. The order is communicated to the lead B-52 bomber, commanded by Major T. J. "King" Kong (Slim Pickens). We see the bored crew passing time reading *Playboy* magazine and shuffling cards. When the code for condition R is received by the radio operator and confirmed, Kong tells his men they'll be going toe-to-toe with the Rooskies in "nookular" combat. The music under the scene is a stirring rendition of "When Johnny Comes Marching Home." After putting on his ten-gallon cowboy hat, Kong lets his crew know that the folks back home are counting on them and that there could be special citations and awards for them regardless of race, color, or creed.

Each lead actor in the film portrays his role as a cartoon character, with animated gestures and facial expressions. Their dialogue can be imagined as a cartoon balloon floating above their heads, just as in a comic strip. They are all clownish figures interacting on a proscenium in a portrayal of a serious circumstance made comical by their gross ineptitude and folly.

Receiving a telephone call alerting him to the situation created by General Ripper, General Buck Turgidson (George C. Scott) is enjoying a tryst in his hotel room with his secretary, Miss Scott (Tracy Reed), who answers the phone and tells the caller the general is unavailable. After off-camera grumbling from the bathroom, Turgidson finally comes to the telephone. Hanging up, he announces that he is going to the War Room, even though it's 3:00 A.M. Disappointed, Miss Scott says that she is not tired, and Bucky replies:

I know how it is, baby. Tell you what you do. You just start your countdown, and old Bucky'll be back here before you can say—Blast Off!

The movie effectively inter-cuts scenes between Ripper's Burpelson Air Force Base, Kong's B-52 bomber, and President Merkin Muffley in the War Room. After Ripper orders the confiscation of radios, ostensibly under the guise of security reasons but really to protect his insane pursuit of nuclear war with the Soviet Union, Mandrake turns on a portable transistor radio and hears ordinary musical broadcasts and not civil defense alerts. He immediately goes to see Ripper to recall the bombers and is locked in his office and invited to drink grain alcohol and rainwater. In his mad paranoia, Ripper is concerned about the contamination of his bodily fluids by the commies and their insidious plan to fluoridate the drinking water in the U.S. As Captain Lionel Mandrake, Peter Sellers is the master of understatement and British savoir faire. He reasons that it will create "a bit of a stink" if the bombs are dropped. Having served in the Royal Air Force during World War II, Sellers performed excellent impersonations of his superior officers, using his talent to gain access to the officers' club. Most likely he used his experience as a mimic to portray Captain Mandrake.

The War Room scenes in *Dr. Strangelove* are a testament to Kubrick's fascination with detail and authenticity. Even in today's sophisticated marketplace of over-the-top digital special effects, the War Room is an impressive array of technology and a convincing setting for the confrontation with the Russians.

Facing the grim situation brought about by the psychotic General Ripper, President Muffley engages General Turgidson in pursuing alternatives to recall the bombers once they reach their fail-safe points. Acknowledging that the B-52 squadron has proceeded from those points, Turgidson presents a scenario urging the aggressive bombing of Soviet missile silos with the U.S. superiority of three-to–one, and anticipating that civilian casualties from the few rogue Soviet missiles would be acceptable, with an estimate of ten to twenty million people killed.

Deciding to send troops to the sealed-off Burpelson Air Force base and confront General Ripper to obtain the code that would enable the recall of the bombers, President Muffley also decides to brief the Russian Ambassador, Alexei De Sadesky (Peter Bull), about the situation in the War Room. Calling it an outrageous breach of national security, General Turgidson protests De Sadesky's presence in the War Room and eventually tackles the ambassador, whom he discovers photographing the interior with a secret camera. In an ironic twist of language, Muffley incredulously reprimands the men for daring to fight in the War Room.

With the help of Ambassador De Sadesky President Muffley attempts to track down Soviet Premiere Dmitri Kisoff, who can only be reached at his private number, while De Sadesky warns Muffley that the premier is drunk. The dialogue in the conversation between Muffley and Kisoff is a delicate attempt by the American president to engage the premier with the patience and understanding, as though he were talking to a child. It's a clever, funny scene that showcases the talent of Peter Sellers. He begins by telling Premier Kisoff that one of the base commanders did a "silly" thing and ordered his planes to attack your country. When Kisoff responds, Muffley says that he is very sorry and is not calling just to say "hello." After a pause, Muffley must assuage the sensitive Soviet premier by assuring him that he enjoys calling to say "hello" and that it is a friendly conversation. This is followed by an exchange wherein the leaders each profess they are more sorry about the situation than the other, matching the intensity of their mutual regrets. After the conversation ends, Ambassador De Sadesky informs Muffley and the rest of the personnel in the War Room about the Russian Doomsday Machine that will destroy all human, animal, and plant life on Earth in response to an attack.

The scene is memorable because of the profound talent Sellers displays in creating a conversation with a fictional character who never appears on-screen. His performance is nuanced with intonations and body language that present a reality presumed by the audience, making the scene believable.

The action is heightened as Burpelson Air Force base is taken by an opposing American force, Ripper commits suicide, and Mandrake identifies himself to Colonel "Bat" Guano (Keenan Wynn), commander of the rescue force who doesn't recognize his strange uniform. Having cleverly deciphered what could be the recall code from doodles written by Ripper, Mandrake desperately wants to phone them in. Suspecting that he is a "pervert," Guano reluctantly allows Mandrake to use the pay telephone to call the president but, realizing he is short of change, Mandrake attempts a collect call but is refused. Then he orders Guano to shoot the lock off a nearby Coca Cola machine and he reluctantly does so, warning Mandrake that he could be held responsible for destroying corporate property.

There is a brief celebration in the War Room as the recall code is communicated to the remaining bombers, but then Premier Kisoff calls to let Muffley know that one of them, Kong's plane, did not turn back and is pursuing its mission. Once again, Muffley must calm down the hysterical premier, and he advises him to use all of his resources to destroy the plane. In the interim, Kong's damaged plane is losing fuel and is unable to reach its primary or secondary targets. Attempts to drop the bomb are thwarted by a stuck door and Kong goes below to fix it. He straddles the bomb with both legs and, after fiddling with the wiring, the door opens and the bomb falls out with Kong riding it like a bucking horse and waving his cowboy hat in glee.

In the War Room, Dr. Strangelove presents his plans for saving at least some of the human race by digging mine shafts deep below the Earth and using computer selection methods to choose the inhabitants, mandating a ratio of ten women for every man. The end of the film is a visual cacophony of hydrogen bomb mushroom clouds accompanied by the song, "We'll Meet Again Some Sunny Day."

Initially, Stanley Kubrick intended to make a serious film based on a book entitled *Red Alert* by Peter George, a Royal Air Force officer. After a great deal of research and reading, he decided to produce a dark comedy, a bold satire that was eerily accurate. At the time of the movie's release, a squadron of twelve B-52 bombers code-named "Chrome Dome" was airborne just outside Soviet air space, ready to attack when ordered. General Ripper's character was modeled after the real cigar-chomping General Curtis LeMay, the head of the Strategic Air Command in the 1950s and the Pentagon's Air Force Chief of Staff in the early 1960s. He was a vocal critic of civilian political leadership and articulated an aggressive posture toward the Russians. As for the Dr. Strangelove character, many critics concluded that he was modeled after Herman Kahn, a vocal nuclear strategist at a think tank called the Rand Corporation who postulated survivor rates and hypothesized about the viability of mine shafts as a survival tool in his book, *On Thermonuclear War* (http://www.nytimes.com/2004/10/10/movies).

IN THE HEAT OF THE NIGHT (1967)

PRODUCER/DIRECTOR: Norman Jewison (director), Walter Mirisch (producer)
WRITERS: Sterling Silliphant, John Ball (novel)
CAST: Sidney Poitier (Detective Virgil Tibbs), Rod Steiger (Chief Bill Gillespie), Warren Oates (Sam Wood), Lee Grant (Mrs. Leslie Colbert), James Patterson (Purdy), Quentin Dean (Delores Purdy), and Larry Gates (Eric Endicott)
CINEMATOGRAPHY: Haskell Wexler
MUSIC: Quincy Jones
LENGTH AND RATING: 109 min; NR

In addition to the compelling performances of the two leads in the film *In the Heat of the Night*, Police Chief Bill Gillespie (Rod Steiger) and Philadelphia homicide officer Virgil Tibbs (Sidney Poitier), the film evokes a rich atmosphere of southern prejudice embedded in the culture of Sparta, Mississippi. As the title implies, the heat appears to languish over the action as it descends in a thick veil, creating a funereal shroud over the events and characters as they are rousted from their slumber by the murder of a northern industrialist, Philip Colbert (uncredited), who is planning to build an integrated mill in Sparta. The entire mood is evocative of a laid-back community where nothing is more important than Officer Sam Wood (Warren Oates) in his cruiser, making his late-night rounds, pausing to see a young woman undress and stopping by the local greasy spoon for a wedge of his favorite pie. As for Chief Bill Gillespie, he has his own demons to face, including the squeaky air conditioner in his office. These, of course, are the minutiae the inhabitants have settled into, until Wood discovers Colbert's dead body. Chief Gillespie is at the scene when the doctor announces that the victim's skull has been caved in. As the chief surveys the crime scene, he asks the young photographer if he has taken homicide pictures before, and the photographer notes that at least this subject won't be moving. Demonstrating his leadership, Gillespie instructs the photographer to cover every angle and orders Sam Wood to check both sides of town, including the depot and the pool hall, even though it closed at 1:00 A.M.

Hoping to make a quick arrest because of the stature of the victim, Wood picks up Virgil Tibbs at the train station, convinced he's the killer because he's black and has a considerable amount of money in his wallet. In the course of apprehending Tibbs, Wood repeatedly refers to him as "boy," telling him to spread his fingers so he can count all ten and warning him not to move or he'll "clean his plough." The first meeting between Gillespie and Tibbs sets the tone for the unfolding action. As the scene opens, Gillespie is bent over the office window air conditioner with his ear near the fan, listening to the annoying squeak. As he rises he looks toward the desk and sees the wallet that Wood has tossed there, its contents exposed. Easing the tension, he asks Wood when he requested that the air conditioner be oiled and tells him to remind Courtney, who was told to do it. Asked to leave by the chief, Wood then expresses concern about the prisoner. When Gillespie learns the name of his suspect, he laughs and says they won't have any trouble with Virgil. After Wood exits, Gillespie asks, "What you hit him with?" and Virgil responds, "Hit whom?" Gillespie wants to know what a northern boy is doing all the way down there, and Virgil says he was just waiting for the train.

This exchange reveals the competitive edge of the two men as they each stake a claim on the reliability of the train schedule. Gillespie tells Virgil there are no trains at that time in the morning and Virgil knowingly responds that there is one, the 4:05 A.M. to Memphis, Tuesdays only. Gillespie responds smugly, "You say," and then the train whistle sounds. Proven wrong, Gillespie sits on his chair and raises his feet on the desk, assuming the role of policeman and interrogator, telling Virgil that he tries to run a clean, safe town, where someone can sneeze and not get his brains beat out. Playing the good cop, he asks Virgil to tell him how he killed Mr. Colbert and says that after his confession he'll feel a lot better. Virgil responds by telling him that he was visiting his mother and waiting for the train to leave. Then Gillespie switches to his bad cop character and tells Virgil that he killed the most important white man in the town and picked up only a couple hundred dollars. Responding to the accusations, Virgil informs the chief that he earned the money working ten hours a day, seven days a week. Angry, Gillespie tells Virgil that the colored can't earn that kind of money and that it's more than he makes in a month. This, of course, compares the two men and the perception that blacks are inferior and can't possibly have a job that earns more than a white. Resisting his insinuations, Tibbs tells Gillespie that he earned the money working in Philadelphia, Pennsylvania, as a police officer, not Philadelphia, Mississippi, as the police chief suggests, and he tosses his badge on the desk. The competitive jockeying between the two men continues when Tibbs volunteers to pay for the telephone call to his chief to confirm his identity and Gillespie sarcastically "swoons" over the salary he earns in Philadelphia, telling Woods not to ruffle him.

In the conversation with Tibbs' chief in Philadelphia, Gillespie learns that he is the department's number one homicide detective. Once again, the southern chief is sarcastic about Tibbs and his expertise, thanking his Philadelphia counterpart for offering such a powerful piece of manpower, but adding that he must decline the offer. After the conversation, Gillespie asks Tibbs to look at the body, as an expert, and he initially declines, saying he has a train to catch, but then is reminded that it doesn't leave until noon.

Eventually they make an unlikely team, although they do share many of the same attributes and characteristics. Both men are competitive and devoted to their work, sacrificing their personal lives for their jobs. They must prove themselves as worthy: Tibbs to the prejudiced views of white southerners, who still treat blacks as chattel, and Gillespie to the town he has served and which may not want him any longer.

After Tibbs examines the body, the police arrest Harve Oberst as their prime suspect because he has Colbert's wallet. He tells them he picked it up after finding Colbert dead in the alley. After a quick examination of the suspect, Tibbs confirms his innocence by telling Gillespie that the murderer was right-handed and Oberst is a lefty, but the chief refuses to listen and demands to see the lab report Tibbs has compiled on the victim. When Tibbs refuses to hand it over, Gillespie locks him in a cell with Harve Oberst. During the time he spends with Oberst, Tibbs learns that he has a pool hall alibi at the time of Colbert's death and still has chalk dust under his fingernails. In addition, the body was moved from where the murder took place. As a result, Gillespie reduces the murder charge to theft and the hunt for the killer continues.

Demanding that Virgil Tibbs be kept on the case, Mrs. Colbert (Lee Grant) threatens to pack up her engineers and leave Sparta if he is not a part of the investigation. Once again, Tibbs reluctantly agrees after Gillespie poses it as an opportunity to show white people how smart he is.

In one of the most compelling scenes in the film, Gillespie and Tibbs visit Eric Endicott, a rabid racist and the wealthiest man in Sparta. After Tibbs finds osmunda, or fern root, inside Colbert's car, they question Endicott in his greenhouse as he compares the Negro to the care and feeding of the epiphytics orchid. When Endicott slaps Tibbs in the face because he is insulted by the line of questioning, Tibbs slaps him back. Word spreads about the incident and as Tibbs is driving he is forced to the side of the road and threatened by a group of rednecks who are dispersed by Gillespie and his deputies.

Although Gillespie wants Tibbs to leave Sparta because of the threat to his life, he refuses and instead they ride with Officer Sam Wood on his night patrol, recreating the route he took on the night of the murder. Suspecting Wood of the murder, Gillespie checks Wood's bank account, which reveals a recent large deposit which he explains as three years of "matching quarters and halves." On that evidence Gillespie locks Wood in a cell, but Tibbs says he is innocent because Colbert was killed at the factory site and then driven in his own car to where he was found. He could not have driven two cars at the same time that evening. Gillespie thinks he has caught his murderer: "I got the motive which is money, and the body which is dead." Tibbs, however, convinces the chief to allow him to stay in Sparta until the next morning so that he can identify Colbert's true murderer, knowing from the evidence that Sam Wood is not guilty.

In a moving scene, Gillespie allows Virgil Tibbs inside the inner sanctum of his home. He admits that Virgil is probably the only other human being beside himself to enter. For just a moment, Gillespie forgets the issue of race and speaks to Virgil as an equal, asking if he ever married and if he gets lonely. When he responds that he gets no lonelier than the chief, Gillespie refers to him as a black boy, telling him not to get smart and that he doesn't need his pity. It is indeed a telling moment as Gillespie allows his guard to drop, revealing his most sensitive side and admitting to feelings he has never expressed to anyone, especially a black. He also does not want to appear weak and so immediately reverts to a more hardened demeanor when he suspects that Tibbs may be expressing compassion for him.

Following up on a lead, Tibbs visits Mrs. Bellamy, known in the community as Mama Caleba, a black woman who is the local abortionist, to learn the identity of the man paying for Delores Purdy's abortion. At first Mama distrusts Tibbs, asking why he's working for "Mr. Charlie." In his attempt to assure Mama that he is not interested in giving her up to the police, Tibbs tells her that the man has a lot more money than the one hundred dollars he is paying for the abortion because he killed Mr. Colbert. When she is still reluctant, Tibbs reminds her that in prison there are two kinds of time, white time and colored time, and colored time that is the worst kind you can do. Mama relents and tells Tibbs that Dolores is visiting her that evening to have an abortion. When Dolores arrives she immediately runs away, with Tibbs in pursuit. Once outside he grabs her and as they struggle, Ralph appears, holding a gun and joined by an angry group of rednecks led by Purdy, Dolores's brother, who are after Tibbs. Threatened by both Ralph and the rednecks, Tibbs tells Purdy to check his sister's purse. When he finds the money for the abortion and learns that Ralph is the father of the child, he menaces Ralph, who shoots Purdy dead.

In the last scene at the train depot, Gillespie, carrying Virgil's luggage, turns to him and after their goodbyes says, "Virgil? You take care. You hear?" Those last words uttered by Gillespie are a vindication for Virgil Tibbs that he has earned the chief's gratitude.

The film was nominated for seven Academy Awards and received five Oscars for Best Picture, Best Actor (Rod Steiger), Best Screenplay (Sterling Silliphant), Best Sound, and Best Film Editing.

BONNIE AND CLYDE (1967)

PRODUCER/DIRECTOR: Arthur Penn (director), Warren Beatty (producer)

WRITER(S): David Newman, Robert Benton

CAST: Warren Beatty (Clyde Barrow), Faye Dunaway (Bonnie Parker), Michael J. Pollard (C. W. Moss), Gene Hackman (Buck Barrow), Estelle Parsons (Blanche), Denver Pyle (Frank Hamer), Dub Taylor (Ivan Moss), Evans Evans (Velma Davis), Gene Wilder (Eugene Grizzard)

CINEMATOGRAPHY: Burnett Guffey

MUSIC: Charles Strouse

LENGTH AND RATING: 112 min; R

The gangster movie has a rich tradition in American film, with stars like Edward G. Robinson as *Little Caesar* (1931) striking box office gold. But several changes in the 1960s created a revisionist approach to the genre, enabling it to capitalize on a realistic depiction of sex and violence. Perhaps the most profound change was in the rating of movie content that was overseen by the Hays Office. Two movies, *The Pawnbroker* (1964) and *Alfie* (1966), released in the 1960s without the Production Code seal, were box office successes and this helped to negate the power of the code. A new code policy was adopted by the

Gene Hackman (as Buck Barrow), Estelle Parsons (as Blanche), Warren Beatty (as Clyde Barrow), Faye Dunaway (as Bonnie Parker), and Michael J. Pollard (as C. W. Moss). [Warner Bros./Photofest]

145

Motion Picture Association of America (MPAA) in 1968, when it discontinued issuing certificates and implemented a letter-oriented rating system: (G) for general audiences, recommended for all ages; (M) for mature audiences over the age of sixteen; (R) restricted to anyone under the age of sixteen and required accompaniment by a parent or guardian; and the ultimate (X) rating, barring anyone under the age of sixteen. After some time, the code system was amended, raising the age for (R) and (X) films while replacing the (M) with (PG) which indicated that parental guidance was suggested.

As a result of the change in the rating system, movies could be more expressionistic and stylized while addressing issues of sexuality and violence. A new generation of film directors was poised to create movies that departed from traditional American cinema by stretching the creative canvas and defining its values in new and compelling ways. They were part of a breed of directors that used innovative techniques, reorienting the dimensions of character and making heroes of what were formerly viewed as villains, as in Arthur Penn's *Bonnie and Clyde*. These were the anti-heroes who were embraced by a disillusioned younger generation who had little faith in the establishment but were enamored with the courage and convictions of these new heroes.

These directors broke the established rules of structure and design, working with jump cuts, slow motion, screen splitting, color distortion, and motivated sound. In *Bonnie and Clyde*, the average length of a shot was four seconds. They used light as a tool to enhance the narrative and favored shooting on location instead of the contrivance of a soundstage. This technical dimension was attributed to the French New Wave-style of filmmaking and indeed, before Arthur Penn assumed the reigns as the film's director, François Truffaut and Jean-Luc Godard, two of the foremost established New Wave directors, were asked to direct *Bonnie and Clyde* but each declined.

After *Bonnie and Clyde* opened in the autumn of 1967, it received mostly negative reviews from influential critics such as Bosley Crowther of the *New York Times*, who wrote in his April 14, 1967, column that the movie was "sentimental claptrap" and "a cheap piece of bald-faced slapstick comedy." He denigrated the violence in the film as "tasteless":

> his blending of farce with brutal killings is as pointless as it is lacking in taste, since it makes no valid commentary upon the already travestied truth. And it leaves an astonished critic wondering just what purpose Mr. Penn and Mr. Beatty think they serve with this strangely antique, sentimental claptrap, which opened yesterday at the Forum and the Murray Hill. (*New York Times, Bonnie and Clyde*, Bosley Crowther April 14, 1967)

The film quickly closed and after a period of reassessment was hailed as a masterpiece and then rereleased. It was nominated for ten Academy Awards while costing $3 million to produce and earning $24 million for Warner Brothers in domestic licensing and grossing more than $70 million worldwide. The characters were fictionalized composites of the real-life Clyde Champion Barrow and Bonnie Parker. When they met in Texas in January 1930, Bonnie was 19 and married to a man in prison for murder, and Clyde was 21. She helped him escape from jail and after Clyde was paroled they went on their crime spree. By the time they were ambushed and killed by Texas Rangers and local sheriffs in 1934, they had committed thirteen murders along with robberies and burglaries. The film presents a romanticized version of the couple, departing from their characterization of social deviants by making them sympathetic characters rebelling against authority. In actuality, the couple, along with Clyde's brother Buck and accomplices Raymond Hamilton and, later, William Hamilton Jones, were cold-blooded, ruthless killers who savagely murdered law enforcement officers and civilians.

After the sepia-toned introductory scenes showing family photographs of the real Clyde Barrow and Bonnie Parker, the portraits change to the two stars, Warren Beatty and Faye Dunaway, who portray the film version of the couple. They meet in West Dallas, Texas, when Clyde tries to steal the Parker family car. As Bonnie is in her bedroom, nude, and preparing to dress for her job as a waitress, she discovers Clyde and runs out of the house to meet him. During a walk into the desolate town, they engage in social and sexually aroused banter and while drinking a Coke Clyde shows Bonnie his gun. The gun is a phallic symbol, representing an extension of Clyde's impotent sexuality, and it is caressed by Bonnie, who is sexually repressed. To demonstrate his bravado and manhood, Clyde robs the local grocery while Bonnie voyeuristically observes the act from outside the store. She joins him in the getaway, hugging and kissing him as he drives, and when he stops the car he tells her that he is no lover boy and never saw a percentage in it, while denying that he likes boys. Upset by this revelation and unable to release her sexual repression, Bonnie asks to be taken home but Clyde convinces her that she is just like him, with their common desire for excitement and notoriety. Later, in a local diner, Clyde impresses Bonnie by giving her an abbreviated biography about her life up until the time they met. He tells her how she dated some of the truckers who stopped at the greasy café, where she was a waitress, knowing that all they were interested in was getting into her pants. And how every day she wondered how to change her life, and now she had the answer.

Demonstrating Clyde's ineptness and false bravado, a number of robberies fail to be consummated. The first bank he chooses to rob has failed and there is no money to take. When he robs a grocery store, the butcher wrestles him to the ground and Clyde wonders why the man acted so violently toward him. At the second bank robbery, their new dim-witted getaway driver, C. W. Moss (Michael J. Pollard), legally parks in a nearby spot between two other cars, and when Bonnie and Clyde find him he struggles to maneuver out of the spot but gets stuck in traffic, which slows them down and allows the elderly bank manager to leap on the sideboard of the car. Clyde shoots him dead in the face.

After hiding out in a movie theater watching the Busby Berkeley-choreographed Warner Brothers film *Gold Diggers of 1933*, they return to their cheap motel, where Bonnie sings and dances to the song, "We're In the Money." Worried about Bonnie's safety and the realization that he is wanted for murder, Clyde urges her to return home but she refuses and is touched by his concern. They lie on the bed together but once again Clyde cannot consummate the relationship.

Soon they are joined by Clyde's older brother and ex-convict Buck (Gene Hackman) and his hysterical wife, Blanche (Estelle Parsons), the daughter of a preacher, and they all decide to take a vacation to Joplin, Missouri, where they must eventually shoot themselves out of a police ambush by breaking through the garage as Blanche incessantly screams and Buck kills a police officer. Speeding away from the carnage, Blanche is left behind and they must circle back to pick her up. There is a tense relationship between Bonnie and Blanche and when Bonnie presses Clyde to get rid of Blanche and Buck, he resists and she denigrates him for his peculiar ideas about making love. Clyde is clearly hurt by her harsh words, and Bonnie apologizes to him.

As they continue their run through the Southwest, the Barrow gang reads about their exploits in local newspapers, and they start to believe in the mythology that now surrounds them. There is a montage of their exploits, accompanied by rhythmic banjo music, along with victims and witnesses detailing their narrow escapes as they bask in the glow of being victims of the Barrow gang, and the fame it brings.

They contribute to the documentation of their exploits when Clyde captures Texas Ranger Captain Frank Hamer (Denver Pyle) and makes him pose with Bonnie and Clyde for pictures as she provokes Hamer by kissing him on the lips. (In reality, Hamer did not confront the Barrow gang until the day of the ambush.) Their intention is to embarrass him by sending the picture to the newspapers. After Bonnie's passionate kiss on Hamer's lips, he spits in her face and Clyde jumps him as Buck restrains his brother and they put Hamer in a rowboat and set him afloat. Tensions continue between Bonnie and Blanche when the meager take of a bank robbery is divided and Blanche demands her share. This is an affront to Bonnie, who feels she doesn't deserve it.

In a scene that provides some comic relief and confirms the iconic status of the gang, they kidnap a couple, Eugene Grizzard (Gene Wilder) and his fiancée Velma Davis (Evans Evans), who are making out on Velma's porch as the gang steals Eugene's car. Filled with bravado, Eugene goes after the bandits but when Velma cautions that they could be violent, they turn around only to be pursued by the Barrows. Urging Velma to go faster— "Step on it, Velma!"—the gang catches up with them and they join them in Eugene's car. They become friendly with the gang, enjoying eating with them and thinking about how they will be admired by their friends for associating with the Barrow gang. During the conversation, Velma admits that she is thirty-three years old and Eugene appears surprised by this revelation. As they share takeout hamburgers in the car, Eugene boldly indicates that he ordered his well-done and demands to know who is eating his burger. When C. W. holds his up with an obvious missing bite and offers it to Eugene, he good-naturedly declines. The good times with Eugene and Velma end when Bonnie learns that Eugene is a mortician, and the couple is left in the dark on the side of a road.

In a moving scene, Bonnie gets her wish and is reunited with her family in an abandoned quarry. It is shot with a reddish hue in soft focus, creating a dreamlike image.

This could be any family get-together, as children play and the adults enjoy the conversation and familial bonding of a picnic. But there is nothing ordinary about it, as it appears like a living wake for the Barrow gang, whose ultimate fate is known to all. The relatives show their scrapbook and Clyde assures Mother Parker that he and Bonnie will be settling down near her. The scrapbook is a symbol of their notoriety and will be their legacy after they are killed. Mother Parker advises Clyde to keep running, because if they live near her they will surely be killed. Knowing that it is the last time she will see her mother, Bonnie gives her a necklace as a memento.

At their next stop at a tourist court in Platte City, Iowa, all of them are almost killed. Bickering in their cottage, Bonnie asserts her need for privacy and Clyde sends Blanche and C. W. out for fried chicken. A patron notices a gun in the front of C.W.'s pants as he and Blanche pay for their takeout, and calls the sheriff.

What comes next is a violent confrontation. The police arrive, in force, and attack the apartment as Bonnie and Clyde spray the perimeter with bullets from a machine gun and C. W. tosses hand grenades at an armored police vehicle. Using a mattress for cover, Buck manages to release the brake on a police car, allowing it to roll and provide cover for the gang's getaway, but he is mortally wounded in the head as Blanche screams. She and

Buck are left behind, and during their escape Clyde is wounded in the shoulder and after abandoning the car, Bonnie is shot while wading through a stream. They are rescued by C. W., who steals a car and stops for water at a shanty town that mimics John Ford's memorable 1940 film, *The Grapes of Wrath*. They are treated reverentially as a crowd gathers around, eager to see and touch these notorious figures. These people, who have nothing, provide them with water and soup as C. W. drives to his family home in rural Louisiana. Although Ivan Moss (Dub Taylor) greets the outlaws and extends his indefinite hospitality, he berates his son for the tattoos on his chest and for listening to white-trash Bonnie Parker. In a touching scene filmed in a country field, Clyde finally consummates his relationship with Bonnie and awkwardly asks her about his performance. She, of course, acknowledges that he was just perfect. Questioning Blanche, Hamer learns C. W.'s last name and easily determines the location of Bonnie and Clyde. Secretly, Ivan (Malcolm) makes a deal with Hamer to ambush the couple in exchange for his son's leniency. The next day Bonnie and Clyde drive into town and wait for C. W. to finish shopping at the hardware store. When Clyde sees a police car he slowly moves his car, picks up Bonnie, who has purchased a small ceramic doll figurine, and indicates that they will return later to pick up C. W., who earlier was told by his father not to return to the car. As they drive down a country road, sharing bites of a juicy pear, they see Ivan, also known as Malcolm, waving them down, feigning a flat tire on his truck. Clyde leaves the car and through fast-paced editing Malcolm notices a jalopy, driven by a couple of black men, coming down the road. A flock of birds suddenly erupts into the sky, the brush moves, and Malcolm dives under his truck. Suddenly, Clyde realizes the danger and he and Bonnie exchange a passionate, fearful look as they are riddled with bullets, their bodies performing a "ballet of death" in one of the most gruesome and famous death scenes in film.

THE GRADUATE (1967)

PRODUCER/DIRECTOR: Mike Nichols (director), Lawrence Turman (producer), Joseph E. Levine (executive producer)

WRITER(S): Charles Webb (novel), Calder Willingham (screenplay), Buck Henry (screenplay)

CAST: Anne Bancroft (Mrs. Robinson), Dustin Hoffman (Benjamin Braddock), Katharine Ross (Elaine Robinson), William Daniels (Mr. Braddock), Murray Hamilton (Mr. Robinson), Elizabeth Wilson (Mrs. Braddock), Buck Henry (Room Clerk), Brian Avery (Carl Smith), Walter Brooke (Mr. McGuire), Norman Fell (Mr. McCleery)

CINEMATOGRAPHY: Robert Surtees

LENGTH AND RATING: 105 min; PG

The graduate, Benjamin Braddock (Dustin Hoffman), was a model for the disaffected youth of the sixties who were disillusioned with the Vietnam War. These were the times when college students marched, chanted, burned their draft cards, and, in some cases, violently opposed the war. Braddock, then, is the symbol of those who rejected the traditions of their elders while trying to make sense of a chaotic world steeped in the mistakes of an older generation.

Using the visual metaphors of film and the resonating lyrics of Simon and Garfunkel's music, director Mike Nichols paints a portrait of a wandering youth turning away from the values of his parents but confused about his own direction. His sense of bewilderment is immediately communicated when he is seen alone on a moving airport walkway and the music and lyrics from *The Sounds of Silence* are heard in the background:

People talking without speaking
People hearing without listening

In the next scene, Benjamin is at his parents' Los Angeles home, in his bedroom staring at a fish tank. Director Mike Nichols uses a number of frame-within-a-frame shots to establish Benjamin's feeling of entrapment. He is framed by the fish tank as he gazes into it, and when Mrs. Robinson (Anne Bancroft) appears at his room, she is framed by the open doorway. This framing technique is repeated by Nichols as a metaphor throughout the film. Downstairs, Benjamin awkwardly mingles with the guests his parents have invited to celebrate his graduation and homecoming; he is embarrassed by their attention and the recitation of the college honors he has earned. Outside at the pool, he is approached by a family friend, Mr. McGuire (Walter Brooke), who utters one of the famous lines in the film, "plastics." When he returns to his room, Mrs. Robinson appears in the doorway, feigning to be looking for the bathroom. Although Benjamin mentions that he would prefer to be alone, she asks him to drive her home because her husband has already left, taking the car. Offering the keys to his new Alfa Romeo, a graduation gift from his parents, Mrs. Robinson tosses them into the fish tank and says she doesn't know how to drive a foreign stick shift. Once in her house, she leads him out to the sunporch, beginning her seduction. In a famous scene, Benjamin, framed by a crook in her arched leg, says:

Mrs. Robinson—you're trying to seduce me, aren't you?

He reluctantly follows her up to daughter Elaine's bedroom. There, a naked Mrs. Robinson offers herself to Benjamin any time he feels the desire. The seduction attempt ends when the screech of a car is heard and Mr. Robinson (Murray Hamilton), who is also a business partner with Ben's father, enters the house, sits with a nervous Benjamin in the sunroom, and has a fatherly chat, urging him to sow some wild oats and have a few flings during the summer.

In another scene that symbolizes Benjamin's detachment from his family's upper-class lifestyle, he models a scuba diving outfit at the twenty-first birthday party his parents give him and sees their faces distorted through the mask. He blocks everyone out by diving into the pool and sinking under the water.

His affair with Mrs. Robinson begins in an awkward and funny scene as Benjamin nervously checks into the Taft Hotel, reserving a single room and declining the clerk's offer of a porter to escort him and carry his bags to the room. Once inside, he immediately hangs the DO NOT DISTURB sign on the outside of the door and nervously watches Mrs. Robinson undress, offering her hangers, "wood or wire," for her dress. Fearing the consequences, he wants to leave, but Mrs. Robinson goads him into staying by preying on his feelings of inadequacy as a virgin. The liaison continues as Benjamin sinks deeper into his malaise; this is symbolized by his floating aimlessly in his parents' pool, wearing black sunglasses. There is an inter-cut scene in which Benjamin leaves the pool and walks out of the hotel bathroom and to the bed where Mrs. Robinson waits. His frustrated father confronts him about his aimless detachment while his mother suspects he is having an affair and asks her son not to lie about it. Determined to try to connect with someone, he attempts to engage Mrs. Robinson in conversation before having sex. This leads to a discussion about Mrs. Robinson's daughter, Elaine (Katharine Ross), a taboo subject for her. The conversation becomes tense when Benjamin threatens to ask Elaine out and is angered by her implication that he is not good enough for her daughter.

On the verge of breaking off the relationship, he apologizes and they return to the status quo…until his parents arrange a date for him and Elaine.

Hoping to alienate Elaine on their date, Benjamin acts rudely and takes her to a strip club. Upset, she starts to cry and runs out, followed by Benjamin, who apologizes and tells her that she is the only good thing that has happened to him. They wind up at the Taft Hotel for a drink where, in a very funny scene, Benjamin is recognized as Mr. Gladstone. Realizing the awkwardness of the situation, Benjamin whisks Elaine out of the hotel but she confronts him with the question of having an affair and he admits to having one with an older married woman, but says it's over. The next day, when he arrives at the Robinson house to pick up Elaine for a drive, Benjamin is confronted by Mrs. Robinson, who threatens to tell her daughter about their affair if he doesn't leave. Angry, he races up to Elaine's room and tells her the truth as Mrs. Robinson stands beside them. Shocked, she orders him out.

After clandestinely observing Elaine as she leaves for college in Berkeley, Benjamin tells his parents he is going to marry her. Excited, they want to share the news with the Robinsons but at Benjamin's urging they do not call. He admits that she doesn't know and or even like him. His parents are perplexed as Benjamin leaves for the 400-mile drive. Arriving at Berkeley, he starts to stalk Elaine, accompanying her on a date to the zoo, where she is meeting Carl Smith (Brian Avery), a medical student. Finally, Elaine confronts Benjamin in his boardinghouse room, and although she is upset by the truth, she realizes that his affair was her mother's fault and that he didn't rape her. Ordered to leave by the landlord, she tells him to stay until he has formulated more definitive plans. That evening, she returns to his room and asks him to kiss her, and Benjamin presses her to get married. During the next scenes he hounds her about marriage as she evades him, finally leaving him a letter expressing her love but saying that such a union will be hopeless. He drives to Los Angeles, confronts Mrs. Robinson, who calls the police, and learns that Elaine is getting married. He returns to Berkeley, finds out the wedding is in Santa Barbara, drives there, runs out of gas a few blocks from the church, and makes a desperate run to rescue Elaine. Gazing down from the balcony, he pounds on the glass, shouting her name as her parents and guests make angry, contorted faces at him. He rushes down, wrestles with Mr. Robinson, grabs Elaine, and seizes a gold crucifix, using it as a prod to fend off the attacking herd of guests. They run out the chapel door and Benjamin uses the crucifix as a dead bolt, locking the guests inside. They board a municipal bus, Elaine still dressed in her wedding gown, and the other riders watch them move toward the back. The last scene shows them giddy with excitement at first, but as the bus moves along the expression on their faces changes to one of uncertainty and apprehension.

The film was very popular and it resonated with the youth movements of the sixties. It articulated the generation gap that was often blamed for the lack of communication between parents and their children. It also explored issues of gender and sexuality, such as adult male virginity and its presumption of innocence and embarrassment. There was also Benjamin's romantic pursuit of Elaine, which bordered on what is now defined as stalking. In our current age of information overload and the Internet, Benjamin's behavior clearly violates the presumption of privacy and would probably result in an order of protection prohibiting him from coming within a defined distance of Elaine.

In his December 22, 1967, *New York Times* review of *The Graduate*, Bosley Crowther writes:

> ...one of the best seriocomic social satires we've had from Hollywood since Preston Sturges was making them. For in telling a pungent story of the sudden confusions and dismays of a bland young man fresh out of college who is plunged headlong into the intellectual vacuum of his affluent parents' circle of friends, it fashions a scarifying picture of the raw vulgarity of the swimming-pool rich, and it does so with a lively and exciting expressiveness through vivid cinema.

The film was nominated for seven Academy Awards and received one, Best Director for Mike Nichols.

2001: A SPACE ODYSSEY (1968)

PRODUCER/DIRECTOR: Stanley Kubrick

WRITER(S): Stanley Kubrick, Arthur C. Clarke

CAST: Keir Dullea (Dr. Dave Bowman), Gary Lockwood (Dr. Frank Poole), William Sylvester (Dr. Heywood R. Floyd), Daniel Richter (Moon-Watcher), Leonard Rossiter (Dr. Andrei Smyslov), Margaret Tyzack (Elena), Robert Beatty (Dr. Ralph Halvorsen), Sean Sullivan (Dr. Bill Michaels), Douglas Rain (HAL 9000—voice), Frank Miller (Mission controller—voice)

CINEMATOGRAPHY: Geoffrey Unsworth

MUSIC: Patrick Moore, musical consultant (uncredited); Frank S. Urioste, music editor (uncredited)

LENGTH AND RATING: 160 min (Premier cut, 1972) 141 min; G

Perhaps the most lasting legacy of Stanley Kubrick's masterpiece, *2001: A Space Odyssey*, is its poetic allegory of humankind's future in a time of consuming technology. Viewing the film in the context of today's technological environment is a lesson in Kubrick's determination to visualize the future and the implication of man's inability to grasp the consequences of being vulnerable and victimized by artificial intelligence. Meticulous to the point of obsession, Kubrick divorced himself from the constraints of the American studio structure, moving to England and becoming his own producer, which gave him complete artistic control over his films, from script to post-production. As an artist he was methodical, overseeing every frame of his films and ensuring the utmost of accuracy without regard to time or budget. When Douglas Trumball found an experimental cinematic means depicting the stargate segment, to create an image visualizing travel from one dimension to another, Kubrick gave him carte blanche to pursue it. This film is a symbolic expression of Kubrick's devotion to his art. He used every tool available at the time to paint a vivid portrait of the future, with the caveat of attempting to understand humankind's past within this context.

Articulating his vision about the infiniteness of space, Kubrick uses America's Apollo space program as a means to embark from. Its goal was to land humans on the moon and return them safely to Earth. This was accomplished on July 20, 1969, when the Apollo 11 mission landed on the moon and astronauts Neil Armstrong and Buzz Aldrin became the first to walk on its surface.

While the American space program influenced Kubrick's work, it did not provide him with the material he needed to visualize space travel and the technology of the future. A 1955 film, George Pal's *Conquest of Space*, provided Kubrick with a sense of direction that helped in his imaginary pursuit of this imagery. In Pal's film there is rotating wheel, or earth station, that Kubrick adapts to *2001*, and he creates a poetic image of it floating and rotating in space accompanied by the "Blue Danube Waltz" by Johann Strauss.

In the *Dawn of Man* opening sequence, Kubrick transports his audience to a prehistoric world and a tribe of apelike men who huddle together in a cave. When dawn arrives the next morning, they discover a black monolith, which at first they fear and then hesitantly touch. In the following sequence, the leader of the tribe sorts through the dry bones of an antelope, slowly picks out a straight one, and uses it as a tool to crush the animal's remains. He has discovered a weapon, implying that he has also attained intelligence. Exuberantly waving the bone over his head, he exults in his discovery, and to the music of Strauss's *Also Sprach Zarathustra* he learns to hunt and fells various animals. This is followed by the apelike man defending his water hole by beating back the transgressor with his newfound weapon and hurling it into the air as a jump-cut quickly moves the action forward three million years, to a space vehicle and an orbiting space station wheel accompanied by the music of Strauss's *Blue Danube Waltz*.

The movie is a visual symphony, with the first dialogue not heard until twenty-five minutes into the film and totaling about forty minutes of actual speech throughout the entire movie. Part of the dynamic of the film is its music, which includes classical compositions by Strauss and Aram Khachaturian (*Gayane's Adagio* from the Gayaneh ballet suite), along with modern classical composer Gyorgy Ligeti, using extracts from his *Requiem* (the Kyrie), *Atmospheres*, *Lux Aeterna*, and *Aventures*.

Kubrick addresses a number of themes in *2001: A Space Odyssey* that have a great deal of relevance to modern times. In the character of the HAL 9000 computer, he delves into the challenge of creating artificial intelligence and its implications for the future of humankind. Indeed, as the world embraces the integration of computers it also faces new vulnerabilities, which raises the question of who is in control, man or machine. There are references to technological innovations that are commonplace today, including videophones, and Kubrick's commitment to scientific accuracy validates his assumptions about space travel. In the film, the HAL 9000 computer sings "Daisy Bell" as he is disconnected by astronaut David Bowman (Keir Dullea). HAL's synthetic speech was an actual rendition of a computer voice that author and scientist Arthur C. Clarke had witnessed at Bell Labs in 1962. While visiting a friend, Clarke was treated to a demonstration by physicist John Larry Kelly, Jr., who used an IBM 704 computer to synthesize speech and recreate the song "Daisy Bell" with an accompaniment by Max Matthews. Impressed, Clarke used it in his novel and the screenplay for *2001*.

The film also evokes the premise of the possibility of extraterrestrial life on other planets. On April 2, 1968, the film premiered at the Uptown Theatre in Washington, DC, and was followed by an April 3, 1968, showing at the Capital Theater in New York

City. At the New York screening, Kubrick spoke about the possibility of life on other planets, alluding to its likelihood given the existence of 100 billion stars along with 100 billion galaxies. He visually relates that possibility at the beginning of the film, during the *Dawn of Man* sequence when the apelike men discover the black monolith which is symbolic of an intelligent life form that existed millions of years ago. Kubrick uses a stunning shot of the apelike man, who has discovered a bone and is using it as a weapon, hurling it above his head. Then, he cuts to the blackness of endless space and a shuttle vehicle in the shape of that bone, moving toward a revolving space station. In a seamless transition Kubrick, visually articulates Darwin's theory of evolution as a portrait of scientific virtue. This imagery also suggests the philosophy of Nietzsche, who viewed evolution as moving from ape to human to superman.

In a 1968 *Playboy* magazine interview, Kubrick clearly defined *2001* as a film about the concept of God but conditioned his statement by saying that he was not a believer in any earthbound monotheistic religions and the traditional anthropomorphic image of God. However, he believed that a scientific definition of God could be created.

Rejecting various hypothetical interpretations of his film, Kubrick was adamant in denying any "official" meanings, stating that his movie is a "nonverbal experience," as evidenced by only forty minutes of dialogue in two hours, forty minutes (premiere cut, re-released in 1971 at 141 minutes) of film. He wanted the audience to be able to speculate on the philosophical and allegorical meaning of the film without presenting them with a "verbal road map." When Kubrick was asked to share his interpretation with the viewer of the film, he refused, saying it would, "shackle him to a *reality* other than his own."

When Arthur C. Clarke, the famous British science fiction writer and author of the novel *2001: A Space Odyssey*, who collaborated with Kubrick on the script for the film, mentioned that they had failed if anyone understood it after a single viewing, Kubrick disagreed. He noted that the initial reaction to the film should be instantaneous and visceral, which would not require additional screenings. However, he admitted that further appreciation of any good film could be enhanced by subsequent viewings, and that a film could be considered a work of art. He cited music, paintings, and books that required more than one contact experience, and was happy to acknowledge that the attitude toward film was changing toward a new appreciation of its artistic merits.

After the release of *2001: A Space Odyssey*, a number of New York–based, nationally known reviewers were highly critical of the film. Indeed, on his way from England to New York on the *Queen Elizabeth*, Kubrick was still editing the film, and he sat in the projection booth at each screening, subsequently deciding to cut nineteen minutes.

The New York critics, including Pauline Kael, Stanley Kauffmann (*The New Republic*), Renata Adler (*The New York Times*), Andrew Sarris (*The Village Voice*), John Simon (*The New Leader*), and Judith Crist (*New York Magazine*) used language like "unimaginative," "dull," "hypnotic and immensely boring," "grim," and "a regrettable failure." However, after a second viewing, Sarris reversed himself, calling *2001* a work of art and Kubrick a major artist. Other, and in some cases younger, reviewers embraced the film as "unforgettable," "a milestone," "the world's most extraordinary film," and "a brilliant intergalactic satire on modern technology."

One fan who expressed a particular affection for the film is the late Pope John Paul II, who held a special screening of *2001* that same year. In 1999, he included *2001* among forty-five films suitable for viewing by the faithful.

The film was released in 70-millemeter wide-gauge prints and scheduled for reserve seating at many movie theaters around the world. In Los Angeles, the film played for 103 weeks as an exclusive area release. It earned close to $57 million in domestic box office gross, with a worldwide gross in excess of $190 million on a production budget of $12 million (http://www.imdb.com/title/Hoo62622/business).

The progression of the narrative interfaces the complex world of technology with the development of the plot as Dr. Heywood R. Floyd (William Sylvester), a scientist administrator, travels to the moon base crater, Clavius, which houses American astronauts. In the visualization of Dr. Floyd's trip, Kubrick makes it appear ordinary with familiar signs and corporate logos such as Pan Am (now defunct) and Orbiter Hilton, and he reminds the audience that while we are grounded in earthbound corporate logos, Dr. Floyd is in space, as a sign directs, "Caution: Weightless Condition." While Dr. Floyd is in the waiting area preparing to continue his journey, the routine of space travel is reinforced by an announcement over the loud speaker that a woman's blue cashmere sweater was found in the restroom and will be available to be claimed in the manager's office.

Once again, Kubrick attempts a semblance of normalcy when Dr. Floyd uses a videophone to call his daughter, Squirt, millions of miles away on Earth, and wish her happy birthday. In the 1960s, AT&T demonstrated its Picturephone product and service at Expo 67, the International World's Fair held in Montreal, Canada, in 1967. With today's computer interface and the use of a webcam, the realization of video telephony has become more commonplace and is a remarkable tribute to Kubrick's prescience. Another technological realization in today's security environment is the Voice Print Identification Test that Dr. Floyd takes to secure his clearance. As of this writing, many forms of security tests exist, including voice prints and retina scans.

The reasons for Dr. Floyd's trip are slowly revealed by a conversation he has in the waiting area with Russian scientists, who are returning from their sector of the moon. They ask him why there has been no telephone contact for ten days with the American moon base on the crater Clavius. They speculate that there may be an epidemic, which is the cover planted by the Americans for Dr. Floyd's trip. His reaction to the Russians is evasive and he deliberately excuses himself to continue his journey.

Upon reaching Clavius, Dr. Floyd makes a top secret presentation to scientists there about the discovery of a second monolith found on the crater. An expedition of men dressed in space suits led by Dr. Floyd proceeds to the crater and descends into the vast cavern, where the monolith appears, encircling it; they are awed by its appearance. In an action similar to the apelike man millions of years before him, Dr. Floyd reaches out his gloved hand to touch the object, which suddenly emits an ear-piercing radio signal apparently aimed at the planet Jupiter.

The discovery of the monolith leads to the Jupiter mission aboard the spaceship *Discovery*, a manned vehicle with a crew of five, three of whom are asleep in hibernation. The others are Mission Commander Dave Bowman (Keir Dullea) and Astronaut, Executive Officer Dr. Frank Poole (Gary Lockwood). As the two men eat their space dinner, they sit silently, watching a BBC interview with them prior to leaving on the mission. The interview provides some interesting exposition about the need to have part of the crew in hibernation, its scientific explanation, and comments from HAL, the computer that oversees every function of the ship and its occupants. Perhaps the most engaging and suspicious of the characters, HAL calmly praises his abilities as being perfect and infallible, which include working with Dave and Frank. His voice (that of Douglas Rain) is calm and yet troubling because it appears empty and soulless. When the BBC interviewer asks Dave if HAL has emotions, he replies that he was programmed with them but is unsure if he has true feelings.

In the routine of space, Kubrick demonstrates the life of tedium experienced by Bowman and Poole as they acquiesce to HAL's supremacy over all aspects of the *Discovery*. In a chess match with HAL, Poole easily succumbs to the machine's superiority. After a probing conversation with Dave about the secretive nature of the mission, HAL announces that there will be a major malfunction of the AE35 communications component within seventy-two hours, and Dave goes on an EVA (extra-vehicular activity) to replace the unit. Neither Dave nor Frank know the true nature of the mission, which is only known to HAL, who suspects that the astronauts may try to abort it and decides that he must protect the integrity of the mission.

Communicating with Mission Control in Houston, Dave and Frank learn that the twin HAL 9000 computer on Earth indicates that Discovery HAL has made an error in predicting that the AE35 communications component will fail. HAL attributes the anomaly to "human error." This revelation shocks Dave and Frank because HAL controls every aspect of the *Discovery*'s operation, thus he controls them as well. They remove themselves to a pod where HAL cannot overhear their conversation as they strategize about their options and decide to put the original AE35 unit back in place and disconnect HAL. Any attempt to disconnect HAL is fraught with danger because a HAL 9000 computer has never been disconnected. This is a telling scene as Kubrick demonstrates the paranoia of the two astronauts, who must hide from the omnipresent computer and engage in a surreptitious plot to compromise his oversight. But of course HAL is smarter, and while he cannot overhear what the men say, his eye-like lenses can read their lips and discover how they plan to deactivate him. This is a classic rendition of "man against machine," and Kubrick brilliantly addresses it in a visual contretemps that evokes the mysteries of machine intelligence and how much freedom man will yield to computers.

Unsuspecting of HAL's diabolical intentions, Frank exits the *Discovery*, and while he is on an EVA to install the original AE35 unit, HAL uses a space pod as a weapon to sever his oxygen cord and thrust Frank into space, suffocating him. In a vain rescue attempt, Dave, leaving behind his space helmet, enters a pod and retrieves Frank's body. When he asks HAL to open the bay doors, the computer refuses the command and terminates the conversation with Dave. This exchange once again demonstrates how man can be victimized by intelligent machines.

Unlike HAL, who has been programmed to perform like a human but does not have a brain, Dave has the unique capabilities of human intuition and the ability to address a problem with a creative solution, albeit a risky one. He releases Frank's body and uses the pod to open the *Discovery's* emergency air locks, thus exploding himself inside, releasing the oxygen and surviving the ordeal without his space helmet. In doing so he has contradicted HAL's admonition that such an attempt would be "difficult."

For now, man is victorious over machine, and Dave systematically disconnects HAL's functions, as evidenced by its voice regression and return to an infantile state. Now Dave, severed from HAL's interface, pursues the mission to Jupiter. While in the *Discovery* he sees the third monolith orbiting in space and exits his spaceship, entering the pod to continue his journey. As the pod enters deep space and speeds through various galaxies, a vibrant display of pulsating, colored light races past Dave Bowman's eyes, accompanied by a cacophony of sound that creates a hallucinogenic canvas of sight and sound.

The final scenes of the movie are an allegorical essay on the meaning of life and its evolution from embryo, to child, to old age and death, and a rebirth or resurrection of the embryonic fetus, floating through infinite space, symbolic of the eternal endurance of humanity and the essence of faith as a sustaining value in the timeless progression of life.

As Dave Bowman confronts life's evolution, Shakespeare's literary algorithm articulates the seven ages of man in his play, *As You Like It*. From the "mewing and puking infant," to the school boy, lover and soldier, to the wise justice, then the older man, "with spectacles on nose," and "his big manly voice turning again toward childish treble."

Observing a surrealistic bedroom scene, starkly white but furnished in period French baroque, Dave Bowman watches himself as an older man eating dinner. Then he is dying in bed, and as life leaks away he raises his wizened finger to point at the fourth black monolith at the foot of his bed, and then he morphs into the star embryonic fetus. The floating fetus is humankind's testament to all intelligent life as the enduring virtue of its creative design and its devotion to the eternal spirit of the universe.

The 2001 film *A-I: Artificial Intelligence*, directed by Steven Spielberg, was influenced by Stanley Kubrick's vision and concern about the future and the role of computers and robots.

PLANET OF THE APES (1968)

PRODUCER/DIRECTOR: Franklin J. Schaffner (director), Arthur P. Jacobs (producer)
WRITER(S): Michael Wilson (screenplay), Rod Serling (screenplay), Pierre Boulle (novel)
CAST: Charlton Heston (George Taylor), Roddy McDowall (Cornelius), Kim Hunter (Zira), Maurice Evans (Dr. Zaius), James Whitmore (President of the Assembly), James Daly (Honorious), Linda Harrison (Nova), Robert Gunner (Landon), Lou Wagner (Lucius), Woodrow Parfrey (Maximus)
CINEMATOGRAPHY: Leon Shamroy
MUSIC: Jerry Goldsmith
LENGTH AND RATING: 112 min; NR

Planet of the Apes is a superb science fiction drama that combines the best aspects of film production values, narrative storytelling, makeup design, and acting into a seamless parable about racial prejudice, domination, subversion, and intolerance. The irony, of course, is the subjugation of humans by an intelligent species of simians (apes), who ironically possess a similar culture to that of humans. But, while they espouse similar values, they clearly mimic the inherent prejudice that is part of the fabric of mankind.

The film is an adaptation of Pierre Boulle's novel *La planete des singes*. He also wrote *Le pont de la rivière Kwai*, which became the hugely popular and successful film *The Bridge on the River Kwai*. The talented television writer and creator/host of the hit television series, *The Twilight Zone*, Rod Serling wrote the first draft of the script, which included an anti-nuclear theme, and Michael Wilson, who wrote the screenplay for *The Bridge on the River Kwai,* did the final draft, which made reference to political allegory.

The narrative story arc and exposition for *Planet of the Apes* is quickly established by Captain George Taylor (Charlton Heston), the astronaut who commands the space vehicle hurtling through the universe, traveling at the speed of sound across the time barrier and catapulting the crew thousands of years into the future. This verifies Dr. Otto Hasslein's theory of time travel at light speed, because the astronauts left Earth in 1972 but the chronometer now reads November 25, 3978. Before injecting himself with a long-term sleeping drug, Taylor, puffing away on a cigar, is absorbed in his own self-righteous assessment of the evils of mankind. He's a cynical opportunist escaping from the earthbound sanctimony of unethical leadership and the misguided brinkmanship of greedy world powers.

But once again man is not perfect, and the ship crashes into the water and desolate, arid land mass of the Forbidden Zone on a foreign planet. The crew, Landon (Robert Gunner) and Dodge (Jeff Burton), quickly abandon ship, leaving behind the sole female crew member, who has died and aged in her sleeping pod due to an oxygen malfunction. She was to be the mission's Eve, procreating the species on a distant planet. When the three men reach land, Landon plants a miniature American flag on the shoreline and Taylor laughingly disdains his crewmate's actions. Soon, they discover plant life, which leads them to a verdant land area with a lush, flowing waterfall that invites them to bathe. They became aware of something lurking in the brush, stealing their clothes, and as they pursue, recovering some of their garments, they come upon a tribe of humans in loin cloths and rags, savagely foraging for food. Watching from a distance, Taylor arrogantly observes that if this is the best they have to offer, they'll be running the planet in six months. Taylor's statement is an affirmation that, although he disdains the corrupt leadership on Earth and is looking for a better place, he is not above using the same means to take advantage of those who are vulnerable. In other words, he is a hypocrite.

What appears to be an idyllic scenario is interrupted by the horn of a hunt, and the group of humans becomes the hunted, pursued by manlike apes riding horses, wielding nets, and armed with rifles. It is a chaotic scene as the humans attempt to escape the grip of the apes by dodging and leaping; however, they are frustrated by the fleet-footed mounts the apes ride and by the weapons they yield. Attempting to escape, Taylor runs with the others and, just before he is wounded in the throat, he sees his fellow astronaut shot and killed.

What follows is the revelation that Taylor is a thinking and speaking human being who may be the missing link in the ape kingdom's evolutionary cycle. Calling him "bright eyes," he is befriended and studied by scientist/animal behaviorist Zira (Kim Hunter), who enlists her boyfriend, archeologist Cornelius (Roddy McDowell), in her effort. Her nemesis is Dr. Zaius (Maurice Evans), a clever orangutan who quotes ape scripture in his quest to silence any attempt at revealing the truth as heretical, because he is well aware that ape culture is descendent from humans. Indeed, as Taylor recovers from his throat wound, he cannot speak and instead writes words in the dirt. Caged with a savage human, they fight as the savage erases the message, and as Dr. Zaius walks by, he scratches out the remaining words with his cane. He must preserve the secret of his civilization and protect ape culture from the human beasts that destroyed their own race.

When they first come upon the savage humans, Taylor notices a beautiful young woman named Nova (Linda Harrison). Eventually, Zira cages them together so they can mate, innocently chuckling at this prospect. When they attempt to forcibly remove Taylor from the cage so that he can be castrated, he escapes and runs wild in the village. During this time, the audience is exposed to the routines of ape culture, which are very human. For example, Taylor intrudes into a eulogy at a funeral and then winds up in a natural history museum, where he sees fellow astronaut Dodge stuffed as an exhibit.

Clever lines in the film mimic the adages humans use in everyday colloquialisms, such as "I never met an ape I didn't like," "Human see human do," and "All men look alike to most apes." And there are the lingering biases in ape culture, as one chimp notes that the quota system was abolished.

Appearing before a tribunal, Taylor is declared to have no rights under ape law, and that God has created the ape in his own image. Although Zira and Cornelius attempt to defend him, they are mocked and threatened for advocating theories like evolution, which contradict the "faith." Attempting to have a statement read in to the record and asserting that he came from a distant planet in another galaxy, Taylor is led outside to identify his crewmate, Landon, who was rounded up with the others during the hunt. He excitedly acknowledges Landon but is tragically disappointed when he sees a visible scar on the side of his head, revealing that he has undergone a lobotomy.

Attempting to prove the existence of a previous human culture and confirm the theory of evolution, Cornelius and Zira, under threat of being accused of heresy, embark on a journey to a cave in the Forbidden Zone, where Cornelius had previously discovered human artifacts. They take Taylor and Nova with them in an effort to save him from being destroyed by Dr. Zaius. Once in the cave they are joined by Dr. Zaius, and although the artifacts and bones are of human origin, Dr. Zaius denies their legitimacy. When Nova picks up a doll shaped like a human baby, Zaius once again dismisses it and remarks that his grandchildren play with such dolls. However, when the doll cries "ma, ma," Taylor questions why an ape would make such a doll.

After holding Dr. Zaius hostage to avert the onslaught of the ape army, Taylor and Nova mount a horse and ride away to their destiny along the shore. He asks Zira, Cornelius, and Lucius to join them but they choose to remain with their culture. As they ride, Taylor comes upon a monument to the past: the rubble of the Statue of Liberty. He realizes he has been on Earth the whole time, albeit in the future, and curses the human race for destroying itself.

The film was well-received by critics and audiences, with a box office of more than $32 million and a production budget of just over $5 million. In her *New Yorker* review of February 17, 1968, Pauline Kael writes:

> *Planet of the Apes* is one of the best science-fiction fantasies ever to come out of Hollywood. That doesn't mean it's art. It is not conceived in terms of vision or mystery or beauty. Science-fiction fantasy is a peculiar genre; it doesn't seem to result in much literary art, either. This movie is efficient and craftsmanlike; it's conceived and carried out for maximum popular appeal, though with a cautionary message, and with some attempts to score little points against various forms of establishment thinking. These swifties are not Swift, and the movie's posture of superiority is somewhat embarrassing. Brechtian pedagogy doesn't work in Brecht, and it doesn't work here, either.

At best, this is a slick commercial picture, with its elements carefully engineered—pretty girl (who unfortunately doesn't seem to have had acting training), comic reliefs, thrills, chases—but when expensive Hollywood engineering works, as it rarely does anymore, the results can be impressive. Schaffner has thought out the action in terms of the wide screen, and he uses space and distance dramatically.

As a science-fiction film, *Planet of the Apes* succeeds in being both entertaining and allegorical in its purpose. It evokes the self-centered egoism of human nature that assumes that man is the center of the universe. As a parable, it presents its audience with a moment of introspection about the fragility of life and the purpose of humankind.

EASY RIDER (1969)

PRODUCER/DIRECTOR: Dennis Hopper (director), Peter Fonda (producer)
WRITER(S): Peter Fonda, Dennis Hopper, Terry Southern
CAST: Peter Fonda (Wyatt), Dennis Hopper (Billy), Antonio Mendoza (Jesus), Phil Spector (Connection), Mac Mashourian (Bodyguard), Warren Finnerty (Rancher), Tita Colorado (Rancher's Wife), Luke Askew (Stranger on Highway), Luana Anders (Lisa), Sabrina Scharf (Sarah), Jack Nicholson (George Hanson)
CINEMATOGRAPHY: László Kovács
MUSIC: Mike Deasy (uncredited)
LENGTH AND RATING: 95 min; R

"A man went looking for America and couldn't find it anywhere?" The year this film was released, John Lennon of The Beatles recorded his song, "Give Peace a Chance," and the group released its *Abbey Road* album. Students at Harvard University occupied the administration building, and it was a difficult year for Senator Edward Kennedy, who drove off a bridge on Chappaquiddick Island, killing a young campaign aide to Robert Kennedy, Mary Jo Kopechne. There was also the tragic and bizarre murder of Sharon Tate, the wife of director Roman Polanski, and her friends Abigail Folger, Wojciech Frykowski, and Jay Sebring and the caretaker for their Los Angeles home, Steven Parent. At the time of her death, Ms. Tate was eight months pregnant. In November, the innovative children's program *Sesame Street*, produced by Children's Television Workshop, premiered on public television, and noted investigative journalist Seymoure Hersh broke the story of the Vietnam My Lai massacre. And a tribute to the end of the 1960s was the "Woodstock West" free concert hosted by the Rolling Stones at Altamont Speedway in Northern California, attended by 300,000 people and filmed by distinguished documentary filmmakers Albert and David Maysles, later to be released as *Gimme Shelter*, a landmark concert film.

American youth felt disenfranchised and were disillusioned with their leaders and policy agendas. The timing was right for a counterculture movie and *Easy Rider* presented an iconoclastic view of America and its lost virtue. The two characters Wyatt, Captain America (Peter Fonda), and Billy, Wild Bill Hickok (Dennis Hopper, director of the film), were the archetypes of youth searching for life on the crossroads of America. Their long hair and clothing identified them as "hippies" as they took to the roads of America, scoring a cocaine deal in California and using some of the cash to buy their "bikes" and finance their trip to New Orleans in time for Mardi Gras. After picking up the cocaine in Mexico, riding on old motorcycles and dressed in nondescript clothing, they are transformed into iconic symbols of the counterculture.

Soon, the audience becomes aware of the conflict between them and mainstream society. Their clothing betrays them, with Wyatt wearing tight leather pants, his motorcycle emblazoned with the Stars and Stripes on the gas tank, and on his helmet, with an image of the American flag on the back of his jacket. In his attire Billy is less pretentious and more subdued, with a buckskin jacket and a floppy leather hat that seems to fit his cowboy image that's complemented with a bushy moustache. Looking for a room to spend the night, they pull up to a motel displaying a lit "vacancy" sign, get the door slammed in their face, and before they leave the proprietor has turned on the "no vacancy" sign.

Needing to repair Wyatt's flat tire, they stop at a ranch and are welcomed by the owner/rancher (Warren Finnerty), his Mexican wife, and their brood of children. Their appearance and mode of transportation doesn't provoke or offend the family; indeed, the rancher is impressed with Wyatt's motorcycle. They are invited to the family dinner at a long outside table and are incorporated into the family dynamic. Although their lifestyle is nomadic, uprooted, and independent, they respect the virtues of the rancher's work ethic and his family values. But they soon realize that at this point in their lives, the responsibilities and obligations of family life are not a priority, so they continue on their road journey.

There is an interesting confrontation after Wyatt picks up a hitchhiker (Luke Askew) and they go to a gas station to fill their tanks. After the sale of the cocaine, Wyatt had stuffed the remainder of the cash into a plastic tube and hid it in his teardrop gasoline tank. At the station, Billy nervously watches as the hitchhiker fills the tanks and expresses his concern about a stranger possibly discovering their stash. Although he respects the rigors of the work ethic, Billy nevertheless embraces the concept of wealth and its associated comforts. He is assured by Wyatt that their money is safe, and after the hitchhiker pays for the gasoline they ride on, making camp on a Native American burial ground, where Billy is chided by the stranger for not showing enough respect toward the dead.

When they arrive at the stranger's commune, they are accepted by the group but Billy's greeting is less hospitable and he becomes uncomfortable and anxious to leave. The audience also learns that the commune's circumstance is less than idyllic due to a shortage of food after a harsh winter that resulted in many of the members leaving. After sharing dinner with the commune members, Wyatt and Billy give a lift on their motorcycles to two of the women and later skinny-dip with them in the hot springs. When they return, the stranger offers them some LSD and tells Wyatt to use it wisely with the right people at the right place. Wyatt begins to experience an inner conflict of whether to stay at the commune and develop a relationship with Lisa, the girl from the hot springs, or continue on his journey with Billy. In the end, although the commune offers him a refuge, he is compelled to move on.

When they arrive in Las Vegas, Mississippi, Wyatt and Billy inadvertently join a parade down Main Street and are arrested and thrown in jail for "parading without a permit." At this point the narrative turns toward a new character arc with the introduction of George Hanson (Jack Nicholson), a young alcoholic American Civil Liberties Union (ACLU) lawyer who has compromised his professional career because of drunkenness.

He tells Wyatt and Billy that he can get them out of jail with his political connections as long as they haven't killed anyone … white, and they're released for twenty-five dollars.

Frustrated by the small-town, redneck mentality he must endure, George confides to Wyatt and Billy that he always wanted to go to Mardi Gras but never got there, and then entices them into allowing him to join them because the governor of Louisiana told him about the best whorehouse in New Orleans, "Madame Tinkertoy's House of Blue Lights," where the ladies are "U.S. Prime." As the more suspicious of the two, Billy's acceptance of George and welcoming of him on their three-day trip to New Orleans on the back of Wyatt's motorcycle, wearing a football helmet no less, provides a cultural determinant that defines the men as equal opportunity hippies.

At another campfire site, Wyatt gives a reluctant George a marijuana joint, but because of his alcohol addiction he fears the possibility of moving on to harder drugs, a fallacy that was widely disseminated at the time. He smokes the joint and then embarks on a treatise about UFOs and the Venutians who live among the humans on Earth. This is interesting within the context of the action that follows, as George tells them that within the alien culture there are no leaders, no wars, and no monetary system; indeed, each man is a leader, an equal. But this is not the case for Wyatt and Billy, who are viewed by their own society as aliens and feared because they are different. As George said, the Venutians integrate into human society because they look like ordinary people. That is not the case for Wyatt and Billy, who dare to be different.

An even more eloquent George presents a compelling discourse at the next campfire setting, after the party of three has been rudely treated at a local café, where they are refused service. A deputy sheriff, along with a redneck construction worker, mock and belittle them because of their appearance, and several of the customers take part in the verbal abuse. The men are received on more friendly terms by several teenage girls, who congregate around them as they mount their motorcycles to leave, begging for a ride. Fearing trouble, the three quickly exit.

Sitting around the campfire, George contemplates the previous events and tells Billy and Wyatt that they are feared not for who they are but for what they represent, and they embody the spirit of freedom. For most people, freedom is a reach because they are bought and sold in the marketplace. Talking about it is not living it, and George is prescient when he says that trying to tell someone he is not free will cause him to kill and maim to prove that he is, and that makes him dangerous. That night, the three men are attacked by baseball bat-wielding thugs from the café, an incident that culminates in George's murder and a bruised Wyatt and Billy.

As homage to their friend, they visit Madame Tinkertoy's House of Blue Lights in New Orleans and then join the Mardi Gras celebration with two prostitutes, sharing the LSD in a cemetery. There is a religious theme to their trip as they hallucinate the subtext of their lives and cast themselves into a purgatory of guilt, fear, and death.

After New Orleans, the two continue their road trip to Florida and have their last campout together. While Billy is elated they have "made it" and will retire to Florida, Wyatt, always the more introspective of the two, says they "blew it."

He repeats himself and then wishes Billy a good night. In his response, Wyatt may have been contemplating the worth of their trip in relation to its emotional cost—the murder of their friend, George, their station as outcasts from society and, based on Wyatt's bad LSD trip, his hatred for his mother and his longing for family and community, which he rejected but was attracted to at the commune.

In the ending sequence, Wyatt and Billy are riding down a country road to the music of Bob Dylan's "It's All Right Ma (I'm Only Bleeding)," performed by Roger

McGuinn, when a truck carrying two hostile locals pulls alongside Billy with the intention of scaring him, and after threatening to blow his brains out Billy defiantly raises his midde finger, the man aims his rifle and, after asking about getting a haircut, fires, mortally wounding him. As Wyatt races for help, the truck turns around, another shot is fired, and the final image on the screen is of Wyatt's exploding, burning motorcycle. The two have become victims of their own fate, hated because they were different and punished for their beliefs.

The sound track in *Easy Rider* is a tribute to the artists of that generation and features the music of Steppenwolf, Smith, The Byrds, The Holy Modal Rounders, Fraternity of Man, The Jimi Hendrix Experience, The Electric Prunes, and Roger McGuinn.

OUTLAWS

Butch Cassidy and the Sundance Kid (1969)
The Wild Bunch (1969)

Although released the same year with the western theme of iconic outlaws who have become anachronisms in a changing world, *Butch Cassidy and the Sundance Kid* and *The Wild Bunch* defined their characters in sharply different ways. In his world, Butch Cassidy, with an air of gloom, notes the passing of an another era to one that is more conscious of utility and not beauty. He has gotten older and feels out of place in a world that is changing more quickly than he can adapt. His life has been spent avoiding confrontation and taking the path of least resistance. But, the societal changes that are manifesting themselves on American culture present issues he must face to survive.

In *The Wild Bunch*, considered by many to be a masterpiece, the audience is exposed to the exceptional violence that was a part of the West and its portrayal of characters that are defined by the rituals of devotion and loyalty to their comrades in arms. It is an allegory about men who lived by their own code of frontier justice, surviving by their grit, brawn, and instinct. The opening scene of the film is a gruesome confrontation between two opposing outlaw groups involving a brutal gunfight that kills many of the town's innocent civilians. After fleeing from the carnage with their saddlebags of loot from the bank robbery, the leader of the bunch, Pike Bishop (William Holden), discovers that their "treasure" is a worthless load of washers planted by his former friend-turned-railroad-bounty hunter Deke Thornton (Robert Ryan). As they ruefully ponder their wasteful effort, the men face the stark reality that they are getting older, and Pike contemplates a future without their guns.

Other similarities exist between the characters in these two distinctive films. They're not entirely ruthless and they do have some sense of decency. Both bands of outlaws rob trains, and that makes Butch and Sundance, along with Pike Bishop and his "bunch," potential targets by the railroad barons who want to stop their looting and destruction. They face the dilemma of giving up the only life they know or pursuing their thievery in countries that may be more conducive to their tactics.

BUTCH CASSIDY AND THE SUNDANCE KID (1969)

PRODUCER/DIRECTOR: George Roy Hill (director), John Foreman (producer)
WRITER(S): William Goldman
CAST: Paul Newman (Butch Cassidy), Robert Redford (The Sundance Kid), Katharine Ross (Etta Place), Strother Martin (Percy Garris), Henry Jones (Bike Salesman), Jeff Corey

(Sheriff Bledsoe), George Furth (Woodcock), Cloris Leachman (Agnes), Ted Cassidy (Harvey Logan), Kenneth Mars (Marshal)
CINEMATOGRAPHY: Conrad L. Hall
MUSIC: Burt Bacharach
LENGTH AND RATING: 110 min; M

The opening scene is an apt beginning for a movie that establishes the motivation of its characters in a succinct, visual portrait. It presents a silent-film version of projected scenes, in sepia tones, of the "Hole in the Wall Gang" along with the clickity-click sound of the projector. The images shift to the present–day of the story, still colored in sepia tones. Demonstrating the changing times, Butch Cassidy (Paul Newman), surveys a new bank, noting its modern security provisions, including an electric alarm bell, heavy-duty safes and strong latches, window shutters, and a security guard. He laments the changing times and asks about the old beautiful bank and is told that it sustained too many robberies, and he responds that it's a small price to pay for what was its beauty. The next scene in the saloon defines the characters' moods and temperament as the audience is introduced to the Sundance Kid (Robert Redford), engrossed in a card game and challenged by the other gambler for cheating. He is told to relinquish his winnings and leave the saloon. Attempting to mediate the situation in a peaceful manner that would avoid a gunfight, Butch admonishes Sundance that he doesn't know how fast on the draw the gambler is, and that everyone gets older, using himself as an example of being over-the-hill. Angered by the implication that he cheated, Sundance tells Butch that he did not cheat and will only leave if he is asked to stay by the other gambler. Negotiations fail and Sundance stands up for his showdown with the challenger who, after learning the identity of the man he accused of cheating, demures from drawing on him. Acquiesing to Sundance's request, the challenger asks them to stay, so of course they must be on their way, and as they leave Sundance is asked how fast a draw he is and he demonstrates by shooting the belt and gun holster off the waist of the challenger. This scene establishes the main characters and their motivations and shows that Butch is well aware of the passing of time and the changing times.

As the image turns from sepia tones to color, the two men return to their hideout and the Hole in the Wall Gang, where Butch learns that during his absence his leadership has been challenged by loutish gang member Harvey Logan (Ted Cassidy). Befitting his character, Butch tries to talk himself out of fighting Harvey for leadership of the gang and enlists News Carver (Timothy Scott) to read the press clippings about the gang and its leader. But Harvey's plan to rob the Union Pacific Flyer railroad is more attractive to them than Butch's idea of robbing another bank.

As Harvey Logan prepares to settle the leadership issue with a knife fight, Butch agrees but only after they determine the rules. Disputing the notion of rules in a knife fight, Harvey wants to begin, and Butch gives him a swift kick in the groin followed by a two-handed punch in the jaw, bringing him to the ground and effectively settling the matter of leadership.

As a movie, *Butch Cassidy and the Sundance Kid* could be labled an anti-western, mocking some of the traditional visual clichés of the western genre with its tongue–in-cheek humor and clever dialogue. Compared to the "ballet of violence" in *The Wild Bunch* and the hard-edge outlaws of that movie, Butch and his gang are comic, child-like figures playing a game of cops and robbers and wanting to leave when they are tired. Even the employees working for the railroad feel a kinship with Butch, with some more cooperative and others mildly reluctant to hand over the money. The gang's ineptitude has a funny spin when, during the second train robbery, they plant too much dynamite and blow up the railroad car, the safe, and its contents. The owner of the railroad, E. H. Harriman, has hired a super-posse to track and kill Butch, and they arrive on a second train mounted on horses that leap from the railroad cars in pursuit of Butch and Sundance. Although they really don't want to hurt anyone, the rules of the game suddenly change as the two outlaws are incessestantly tracked by the posse.

Exhausted from the chase, Butch and Sundance have tried every ruse to throw off their pursuers, even mounting the same horse to confuse them, but it does not succeed. Eventually, Butch correctly concludes that the only men capable of such tracking ability are the Indian Lord Baltimore and Sheriff Joe Lafore. The super-posse successfully pins them down at the edge of a cliff by the river and the two oulaws debate the merits of jumping. In a humorous exchange, Sundance admits he can't swim and Butch laughs, saying the fall will probably kill him, and they jump.

They return to the home of Etta Place (Katharine Ross), Sundance's schoolteacher lover, and ready themselves to depart for New York City. Prior to their arrival in New York, Butch, whose real name was Robert LeRoy Parker, and Sundance, whose name was Harry Longabaugh, hold up a train near Wangner, Montana, netting $65,000. There is historical documentation that Etta and Sundance checked into Mrs. Taylor's boardinghouse at 234 East 12th Street and that Butch joined them later, checking in under his alias, James Ryan. The three go sightseeing in New York, visiting Coney Island. At a Broadway photography studio, Sundance and Etta have their picture taken, which is later used by Pinkerton detectives in their pursuit of the pair. In that photograph, Etta is wearing a Tiffany lapel watch, which may have been bought for her by Butch Cassidy. There is a Tiffany receipt for such a watch, purchased by James Ryan on February 4, 1901, for $40.10, but the date is one year earlier than their presence in New York City. They sail for Buenos Aires and there take up ranching for a short time, but soon return to robbing banks and trains in Argentina, Chile, and Bolivia (http://select.nytimes.com/search).

The film documents their visit to New York in a creative sepia-toned montage of tintype photographs of Butch, Sundance, and Etta frolicking in turn-of-the-century New York City. They board a steamship for South America and disembark in Bolivia, and although they are somewhat disappointed with their first impressions of the barren, hard scrabble texture of the country, Butch tries to cheer up a despondent Sundance by telling him their money can go a lot further, and he tells Etta that he'll feel better after he robs a few banks. In several humorous scenes, the inept bandits attempt bank robberies unable to speak Spanish, and Etta coaches them in several "work-related" phrases. Fearing they may be pursued in Bolivia by the same super–posse, Butch and Sundance decide to go straight but fail as payroll guards when their eccentric, "colorful" boss Percy Garris (Strother Martin) is killed during an ambush and they recover the money by killing all of the bandits and decide there are no benefits to an honest job. After Etta leaves they resume their bank robbing activities, and while eating in a restaurant a stable boy recognizes their mule's brand and alerts the authorities, who amass around the village, surrounding the bandits with hundreds of uniformed armed soldiers. They are wounded as they run for more ammunition and take cover in an empty house. Inside, they argue about their situation and Butch wants to tell

Sundance about his latest great plan but Sundance doesn't want any part of it. However, Butch tells him about Australia, where they speak English, have luscious women and banks, and beautiful beaches where Sundance can learn to swim. He appears to interest Sundance, except for the swimming aspect, and the two men get ready to run for the horses when Butch has a sudden fearful realization that Lafore is outside. When Sundance assures him that he is not, Butch is relieved, thinking that they can easily deal with the present situation. As they run outside, poised to fire, their image is freeze-framed with the sound of loud gun shots, and the color changes to a sepia tone as the camera zooms out. The movie ends with the two likeable outlaws meeting their demise without the audience having to witness their gruesome deaths. As such, they are eternally immortalized in the last frame of the film as Butch and Sundance, iconic figures of the fading West steadfastly clinging to their traditions and resisting the changes they eventually must succumb to.

THE *WILD BUNCH* (1969)

PRODUCER/DIRECTOR: Sam Peckinpah (director), Phil Feldman, Roy N. Sickner (producers)
WRITERS: Walon Green, Sam Peckinpah, Roy N. Sickner
CAST: William Holden (Pike Bishop), Ernest Borgnine (Dutch Engstrom), Robert Ryan (Deke Thornton), Edmund O'Brien (Sykes), Warren Oates (Lyle Gorch), Jamie Sanchez (Angel), Ben Johnson (Hector Gorch), Emilio Fernandez (Mupache), Strother Martin (Coffer)
CINAMATOGRAPHY: Lucien Ballard
MUSIC: Jerry Fielding
LENGTH AND RATING: 145 min; R

In his February 1969 review, *New York Times* critic Vincent Canby called this film "very beautiful" and "the first truly interesting, American-made western in years." The director Sam Peckinpah said: "I was trying to tell a simple story about bad men in changing times. *The Wild Bunch* is simply what happens when killers go to Mexico. The strange thing is that you feel a great sense of loss when these killers reach the end of the line" (http://www.geocities.com/paulinekaelreviews/w3.html).

Noted film critic Pauline Kael said the film had the poetic force of Kurosawa's *The Seven Samurai*. She also said the director, Peckinpah, had contradictory feelings about the aesthetics of violence and called the deaths as depicted in the film "voluptuous, frightening, and beautiful." She added that Peckinpah poured new wine into the bottle of the western and then "he explodes the bottle; his story is too simple for this imagist epic" (http://www.geocities.com/paulinekaelreviews/w3.html).

Known to some critics as the poet of violence, Sam Peckinpah's body of work, which also includes the contemporary violence of *Straw Dogs* (1971), has influenced many modern filmmakers, including Kathryn Bigelow, Martin Scorsese, Quentin Tarantino, and John Woo. A student of John Ford westerns, Peckinpah takes his mentor's ideology of the heroic frontier hero and casts a violent shroud over its traditions. Indeed, before the first bloody ballet in the town of San Raphael, Texas, also called Starbuck, the South Texas Temperance Union is holding an outdoor tent meeting, and Mayor Wainscoat (Dub Taylor) is preaching against the evils of drink and quoting liberally from the Bible. Then the Temperance Union band plays "Shall We Gather at the River," which John Ford used as a symbolic reference to death in movies like

The Searchers (1956) and which serves as a prelude to the relentless violence that is about to unfold on the screen. A reference to the hymn is used again when the Wild Bunch gang leaves the Starbuck bank after stealing what they thought is the railroad payroll, leaving behind Crazy Lee (Bo Hopkins), who terrorizies the remaining bank employees and a woman hostage, forcing them to march around singing, "Shall We Gather at the River."

They are the target of a bounty hunter ambush organized by Pat Harrigan (Albert Dekker) of the railroad, whose character is modeled after railroad financier E. H. Harriman (also referenced in *Butch Cassidy and the Sundance Kid*), led by Pike's former friend and gang member Deke Thornton (Robert Ryan). Realizing the entrapment, Pike Bishop (William Holden), the leader of the *Wild Bunch*, uses the marching temperance citizens as shields in making their escape, which results in a frenzied gun battle, in real-time and in slow-motion, that vividly portrays the citizens, men, women, and children, caught in the symphony of violence.

Disgusted with the sheer enormity of death, Deke tells Harrigan that next time, he had better plan his massacre more carefully. He is also angry over the band of trigger-happy misfits that Harrigan has organized as his posse. However, he is caught in the dilemma of being paroled out of a Yuma prison by Harrigan, with the agreement that he hunt down Pike Bishop and kill him in thirty days. This establishes another conflict in the film between former best friends Pike and Deke, who have become adversaries, each man searching for the means to an end.

After escaping the ambush in Starbuck, the gang retreats to Mexico to divide up the stolen treasure. They meet up with the whiskered and aging Sykes (Edmond O'Brien), a former gang member who is watching the fresh horses, when the Gorch brothers, Lyle (Warren Oates) and Tector (Ben Johnson), propose not to share with Sykes because he wasn't on the raid, nor with Angel (Jamie Sanchez), the Mexican, because it was his first outing with the bunch. Immediately standing up to the Gorch brothers, Pike Bishop assails their greed and challenges them to test his leadership. They back down, cut open the saddlebags, and find the worthless silver washers. After dealing with the frustrations of being "had" by Harrigan, Thornton, and the railroad, Pike talks about the next job, possibly a bank or a payroll. Acknowledging that it's not getting any easier, Sykes mentions their getting older and Pike speaks about putting down their guns because their time is coming to an end.

A parallel campfire scene between Thornton and Pike reveals some of the emotional backstory between the characters. As Thornton sits at the campfire with his misfit posse, including Coffer (Strother Martin), he is asked about Pike, and Thornton describes him as being the best, having never been caught. At Pike's campfire, while talking with Dutch (Ernest Borgnine) he speaks about one last good "score" and then "backing off," or retiring. Surprised, Dutch asks what he's thinking of doing. That's when Pike shares his idea of stealing the payroll of General Pershing's troops, who are defending the U.S. border against Mexican revolutionaries like Pancho Villa. Hearing the idea, Dutch feels that such information is hard to get and that pulling it off would be difficult, but Pike is confidant they can accomplish it.

In a revealing flashback, the circumstances of the animosity between Pike and Deke are exposed. Both men are enjoying the favors of prostitutes in a bordello and Pike, expecting a bottle of champagne, dismisses Deke's fear after hearing a knock on the door. Deke's fear is realized when an armed Pinkerton detective bursts in,

wounding Deke. Pike escapes through a window, leaving his friend to face the consequences of his capture.

After a respite in Angel's village, the bunch enters Agua Verde, where the corrupt
Mexican Generalissimo Mapache (Emilio Fernandez) and his Federales troops are
headquartered. They have ventured there to sell their extra horses, but the tension
rises when Angel sees his former girlfriend, now Mapache's mistress. As she cavorts in
the generalissimo's lap, Angel fires his gun, killing her. In the confusion that follows,
the Federales assume the shot was aimed at Mapache, and Pike and his men raise their
hands away from their weapons in a gesture of submission.

After convincing Mapache and his cohorts that the killing was the action of an
impetuous, hot-headed, jealous lover, the gang enters into an arrangement with Mapache to steal an army shipment of rifles and ammunition in return for $10,000 in gold.
Demonstrating a loyalty to his "troops," Pike negotiates with Mapache for Angel's
return as an essential member of the team and the generalissimo agrees, dismissing
Angel as insignificant. However, Angel refuses to join them in the raid, providing
weapons for Mapache to kill innocent villagers. With the help of Dutch, Pike agrees to
allow Angel to "steal" one case of rifles and ammunition for the resistance; in return,
Angel must relinquish his share of the gold.

Speculating that the Wild Bunch will attack the troop train carrying the rifles,
Deke Thornton and Harrigan plan for an ambush. Thornton is wary about using the
"trash" that Harrigan hired and wants additional good men, but Harrigan refuses.

Another flashback provides more detail about Pike's past, when the circumstance
of his leg injury is revealed. He had been romantically involved with a married woman
whose husband had deserted her, and was shot in the leg when the husband unexpect-
edy returned one evening, killing his wife and wounding Pike. This scene provides
depth to Pike's character, revealing his guilt, passion, and sense of loss for what "could
have been." Contemplating his past failures, both personal and professional, Pike tells
Dutch that it's their last job together and that they have to do it well.

As the train stops to replenish its water, the Wild Bunch stealthily scurries from
the tracks underneath and, without alerting the troops, Thornton, or the bounty hunters, Angel disconnects the open car, carrying the weapons from the rest of the train,
and it separates, chugging off. Anticipating their attack, Thornton has horses waiting in
the cars and the mounted posse jumps off the train, giving chase. The army troops cannot seem to mount their horses and are mired in the muddled confusion of the theft.
And, as the posse crosses a river, Pike blows the bridge out from under them and the
riders and their mounts fall in slow-motion into the water. There is a tense moment
after the weapons are loaded onto a wagon when it falls into a hole on the bridge and
has to be hauled out before the bridge is blown.

The action proceeds quickly to Mapache's unsuccessful defense against Pancho Villa's
troops, which causes him to retreat while eagerly awaiting his supply of weapons. Moving
over the rocky terrain with the wagon, Angel's rebel friends stealthily surround the Wild
Bunch, and the case of rifles and ammunition are given to them. Outmaneuvering the
generalissimo, Pike, suspecting their intent to steal the weapons, threatens to dynamite
the wagon carrying them after being confronted by his troops.

Seasoned in the art of negotiation, Pike arranges the delivery of the first shipment
of weapons for $2,500 in gold and then sets the terms for further shipments that are
hidden in the hills and can be retrieved only after payment is made. When Dutch

appears to pick up the last payment for the rifles, he is questioned about the number of cases. He lies and says sixteen, explaining that one was lost in transit. But Mapache knows otherwise and accuses Angel of stealing it, then takes him prisoner. Outnumbered and outgunned, Dutch has no choice but to submit to their demands, and he abandons Angel to them. He is guilt-ridden because Angel saved his life when he fell between the railroad cars during the attack on the train.

Pursued by Deke Thornton and the bounty hunters who wounded Freddie Sykes, Pike makes the fateful decision to return to Mapache's camp, knowing that Thornton will not follow. As the bunch rides in they are greeted by a drunken, carousing generalissimo and his troops, who are celebrating their newfound arms (including a machine gun) while dragging Angel on a rope behind his open-air automobile. They are invited to participate and the men pair up with their whores as Pike chooses a young woman with a baby who makes him think about the family he never had. Dutch is the only member of the gang who remains aloof to the revelry, instead sitting and whittling on a piece of wood, thinking about Angel. After leaving the woman, Pike becomes determined to rescue Angel and live up to his commandment of loyalty and allegiance, which he preached but did not practice.

They confront Mapache and offer gold in return for Angel, but the corrupt generalissimo responds by cutting his throat. Pike and the bunch respond by killing Mapache and his key lieutenants. Although they are badly outnumbered, the troops are momentarily stunned by the actions of the four gunmen and, after a pause, a lengthy and bloody battle ensues. This scene is one of the most violent, vivid, blood-soaked, and cathartic gunfights ever filmed, with blood spurting everywhere as the bunch uses grenades, a machine gun, and standard weapons to kill their opponents. They fight valiantly but eventually succumb to the superiority-in-numbers of the Federales. In a revealing moment, Pike turns his back on a whore and she shoots him. He then turns around, utters the expletive "bitch," and kills her. As Pike and Dutch lay wounded on the ground, Pike calls Dutch a lazy bastard and he grabs the machine gun, with Dutch at his side. He becomes a killing machine, relentlessly shooting everything that moves. In the end, a shot fired by a small boy in a poorly fitting uniform drops Pike, and soon Dutch succumbs, calling Pike's name. The two old gunfighters are dead, and the irony for Pike is that two of his most fatal wounds were caused by a woman and a small boy, symbolizing his unfulfilled desire and the emptiness of his emotional life.

The final moments of the film provide a resolution of the conflict between Pike, Deke Thornton, and the bounty hunters. The dysfunctional posse descends on the corpses to rob them of their possessions and then slings their remains over horses. Seeing his friend Pike, Thornton takes his gun as a memento, something of their past that he can cherish. Exhausted, Thornton rests outside the gates of the compound as the bounty hunters ride away. He is confronted by Sykes, who was rescued by the revolutionaires, and offers him an opportunity to ride on with them, acknowledging that it may not be the same as before, but it will do. He accepts the offer to join in the fight to free Mexico with a new "gang," while in the distance they hear gunfire, signaling the demise of the misfit posse. For Deke Thornton and Sykes, a new chapter awaits.

The violence in *The Wild Bunch* shocked and disgusted some audiences when it was released in 1969. Since then, however, it has been recognized as a quintessential example of American art that explores themes of integrity, honor, loyalty, and the iconic state of America's western heroes. Director Sam Peckinpah and his film editor, Louis

Lombardo, used the optical technical tools available to them at the time to produce a montage of images in standard- and slow-motion that contextualized the violence as part of the conflicted emotions of the main characters who embody an independent outlaw spirit, but possess a sense of humanity that sustains an altruistic feeling toward the downtrodden.

In filming the violent action sequences, perhaps six cameras were used, with various focal-length lenses. For the montages, they combined footage shot at standard- and slow-motion speeds to create a vivid sense of the action on the screen. There were 3,642 cuts in the film, which surpassed the number of edits in Eisenstein's "The Odessa Steps" sequence in *Battleship Potemkin* (http://www.filmreference.com/Films-Vi-Wi/ The-Wild-Bunch.html).

MEDIUM COOL (1969)

PRODUCER/DIRECTOR: Haskell Wexler (director), Tully Friedman (producer), Haskell Wexler (producer), Jerrold Wexler (producer)

WRITER(S): Haskell Wexler

CAST: Robert Forster (John Cassellis), Verna Bloom (Eileen), Peter Bonerz (Gus), Marianna Hill (Ruth), Harold Blankenship (Harold), Charles Geary (Buddy), Sid McCoy (Frank Baker), Christine Bergstrom (Dede), William Sickinger (News Director Karlin), Robert McAndrew (Pennybaker)

CINEMATOGRAPHY: Haskell Wexler

MUSIC: Mike Bloomfield

LENGTH AND RATING: 111 min; X

Cinematographers possess a subjective eye that views film as a canvas for telling a story that entertains and engrosses the audience in the drama of the narrative. For Haskell Wexler, the noted award-winning cinematographer, both truth and fiction are layered in every story, and those portraits help to define and nourish the mise-en-scène. His career has been built on the excellence of his technical work and by the socially aware themes of his films. These interests converged in 1968, with the movie *Medium Cool*, which thrust actors into the drama of real-life and real people into the realm of fiction.

The story evolves around the political and racial turbulence of the time and focuses on the fictional character John Cassellis (Robert Forster), a television news cameraman for Channel 8 in Chicago who loves shooting film more for its technique than its content, and who is dispassionate about his subjects. This sense of detachment is portrayed in the beginning of the film, when he and his soundman, Gus (Peter Bonerz), come upon an automobile accident scene. They record the image of the moaning victim and the wrecked car, and only after memorializing the event on camera do they call for an ambulance. At a cocktail party, a number of news camera people discuss the purpose and safety of their work, along with the power of television to tell a compelling story.

Looking for a gripping feature story, Cassellis interviews a black Chicago taxi driver who, after finding $10,000 in his cab, turns it in to the police only to face tough, accusatory questioning. Hoping to find out more about the driver, John tracks him down to a black section of Chicago, hoping to do an in-depth profile on him. However, he and Gus are greeted by hostile and militant friends of the driver, who are suspicious that

Gus is an undercover policeman, and they deliberately make him feel threatened so that he returns to the car. Unsuccessful in his attempt to get the taxi driver to cooperate, John is blocked from leaving the apartment while an actress, also black, wants to know why she doesn't get any roles and the men tell him that the media establishment, of which he is a part, does not represent them. It doesn't tell their story and while their bitterness, suspicion, and hostility resonates with him, John anxiously looks at his watch, trying to get to the next story, ignoring their claims and remaining aloof to their plight.

Visually, Haskell Wexler captures the gritty poverty of the city's ghettos, where children in torn clothes play among the garbage and in the streets. His camera unflinchingly views the discordant times of military preparedness and antiwar demonstrators. Intercut in the film is a sequence shot at a national guard base, where guardsmen are being trained to confront civil disobedience at the Chicago Democratic Convention. The men are preparing to confront the demonstrators and maintain order with their chosen weapons, which include batons and tear gas. The actors are thrust into the real action among the training soldiers, moving from fiction to reality.

These transitions also involve the other actors, including John's new love interest, Eileen (Verna Bloom), a teacher from Appalachia, West Virginia, and her son, Harold (Harold Blankenship). They meet when John mistakes Harold for a vandal near the Channel 8 station wagon as he and Gus walk toward the car in a parking lot. After John gives chase, he retrieves a wicker basket containing a homing pigeon with the boy's address. He tracks down Harold and visits his apartment, returning the pigeon while meeting and striking up a conversation with the boy's attractive mother, Eileen.

In another scene, John and Gus visit a gun club with a shooting range and interview the owner, played by Peter Boyle. During the filming, a Caucasian woman holding a gun walks in and asks a question about its operation. The effect provides a sense of fear on the part of white society as they respond to this chaotic, unruly time of civil unrest, not trusting law enforcement to protect them from harm.

A turning point for John occurs when he learns that station management has been supplying the FBI with film he has shot, thus compromising his integrity as a journalist. Ultimately, he is fired because he has angered station management by venturing into controversy, filming stories in the black ghettos and other poor sections of Chicago.

He begins a relationship with Eileen and Harold, having dinner with them and taking Harold to visit a large pigeon reserve, then returning with him to his apartment. The two have a lot in common, including that they are somewhat rootless in their search for meaning and identity. Eileen, a Vietnam War widow, has moved from Appalachia to Chicago, and John, fired from the job he loves, begins to assess his work within the context of the turbulent times.

At the Chicago Democratic convention in 1968, John works as a freelance cameraman, covering the protests and antiwar demonstrations. The scenes are chilling as Haskell Wexler depicts the brutality of the police and the National Guard troops as they confront the chanting demonstrators, beating and bloodying them with their batons. The protests are integrated into the substance of the narrative as Eileen goes searching for Harold, who is missing from their apartment. Wearing a bright yellow dress, she walks among the demonstrators, looking for Harold and bearing witness to the chaotic cruelty of the moment. Once again, fiction intrudes on the theater of reality as Eileen becomes part of the unfolding events, succumbing to the demands of the National Guard troops. Inside the convention hall, John is filming and watching the political drama as protestors are ejected and journalists, including Dan Rather and Mike Wallace of CBS News, are "roughed up."

Still desperately trying to locate her son, Eileen finds Gus, who communicates via radio with John, and the two set out to search for Harold in the Channel 8 station wagon. The car suddenly veers off the road, tumbling and crashing, and over the shot of the mangled, smoking automobile, the audio from a news report mentions the crash, naming John as one of the victims rushed to the hospital. It also mentions an unidentified female passenger, who died. Another vehicle passing the wreck slows down for pictures without stopping to help, an ironic twist on John's preoccupation with shooting film while ignoring the plight of his subjects.

As a film, *Medium Cool* is an expressive work that depicts a time in history that challenged the civil rights of all Americans. As a cinematographer, Haskell Wexler had impeccable credentials, having won an Academy Award for *Who's Afraid of Virginia Woolf?* Its imagery was so forceful and disturbing that Paramount Pictures asked him to edit the scenes of police brutality but he refused. The film wasn't released until a year after its completion and was given an X rating by the Motion Picture Association of America (MPAA) because it contained a nude scene. However, Wexler maintains that the film was labeled X because of its political content.

 MIDNIGHT COWBOY (1969)

Producer/Director: John Schlesinger (director), Jerome Hellman (producer)
Writer(s): Waldo Salt (screenplay), James Leo Herlihy (novel)
Cast: Dustin Hoffman (Ratso), Jon Voight (Joe Buck), Sylvia Miles (Cass), John McGiver (Mr. O'Daniel), Brenda Vaccaro (Shirley), Barnard Hughes (Towny), Ruth White (Sally Buck - Texas), Jennifer Salt (Annie - Texas), Gilman Rankin (Woodsy Niles - Texas), Gary Owens (Little Joe - Texas)
Cinematography: Adam Holender
Music: John Barry
Length and Rating: 113 min; X

British director John Schlesinger's first American film, an adaptation of Leo Herlihy's 1965 novel, required an instinctive sense of the cultural climate of the time and a textured understanding of the detachment felt by many Americans. The film is a study of two lonely people mired in lives of neglect and without the nurturing support of family. They are indeed outcasts like Butch and Sundance, Bonnie and Clyde, and Pike Bishop, but unlike those characters, Joe Buck (Jon Voigt) and Ratso Rizzo (Dustin Hoffman), are invisible within the urban mileu of New York City.

Through various flashbacks, a backstory is established on Joe Buck, for the most part abandoned by his mother and raised in a small Texas town by his grandmother, Sally Buck (Ruth White), who left him frozen TV dinners and a dollar for a movie while she went out on "dates" with various new beaus. It also establishes his youthful relationship with the insecure Annie (Jennifer Salt), who constantly reminds Joe that he's the only one for her. They are a sexually active couple, and one night as they are being intimate in a parked car, they are both hauled out and raped by Texas hoodlums.

The pleasurable scenes of their lovemaking are evoked by Joe as he escapes from the tawdry life of a hustler, as when he has liaisons with a young student in a movie theater. This violent episode is visualized when Joe is agitated, as when he meets a guilt–ridden, aging homosexual and beats him up, stealing his money to buy two bus tickets for himself and Ratso to Miami, Florida.

Although Joe perceives himself as a blonde Adonis with marketable skills as a male hustler with a gruff exterior, it is quickly established that he is a polite and compassionate young man. On the bus to New York, he gives a piece of gum to a young girl traveling with her mother and lowers the brim of his cowboy hat, scrunching his face toward her. He addresses all women as ma'am and is both accommodating and respectful. When the young gay student in the movie theater tells Joe that he's broke and can't pay, they struggle over the watch he's wearing and the student pleads that he cannot return home without it because his mother would be distraught. Towering over the student, Joe can easily take the watch but he doesn't and instead leaves the men's room without harming the boy.

Leaving his drab Texas room, Joe postures before the mirror and heads down to his dishwashing job at Miller's restaurant. He is expected to begin his shift at 4:00 P.M. but instead asks for his last paycheck. His naiveté and idealism are in direct opposition to Enrico "Ratso" Rizzo, an urban denizen weasel with a tubercular cough, a limp, and a nasal voice that is part of the coarse underbelly and the detritus remains of the inner city. Although Joe tries to appear as a tough cowboy, Ratso, whose instincts have been honed by a lifetime of grifting, conning, and lying, recognizes that Joe is a nice guy.

Riding a bus nearing New York City and sitting next to a nun, Joe listens to a portable radio that picks up WABC, a local New York radio call-in station that features women discussing the attributes of an ideal man, and after hearing their commentary he howls, thinking the descriptons fit him like a glove.

Once in New York, Joe's first encounters with potential female "clients" are a comedy of errors. One woman summarily dismisses him, saying he should be ashamed of himself, while another, Cass (Sylvia Miles), is a prostitute in a fancy Park Avenue apartment who invites Joe up for a free tryst and is outraged when he asks to be paid for his services. Following her rage are tears, which Joe succumbs to, half-heartedly joking that he wasn't really asking her for money. He offers Cass cab fare to her next date and she helps herself to a twenty-dollar bill from his wallet. These scenes quickly establish that Joe Buck is not cut out to be a hustler, that he is slow-witted but compassionate.

He meets Ratso in a crummy bar and the hustler immediately becomes the hustled. Impressed by Ratso's urban shrewdness, Joe immediately agrees to his offer of management. For a modest fee, Ratso agrees to arrange for Joe to meet O'Daniel (John McGiver), a pimp with a client list of wealthy women with social stature. He, of course, turns out to be a Bible-thumping, psychotic fraud, and this causes Joe severe flashbacks to the day he was baptized, and he flees. Evicted from his room and down on his luck, he runs into Ratso at a local diner. Fearing physical harm, Ratso takes the loose change from his pocket and then offers Joe shelter at his apartment in a condemned building.

These two men, the good-looking golden boy from Texas and the slimy, unkempt, and limping conman from the Bronx, have a great deal in common. They both have led lives of neglect while surviving on the edge of society, and they have dreams that may be unrealistic but are nevertheless enduring. And they have their demons. Joe's are his nightmarish flashbacks of the rape, which put Annie in an asylum. And Ratso, who wants to be called by his given name Enrico or Rico, dreams of respect and going to Florida, his halcyon for curing his limp and turbuculosis. He carries the shame of his illiterate father, Dominic, who was a shoeshine boy barely scraping together a living.

Just as Joe's business starts to improve after servicing (with some pre-Viagra delay) Shirley (Brenda Vaccaro), a society woman who starts to network with her friends for Joe's services, he returns to their hovel to find Ratso deathly ill. He hustles the elderly, self-loathing gay executive stealing his money and he and Ratso board a bus for Miami. On the bus, the relationship between the two men becomes poignant, with Joe caring for Ratso and making sure he's covered with blankets and buying him new clothes after he wets himself in an "unscheduled" rest stop. Eagerly searching for the respect he desires, Ratso reminds Joe that when they reach Miami he wants to be known as Rico, beginning his new life with dignity. Just outside Miami, Rico dies, and as the people on the bus stretch to ogle at him after being reassured by the driver that "it's just a little illness," Joe places his arm around his friend, holding him close and protecting Rico from their prying eyes.

In his May 26, 1969, *New York Times* review of *Midnight Cowboy*, Vincent Canby describes the film as, "tough and good in important ways." He also portrays the gritty Manhattan world of Joe and Ratso: "As long as the focus is on this world of cafeterias and abandoned tenements, of desperate conjunctions in movie balconies and doorways, of catsup and beans and canned heat, *Midnight Cowboy* is so rough and vivid that it's almost unbearable" (http://www.movies.nytimes.com/movies/review).

The sixties was a time of alienation and distrust, and in *Midnight Cowboy*, two lost souls found each other in a confused world of hedonistic pleasure and detachment. They form an unlikely bond, caring for each other in the midst of turbulence and agonizing despair.

The film won Academy Awards for Best Picture (the first X-rated film to earn that distinction), Best Director (John Schlesinger), and Best Screenplay (Waldo Salt, a formerly blacklisted writer).

6 Platform Shoes, Pet Rocks, Disco, and a Dysfunctional Presidency, 1970–1979

"In the United States today, we have more than our share of the nattering nabobs of negativism." Known as President Nixon's hatchet man, Vice President Spiro Agnew was the alter ego of the president, spewing forth alliterated phrases (such as "nattering nabobs," written by speechwriter William Safire) condemning liberals and antiwar protestors. He was accused of taking bribes while he was governor of Maryland, and he resigned the office of vice president in 1973 (succeeded by Gerald Ford), a harbinger of Nixon's disgraced departure from office. However, in 1972, Nixon made an historic trip to China, the first American president to visit the country. As a result of that trip and his meeting with Mao Zedong, the U.S. eventually withdrew from Vietnam and forged new political and trade alliances with China.

It was a time when Americans doubted their leaders, as four antiwar student demonstrators were killed and nine wounded by the Ohio National Guardsmen patrolling the campus of Kent State University. In 1971, the top secret *Pentagon Papers* were released, discrediting Nixon's war policies in Vietnam. And, in 1970, the first Gay Pride march was held in New York City. In 1973, America reeled as energy prices skyrocketed from the first Arab oil embargo, demonstrating a newly empowered Middle East, and abortion was legalized under *Roe v. Wade*. After enduring withering condemnation over Watergate, Nixon resigned in 1974 and Gerald Ford replaced him.

The 1972 summer Olympics in Munich, Germany, were a cause for celebration and a time for mourning. American swimmer Mark Spitz won seven gold medals, and the tragic massacre of eleven Israeli athletes by the terrorist Black September group would be a haunting legacy of Olympic competition. Baseball welcomed a new champion in 1974, when Hank Aaron broke Babe Ruth's home run record, and in 1973 Roberto Clemente was the first Latino to be inducted into the Baseball Hall of Fame. The first *Star Wars* movie was released in 1977, and that same year, about three decades before the television hit *Dancing with the Stars*, the movie *Saturday Night Fever* became the rage, catapulting actor John Travolta to stardom. Ordinary heroes were celebrated in the movies *Rocky*, starring Sylvester Stallone, and Steven Spielberg's *Jaws*, which featured a menacing killer shark and a water-challenged sheriff played by actor Roy Scheider. As a film that changes behavioral patterns of an audience and imposes a high level of fear, *Jaws* ranks equal to Alfred Hitchcock's *Psycho*.

The entertainment industry was revolutionized by the introduction of the video cassette recorder in 1975, and the invention of the first microprocessor, the Intel 4004, in 1971 would serve as a harbinger to the coming technological revolution which would create a new information order, including computers, cell phones, and PDAs.

In 1979, America's worst nuclear energy accident occurred at the Three Mile Island Unit 2 (TMI-2) nuclear power plant near Middletown, Pennsylvania. Although there were no deaths or injuries, the potential hazard of a partial-core meltdown and the serious errors made by the plant technicians launched an investigation that resulted in regulatory oversight modifications. The irony is that just twelve days before the Three Mile Island accident, on March 16, the film *The China Syndrome*, starring Jane Fonda and Michael Douglas, was released depicting an incident remarkably similar to the one that occurred near Middletown.

PATTON (1970)

PRODUCER/DIRECTOR: Franklin J. Schaffner (director), Frank McCarthy (producer)
WRITER(S): Ladislas Farago (book), Omar N. Bradley (book), Francis Ford Coppola (screen story), Edmund H. North (screen story)
CAST: George C. Scott (Gen. George S. Patton, Jr.), Karl Malden (Gen. Omar N. Bradley), Stephen Young (Capt. Chester B. Hansen), Michael Strong (Brig. Gen. Hobart Carver), Carey Loftin (Gen. Bradley's driver), Albert Dumortier (Moroccan Minister), Frank Latimore (Lt. Col. Henry Davenport), Morgan Paull (Capt. Richard N. Jenson), Karl Michael Vogler (Field Marshal Erwin Rommel), Bill Hickman (Gen. Patton's driver)
CINEMATOGRAPHY: Fred J. Koenekamp
MUSIC: Jerry Goldsmith
LENGTH AND RATING: 170 min; PG

Movies about wars take on various dimensions that sometimes create revisionist history, sustaining the glories of the past. In the end, war movies such as *Saving Private Ryan* (1995), *Platoon* (1986), and *The Bridge on the River Kwai* (1957) are about sacrifice, patriotism, and heroes. They are also about winning, with the spoils of war going to the victors.

There was little doubt that America's participation in World War II was a noble effort to save the world from tyranny and preserve democracy. Therefore, by definition, US troops and their allies could be immortalized on film as iconic heroes destined for eternal homage.

Patton takes the heroism and glory from earlier war movies and integrates those qualities into one character, General George S. Patton. He's a hero, with many faults, but as a general he is dedicated to his troops, his country, and his God. His personality was very complex, and although he was a devout Christian, Patton believed in reincarnation and that he had been a general leading troops to battle in ancient times. Although dyslexic (he didn't learn to read until the age of twelve), Patton was an avid reader. He loved drama and cut a dramatic figure in his custom tailored uniforms and vintage, ivory-handled revolvers: a Smith & Wesson .357 Magnum and a Colt .45 (circa 1873). But what drives this film's narrative is the Shakespearean construct of the tragic hero, one who, despite his brilliance and fortitude, is bent on self-destructiveness.

The film was released during America's unpopular war in Vietnam. Although President Nixon had pledged to bring the troops home and committed to replacing

American GIs with Vietnamese soldiers, on April 30, 1970, he announced on national television that the U.S. Army had invaded Cambodia to stop the North Vietnamese military from supplying their troops in the south. The following month, on May 4, 1970, during student demonstrations against the Cambodia invasion held on the campus of Ohio's Kent State University, four students were killed and nine wounded when National Guardsmen fired on the crowd. It was a moment of anguish for Americans, who had to deal with the loss of innocence and faith in their leaders.

Americans were desperately searching for meaning, purpose, and a sense of legitimacy. When *Patton* was released, it served as a reminder of a great nation's call to arms, serving the greater good of humankind. It was also a tribute to an American hero who embodied the spirit and idealism that had been buried in the morass of Vietnam.

True to the spirit of the film and its main character, the opening scene establishes the gritty substance of the man as he walks up from behind the stage, in his tailored uniform and metal helmet, saluting the troops before him as a bugle sounds. He holds the salute and the scene is intercut with close-ups of his numerous medals and service awards, his cavalry riding whip, knee-high leather riding boots, and ivory handled gun. This is a defining scene, as Patton appears before a huge American flag, its red, white, and blue colors bathing its subject in a giant hue of patriotism. His opening remarks to the troops reveal a great deal about his character as he admonishes, "No bastard ever won a war by dying for his country, he won it by making the other poor dumb bastard die for his country." And then he tells them that Americans love to fight and love the sting of battle. He continues by letting the troops know that Americans love a winner and will not tolerate a loser and that they play to win all the time. Then he proclaims that Americans have never lost and will never lose a war. He lets the troops know that he pities the soldiers who are going to fight because they are not only going to shoot them but will cut out their living guts and use them to grease the treads of their tanks, murdering the Huns by the bushel. He goes on to warn them that he will not tolerate any messages that they are holding a position; his strategy is to keep advancing. He then tells the gathered soldiers, "I will be proud to lead you wonderful guys into battle any time, anywhere."

This opening scene and its dialogue provide a mesmerizing portrait of a career soldier: his patriotism, dedication, bravery, discipline, and will to win. It also establishes the character and tone of the film and is a harbinger of the narrative and action to unfold on the screen. It adheres to the classical elements of the Hollywood war film, which portrays the American soldier as an icon of heroism, representing the best of American idealism. In addition, it provides a sympathetic view of the American cause, offering a sound rationale for going to war: protecting the ideals of democracy while fighting the horrors of tyranny.

The films made about World War II were a tribute to the bravery and fortitude of the American fighting man. They were a testimony to the soldier's spirit, compassion, and determination to protect and serve. There was no doubting the American cause as a just one, unlike those films addressing Vietnam and the wars in Afghanistan and Iraq.

The culture of American war films can be categorized into a number of genres and sub-genres, including realistic docudrama, naval and submarine battles, infantry, the Civil War, antiwar, prisoners of war, revisionist historical analysis, returning veterans and disabled veterans, the enemy's story, and many more. Many of these movies reflect the political climate of the time, mirroring American attitudes during times of war and peace. This is what makes *Patton* so interesting. Released during a time of protest over America's role in Vietnam and Indochina, *Patton* presents a contrarian point of view of classic military might and heroism. Indeed, it is a vivid portrayal of a soldier who felt destined to fight in the most epic of battles, demonstrating the virtues of patriotism, teamwork, discipline, and leadership, rallying the troops to defeat the enemy.

The film follows Patton's command of troops from North Africa to Sicily and as he leads the Third Army across Europe through France and into Germany. In thirty-eight days, he leads the American Seventh Army while General Sir Bernard Montgomery leads the British Eighth Army to conquer Sicily. As the leader of the Third Army on the western front, his troops of armor and infantry roar through six countries, France, Belgium, Luxembourg, Germany, Czechoslovakia, and Austria, and capture more than 750,000 Nazis while killing or disabling 500,000 other enemy troops. On March 22, 1944, Patton leads the Third Army across the German Rhine River and attacks without the cover of air or artillery, surprising the enemy by landing on the east bank without a single casualty. While many of these heroic battles are depicted in the film, they are just part of the story about Patton, the man, his strength and his foibles as a soldier trained in the classic form of battle, troubled by modernization and the politics of war. His fighting spirit and dedication to his troops are a theme of the film as it profiles his determination to win. He was also a poet who decreed that his poetry could not be published until after his death, and was also noted for his fierce public comments like, "We shall attack and attack until we are exhausted, and then we shall attack again." Such comments earned him the nickname "Old Blood and Guts."

As the film *Patton* demonstrates, the general had little patience for malingerers or shirkers and was dedicated to military decorum and discipline. He also had a reverence for bravery and little tolerance for cowardice. This is established in two field hospital scenes, one where he tells doctors to remove soldiers with self-inflicted wounds because they do not deserve to be among the brave, injured men, and in another when he slaps a young shell-shocked soldier with his leather riding gloves (in reality, Private Charles H. Kuhl, L Company, 26th Infantry, 1st Division), accusing him of being a yellowbelly and ordering him back to the front. Later, medics determine that the soldier is suffering from dysentery and malaria. Apparently, during the Sicilian campaign, Patton slapped another soldier, Private Paul G. Bennet. These incidents, along with impolitic political comments, delayed congressional approval of his fourth star and resulted in his being relieved of command of his beloved Third Army (*New York Times* 1945, p. 5.).

The movie captures the personality of a soldier and leader of mythic proportions, one of the most respected, revered, and maligned military generals of all time. In his February 5, 1970, review of the film, Vincent Canby writes about the spectacle of the film and its controversial subject:

It's both fascinating and appalling the sort of extravagant technically superior spectacle that only a big Hollywood movie company could afford to make, and the story of a man about whom only the Establishment could become genuinely sentimental. Patton, the movie keeps telling us, is "a magnificent anachronism," "a 16th-century man lost in the 20th century," a man who damn well loved war, was surprised and somewhat taken aback when men near to him were killed, who wrote poetry, quoted the Bible, had the political instincts of a California grape and was, according to those who knew him best, basically decent.

🎥 *M*A*S*H* (1970)

PRODUCER/DIRECTOR: Robert Altman (director), Ingo Preminger (producer)

WRITER(S): Richard Hooker (novel), Ring Lardner, Jr. (screenplay)

CAST: Donald Sutherland (Capt. Benjamin Franklin "Hawkeye" Pierce), Elliott Gould (Capt. "Trapper John" McIntyre), Tom Skerritt (Capt. Augustus "Duke" Forrest), Sally Kellerman (Maj. Margaret "Hot Lips" O'Houlihan), Robert Duvall (Maj. "Frank" Burns), Roger Bowen (Lt. Col. Henry Blake), Rene Auberjonois (Father Mulcahy), David Arkin (SSgt. Wade Douglas Vollmer), Jo Ann Pflug (Lt. Maria "Dish" Schneider), Gary Burghoff (Cpl. Walter "Radar" O'Reilly)

CINEMATOGRAPHY: Harold E. Stine

MUSIC: Johnny Mandel

LENGTH AND RATING: 116 min; R

Heroism in the 1970s was measured within the context of a time of protest, a feeling of disenfranchisement, and a lingering suspicion of the military industrial complex. In *Patton*, audiences learned about the exploits of a fearless Amercian general and his respect for the virtues of the military and its creed. The film *M*A*S*H*, however, presented an irreverent and iconoclastic look at war from the perspective of those who condemned and villfied its pretensions, traditions, pecking order, and ranks.

*M*A*S*H* is just one piece of the creative work of director Robert Altman, who had a profound influence on film. The 1970s provided an opportunity for Altman to define his "voice" by producing films that were irreverent, satirical, and sometimes troubling. In addition to *M*A*S*H*, he produced a staggering fifteen films in the 1970s, including *Brewster McCloud* (1970), *McCabe and Mrs. Miller* (1971), *Images* (1972), *The Long Goodbye* (1973), *Thieves Like Us* (1974), *California Split* (1974), *Nashville* (1975), *Buffalo Bill and the Indians* (1976), *Sitting Bull's History Lesson* (1976), *Three Women* (1977), and *Quintet* (1979).

Altman defied traditional film genres, deconstructing them to fulfill his vision and voice. His subject could be very personal and intimate or it could be a study of an American institution (for example, the military in *M*A*S*H*) and a portrait of its dysfunction. As younger directors (Altman was 45 when he made *M*A*S*H*) embraced the stylistic rebellion against the hallowed traditions of filmmaking, Altman had already devoted a lifetime to articulating his disdain for those values. He began his career in industrial films and then moved to episodic television (*Maverick, Lawman, Peter Gunn, Bonanza, Hawaiian Eye, Route 66*) before making feature films (*The Delinquents*, 1957; *Countdown*, 1968; *That Cold Day in the Park*, 1969). Altman thrived on innovation, collaboration, and improvisation. Always seeking new ways to tell a story, he developed the technique of multi-layered sound, which gave an added sense of reality to his films. He railed against the mythology of various cinematic genres, redefining them with a desperate sense of reality as he did in the film *McCabe and Mrs. Miller* (1971). Altman explained his attitude as a kind of rebellion against clichés, saying that he didn't like Westerns, and he "pictured a story with every Western cliche in it." He also wanted to look at it "through a different window," but "still wanted to keep the poetry in the ballad." (Lyman, Rick. 2006. "Robert Altman, Icono-clastic Director, Dies at 81." *New York Times*, November 21).

In addition to *M*A*S*H*, Altman's *Nashville* is considered a brilliant ensemble film involving twenty-four chartacters whose lives weave in and out of the narrative. Film critic Pauline Kael described the film as "an organic style of movie making" and said that it was "an evolutionary leap" using a multiple-track sound system and telling a story "without the clanking of plot."

Of all the films Altman produced, *M*A*S*H* was his most significant because of its critical and box office success. Although the subject is the rebellious doctors Haweye Pierce (Donald Sutherland), Duke Forrest (Tom Skerritt), and Trapper John McIntire (Elliot Gould) working at a Mobile Army Surgical Hospital during the Korean War, its release in 1970, during America's conflict in Vietnam, embraced the sentiments of a war-weary and suspicious American public.

It's an irreverent view of military bureaucracy, incompetence, and waste and the doctors who rebel against the status quo. In the film, Altman and screenwriter Ring Lardner, Jr. poke fun at other "hallowed" institutions, including marital fidelity, religion, and race relations. The conflict in the film exists between surgeons Hawkeye Pierce, Duke Forrest, and Trapper John McIntire, and the rigid military protocol propagated by Major Frank Burns (Robert Duvall) and the new head of nursing, Major Margaret "Hot Lips" O'Houlihan (Sally Kellerman). As surgeons, they are devoted to their craft and are experts in their speciality. The operating room scenes in the film have a compelling real-ism but the harsh reality is mediated by a cavalier yet caring atmosphere punctuated by sexual entendres that provide relief from the bleakness of the task at hand. And, life and death decisions are made with certainty and some detachment, as when Duke Forrest asks Father Mulcahy (Renee Auberjonois), who is administering last rites, to leave the dying soldier's side and assist him by holding a surgical instrument for another soldier. His rationale is that the effort must be placed to aid the living and not the dying.

Adding to a dimension of farce are the frequent fumbled announcements over the public address system, such as the broadcast for Yom Kippur holiday services that must be postponed to Sunday (the holiday must be observed on a particular day). These serve as a metaphor for the insanity of the environment, with its constant influx of helicopters laden with wounded soldiers requiring urgent medical assistance.

To relieve the tension, the doctors, nurses, and staff occupy themselves by making Majors O'Houlihan and Burns the victims of their practical jokes. In one scene, a microphone is surreptitiously placed in Major O'Houlihan's quarters to monitor her and Burn's lovemaking and is then fed through the public address system to broadcast their passionate liaison to the entire camp, including the operating room, resulting in her nickname "Hot Lips." In another scene, Duke Forrest claims that Major O'Houlihan's blonde hair is dyed and places a twenty-dollar bet to confirm his suspicion. The issue that must be resolved is a means to determine her true hair color. A clever scheme is devised to expose Major O'Houlihan as she showers, and the doctors, nurses, and staff encamp on lawn chairs, awaiting the appropriate moment when the sides of the tent are raised, exposing her to a leering and applauding crowd.

Although the surgeons may appear selfish and preoccupied with their libidos, their devotion to medicine and their patients is sustained through their actions. When Hawkeye Pierce and Trapper John McIntire are summoned to Tokyo to operate on the wounded son of a congressman, they call themselves "The Pros from Dover" and, dressed in golfing attire, they "invade" the hospital, disregarding protocol, demanding the latest "pictures" on their patient, and asking for a nurse to assist who will keep her tits out of the way. Appalled at their presumption, the colonel in charge threatens them with arrest and they use their wit to blackmail him with a threatened call to the congressman, whose son's life they have saved. When Hawkeye and Trapper are asked by a colleague to treat the sick baby of a local geisha, they immediately respond by removing the child to the military hospital and performing surgery to the objections of the colonel and the head nurse.

Some of the most irreverent moments in the movie are the scenes featuring Captain Walter Waldoski (John Schuck), aka "painless" and known as the best-equipped dentist in the army, and his loss of faith in his sexual prowess. His announcement of impending suicide is greeted under the guise of aloofness by his friends and colleagues, who arrange to assist him in their attempt to reinvigorate his confidence. To authenticate the ruse, Hawkeye Pierce asks Father Mulcahy to offer Waldoski absolution, but the gentle and confused priest initially demures because he cannot save the soul of someone who is about to commit suicide, but finally he concedes. The action then moves to the evening when the surgeons, staff, and Waldoski are seated and arranged like the painting of the "Last Supper" and then "painless" is placed in an open coffin and given the black suicide pill (a sleeping pill) as the spectators walk by, offering him their best wishes and handing him mementos for his journey to the ever after. When Waldoski is asleep, they move him into a tent and Pierce enlists his nurse girlfriend, who is returning home the next day and assumes one last liaison with him, to sleep with Waldoski. She resists but acquieces when Pierce raises Waldoski's sheets to reveal his above-standard "equipment."

The film is a testament to challenging authority and the traditions of organized institutions, including the military, government, religion, and marriage. Although its setting is Korea, the theme has a timeless relevancy to America's leadership in the post-World War II world. War is never pretty and its visual imagery is fraught with controversy and concern. It's never pleasant to witness soldiers in body bags or the severely wounded who have lost limbs or suffered blindness. Robert Altman bathes his satire within the context of humor, which makes an even more profound statement on the destructiveness of these ritualistic moral constructs. It is a timeless portrait of disdain for the ineptness of leadership and the costs endured.

A CLOCKWORK ORANGE (1971)

Producer/Director: Stanley Kubrick

Writer(s): Stanley Kubrick (screenplay), Anthony Burgess (novel)

Cast: Malcolm McDowell (Alex), Patrick Magee (Mr. Alexander), Michael Bates (Chief Guard), Warren Clarke (Dim), John Clive (Stage Actor), Adrienne Corri (Mrs. Alexander), Carl Duering (Dr. Brodsky), Paul Farrell (Tramp), Clive Francis (Lodger), Michael Gover (Prison Governor)

Cinematography: John Alcott

Music: Wendy Carlos (composer, electronic music)

Length and Rating: 136 min; X

Based on the Anthony Burgess novel, Stanley Kubrick's film, *A Clockwork Orange*, presents a picture of a crumbling, sadistic society that has forsaken the rule of order and violated its citizens by neutering their constructive individualism while

Malcolm McDowell (as Alexander de Large). [Warner Bros./Photofest]

compromising their values. It portrays violence in a somewhat detached manner as its main character Alex de Large (Malcom McDowell) pursues his bizarre fantasies in the real world, leading a gang on a rampage of random violence and brutal rape.

Film critic Pauline Kael notes that the number of rapes and beatings are devoid of any sensuality and bemoans the repellent state of Stanley Kubrick, the "clean-minded pornographer." She writes:

> Is there anything sadder—and ultimately more repellent—than a clean-minded pornographer? The numerous rapes and beatings have no ferocity and no sensuality; they're frigidly, pedantically calculated, and because there is no motivating emotion, the viewer may experience them as an indignity and wish to leave.
>
> The movie's confusing—and, finally, corrupt—morality is not, however, what makes it such an abhorrent viewing experience. It is offensive long before one perceives where it is heading, because it has no shadings. Kubrick, a director with an arctic spirit, is determined to be pornographic, and he has no talent for it. ("Strangely Strangelove," *The New Yorker*, January 1972)

The title of the film has its origins in British culture and Cockney slang. As a clockwork, it could mean an artificial robot, and orange could refer it to an orangutan, an ape-like animal. The slang reference is "as queer as a clockwork orange," which indicates abnormal or bizarre internal behavior while outwardly human appearance parades as normal. The film is based on the Anthony Burgess novel, which created a lingua franca of punk vocabulary, a blend of English and Russian slang. The irony is that in modern rap/gang culture there is a vibrant language that defines their essence within a hierarchy of their behavioral dynamic.

In the opening scene of the movie, a close-up of Alex reveals a figure with cast-down blue eyes and one false eyelash (upper and lower), with a menacing stare. The camera slowly zooms out, revealing his gang of "droogs," which include Georgie (James Marcus), Dim (Warren Clarke), and Pete (Michael Tam). They are drinking drug-spiked milk ("milk plus") in the Korova Milkbar, surrounded by nude female mannequins in various submissive postures. In his own voice, Alex introduces his "crew" and tells of the brew they are drinking, which will "sharpen you up and make you ready for a bit of the old ultra-violence." Wearing white suits, suspenders, black combat boots, derbies, and external athletic supporters they are ready for an evening of lustful random acts of violence, including beating an old drunk who decries the breakdown of law and order and the abuses by the youth toward the older generation. Then Alex and his droogs come upon a rival gang, Billyboy and his four droogs dressed in partial Nazi uniforms, at the abandoned casino about to gang rape a young victim, or as Alex describes, "a little of the old in-out." At that moment, Alex prefers to fight rather than rape and the two gangs go at it until the wail of a police siren forces them to flee in a stolen sports car. In one of the most vivid and disturbing scenes in the film, Alex and his boys descend on the upper-class country home of writer Frank Alexander (Patrick Magee) and his wife (Adrienne Corri) and gain entrance ("home invasion" in today's parlance) by feigning a terrible accident. Once inside they terrorize the couple, beating Frank while raping his wife in his presence. The stylized rape scene is accompanied by Alex wearing a phallic nose and singing the lyrics to "Singin' in the Rain" while slowly cutting away her skin-tight one-piece red suit. He first cuts two holes for each breast and then cuts up the pant leg, removing the entire suit to expose her naked body, and then performs the "old in-out."

The next day Alex tells his mother Em (Shelia Raynor) that he has a pain in his Gulliver and cannot go to school. Later in the morning, there is a surprise visit from his social worker, Mr. Deltoid (Aubrey Morris), who appears to have a sleazy attraction to Alex and questions him about the attack on Billyboy and his droogs the night before. Remaining calm and cool, Alex denies any association with the event. Surprised by the appearance of his droogs in the lobby of his apartment building, Alex confronts their mutinous behavior by attempting to assert himself as their leader. Later, while walking along the flatbox marina, Alex takes action, battering Georgie and Dim and throwing them in the water, thus reasserting his leadership.

His droogs gain their revenge by setting Alex up for a home invasion of the Woodmere Health Farm, run by Miss Weathers (Miriam Karlin). Attempting the same entry technique as the night before by feigning a tragic accident, they are denied access by Miss Weathers, who recognizes the ruse from newspaper accounts of the earlier attacks and notifies the police. After gaining entry through an upstairs window, Alex confronts a defiant Miss Weathers and wards off her attacks with a fully realized model of a penis with testicles. He smashes her head, killing her with a Beethoven statue and, hearing a police siren, meets his droogs out front and they bash him with a bottle of milk, knocking him down. He is sentenced to fourteen years in prison but is chosen by the government for a reclamation conditioning experiment called "aversion therapy" that is the hallmark of their plan to save money and address prison overcrowding by changing the violent behavior patterns of criminals.

Drugged and forced to watch violent and sexually erotic films, Alex is eventually cured and becomes a soulless being devoid of character and personality. There is an inadvertent side effect of the therapy, as Beethoven's Ninth Symphony, fourth movement, is played under a violent film: Although an avid fan of the composer, Alex can no longer tolerate that piece of music.

After his release from prison, Alex must confront the people from his violent past.

Upon his return home, his finds that his parents have rented his room to a young male lodger who has taken Alex's place as their surrogate son, and he is cast out. He meets the old drunk on the street and is beaten up by him and his cronies and is saved by two policemen, who turn out to be his former droog buddies, Georgie and Dim, who take him out to the country, beat him, and hold his head under water in a trough. Fleeing, he winds up at the Alexander home and is taken in by the wheelchair-bound Mr. Alexander and his manservant. At first he goes unrecognized but after hearing him sing "Singin' in the Rain," Alexander remembers who he is. They give him dinner, spike his wine, and with friends who want to embarrass the government, lock him in an attic room, playing Beethoven's Ninth Symphony, fourth movement. Unable to endure listening to the music, Alex crashes through the window but survives and is nursed back to health in a private hospital ward. The government has taken a renewed interest in him and he is visited by the Minister of the Interior, who apologizes for the misguided aversion therapy and strikes a bargain with Alex, offering him a high-paying job if he'll work with the party. They strike a bargain and the press enters, along with several large floral arrangements and two giant audio speakers that blast the music of "Ode to Joy," from Beethoven's Ninth.

In the final scene, Alex is seen cavorting in the snow with a naked woman, being watched and politely applauded by proper Victorian ladies and gentlemen. Then the viewer hears this voice-over by Alex: "I was cured all right."

Alex has been transformed from victim to hero, becoming the poster boy for the government and cashing in on their need for his forgiveness and support and exposing their hypocrisy. He is no longer a robot and has reclaimed his sexuality and violent behavior. There is redemption and forgiveness in his return to free will, no matter what the consequences may be.

In his *New York Times* review of December 20, 1971, Vincent Canby calls the movie "brilliant," "beautiful," and "a tour de force of extraordinary images, music, words and feelings." He also writes that the film "dazzles the senses and the mind, even as it turns the old real red vino to ice."

THE FRENCH CONNECTION (1971)

PRODUCER/DIRECTOR: William Friedkin (director), Philip D'Antoni (producer)
WRITER(S): Ernest Tidyman (screenplay), Robin Moore (book)
CAST: Gene Hackman (Jimmy Doyle), Fernando Rey (Alain Charnier), Roy Scheider (Det. Buddy Russo), Tony Lo Bianco (Sal Boca), Marcel Bozzuffi (Pierre Nicoli), Frédéric de Pasquale (Devereaux), Bill Hickman (Mulderig), Ann Rebbot (Marie Charnier), Harold Gary (Weinstock), Arlene Farber (Angie Boca)
CINEMATOGRAPHY: Owen Roizman
MUSIC: Don Ellis
LENGTH AND RATING: 104 min; R

The director of *The French Connection*, William Friedkin, acknowledged a debt to the French New Wave films of the 1950s and 1960s, along with the American classics of the 1930s, '40s, and '50s, saying that his work and the work of other directors in the 1970s was a synthesis of these cinematic styles. This film is mostly about Jimmy "Popeye" Doyle (Gene Hackman) and his partner, Buddy "Cloudy" Russo (Roy Scheider), New York City narcotic detectives who use some very unorthodox means to track down drug dealers and smugglers. The film portrays Popeye as a tireless crusading cop with an attitude and willing to use any means at his disposal to catch the bad guys and punish them.

It is a richly textured film that portrays a city in decline, with the criminals having an advantage while the police struggle to keep up. Although Popeye Doyle has many character flaws, including being a racist, he is relentless in tracking down the users, pushers, and other social miscreants.

The film is based on Robin Moore's book *The French Connection: A True Account of Cops, Narcotics and International Conspiracy*. The book documents the tireless investigation by New York City narcotic detectives Eddie Egan (Doyle) and Sonny Grosso (Russo), who act on a hunch to uncover what was probably the largest drug bust in New York City history. The screenplay was written by Ernest Tidyman and produced by Phillip D'Antoni, who also produced the film *Bullit* (1968), starring Steve McQueen, who played a no–nonsense, free-spirited San Francisco detective. Both films offered break out roles for their stars, as well as realistically choreographed car chases, and *The French Connection* was the third-highest grossing film of 1971.

Many film reviewers cite the gritty naturalism of the film that gives the character settings and situations a vivid sense of realism. It's not surprising that the film has a cinema verite look to it because Friedkin had worked in documentaries and made extensive use of handheld cameras. Scenes were shot on the streets of New York City and in the French city of Marseilles, both of which provide a unique kind of authenticity. To achieve this look and feel, Friedkin minimally rehearsed his actors, relying more upon their instincts and their freedom to ad-lib. Also, Hackman and Scheider spent a few weeks with Egan and Grosso, accompanying them on drug raids to bars. In one of many memorable scenes, the two detectives enter a Brooklyn bar and Doyle grabs a man who is leaving, pushes him back inside, and unplugs the jukebox, announcing:

Alright, Popeye's here. Put your hands on your head, get off the bar, and get on the wall.

As the "patrons" move from the bar to the wall, vials of drugs and assorted pills drop to the floor. Doyle confronts a man who drops a vial, telling him to pick it up and asking, "What's my name?" The man responds with"Doyle" and the detective responds with "What?" and the man corrects himself by saying "Mister Doyle." Then Popeye utters his signature line "you pick your feet?" and shoves the man back against the wall. Tough-guy Popeye takes his porkpie hat off and moves his hand under the extended lip of the bar, collecting additional drugs and paraphernalia. Two men are arrested and told to lock themselves in separate telephone booths. Seeing his "snitch," Popeye rousts him and takes him into the bathroom for information. The snitch tells him that there's a big shipment of drugs coming in to New York and everyone's going to get well. To validate the interaction, Popeye punches the snitch in the mouth and roughs him up in front of the other patrons in the bar.

The film pays homage to the crusading cop who lives for the job and has no personal life. Following a hunch, Popeye and Russo tail Sal Boca (Tony Lo Bianco) and his wife Angie (Arlene Farber), small-time hoodlums who are entertaining other notable thugs at an East-side Manhattan club. To Popeye the table is "definitely wrong" and the pursuit begins.

The movie's opening scene is a harbinger of the kinetic action to come, as well as an introduction to the characters. The parallel cutting between Marseille and New York City displays a contretemps of similarities and compelling distinctions, with the two cities sharing a worn, decaying look. In Marseille, hit man Marcel Bozuffi (Pierre Nicoli), partner of the mastermind criminal Alain Charnier (Fernando Rey), is tracking a French detective and confronts him in the hallway of his building, shoots him in the face, and tears a piece from the baguette the detective has just purchased. In New York, Popeye is undercover as a street Santa Claus while Russo is posing as a "dirty water" hot dog man and they both chase a fleet-footed black man, whom they suspect of dealing drugs.

The plot centers on a shipment of heroin (the drug du jour of the seventies) hidden in the rocker panels of a Lincoln Continental and unwittingly escorted by French television star Henri Devereaux (Frederic de Pasquale). As the narrative progresses, the boring routine of police surveillance is seen as the two detectives wait outside in the cold to follow their subjects. The New York City subway is also featured in the film as Popeye follows the debonair Charnier underground and is finally outwitted by the French man, who waves from the window of a departing subway car. In the movie's other subway scene, and one of the most famous chase segments in American film, the hit man tries to ambush Popeye from the rooftop of his building while he is walking toward his apartment. Popeye chases him on foot to a Brooklyn elevated subway line but the man eludes him and he flags down a car and races under the "El" to catch his suspect. He continues pursuit in the car as the hit man shoots a cop on the train, along with the conductor after ordering the motorman to pass the next station. Succumbing to the tension, the motorman suffers a heart attack, the subway train crashes, and the stunned hit man makes his way to the elevated station and, descending the stairs, is greeted and shot dead by Popeye Doyle.

The movie ends when the police surround the meeting point for the heroin sale and Popeye searches a slimy, wet, abandoned warehouse for Charnier and in the process accidentally kills Mulderig (Bill Hickman), an FBI agent assisting on the case. After a shot fires, the screen goes black and images of the key criminals and results of the prosecution are shown, with most of the key players receiving reduced or no sentences. Sal Boca is killed in the shoot-out.

In writing about the movie, Pauline Kael condemns *The French Connection* as "total commercial opportunism passing itself off as an Existential view." However, she also describes it as a "slam-bang thriller."

> A hugely successful slam-bang thriller that zaps the audience with noise, speed, and brutality. It's certainly exciting, but that excitement isn't necessarily a pleasure. The ominous music keeps tightening the screws and heating things up; the movie is like an aggravated case of New York. It proceeds through chases, pistol-whippings, slashings, murders, snipings, and more chases for close to two hours. This is what's meant to give you a charge.

In Roger Greenspun's October 8, 1971, *New York Times* review, he praises the film as "a very good new kind of movie," despite its familiar story arc of cops and crooks, with thrills and chases, and lots of shoot-'em-up. He also writes about the film's "magnificent speed" and central characters who appear and disappear in and out of the city's mass.

The influence of *The French Connection* would be seen in films and television programs for decades to come as they adopted the cinema verite look and cast the streets of cities like New York, Miami, San Francisco, Baltimore, and Boston as prominent characters.

SHAFT (1971)

PRODUCER/DIRECTOR: Gordon Parks (director), Joel Freeman (producer)

WRITER(S): Ernest Tidyman, John D. F. Black

CAST: Richard Roundtree (John Shaft), Moses Gunn (Bumpy Jonas), Charles Cioffi (Vic Androzzi), Christopher St. John (Ben Buford), Gwenn Mitchell (Ellie Moore), Lawrence Pressman (Sergeant Tom Hannon), Victor Arnold (Charlie), Sherri Brewer (Marcy), Rex Robbins (Rollie), Camille Yarbrough (Dina Greene)

CINEMATOGRAPHY: Urs Furrer

MUSIC: Isaac Hayes, J. J. Johnson

LENGTH AND RATING: 100 min; R

Although many scholars and critics cite the year 1971 as a critical turning point in the validation of blacks in creative, production, and directorial roles in film, the legitimization of black heroes in film appeared earlier. Although Rex Ingram as Sergeant Major Tambul of the 4th Sudanese Batallion fighting the German Afrika Corps. in the 1943 film, *Sahara*, may be defined more as an action hero by white audiences than black, his portrayal was a depature from the more provincial roles given black actors. In a role that helped to define blacks as agents of their own destiny and equal to whites in intelligence, charm, and wit, Sidney Poitier as Philadelphia police detective Virgil Tibbs in the film *In the Heat of the Night* (1967) is an outstanding example. In a portrayal that preceeded Richard Roundtree's in *Shaft*, Tibbs displayed his charm, and arrogance, in the face of bigoted white southerners. When he returned the slap of white racist Eric Endicott you could hear the audiences' collective gasp.

As the iconic, homogonized black man acceptable to white society, Poitier embodied these values in other hit films, including *Guess Who's Coming to Dinner* (1967) and *To Sir, With Love* (1967). These films were produced by studios whose leadership was dominated by whites and white creative artists. However, they marginalized the black audience, which in 1970 accounted for 15 percent of the population but was 30 percent of the national first-run film audience.

A new definition in black filmmaking defined an alternative culture that reflected the attitudes of blacks and how they were portrayed on screen, and was described as *blaxploitation*, which referred to production and merchandising. This alternative black cinema was manifested in various ways, including black produced and directed work, black work but controlled by whites, and "white controlled white works using blacks for blacks." As Brandon Wander explains in *Black Dreams: The Fantasy and Ritual of Black Films*: "Black films, despite their shoddiness, are creating a black mythology. Each film is a ritual, a morality play, recognized and appreciated by the audience" (Wander, *Film Quarterly*).

He also notes that black and white film critics spend their time "attacking the shortcomings of black cinema" rather than delving in to the substance beneath the surface. These films were also a product of the black radicalism of the sixties and seventies. In his essay, Wander cites the popular black films of the era, *Superfly* (1972), *Hit Man* (1972), *Black Caesar* (1973), *Sweet, Sweetback* (1971), and *The Education of Sonny Carson* (1974), saying that the "ebony mythology of these films should explain black society's relation to white society, at least in filmic terms."

Although these films may have had some content appeal to the mass consumption of sex and violence, there were talented and creative individuals associated with them. Distinguished *Life* magazine photojournalist Gordon Parks, who directed the critically acclaimed semiautobiographical film *The Learning Tree* (1969), also directed *Shaft*. The screenplay was written by Ernest Tidyman (*In the Heat of the Night*), a Caucasian, and John D. F. Black and adapted from Tidyman's novel *Shaft*.

The film, budgeted at $1.125 million, was a runaway hit, grossing $12 million and earning an Academy Award for Best Music, Song, the "Theme from *Shaft*," composed by jazz musician Isaac Hayes. Historian Donald Bogle writes about how *Shaft* surprised the MGM studio:

> This little picture, which its studio, MGM, thought might make a little money, instead made a mint—some $12 million within a year in North America alone—and single-handedly saved MGM from financial ruin. (http://www.blackfilm.com/0107/features/may1_Blaxsp_1.shtml) (http://www.tcm.com/thismonth/article.jsp?cid=133220&mainArticleId=133204)

As John Shaft, actor Richard Roundtree was a suave, cool, and defiant New York City private detective who was equally uncooperative and abusive to prying cops, black Harlem hoods, and tough Mafia gangsters. From his first moments on the screen, strutting through New York City's Times Square, Richard Roundtree's Shaft exudes a confidence, style, and arrogance that captured the mood of the time. In agreeing to find the kidnapped daughter of Bumpy Jonas (Moses Gunn), a prominent Harlem gangster, Shaft sets his own terms and feeds police Lieutenant Vic Androzzi (Charles Cioffi) only enough information to appease his inquiry. Although he and Androzzi appear to have an adversarial relationship, the two men have a mutual respect for each other.

In the course of locating Bumpy's daughter, Shaft enlists the aid of a black militant group, outsmarts two mafia goons who are staking out his apartment from a Greenwich Village bar, makes love to two women, one black, one white, and, in a daring raid, rescues the kidnapped girl from the bad guys.

Writing in the *New York Times* on July 11, 1971, critic Vincent Canby finds *Shaft* to be a film that identified an audience and understood the realities of entertainment, saying that while not a great film it was very entertaining:

> In the case of *Shaft*, the vitality is so freshly vulgar, so without solemnity except for its observance of private-eye conventions (which are not exactly solemn to start with), that the movie becomes the kind of entertainment to which any audience—black, white or you-name-it—can respond. I suppose it's the same sort of vitality that kept black audiences responding to white, assembly line–movies during all of those decades past when to be black was not so beautiful, just invisible. (Canby *New York Times*)

🎥 *DELIVERANCE* (1972)

PRODUCER/DIRECTOR: John Boorman

WRITER(S): James Dickey

CAST: Jon Voight (Ed), Burt Reynolds (Lewis), Ned Beatty (Bobby), Ronny Cox (Drew), Ed Ramey (Old Man), Billy Redden (Lonnie), Seamon Glass (First Griner), Randall Deal (Second Griner), Bill McKinney (Mountain Man), Herbert "Cowboy" Coward (Toothless Man)

CINEMATOGRAPHY: Vilmos Zsigmond

MUSIC: Michael Addiss (banjo); Billy Redden (uncredited)

LENGTH AND RATING: 109 min; R

"This is the weekend they didn't play golf." Such was the tag line for the film's promotional marketing campaign. A great deal has been written about the theme and meaning of the film as an allegory to the turbulence of the time of its release and its relevance to current events. Author James Dickey, who wrote the 1970 novel and adapted it for the screen, was passionate about preserving the environment from destruction and interested in exploring the relationship between man and nature and their respective redeeming values. It was also viewed as an allegory about America's involvement in Vietnam, its rape of the country's natural resources, and intrusive involvement and unexpected resistance by the country's inhabitants. Recently, the author's son, Christopher Dickey, wrote about the film's compelling theme and how it is reflected in America's current involvement in Iraq. He wrote that Lewis (Burt Reynolds) "loves to flirt with extinction. To come near death, then survive." He also

Burt Reynolds (left), as Lewis Medlock. [Warner Bros./Photofest]

189

commented that "the role of government—of civilization—is to curb our sense of personal license when civilized society is under pressure from anger and fear" and blamed Bush and Cheney for pursuing a "war with Iraq at all costs and as an end to almost all constraints" (http://www.newsweek.com/id/53461/page/2).

There are four characters in the movie whose resolve, determination, morality, and self-esteem are tested in the harsh natural environment of the river they have chosen to challenge. It's not just the river and its turbulent rapids they must endure; they also have to face their own vulnerabilities and insecurities.

The trip is organized by Lewis Medlock (Burt Reynolds), who is in the real estate business and the most macho of the group, with his muscular physique, arrogant demeanor, and sense of adventure. He's a survivalist with a talent for using a bow and arrow, and when asked by one of the native hillbillies why he wants to go canoeing down the Cahulawassee River, he answers, "Because it's there." In a foreboding response, the "local" responds, "It's there all right. You get in there and can't get out, you're gonna wish it wasn't." The other men on the weekend trip are professionals who live in suburbia. Bobby Trippe (Ned Beatty), a single insurance and mutual funds salesman referred to as "chubby" by Lewis, appears to be the most vulnerable of the group. The other two have wives and children: Ed Gentry (Jon Voight), a pipe-smoking gentleman who runs an art service and has a hunting bow, and Drew Ballinger (Ronny Cox), a guitar-playing sales supervisor who is the most virtuous of the group.

For Lewis, the trip is viewed as the last opportunity to experience the natural habitat of the Cahulawassee River and its raging white rapids. In his response to Bobby, Lewis lets the others know about his passion for the environment. However, they feel that his emotional response is too overzealous:

> … because they're buildin' a dam across the Cahulawassee River. They're gonna flood a whole valley, Bobby, that's why. Dammit, they're drownin' the river …
> Just about the last wild, untamed, unpolluted, unfucked up river in the South.

Several scenes in the film provide a lingering sense of what may happen to the men on their trip down the river. The party has arrived at a backwoods community to enlist drivers to take their two cars down to Aintree, where the men will disembark after their trip. In a particularly entertaining and defining cinematic moment, Drew starts strumming his guitar and a young, deformed albino hillbilly responds with chords on his banjo. Soon the two are engaged in "Dueling Banjos," with Drew feverishly trying to keep up and finally admitting defeat. This scene could be construed as a metaphor for the film, with the men being charmed by the calm of the river and subsequently trying to meet the challenge of both the human and natural hostile environment.

In another scene, Lewis bargains with the Griner brothers over the fee for driving the cars to Aintree, and makes mild-mannered Ed uncomfortable with his aggressive haggling. They finally set out for the river, with Lewis driving one of the cars, followed by the Griners and Drew. He puts the "pedal to the metal" in the backwoods, with Ed cringing at his side as they race through the brush, Lewis bragging that he can find the river but instead turning onto a dead–end and earning the derisive laughter of the Griners. He eventually rights himself and the men begin their journey.

After the first day, the men make camp on the riverbank and Lewis demonstrates his skill with the bow by shooting fish with an arrow. In the evening, Ed, Bobby, and

Drew share some liquor, and Lewis, who doesn't drink, goes off to investigate a strange sound he may have heard. He returns, saying he didn't find anything. The next morning, Ed rises early and stalks a deer with his bow and arrow, trying to imitate Lewis. When he takes aim for the kill, his hands shake violently and he fails to hit the animal, the arrow instead landing in a tree trunk. Compared to Lewis, Ed appears weak and lacking the fortitude to hunt and kill.

The next day Ed, paired with Bobby in the canoe, pulls to the side of the riverbank to wait for Lewis and Drew to catch up. They try to rest but are confronted by two hillbilly perverts armed with a shotgun and a knife. Sensing they may be in trouble, Ed attempts to be polite and cordial, addressing them as gentlemen and asking, "What do you require of us?" Attempting to talk his way out of the situation, Ed makes matters worse by letting the hillbillies know that if they have an illegal still for making whiskey they won't tell anyone, and Bobby concurs. But these men have other intentions, and they tie Ed to a tree with his own belt and he is guarded by the tall, toothless hillbilly with the shotgun. The other man forces Bobby to strip naked, mounts him on the back, forcing him to squeal like a pig, and then sodomizes him. During this time, Ed cringes and struggles but cannot free himself to aid Bobby. He does notice Lewis and Drew quietly approaching the riverbank in their canoe, Lewis taking aim with his bow and shooting the arrow through the back of the hillbilly as the toothless man drops his shotgun and runs away.

After the incident, Lewis calmly confirms that the hillbilly is dead, proudly announcing it as a "center shot," and then asks the group what they should do with the body. This sets off a debate about the American judicial system, with Drew arguing that they should notify the sheriff about what happened and Lewis responding that if they do, they'll be judged by other hillbillies in the jury, who are all related. However, Drew passionately insists that they follow the rule of law, while Lewis urges that they can walk away without being connected to the murder: "We gotta get rid of that guy! Anywhere, everywhere, nowhere." He tells them there is going to be a lake and that being buried in a lake is about as buried as you can get. Cleverly using Drew's belief in democracy and the law, Lewis asks for a vote, which supports his plan to get rid of the body.

After burying the body, they set off down the river and as they approach the rapids, Ed, paired with Drew in a canoe, tells him to put on his life jacket. Suddenly, Drew, the point person in the canoe, jolts his head and falls into the water and both canoes collide with the rocks, throwing Lewis, Ed, and Bobby into the raging rapids. This is the turning point in the narrative as Lewis is severely injured with a broken leg and busy "licking his wounds" and crying in pain while Ed must assume leadership. They take refuge in a gorge and, fearing they will be ambused by the same man who shot Drew, Ed climbs the precarious cliff and rests from exhaustion until the next morning. After waking he sees a hillbilly with a shotgun and shakes while taking aim, releasing the arrow while falling on his side and injuring himself on a quivered arrow. The man approaches Ed and aims the shotgun barrel at point-blank range, then suddenly fires at the ground, falling down dead. Feverishly checking the mouth of his victim, Ed attempts to confirm his identity as the toothless hillbilly who had terrorized them in the backwoods.

In a treacherous descent from the cliff, Ed carefully lowers himself and the body of the hillbilly and then in a mishap with the rapelling rope, he scrapes the rock and falls into the water. As the leader, he decides to bury their latest casualty in the river and then they continue down stream, with Lewis straddled in the canoe, his leg in a splint. On their way, they discover Drew's contorted body and Ed decides to submerge and bury him to avoid any inquiries as to the cause of death.

Sucessfully reaching Aintree, Lewis is brought to a hospital while Ed and Bobby are put up in a rooming house. Taking charge, Ed tells the cowardly Bobby that they must agree on the story that their accident and Drew's drowning occurred at the bottom of the river to prevent law enforcement from looking upriver. Doubts are raised by Sheriff Ed Bullard (James Dickey) and Deputy Queen (Macon McCalman), especially after the remnants of the other canoe are found upstream. The deputy urges the sheriff not to let them go because there is a missing hunter related by marriage to the deputy sheriff. Visiting the hospital, Ed and Bobby see Lewis, who has feigned being unconscious, and when told that they had to change their story he winks and tells them he doesn't remember anything.

The men are released and given a stern warning by Sheriff Bullard, who tells them never to return because he would like to see the town die peacefully. Reunited with his wife and son, Ed has a nightmare of the dead mountain man's hand protruding from the water in the lake, pointing into the air.

THE GODFATHER (1972)

PRODUCER/DIRECTOR: Francis Ford Coppola
WRITER(S): Mario Puzo (novel, screenplay), Francis Ford Coppola (screenplay)
CAST: Marlon Brando (Don Vito Corleone), Al Pacino (Michael Corleone), James Caan (Santino "Sonny" Corleone), Richard S. Castellano (Peter Clemenza), Robert Duvall (Tom Hagen), Sterling Hayden (Capt. McCluskey), John Marley (Jack Woltz), Richard Conte (Don Emilio Barzini), Al Lettieri (Virgil "The Turk" Sollozzo), Diane Keaton (Kay Adams)
CINEMATOGRAPHY: Gordon Willis
MUSIC: Nino Rota
LENGTH AND RATING: 175 min; R

American movie audiences and television viewers have had a long fascination with the exploits of gangsters, whether fictional characters on screen or their real-life counterparts like the "Teflon Don," John Gotti. Earlier in this book, the gangster genre films of the 1930s were discussed, citing *Little Caesar* (1930) and *The Public Enemy* (1931), respectively starring tough-guy actors Edward G. Robinson and James Cagney. Throughout the cultural evolution of American film directors and writers sought to redefine the essence of the gangster by painting a more sympathetic and distinctive portrait of him on the screen, and it was Francis Ford Coppola who articulated this artistic vision with a voice that was utterly unique and distinct. His *Godfather* trilogy is the epic saga of the immigrant's search for recognition in a land of opportunity and his longing for acceptance as he resists the assimilation that threatened his legacy and traditions. The only other gangster film that could qualify as an epic and compare to the *Godfather* trilogy is Sergio Leone's *Once Upon A Time in America* (1984).

Critics praised the film, and Vincent Canby, in his March 16, 1972, *New York Times* review, noted that, "Francis Ford Coppola has made one of the most brutal and moving chronicles of American life ever designed within the limits of popular entertainment."

Another respected critic, Pauline Kael, addressed the movie's "new tragic realism" when she wrote:

> A wide, startlingly vivid view of a Mafia dynasty, in which organized crime becomes an obscene nightmare image of American free enterprise. The movie is a popular melodrama with its roots in the gangster films of the 30s, but it expresses a new tragic realism, and it's altogether extraordinary. (http://www.geocities.com/paulinekaelreviews/g3)

In one of the most remarkable expository opening scenes in cinema, the audience is taken to an Italian-American wedding where the characters are introduced and the essence of the theme and the profile of Don Vito Corleone (Marlon Brando) are established. Like a king or the Pope, Don Vito engages in the age-old Sicilian ritual of granting favors on the day of his daughter's wedding. The undertaker, Amerigo Bonasera (Salvatore Cositto), has come to the Don to ask for justice in the brutal beating and attempted rape of his daughter. But the Don is annoyed that Bonasera never sought his counsel or offered friendship, even though his wife is the godmother to his daughter. Finally, Bonasera does what is expected and in a religious gesture, he bows to the Don, kissing his hand and calling him "Godfather." He has paid tribute to Don Vito and receives the gift of justice on the wedding day of the Don's daughter.

The wedding provides a perfect setting to introduce the players in this story of rivalry, greed, power, vindication, family, and assimilation. In addition to Don Vito, there is his wife Carmella (Morgana King); Tom Hagen (Robert Duvall), his adopted son and attorney (consigliere); and his four birth children: hot headed and presumptive heir-apparent Santino, Sonny (James Caan), Fredo (John Cazale), the weakest of the children, Connie (Talia Shire), the petulant bride who is marrying Carlo Rizzi (Gianni Russo), a negligible small-time bookie with greater aspirations than brains, and war hero and Marine Captain Michael (Al Pacino), who appears to be the most assimilated of the clan and is accompanied by his very WASP-ish girlfriend, Kay Adams (Diane Keaton). Other characters include a loyal but simple hit man Luca Brasi (Lenny Montana), Salvatore Tessio (Abe Vigoda), and Clemenza (Richard Castellano), who are part of the extended Corleone family.

The importance Don Vito places on family, loyalty, and manliness is vividly portrayed in two scenes. His famous godson, crooner Johnny Fontane (Al Martino), asks the Don for his help in getting a role in a movie that he has been denied. He whines and is reprimanded by the Don for being unmanly and then asked if he spends time with his family (this is directed more at the Don's philandering, married son, Sonny, than at Johnny), and he replies that he does. The importance of family is reiterated by Don Vito Corleone, who says that a real man spends time with his family. Fealty to the family's interests are boldly portrayed when the Don meets with Virgil Sollozzo (Al Lettieri), a member of the Tattaglia family who is negotiating for a one-million-dollar loan to support the growth of his heroin trade. In return, he advises that he will give the Corleones thirty percent of the business. The deal is not just about money, as Sollozzo covets the important network of political and law enforcement connections the Corleone family has nurtured over the years. Although he has been advised by Tom Hagen that it is a sound strategic move, one endorsed by his son, Sonny, Don Vito graciously turns down the offer, unwilling to threaten the business connections in gambling and prostitution that he has struggled to sustain over the years because his "friends" view them as "minor vices." However, when Sonny remarks that if the Tattaglias will guarantee the loan, speaking out of turn, he is mildy rebuked publicly and then sternly reminded in private never to tell anyone outside the family what he's thinking.

Although Michael vows to Kay at his sister's wedding that the people she was meeting and the business they conducted were not about him or his interests, he, of course, becomes the ruthless head of the family. In Las Vegas, where his brother, Fredo, has been sent in the diminished capacity to oversee the family's casino interests, Michael meets with Moe Greene (Alex Rocco), a majority owner to buy out his interests in the casino business by "making him an offer he can't refuse." When the men meet, Greene summarily rejects Michael's offer, insulting his efforts. After the meeting, Fredo argues that Greene should not have been approached by Michael in the manner he chose and he is reprimanded by Michael and sternly warned never to take sides with anyone against the family. Once again, the devotion to family is a compelling requisite for the Corleones.

After returning from Las Vegas, Michael meets with his father to set his grand scheme of moving to Las Vegas and entering the legitimate gambling business and settling the family's affairs in New York. His father is now his most trusted adviser, and he warns Michael how his nemesis, Don Emilio Barzini (Richard Conte), will attempt to assassinate him and compromise one of the Corleone family's most trusted lieutenants, who is later revealed to be Tessio.

In the memorable baptism scene of the son of his sister, Connie, which occurs after the death of Don Vito, in one sweeping gesture Michael rids himself of all the opposing family leaders, including Moe Greene and Barzini, as their assassinations are intercut with the religious baptism ritual of the Catholic Church. On that day, Michael's final vengeance is taken out on his brother-in-law Carlo, who sets Sonny up for assassination as Clemenza garrots him from the back seat of a car.

In the final scene, which has forceful religious overtones, Kay asks Michael if he was responsible for Carlo's death, and although he is annoyed by her questioning about "matters of business," he lies and says "no." Satisfied with her husband's answer, Kay leaves and observes Michael in his office, surrounded by his loyal lieutenants who pay their respects by bowing and kssing his hand. He has proven his courage and shrewd leadership. As Kay watches the door to Michael's office being closed, she sees that that gesture is symbolic of her role as a wife and mother who will always be on the fringe of her husband's life. As Don Vito told his son Michael, "Women and children can be careless but not men."

The film won three Academy Awards for Best Picture, Best Actor for Marlon Brando (who refused to accept), and Best Adapted Screenplay for Mario Puzo and Francis Ford Coppola. It earned $134 million, making it the top-grossing film of the year.

THE GODFATHER PART II (1974)

PRODUCER/DIRECTOR: Francis Ford Coppola
WRITER(S): Mario Puzo (novel, screenplay), Francis Ford Coppola (screenplay)
CAST: Al Pacino (Don Michael Corleone), Robert Duvall (Tom Hagen), Diane Keaton (Kay Corleone), Robert De Niro (Vito Corleone), John Cazale (Fredo Corleone), Talia Shire

(Connie Corleone), Lee Strasberg (Hyman Roth), Michael V. Gazzo (Frankie Pentan-
geli), G. D. Spradlin (Senator Pat Geary), Richard Bright (Al Neri), Gastone Moschin
(Don Fanucci)
CINEMATOGRAPHY: Gordon Willis
MUSIC: Nino Rota and Carmine Coppola
LENGTH AND RATING: 200 min; R

The depth and breadth of this film in many ways emulates the ideals of leadership and
conflict as portrayed in Homer's *Iliad* and the adventurous journey so beautifully told
in the *Odyssey*. They address themes similar to those portrayed in *The Godfather Part I*,
about the struggle for leadership, the power of fate, life's journey, and the meaningless
virtues of conflict and plunder. These are enduring themes that reach a stunning rhapsody of heightened drama in *The Godfather Part II*.

In many ways this film is a visual poem, with imagery that takes on the passion of
literary language and art. It is both a prequel and sequel that weaves a tale about the
coming to America of nine-year-old Vito Andolini who, after his father, older brother,
and mother are killed by local Mafia head Don Francesco Ciccio (Giuseppe Sillato) as
revenge for an insult, is secretly smuggled out of Sicily and travels alone in steerage to
New York City. At Ellis Island, where the attendants had to process thousands of immigrants, Vito's surname is confused with the Sicilian town he's from, and he is quaran-
tined for three months with smallpox.

The story of Vito Corleone (Robert De Niro) runs parallel to and is intercut with
scenes from the 1950s that depict Michael as the Don, heading the family in Nevada,
celebrating his son Anthony's holy communion. Once again religion is a powerful
theme in this epic film, as it opens with a Sicilian funeral procession for Vito's father,
continues with the rituals of 1950s communion in Nevada, and moves back in time to
the crowded streets of New York's Little Italy during the feast of San Gennaro with its
religious procession during which Vito murders the corrupt, greedy Don Fanucci and
ascends to the throne as the new Don.

At the compound during his son's communion, Michael conducts "business" as his
father did during his daughter's wedding. In a tense meeting with Nevada Senator Pat
Geary (G. D. Spradlin), Geary insults Michael and his Italian heritage and solicits a
bribe of $250,000 plus five percent of the monthly gross from the four Corleone casinos
for allowing the family to consolidate its Nevada gambling interests. Acknowledging
that a Nevada gaming license is less than $20,000, Michael rejects Geary's offer and
accuses him of being part of the same hypocrisy, but warns him never to relate it to his
family. Interestingly, the senator may despise the Corleones but he is willing to do
business with them. While he espouses the virtues of decent Americans and condemns
the Corleone family's dishonesty, Geary is no different from them, compromising his
public trust in an attempt to extort money.

The theme of family is also important to this film, as is evident when Michael meets
with his sister, Connie, who introduces him to her soon-to-be third husband and he
chastises her for not spending enough time with her children. Later, on the dance floor,
Fredo's wife Deanna (Mariana Hill) drunkenly dances suggestively with another man
and on Michael's orders is subdued and removed from the party. In a meeting with
Frankie Pentangeli (Michael Gazzo), who is still married to the old traditions of the

195

Mafia and rejects assimilation, he is reminded by Michael that his family is still called Corleone and he must run it that way.

After an assassination attempt, Michael meets with Jewish criminal mastermind Hyman Roth (Lee Strasberg) in Miami Beach, Florida. Modeled after the infamous Meyer Lansky, Roth is an unassuming man living in modest surroundings, eating tuna fish sandwiches for lunch, and hatching a grandiose scheme for gambling casinos in Cuba.

Later, Michael meets Roth and representatives of major businesses in Havanna, and Fredo arrives carrying a suitcase filled with two million dollars in cash for a government bribe. During the trip, Michael confirms that it was Roth who tried to kill him and he also learns it was his brother, Fredo, who set him up. An attempt in a hospital on Roth's life by Michael's bodyguard is interrupted and the bodyguard is killed. Another assassination attempt in New York on Frank Pentangeli is interrupted by a patrolling police officer.

The Cuban revolution intrudes on the family business and Michael leaves Cuba to return home to Nevada, only to learn that his wife, Kay, has lost their unborn child. At a Senate hearing on organized crime with Frank Pentangeli as a key witness against Michael, he and other witnesses recant their accusations. Although Michael has consolidated his power, he is powerless in sustaining his nuclear family. Telling Michael that she aborted his child, Kay leaves but Michael retains custody of his children. Suspicious and alone, after his mother's death Michael orders the murder of his brother Fredo.

In attending to the family business, Michael Corleone sacrifices his familial bonds for the sake of insuring and consolidating his power. Like other powerful men, he has isolated himself from the world of ordinary mortals and rules from a bully pulpit of arrogance, greed, and revenge.

In her review, critic Pauline Kael spoke of the richness and fullness of the film:

The daring of PART II is that it enlarges the scope and deepens the meaning of the first film. Visually, PART II is far more complexly beautiful than the first, just as it's thematically richer, more shadowed, fuller. The completed work, contrasting the early manhood of Vito (Robert De Niro) with the life of Michael, his inheritor (Al Pacino), is an epic vision of the corruption of America. (http://www.geocities.com/paulinekaelreviews/g3)

The film was nominated for eleven Academy Awards and won six: Best Picture for producer/director Francis Ford Coppola, Best Supporting Actor (Robert De Niro), Best Adapted Screenplay (Mario Puzo and Francis Ford Coppola), Best Art Direction/Set Decoration, and Best Original Dramatic Score (Nino Rota and Carmine Coppola).

AMERICAN GRAFFITI (1973)

PRODUCER/DIRECTOR: George Lucas (director), Francis Ford Coppola (producer)
WRITER(S): George Lucas, Gloria Katz, Willard Huyck
CAST: Richard Dreyfuss (Curt Henderson), Ron Howard (Steve Bolander), Paul Le Mat (John Milner), Charles Martin Smith (Terry "The Toad" Fields), Cindy Williams (Laurie

Henderson), Candy Clark (Debbie Dunham), Mackenzie Phillips (Carol), Wolfman Jack
(XERB Disc Jockey), Bo Hopkins (Joe Young), Manuel Padilla, Jr. (Carlos)
CINEMATOGRAPHY: Jan D'Alquen, Ron Eveslage
MUSIC: Kim Fowley (music producer), Karin Green (music coordinator)
LENGTH AND RATING: 110 min | 112 min (re-release) (1978); PG

It was the year that New York City's World Trade Center opened and New York Yankee
Ron Blomberg became Major League Baseball's first designated hitter. The Vietnam War
ended and Pink Floyd's landmark album, *Darkside of the Moon*, was released. In that year,
Robert Metcalf, a researcher at the Xerox headquarters in the Palo Alto Research Center
wrote a memo about developing the Ethernet to connect a network of computers in a
single building, thus helping to usher in the age of personal computing. And a young
filmmaker named George Lucas, with one previous film credit (*THX 1138*, 1971), captured the mood and culture of early 1960s American teenagers in *American Graffiti*.

Capturing the essence of a cultural era can be a daunting experience for writers and
filmmakers desperate to portray and evoke the mood of the time. Director George Lucas
was able to accomplish this by defining the pulse of that time, combining the music of
the era with the popular pursuits of "romance, racin, and rock 'n' roll." The movie articulates the conflicts and challenges these teens face as they make the transition from a
carefree youth to the reality of adulthood. The main characters reflect this dynamic of
change and include Steve Bolander (Ron Howard), the clean–cut, all-American boy who
can't wait to leave for the university the next day with his friend Curtis Henderson
(Richard Dreyfuss) and get out of what he describes as "this turkey town." Curtis, who
has earned a scholarship, is less confident and more insecure about leaving, and Steve
berates him, saying that he can't remain seventeen forever like John Milner (Paul Le
Mat). For John, who graduated from high school two years earlier, being an auto
mechanic, driving a hot rod, dating, and drag racing are his life and he has no illusions
about altering it. Since Steve is leaving for college, he must address his imminent
departure with his girlfriend, Laurie Henderson (Cindy Williams), Curtis' younger sister
who longs for his commitment and is devasted when Steve suggests that they date other
people while he's away at college. She removes his class ring from around her neck, saying that she can't expect him to behave like a monk while he's away. There is also Terry
Fields (Charles Martin Smith), nicknamed "the toad," a nerd who wears glasses and
drives a Vespa motor scooter. His stature goes up a notch when Steve entrusts his white
1958 Chevy Impala to him while he's away at college. However, as he cruises on the
strip, he forgets that he's in reverse and smashes into the car behind him, blaming the
adult at the wheel and speeding away to avoid the consequences.

The action in the film takes place from evening to early morning as the main characters confront their conflicts and desires. Struggling with the decision to travel east
the next morning to attend college, Curtis is lost as he attempts to reconcile his feeling
of insecurity with the need to make the transition to adulthood, which means leaving
his friends and family behind. While riding as a passenger in his sister Laurie's car, a
sporty two-door Thunderbird pulls up parallel and a beautiful blonde mouths the
words "I love you" at him. This event precipitates Curtis' desperate search for the girl,
which is actually his quest to find himself and the adventures he confronts along the
way. Meeting up with the Pharoahs, a local gang of hoodlums led by Joe (Bo Hopkins),
he is accused of scratching their car, which he's sitting on while watching *The*

Adventures of Ozzie and Harriet on an appliance store television set, and is thus forced to accompany them on their mini crime spree. After he demonstrates his courage and ability to talk his way out of difficult situations, he's encouraged to meet with the group the following evening, but he expresses his doubts to them, expecting to leave in the morning. Desperate to find the blonde girl, he drives to the local radio station and asks DJ Wolfman Jack to broadcast a dedication, leaving the number of a pay phone for her to call.

Another theme in the movie is the strain placed on love and the reality of losing someone. This develops as Laurie and Steve attempt to deal with the demands on their relationship as they argue at the freshman hop and are forced to dance together under the spotlight as Steve is honored as the former class president and Laurie as the new head cheerleader. Dancing to the ballad of "Smoke Gets in Your Eyes" by The Platters, Laurie reminds Steve how she had to be the aggressive party in their relationship, kissing him before he kissed her, and then she cries on his shoulder. Parked in Laurie's Edsel, Steve tries to convince her to have sex but she resists, throwing him out of her car. Sitting alone in Mel's Diner, Steve is propositioned by Budda (Jana Bellan), one of the roller-skating carhops, and initially he accepts her offer to meet but then reneges. Passing by outside, Laurie sees the pair talking and then joins Falfa (Harrison Ford) in his Chevy, who has challenged John to a race. Learning about the drag race, Steve rushes to the scene in time to see Falfa's car crash and roll over into a ditch and watch as the two escape before it bursts into flames. As the car burns, Steve and Laurie embrace and she begs him not to leave her and he promises to stay.

While cruising on the Strip, Terry picks up a flaky blonde, Debbie Medway (Candy Clark), and brags to her about his nickname, "Terry the Tiger," the other car (a jeep) he uses for hunting, and the horses he's owned. They embark on a series of misadventures, including witnessing a liquor store robbery as Terry tries to get an adult to buy him a pint of Old Harper. They then make out by a canal and discover that Steve's car has been stolen. They find the car and take a beating from the two hoods who stole it. In the end, they are rescued by John. Later that evening, Terry admits that he doesn't own the car and instead drives a scooter. Debbie tells Terry how she had a great time with him and that she loves motorcycles, and a scooter is close enough. Then she kisses him and tells him to call her, and Terry learns that Debbie likes him for who he is and not for the web of lies he told her.

As for John Milner, he winds up picking up Carol Morrison (Mackenzie Phillips), a thirteen-year-old foisted on him as a joke by a group of girls in another car. Although he is initially embarrassed to be with her, John eventually warms up to the young brat, taking her to the auto junk yard, cruising with her, and finally taking her home and giving her his gear shift knob, which she excitedly equates with a ring. His life is aimless, consisting mostly of defending his title as drag-racing king of the valley. However, reality confronts him when, after Falfa crashes, John tells Terry that if Falfa's tire hadn't blown he would have beaten him.

Camped out in his car by the pay phone, Curt is awakened by its ring and on the other end is the blonde girl. She tells him she might see him that evening cruising on Third Street, but knowing he won't be there he pleads to learn her name but she hangs up. The next morning at the airport, Curt is seen off by his parents, Steve, Laurie, John, and Terry. As the plane ascends, he looks out the window and sees a Thunderbird following in its the path.

In his *New York Times* August 13, 1973, review, Roger Greenspun notes how *American Graffiti* never exploits nostalgia:

> *American Graffiti* exists not so much in its individual stories as in its orchestration of many stories, its sense of time and place. Although it is full of the material of fashionable nostalgia, it never exploits nostalgia. In its feeling for movement and music and the vitality of the night—and even in its vision in white—it is oddly closer to some early Fellini than to the recent American past of, say, *The Last Picture Show* or *Summer of '42*.

The film was shot in a month of evenings on location in Petaluma, California. The classic rock 'n' roll music was an important part of the film and helped to evoke the period, claiming ten percent of the production budget. The film's production budget was $777,000, with a total domestic gross of $115 million and worldwide gross of $140 million.

THE EXORCIST (1973)

PRODUCER/DIRECTOR: William Friedkin (director), William Peter Blatty (producer)
WRITER(s): William Peter Blatty
CAST: Ellen Burstyn (Chris MacNeil), Max von Sydow (Father Merrin), Lee J. Cobb (Lt. Kinderman), Kitty Winn (Sharon), Jack MacGowran (Burke Dennings), Jason Miller (Father Karras), Linda Blair (Regan), Reverend William O'Malley (Father Dyer), Barton Heyman (Dr. Klein), Peter Masterson (Dr. Barringer, Clinic Director)
CINEMATOGRAPHY: Owen Roizman
MUSIC: Steve Boeddeker
LENGTH AND RATING: 122 min; R

Degrees of fright can capture the mood of a person, whether they are reading a book or watching a film. Films have a rich tradition of manipulating the visual and auditory components of storytelling by infusing images with subtle or obvious manifestations of evil. What is most fascinating about the success of these movies is the very texture and fabric of evil they represent. A number of horror genres can be categorized as narrative forms that communicate fear within the context of specific themes. One theme that has endured in popularity is possession, and its relationship to evil as inspired by the devil. In the 1914 Yiddish play *The Dybbuk*, by S. Ansky, a young bride-to-be is possessed by an evil spirit. The play was adapted to the screen in 1937 and directed by Michal Waszynski.

The theme of demonic possession in literature and the movies has been adapted to various forms that have at times manifested into political commentary. In Authur Miller's play *The Crucible*, about the Salem witch trials, the allegation of possession and heresy, and false accusations, were an allegory about the McCarthy era and the Red Scare. One of the most successful movie franchises treats the cult of vampires. Based on the seminal 1897 novel *Dracula* by Bram Stoker, its adaptation to the movies began with the 1922 silent German expressionistic film *Nosferatu*, directed by F. W. Murnau and starring Max Schreck. Unable to secure the rights to Stoker's novel, Murnau changed the name of the title in German to *Nosferatu eine Symphonie des Grauens* ("Nosferatu, a Symphony of Horror"). The first Dracula film to be an authorized adaptation of Stoker's novel was *Dracula* (1931), produced by Carl Laemmle, Jr., directed by Tod Browning, and starring Bela Lugosi, with cinematography by Karl Freund and released by Universal.

The 1968 *Rosemary's Baby*, directed by Roman Polanski, starring Mia Farrow and John Cassavetes and based on Ira Levin's best-selling novel, was a box office and critical success. Perhaps one of its most effective techniques is making the ordinary and taking it to extraordinary circumstances. In this case, an ordinary young couple in love and conceiving a child are befriended by elderly and somewhat eccentric neighbors who happen to be devil worshippers.

Interestingly, *The Exorcist* follows a similar arc, as the mother of the possessed victim, Chris MacNeil (Ellen Burstyn), is an actress shooting a movie on location in Washington, DC, and in *Rosemary's Baby* the husband is an actor. The demonic possession inhabits Chris's twelve-year old daughter Regan (Linda Blair).

The film is based on the 1971 best-selling novel *The Exorcist* by William Peter Blatty, who based the story on the supposed 1949 exorcism of a fourteen-year-old boy whose pseudonym is Robbie Mannheim. The boy lived in Cottage City, Maryland, and his exorcism was performed by the Jesuit Catholic priests Fr. William S. Bowdern, Fr. Raymond McBride, and Fr. Walter H. Halloran, with a diary kept by Fr. Bishop. The events were chronicled in the 1993 book *Possessed: The True Story of an Exorcism*, by Thomas Allen, and produced as a 2000 television movie with the same title, directed by Steven De Souza and starring Timothy Dalton as Father Bowdern. The theatrical feature film *The Exorcist* was directed by William Friedkin, who also directed *The French Connection* (1971).

The film begins with two distinct signs of foreboding. The first takes place at an archaeological dig in Iraq, where Father Lanklester Merrin (Max von Sydow), a Jesuit priest and archaeologist, has uncovered an ancient gargoyle of the demon Pazuzu. He senses the inherent evil of the devil as he confronts the large, stone rendering of the demon. Next, a stark cut to the trendy Georgetown community in Washington, DC, finds actress and divorced mother Chris MacNeil responding to scurrying sounds in the attic of her home. As she walks upstairs to her daughter Regan's bedroom, she finds the child uncovered, the window wide open, and feels the cold in the room. Attributing the noise to rats in the attic, she instructs Karl (Rudolf Schundler), her housekeeper, to bait traps.

The characters have their own demons to face. Chris is upset about her divorce and its effect on Regan, and Father Damien Karras (Jason Miller), a psychiatrist as well as a priest, must minister to peers who question their faith, which causes him to doubt his own. He must also endure the guilt of leaving his sick mother in a crumbling New York City tenement apartment, and reconcile the blame of his uncle, who admonishes him for becoming a poor priest instead of a successful, wealthy psychiatrist. For Regan, the divorce of her parents has had a disturbing impact, and she fantasizes about her mother marrying the director of her film, Burke Dennings (Jack MacGowran). On her birthday, Regan surreptitiously overhears her mother cursing the long-distance telephone operator as she attempts to reach Regan's father in Rome; he hasn't bothered to call his daughter on her birthday. She is a lonely child with no playmates her age except for an imaginary friend and eerie disciple, *Captain Howdy*. The next morning, Chris finds Regan in her bed, complaining that the bed is shaking. This incident is a harbinger of the horror to come.

The first manifestation of Regan's bizarre behavior comes at a dinner party in their home, when she appears in a nightgown, urinates on the carpet, and warns an astronaut guest that he is going to die on his next trip into space. Making an effort to assure her daughter that she is just responding to the move from Los Angeles to Washington, DC, Chris bathes Regan and tells her it's just nerves, and that taking her medication will help.

In one of the most controversial scenes in the movie, a Jesuit priest discovers a statue of the Virgin Mary on the campus of Georgetown University, which is near Chris and Regan's home. The statue has been desecrated with red paint and the addition of a long penis. This is symbolic of the spiritual possession lingering next door. After the death of his mother, Father Karras has a wave of guilt over his inability to be with her when she died. This guilt makes him vulnerable to the devil's mocking behavior through the manifestation of Regan's body. When Regan's bed violently shakes up and down, Chris realizes that something very bizarre is happening to her daughter. After consulting with physicians, who conduct a myriad of tests on Regan with negative findings, they advise Chris to pursue an exorcism. This leads her to contact Father Karras who, after interviewing the possessed Regan, who speaks in tongues, submits evidence to his superiors and they approve and contact Father Lanklester Merrin to lead the exorcism, assisted by Father Karras.

As a subplot, there is an investigation by homicide detective Lt. William Kinderman (Lee J. Cobb) into the sudden death of film director Burke Dennings, who was hurled down a flight of steps with his head twisted around. Then there is the investigation of the desecration of the Virgin Mary statue. He interviews Father Karras and Chris, becoming convinced that there are some strange occurrences involved.

In the climactic scene of the movie, the two priests conduct a ritual exorcism and Regan spews bile, epithets, and curses at them, assuming the image and tone of Father Karras' mother. Exhausted, they take a break, and when Karras returns he sees Lanklester slumped over, dead of a heart attack. Sacrificing himself to save Regan, Karras challenges the demon to take him, and after he is possessed he struggles to sustain enough self-control to prevent himself from killing the child by hurling himself through the window to his death on the steps outside.

The last scene of the movie shows a normal Regan, who remembers nothing of her ordeal, and her mother leaving Washington. For now, evil has been defeated.

Audience reaction to the R-rated movie was varied, with some theatergoers vomiting and fainting. When the film's R rating was challenged, Jack Valenti, then president of the Motion Picture Association of America, defended it, arguing that the film's ability to influence the imagination and suggest the horrors that are a product of the audiences' fantasy did not validate punishing the film with a harsher rating. The 1973, U.S. gross box office for *The Exorcist* was $204,632,868, and the worldwide total box office gross was $402.5 million on a budget of $12 million.

CHINATOWN (1974)

PRODUCER/DIRECTOR: Roman Polanski (director), Robert Evans (producer)

WRITER(S): Robert Towne

CAST: Jack Nicholson (J. J. "Jake" Gittes), Faye Dunaway (Evelyn Cross Mulwray), John Huston (Noah Cross), Perry Lopez (Lieutenant Lou Escobar), John Hillerman (Russ

Yelburton), Darrell Zwerling (Hollis I. Mulwray), Diane Ladd (Ida Sessions), Roy Jenson (Claude Mulvihill), Roman Polanski (Man with Knife), Richard Bakalyan (Detective Loach)
CINEMATOGRAPHY: John A. Alonzo
MUSIC: Jerry Goldsmith
LENGTH AND RATING: 131 min; R

What turned out to be an obscure yet compelling historical event in the city of Los Angeles, the Owens River Valley scandal of 1908, which concerned land speculation and water rights involving a group of unprincipled yet powerful businessmen, who diverted the Owens River to irrigate arid land in the San Fernando Valley, making it worth millions of dollars more than they paid for it, provided the narrative foundation for *Chinatown*, one of the great film noir detective stories. Based on the conniving and compulsive ambition of self-taught engineer William Mulholland, the designer and engineer of the Los Angeles Aqueduct, the Owens Valley was starved of water when Mulholland and his conspirators purchased critical land and water rights in the Owens Valley.

The 1930s mood and flavor of *Chinatown* is evoked by the haunting music of composer Jerry Goldsmith, the rich cinematography of John A. Alonzo, and the dialogue and characterizations written by Robert Towne. In his role as private detective J. J. "Jake" Gittes, actor Jack Nicholson portrays a jaded but smooth-talking, confident, and self-assured operative, a former Los Angeles cop whose métier is matrimonial work. This is established in the first scene when he shows his fisherman client, Curly (Burt Young), photographs of his wife having sex with another man, and while Curly is upset, for Jake it's just another case. His next client, who is posing as Evelyn Mulwray, wife of the chief engineer of the Los Angeles Water and Power Company, Hollis Mulwray (Darrell Zwerling), hires him to follow her husband, who she believes is having an extramarital affair. She is, however, an imposter whose real name is Ida Sessions (Diane Ladd), a prostitute hired to discredit Mulwray and ensnare Jake Gittes into discovering a plot by Noah Cross (John Huston), Mulwray's former partner in the water company before it was sold to the city of Los Angeles to divert water into the arid land of the San Fernando Valley, making Cross even richer.

As he begins his investigation of Mulwray, Jake inadvertently stumbles into the politics of water, as the city of Los Angeles is experiencing a brutal drought. He discovers a large volume of water being diverted into the Pacific Ocean through a run-off pipe. Trailing him, Jake photographs Mulwray and his alleged girlfriend at an apartment complex and rowing a boat together in a park. The photographs are published in a local newspaper, provoking a scandal, and Jake is visited by the real Mrs. Mulwray (Faye Dunaway) and her lawyer, threatening a legal suit.

Hoping to find Mulwray in his office, he is seen by Russ Yelburton (John Hillerman), Mulwray's deputy, and introduced to Claude Mulvihill (Roy Jenson) the water company's bully hired to protect them from threats by the farmers in the valley, who are being starved for water. But Jake and Mulvihill have a previous history and go back to when Mulvihill was a corrupt sheriff in Ventura County.

After visiting with Evelyn Mulwray, who raises Jake's suspicion when she readily agrees to drop the lawsuit, he looks for Mulwray, finds him dead from drowning at the Oak Pass Reservoir, and is confronted by his former police colleague and partner in

Chinatown, detective Lou Escobar (Perry Lopez) and another detective, Loach (Richard Bakalyan). In Escobar's office, Jake corroborates Evelyn's story about hiring him (although it's a lie), thus establishing a bond between them. Wanting to learn more about Mulwray's death, he visits the morgue and talks to Morty (Charles Knapp), the mortician, and is now more intrigued by the drowning death of a homeless man living under the Hollenbeck Bridge. He refutes Morty's fundings by telling him it's dry there.

In the evening, Jake visits the reservoir and is nearly killed by the rushing water being siphoned off to convince the locals there is a drought. He's confronted by Mulvihill and a short, knife-wielding hoodlum (director Roman Polanski), who puts the blade of his knife in his nose and slices a nostril, warning him not to be too nosy. Eventually, Jake learns that Evelyn is Noah Cross's daughter and that he and her husband were once partners in the water company. Still, Jake senses that Evelyn is not telling him the entire truth, and she "admits" to having had affairs with men, knowing the woman her husband was with, and thus not being upset about the relationship.

The clues begin to add up as Jake pursues his investigation and the audience tries to keep track of them. There is the homeless man who "drowned" in a dry drainage ditch, Evelyn's emotionless reaction to the loss of her husband, a glaring object in the saltwater pond on Evelyn Mulwray's estate, a call to Jake from the female impersonator declaring her innocence and telling him to check the obituary column of the newspaper, and the revelation that Hollis Mulwray had salt water in his lungs.

Trying to understand the relationship between Evelyn, her father, and Hollis Mulwray, Jake meets with Noah Cross at the Albacore Club. After Noah inquires if Jake has slept with his daughter, he warns the detective that he doesn't know what he's dealing with. Surprised that his daughter has hired him because he suspects Mulwray was murdered, Cross hires Jake to find Hollis Mulwray's lover. Of course, Jake is in the midst of a sordid family affair and unwittingly becomes a victim of the father and daughter intrigue. After visiting the hall of records, he learns that large tracts of land in the valley have been sold in the last few months to a number of individuals. He visits an orange grove in the valley and, after entering an area posted with a NO TRESPASSING sign and crashing his car into a tree, he struggles with the owner and his sons, who tell him that the corrupt officials are blowing up their water tanks and poisoning their wells in an attempt to force them to sell their land. After another struggle, he is knocked unconscious and when he awakes, Evelyn Mulwray is there to help.

He tells her that her husband discovered the plot to build a dam that would not provide water to Los Angeles but divert it to the valley, where investors had purchased land on the cheap and stood to reap a fortune thanks to the diversion, and that's why Hollis Mulwray was murdered. Checking the obituary article torn from the newspaper against the page he tore from the hall of records on land sales, Jake learns that the deceased died a week before he purchased the land. This leads Jake and Evelyn to the Mar Vista Rest Home, where they discover the identities of many elderly residents whose names have been used as straw buyers to purchase the valley land. Discovered by Mulvihill and the knife-wielding hoodlum, Jake subdues Mulvihill in a fight as Evelyn speeds her car to his rescue. They wind up at her estate, where they make love and she tries to find out more about him, but Jake is reluctant to discuss his police work in Chinatown and the woman he failed to save. She also warns Jake that her father is a very crazy and dangerous man. A phone call interrupts their liaison and Evelyn rushes out and Jake follows her to a small house. There he sees a blonde woman who matches the description of the woman with Mulwray and he assumes that Evelyn and her Chinese butler are holding her captive. She convinces Jake that the woman is her sister and declines Evelyn's offer to return home with her.

On an anonymous telephone tip, Jake is lured to the home of Ida Sessions and finds her dead. He is met by Lieutenant Escobar and Detective Loach, and they hatch their own preposterous story that Sessions hired Jake to extort Hollis Mulwray, and it was Evelyn Mulwray who murdered her husband and was paying off Jake. After denying the allegations, Jake promises to appear with Evelyn at Escobar's office in two hours.

He visits the Mulwray estate, but Evelyn is not there, and it appears that the house is being closed up, with the maid covering the furniture. He goes out to the pond and asks the gardener to retrieve a shiny object, which turns out to be a cracked pair of spectacles. Then he rushes to the address where he discovered the woman and finds Evelyn, the blonde woman, and her Chinese butler with luggage, preparing for an imminent departure. He telephones Escobar and tells the lieutenant to meet him at the address. Then he slaps Evelyn until she blurts out the truth that Katherine (Belinda Palmer), the blonde, is both her daughter and her sister, the product of an incestuous affair with her father, Noah Cross. Shocked and believing in Evelyn's innocence, Jake advises them to meet him at the butler's address in Chinatown. As an afterthought, Evelyn mentions that the spectacles found in the pond did not belong to Hollis because he didn't wear bifocals.

In a clever ruse, Jake pretends to take Escobar to Evelyn but instead guides them to the home of the fisherman, Curly; there, he surreptitiously escapes by hiding in Curly's truck and persuades him to go to Chinatown to pick up Evelyn and Katherine, assisting in their escape.

In a showdown with Cross at Evelyn's estate, Jake confronts him with the cracked eye glasses that belong to him as evidence that he murdered Mulwray. Admitting that he is the perpetrator of the land-grab scheme, Cross proudly presents his vision of a Los Angeles incorporated with the valley and demands that Jake take him to Katherine, the only daughter he has left.

The final scene is the only setting in Chinatown, and when Jake arrives, his assistants Walsh and Duffy (Joe Mantell and Bruce Glover) are handcuffed and Jake is handcuffed to Detective Loach. As he tries to explain to Escobar that Noah Cross is responsible for Mulwray's murder and is also behind the water and land scandal, Cross approaches Evelyn, pleading with her to see his daughter. She adamantly refuses, then shoots her father in the arm and speeds away. Shots are fired and the car stops with its horn blowing, and as Jake rushes to open the door Evelyn's body falls out; she has been fatally shot in the back of the head. Ordering everyone to be released, Escobar tells Walsh and Duffy to take Jake home. And in the famous last line of the film, Walsh tells Jake: "Forget it, Jake. It's Chinatown!"

Chinatown is a classic film noir fable with mysteries, lies, and conspiracy that lead to tragic circumstances. It is also about greed and the arrogance of power and the futility of attempting to thwart its ultimate resolution. It was released during the Nixon Watergate revelations that in many ways matched the intrigue of the film. That same year, Patricia Hearst, a granddaughter of newspaper scion William Randolph Hearst, was kidnapped by the Symbionese Liberation Army and then participated in a bank robbery. After serving two years in prison, her sentence was commuted by President Jimmy Carter and later she was pardoned by President Bill Clinton. Her grandfather could have been an inspiration for Noah Cross, and the commutation and pardon of his granddaughter is a reflection of power, wealth, and "justice."

BLAZING SADDLES (1974)

PRODUCER/DIRECTOR: Mel Brooks (director), Michael Hertzberg (producer)
WRITER(S): Mel Brooks (screenplay), Norman Steinberg (screenplay), Andrew Bergman (screenplay), Richard Pryor (screenplay), Alan Uger, Andrew Bergman (story)
CAST: Cleavon Little (Bart), Gene Wilder (Jim), Slim Pickens (Taggart), Harvey Korman (Hedley Lamarr), Madeline Kahn (Lili Von Shtupp), Mel Brooks (Governor William J. Lepetomane/Indian Chief), Burton Gilliam (Lyle), Alex Karras (Mongo), David Huddleston (Olson Johnson), Liam Dunn (Rev. Johnson)
CINEMATOGRAPHY: Joseph F. Biroc
MUSIC: John Morris
LENGTH AND RATING: 93 min; R

It takes a special ability and talent to create parody, which can be a difficult challenge in literature and the visual arts. Literature has a rich tradition in the art of parody, as when Aristophanes parodied the plays of Euripedes, and Cervantes mocked the age of chivalry in his classic *Don Quixote*. In film, parody is a satire of either a genre or a specific film which may feature scatological, gross, and vulgar humor, stereotypes, and sexual innuendo. Two of the greatest directors to engage in parody are Woody Allen, who directed *Bananas* (1971), *Everything You Always Wanted to Know About Sex but Were Afraid to Ask* (1972), *Sleeper* (1973), and *Love and Death* (1975), and Mel Brooks, although others such as Blake Edwards and his *Pink Panther* franchise are enduring examples of the genre.

In *Blazing Saddles*, Mel Brooks indirectly satirizes the work of the great authors and filmmakers of America's Old West, among them Zane Grey and John Ford, who paid tribute to the heroism and sacrifice of the settlers. Brooks does a send-up that includes cowboys eating beans to a chorus of farting around a campfire, lots of racist humor, and references to idiomatic racial expressions. However, using the theme of the western's traditional good guy (white) and bad guy (black), he is able to transcend images of hostile racism by making fun of white bigots, historical cinematic references to blacks (Stepin' Fetchit, the world's laziest man, portrayed by Lincoln Perry), and transforming a black man, Black Bart (Cleavon Little), into the hero of the film.

The plot is a simplistic treatment of iconic western themes. A wholesome town, Rock Ridge is populated by whites petitioning idiotic sex-crazed Governor William J. Lepetomane (Mel Brooks) for a new sheriff after being attacked by a posse trying to drive them off their land, which will become very valuable when the railroad comes through. The governor and his corrupt attorney general, Hedley Lamarr (Harvey Korman), scheme to reprieve Black Bart from the gallows and send him to Rock Ridge as the new sheriff, hoping he will alienate the bigoted townsfolk and cause them to leave.

The people of Rock Ridge, anxiously awaiting the sheriff's arrival, have decked out the town with a podium and planned a reception with speeches and a brass band.

As he rides in and they see he's black, they try to kill him but he cleverly threatens to blow his own head off by aiming the gun on himself. Safely in the jail, he meets the gunslinger called the Waco Kid (Gene Wilder) and eventually they join forces, winning over the town and defending it from the murdering posse led by Hedley Lamarr.

In an attempt to corrupt Black Bart and blackmail him, Lamarr arranges for Lili Von Shtupp (Madeline Kahn) to seduce him. She's a saloon singer and Kahn does a hilarious, lisping parody ("I'm Tired") of Marlene Dietrich's "Falling in Love Again," from *Der blaue Engel* (*The Blue Angel*, 1930). The western reference is to Dietrich's portrayal of the saloon singer "Frenchy" in the film *Destry Rides Again* (1939).

The seduction includes anatomical humor alluding to the male genitalia and breathless confirmation by Von Shtupp, who is seduced by Bart. To save the town from the marauding outlaws rounded up by Lamarr, Bart enlists the chain gang working on the railroad to build an exact replica. After the outlaws ride in to the fake Rock Ridge, they are subdued by exploding dynamite, which the Waco Kid sets off with a single shot from his revolver.

The film's final scenes are a jumbled, chaotic brawl that spills out to a Warner Brothers Hollywood lot. Inside a soundstage is a Busby Berkeley-like set, with gay male dancers directed by Buddy Bizarre (Dom DeLuise). The *Blazing Saddles* actors break through the wall and fight with the gay dancers, which eventually has them bursting into the studio commissary. It ends as a movie within a movie as Hedley hails a taxi and is driven to Grauman's Chinese Theatre, settling into a seat only to leave when he sees that the movie is *Blazing Saddles*. Once outside, he is shot in the groin by Bart and then falls into wet cement, writing his name followed by a dollar sign. Bart and Waco join forces heading to "Nowhere Special," dismounting from their horses and entering a chauffered limousine that drives into the sunset.

This film, and Mel Brooks' style, influenced the work of other producer/directors, including the Ferrelly brothers (*Dumb and Dumber*, 1994, and *Shallow Hal*, 2001). The reviews for the film were mixed, with Pauline Kael commenting, "Mel Brooks' comedy of chaos, with a surfeit of chaos and a scarcity of comedy" (http://www.geocities.com/paulinekaelreviews/b6.html).

Vincent Canby of the *New York Times* referred to it as "low burlesque":

Blazing Saddles, which opened yesterday at the Sutton Theater, is every Western you've ever seen turned upside down, and inside out, braced with a lot of low burlesque, which is fine. In retrospect, however, one remembers along with the good gags the film's desperate, bone-crushing efforts to be funny. One remembers the exhaustion, perhaps because you kept wanting it to be funnier than it was. Much of the laugher Mr. Brooks inspires is hopeful, before-the-gag laugher, which can be terribly tiring. (Canby, 1974, *New York Times*)

Roger Ebert called the film's structure "a total mess" but praised its ability to provoke laughter: "*Blazing Saddles* is like that. It's a crazed grab bag of a movie that does everything to keep us laughing except hit us over the head with a rubber chicken. Mostly, it succeeds. It's an audience picture; it doesn't have a lot of classy polish and its structure is a total mess" (http://rogerebert.suntimes.com).

In retrospect, Mel Brooks' humor in *Blazing Saddles* broke through the arcane measure of political correctness and laid bare the truth about liberal racism and sexism within the dynamic of American society. It mocks the civility of inappropriate language and bodily functions, providing the ultimate equalizer, which is human frailty.

YOUNG FRANKENSTEIN (1974)

PRODUCER/DIRECTOR: Mel Brooks (director), Michael Gruskoff (producer)
WRITER(S): Gene Wilder, Mel Brooks
CAST: Gene Wilder (Dr. Frankenstein), Peter Boyle (The Monster), Marty Feldman (Igor), Cloris Leachman (Frau Blücher), Teri Garr (Inga), Kenneth Mars (Inspector Kemp), Richard Haydn (Herr Falkstein), Liam Dunn (Mr. Hilltop), Danny Goldman (Medical Student), Oscar Beregi Jr. (Sadistic Jailor), Madeline Kahn (Elizabeth)
CINEMATOGRAPHY: Gerald Hirschfeld
MUSIC: John Morris
LENGTH AND RATING: 106 min: PG

Although Mel Brooks' *Young Frankenstein* is a parody of the original 1931 *Frankenstein* directed by James Whale, it also pays homage to the cinematic traditions of horror in the movies that *Frankenstein* and *Dracula* established. In its beautifully toned, black-and-white cinematography, use of optical wipes, and setting and laboratory of the orginal 1931 film, Brooks pokes fun but with a certain amount of reverence.

The grandson of Dr. Victor Frankenstein, Dr. Frederick Frankenstein (Gene Wilder) is an eminent scientist, brain surgeon, and medical school professor who inherits his grandfather's castle. One of the running jokes in the film is Frederick's insistence in having his surname pronounced STEEN, not STEIN, in an effort to disassociate himself from his "raving" grandfather. At the train station awaiting his departure, Frederick says good-bye to his fiancée, Elizabeth (Madeline Kahn), recalling the cliché of every fog- and smoke-bound train departure scene from the early movies. He wants to embrace and kiss Elizabeth, but she demurs, concerned about her makeup and wrinkling her clothing.

Arriving in Transylvania, (the setting for *Dracula* and not the Bavaria of the original *Frankenstein*), Frederick is met at the train station by Igor (Marty Feldman), whose name is pronounced eye-gor and who denies having an obvious hunchback, which shifts position throughout the film. He informs him that his grandfather worked for Frederick's, but since then rates have gone up. Leading him to his transport, a horse-drawn wagon filled with hay, Frederick meets the lovely Inga (Teri Garr), his new lab assistant.

Arriving at the castle, he is greeted by the dour, fearful Frau Bleucher (Cloris Leachman), who causes the horses to whinny every time her name is mentioned. Sending up another cinematic cliché, Frederick and Inga find the hidden door, disguised as a bookcase, locating his grandfather's laboratory.

As in the original *Frankenstein*, Igor drops the "good brain" and exchanges it for a brain marked "abnormal." When the roaring monster (Peter Boyle) awakens, Frederick initiates a game of charades to communicate the need for Inga and Igor to inject him with a sedative. This funny gag occurs again, when the monster attempts to strangle Frederick.

In a reference to a famous scene in the movie *King Kong* (1933), the monster becomes agitated when a lightbulb explodes after he performs a soft-shoe number of "Puttin' on the Ritz" with Frederick onstage before an audience. In *King Kong*, this event provides the catalyst for Kong to break free of his chains and go on a rampage in New York City.

In another parody of the original *Frankenstein*, when the monster meets a little girl, instead of accidentally drowning her as he does in the original, she is suddenly catapulted off a seesaw, flies through her bedroom window, and is tucked into bed by her concerned parents.

After the monster kidnaps Elizabeth, he is able to earn back her trust and love thanks to his prowess in the bedroom. At the end, Frederick has normalized the monster by sharing his brain and calmed the mob, led by Police Inspector Hans Wilhelm Friederich Kemp (Kenneth Mars, modeled after Dr. Strangelove), who wants to kill the beast. The resolution of the film has Elizabeth married to the monster, who sits reading *The Wall Street Journal*. Frederick marries Inga.

In *Young Frankenstein*, Mel Brooks was deferential to the traditions of early monster movies and their impact on film culture and history. Many critics agreed that Brooks' film was funny, but in its parody respectful to the theme. In his *New York Times* review, Vincent Canby notes that the film was more disciplined and controlled, and Pauline Kael said that it could make you laugh helplessly:

> Although it hasn't as many roof raising boffs as *Blazing Saddles*, it is funnier over the long run because it is more disciplined. The anarchy is controlled. Mr. Brooks sticks to the subject, recalling the clichés of horror films of the nineteen-thirties as lovingly as someone remembering the small sins of youth. (Canby, "*Young Frankenstein*")

> A farce-parody of Hollywood's mad-scientist movies. You have to let this Mel Brooks comedy do everything for you, because that's the only way it works. If you accept the silly, zizzy obviousness, it can make you laugh helplessly. (http://www.geocities.com/paulinekaelreviews/xy)

In his review, Roger Ebert praised Mel Brooks because he could make the audience laugh when they should have been offended:

> In his two best comedies, before this, "The Producers" and "Blazing Saddles," Brooks revealed a rare comic anarchy. His movies weren't just funny, they were aggressive and subversive, making us laugh even when we really should have been offended. (Explaining this process, Brooks once loftily declared, "My movies rise below vulgarity.") (http://rogerebert.suntimes.com)

THE CONVERSATION (1974)

PRODUCER/DIRECTOR: Francis Ford Coppola

WRITER(S): Francis Ford Coppola

CAST: Gene Hackman (Harry Caul), John Cazale (Stan), Allen Garfield (William P. "Bernie" Moran), Frederic Forrest (Mark), Cindy Williams (Ann), Michael Higgins (Paul),

Elizabeth MacRae (Meredith), Teri Garr (Amy Fredericks), Harrison Ford (Martin Stett),
Mark Wheeler (Receptionist)
CINEMATOGRAPHY: Bill Butler
MUSIC: David Shire
LENGTH AND RATING: 113 min: PG

Profoundly disturbing when Francis Ford Coppola produced this film, during the Watergate era and with a purpose that clearly resonates in today's world of intrusion and identity theft, *The Conversation* is a parable on the sacrifice of privacy and its resulting consequences. The main character is surveillence expert and master "bugger" Harry Caul (Gene Hackman.) Harry's reputation has secured him a reverence in the professional community that endures from coast to coast. He is consumed with protecting his privacy, with numerous locks on his apartment door and little revealed about his life. When a neighbor greets him with happy birthday wishes and Harry then enters his apartment to discover a gift-wrapped bottle of wine from his landlady, Mrs. Evangelista, he becomes annoyed that she has entered his apartment and calls her from his unlisted telephone that he hides in a desk drawer to complain about her intrusion. The irony is that while Harry's reputation has followed him from New York to San Francisco, he is woefully inadequate in protecting his own privacy.

With the help of his assistant, Stanley (John Cazale), and others, Harry has just finished a complex audio surveillance of a young couple, Ann (Cindy Williams) and Mark (Frederic Forrest), walking in San Francisco's City of Paris Park during the lunch hour. He has been hired by the mysterious Director (Robert Duvall) to eavesdrop on his wife, whom he suspects of being unfaithful.

For Harry Caul, life is lonely and destitute, with no friends, a fleeting relationship with a woman, and his only entertainment listening to jazz records as he accompanys the music with his saxophone. While listening to the tape recordings, Harry scolds Stanley for asking too many questions and using the Lord's name in vain. In another scene, when Harry surreptitiously visits Amy (Teri Garr), his mistress, on his birthday, she tells him how little she knows about him and badgers him with questions. He lies when he tells her that he's a freelance musician and is annoyed by her probing questions. Finally, Amy tells him that she won't be waiting for him any longer and he leaves, knowing the relationship has ended. When Harry tries to reconnect with her, he finds that her phone has been disconnected.

He is haunted by a surveillance job in New York City that resulted in the murder of three innocent people. Although he outwardly expresses that his only job is to deliver recordings, he is guilt-ridden over the incident. After arranging a meeting to submit the tapes and collect his $15,000 fee, Harry refuses to give the tapes to the Director's assistant, Martin Stett (Harrison Ford), and insists on dealing with his client directly. He is warned by Stett not to interfere because somebody could get hurt. As he leaves the building, he sees the young couple together.

Later he returns to his workshop, located in a desolate warehouse, and continues to listen to the tape. As a result of his surveillance of the young couple and his technical expertise, he hears Mark say on the tape, "He'd kill us if he got the chance," and then a reference to a 3:00 p.m. Sunday rendezvous in room 773 at the Jack Tar Hotel. His worry over the welfare of Mark and Ann is evident in a church confessional scene, when he attempts to absolve himself of petty sins and then briefly alludes to his work and concern, then abruptly leaves.

At a surveillance convention of hardware and experts at the St. Francis Hotel, Harry is a celebrity with vendors eager to solicit his endorsement. Stopping by a video booth demonstrating surveillance cameras, he notices Martin Stett following him. After a confrontation, Stett instructs Harry to deliver the tapes to the Director that Sunday at 1:00 p.m. Later, he stops by the booth of Moran and Associates, meeting the slimy technology salesman, William T. "Bernie" Moran (Allen Garfield). The loud and overly gregarious Moran, a contrast to Harry's introversion, offers him a free pen, which he places in Harry's breast pocket. Surprised to see Stanley working Moran's booth, Harry admonishes him not to divulge any of his trade secrets.

In an uncharacteristic role, Harry invites Moran, Stanley, Meredith (Elizabeth MacRae), Moran's sexy booth "eye candy," and a group of friends to his workshop. As they drink and cavort, Moran extols the virtues of Harry's expertise and his own, even suggesting that they become partners. They share exploits with Stanley, telling him about Harry's ingenious planting of microphones. However, things become tense when Moran raises the resulting murders of Harry's New York City job, to which Harry responds that all he did was turn the tapes in.

The party scene reaches a climax after Moran plays a recording of Harry discussing his intimate feelings with Meredith, a conversation caught by the pen microphone that Moran had planted in Harry's breast pocket. He has bugged "the bugger" and Harry orders everyone to leave except Meredith. She stays behind to "comfort" Harry, and when he wakes from a restless sleep the next morning he discovers that the tape is missing.

He attempts to call the Director at his company, but is told that someone will return his call. The call is indeed returned on Harry's hidden, unlisted telephone, and he is told by Stett that the company has a complete dossier on him, and to bring the photographs, meet the director, and collect his fee.

In the office, Harry asks the Director what will happen to Ann, the Director's wife, and he is asked to take his money and count it outside. In a daring move, Harry checks in to a room adjoining room 773 at the Jack Tar Hotel. Using the tools of his trade, he drills a hole in the bathroom wall adjacent to the toilet and, hearing Ann's sudden scream through the headphones, he jolts up, imagining the carnage in the room next door.

After curling up in bed with the television tuned to a Flintstones cartoon, Harry breaks into room 773. He hesitantly pulls the shower curtain aside to reveal a clean bathtub and drain. But when he flushes the toilet, it overflows with bloody water and blood-soaked toilet tissue. Shocked, he rushes to the corporate headquarters but is blocked entry by burly security guards. However, he's just in time to see Ann and Mark leave the building, surrounded by reporters who question her about her husband's death and control of the company. Now, Harry imagines what really happened in room 773: the murder of the Director in a manner similar to Hitchcock's shower scene in *Psycho*.

Back at his apartment and playing his saxophone, Harry receives a call from Martin Stett letting him know that he is being watched. He then plays back a recording of what Harry had just played on his saxophone. Determined to find the bugs, Harry dismantles his furniture and strips the walls and floors but is unsuccessful in locating them. In the last scene, Harry sits in the rubble of his apartment, playing the saxophone, a victim of his own trade, stripped of his privacy and his professional ego.

Harry Caul is a character haunted by childhood illness and the deadly consequences of his profession. He is devoid of personality and the ability to engage in personal relationships. It is indeed an irony that Harry lives like a hermit and that his only recreation is the solitude of playing his saxophone and the voyeuristic act of spying on other people. He is detached and aloof, obsessed with protecting himself from the prying eyes of others and sustaining his world of anonymity.

The theme and relevance of *The Conversation* are in many ways prescient to today's concern about violation of privacy and the intrusion and oversight by technology into the home and work place.

Developing the story and completing his screenplay by 1969, Coppola was fascinated to learn that bugging was a profession. Faced with a deadline to complete *The Godfather Part II*, Coppola hired Walter Murch, the brilliant sound and picture editor (http://www.geraldpeary.com/essays/the/the_conversation.html).

In his April 21, 1974, *New York Times* review, Vincent Canby called the film haunting and fastidiously detailed, noting that Gene Hackman's performance was "superb." Roger Ebert described the film as a "...taut, intelligent thriller" (http://rogerebert.suntimes.com).

NASHVILLE (1975)

PRODUCER/DIRECTOR: Robert Altman

WRITER(S): Joan Tewkesbury

CAST: David Arkin (Norman), Barbara Baxley (Lady Pearl), Ned Beatty (Delbert Reese), Karen Black (Connie White), Ronee Blakley (Barbara Jean), Timothy Brown (Tommy Brown), Keith Carradine (Tom Frank), Geraldine Chaplin (Opal), Robert DoQui (Wade Cooley), Shelley Duvall (Marthe aka "L. A. Joan")

CINEMATOGRAPHY: Paul Lohmann

MUSIC: Arlene Barnett, Jonnie Barnett, Karen Black, Ronee Blakley, Gary Busey, Juan Grizzle, Allan F. Nicholls, Dave Peel, Joe Raposo

LENGTH AND RATING: 159 min; R

The word *epic* in literature is usually defined as a long poem that tells the story of gods and heroes and their exploits. One such epic, Homer's *The Iliad*, is often loosely organized, episodic, and has some digressions. Every episode may not be essential to understanding the entire story but it does add a dimension to its substance.

Epic films, such as *Intolerance* (1916), *Birth of a Nation* (1915), *Gone with the Wind* (1939), and, more recently, *The Godfather* saga (1972, 1974, 1990) and *Schindler's List* (1993), have taken compelling historical events and dramatized them for the screen. One could define epics from their narrative content, cast of characters, and running time. Within the context of that definition, and although *Nashville's* running time of over two-and-a-half hours could qualify it as an epic, it has an unconventional narrative structure that evolves around twenty-four characters who bring their own story to an event that brings them all together. The poetry is the country music written or co-written and performed by the actors portraying their characters, creating an enduring dynamic of personalities and events that converge on a canvas of greed, ambition, arrogance, and disdain.

In *Nashville*, Altman has created a "tableau vivant" of characters placed on a ritual-istic canvas that reveals the foibles and desires they have buried within a lifetime of secrecy. The cast of characters is cleverly introduced in a playful, fast-paced montage that quickly cuts to each character and provides a sound-bite on who they are. The film's trailer is like a hard-sell televison commercial that ends with a strong sales message:

> Now, after years in the making, Robert Altman brings you his...Nashville with twenty-four, count'em, twenty-four of your very favorite stars...right before your very eyes without commercial interruption.

Country music provides a central theme and is featured like another character because of the way it weaves through the film, helping to create a common bond between the characters. In this film it's more than just background music; it assumes a part of the character's fabric, adding another dimension to understanding motivation and purpose.

Perhaps Altman's greatest accomplishment is that, unlike traditional character-driven films that define just several leading protagonists, he deftly gives his audience twenty-four of them to follow and care about, even though some gain more prominence than others. More importantly, they seamlessly move through the narrative in a natural, interpersonal way that helps to define who they are and understand their motivation. Most interestingly, the character who brings all of these people together is Hal Phillip Walker (Thomas Hal Phillips), the independent presidential candidate of the Replace-ment Party who never appears on screen but whose voice the audience hears broadcast-ing his campaign message. His ideas about inept political leadership and corrupt lawyers in the seat of government punctuate the film's multi-layered sound track.

The country music celebrities converge on Nashville to perform at the Grand Ole Opry and are solicited by John Triplette (Michael Murphy), Walker's campaign man-ager who is working with one of Nashville's preeminent lawyers, Delbert Reese (Ned Beatty), to cajole some of them to perform at Walker's political rally, to be held at the Parthenon in Nashville. In an attempt to convince country music star Haven Hamilton (Henry Gibson) to perform at the rally, Triplette proposes that Walker could be inclined to endorse him should he be interested in running for governor of Tennessee.

The opening scenes are established by creating a sense of patriotism within the context of celebrating America's Bicentennial. A sound truck broadcasting Walker's message of change and political involvement proceeds down the street, admonishing that the Replacement Party is ready to do some replacing. This is followed by the inte-rior of a recording studio, where Haven Hamilton is recording "200 years," a "solemn" tribute to the Bicentennial replete with hackneyed patriotic language and stanzas that each end with the refrain, "Oh we must be doin' somethin' right to last 200 years." While recording, he is distracted by the presence of Opal (Geraldine Chaplin), a preten-tious British Broadcasting Corporation (BBC) reporter who is producing a documentary and provides some of the characters' backstory by conducting audio interviews with them. Angered that there is a stranger watching him record, Hamilton orders his son, Buddy Hamilton (David Peel), to remove her, and Buddy takes Opal into another stu-dio which is recording a black gospel choir led by a Caucasion woman, Linnea Reese (Lily Tomlin), Delbert's wife. As they watch, Opal describes what she sees as "frenzied," mentions that their behavior is genetic, and says she can imagine being in darkest

Africa watching their dancing, naked bodies. Throughout the film she demonstrates her obnoxious, arrogant behavior, as when she and Linnea are riding in a car together after leaving the Nashville airport and she is told by Linnea that her two children are deaf and Opal blurts out, "How awful."

A catalyst in the film that provides the means for all of the characters to converge at Nashville Metro Airport is the arrival of country music star and local favorite, Barbara Jean (Ronee Blakely), who is returning from convalescing after suffering severe burns. An eager crowd led by Haven Hamilton as the pompous master of ceremonies has gathered to welcome her home, replete with the local high school twirlers and marching band. However, she collapses on her way inside to greet people gathered there and is rushed to the hospital.

In a frantic scene on the highway, the cars leaving the airport collide and swerve after a sofa falls off an open flatbed and a truck carrying a boat swerves to avoid hitting it. This event provides an interesting interlude that allows the audience to get better acquainted with the many personalities involved in the story. Standing in a Volkswagen Beetle, Tom Frank (Keith Carradine), who is part of a folk-rock trio that includes the husband and wife team of Bill (Allan Nicholis) and Mary (Cristina Raines), is taking telephone numbers from various young women. He is an insufferable self-centered womanizer who listens to his own recordings while in bed with Opal and Mary, and he relentlessly calls Linnea, whom he met several months earlier at a recording studio, eventually having a liaison with her. His superficial, cavalier attitude toward the women he sleeps with is reflected in his scheduling women to succeed those he has just bedded down before she has even left his room.

Nashville is a story about fragile egos, hope, fantasies, political determinism, jealously, and manipulation as people pursue their dreams and ideals. Two of the women, Suleen Gay (Gwen Welles) and Albuquerque Winifred (Barbara Harris), are aspiring country music stars consumed by the populist culture of celebrity, and they face a number of obstacles trying to make it on stage. The unfortunate reality for Suleen, the waitress, is that she cannot carry a tune. She is cajoled into performing a reluctant striptease before a male audience of potential Walker donors on the promise of appearing at the Walker benefit at Nashville's famous Parthenon on the same stage as Barbara Jean. After the event she arrives home and her dishwasher colleague and friend from the diner, Wade (Robert Doqui), tries to tell her she cannot sing but she is undeterred. Winifred, who can sing, is running away from her husband, Star (Bert Remsen), and is given a performance slot at the local celebrity drag raceway but her voice is drowned out by the roar and exhaust of the engines. At the end of the film, when Barbara Jean is shot by the troubled drifter Kenny Frasier (David Hayward), a wounded Haven Hamilton thrusts the microphone into Winifred's hands and tells her to sing. She sings "It Don't Worry Me" and is accompanied by the choir and engages the restless audience, preventing a panic. As she sings we see close-ups of women, children, and men in the audience, singing along with her and appearing to put the tragedy behind them. It is an ironic twist to a tragic ending as Winifred is given her chance at fame, a shattered star and one about to shine.

Throughout the film the audience is faced with actors who command their roles so effectively it is difficult to separate the real from the fiction. Indeed, the performances and authoring of many of the songs by the actors creates a unique presence by them not merely performing but living their roles. At times the audience is touched by the emotional vulnerability of the characters, and at others their behavior is abhorrent, manipulative, and destructive. *Nashville* is a microcosm of life that is a revelation about interpersonal relationships that have a shared experience, whether they are mired in celebrity or facing the mundane routines of everyday life.

In his 1975 *New York Times* review, Vincent Canby speaks of the film's well-defined structure and "burst of life" that seems impossible to plan.

He continues by recognizing Lily Tomlin's "spectacular dramatic debut" and calling the film an "immense collaboration, a timely coming together of all sorts of resources" (Canby, Vincent. 1975. *Nashville, New York Times* June 12).

JAWS (1975)

PRODUCER/DIRECTOR: Steven Spielberg (director), David Brown (producer), Richard D. Zanuck (producer)

WRITER(S): Peter Benchley (novel, screenplay), Carl Gottlieb (screenplay)

CAST: Roy Scheider (Police Chief Martin Brody), Robert Shaw (Quint), Richard Dreyfuss (Matt Hooper), Lorraine Gary (Ellen Brody), Murray Hamilton (Mayor Larry Vaughn), Carl Gottlieb (Ben Meadows), Jeffrey Kramer (Deputy Leonard "Lenny" Hendricks), Susan Backlinie (Christine "Chrissie" Watkins), Jonathan Filley (Tom Cassidy), Ted Grossman (Estuary Victim)

CINEMATOGRAPHY: Bill Butler

MUSIC: John Williams

LENGTH AND RATING: 124 min; PG

The best form of horror is the implied anticipation and surprise of a shocking event. This technique is masterfully portrayed in Steven Spielberg's *Jaws*. Based on the novel by Peter Benchley and a screenplay written by Spielberg and Carl Gottleib, *Jaws* features cinematic tributes to the movies the director grew up with and admired.

One of those films may have been John Huston's 1956 film adaptation of the 1851 Herman Melville novel, *Moby Dick*, which starred Gregory Peck as the whale-obsessed Captain Ahab of the whaling ship *Pequod*. Both Quint and Ahab have experienced the majesty and wrath of the beasts they hunt, the white whale and the great white shark, and in turn, each of them realizes and suffers their greatest nightmare.

The power of suggestion is the best tool a film director can use to create a sense of foreboding and fear. Using the elements of music (composed by John Williams) and a subjective camera angle that does not reveal a detailed image of the shark until later in the film, Spielberg sets a tone of heightened terror. A group of teenagers sitting on a beach around a summer bonfire, drinking alcohol and smoking pot, are innocents passing through a lifetime ritual of disobedience and experimentation. This purity is reflected in the New England coastal town of Amity (meaning "friend"), which offers sun, sand, and an ambience of fun and relaxation on a carefree island. It's summertime and the ferry disembarks passengers laden with beach chairs, sand umbrellas, funny hats, ill-fitting bathing suits, and buckets of suntan lotion, the paraphernalia of the summer tourist. The crowds are a symbol of prosperity to the business owners in every seasonal beach resort, including Amity.

The innocence and reverie is disrupted when Chrissie Watkins (Susan Backlinie) tempts a drunken teenage boy to skinny dip in the ocean, and as she runs toward the beach she removes an article of clothing until she is completely naked. She dives into the ocean and swims while her aroused young follower passes out on the beach.

The scene of Chrissie blithely swimming in the dark ocean on a moonlit night evokes both harmony and fear. Water is a ritual symbol in cinema, representing cleansing, purity, and life. It can also prompt fear of the unknown, of what may be lurking beneath the depths of the ocean. An attractive woman swimming also conveys sexuality and beauty. In *The Creature from the Black Lagoon* (1954), Kay Lawrence (Julie Adams) dives off a boat for a leisurely swim and is stalked by a gilled, scaled creature that swims below and parallel to her, a reference to beauty and the beast. In *Tarzan and His Mate* (1934), the beautifully choreographed underwater swimming ballet of Tarzan (Johnny Weissmuller) and Jane (Olympic swimmer Josephine McKim standing in for actress Maureen O'Sullivan) is poetic, sexual, and visually enchanting.

As Chrissie swims, she is also stalked by an unseen creature, which grabs her and speeds through the water as she screams and clings to a floating buoy and a bell that sounds the final death knell of her life. This act serves as the catalyst to a story that interweaves themes of greed, conspiracy, fear, mob psychology, arrogance, and heroism, each sustained by the acting and imagery.

Former New York City cop and Amity Police Chief Martin Brody (Roy Scheider), who has a phobia about swimming or being on the water, has recently relocated to the island with his wife Ellen (Lorraine Gary) and their two young sons.

After discovering Chrissie's mutilated remains and typing an incident report listing the cause of death as a possible shark attack, Brody orders his deputy to make signs warning bathers that the beaches are closed. He is quickly overruled by Amity's mayor, Larry Vaughn (Murray Hamilton), and told by the medical examiner that he must amend his report to indicate that the cause of death was a boating accident.

In a scene filled with tension, Brody is on the beach with his family, anxiously staring into the water. Adults and children are swimming, kicking, and splashing, and a boy is tossing a stick to his dog, who eagerly retrieves it from the water. In an ominous sign, the stick floats on the water and the dog does not return. A young boy floating on a raft is suddenly attacked, and after a panicked retreat from the water by all of the bathers, the only sign of the boy is his mangled raft and the blood-tinged water that washes ashore, to the horror of his mother.

At a raucous town meeting, Brody, along with the town council, presents plans for dealing with the shark and is surprised to learn that while he has requested that the beaches be closed, Mayor Vaughn announces that the closure will last only 24 hours. Grabbing the attention of the room, crusty fisherman and Navy veteran Quint (Robert Shaw, a reference to Melville's Captain Ahab in *Moby Dick*) scratches a blackboard with his nails, silencing the commotion, and offers to catch the shark for $10,000. Because the town has already approved a $3,000 bounty for anyone who catches the animal, Quint's offer is dismissed.

In two scenes that offer comic relief, a couple of men on a pier bait the shark, which pulls the pier out from under them, and one of them barely swim back in time. In another scene, local townsfolk board their boats, dingys, and anything that floats to locate the shark, capture it, and earn the reward. It's a mob scene as they crowd the water and demonstrate their ignorance about navigation. The character of Matt Hooper (Richard Dreyfuss), the marine biologist, enters this scene and later examines Chrissie's remains, clearly stating that a shark was the cause of death, and not a boating accident.

A large captured tiger shark is hauled in and hung up on the pier for a photo shoot and congratulatory remarks by Mayor Vaughn, who is relieved the nightmare is over. Hooper is not convinced, and later that evening he and Brody perform an autopsy that proves the captured shark is not the predator. They embark on Hooper's gadget-equipped research vessel to locate the shark and in the process discover the wreckage of Ben Gardner's boat, and, in a dive, Hooper locates his remains. Insisting that the beaches must be closed, they fail to convince Mayor Vaughn. On the July 4 weekend, the mayor and Chief Brody are both on the beach: Brody keeping watch and the mayor urging a local resident and his family to swim in the deserted ocean. As the beachgoers enter the water, a shark fin appears and Brody orders everyone out of the water, but it turns out to be a prank by two young boys. During the scare, a young woman's voice, crying out that there is a shark in the pond, finally draws Brody's attention and the horror becomes more real, because his son Michael and his friends are there, floating in a sailboat. In the pond, the shark turns over a boat and bites the leg off his victim, then swims toward Michael, who is floating in the water. It's a tense scene, and Brody rescues his son, who is unharmed and taken to a hospital.

Confronted again, the mayor reluctantly agrees to hire Quint and he, Brody, and Hooper join forces for the hunt. These men from such diverse backgrounds bond through this treacherous experience. In a particularly moving night scene aboard Quint's boat, the *Orca*, the men have been drinking and Quint and Hooper are showing off their physiscal scars, each attempting to outdo the other. Finally, Quint reveals his tattoo from the USS *Indianapolis*. His riveting story is historically true, as this ship was torpedoed by a Japanese submarine and sank in the Phillipine Sea on July 30, 1945. It was returning from a top-secret mission after delivering the atomic bomb to the US air base on Tinian Island. It had a crew of 1,196 men, 880 of whom were forced to float in the water, and, after four days, 321 were rescued with some who may have been eaten by sharks. Reasons for the rescue delay and the validity of the shark attacks are disputed, but the relevance to the movie is compelling.

The hunted shark continues to confound its hunters with behavior uncharacteristic for its species. Finally, after the *Orca* has sustained considerable damage, Hooper descends in his shark cage and narrowly escapes. However, when Brody and Quint pull up the badly damaged, empty cage, they fear their friend is dead. In a harrowing scene, the shark attacks the boat and Quint is eaten, his greatest fear. Left alone, Brody throws a compressed air tank into the mouth of the shark and, armed with a rifle, climbs up to the crow's nest and fires a couple of shots, finally hitting the tank, which explodes, killing the shark. Floating in the water on a piece of debris, Hooper finally surfaces and he and Brody paddle back to shore.

The film was a huge financial success and established the importance of the summer blockbuster, after opening in 675 theaters and earning domestic gross box office revenue of $260 million and a worldwide box office in excess of $460 million.

Although a horror film can be very entertaining, few have a lasting emotional impact upon their audience. In *Psycho*, Alfred Hitchcock managed to create enough bone-tingling fear in Janet Leigh's shower scene to frighten people into changing their bathing habits. With *Jaws*, Spielberg altered behavioral patterns toward swimming in the ocean. The film was released in the summer of 1975 and made many summer revelers reluctant to dip their feet into the deep, dark, blue sea.

📽 *ONE FLEW OVER THE CUCKOO'S NEST* (1975)

PRODUCER/DIRECTOR: Milos Forman (director), Michael Douglas (producer), Saul Zaentz (producer)

WRITER(S): Lawrence Hauben (screenplay), Bo Goldman (screenplay), Ken Kesey (novel), Dale Wasserman (play)

CAST: Jack Nicholson (R. P. McMurphy), Louise Fletcher (Nurse Mildred Ratched), William Redfield (Dale Harding), Michael Berryman (Ellis), Peter Brocco (Col. Matterson), Dean R. Brooks (Dr. John Spivey), Alonzo Brown (Miller), Scatman Crothers (Turkle), Mwako Cumbuka (Warren), Danny DeVito (Martini)

CINEMATOGRAPHY: Haskell Wexler

MUSIC: Jack Nitzsche

LENGTH AND RATING: 133 min; R

Based on the 1962 counterculture novel of the same name by Ken Kesey, the film, directed by Milos Forman, expressed a disdain for conformity and authority and articulated a respect and devotion to the freedom of spiritual exploration. As a graduate student in the creative writing program at Stanford University, Kesey also worked as a part-time orderly in a veterans hospital. As a student, he was a human subject in experiments with LSD, under the supervision of Stanford's psychology department, which resulted in hallucinations that contributed to the character development in his novel. Interestingly, the theme of the narrative as seen in the movie is about the revolt by Randle Patrick "Mac" McMurphy (Jack Nicholson) against Nurse Mildred Ratched (Louise Fletcher), the authoritarian figure in a mental hospital ward who represents the status quo.

The question raised in the film is, who are the crazy ones, the patients or their caregivers? A 1975 article published in *General Psychiatry* asserted that mental illness is a myth that doctors attribute to people being labeled as "mentally ill" because they have different aims, and that the phrase "mental illness" is used to make value judgments about how others behave. Such behavior has been described as "an enlightened expression of rebellion against a crazy society." This provides an interesting dynamic and contextual relevance when viewing *One Flew Over the Cuckoo's Nest*.

Dr. Glen Gabbard, the psychiatrist author of *Psychiatry and the Cinema*, has studied the portrayal of mental illness and psychiatry in the movies. In his practice he has dealt with patients who have requested a particular therapy, such as hypnosis, because they saw it in a film (*The Three Faces of Eve* [1957], for example). In the French film *The King of Hearts* (*Le Roi de Coeur*, 1966), starring Alan Bates, the Germans at the end of WWI have booby-trapped an entire town to explode during their retreat, and all of the inhabitants have left except for the patients in a mental hospital. The patients take over the town and prove to be a fun-loving bunch who create a utopian society and raise the question of who is crazy, the patients or the soldiers (Goode, Erica. 2002. "A Conversation with: Glen Gabbard; A Rare Day: The Movies Get Mental Illness Right," *New York Times*, February 5).

When Randle arrives at the mental institution from a work farm prison, his sanity is never questioned. After being evaluated by Dr. Spivey (Oregon State Mental Hospital superintendent Dr. Dean Brooks), the reason for McMurphy's referral is that he is lazy and disobedient. He had been serving a sixty-eight-day sentence for statutory rape. After being placed in the ward supervised by the repressed, rigid, and authoritarian Nurse Ratched, McMurphy's rebellious attitude threatens her dominance over the weak and compliant behavior of her other patients. As a free spirit and unaware that most of his ward-mates are self-committed and can leave the institution at any time, McMurphy's defiance of Ratched's rule of order wins over their admiration.

In several compelling scenes, including a brilliant one where, after being denied the privilege of watching a World Series baseball game after a democratic vote, McMurphy gathers the patients around a dark television screen and creates a fantasy narrative play-by-play that excites his new friends. This happens on the second day after a previous vote had failed to gather adequate support. In a second round of voting, McMurphy manages to have the "mute," the very large Native American Chief Bromden (Will Sampson), raise his hand, but Ratched denies the television privilege by claiming the voting was closed. Grasping at victory, she is dismayed when McMurphy sours her taste for success by rallying the patients around his fanatasy baseball game.

At almost every turn, McMurphy outmaneuvers Ratched. In a very funny scene, he hijacks the institution bus that is carrying his ward mates on a field trip, picks up his girlfriend Candy (Marya Small), and manages to board a charter fishing vessel by posing the inmates as doctors from the institution. The inmates' fears and foibles, although visible during the charter voyage, are managed, and their excitement at being freed from Ratched's bondage is very therapeutic.

When shock therapy fails to control McMurphy's rebellious behavior, he plans an escape to Canada with the Chief, who has been faking his deaf and dumb routine. Bribing the night monitor Turkle (Scatman Crothers), Candy and Rose (Louisa Moritz) enter the hospital to bring liquor for a wild party. During the celebrations, McMurphy convinces Candy to sleep with the stuttering, mother-dominated Billy Bibbit (Brad Dourif) and they are discovered together the next morning in bed, the ward in shambles. As his ward mates cheer Billy for his "conquest," Nurse Ratched admonishes him, saying he should be ashamed of himself, but he defies her by indicating that he's not and is applauded by his friends. Knowing his vulnerabilities, Nurse Ratched cruelly suggests that she will tell his mother about the incident and he pleads for her not to mention it. A few minutes later, Billy is found dead after slitting his throat, and in the ensuing confusion, when McMurphy could have escaped, he instead attacks Nurse Ratched, nearly strangling her to death before being subdued.

After the melee, the scene returns to the ward and to Nurse Ratched, who is wearing a neck brace while attending to her charges. That evening, McMurphy is wheeled into the ward in a catatonic state after having undergone a lobotomy. Realizing his friend is now in a nonfunctioning vegetative state, Chief Bromden places a pillow over McMurphy's face and smothers him. The Chief has found the courage to lift a heavy water fountain, smash it through a window, and break away from Nurse Ratched and the confines of the institution.

In his November 28, 1975, *New York Times* review, critic Vincent Canby describes Jack Nicholson's portrayal of Randle as one filled with "easy grace" and calls the supporting actors "close to briiliant."

> Mr. Nicholson slips into the role of Randle with such easy grace that it's difficult to remember him in any other film. It's a flamboyant performance but not so overbearing that it obscures his fellow actors, all of whom are very good and a few of whom are close to brilliant, including William Redfield (as an egghead patient who talks grave nonsense), Will Sampson (as a deaf-mute Indian) and Brad Dourif (as a young man with a fatal mother complex). (Canby *New York Times*)

In her review, Pauline Kael calls the film adaptation of Ken Kesey's novel "smashingly effective."

> Smashingly effective version of Ken Kesey's novel about a rebel outcast, McMurphy (Jack Nicholson), who is locked in a hospital for the insane. The book was a lyric jag, and it became a nonconformists' bible. Published in 1962, it contained the prophetic essence of the whole Vietnam period of revolutionary politics going psychedelic. (http://www.geocities.com/paulinekaelreviews/o2.html)

Similarities exist to the film *Cool Hand Luke* (1967), which stars Paul Newman as the noncomformist Luke who is imprisoned in a southern chain gang and inspires his fellow prisoners by his rebellion and escape attempts. Both McMurphy and Luke eventually die trying to assert their independence and win their freedom.

One Flew Over the Cuckoo's Nest earned Academy Awards for Best Picture, Best Director (Milos Forman), Best Actor (Jack Nicholson), Best Screenplay (Lawrence Hauben, Bo Goldman), and Best Actress (Louise Fletcher).

ROCKY (1976)

PRODUCER/DIRECTOR: John G. Avildsen (director), Robert Chartoff (producer), Irwin Winkler (producer)

WRITER(S): Sylvester Stallone

CAST: Sylvester Stallone (Rocky Balboa), Talia Shire (Adrianna "Adrian" Pennino), Burt Young (Paulie Pennino), Carl Weathers (Apollo Creed), Burgess Meredith (Mickey Goldmill), Thayer David (Jergens), Joe Spinell (Gazzo), Jimmy Gambina (Mike), Bill Baldwin (Fight Announcer), Al Silvani (Cut Man)

CINEMATOGRAPHY: James Crabe

MUSIC: Bill Conti

LENGTH AND RATING: 119 min; PG

Movies about American boxing have an enduring tradition in American cinema. From *The Champ* (1931) to Clint Eastwood's *Million Dollar Baby* (2004), they have portrayed the sport as an opportunity for upward social mobility while condemning it for its corruption and greed. Perhaps one of the best boxing stories ever written was not created for theatrical films but for televison. Written by Rod Serling, the teleplay *Requiem for a Heavyweight* (1956) was broadcast live on Playhouse 90. It was produced as a movie and released in 1962 with a different cast.

All the movies about boxing have been influenced by previous films and are derivative, including *Rocky*. It's interesting that watching the film more than thirty years after its release, one may wonder how such a poorly made film with a star of very limited acting ability (Sylvester Stallone), who also wrote the screenplay, had such a profound effect on American audiences. The movie was shot on location in Philadelphia in twenty-eight days with a budget of approximately one million dollars, and went on to earn more than $117 million in the U.S.

The film is about Rocky Balboa (the Italian Stallion), an inarticulate two-bit club fighter who is good natured and has an unrealized passion to succeed. Living alone with his turtles and goldfish, he's lonely and shy and trying to get a date with his friend Paulie's (Burt

Young) sister, the equally shy Adrian (Talia Shire), who works in a pet shop. Several turning points in the story establish Rocky as a conflicted character who must recognize the futility of his life and its lack of meaning. At the local gym, run by the crusty old fighter Mickey Goldmill (Burgess Meredith), Rocky learns that his locker has been given to an up-and-coming contender and that his things are now assigned a hook on "skid row." He is told by Mickey that he had the heart to be a much better boxer but instead wasted his opportunity by becoming an enforcer for the sleazy lone shark Tom Gazzo (Joe Spinell). Sent out on a job to collect a debt and ordered to break the thumbs of the debtor, Rocky takes the money but does not enforce the physical punishment. Later, he is warned by Gazzo not to think but to do as he is told. Finally, on Thanksgiving eve, Rocky gets a date with Adrian, taking her ice-skating by bribing the attendant to open the rink for ten minutes. Later, he takes her to his cluttered room where, in a poignant scene, they make love.

When the world champion Bicentennial bout, scheduled in Philadelphia with the reigning champ Apollo Creed (Carl Weathers), is threatened because the challenger has an injured hand, Creed senses an opportunity to merchandise the event by choosing Rocky, an unknown white Philadelphia boxer with a great stage name: Italian Stallion. At first Rocky is reluctant to fight Creed because he believes he is outclassed. He eventually accepts the offer and works with Mickey to train for the fight.

Against all odds Rocky, who never thought of winning but only to "go the distance," knocks Creed down in the first round and continues to challenge the champion until the final fifteenth round. Both fighters are exhausted and Rocky, although losing to a split decision, is triumphant, having persevered and exceeded his expectations.

The success of the movie, which spun off five sequels concluding with *Rocky Balboa* (2006), had to do with America's love for the underdog and an allegiance to heroes who succeed against all odds. It was a "sleeper" hit with an unkown actor and a modestly successful director, John G. Avildsen. It struck the right chord with its audience, who could identify with an ordinary guy who achieves greatness.

In his November 22, 1976, *New York Times* review, Vincent Canby was critical of Stallone's performance, calling it "an impersonation," although he had praise for the other actors:

> Mr. Stallone's Rocky is less a performance than an impersonation. It's all superficial mannerisms and movements, reminding me of Rodney Dangerfield doing a nightclub monologue. The speech patterns sound right and what he says is occasionally lifelike, but it's a studied routine, not a character.

He also mentioned that although the film was shot on location to add to the realism, it seemed fraudulent and he described Stallone's performance as "an unconvincing actor imitating a lug."

In a more positive review, Roger Ebert wrote: "*Rocky* isn't about a story, it's about a hero. And it's inhabited with supreme confidence by a star" (http://rogerebert.suntimes.com).

THE OUTLAW JOSEY WALES (1976)

PRODUCER/DIRECTOR: Clint Eastwood (director), Robert Daley (producer)
WRITER(S): Forrest Carter (book), Philip Kaufman (screenplay), Sonia Chernus (screenplay)

CAST: Clint Eastwood (Josey Wales), Chief Dan George (Lone Watie), Sondra Locke (Laura Lee), Bill McKinney (Terrill), John Vernon (Fletcher), Paula Trueman (Grandma Sarah), Sam Bottoms (Jamie), Geraldine Keams (Little Moonlight), Woodrow Parfrey (Carpetbagger), Joyce Jameson (Rose)
CINEMATOGRAPHY: Bruce Surtees
MUSIC: Jerry Fielding
LENGTH AND RATING: 135 min; PG

Heroes of the West as portrayed in American film evoke rugged independence, lingering disdain for authority, self-righteousness, and trust. Some of the movies offer didactic lessons about loss, vengeance, retribution, and honor. The narratives are sometimes punctuated by an epic quest to right a wrong, locate a missing person, or retreat into the healing solitude of the wilderness.

In *The Outlaw Josey Wales*, actor/director Clint Eastwood creates a fable about a Missouri farmer and veteran of the Confederacy who distrusts an offer of government amnesty, refusing to relinquish his weapons and swear allegiance to the Union. Having lost his wife, son, and farm in a violent raid by the Union redlegs, led by Captain Terrill (Bill McKinney), Josey Wales (Clint Eastwood) joins a band of Confederate guerillas led by Fletcher (John Vernon), hoping to gain his revenge. At the end of the war, Fletcher conspires with the Union to sell out his guerillas, who are then massacred by the unscrupulous Senator Lane (Frank Schofield) when they surrender. These actions serve as a catalyst for Wales to pursue his vengeance while confronting the people who hope to kill him for the generous bounty on his head.

Although consumed with rage, Wales doesn't lose his sense of compassion. His is a quest not just for vengeance, but also for redemption. As with John Ford's western *The Searchers* (1956), which starred John Wayne as Ethan Edwards, a returning Confederate soldier searching for his massacred brother's two daughters, Debbie and Lucy, who were kidnapped by Indians, the story evolves into a morality tale of good versus evil and the fragility of life. Unlike Josey Wales, Ethan is a racist, and his motivation to locate his nieces is driven by a hatred of Indians and his desire to kill the girls because they have suffered the highest indignity and been made impure by the renegades. Many similarities exist between the two movies. As he flees the Union soldiers, Josey, though intitally reluctant to befriend or assist anyone, does so when he aids his wounded friend Jamie (Sam Bottoms); meets the aged "civilized" Cherokee Indian Lone Watie (Chief Dan George) and offers to get him a horse and let him ride with him; saves the Navajo squaw Little Moonlight (Geraldine Keams) from involuntary servitude; rescues Grandma Sarah (Paula Trueman) and her granddaughter, Laura Lee (Sondra Locke), from Comancheros; and makes peace with their chief Ten Bears (Will Sampson). In their powwow, Josey tells Ten Bears that governments don't always treat people fairly and that they don't live together, but people do. Ten Bears agrees that such a truce cannot be guaranteed by a piece of paper, but must come from the honest words of men.

In the final scenes it's not the Indians who attack the new homestead in Santa Rio, Texas, but a posse of redlegs led by Terrill who attempt to kill Josey. Through his compassion for others, Josey has the support of his friends who defend him against his enemies and he succeeds in killing Terrill, ultimately fulfilling his revenge.

At the end of the movie, wounded in his fight with Terrill, Josey enters the Lost Lady Saloon and comes upon two Texas Rangers asking patrons, including Fletcher, about the fate of Josey Wales. They introduce Josey as Mr. Wilson and assure the rangers that the outlaw Josey Wales is dead, signing an affadavit to that effect. Satisfied, the rangers leave. Meanwhile, Josey, blood dripping on his boots from his wound, confronts Fletcher, who denies Josey's death and mentions that he'll search for him in Mexico and when he meets him will say that the war is over. This is Fletcher's way of telling Josey that the hunt has ended, for both sides.

The difference between *The Outlaw Josey Wales* and *The Searchers* is that both movies were defined by their time. For Josey Wales, the 1970s, when the film was released, articulated a time of tolerance and civil rights even as there was a deepening distrust of government. It also reflected a mood of re-enlightenment and hope after the resignation of President Richard Nixon and the election of Jimmy Carter in 1976 (http://www.encyclopedia.com/doc/1G1-97629464).

In his August 5, 1976, *New York Times* review of *The Outlaw Josey Wales*, Richard Eder calls it a "soggy attempt at a post-Civil War western epic" and describes Josey's companions as "stock characters." Although the film isn't perfect, it does resonate with a theme of reconciliation which, then as now, reflected the mood of a changing America.

SPACE: THE NEW FRONTIER

Star Wars (1977)
Close Encounters of the Third Kind (1977)

Science fiction involving themes relating to aliens, outer space, and the movies have an enduring relationship. They also reflected the mood of America in times of stress and insecurity. During Senator Joseph McCarthy's infamous witch hunt to rid America of communists, films such as *It Came From Outer Space* (1953), *The Day the Earth Stood Still* (1951), and *Invasion of the Body Snatchers* (1956) served as allegories on the dangers of condemning people because they are different or have an opposing point of view.

Of course, aliens visiting Earth could either be portrayed as benevolent or evil, attempting to befriend or conquer. The two films, *Star Wars* and *Close Encounters of the Third Kind*, although part of the cinematic heritage of movies articulating extraterrestial experiences, are distinctive in their purpose and design. While both owe tribute to the space films that so richly set the agenda for this theme, each is unique in integrating the past into their own dramatic form.

For director George Lucas, *Star Wars* would turn out to be an otherwordly experience, a fable to transport his audience to a different place and time. As in the *Wizard of Oz*, strange characters, some good, some evil, would inhabit a new world. Just as Dorothy is orphaned and lives on a farm with Auntie Em and Uncle Henry, Luke Skywalker (Mark Hamill) lives on a moisture farm with Uncle Owen Lars (Phil Brown) and Aunt Beru (Shelagh Fraser). Both Dorothy and Luke yearn to be transported away from their surroundings to a more exciting place.

Similarities also exist between the unique characters from the *The Wizard of Oz* and those in *Star Wars*. Although C-3PO is a droid in *Star Wars*, he resembles the Tin Man from the *Wizard of Oz*, and the junk-gathering midget, Jawa, has the same stature as the Munchkins from *Wizard*. After Dorothy runs away she meets Professor Marvel, who in her fantasy is transformed into the Wizard, and the wizard reference is used by Uncle Owen when he refers to Obi-Wan Kenobi (Sir Alec Guinness) who, as the last of the Jedi Knights of the Planetary Round Table, possesses special wizard-like powers.

George Lucas acknowledged he used the theatrical serial *Flash Gordon* and Akira Kurosawa's film *The Hidden Fortress* (1958) to provide a narrative foundation for *Star Wars*. At the beginning of the film, there is a text crawl in a geometric pattern that provides the audience with the backstory about a civil war and the rebel attack. The same stylisitic textual format was used in the foreword for chapter 2 of the "Purple Death" in *Flash Gordon*. There are many other plot and visual references to *Flash Gordon*, including the "Ice Planet" and "Ming the Merciless," who is transformed in *Star Wars* to Grand Moff Tarkin (Peter Cushing). Other visual references in *Star Wars* are the optical vertical and horizontal wipes used in *Flash Gordon*.

In *The Hidden Fortress*, two disagreeable, battle-worn peasants, much like C-3PO and R2-D2, attempt to return home and on their way join General Makabe (Toshiro Mifune), who is escorting the princess of the defeated royal family and her remaining treasure, facing hardship and danger as they pass through enemy territory. The seeds of their adventure, including spear and sword fights, are used as plot devices in *Star Wars*.

Another scene in *Star Wars* is reminiscent of the John Ford western classic *The Searchers* (1956), starring John Wayne. In *The Searchers*, Ethan Edwards (John Wayne) has returned from the Civil War to the Texas homestead of his brother Aaron, his wife Martha (Dorothy Jordan), and their children Lucy (Pippa Scott), Debbie (Lana Wood, younger sister of Natalie Wood), and Ben (Robert Lyden). Leading a posse to track down the Comanches who have killed the settlers' cattle, Ethan realizes they have been duped by the Comanches and that they used the livestock attack as a diversion to raid and murder the undefended settlers. Returning to his brother's ranch, Ethan surveys the smoldering devastation and the murder of Aaron, Martha, and son Ben. His nieces, Lucy and Debbie, have been taken captive by the Comanche Chief Scar.

🎥 *STAR WARS* (1977)

Producer/Director: George Lucas (director), Gary Kurtz (producer)
Writer(s): George Lucas
Cast: Mark Hamill (Luke Skywalker), Harrison Ford (Han Solo), Carrie Fisher (Princess Leia
  Organa), Peter Cushing (Grand Moff Tarkin), Alec Guinness (Ben Obi-Wan Kenobi),
  Anthony Daniels (C-3PO), Kenny Baker (R2-D2), Peter Mayhew (Chewbacca), David
  Prowse (Darth Vader), James Earl Jones (Darth Vader—voice)
Cinematography: Gilbert Taylor
Music: John Williams
Length and Rating: 121 min; PG

In *Star Wars*, after Luke meets with Obi-Wan Kenobi and is urged to learn the power of the Force, he hesitates, and as they drive the landspeeder home they come upon the burned-out remains of the Jawa's base and Luke soon realizes that the two robots, R2-D2 and C-3PO, purchased from them, can be traced back to his Uncle Owen's farm. He rushes home only to find the charred remains of his aunt and uncle following an attack by the Imperial Forces.

The *Star Wars* narrative unfolds with several parallel plots, including the rescue of Princess Leia Organa (Carrie Fisher), imprisoned by Grand Moff Tarkin and Lord Darth Vader. Her hologram message, carried by R2-D2, whom she embedded with the data blueprints for the Death Star battleship, seeking the help of Obi Wan-Kenobi captivates

Mark Hamill (as Luke Skywalker), Carrie Fisher (as Princess Leia Organa), Peter Mayhew (as Chewbacca) and Harrison Ford (as Han Solo). [Lucasfilm Ltd./Twentieth Century Fox Film Corp./Photofest]

Luke as she pleads that the General deliver the plans to her father on the planet Alderaan. A young Luke Skywalker, under the watchful eye of Obi Wan-Kenobi, anxiously learns the mysteries of the Force, practicing with the lightsaber and becoming a Jedi Knight to rescue Princess Leia. As the adventure unfolds, the heroic altruism of Luke and Obi Wan is tainted by the mercenary smuggler Han Solo (Harrison Ford) who, after negotiating an attractive fee, agrees to use his spaceship, the Millennium Falcon, co-piloted by a furry Wookie named Chewbacca (resembling the cowardly lion in *The Wizard of Oz*) to transport Luke and Obi Wan-Kenobi to Alderaan. However, Han has defaulted on a debt owed to Jabba and is confronted in the cantina (a western-style saloon) by bounty hunter Greedo. In a tribute to the movie western saloon gunfights, Han silently unbuckles his holstered gun and blasts the lizard-like bounty hunter. As in the classic movie westerns, the patrons of the saloon momentarily pause and then resume their drinking and talking, ignoring the carnage.

Not trusting Princess Leia to reveal the location of the rebel fortress, Grand Moff Tarkin orders the destruction of Alderaan and the execution of the princess. Trapped by the Death Star tractor beam, the Millennium Falcon is captured by the Imperial Forces, but Han conceals his passengers in a hidden smugglers well, a scene reminiscent from *The Hidden Fortress*. The tractor beam is a fictional device to bring two objects together and may have originated in the 1928 novel *The Skylark of Space* by E. E. Smith and was featured in the television series *Star Trek* (1966-1969). In an effort to rescue Princess Leia, several protracted battle scenes occur as she blasts an escape route through the garbage chutes. When Luke, Princess Leia, Han, and Chewbacca enter the slime, they face challenges with a death threat from a reptile creature in the garbage swamp and two huge garbage compactors that act like a vice, threatening to crush them. A similar scene from the movie *The Getaway* (1972) depicts Doc McCoy (Steve McQueen), a smart, sophisticated thief and his wife, Carol (Ali McGraw), escaping a shoot-out with law enforcement officers by hiding in garbage cans and being picked up by a compactor garbage truck and then dropped onto a landfill.

As they rush to escape in the Millennium Falcon, Obi Wan-Kenobi and his former student, Darth Vader, meet in a duel to the death. Distracting Vader by raising his sword, Obi Wan allows him to cut him in half and he disappears, his empty clothing crumpling to the ground as he urges Luke to run. His spirit has survived and his "force" is transferred to Luke and the others. Although they escape into hyperspace, Vader has placed a homing device on the ship, which Princess Leia acknowledges as the reason for the ease of their departure, thus challenging Han's braggadocio claims of his flying abilites. They are guided to land on the secret rebel base and told their only hope to escape the Death Star is to mount one-man fighter ships to the vulnerable but very dangerous center narrow shaft, creating a chain reaction explosion. Collecting his reward, Han abandons the rebels and Luke joins them in their attack.

As the rebels attack they are blown up by Imperial fighters and their last hope is Luke, who hears Obi Wan's admonition to trust the Force. He does, and is supported by Han Solo in his old spaceship, providing protection for Luke. The movie ends with a ceremony celebrating the victory and honoring rebel heroes Luke Skywalker and Han Solo.

CLOSE ENCOUNTERS OF THE THIRD KIND (1977)

PRODUCER/DIRECTOR: Steven Spielberg (director), Julia Phillips (producer), Michael Phillips (producer)

WRITER(S): Steven Spielberg

CAST: Richard Dreyfuss (Roy Neary), François Truffaut (Claude Lacombe), Teri Garr (Ronnie Neary), Melinda Dillon (Gillian Guiler), Bob Balaban (David Laughlin), J. Patrick

McNamara (Project Leader), Warren J. Kemmerling (Wild Bill), Roberts Blossom (Farmer), Philip Dodds (Jean Claude), Cary Guffey (Barry Guiler)
CINEMATOGRAPHY: Vilmos Zsigmond
MUSIC: John Williams
LENGTH AND RATING: 135 min; PG

"Ordinary people in extraordinary circumstances" and "we are not alone" are the themes that serve as a foundation for this epic science fiction film. It is director Steven Spielberg's tribute to the 1950s films, featuring visits to Earth by aliens both benevolent and hostile. Interestingly, the medium of radio and the dramatization of H. G. Wells' *War of the Worlds* on the October 30, 1938, broadcast of CBS' "Mercury Theatre on the Air," Orson Welles' broadcast, created the first collective panic to a gas attack by Martian invaders. The October 31 *New York Times* ran the headline, "Radio Listeners in Panic, Taking War Drama as Fact." This was followed by the subhead, "Many Flee Homes to Escape Gas Raid From Mars—Phone Calls Swamp Police at Broadcast of Welles' Fantasy" (http://en.wikipedia.org/wiki/Image:WOTW-NYT-headline.jpg).

Spielberg's mythic interpretation of aliens visiting Earth is steeped in the altruism of friendship, as demonstrated in the 1951 film *The Day the Earth Stood Still*, starring Michael Rennie as the alien visitor Klaatu. After his flying saucer lands in Washington and the military is poised to take action, he appears to make an appeal to the people of Earth. However, as he extends a device which turns out be a high-tech gift for the American president, he is wounded by a nervous soldier. Responding to this aggression, Gort, a robot, enters and uses a laser beam to destroy the weapons. In his message, Klaatu informs the world that they must live in peace and if they cannot and their hostilities threaten other planets, then Earth will be destroyed. The film was remade in 2008 with an environmental theme featuring Keanu Reeves as Klaatu.

The phrase "close encounters of the third kind" is a reference to contact with aliens. A close encounter is a sighting, a close encounter of the second kind is physical evidence of an alien landing and, if it's an encounter of the third kind, it refers to contact with aliens. In the movie, several ordinary people see the unidentified flying objects (UFOs), as do two commercial airline pilots who decline to report the incident. In a harrowing scene that takes place at an isolated home in Muncie, Indiana, a single mother, Jillian Guiler (Melinda Dillon), and her young son, Barry Guiler (Cary Guffey), are visited. First, in a humorous fashion with Barry's toys suddenly coming to life and then in a frightening manner as the house, their sanctuary, is invaded by a powerful force punctuated by bright lights. As Jillian desperately clings to Barry, the house comes alive as a vent remotely unscrews and smoke spews out. Finally Barry, who is unafraid and wants to play with his new friends, escapes through a pet door and although she exerts all her energy grabbing his torso, Jillian is overcome from the pressure on the other side.

This scene evokes an episode of *The Twilight Zone* entitled "The Invaders," starring Agnes Moorehead and broadcast on January 27, 1961. She is alone in a remote shack and visited by a flying saucer, which lands in her attic. She uses her wit, strength, and rudimentary weapons of a kitchen knife and an ax to ward off the miniature invaders. Finally, she succeeds, chopping up the flying saucer with her ax. As the vehicle smokes in the aftermath of its destruction, a distress call is made urging others not to counterattack. The final shot is a close-up of the flying saucer and its emblem, "U.S. Air Force

Space Probe No 1." In this instance, earthlings are the invaders creating fear for an inhabitant of another planet.

The narrative in *Close Encounters* gradually builds into a compelling drama as each close encounter is documented. The first instance is in Mexico's Sonora Desert on December 5, 1945, when five Navy PVM Torpedo bombers designated as Flight 19 on a training exercise out of Fort Lauderdale, Florida, go missing and 14 airmen, along with a crew of 13, are lost. The event is historical fact and it is woven into fiction as the planes appear intact in the desert without the crew. In this encounter, the audience is introduced to the French UFO investigator Claude Lacombe (François Truffaut), modeled after notable French UFO expert Jacques Vallee and the cartographer David Laughlin (Bob Balaban), who is hired as Lacombe's interpreter.

The second sighting involving two commercial airline pilots is also part of historical documentation, as there have been many such recorded incidents. The encounter of the third kind is the physical abduction of little Barry Guiler, and although claims have been made about such events they have been met with official government denials.

The movie presents an interesting psychological dynamic for those who have seen the UFOs and are witnesses to their exsistence. One witness is Roy Neary (Richard Dreyfuss), a lineman for the Muncie, Indiana, department of water and power who is sent to investigate a wide blackout and confronts a UFO, which literally shakes him up. Later, he encounters Barry (before his abduction) and Jillian in a near-miss accident, almost hitting the child with his truck. They are among the spectators on a highway awaiting the arrival of the UFOs, and they are not disappointed as three of them descend. For this scene, Spielberg relied on his childhood experience living with his family in Haddonfield, New Jersey, when his father took him to see the Perseid meteor shower.

After Barry is abducted and Roy sees the alien craft, they each have a sunburn, which identifies them and others as eyewitnesses. They also become obsessed with an image which turns out to be Devils Tower, a rock formation in Wyoming that rises 1,267 feet above the Belle Fourche River and is a national monument. For Neary, his obsession with trying to realize the image in his head alienates his family, who abandon him when he removes dirt and plantings from his yard and throws the debris through a window into the living room in order to sculpt what he imagines. This location has been secretly designated by the government as the staging area for the encounter with the aliens.

The movie continues to build with other encounters that help sustain the narrative, including a bizarre sighting of the *Cotopaxi* a tramp steamer, in the Gobi Desert in Mongolia. The freighter and its crew of 35 were lost on December 1, 1925, on a voyage from Charleston, South Carolina, to Havana, Cuba. In the movie, the sight of a ship lying in the sand offers an irony, literally interpreting the phrase "a duck out of water." Earlier encounters include a scene in Dharamsala, India, embracing a deified tone with religious references as worshippers repeatedly chant the same five notes and then point to the sky when asked to identify where the sounds came from. Following up on this, there is a signal picked up from space by the Goldstone Radio Telescope Station consisting of intervals of rapid pulses that represent various numbers in response to a musical combination of pulses that the station had been broadcasting for several weeks. The scientists and technicians are confused by the random numbers until Laughlin interrupts, telling them he used to be a cartographer and that the numbers represent map points of longitude and latitude. After rolling an expensive floor-anchored globe into their work area, they find that the lines of longitude and latitude intersect on the state of Wyoming. The aliens have communicated a rendezvous point for a meeting. Listening to another communication, Lancomb sits at a synthesizer and plays a five-note response to the message.

Obsessed by identifying the image in their minds, Roy and Jill learn from television reports of a train derailment and the spread of a dangerous chemical gas that has been killing animals near Devils Tower, resulting in the evacuation of everyone in the area. The report is a government cover-up to secure the area from onlookers and maintain the secrecy of the meeting with the aliens. Meeting in Wyoming, Jill and Roy are picked up by the military and detained with others who have journeyed to the rendezvous. Attempting to learn what drove Roy and the others to Devils Tower, he is interviewed by Lancombe and Laughlin and eventually placed aboard a helicopter with Jill and the other "intruders" for evacuation. The military commander in charge, Major Walsh, is angry that they were brought into the decontamination area and is told by Lancombe and Laughlin, "We didn't choose this place. We didn't choose these people. THEY WERE INVITED!" In the confusion of the evacuation, Jill and Roy take off their gas masks and escape, along with Larry Butler (Josef Sommer), and begin to climb a side of Devils Tower in a scene that evokes similar imagery in Alfred Hitchcock's film *North by Northwest* (1959). As they climb, Larry succumbs to the sleeping drug that the military is dusting the area with. In the evening, leaving Jill behind, Roy moves closer to the meeting point of the giant runway, where she eventually joins him.

The spectacular ending is a virtual light show accompanied by pulsating musical notes that serves as the primary mode of communication between the humans and their visitors. As the mother ship lands, a group of people begin to exit, including the pilots from Flight 19 and little Barry. A skeletal, spindly looking alien follows and raises its arms in a gesture of peace. It is followed by short, childlike figures with large round heads who circle Roy and lead him onto the ship. After Roy ascends into the spacecraft, the alien and Lancombe approach each other and in a lasting gesture of peace and faith he uses the Zoltan Kodaly hand signals to mimic the musical notes and the alien responds in kind.

Although *Close Encounters of the Third Kind* is a science fiction film, unlike *Star Wars*, which is a fable, it also relies upon whimsical fancy. The musical theme of the film is the well-known song, "When You Wish Upon a Star," from the 1940 Disney animated feature film *Pinocchio*. In his fearless reaction to the aliens, Barry represents a part of the human race, the children, who are untarnished by hate and bias and attracted to the aliens by their innocence. The film addresses many issues, including a distrust of government (Vietnam, Nixon, Watergate) and its deceptions. It also speaks to how America views the world and its desire to learn from others pursuing new frontiers. And the film is a parable about family and parents' devotion to their children. Although Roy leaves his family to board the alien craft and has alienated them with his obsession, he has from his earlier behavior proved that he is a good father and husband. He has been "invited" by the aliens who, with their childlike behavior, recognize him as an innocent with the positive virtues they admire.

Perhaps the film's greatest achievement is its theme of friendship and benevolence in a world fraught with war and hate. It is science fiction that compels the viewer to understand it as an allegory extolling the virtues that Americans hold dear.

VILLAINS AND HEROES

Death Wish (1974)
Taxi Driver (1976)

As a literary thematic form, revenge has a tradition in plays, novels, and film. Several films from the 1970s can be considered as prominent illustrations that created the vigilante genre, creating an enduring form and style. These films are *Billy Jack* (1971), *Dirty Harry* (1971), *Walking Tall* (1973), *Death Wish* (1974), and *Taxi Driver* (1976). Two films, *Death Wish* and *Taxi Driver*, resonated with an American public insecure and somewhat paranoid about violent crime.

🎥 *DEATH WISH* (1974)

PRODUCER/DIRECTOR: Michael Winner (director), Hal Landers (producer), Bobby Roberts (producer)

WRITER(S): Brian Garfield (novel), Wendell Mayes (writer)

CAST: Charles Bronson (Paul Kersey), Hope Lange (Joanna Kersey), Vincent Gardenia (Detective Frank Ochoa), Steven Keats (Jack Toby), William Redfield (Sam Kreutzer), Stuart Margolin (Ames Jainchill), Stephen Elliott (Police Commissioner), Kathleen Tolan (Carol Toby), Jack Wallace (Hank), Fred J. Scollay (District Attorney)

CINEMATOGRAPHY: Arthur J. Ornitz

MUSIC: Herbie Hancock

LENGTH AND RATING: 93 min; R

For successful architect and New Yorker Paul Kersey (Charles Bronson), life has been comfortable. Indeed, in the first scene he is on a Hawaiian beach with his wife Joanna (Hope Lange), where she is doing some cheesecake posing for his photographs. When they return from their vacation, Paul goes back to the office, where one of his associates is talking about the high homicide rate in New York. From the conversation it appears that Paul is a liberal-thinking individual.

In another scene, Joanna and their married daughter Carol (Kathleen Tolan) shop at a local supermarket and ask that the groceries be delivered to the Kersey's Riverside Drive apartment. Three hooligans, who have been acting out inside the market, sneak a peak at the address in the box of groceries, enter the Kersey building from the back entrance, and one poses as the delivery boy. They burst into the apartment after Carol, believing that it is the grocery delivery, opens the door. After getting only a few dollars they brutalize Joanna and rape Carol. At the hospital with his son-in-law Jack (Steven Keats), Paul learns that his daughter Carol will recover from her injuries, although she is in a catatonic state, but his wife has died.

Evolving into a vigilante, Paul defends himself with rolls of quarters in a sock in his first confrontation with a mugger. It unnerves him and he rushes home to calm himself with a tall glass of scotch. Sent to Tucson, Arizona, by his firm to work on a residential housing project, he meets builder Aimes Jainchill (Stuart Margolin), who takes him to a Wild West shoot-out reenactment and then to his gun club. At the gun club, Jainchill gives Paul a 1870s percussion pistol to fire and Paul proves to be a marksman. He reveals that his father was a hunter and he grew up with guns but after a hunting accident that killed his dad he gave them up, became a conscientious objector, and served as a medic in the military. At the airport, Jainchill slips a box into Paul's checked luggage and when he returns to New York he discovers a nickel-plated .32 caliber unregistered revolver. He uses this as his weapon of choice, killing muggers on the streets and in the subways of New York.

As the local New York City newspapers label him the "vigilante," the police commissioner and district attorney secretly acknowledge that crime has gone down since the so-called vigilante has been patrolling the streets and subways of New York. They order Detective Ochoa (Vincent Gardenia) to find the vigilante and order him to leave New York City without prosecuting him, hoping that if the public believes he is still at large it will positively aid in reducing crime.

In a subway platform confrontation with muggers, Paul is cut and his blood type is eventually matched by the police with the blood on the weapon. During a final shoot-out Paul is seriously injured and taken to the hospital, where he is met by Detective Ochoa. He is told to leave New York City "permanently" and the detective tells the gathered press, which suspects that Paul is the vigilante, that he is merely another mugging victim and that the vigilante is still at large.

In the last scene, Paul is met at the the Chicago airport by a new colleague and, seeing a young woman bumped and dropping a package, he goes to assist. While on one knee, he winks at the camera and gestures with his trigger finger as if shooting a gun. That is the defining gesture for the four sequels, *Death Wish II* (1982), *Death Wish III* (1985), *Death Wish IV: The Crackdown* (1987), and *Death Wish V: The Face of Death* (1994). For the most part, the US domestic gross box office for the films remained fairly consistent until the last two features. Starting with *Death Wish* at $22 million, versions two and three were in excess of $16 million, four just short of $17 million, and five just over $1.5 million.

In 1974, *Death Wish* was poorly reviewed and criticized for its violence and brutality. Writing in the July 25, 1974, *New York Times*, film critic Vincent Canby called *Death Wish* "...a despicable movie." He also said the movie would "cheer the hearts of the far-right wing," and that it exploited violence for its own sake.

The movie was based on Brian Garfield's novel, and he criticized the film for its glorification of vigilantism. He viewed vigilantism as an attractive fantasy but felt that such actions would have severe negative effects on society. Interestingly, on December 22, 1984, Bernhard Goetz shot a mugger on a New York City subway after being surrounded by four thugs and was labled by the press as the "subway vigilante." He was acquitted of attempted murder and assault but served 250 days in jail for criminal possession of an unlicensed weapon.

The spectacle of the vigilante was revisted in 2007 by two films: *The Brave One* and *Death Sentence*. In *The Brave One*, Jodie Foster plays Erica Bain, a public radio talk show host of a program called "Street Walk." She is somewhat of a romantic muse until she and her boyfriend, David, out for a walk with their dog in Central Park, are mugged and he is murdered. After recovering from a three-week coma, she buys a 9mm handgun and, like Paul Kersey, begins a reign of vengeance. In a subway scene that bears a striking resemblance to *Death Wish*, she is left alone in the car after other passengers leave in fear at the next stop after being harassed by two surly African Americans. In *Death Wish*, Paul Kersey is reading a newspaper, which the mugger slices in two with a knife. Thirty-three years later the newspaper is out, the iPod is in, and Erica is listening to music. When the mugger begins to caress her with a knife and asks, "You ever been fucked by a knife?" she blows him away, along with his partner. Although she wonders why her hands don't shake and why someone doesn't stop her, Erica Bain is the embodiment of Paul Kersey, living out the *New York Post* headline of the vigilante and consumed by a thirst for revenge.

It is somewhat ironic that Jodie Foster morphs into a bloodthirsty killing machine, taking after her hero, Travis Bickle, who rescued her in a rampage of death when she played Iris, a twelve-year-old New York prostitute in *Taxi Driver.*

🎥 *TAXI DRIVER* (1976)

PRODUCER/DIRECTOR: Martin Scorsese (director), Julia Phillips (producer), Michael Phillips (producer)

WRITER(S): Paul Schrader

CAST: Robert De Niro (Travis Bickle), Cybill Shepherd (Betsy), Peter Boyle (Wizard), Jodie Foster (Iris Steensma), Harvey Keitel ('Sport' Matthew), Leonard Harris (Senator Charles Palantine), Albert Brooks (Tom), Diahnne Abbott (Concession Girl), Frank Adu (Angry Black Man), Gino Ardito (Policeman at Rally)

CINEMATOGRAPHY: Michael Chapman

MUSIC: Bernard Herrmann

LENGTH AND RATING: 113 min; R

The roots of *Taxi Driver* are entwined in the French New Wave, American film noir, and the brutal images of the Vietnam War. The film can be defined as being about failure: personal, cultural, and that of a state, America's arrogance in fighting a war in Southeast Asia. The author of the screenplay, Paul Schrader, while recovering from a gastric ulcer in a hospital, was motivated to write the screenplay for *Taxi Driver* when he read the newspaper coverage of would-be assassin Arthur Bremer, who shot Governor George Wallace, who as result of his injury was paralyzed from the waist down.

In his own way Schrader identified with Bremer, who kept a diary, was isolated, and had been living out of his car. After his marriage failed and the affair with the woman who precipitated the breakup also dead-ended, Schrader was living out of his car, drinking heavily, and hadn't talked to anyone for weeks. For Bremer, his only means to gain the recognition he coveted was to assassinate someone of distinction, and after failing to penetrate President's Nixon's security zone he targeted Governor George Wallace.

In *Taxi Driver*, Bremer becomes Travis Bickle (Robert De Niro), a Marine Vietnam War veteran whose insomnia leads him to a job driving a New York City taxi cab at night... and yes, he'll work anytime, anywhere, including Jewish holidays. His view of New York is laden with hostility and rancor, and he expresses this in his diary when writing that the rain will wash away the squalor and sleaze on the streets, along with the garbage and trash. As he drives the city streets at night, he laments about the animals that come out, the whores, queens, fairies, dopers, the miscreants he holds in contempt, yearning for a ritual cleansing of the sinners. He does this after each twelve-hour shift, cleaning the cab's interior from the trash that has defiled it with cum and blood.

He is alienated and awkward in attempting relationships with other people. Unable to sleep, he visits the Times Square X-rated movie theaters and watches the screen with a dispassionate gaze. When Travis tries to pick up a girl at the concession stand, she

231

threatens to call for help so he demures, buys candy and soda, and retreats into the darkness of the audience. As in his taxicab Travis, even when he is with people, is alone in a world he considers filled with sinners. The only people he has a minimal relationship with are a group of other taxi drivers whom he occassionaly meets for evening coffee. He consults one of them, Wizard (Peter Boyle), and attempts to explain the dark, evil thoughts he's having. Trying to discuss life in a strained, existentialist way, Wizard embarks on a disjointed discussion about why he doesn't own his own cab, why he drives at night, and that people are born, get sick, and die. He tells Travis that he envies his youth and advises him to go out, get drunk, and get laid and then, using his nickname "killer," advises him that he'll be all right.

Several defining moments in the narrative act as a catalyst in setting the motivation for Travis. He meets and pursues beautiful blonde Betsy (Cybill Shepherd), who works in presidential candidate Senator Charles Palantine's (Leonard Harris) Manhattan office. She is a vision of purity, dressed in a flowing white dress, representing the myth of virginal innocence he has created in his mind. After observing her from the insulation of his taxi, he meets Betsy in the office and tells her how lonely she appears and convinces her to have coffee with him. Unable to separate Betsy from his routinized, alienated lifestyle, he takes her to a pornographic movie on their first date and she rushes out, running away from him.

His other meeting with a female is by chance, when Iris (Jodi Foster), a teenage prostitute, suddenly gets into his taxi and tells him to quickly drive away. Before he can react, she is pulled out of the cab by her pimp Sport (Harvey Keitel), who drops a twenty-dollar bill on his seat and tells him to forget about what just happened. In his wanderings, Travis again meets Iris and this time befriends her, attempting to convince her to abandon her lifestyle and return home.

One evening Travis picks up Senator Palantine and his aides on their way to an event. During the ride Travis tells the senator how he feels about the city being an open sewer and how it must be rid of the filth and scum, which should be flushed down the toilet. The senator humors Travis, understanding that he is deranged. In another self-defining incident, Travis who has purchased an array of assault weapons, confronts an armed robber in a convenience store and shoots him, then leaves the unlicensed gun with the store owner and flees.

Deciding to organize his life and get his body into shape, Travis begins a regimen of physical exercise, lifting weights and doing push-ups and pull-ups. Visiting a Palantine rally, he saunters up to a Secret Service agent and asks questions about becoming one. The suspicious agent tries to get personal information about him and then signals another Secret Service photographer to take his picture but Travis melts into the crowd. At home, in one the most famous scenes in film, Travis, wearing a green military fatigue jacket, poses in front of a mirror, posturing as a tough guy and repeating the phrase, "You talkin' to me?" He challenges his imaginary opponent like in a vintage western movie, drawing his gun from a forearm spring-loaded holster.

Realizing his greater mission, Travis begins to set his life in order, writing his parents an anniversary card that articulates his fantasy of living with Betsy and working at a sensitive job with the government. He stuffs five $100 bills into an envelope, which he intends for Iris, thinking that he'll be dead by the time she receives it. Wearing a Mohawk-style haircut, Travis stalks Senator Palantine at a rally with the intent to assassinate him, but after he's seen by a Secret Service agent he flees, barely making his getaway.

In a bloodthirsty scene of retribution and symbolic cleansing, Travis confronts Sport outside Iris' apartment and shoots him in the stomach. He enters the building, shooting the manager, and is wounded in the neck by Sport, whom he kills. Then he is shot in the arm by a Mafioso customer of Iris, whom he shoots in the face and chest. Then, he wrestles with the manager and, after subduing him in front of Iris, he tries to shoot himself under the chin but he's out of bullets. As the police enter he puts his bloody trigger finger to his head and mimics the sound of a shot.

In a world where everyone achieves fame for fifteen minutes, Travis gets his due. The newspapers and television pay tribute to him as a hero who rescued the young Iris from her involuntary servitude. He is lauded as a purveyor of vigilante justice, cleaning the city of its dirt and filth. In the last scene he's the next taxi in line at the St. Regis Hotel and Betsy enters. They say little, talking about Palantine's nomination and she asks how he's feeling. When they reach her apartment Betsy wants to pay the fare but he declines to collect and drives away, taking a last glance of her in the rearview mirror.

In his February 8, 1976, *New York Times* review, Vincent Canby writes that Travis Bickle is fascinating because he is played by an actor who understands the character, otherwise he would be a sideshow freak:

> Travis Bickle—the collaboration of writer, director, and actor—remains fascinating throughout, probably because he is more than a character who is certifiably insane. He is a projection of all our nightmares of urban alienation, refined in a performance that is effective as much for what Mr. De Niro does as for how he does it. Acting of this sort is rare in films. It is a display of talent, which one gets in the theater, as well as a demonstration of behavior, which is what movies usually offer.

In his sick, distorted view of the world that is nuanced by the neighborhoods he drives through and the night people he picks up, Travis is on the outside looking in. His world is a phantasma of grotesque, psychotic Dali-like images and he has internalized his alienation into biblical dogma. He views his sacrifice as a Christ-like gesture and is ultimately vindicated and made a hero by his actions. Like Paul Kersey, who is asked to leave town but never prosecuted, Travis Bickle, unlike Bernhard Goetz, is celebrated for his vigilantism.

The film *Death Sentence* (2007) stars Kevin Bacon, who plays Nick Hume, a middle-class insurance adjuster who avenges the death of his oldest son, whose throat was slashed by a machete-wielding gang member robbing the convenience store the boy has entered. It's an artistic reference to *Death Wish* (written by the same author) and mimics Travis Bickle when Nick shaves his head, wipes out the gang, and then slumps on a sofa.

Although neither *The Brave One* nor *Death Sentence* have the depth or nuance of *Taxi Driver*, it is significant that the theme of the vigilante has once again become conversant in film. It could speak to the insecurity and distrust of government since 9/11 and the paranoia of threat, real or perceived, that has pervaded America (Taubin, Amy. *Taxi Driver*. London: BFI Publishing, 2000).

VIETNAM: THE LOSS OF INNOCENCE

The Deer Hunter (1978)
Apocalypse Now (1979)
Platoon (1986)

In the aftermath of the Vietnam War, several films addressed the futility and agony of the jungle war in Southeast Asia. The 1970s, however, featured two films that were starkly different in chronicling the events in Vietnam and the political dynamics of the war. Interestingly, each of the directors, Francis Ford Coppola (*The Godfather, Apocalypse Now*) and Michael Cimino (*The Deer Hunter, Heaven's Gate*), were auteurs and each was known for his excess and arrogance. Both *The Deer Hunter* and *Apocalypse Now* have distinctive plots that metaphorically cast America's failure in Vietnam within a narrative of camaraderie, defiance, and ecumenical deliverance.

THE DEER HUNTER (1978)

PRODUCER/DIRECTOR: Michael Cimino (director and producer), Michael Deeley (producer), John Peverall (producer), Barry Spikings (producer)
WRITER(S): Michael Cimino (story), Deric Washburn (screenplay), Louis Garfinkle (story), Quinn K. Redeker (story)
CAST: Robert De Niro (Michael), John Cazale (Stan), John Savage (Steven), Christopher Walken (Nick), Meryl Streep (Linda), George Dzundza (John), Chuck Aspegren (Axel), Shirley Stoler (Steven's Mother), Rutanya Alda (Angela), Pierre Segui (Julien)
CINEMATOGRAPHY: Vilmos Zsigmond
MUSIC: Stanley Myers
LENGTH AND RATING: 182 min; R

For the three working-class buddies, Michael (Robert De Niro), Nick (Christopher Walken), and Steven (John Savage), who work together in a steel mill and live in western Pennsylvania in a town steeped in the liturgy of the Russian Orthodox church, their lives are punctuated by the drudgery of their jobs, drinking, and deer hunting. They're also naively idealistic and innocent about going to war and fighting in Vietnam. Their vision of heroism is defined by previous American generations and steeped in a culture that defended American values around the world.

They live and love within the boundaries set by their culture and religion, and Cimino makes a concerted effort to demonstrate these values by depicting the lengthy wedding scene between Steve and Angela (Rutanya Alda). Although Steve's mother doesn't approve of the marriage, knowing that Angela is carrying another man's child, her son is determined to marry the woman he loves. He is noble and also the least worldly of his friends.

After the wedding, an extended group of friends go deer hunting and it becomes very evident that Michael is a leader whom everyone respects. He is a seasoned hunter who patiently stalks his prey, killing the animal with one lethal shot. In Vietnam, he meets Steve and Nick on the field of battle and apparently is the only one in his platoon who has survived an enemy attack. He engages the enemy, and the three friends are captured. In one of the most harrowing scenes of war ever depicted on the screen, the friends are forced by their captors to "play" against each other in a game of Russian roulette with six shot revolvers, spinning the barrel while holding the gun to their head as bets are made. Breaking down, Steve is sent to a floating prison raft where drowning is inevitable. When Michael and Nick face off, Michael convinces his captors to put three bullets in the chamber instead of one and then takes the opportunity to kill them. Although they are picked up by an American helicopter, Nick manages to cling to it while Michael dives into the river to rescue Steve, who fell, and then heroically manages to get his friend back to the American base.

Expecting a homecoming, Michael's friends plan a party, but when he sees their preparations, he asks the taxi driver to take him to a local motel instead. The next morning he visits the home he shared with Nick, which is now occupied by Linda (Meryl Streep), Nick's girlfriend and the woman Michael has longingly desired. He walks her to work, and when she asks that they comfort each other, he leaves and Linda joins him at the motel, where she snuggles up to him and he falls into a dead sleep.

Guilty about leaving Nick behind, Michael returns to Vietnam as Saigon is falling to the enemy. He locates Nick, now a heroin addict, in a remote gambling den, where he is a champion Russian roulette player. Bribing the locals, Michael faces off with him, trying to convince Nick to leave and return home, but the chamber explodes as he pulls the trigger, killing him. At home there is a solemn Russian Orthodox funeral for Nick and afterward the group meets at John's (George Dzundza) restaurant/bar for breakfast. Also present is Steve, whose legs have been amputated and who is in a wheelchair. As John retreats to the kitchen to scramble eggs, he starts to cry and then begins to hum the melody of *God Bless America*. As he enters the room, the others begin to sing and at the end raise their glasses in a toast to Nick. Even after all the sorrow, suffering, and hardship they cling to their patriotic values. They are not the sophisticated literati who debate politics and spout puzzling profundities. Instead, they are the men who went off to fight in Vietnam and their families and communities who sacrificed for them. It was a living room war and it was the Michaels, Steves, and Nicks from the working-class cities and towns who starred in it.

In his December 15, 1978, review Vincent Canby wrote that *The Deer Hunter* is a "breathtaking motion picture," coming close to being an American epic. He also wrote about how the characters react to their experiences and whether or not it raised their level of political consciousness:

> More terrifying than the violence—certainly more provocative and moving—is the way each of the soldiers reacts to his war experiences. Not once does anyone question the war or his participation in it. This passivity may be the real horror at the center of American life, and more significant than any number of hope-filled tales about raised political consciousnesses. What are these veterans left with? Feelings of contained befuddlement, a desire to make do and, perhaps, a more profound appreciation for love, friendship and community. The big answers elude them, as do the big questions.

APOCALYPSE NOW (1979)

PRODUCER/DIRECTOR: Francis Ford Coppola

WRITER(S): John Milius (screenplay), Francis Ford Coppola (screenplay), Michael Herr (narration)

CAST: Marlon Brando (Colonel Walter E. Kurtz), Martin Sheen (Captain Benjamin L. Willard), Robert Duvall (Lieutenant Colonel Bill Kilgore), Frederic Forrest (Jay "Chef" Hicks), Sam Bottoms (Lance B. Johnson), Laurence Fishburne (Tyrone "Clean" Miller), Albert Hall (Chief Phillips), Harrison Ford (Colonel Lucas), Dennis Hopper (Photojournalist), G. D. Spradlin (General Corman)

CINEMATOGRAPHY: Vittorio Storaro

MUSIC: Carmine Coppola, Francis Ford Coppola
LENGTH AND RATING: 153 min; R

In its manifestation of men at war, *Apocalypse Now* is a brutal yet poetic polemic about war and imperialism. It has "good bones," a term often used to articulate the foundation of a movie or play. It was an epic journey for both the filmmaker and the film who, like the beleaguered Odysseus in Homer's *The Odyssey*, endured captivity and hardships after leaving Troy. This film, as well as Oliver Stone's *Platoon* (1986), articulates a sonorous voice about the confusion, futility, and tragedy of the Vietnam War. Although very different in their approaches as anti-war films, they offer compelling images about war and, unlike traditional war films like *The Green Berets* (1968), starring the iconic cinematic hero John Wayne, which was an overt piece of military propaganda with full cooperation from the Johnson administration, these two films had no easily defined heroes, just victims.

Making the film was an epic undertaking for Francis Ford Coppola and, as many critics of *Apocalypse Now* have noted, every dollar he spent is on the screen. Somewhat like Odysseus, Coppola exhibited a similar state of hubris in producing what he described as "the ultimate Vietnam film." The United Artists studio feared the worst in 1978, when the film had already consumed 238 days of shooting over 15 months, at a cost of $30 million, which did not include optical effects, sound dubbing, or the mutiple prints needed for distribution to hundreds of movie theaters. Production was delayed by actor Martin Sheen's (Captain Willard) heart attack, a typhoon, several love affairs, ample drug use, and Marlon Brando's (Colonel Kurtz) ballooning weight gain and notorious lack of preparation (Cowie, Peter. *The Apocalyose Now Book*. Cambridge: Da Capo Press, 2001).

The script was written by John Milius and Francis Ford Coppola and based on Joseph Conrad's 1902 novel *Heart of Darkness*. The novel addresses the evils of colonization and imperialism, making an example of the African Congo under the rule of King Leopold II of Belgium, who ran the country of the Congo Free State and in 1892 authorized Belgians to hunt for unlimited ivory without having to trade with the Africans.

In *Heart of Darkness*, Marlow is commissioned to travel by boat up the Congo River to gather ivory and transport it downriver. However, his real mission is to capture and return Kurtz, the head of the station that harvests the most ivory, because he has evolved into a savage within the darkness. The local natives worship him and in a gesture toward his leadership, Kurtz has placed the human heads of rebels on poles around his encampment.

The narrative was adopted for *Apocalypse Now* and the scene shifted to "the colonization" of Vietnam by Americans and the futility of the mission. Like Marlow in *Heart of Darkness*, Captain Willard, an intelligence officer, is given a mission to travel by boat up the Nung River (Mekong River) to Cambodia with a military crew and "terminate with extreme prejudice" Green Beret officer Colonel Walter E. Kurtz, who has created his own feudal fighting force of Montagnard tribesman, who worship him as a deity as he disregards and flaunts the traditional military chain of command.

In the opening scene, the audience is introduced to Willard as he wakes up from an alcoholic stupor to the sound of whirring helicopter blades and a vision of red-hot flames of incendiary napalm in a psychedelic sequence accompanied by the song "The

End" by The Doors. In his mental narrative, he reveals that he has returned to a second tour of duty in Vietnam and his conflicted attraction to the war. When at home he longs for the jungle and when in the jungle he pines for home. His silence with his wife was broken only when he said "yes" to her request for a divorce. To the audience, Willard is the first casualty of the movie. He is brought before his superiors and lectured about the rational and irrational, about good and evil, that sometimes even with the best of intentions evil wins out, and then told to terminate Kurtz, whose insane dictatorship has jeopardized America's interests in Vietnam. And he learns from the CIA operative present at the meeting that the mission doesn't exist, now or ever.

He is assigned to a Navy PBR (plastic patrol boat) with a crew that includes Jay "Chef" Hicks (Frederic Forrest), a dope-smoking machinist and cook; Lance B. Johnson (Sam Bottoms), a famous California surfer; "Mr. Clean" Tyrone Miller (Laurence Fishburne), a Gunners Mate Third Class; and Chief Phillips (Albert Hall), Chief Quartermaster and NCO.

They are a motley crew on an unknown mission and as they travel the river, the "heart of darkness" enters their souls. During the journey Willard reads the top-secret file on Kurtz and after reviewing his distinguished service record, which includes numerous decorations, including third generation at West Point and top of his class, he wonders why the generals would want such a heroic figure terminated.

In one of the most memorably jingoistic battle scenes on film depicting the arrogance, cruelty, and "fog of war," Willard and his crew meet with his escort, Lieutenant Colonel Bill Kilgore (Robert Duvall) of the Ninth Air Cavalry. Like the character portrayed by George C. Scott in the film *Patton*, co-written by Francis Ford Coppola, Kilgore is a relic of the Army who lives to fight another day. He wears a western-style horse soldier Stetson cavalry hat with crossed swords, a yellow tunic, and has a bugler play before and after each engagement with the enemy. Like Patton he stands tall when his soldiers run for cover as enemy shells explode around him.

When Kilgore and Willard meet, the colonel is engaged in "mopping" up after attacking the enemy. He places death cards on the bodies of the VC and civilians as a mark of distinction and recognition of who was responsible for their demise. Always the soldier and respectful of his enemy, when South Vietnamese troops deny water to a dying Vietcong fighter, he pushes them away and offers water from a canteen. But, he abruptly turns away when he is informed that Lance Johnson, the surfer, is present and goes to meet him. That evening at a "beach party" with steaks and beer for his troops, Willard shows Kilgore his destination and at first he hesitates because it's "Charlie" territory and then changes his mind when he's told the area has great surfing. When a concern is raised about surfing in hostile waters, Kilgore responds, "Charlie don't surf."

The village about to be devastated appears to be blissfully peaceful but then singing school children are frantically herded away at first sight of the Huey helicopters. The villagers and VC quickly spring into action in a coordinated effort to arm and defend themselves. To the musical accompaniment of Richard Wagner's "Ride of the Valkyries," from the opera *Die Walkure*, blaring from a loudspeaker, the helicopters, in a stunning formation, fire rockets, blasting the village as armed soldiers strafe the village with machine gun fire. During the attack, over the radio Kilgore compliments his teams on good kills, promising a case of beer to the men, and when a woman on the ground tosses a bomb into a helicopter evacuating the wounded, Kilgore cries out, "the fucking savages" as another helicopter swoops down and kills her. Of course the irony is the savagery that war breeds and the depth of hypocrisy that clouds the reasons for killing each other.

To secure the area and make it safe for surfing, Kilgore calls for a napalm strike, urging the flying scout to, "Bomb it to the Stone Age son." After the attack, Kilgore waxes poetic and says, "I love the smell of napalm in the morning.... Smells like victory." And like Patton he ruefully acknowledges that, "Some day this war's gonna end." But to the relief of Lance, the naplam has altered the wind pattern. Kilgore apologizes for the poor surfing conditions and after a helicopter drops their boat into the water the men quickly board and sail away.

When the boat puts into the Hua Phat supply depot, the sergeant in charge is busily distributing supplies for a few bucks on the side and at first declines Willard's request for diesel fuel because there is no destination for the mission. He grabs the sergeant, showing him papers that the mission is classified, and he apologizes, offering the men a front-row seat for the Playboy Bunny USO show, along with a free bottle of bourbon for Willard. When the helicopter touches down and the Bunnies arrive dressed in skimpy costumes, bumping and grinding to the song "Suzie Q" on the helicopter landing pad, the men go wild and a near riot causes the women to board the helicopter and hastily depart.

In a horrific and tragic scene that depicts the cruelty and callousness of war and the dehumanization of the fighting men, the chief, despite Willard's protests, decides to board and search a civilian sampan for contraband. He orders Chef, who goes reluctantly to search the boat as all the men on board their patrol boat nervously hold and aim their weapons. Although Chef repeatedly shouts there's nothing suspicious, the tension builds as the chief orders him to keep searching and then a young girl suddenly moves to a can and hell breaks loose as the soldiers fire, murdering the people on the boat. It's a chaotic event that typifies the insanity of the Vietnam War, and the soldiers are remorseful after they find a puppy in the can that the girl was reaching for. In a gesture of compassion, the chief wants to take the girl, the wounded lone survivor, to "friendlies" for medical care. Unwilling to divert the boat from his mission, Willard shoots the girl through the heart and reminds the chief of his warning not to stop the sampan.

In another scene that depicts the confused insanity of war, their patrol boat cruises by the Do Lung Bridge during an eerie evening psychedelic bombardment by the Vietcong. In an effort to find the commanding officer, Willard approaches an African American soldier who seems to think that Captain Willard is in charge. Another soldier identifies Willard and gives him mail (the crew also receives mail) that contains a secret dossier informing him that a Captain Richard Colby (Scott Glenn) was sent on an identical mission to terminate Kurtz and is now believed to have joined him. As they depart the area, desperate soldiers are seen jumping into the water with suitcases, hoping to board the patrol boat for rescue. This compelling image shows the hopelessness and desperation of men facing death.

As they continue into Cambodia, the crew reads their mail and in a poignant scene, Clean is listening to an audiotape his mother sent when they come under Vietcong attack and the youngest crew member is killed. The audiotape continues, with the voice of his mother urging him to stay out of harm's way. Everyone on board is upset and traumatized. As their boat continues upriver in the fog it is attacked by a hail of arrows and the crew fires into the jungle as Willard shouts to cease fire, that it is only a scare tactic. The chief is killed by a spear through his back and in his dying breath grasps Willard, who subdues him.

The local natives escort the men to Kurtz's encampment, which is populated by the Montagnards and grotesque displays of hanging dead bodies and decapitated heads. They meet a crazed photojournalist (Dennis Hopper), who incessantly babbles about the greatness of Kurtz as a deified figure. Concerned about their security, Willard asks Chef to stay behind on the boat and gives him coordinates for an air attack if he does not return with Lance. In the encampment, Willard is wrestled in the mud and taken to Kurtz and asked if he's an assassin and then told by Kurtz that he is merely an errand boy sent by grocery clerks to collect a bill. He is then imprisoned in a bamboo tiger cage surrounded by decomposing bodies. While Willard is a prisoner, Kurtz delivers Chef's severed head, dropping it onto his lap, which elicits a soul-shattering cry.

After being taken to Kurtz, Willard listens to his incoherent monologues but recognizes the brilliance and loyalty of this deranged Green Beret officer and becomes conflicted in his mission. Ultimately he realizes that Kurtz has doomed himself by his aberrant behavior and that he must carry out his mission. He surreptitiously enters Kurtz's compound and as the colonel is babbling into the microphone of a tape recorder, Willard attacks him with a machete, hacking at him as the scene is cross-cut with one of the native's ritual slaughter of a water buffalo as a sacrifice to the gods. Having assassinated Kurtz, the natives recognize Willard as their new leader but he resists the temptation to be their new god. Instead he leads Lance, who is stoned, back to the patrol boat for their journey.

The film is a study of good and evil and how men can become corrupted and debased by the rule of war. Survival is a basic instinct that can consume the soul and provide a rationale for irrational behavior, as soldiers nervously embrace their weapons as tools that will deliver them from their horror. In *Apocalypse Now*, director Francis Ford Coppola dares to tell the audience that Vietnam, like all wars, takes on a surreal iconography that breaks down into chaos, vengeance, and retribution.

In his August 15, 1979, *New York Times* review, Vincent Canby praises the film as a "stunning work," and calls many of the sequences "spellbinding," comparing the film to David Lean's *Bridge on the River Kwai*. Another critic wrote in his June 1, 1979, review that the film is a "masterpiece" and a "...grand and grave and insanely inspired gesture of film making—of moments that are operatic in their style and scope" (ttp://rogerebert.suntimes.com/apps/pbcs.dll/article?AID=/19790601/REVIEWS/41214002/1023).

As for Coppola, he viewed his work as such:

My film is more of an "anti-lie" film, in that the fact that a culture can lie about what's really going on in warfare, that people are being brutalized, tortured, maimed and killed, and somehow present this as moral is what horrifies me, and perpetuates the possibility of war. (http://www.wsws.org/articles/2001/aug2001/apoc-a25.shtml)

PLATOON (1986)

PRODUCER/DIRECTOR: Oliver Stone (director), Arnold Kopelson (producer)

WRITER(S): Oliver Stone

CAST: Tom Berenger (Sgt. Bob Barnes), Willem Dafoe (Sgt. Elias Grodin), Charlie Sheen (Pvt. Chris Taylor), Forest Whitaker (Big Harold), Francesco Quinn (Rhah), John C.

McGinley (Sgt. Red O'Neill), Richard Edson (Sal), Kevin Dillon (Bunny), Reggie Johnson (Junior Martin), Keith David (King)
CINEMATOGRAPHY: Robert Richardson
MUSIC: Georges Delerue
LENGTH AND RATING: 120 min; R

Although discussion of this film may appear out of context as film analysis has thus far been organized by decade, it is appropriate because of the "good vs. evil" contextual themes of both *Apcalypse Now* and *Platoon*, directed by Oliver Stone. The other similarity is of course father (Martin Sheen) and son (Charlie Sheen) in starring roles in each of their respective Vietnam war films. For director Oliver Stone the movie is autobiographical and represents his perspective as Chris Taylor (Charlie Sheen), a privileged young "grunt" in Vietnam. He's a "cherry" and none of his platoon mates care enough to learn his name because of the likelihood of his being killed in the first few weeks of a tour. That stark reality is quickly visualized as Chris disembarks from a transport plane with other new recruits and he sees the body bags of casualties being transported. Soon, he is another face in a crowd of anonymous combat infantrymen, most of them forgotton to the world even before being sent to the jungle.

His idealism as a college dropout volunteer infantryman is quickly tested as he writes to his grandmother about his exhaustion and the mistake he made by enlisting. However he is counseled by Sergeant Elias (Willem Dafoe) who represents the altruistic good soldier as opposed to Sergeant Barnes (Tom Berenger) who is consumed with the rage of survival and after an evening ambush that kills the oafish new recruit Gardner (Bob Orwig) refers to the dead soldier as "a lump 'o shit" warning the men that they too can get a "...trip out of the bush...in a body bag." It is Elias who mentions offhand to Barnes that if Gardner just had a few more days to learn something he might still be alive. And it is Elias who cares enough about the new recruit Taylor to instruct him to lighten the load of his knapsack discarding the items that don't need to be carried. He shows compassion and bravery.

As in *Apocalypse Now* the members of Taylor's platoon are a heterogeneous group of men and boys, black and white, rednecks and dopers who at times appear to be fighting a battle among themselves just as the two sergeants are fighting a war of morality and decency. Attracted to the smoking dopers which includes Elias, Chris finds a comraderie with their spirit as opposed to the "juicers" and rednecks aligned with Barnes.

Just like in *Apocalypse Now* and the wanton killing of innocent victims on a sampan, *Platoon* evokes its own horror when the troops enter a village that appears to be a VC stronghold, threatening and killing the civilians (reference to My Lai). The Americans bomb the tunnels and, in a confrontation with a mother and son who Chris orders out of hiding, he vents his rage by firing at the man's feet making him dance. When he stops, realizing the terror of his actions, Bunny (Kevin Dillon) a southern redneck advises Chris "to do" the young man. Before leaving, Bunny uses the butt of his weapon to strike the man in the face and then smashes his skull causing blood to spurt on Chris. Then in an amazed and guiltless remark Bunny mentions how the skull came apart and exposed the man's brains. During a parallel scene Barnes attempts to get information about VC and harshly interrogates a scared villager. The man's wife intercedes whining and the translator Lerner (Johnny Depp) can barely keep up with her rapid dialogue. Finally Barnes fires a round into her forehead killing her. Then he takes the man's daughter hostage holding the barrel of a gun to her head as their Lieutenant Wolf, who is intimidated by Barnes, looks on helplessly. As Elias enters the scene he tells Barnes that he's not a firing squad and the two men fight; good against evil. Just before the men leave the village Taylor comes upon several of them gang-raping a young Vietnamese girl. He intercedes, disgusted by their lack of humanity and decency, and his actions are observed by Sergeant Elias.

When the men return to the base, Elias complains to the captain about Barnes and the killing of innocent civilian. Their commanding officer assures them that there will be an investigation. In the bush the platoon walks into an ambush by the North Vietnamnese Army (NVA) and is under siege taking casualties. Understanding their predicament and trying to avoid being boxed in by the enemy, Elias volunteers to circumvent their counterattack by backtracking in the jungle and taking three men with him, including Taylor. He engages the enemy, surprising them by his tactics and resulting in the evacuation of the troops. When Barnes, under the guise of finding Elias, confronts him the two men face each other and as Barnes raises his weapon Elias breaks into an innocent smile. Then Barnes pauses and Elais realizes he's going to shoot and Barnes fires off three rounds. When Taylor sees Barnes, he asks about Elias and learns that he is dead and is ordered to return to the landing zone for evacuation. As the helicopter flies off, Taylor sees Elias being chased by the NVA. Elias is shot repeatedly as he continues to run, until he takes his last breath, extending his arms and reaching to the sky in a Christ-like pose. On the helicopter Taylor and Barnes exchange a knowing look, and back at the base camp dope den, Taylor tells his comrades how Barnes killed Elias and that he should be killed. Eavesdropping on their conversation, Barnes enters; Taylor jumps him but is no match for the veteran soldier, who whips out a knife and is poised to strike. Barnes is warned by others and decides instead to slash Taylor's cheek.

Ordered into battle, the platoon faces their most difficult confrontation with the NVA as their position is overrun by the enemy and the captain orders an air strike on their location taking responsibilty for the casualties of American troops. Just as the bombs and napalm fall, Barnes tries to kill Taylor, his last witness to murder, when he is blown off by the attack. The next morning as Taylor awakes he sees Barnes stirring and aims his rifle at him as the sergeant prods him to pull the trigger, and Taylor obliges, killing him.

Unlike *Apocalypse Now*, which was one man's quest upriver to find salvation, *Platoon* is one man's search for his identity. In this film the harsh brutality of jungle warfare is depicted in a gritty way showing the cruel reality of fighting off ants, leeches, and jungle rot along with the enemy. In the end Chris Taylor has learned more about who he is by forming lasting bonds with other men whom he would never have met outside the jungle. He has also rediscovered his own decency which he temporarily lost in the "fog of war."

In his December 30, 1986, *Chicago-Sun Times* review of *Platoon* film critic Roger Ebert wrote about the energy and sense of adventure of war movies making combat look like fun.

It was François Truffaut who said that it's not possible to make an anti-war movie, because all war movies, with their energy and sense of adventure, end up making combat look like fun. If Truffaut had lived to see *Platoon*, the best film of 1986, he might have wanted to modify his opinion. Here is a movie that regards combat from ground level, from the infantryman's point of view, and it does not make war look like fun. (http://www.toptenreviews.com) (http://rogerebert.suntimes.com)

In Vincent Canby's December 19, 1986, *New York Times* review of *Platoon*, he mentioned that the film is a singular achievement and possibly the best work about the Vietnam War. He also discussed the film's successful use of narrative order.

Another measure of the film is the successful way Mr. Stone has managed to create narrative order in a film that, at heart, is a dramatization of mental, physical and moral chaos. *Platoon* gives the impression at first of being only a little less aimless than the men, whose only interest is staying alive or, as Chris Taylor puts it, of remaining "anonymous," meaning safe.

SATURDAY NIGHT FEVER (1977)

PRODUCER/DIRECTOR: John Badham (director), Robert Stigwood (producer)
WRITER(S): Nik Cohn (magazine article "Tribal Rites of the New Saturday Night"), Norman Wexler (screenplay)
CAST: John Travolta (Tony Manero), Karen Lynn Gorney (Stephanie Mangano), Barry Miller (Bobby C.), Joseph Cali (Joey), Paul Pape (Double J.), Donna Pescow (Annette), Bruce Ornstein (Gus), Julie Bovasso (Flo Manero), Martin Shakar (Frank Manero, Jr.), Sam Coppola (Dan Fusco)
CINEMATOGRAPHY: Ralf D. Bode
MUSIC: Barry Gibb, Maurice Gibb, Robin Gibb
LENGTH AND RATING: 118 min; 1977–R, then re-rated in 1979 as PG

The story was taken from a 1976 *New York* magazine article, "Tribal Rites of the New Saturday Night" by British journalist Nik Cohn which he later admitted fabricating. However, the movie took the world by storm heightening the zeal for disco fever and making Tony Manero (John Travolta), the former sweathog Vinnie Barbarino on the 1970's sitcom *Welcome Back Kotter*, into a movie star of global dimensions. Why did a movie about an ordinary 19-year-old Italian Catholic boy growing up in Bay Ridge, Brooklyn, New York, and featuring a soundtrack by the Bee Gees strike gold at the box office earning a worldwide gross of $282,400,000 and was one of the most successful movie soundtracks of all time?

For young and old audiences the message in the film was about hope and the search for self-identity and a better life. In Tony Manero (John Travolta) the world saw an Everyman plodding along in a universe of endless routine and boredom. Working in a hardware store selling paint Tony is a personable clerk of no special distinction accommodating the needs of customers. But on Saturday nights at the disco club he's transformed into the prince of the dance floor as the crowd parts to witness his virtuoso performance.

At home Tony is a nonentity treated with disinterest by his mother who dotes on her priest son, Tony's brother Father Frank Manero, Jr. (Martin Shakar) and disdain by his unemployed father, who mocks Tony's $4.00 weekly raise. His dancing is the only thing that makes him different and separates Tony from the pack of his friends and the people he works with. When he asks his boss Dan Fusco (Sam Coppola) for an advance

Karen Lynn Gorney and John Travolta. [Paramount Pictures/Photofest]

on his salary to buy a new disco shirt he adamantly refuses citing store policy. Following up that request later, needing a day off to move his dance partner Stephanie (Karen Lynn Gorney) from Brooklyn to her new Manhattan apartment Tony quits his job when he is denied the day off.

Training for a dance competion Tony first chooses Annette (Donna Pescow) who is in love with him although he doesn't feel the same toward her. Then, after seeing Stephanie dance at the club, he abruptly drops Annette and partners with Stephanie who is slightly older. Presenting herself as a worldly woman working in Manhattan, Stephanie attempts to characterize herself as a sophisticated New York single mingling with the upper crust, who hold people like Tony in contempt. However, her behavior is a charade as she attempts to mask the insecurity she feels as someone deficient in education and social skills. But, as a typist, she has a skill other than dancing that can move her to the next level offering her a door to exit the tunnel of mediocrity. Meeting Stephanie helps Tony understand the lack of direction in his life. And although he would like to have a sexual relationship with Stephanie he realizes that he must respect her decision not to engage him and to stop treating women as victims and objects of desire.

There are several critiical arcs in the story that help Tony redefine the purpose of his life. His brother, to the horror of his mother, leaves the priesthood, his boss wants to rehire Tony offering him a raise and telling him of the future and how many decades his workers have been with him, his friend Bobby C. (Barry Miller) who has impregnated his girlfriend and throughout the movie seeks advice about his dilemma falls off the Verrazano Narrows Bridge as the boys are horsing around, and although he and Stephanie win the dance contest and the prize money Tony realizes that the Puerto Rican couple who placed second were better dancers and he takes the statue and the prize money and gives it to them. He has grown into a man with a conscience and a vision for a life beyond the hardware store and the dance floor. The last scene of the film evokes a discovery as Stephanie allows him to enter her apartment after he assures her that he will not attempt any romantic initiatives and they talk like grown-ups about the future.

In her review of the film, Pauline Kael noted the "pop rapture" of *Saturday Night Fever:*

> It's Tony's pent-up physicality—his needing to dance, his becoming himself only when he dances—that draws us into the pop rapture of this film. The mood, the beat, and the trance rhythm are so purely entertaining, and Travolta is such an original presence, that a viewer spins past the crudeness in the script (by Norman Wexler, based on Nik Cohn's June 7, 1976, *New York* cover story, "Tribal Rites of the New Saturday Night"). (http://www.geocities.com)

ANNIE HALL (1977)

PRODUCER/DIRECTOR: Woody Allen (director), Charles H. Joffe (producer), Jack Rollins (producer)

WRITER(S): Woody Allen, Marshall Brickman

CAST: Woody Allen (Alvy Singer), Diane Keaton (Annie Hall), Tony Roberts (Rob), Carol Kane (Allison), Paul Simon (Tony Lacey), Shelley Duvall (Pam), Janet Margolin

(Robin), Colleen Dewhurst (Mrs. Hall), Christopher Walken (Duane Hall), Donald Symington (Mr. Hall)
CINEMATOGRAPHY: Gordon Willis
LENGTH AND RATING: 93 min; PG

The scholarly article, "An Analysis of Three Expected Intimate Relationship States: Commitment, Maintenance and Termination," written by Robert B. Minda and published in the *Journal of Social and Personal Relationships*, appears to follow the narrative structure of Woody Allen's *Annie Hall*. The various states include: expected commitment, expected maintenance, and expected termination. In the opening scene of *Annie Hall*, the audience learns that comedian Alvy Singer's (Woody Allen) year-long relationship with Annie Hall (Diane Keaton) has ended and the remainder of the film is devoted, in flashback and present-day narrative, to understanding the complex relationship of these two characters.

The film takes the audience on a journey through Singer's life, from his childhood growing up under the Coney Island roller coaster, where his father ran the bumper car concession, to his elementary school, where he was precocious enough to kiss a girl in class, to early therapy with a psychiatrist because he learns the universe is expanding and that one day it will break apart so there is no point to doing homework. He's neurotic, insecure, paranoid, obsessive, consumed with phobias, and somewhat delusional, which magnifies his Jewish feelings of persecution. Strolling on a Manhattan sidewalk with his actor friend Rob, (Tony Roberts), Alvy relates an earlier conversation he had with an NBC television network executive about lunch, which he suspected was anti-Semitic. When asked if the executive had eaten, Alvy hears the response as "No JEW?" not "Did you?" This is typical of Alvy, who has developed a myriad of complexes that affect his relationships with women (two marriages, two divorces), his career (flying out to Los Angeles to present an award, becoming consumed by fear making him sick, and recovering after the producers find another presenter), and loving Annie and attempting to maintain the commitment (but when she moves in with him he urges her to keep her own apartment and is willing to pay her rent).

This is perhaps as close to an autobiographical film about Woody Allen as any he's made. In *Annie Hall*, there's a clip from Allen's appearance on the *Dick Cavett Show* and the fact that Woody and Diane (who was born Diane Hall with the nickname "Annie") had a relationship gives more credence to the autobiographical nature of the film.

When they meet on a Manhattan tennis court, Annie appears even more insecure than Alvy. She is a girl from Chippewa Falls, Wisconsin, narrow-minded, from a WASP family, and interested in pursuing a singing career in the big city. Soon, they are engaged in a relationship and Alvy serves as her mentor, instructing Annie on what to read and which movies to see. One of the most hilarious scenes in the movie occurs when they are waiting in line at a Manhattan movie theater. Annie has arrived late, and Alvy blames her mood on having her period, which Annie denies. Being two minutes late for Bergman's *Face to Face* (1975), Alvy refuses to enter so they finally arrive on another line at a movie theater featuring Marcel Ophul's *The Sorrow and the Pity* (1969). Behind them is an obnoxious, pretentious man pontificating to his date about Fellini's films and how indulgent a director he is. He then moves on to a discussion about the cult media guru and Canadian philosopher Marshall McLuhan (author of the phrase "Hot and Cool" media) and validates his assumptions by saying that he teaches at Columbia University. He also steps in front of the camera, saying that it's a free country and he can give his opinion. Despising the gibberish of the pseudo-intellectual, Alvy (as he often does in the movie) steps out and talks directly into the camera to the audience, venting about getting stuck in a movie line with such an obnoxious person. Then he confronts the guy by reaching behind a cardboard theater sign and bringing out the real Marshall McLuhan, who refutes everything the man has said and wonders how he ever got to teach at Columbia. Of course, Alvy relishes this fantasy.

In another funny scene, Alvy visits the WASP-ish Hall family, dining with them at a traditional Easter meal of ham. To a Jew ham is forbidden as part of kosher dietary law. They engage in proper, polite conversation and Alvy envisions Grammy Hall (Helen Ludlam) as seeing him as a Hasidic rabbi dressed in black with a beard. They are the realization of Alvy's anti-Semitic paranoia. In a clever split screen, the audience sees the sedate, well-mannered Hall dinner compared to the Singer family's brash, loud, shouting, ill-mannered gathering. They also engage in cross–dialogue, with Mrs. Hall (Colleen Dewhurst) asking Mrs. Singer (Joan Newman) how they spend the holidays and the response that they fast. When they don't understand, Mr. Singer (Mordecai Lawner) explains: no food and it's atonement for sins. Again the goyim don't understand and ask what sins and Mr. Singer replies that they don't understand the concept either.

Interestingly, there is a similarity between *Saturday Night Fever* and *Annie Hall*, as both Tony and Alvy learn about friendship and love with women who have grown professionally and moved on to relationships with others. This was the decade of the seventies, where sex did not lead to commitment, somewhat analogous of the relation-ship marketplace today.

In his April 21, 1977, *New York Times* review, Vincent Canby writes about *Annie Hall* as a comedy about urban love and incompatability:

> In this fashion, Woody Allen introduces us to the particular concerns of his fine new film, *Annie Hall*, a comedy about urban love and incompatability that finally establishes Woody as one of our most audacious filmmakers, as well as the only American filmmaker who is able to work seriously in the comic mode without being the least bit ponderous.

ALIEN (1979)

PRODUCER/DIRECTOR: Ridley Scott (director), Gordon Carroll (producer), David Giler (producer), Walter Hill (producer)

WRITER(S): Dan O'Bannon (story, screenplay), Ronald Shusett (story)

CAST: Tom Skerritt (Dallas), Sigourney Weaver (Ripley), Veronica Cartwright (Lambert), Harry Dean Stanton (Brett), John Hurt (Kane), Ian Holm (Ash), Yaphet Kotto (Parker), Bolaji Badejo (Alien), Helen Horton (Mother - voice)

CINEMATOGRAPHY: Derek Vanlint

MUSIC: Jerry Goldsmith

LENGTH AND RATING: 117 min; R

The genre of the horror film and its sci-fi counterpart has as its historical antecedent the films of the 1950s and '60s that defined their narrative structure, style, and story line. The mammoth 800-foot-long mining spaceship *Nostromo* (named after a character in a 1904 Joseph Conrad novel), hauling 20 million tons of raw mineral ore, with three decks and a crew of seven, is a long way from Earth. The crew consists of Captain Dallas (Tom Skerritt), Warrant Officer Ripley (Sigourney Weaver), Navigator Lambert (Veronica Cartwright), Engineering Technician Brett (Harry Dean Stanton), Executive Officer Kane (John Hurt), Science Officer Ash (Ian Holm), later revealed as humanoid, Chief Engineer Parker (Yaphet Koto), and a cat named Jonesy. The crew has been in hypersleep to preserve the ship's resources for their journey home and they are awakened prematurely by their onboard computer, "Mother." There is a signal from a distressed spacecraft and the mission has been rerouted to a desolate planet in an effort to investigate the source of the signal. The audience gains a sense of the crew's isolation within the cavernous *Nostromo* and again when they enter and launch their shuttlecraft, *Narcissus*, to visit the unknown planet. Two crew members, Parker and Brett, the technicians, have voiced their dissatisfaction over the unequal half-bonus shares they receive while the other crew members are entitled to full shares. When Captain Dallas tells the crew they will be launching an expedition to the planet, Parker demures, saying that his contract does not include rescue missions but for more money he will oblige. He is reminded by science officer Ash that company policy requires they investigate possible intelligent origin, with the penalty of total forfeiture of shares if they do not comply.

Many similarities exist between *Alien*, directed by Ridley Scott, and the 1951 sci-fi film *The Thing from Another World* ("the Thing" was portrayed by James Arness, star of the television series *Gunsmoke*). In this film, the group is a US Air Force re-supply crew based in Anchorage, Alaska (also cold and desolate), that is requested by Dr. Carrington (Robert Cornthwaite), the lead scientist working at Polar Expedition Six in the Arctic, to investigate an aircraft, a flying saucer, that has crash-landed nearby. Just as in *Alien*, the crew is placed in danger by "mad" scientists (Ash, Carrington) who are willing to risk the lives of colleagues to save the alien specimen for study and research.

In *Alien*, the shuttlecraft has a difficult time landing and requires repairs by Parker and Brett. Leaving the shuttle in space suits, Captain Dallas leads a three-man crew, along with Kane and Lambert, to investigate. Both Ripley and Ash remain onboard the *Narcissus* to monitor the progress of the expedition while Brett and Parker make repairs to the shuttlecraft. In an eerie, cavernous alien spacecraft Kane is lowered into a field of gestating alien eggs as Ash views the images, sometimes interrupted by interference, from video cameras mounted on their helmets. After reviewing the coded messages from Mother, Ripley concludes that the information is not an SOS but a warning, and she transmits her concerns to Ash, who rejects her plan to leave the shuttle and warn the expeditionary crew.

Soon Kane gets close enough to the leathery egg pod to report that there is organic life and movement. It opens and suddenly attacks him, sticking to his helmet. This scene is similar to one in the 1958 horror sci-fi movie *The Blob*, starring Steve McQueen. After a meteor lands in a Pennsylvania town, a man living nearby investigates, using a stick to explore the meteor, which suddenly breaks open to reveal a gelatin-like mass that moves up the stick and attaches to the man's hand. Eventually, the

Blob consumes the man, along with the doctor and nurse whom he has rushed to for help.

In *The Thing from Another World*, the crew digs out a body encased in ice and although the scientists want to thaw out the specimen immediately, Captain Hendry decides to wait for instructions from Anchorage. Just as in *Alien*, the crew is too far away from Earth for transmissions and the same is true for the Arctic expedition because a storm has disrupted their communication. However, as a guard watches over the ice-encased specimen he inadvertently drapes it with an electric blanket that defrosts the ice and revives the bloodthirsty space invader.

Attempting to return to the ship with the ailing Kane, Captain Dallas requests that Ripley open the hatch but she refuses, assuming command because of the stated quarantine policy and the threat to the lives of the rest of the crew. Allthough Captain Dallas repeats his order, she again refuses but Ash overrides her and opens the hatch. Later, in a tense meeting with Ash, she reminds him that when Dallas and Kane are off the ship she is the senior officer. She also tells him she is suspicious of his motives.

Later, Ash summons Dallas and Ripley to the infirmary for them to see that the creature lodged on Kane has disappeared. There is a dead carcass from the creature that Ash wants preserved for further study but Ripley wants destroyed. Once again tension builds as Dallas agrees with Ash and Ripley reprimands him. Learning that Ash was a last-minute replacement for Captain Dallas' usual science officer makes Ripley even more suspicious.

In a famous dinner scene, before entering hypersleep the crew engages in carefree conversation as Kane exhibits a prodigious appetite when suddenly the creature, which has been using his body as a host, bursts through his chest and scampers away. In another 1950s classic film, *Invasion of the Body Snatchers* (1956), alien pods take possession of sleeping humans, using their bodies as hosts to grow into identical forms and then killing off the original human form. The remainder of *Alien* is about the pursuit of the creature aboard the *Nostromo* as it mutilates each crew member one at a time until Ripley is the only one left alive. At the action-packed, tension-laden end of the film, Ripley sets off the *Nostromo*'s self-destruct timer and attempts to rush toward the shuttlecraft but is temporarily thwarted by the alien creature, stops to rescue Jonesy, and finally reaches the shuttle, blasting off in the nick of time. However, the alien has attached itself to the shuttlecraft and through her ingenuity and fortitude Ripley dons a space suit, opens an air lock, and blasts the creature into space.

The suspenseful ending and the survival of Ripley as a female action adventure hero owes tribute to the theatrical movie serial *The Perils of Pauline* (1914) and to John Carpenter's *Halloween* (1978). In the silent-era, twenty-episode *Perils of Pauline*, Pauline (Pearl White) was one of the first female action adventure heroes as she, week after week, is placed in one death-defying, precarious situation after another, with the cliff-hanger being her rescue in the following episode. In John Carpenter's *Halloween*, Laurie Strode (Jamie Lee Curtis) heroically battles the maniac murderer Michael Myers and survives, protecting her babysitting charge, young Tommy Doyle. Director John Carpenter pays tribute to the 1950s and the film *The Thing from Another*

World by featuring it on television as a Halloween treat for Laurie and Tommy to watch.

There were three sequels to the *Alien* franchise, with Sigourney Weaver reprising her role as Ripley in each: *Aliens* (1986), directed by James Cameron, *Aliens 3* (1992), directed by David Fincher, and *Alien Resurrection* (1997), directed by Jean-Pierre Jeunet. These were followed up by two *Predator* and two *Alien vs. Predator* films.

7 Bits, Bytes, and Boomers, 1980–1989

The decade of the 1980s was distinguished by the presidency of Ronald Reagan (1981–89) and his economic and foreign policy initiatives. During his time in office, he was in relentless pursuit of the Soviet Union, calling it an "evil empire" and challenging its leader by saying, "Mr. Gorbachev, tear down this wall," referring to the Berlin Wall that separated West and East Germany. He derided the role of big government and believed power came from the people.

This was the time of the "me generation" and the eccentric indulgence by baby boomers and a prodigious increase in their offspring. The era was also marked by a greater degree of tolerance toward people of color and same-sex couples. Along with no-fault divorce and the adopted title of Ms., women embraced the professions and power-dressed. They were Yuppies (young urban professionals) and Yummies (young urban mothers) adapting to families and jobs.

The 1980s, in many ways, was defined by trends in consumer technology. The age of portable and self-directed entertainment beckoned with the arrival of Sony's Walkman, and VHS videocassette recorders and cassette players. It was also the beginning of mobile telephone communication and personal computing, with the debut of the Motorola DynaTAC 8000X, the personal computer, and the Apple Macintosh. It was the age of surrogate mothers and the battle for "Baby M," and the prime-time television soap opera, *Dallas*, which created the popular buzz words, "Who shot JR?" And there were two critical launches: the first space shuttle and Pac-Man.

The eighties were also defined by movies of fantasy, substance, style, and a political dynamc that included *Raiders of the Lost Ark* (1981), *Blade Runner* (1982), *Back to the Future* (1985), *El Norte* (1983), and *The Thin Blue Line* (1988). The film *El Norte*, although released in 1983, holds particular significance because of its relevance to the current immigration debate, and *The Thin Blue Line*, a 1988 documentary about a miscarriage of justice that is still timely because of the number of guilty verdicts overturned by DNA evidence as a result of Barry Scheck's Innocence Project.

Although films about boxing have a long Hollywood tradition there are only a few that stand out as prominent achievements within the genre, and two of great distinction are *Raging Bull* and *Million Dollar Baby*. While each has a unique voice, they share similar themes that make them suitable for comparison even though their release is separated by almost twenty-five years.

🎥 *RAGING BULL* (1980)

PRODUCER/DIRECTOR: Martin Scorsese (director), Robert Chartoff (producer), Irwin Winkler (producer)

WRITER(S): Jake La Motta (book), Joseph Carter (book), Peter Savage (book), Paul Schrader (screenplay), Mardik Martin (screenplay)

CAST: Robert De Niro (Jake La Motta), Cathy Moriarty (Vickie Thailer), Joe Pesci (Joey La Motta), Frank Vincent (Salvy Batts), Nicholas Colasanto (Tommy Como), Theresa Saldana (Lenore), Mario Gallo (Mario), Frank Adonis (Patsy), Joseph Bono (Guido), Frank Topham (Toppy)

CINEMATOGRAPHY: Michael Chapman

MUSIC: Jim Henrikson (music editor), Robbie Robertson (music producer)

LENGTH AND RATING: 129 min/; R

Although these films share a common subject matter, boxing, and while *Raging Bull* (directed by Martin Scorsese) is biographical and *Million Dollar Baby* (directed by Clint Eastwood and discussed in Chapter 10) is fictional, they do share common elements, including their distinguished directors. Both films made a significant cultural contribution to the decade in which they were released and demonstrated the compelling theme that so often pervades boxing films; that, according to Joyce Carol Oates, is "America's tragic theater." The stories are usually about some disadvantaged, poor street kid who uses the ring to gain status and wealth but has a difficult time adapting to the fame, fortune, and greed of the sport. When Clint Eastwood pitched his idea to Warner Brothers, his studio of record, they initially had little interest in the project, even with a director of his stature associated with it. However, Eastwood told the Warner executives that the film is a father-daughter love story: (http://www.usfca.edu/~southerr/boxing.html) "I told them it's not a boxing movie. It's a love story that just happens to take place on the periphery of the boxing world—a father-daughter love story" (http://www.brightlightsfilm.com/47/clint.htm).

Indeed, many of the classic American boxing movies are love stories, such as *City For Conquest* (1940), which starred James Cagney and Ann Sheridan as his dancer girlfriend. For Cagney, the truck driver who plays Danny Kenny, boxing is a means to providing money for his composer brother Eddie's (Arthur Kennedy) music lessons. However, as a result of his fighting he tragically goes blind. As Joyce Carol Oates notes, many of the boxing films are indeed tragic, with themes and characters that rival Shakespeare for their needs and faults. In *Body and Soul* (1947), starring John Garfield, who plays boxer Charlie Davis, success has cost him his dignity while the sleaze of boxing's underworld is vividly revealed. In that movie, Charlie is paid to take a "dive," not unlike Jake La Motta, the character portrayed by Robert De Niro in *Raging Bull.* In the 1956 film *The Harder They Fall*, also about boxing corruption and adapted from the Bud Schulberg novel, Humphrey Bogart portrays Eddie Willis, a journalist hired as a publicist for corrupt fight promoter Nick Benko (Rod Steiger), who fixes fights for a tall young fighter who isn't aware until he becomes a contender that all of his matches have been thrown. The story has factual relevance to Italian fighter Primo Carnera, whose manager was associated with the mob, and it was believed that most of his bouts were fixed. After retiring from the ring, Carnera became a professional wrestler and was a main attraction at various events. His story may have some relationship to one of the most poignant boxing films ever made, the 1956 Playhouse 90 television drama *Requiem for a Heavyweight*, written by Rod Serling and starring Jack Palance as the washed-up fighter Mountain McClintock who, after a doctor bars him from boxing because of a severe eye injury, resorts to the embarrassment of becoming a wrestler in order to help pay his corrupt father-figure manager Maish's (Keenan Wynn) gambling debts. It was made into a theatrical feature film in 1962 starring Anthony Quinn as Mountain McClintock and Jackie Gleason as Maish.

In a 2005 interview about the film *Raging Bull*, Scorsese discussed the fight sequences and how they were filmed from the boxer's persepective inside the ring instead of outside. He also revealed that he was not a fan of boxing:

> We went a bit over schedule...I think, five weeks over, because of shooting the boxing scenes. They were very intricate...and I never was a fight fan, so I designed the fight scenes a certain way, all from the point of view of the fighter inside the ring, not outside—that sort of thing. So we just kept sorta stumbling along and— and making the best picture we could make. (http://www.cbsnews.com/stories/2005/02/04/earlyshow/contributors/lauriehibberd/main671694)

Like Scorsese, one does not have to be a fan of boxing to understand that *Raging Bull* is not so much a film about boxers but rather a character study about the struggle for recognition and success and the self-destruction that can lead to failure. Most heroes are flawed, and Jake La Motta was a tragic figure who alienated his family and friends through a consuming sense of paranoia. From the opening of the film, the audience immediately learns about the corrupt nature of boxing and experiences La Motta's volatile personality. As Jake's younger brother Joey (Joe Pesci) walks to Jake's Bronx apartment, he is accompanied by the small-time hood Salvy (Frank Vincent), who asks Joey to talk to his brother about being managed by mob leader Tommy Como (Nicholas Colasanto), who can arrange a title bout. In his last fight, with a boxer named Reeves, the outcome was "fixed," declaring a unanimous decision for Reeves even though La Motta knocked him down to the mat three times. This scene parallels another in Jake's apartment, as he sits in the cramped kitchen waiting for his first wife Irma (Lori Anne Flax) to cook a steak and then chides her for overcooking it. Frustrated, she stabs it with a fork, removes it from the pan, and drops it on his plate, and he responds by turning over the table and its dishes. His wife runs into the bedroom and there are crashing sounds from objects she throws.

For Jake, being his own man and asserting his independence is an essential part of his character. At the gym he pummels Joey while sparring in response to seeing Salvy and two of his cronies watching them fight. Later, Joey tells Jake that they came because Tommy, the boss, sent them to help Jake and his career. Angry at his brother, Jake lets him know he doesn't need any help nor does he want to share any of his winnings with the mob.

In a scene at the community pool, Jake reveals his obsessive-compulsive personality. He spots Vicki (Cathy Moriarty) and wants to know everything about her and whether Joey had slept with her. His questioning is insistent and abusive, and at the Annual Summer Dance he follows Vicki outside as she is escorted by Salvy, who drives away with her in a beautiful convertible. In another scene, Jake drives up to the pool in his own convertible and is officially introduced to Vicki by Joey. They eventually marry and have children, but Jake's insecurity makes him suspicious about Vicki's fidelity to him and their marriage, and he suspects her of having affairs with various men, including his brother. He becomes more violent, beating Vicki and his brother and taking his anger out by brutalizing his opponents in the ring. When Vicki mentions that a young fighter named Tony Janiro (Kevin Mahon) is handsome, Jake assumes she is attracted to other men and in the boxing ring pulverizes his opponent's face. Slowly, Jake descends into a state of paranoia, suspecting Vicki of various infidelities and brutalizing the people dearest to him. Soon, Jake must be unfaithful to himself by agreeing to deliberately lose (take a dive) in a bout with Billy Fox (Ed Gregory). As a result, the prize money is suspended while the authorities investigate.

Despite himself, Jake La Motta becomes a champion but eventually loses the crown to his longtime nemesis, Sugar Ray Robinson. He has alienated his wife, who has divorced him and has custody of their children, his brother Joey, and his fans, who desert him after he is convicted on a morals charge for solicitation of minors for prostitution in his rundown Miami nightclub. At the end of his life, he's reduced to telling lame jokes, introducing strippers in seedy nightclubs, and after a chance Manhattan meeting with his brother Joey, it appears as if he is no longer blinded by his distrust and insecurity.

TOOTSIE (1982)

PRODUCER/DIRECTOR: Sydney Pollack (director, producer), Dick Richards (producer)

WRITER(S): Don McGuire (story), Larry Gelbart (story), Murray Schisgal (screenplay), Larry Gelbart (screenplay)

CAST: Dustin Hoffman (Michael Dorsey), Jessica Lange (Julie Nichols), Teri Garr (Sandy Lester), Dabney Coleman (Ron Carlisle), Charles Durning (Leslie "Les" Nichols), Bill Murray (Jeff Slater), George Gaynes (John Van Horn), Geena Davis (April Page), Doris Belack (Rita Marshall), Ellen Foley (Jacqui)

CINEMATOGRAPHY: Owen Roizman

MUSIC: Dave Grusin

LENGTH AND RATING: 116 min; originally rated R, then switched to PG on appeal

Tootsie is a cross-dressing comedy about a struggling New York City actor who dresses as a woman to land a role in a soap opera and becomes a star. As an actor with the reputation for being difficult, Michael Dorsey (Dustin Hoffman) pursues his goal of becoming successful while ignoring the emotions of the people who care about him. This includes his insecure friend and, later, girlfriend Sandy (Teri Garr), who has auditioned for the soap part that Michael is chosen for as "Dorothy Michaels." Then there are Julie (Jessica Lange), an attractive actress playing a nurse on the same soap, *Southwest General Hospital*, whom Michael befriends as Dorothy but fails to impress as Michael Dorsey, and Jessica's father, Les (Charles Durning), who becomes romantically interested in "Dorothy." The film also addresses the empowerment of women and their ability to confirm their own convictions of truth, beauty, and goodness, which Sandy and Jessica have difficulty doing but that Michael, playing the surrogate woman "Dorothy Michaels," achieves with great success, as a man. As "Dorothy Michaels," Michael Dorsey is given the opportunity to prove to himself and those around him that he has the ability to succeed despite his previous failures.

When Dustin Hoffman, as Michael Dorsey, then as Dorothy Michaels, dresses as a woman to get a job, he enters a world of cinematic cross-dressing and transgender. American films and television have used this concept successfully in comedy and drama. Perhaps the most famous of the cross-dressing comedies was *Some Like It Hot* (1959), starring Tony Curtis (Joe) and Jack Lemmon (Jerry) as two down-on-their-luck musicians during the Prohibition era who pose as women to get a gig with an all-women band bound for Florida. Joining up, they meet the voluptuous ukelele player Sugar Kane Kowalczyk (Marilyn Monroe). The success of this film provided opportunities for other comedies to explore the dynamics of male characters masquerading as women and vice versa. In the film *La Cage Aux Folles* (1978), gay nightclub manager Renato (Ugo Tognazzi) and his star female impersonator attraction and long-term lover Zaza (Michel Serrault), pose as husband and wife to provide Renato's son Laurent with "normal" parents to meet his future conservative father-in-law, while in *Victor/Victoria* (1982) Julie Andrews portrays the starving Victoria, who teams up with a gay man, Toddy (Robert Preston), and becomes a man "impersonating" a female impersonator. As *Mrs. Doubtfire* (1993), Robin Williams poses as a stern but loving matronly housekeeper so that he can be with his children, who are living with his ex-wife Miranda (Sally Field). These issues of sexuality become more profound in films like *Boys Don't Cry* (1999) and *The Crying Game* (1992).

Each character, Michael Dorsey and Frank Galvin, becomes obsessed with the opportunity to prove to themselves and to those around them that they have the ability to succeed despite their previous failures.

Courtroom dramas have been a staple of American cinema and have revealed the best and the worst of our system of jurisprudence. In *To Kill a Mockingbird* (1962) and *12 Angry Men* (1957), the issue of racism was addressed within the context of a courtroom drama. Some films addressed child custody battles, among them *Kramer vs. Kramer* (1979), while others, like *The Caine Mutiny* (1954) and *A Few Good Men* (1992), put the military on trial. One of the most famous and compelling courtroom dramas was *Judgment at Nuremberg* (1961), which depicted the war crime trial of Nazi Ministry of Justice officials before a four-judge panel.

THE VERDICT (1982)

PRODUCER/DIRECTOR: Sidney Lumet (director), Richard D. Zanuck (producer), David Brown (producer)
WRITER(S): Barry Reed (novel), David Mamet (screenplay)
CAST: Paul Newman (Frank Galvin), Charlotte Rampling (Laura Fischer), Jack Warden (Mickey Morrissey), James Mason (Ed Concannon), Milo O'Shea (Judge Hoyle), Lindsay Crouse (Kaitlin Costello), Ed Binns (Bishop Brophy), Julie Bovasso (Maureen Rooney), Roxanne Hart (Sally Doneghy), James Handy (Kevin Doneghy)
CINEMATOGRAPHY: Andrzej Bartkowiak
MUSIC: Johnny Mandel
LENGTH AND RATING: 129 min; R

For Frank Galvin (Paul Newman), a once-successful lawyer, personal and professional confidence come from a bottle. He has lost his friends, family, and respect as a result of a scandal involving jury tampering, which almost resulted in his being disbarred. Only one person, old-time lawyer Mickey Morrissey (Jack Warden), still believes in him.

He's given an opportunity to represent the family of a young woman admitted for a routine childbirth to a Boston Catholic hospital but who ends up with a catastrophic brain injury. Initially Galvin decides, like the "ambulance chaser" he's become, to settle quickly and take the money and run. But after visiting his client in the hospital and snapping several Polaroids, he's devasted at the injuries the doctors and hospital caused. Now, instead of money being his primary concern, he views the case as his salvation and selfishly pursues it for his redemption. In doing so he neglects the family of the victim as he risks their claim against the archdiocese, who hires a brilliant law firm headed by the suave, urbane Ed Concannon (James Mason). They cleverly plant a female lawyer, the recently divorced Laura Fischer (Charlotte Rampling), to develop a romantic interest in Frank Galvin, revealing his strategy and tactics to the opposition. She is prompted into this role because of her desire to validate her own worth and empowerment as a woman by returning to the practice of law.

The Verdict provides a compelling story about courage, vindication, and fortitude in the face of overwhelming odds. It is also about how people can become disillusioned with the "system," as when Frank, after requesting a postponement, is told by Judge Hoyle (Milo O'Shea) that he has no sympathy for him because he didn't take the money and run like a thief. Or, when the admitting hospital nurse Kaitlin Costello (Lindsay Crouse) is found by Frank in New York City and admits under oath that she was forced by the doctor to change information on the admitting record of the patient and screams, "Who were these men? Who were these men? I wanted to be a nurse."

THE HUNT

Blade Runner **(1982)**
The Terminator **(1984)**

As a film noir futuristic detective story, Ridley Scott's brilliant and sensually evocative film *Blade Runner*, set in Los Angeles in the year 2019, was influenced by Fritz Lang's silent film *Metropolis* (1926), set also in a futuristic city where machines rule the routinized lives of workers. Both films question how technology will impact human values, interpersonal relationships, and survival in a world objectified by a culture devoured by pretensions and devoid of substance. The noted scholar and critic Scott Bukatman has written that *Blade Runner* incorporates panorama and obscurity into shifting fields of the kaleidoscope:

> Like the best science fiction stories and city films, *Blade Runner* incorporates at once the magisterial gaze of the panorama, the sublime obscurity of the phantasmagoria and the shifting fields of the kaleidoscope. *Blade Runner*'s elaborate *mise-en-scène* and probing cameras create a tension that is fundamental to a period of inexorably advancing technological change. The inescapable and immersive city becomes a synecdoche for, and distillation of, all these unsettling technologies that continue to pervade lived experience. The film's aesthetic and its narrative underpinnings magnify and enhance the admixture of anxiety and delirium inherent in its experience. Its instability induces the epistemological and ontological uncertainties—the

Harrison Ford (as Rick Deckard). [Warner Bros./Photofest]

crises of knowing and being—that it narrates and theorizes. Seeing is everything in *Blade Runner*, but it guarantees absolutely nothing. (http://www.depauw.edu/sfs/reviews_pages/r75.htm)

BLADE RUNNER (1982)

PRODUCER/DIRECTOR: Ridley Scott (director), Michael Deeley (producer), Charles de Lauzirika (producer)

WRITER(S): Philip K. Dick (novel), Hampton Fancher (screenplay), David Webb Peoples (screenplay)

CAST: Harrison Ford (Rick Deckard), Rutger Hauer (Roy Batty), Sean Young (Rachael), Edward James Olmos (Gaff), M. Emmet Walsh (Bryant), Daryl Hannah (Pris), William Sanderson (J. F. Sebastian)

CINEMATOGRAPHY: Jordan Cronenweth

MUSIC: Vangelis

LENGTH AND RATING: 117 min; R

The 2019 Los Angeles that Ridley Scott depicts in *Blade Runner* is a dystopian universe that belches out steam in a dark shadowy city where the constant rain signifies a breakdown in the environment and the crowded streets and alleys populated by Asians speaking the slang of "cityspeak" resemble the bazaars and marketplaces of biblical cities. Huge electronic billboards that weave a mesmerizing marketing message advocate the virtues of drinking Coca-Cola and Budweiser beer, with blimps promoting escape from this melancholy existence to Off World colonies where the promise of life in a hospitable climate assisted by a humanoid replicant is an attractive alternative, but only for those who are fit.

Like many of his film noir detective counterparts, Rick Deckard (Harrison Ford), a retired, divorced ex-cop Blade Runner, or bounty hunter, at first rejects the assignment of hunting six escaped androids or replicants, Nexus 6 models with an embedded life span of four years who have hijacked a shuttle to Earth, killed its crew, and are determined to meet their "maker," Eldon Tyrell (Joe Turkel), at the Tyrell Corporation to extend their lives. They are the most advanced form of humanoid replicants and difficult to identify as non-humans even with the "Voigt-Kampff Empathy" test.

THE TERMINATOR (1984)

PRODUCER/DIRECTOR: James Cameron (director), Gale Anne Hurd (producer)
WRITER(S): James Cameron, Gale Anne Hurd
CAST: Arnold Schwarzenegger (The Terminator), Michael Biehn (Kyle Reese), Linda Hamilton (Sarah Connor), Paul Winfield (Lieutenant Ed Traxler), Lance Henriksen (Detective Hal Vukovich), Bess Motta (Ginger Ventura), Earl Boen (Dr. Peter Silberman), Rick Rossovich (Matt Buchanan), Dick Miller (Pawnshop Clerk), Shawn Schepps (Nancy)
CINEMATOGRAPHY: Adam Greenberg
MUSIC: Brad Fiedel
LENGTH AND RATING: 108 min; R

In *The Terminator*, similar themes are shared with *Blade Runner* in that both films evolve around a hunt. In *Blade Runner* the search is a complex narrative outwardly involving the hunt for the wayward replicants; however, it also manifests itself into an inquiry toward the meaning of life. For Rick Deckard can kill and retire the replicants but then falls in love with Rachael (Sean Young), who is a replicant, and at the end of the movie realizes that he, too, is a machine, with implanted memories and emotion, but a replicant nevertheless who may also want to exist as a human.

Although stylistically *The Terminator* does not evoke a similar mileu or the noir story line of *Blade Runner*, its theme addresses a future of machines that rule humanity, not unlike the threat of the Nexus-6 replicants in *Blade Runner*. But *The Terminator*, although having a futuristic plot, is more of a survivalist action adventure movie. Just as Deckard must hunt down and kill the escaped replicants, the Terminator (Arnold Schwarzenegger), a cyborg, is sent to Earth in 1984 from the future year of 2029 to kill Sarah Connor (Linda Hamilton), the birth mother of John Connor, who is leading the human revolt, circa 2029, against the machines. A human from the future, Kyle Reese (Michael Biehn) is sent by John Connor to protect his mother and father her child. The film once again establishes the creative use of time travel (or temporal anomalies) as a legitimate plot device, along with defining the invincibility of the cyborg. Many films have used time travel as a plot device, including *The Time Machine* (1960), based on the H. G. Wells novel, *Planet of the Apes* (1968), and *Back to the Future* (1985), but in *The Terminator* it takes on the new twist of a monster-like machine from the future that relentlessly pursues its victim in the present.

In *Blade Runner*, Deckard is also in single-minded pursuit and although he manages to eliminate the replicants he is severely outmatched by their strength and intelligence, just as Sarah, Kyle, and the Los Angeles law enforcement community are no match for the Terminator. The life and death struggle in both movies is tense, physical, and purposely imaginative, as mere mortals must do battle with robot creatures, replicants, and cyborgs, which display a cunning for survival matched with superhuman strength. These creatures mimicking human behavior take on the best and worst characteristics of people. In *Blade Runner*, Rachael is convinced she is human because of the memories she has of her family and childhood. But corporate arrogance and deceit in the form of Eldon Tyrell of the Tyrell Corporation, in a quest to replicate human beings, has programmed the Nexus-6 replicants with memories, emotions, and skills, like playing the piano, that create an overwhelming desire enticing them with human virtues that cruely remain out of their reach.

In *The Terminator* Kyle explains the sophistication of the new cyborgs to Sarah compared with the earlier 600 series that had rubber skin and were easier to identify. The new 600-model has living skin, with sweat, and even bad breath. In both *Blade Runner* and *The Terminator*, these robots have become a threat to humankind in their attempt to enslave their masters and aspire to longer operating lives. Some critcs have labeled *The Terminator* as an action adventure film based on a formulaic definition of comic books and their heroes being transposed to the screen. While there may be some substance to that argument, because of the mammoth portrayal of the cyborg by actor Arnold Schwarzenegger and the somewhat campy nature of the dialogue ("I'll be back") there are still themes being addressed that are more relevant today than in 1984. We are a culture that has become totally dependent upon machines driven by computers that support and in some cases dictate behavioral dynamics. The film clearly points to the dominance of machines in American culture. As Kyle rests in his car next to a construction site with heavy equipment in operation, it is a reference to the dominance of machines that rule the future, and he wakes from a troubled dream with a start as a light from a large construction crane falls on his eyes. At the end of the movie, Sarah manages to terminate the cyborg, after Kyle's death, in an automated manufacturing facility by activating a hydrolic crusher.

The physical features of the human eye play an important role in each of these films and may be a reference to the search for a human soul. In *Blade Runner*, the lie detector test, the Voigt-Kampff machine, is based on a series of questions, with reactions monitored by a retina scan of the eye, while the eyes of replicants creator Dr. Eldon Tyrell are magnified by large lenses in his glasses, giving him a lizardly look. Other references to vision and the importance of eyes in *Blade Runner* include the visit by renegade replicants Roy and Leon to the workshop of Hannibal Chew (James Hong), who manufactures the eyes for the Tyrell Nexus 6 replicants. Later, when Roy and Pris (Daryl Hannah), with the help of J. F. Sebastian (William Sondenon), gain access to Tyrell's private apartment, the confrontation ends with Roy plunging his fingers into Tyrell's eyes, killing him. (This is a reference to Shakespeare's *King Lear* and the plucking out of Gloucester's eyes by Cornwall.)

In *The Terminator*, the cyborg's eyes appear to be part of his cosmetic façade. This is demonstrated in a scene where the cyborg returns to his room to repair himself, removing one eye and before leaving donning a pair of sunglasses. He has demonstrated his visual acuity by processing images displayed on an internal screen.

There is also a literary basis for *The Terminator* and *Blade Runner* in the short story "The Most Dangerous Game" by Richard Connell. The narrative is about a big game hunter who cares only about the hunt but becomes the human quarry of a madman in the Amazon jungle who is bored by conventional game and pursues humans as his prey. In *Blade Runner*, Deckard is assigned to hunt down the replicants but becomes the hunted when the replicant Roy Batty (Rutger Hauer) pursues him, and although he can kill the Blade Runner he instead displays the very human characteristic of compassion and saves Deckard from falling off the roof, yelling "Kinship." As his own life slips away, Roy speaks of his own very human memories, not those implanted by others, as a combat replicant, a soldier:

> I've seen things you people wouldn't believe. Attack ships on fire off the shoulder of Orion. I watched C-beams glitter in the dark near the Tanhauser gate. All those moments will be lost in time like tears in rain. Time to die.

Both *Blade Runner* and *The Terminator* end with suggestions of hope, as Deckard and Rachael follow their human instinct of love and a pregnant Sarah leaves the present world, preparing for Armageddon and its future.

ADVENTURE

Raiders of the Lost Ark **(1981)**
E.T. **(1982)**
Back to the Future **(1985)**

Perhaps the greatest serial franchises in contemporary film are James Bond (007), *Star Wars*, *Back to the Future*, and *Raiders of the Lost Ark*. When George Lucas and Steven Spielberg collaborated on *Raiders of the Lost Ark*, they paid homage to the action adventure serial films of the silent era (*Perils of Pauline*, 1914), and those sound serials of the 1940s based on the comic book adventures of Flash Gordon, Zorro, Dick Tracy, and many others that ended in cliff-hangers. In *Raiders of the Lost Ark*, Indiana Jones (Harrison Ford) is a swashbuckling archaeologist (loosely modeled after the showman, amateur archeologist Giovanni Belzoni, 1778–1823). He is fearless (except for snakes), smart, handsome, clever, resourceful, and victorious against evil. In many ways the *Raiders* franchise reflects the same themes of danger and the attention to special-effects-driven creative action sequences of the *James Bond* film franchise.

Starting in 1962 with *Dr. No*, the James Bond franchise is one of the most successful contemporary series based on a single theme and character. As this book goes to press, there have been twenty-two Bond films, with the latest entry, *Quantum of Solace*, released in 2008. They are based on the British secret service agent character created by author Ian Fleming. The first actor to portray Agent 007 in "official" Bond films was Sean Connery (1962–67, 1971, and in 1983 the "unofficial" Bond film, (*Never Say Never Again*), and he was followed in chronological order by: George Lazenby (1969, one feature), Roger Moore (1973–1985, seven features), Timothy Dalton (1987–89, two features), Pierce Brosnan (1995–2002, four features), and Daniel Craig (2006–08, two features.) The inflation-adjusted total box office gross for the Bond series exceeds $11 billion.

American actor Barry Nelson was the first to portray James Bond in the 1954 one-hour television adaptation of Ian Fleming's novel *Casino Royale*, which appeared on the episodic television series entitled *Climax!* (CBS 1954–58), hosted by William Lundigan and featuring the actors Peter Lorre and Linda Christian. As an early television drama, the episode captured the essence and mood of the subsequent Bond feature films, although Nelson wasn't quite as suave, charming, and refined as his subsequent counterparts; but then, he was the only American actor to portray Agent 007.

RAIDERS OF THE LOST ARK (1981)

PRODUCER/DIRECTOR: Steven Spielberg (director), Frank Marshall (producer)
WRITER(s): George Lucas (story), Philip Kaufman (story), Lawrence Kasdan (screenplay)
CAST: Harrison Ford (Indiana Jones), Karen Allen (Marion Ravenwood), Paul Freeman (Dr. Rene Belloq), Ronald Lacey (Major Arnold Toht), John Rhys-Davies (Sallah), Denholm Elliott (Dr. Marcus Brody), Alfred Molina (Satipo), Wolf Kahler (Colonel Dietrich), Anthony Higgins (Gobler), Vic Tablian (Barranca)
CINEMATOGRAPHY: Douglas Slocombe
MUSIC: John Williams
LENGTH AND RATING: 115 min; PG

For *Raiders of the Lost Ark*, Spielberg and Lucas used the Bond franchise as a template for the start of a successful film series. This included the design of unique opening title sequences, clever "campy" dialogue, shrewd villains, and exciting, dramatic special effects. For example, just like in many Bond films, *Raiders of the Lost Ark* opens with a momentous action sequence as Indiana Jones, with the aid of a native guide, attempts to collect a priceless jeweled gold figurine of a head resting on a pedestal inside an ancient jungle temple rigged with an assortment of deadly guardians. After testing the hazards and deflecting them, he cautiously moves toward the gold idol. However, before lifting the head from its pedestal he cleverly switches it for a bag of sand of approximate weight, thinking he has outsmarted the ancients. Instead, the pedestal lowers and he and his native guide Satipo (Alfred Molina) face imminent death as poisonous darts and arrows fly and the walls begin to cave in. A huge pit forms and Satipo uses Indiana's whip to jump over it but when Indiana asks for the whip Satipo refuses unless he is given the priceless idol. After Indiana tosses the idol to him, Satipo betrays him, drops the whip, says good-bye, and leaves the temple. In a scene blocked like a cliff-hanger, facing imminent death, Indiana takes a running leap and jumps across the divide but, landing short, he must cling to the dirt edge, managing to raise himself up with the aid of a decrepit vine and then is able, by mere inches, to slide under a vertical stone door as it shuts. As for Satipo, his betrayal is rewarded by spears through his head and Indiana once again takes possession of the idol and then faces a huge boulder as it spins toward the entrance of the cave; he manages to leap out just before the boulder seals the cave. Once outside he meets his nemeis, the evil, shrewd, French archaeologist Rene Belloq (Paul Freeman), who is chaperoned by a group of warrior natives. In another breathless scene, Indiana manages to run from Belloq and the natives to a seaplane idly resting on the water, and as he swims toward it he shouts to the pilot to start the engines. He grabs one of the pontoons, slides into the cockpit, and nearly jumps out of the plane upon encountering Reggie, the pilot's pet snake.

There's an interesting parallel between between the idol scene in *Raiders of the Lost Ark* and other "heist" movies, such as *The Asphalt Jungle* (1950), *Topkapi* (1964), and the more contemporary *The Bank Job* (2008), where elaborate and painstaking plans to steal the loot sometimes fail. Throughout *Raiders of the Lost Ark*, as Indiana Jones and Marion Ravenwood (Karen Allen) try to find the Ark of the Covenant, they are endlessly placed in precarious and life-threatening situations as they are pursued by Belloq and the Nazis. It is indeed the ultimate action adventure fantasy featuring a hero and his damsel, who is sometimes in distress. *New York Times* movie critic Vincent Canby notes in his June 12, 1981, review that "it evokes memories of moviegoing of an earlier era but that possesses its own, far more rare sensibility."

Canby also says, "*Raiders of the Lost Ark* is off and running at a breakneck pace that simply won't stop until the final shot…" And he adds:

> To get to the point immediately, *Raiders of the Lost Ark* is one of the most deliriously funny, ingenious, and stylish American adventure movies ever made. It is an homage to old-time movie serials and back-lot cheapies that transcends its inspirations to become, in effect, the movie we saw in our imaginations as we watched, say, Buster Crabbe in *Flash Gordon's Trip to Mars* or in Sam Katzman's *Jungle Jim* movies. (http://www.nytimes.com/1981/06/12/movies)

A movie that had several adaptations and in its 1985 version parodied *Raiders of the Lost Ark* was *King Solomon's Mines*. Starring Richard Chamberlain as Allan Quatermain, the African big-game hunter, and Sharon Stone as Jesse Huston, it is loosely based on H. Rider Haggard's 1885 novel. However, Quatermain is dressed like Indiana Jones, replete with khaki jungle attire and wide-brimmed fedora and he manages to fall in love and get himself and Jesse out of some close calls. Two other films with similarities to *Raiders of the Lost Ark* are *Romancing the Stone* (1984), directed by Robert Zemeckis and starring Michael Douglas and Kathleen Turner, and its sequel *The Jewel of the Nile* (1985), with the same stars but directed by Lewis Teague.

There have been four Indiana Jones movies: *Raiders of the Lost Ark* (1981), the prequel *Indiana Jones and the Temple of Doom* (1984), *Indiana Jones and the Last Crusade* (1989), and *Indiana Jones and the Kingdom of the Crystal Skull* (2008). The first three movies earned a worldwide box office total in excess of $1 billion.

E.T. (1982)

PRODUCER/DIRECTOR: Steven Spielberg (director, producer), Kathleen Kennedy (producer)
WRITER(S): Melissa Mathison
CAST: Henry Thomas (Elliott), Dee Wallace (Mary), Robert MacNaughton (Michael), Drew Barrymore (Gertie), Peter Coyote (Keys), K. C. Martel (Greg), Sean Frye (Steve), C. Thomas Howell (Tyler), David M. O'Dell (Schoolboy), Richard Swingler (Science Teacher)
CINEMATOGRAPHY: Allen Daviau
MUSIC: John Williams
LENGTH AND RATING: 115 min; PG

The theme of pursuit, childhood loneliness, and displacement in action adventure fantasy movies is also evident in *Back to the Future* and *E.T.* These films, which Spielberg was associated with as a producer (*Back to the Future*) and director (*E.T.*), share a fairy-tale

Drew Barrymore (as Gertie) with ET. [Universal Pictures/Photofest]

theme similar to *Peter Pan* and *The Wizard of Oz*. Children have a self-centered view of the universe and contextualize themselves at its center. For example, when children look at the sun or the moon while traveling in a car, their response is that it's following them. Both *E.T.* and *Back to the Future* are two child-centered films contextualizing their fears and fantasies. Adults are treated as dismissive, bungling, threatening, or suspicious.

In the *Wizard of Oz*, Dorothy is a lonely girl living in Kansas who, in an attempt to protect her dog from being taken, runs away from home. But Dorothy is a dreamer who looks at the sky and sings "Somewhere Over the Rainbow," evoking the fable of a child's lullaby, in a land where skies are blue and dreams that you dream can come true. And her wishes are realized when she is transported to the Land of Oz (her Neverland) and meets her new loving friends, who help her triumph over the evil witch.

"Nothing that happens after we are twelve matters very much." This quote is from Sir James Matthew Barrie, author of *Peter Pan*, a character related to the Greek god of shepherds and associated with the hunt and fertility. In Greek mythology, Pan was depicted with the head of a horned, bearded man and the legs and tail of a goat. In Barrie's story, Peter Pan takes on the playful qualities of the Greek god as the boy who would never grow up, and everyone remains young forever in the playful mythological world of Neverland, where good always triumphs over evil. Both as a play and in the 1955 and 1960 television adaptations, the story of Peter Pan captivated audiences throughout the world. Many of the themes associated with Peter Pan, surrounding the myths and fears of children, became part of contemporary cinema.

In *E.T.*, the parables and themes of these two children's classics are given a contemporary look as Elliot (Henry Thomas), the lonely child of a single-parent home, befriends an alien who is left by a group of botanists from outer space who were collecting samples of Earth's vegetation. He becomes the creature's mentor and protector, developing a bond of trust, friendship, and love. When Elliot first encounters E.T., he tempts the alien by dropping pieces of Hershey's Reese's Pieces, forming a path to his house, and then he uses the same technique to lure him up to his bedroom. This is a reference to the fairy tale "Hansel and Gretel," where after the two children are abandoned by their father, Hansel on their first trip drops pebbles, which lead them back to their home but on the second trip drops bread crumbs which are eaten by the birds.

In *E.T.* adults are seen as threatening figures as they are viewed from the waist down, hunting for the alien. Determined to protect E.T. from being found and dissected, Elliot acts out his concerns in school by releasing all of the frogs his class is readying for dissection. Eventually, the authorities locate E.T. and seal off Elliot's home in a bizarre scene of clinical hostility and after his heart stops as they are about to freeze him he miraculously comes to life. To save E.T., who wants to return home, Elliot enlists the aid of his friends, who on their bicycles race against the authorities to the forest, where the spaceship has a rendezvous to pick up their misplaced colleague. During this scene, when Elliot, who is carrying E.T. in a bicycle basket, and his friends are blocked by gun-toting agents, they become airborne, riding their bicycles and looking down on the ground below. In the end, E.T. must return home but as in any good fairy tale, just like in *The Wizard of Oz*, good triumphs over evil and Elliot has learned the feelings of love and loss.

In his June 11, 1982, *New York Times* review, Vincent Canby refers to *E.T.* as "a children's classic of the space age."

The film, directed by Mr. Spielberg and written by Melissa Mathison from an idea of Mr. Spielberg, freely recycles elements from all sorts of earlier children's works, including *Peter Pan* and *The Wizard of Oz*. *E.T.* is as contemporary as laser-beam technology, but it's full of the timeless longings expressed in children's literature of all eras. (http://www.nytimes.com/1982/06/11/movies/moviesspecial)

BACK TO THE FUTURE (1985)

PRODUCER/DIRECTOR: Robert Zemeckis (director), Neil Canton (producer), Bob Gale (producer)
WRITER(S): Robert Zemeckis, Bob Gale
CAST: Michael J. Fox (Marty McFly), Christopher Lloyd (Dr. Emmett Brown), Lea Thompson (Lorraine Baines McFly), Crispin Glover (George McFly), Thomas F. Wilson (Biff Tannen), Claudia Wells (Jennifer Parker), Marc McClure (Dave McFly), Wendie Jo Sperber (Linda McFly), George DiCenzo (Sam Baines), Frances Lee McCain (Stella Baines)
CINEMATOGRAPHY: Dean Cundey
MUSIC: Alan Silvestri
LENGTH AND RATING: 117 min; PG

Time travel, a teenager's shame for his weak-willed father, and his sense of displacement is the theme of *Back to the Future*. In the film, Marty McFly (Michael J. Fox) is accidently transported in his scientist friend Dr. Emmet "Doc" Brown's (Christopher Lloyd) DeLorean time machine, going from 1985 to his 1955 hometown of Hill Valley, California. Wearing a cool-weather sleeveless vest, his 1985 wardrobe perplexes the 1955 townsfolk, who think it's a life preserver. Meeting his mother, Lorraine (Lea Thompson), and his father, George (Crispin Glover), as teenagers, along with the generational bully Biff Tannen (Thomas F. Wilson), Marty is an obstacle to his parents meeting and falling in love. His teenage mother becomes infatuated with him, and if Marty cannot succeed he and his siblings could be "erased" forever from existing (as depicted by a family photograph Marty carries with him).

Just as the present adult bully in 1985, Biff is the teenage town bully in 1955 and after Marty coaches his teenage father on how to rescue his mother from "making out" with him in a car, Biff interrupts the scenario and his friends haul Marty away, locking him in the trunk of a car. When George arrives at the prescribed time, instead of finding Marty he faces Biff manhandling Lorraine and, collecting his courage, punches Biff and knocks him out, then takes her to the dance, where they fall in love.

Transporting Marty back to 1955 provides ample opportunity to poke fun at the quaint world of the 1950s, as he demonstrates the language and technology of the 1980s. He is able to connect the video camera to Doc's televsion set so that they can view the last moments before the time machine entered a time warp. Using the popular 1980s slang word "heavy," he confuses Doc who, in his scientific mind, connotes the word with gravity. In a clever and funny scene, Marty escapes from Biff and his cronies by yanking a 1950s wooden scooter crate mounted on roller skate wheels from a child, separating it from the box, and using it as a skateboard. He confounds the goons chasing him in Biff's vintage convertible when he hangs to the front hood of the car on his skateboard. Thinking they have finally cornered Marty, he jumps up onto the car, goes over the heads of the goons, and lands back on the skateboard, which has traveled underneath, to the rear of the moving car. Too late to stop, the car crashes into a truck carrying manure, which dumps its load on top of Biff and his goons.

As in E.T., Marty's objective is to return home after bringing his teenage parents together. But there are complications, as there is no plutonium available to power the time machine in 1955. However, knowing the exact time and date when lightning will strike the clock tower, Doc is able to compute the gigawatts to power the time machine and rigs a contraption to harness the electricity. The tension builds as the DeLorean stalls when Marty starts it, and Doc dangles precariously from the clock tower. After finally getting the car started, Marty races toward the destination point while Doc pulls on the wire, which is caught on a branch, attempting to plug it in. As he pulls the extension separates from another plug lower to the ground and in a last-minute rescue attempt before the lighning strikes he glides down the wire on a ring and, with a bolt of lighting striking and electric current flowing, manages to make the connection.

When Marty wakes up in his bed the next morning he sees that his family has been transformed from dysfunctional to normal. His father has become a successful novelist, his mother an attractive, svelt woman, and Biff is the lackey waxing the cars and delivering packages.

Both Elliot, the child in E.T., and Marty long for inclusion in their respective subgroups. With his brother's older friends, Elliot is excluded from playing "Dungeons and Dragons," and after auditioning for the school dance Marty's band is rejected by the high school administrators. A teacher in Marty's high school, Mr. Strickland (James

Tolkan), warns him that "no McFly ever amounted to anything in the history of Hill Valley." But eventually Marty plays at a school dance, albeit in 1955, doing a blow-out solo, and Elliot becomes the soul mate of E.T., both of them earning the respect of their peers. These two films are both science fiction fantasies that rely on the suspension of reality that is easily invoked by children, as in *Peter Pan*, taking them to worlds beyond adult control, where they can choose their own destiny.

The concept became a trilogy, with two additional *Back to the Future* movies, *Part II* (1989) and *Part III* (1990), and a total domestic box office of about $400 million.

DESIRE, SEXUALITY, AND NONCONFORMITY

Return of the Secaucus Seven (1980)
El Norte (1983)
Sex, Lies, and Videotape (1989)

Three films in the 1980s captured the sensibilities of the personal films of the 1960s and 1970s, in the tradition of actor/filmmaker John Cassavetes (*A Woman Under the Influence*, 1974). They were independent films that were expressive of rituals, desire, sexuality, and nonconformity.

RETURN OF THE SECAUCUS SEVEN (1980)

PRODUCER/DIRECTOR: John Sayles (director), William Aydelott (producer), Jeffrey Nelson (producer)
WRITER(s): John Sayles
CAST: Bruce MacDonald (Mike Donnelly), Maggie Renzi (Katie Sipriano), Adam LeFevre (J. T.), Maggie Cousineau (Frances Carlson), Gordon Clapp (Chip Hollister), Jean Passanante (Irene Rosenblue), Karen Trott (Maura Tolliver), Mark Arnott (Jeff Andrews), David Strathairn (Ron Desjardins), John Sayles (Howie)
CINEMATOGRAPHY: Austin De Besche
MUSIC: Mason Daring, Tim Jackson, Bill Staines, Guy Van Duser
LENGTH AND RATING: 110 min; R

In the John Sayles film *The Return of the Secaucus Seven*, seven college friends who were political activsts in the 1960s have a weekend reunion at the New Hampshire home of Katie (Maggie Renzi) and Mike (Bruce MacDonald), who are now teachers. The movie examines the strain of interpersonal relationships between the friends as the dynamic of their romantic couplings and ideals have changed. Tensions develop as partners change and while witnessing these events Katie begins to question the durability of her relationship with Mike.

The film exposes the residual counterculture sensibility that the characters once felt and reveals the more mature view of their future. An interesting dynamic is the introduction of a character unknown to the group, Chip (Gordon Clapp), because he is Irene's (Jean Passanante) latest boyfriend. There is anticipation by the group and by Chip pertaining to "fitting in" with Irene's friends. Also present is J. T. (Adam Lefevre), Irene's previous boyfriend. Reflecting the sexual freedom of the sixties and seventies, Irene reminds Chip that she has had many boyfriends. Both Irene and Chip are employed by a liberal Washington senator, and their mocking degradation of him reveals a mature sarcasm that has surfaced since their "heady" activist college years.

Additional tension is created by the sudden arrival of Maura (Karen Trott), an aspiring actress who has ended her long-term relationship with Jeff (Mark Amott), a substance abuse counselor, by abandoning him at a celebration at his parents' home. She had previously indicated that she couldn't make the reunion and surprises everyone when she suddenly turns up without Jeff. After the group absorbs the news of their breakup, Maura becomes attracted to J. T. and they have sex together on the night of her arrival. The next day Jeff shows up, announcing that he left the party at his parents' home early. When Jeff learns that his best friend J. T. had slept with Maura, he takes out his anger on the basketball court by knocking J. T. down several times.

What becomes evident from the characters in the film is the difficulty they have accepting the reality that they are getting older. This is personified when they all gather around a birthday cake decorated with a guitar to celebrate J. T's thirtieth birthday. They debate the effect it may have on him and decide not to surprise him with it.

There is, however, a very revealing portrait of two characters in the film, Ron (David Strathaim) and Howie (John Sayles), two of Mike's friends who never left the small New Hampshire town. They stayed after graduating from high school, taking on hourly jobs. As a single man, Ron jokes about the lack of romantic prospects during the winter and the routine of small-town life. He's very realistic about his future and the respect he receives as the area's expert auto mechanic. He won't move away because he is a valued citizen. Indeed, he proves to be very attractive to Fran (Maggie Cousineau), another group member and medical student who for years has quietly carried a torch for J. T., an untalented musician on his way to Los Angeles to break into the music business. They eventually check in to a motel, where Howie works as a desk clerk. For Fran, Ron poses less of a threat and is frankly, in his own childish way, more mature than J. T. and most other men she has met.

For the women in the group, Howie, who is married and has three small children, presents a formidable challenge. They are getting older but cannot face the commitment and dedication of parenthood. In a local tavern with his friends Ron and Mike, Howie speaks of the sacrifice it takes to care for his family but concludes it's worth it. He demonstrates to the others that life is a progression of relationships and responsibilities that can be very fulfilling.

The film serves as the inspiration for other ensemble, personal-character-driven films, especially *The Big Chill* (1983), directed by Lawrence Kasdan. Whereas *The Return of the Secaucus Seven* was made on a budget of $60,000, the budget for *The Big Chill*, which features movie stars like Glenn Close, Kevin Kline, and Kevin Costner (all his scenes were cut), was approximately $20 million. The theme is identical to the Sayles film, with several University of Michigan friends coming together at the home of Sarah (Glenn Close) and Harold (Kevin Kline) for the funeral of their friend Alex, who commited suicide.

EL NORTE (1983)

PRODUCER/DIRECTOR: Gregory Nava (director), Trevor Black (producer), Bertha Navarro (producer), Anna Thomas (producer)

WRITER(S): Gregory Nava (story), Anna Thomas (writer)

CAST: Zaide Silvia Gutiérrez (Rosa Xuncax), David Villalpando (Enrique Xuncax), Ernesto Gómez Cruz (Arturo Xuncax), Lupe Ontiveros (Nacha), Trinidad Silva (Monte), Alicia del Lago (Lupe Xuncax), Abel Franco (Raimundo), Enrique Castillo (Jorge), Tony Plana (Carlos), Diane Cary (Alice Harper)

CINEMATOGRAPHY: James Glennon

MUSIC: The Folkloristas, Malecio Martinez, Linda O'Brien, Emil Richards

LENGTH AND RATING: 139 min; R

A profoundly emotional film, *El Norte*, directed by Gregory Nava with a screenplay by Nava and his wife, Anna Thomas, tells the story of the modern-day immigrant experience of Central Americans illegally crossing borders and the danger and struggles they encounter trying to enter the United States. Although the film is twenty-five years old, it is a timely statement on the current American debate concerning immigration.

It features two youthful characters, Enrique Xuncax (David Villalpando) and Rosa (Zaida Silvia Guitierrez), in roles as brother and sister. They are indigenous peasants from Guatemala who flee their village when their father is killed by soldiers because he is a leader in organizing the poor natives against their subordination by the wealthy and a corrupt government. After their father is murdered and his severed head hung from a tree, their mother is rounded up with the others and taken away. As the authorities hunt for Enrique, he takes refuge in the mountains and returns to find his sister and they both flee to El Norte (the north).

The film is divided into three acts: "Arturo Xuncax," "Coyote," and "El Norte." In the first act, the audience is introduced to the Xuncax family and their patriarch Arturo (Ernesto Gomez). As he leaves to attend a political meeting, his wife asks him not to go and Enrique runs after him, pleading that he should stay home. But Arturo explains to his son that he must go because the rich see only a peasant with strong arms. After hearing gun shots, Enrique runs to the meeting place and is attacked by a soldier left for dead, whom he kills. A hunted man, he hides in the mountains and eventually reunites with Rosa, and they run away together.

In the second act, after a long journey and a grueling bus trip, they arrive in Tijuana, Mexico, looking for a man recommended by a village friend who could help them cross the border into California. Unable to locate him, they befriend another man who arranges to meet them that evening and guide them across the border. Instead, he leads them into the woods and attacks Enrique, thinking he has a lot of money. They ward off their attacker, who later bemoans that he sustained a beating after learning that Enrique had a mere twenty dollars. Picked up by the American border patrol, Enrique manages to convince an agent who suspects they are not Mexican by peppering his Spanish with the word "fuck," and they are returned to Tijuana. Finally, Enrique locates the man recommended for the border crossing and, after selling their mother's silver necklace to finance their trip, he directs them to an abandoned sewer pipe, which he asserts is the safest way to cross. However, he warns them that its perils are the stench and muck they must crawl through. In a harrowing sewer pipe scene, Enrique and Rosa are attacked by a brood of rats that crawl over and under them, realizing one of Rosa's greatest fears. Finally reaching the end, their coyote appears with sandwiches and takes them to a run-down San Diego motel that houses illegal immigrants.

In the third act, "El Norte," the coyote bargains with Monte Bravo (Trinidad Silva), who runs the labor pool, for their services. Bravo has too many male day laborers and only offers a retainer for Rosa. At a garment factory, Rosa meets Nacha (Lupe Onti-veros), a wise illegal immigrant who teaches her how to press fabrics. When immigra-tion agents raid the factory, Nacha guides Rosa to safety. Later she explains that whenever she takes a job, one of the first things she does is plan several escape routes. They team up to clean houses and in a funny scene receive instructions from a gringo woman on the complex operation of a digital washer/dryer. While working in a posh res-taurant/catering hall, Enrique is promoted from busboy to waiter, which enrages the Chi-cano passed up for the job, even though he is legal. Acting on his jealous anger, he calls the department of immigration and they raid the restaurant and, with the help of a friend, Enrique barely manages to escape. In the interim, Enrique and Rosa enroll in adult education English classes and become conversant. And Monte has a terrific job offer from a Chicago factory owner, but Enrique declines it because he cannot leave Rosa.

After he loses his job, Enrique finds the woman from Chicago and tells her he wants the opportunity and she arranges for him to travel with her that evening. How-ever, Rosa is taken to the hospital with a rash, which is diagnosed as typhus. Rushing to find him, Nacha tells Enrique that Rosa is gravely ill but he continues to pack for his trip, ignoring her pleas. Intercut are scenes of Enrique and the airport as the woman boards and the plane leaves without him. The emotional bond between Enrique and Rosa has drawn him to the hospital, and he is there when she dies.

Back at the motel, Enrique lines up with the rest of the day laborers, shouting that he has strong arms to do the work. He is taken to a work site where he digs ditches. Paausing for a moment, he recalls the village of his youth and the words of his father about a peasant's strong arms.

The directors describe their film as addressing human values rather than political ideologies. They wanted to illustrate the plight of the hundreds of thousands Central American refugees living in Los Angeles in a way that would make a statement about the immigrant experience:

> Any issue would be better served by an involving and dramatic story than a lec-ture: Nobody goes to movies to hear a lecture. We didn't want "El Norte" to look like a docu-drama, or have any stylistic elements that would remind people of journalism or "rough-around-the-edges" documentary. The style we aimed for is the dream realism that comes from the Mayan culture. (http://movies.nytimes. com/movie)

SEX, LIES, AND VIDEOTAPE (1989)

PRODUCER/DIRECTOR: Steven Soderbergh (director), John Hardy (producer), Robert F. Newmyer (producer)

WRITER(S): Steven Soderbergh

CAST: James Spader (Graham Dalton), Andie MacDowell (Ann Bishop Mullany), Peter Gallagher (John Mullany), Laura San Giacomo (Cynthia Patrice Bishop), Ron Vawter (Therapist), Steven Brill (Barfly), Alexandra Root (Girl on Tape), Earl T. Taylor (Land-lord), David Foil (John's Colleague)

CINEMATOGRAPHY: Walt Lloyd

MUSIC: Cliff Martinez

LENGTH AND RATING: 100 min; R

This was Steven Soderbergh's debut film and a remarkably profound statement by a young director on interpersonal relationships and human sexuality. The film addresses themes of insecurity, jealousy, arrogance, and impotence (sexual and emotional) among four people: husband and wife Ann and John Mullany (Andie MacDowell, Peter Gallagher), Ann's sister Cynthia (Laura San Giacomo), and John's college friend Graham (James Spader), who has come to visit them and find an apartment in Baton Rouge, Louisiana.

Although they were close in college, John and Graham now have little in common. As a successful lawyer, John personifies a yuppie mentality and is having an affair with Ann's sister, Cynthia. The two sisters have a tense relationship steeped in jealousy: Ann feels that Cynthia is too loud and extroverted while Cynthia is critical of Ann's straitlaced behavior and is envious of her marriage to John. The affair between Cynthia and John is punctuated by her need to demonstrate superiority over Ann and control over him. She controls John and fulfills her needs on demand, sending him away when her mood changes. As for Ann, she is sexually repressed and in therapy appears to be obsessed by things over which she has no control, such as the amount of garbage accumulating in the world. When asked by her therapist about her relationship with John, she answers that it's fine but that lately she doesn't want him to touch her.

When Graham visits he changes the dynamics of these relationships. He's the opposite of John, with his shaggy, long, boyish hair and casual dress. He attracts both Ann and Cynthia and has the talent to ask probing questions without appearing to be obvious. However, Graham has an unusual passion: he videotapes women answering intimate questions about sex. He is sexually impotent with women and uses these videotaped "confessions" for arousal.

After learning about Graham's condition and his videotaping project, Ann withdraws from their blossoming friendship. Intrigued by him, Cynthia, though uninvited, visits and agrees to be videotaped and masturbates on camera. Eventually, Ann learns about John's affair with Cynthia when she finds an earring that jams the vacuum as she is cleaning her bedroom. Ultimately, Ann returns to Graham, turns the camera on him, and they move to the couch, where they make love.

Although the plot may be as familiar as a daytime serial drama and the script is heavy with dialogue, Soderbergh's film is a vivid psychological drama that provides its audience with substantive characters, resonant performances by its actors, and an interesting plot device, as the camera becomes another character. All of the characters interact with the camera, either by performing for it, watching the tapes, or using it as a tool for their own self-discovery.

In her August 4, 1989 *New York Times* review, Caryn James describes the film as a "Liaisons Dangereuses" for the video age in which the video camera becomes a central player:

> Soderbergh's astonishing first film is a "Liaisons Dangereuses" for the video age, a rich, absorbing tale of sexual greed and fear, love and betrayal, in which Graham's camera becomes a central player. It is an intricate dance of constantly changing partners, whose connections are based on truth, self-denial and outright deception. (http:// movies.nytimes.com/movie)

The production budget for *Sex, Lies, and Videotape* was just over $1 million and it earned approximately $25 million during its initial box office release, making it the most successful independent film of the eighties.

THIS IS SPINAL TAP (1984)

PRODUCER/DIRECTOR: Rob Reiner (director), Karen Murphy (producer)
WRITER(S): Christopher Guest, Michael McKean, Harry Shearer, Rob Reiner
CAST: Rob Reiner (Marty DiBergi), Kimberly Stringer (Heavy Metal Fan), Chazz Dominguez (Heavy Metal Fan), Shari Hall (Heavy Metal Fan), R. J. Parnell (Mick Shrimpton), David Kaff (Viv Savage), Tony Hendra (Ian Faith), Michael McKean (David St. Hubbins), Christopher Guest (Nigel Tufnel), Harry Shearer (Derek Smalls)
CINEMATOGRAPHY: Peter Smokler
MUSIC: Christopher Guest, Michael McKean, Rob Reiner, Harry Shearer
LENGTH AND RATING: 82 min; R

The concert film is a cinematic journey profiling the highlights of a band's concert tour. It has a forty-year history that began with the film *Monterey Pop* (1968). In some cases it evokes a stark reality of the interactive dynamic of the band members, their fans, and the venue. This was the case for the Maysles' *Gimme Shelter* (1970), which chronicled the 1969 US concert tour of the Rolling Stones and the disastrous Altamont Free Concert. The year 2008 featured three concert films: *U2 3D*, *Hannah Montana and Miley Cyrus: Best of Both Worlds Concert*, and Martin Scorsese's Rolling Stone concert film, *Shine a Light*. Indeed, Scorsese made one of the definitive concert films, *The Last Waltz* (1978).

The essence of *This Is Spinal Tap* is that it takes the narrative style of the concert film and creates a satire mocking its values and the etiquette of rock culture. To this end director Rob Reiner created his own rock legends in the band members of Spinal Tap, providing them with a history and a sentiment of their journey as they decline into the oblivion of cultural ennui.

As one of the writers and the director of the film in reality and in fiction, Reiner assumes the character of Marty DiBergi, the documentary filmmaker who captures the Spinal Tap American tour as the band faces canceled dates and downsized venues, including a theme park, where they take second billing to a puppet show, and a military base, where they are a last-minute replacement and the audience covers their ears as they play and sing. The band members David St. Hubbins (Michael McKean), Nigel Tufnel (Christopher Guest), Derek Smalls (Harry Shearer), Mick Shrimpton (R. J. Parnell), and Viv Savage (David Kaff) create a dynamic presence that reflects the pretensions, jealously, pettiness, and stupidity that can be a part of the rock culture.

The band and its members pursue the fiction of a concert tour as Sir Denis Eton-Hogg (Patrick MacNee), the pompous head of their record label, rejects the cover artwork for their latest album, "Smell the Glove." When the band finally receives the album it is in a stark, all-black jacket with no artwork. Their band manager, Ian Faith (Tony Hendra), tries to put a positive spin on it by noting that the album acts like a mirror. There are many funny moments, including the band getting lost on the way to the stage in the subterranean basement of their concert venue, and Nigel trying to reconcile the geometry of small pieces of bread with larger pieces of cold cuts.

Director Rob Reiner described the film as a "mockumentary" and it is a stunning example of the genre. It accomplishes this by the serious posture taken by the actors as they attempt to salvage their legacy amidst the harsh review of critics, "...they are treading water in a sea of retarded sexuality and bad poetry." They face the obstacles of an interfering girlfriend, a disastrous and silly attempt at a makeover as they perform as Druids on stage with a pathetically small Stonehenge replica and dancing dwarfs, and the breakup of Spinal Tap founders Nigel and David.

In her March 2, 1984, *New York Times* review, film critic Janet Maslin writes that the film is almost indistinguishable from the real thing and is quite hilarious:

> It's much too affectionate for that. And it stays so wickedly close to the subject that it is very nearly indistinguishable from the real thing.
>
> There's an in-joke quality to the film, one that will make it all the more hilarious to anyone at all knowledgeable about either the esthetic or the business aspects of pop music. However, you need not have heard a band like Spinal Tap to find its story highly amusing. (http://movies.nytimes.com/movie/review)

The parody of *Spinal Tap* influenced later films, like *CB4* (*Cell Block 4*, 1993), starring Chris Rock, which was described as a "rapumentary" about a fictional rap group with their rise to cult status described by a director, much like *Spinal Tap*.

HOOSIERS (1986)

PRODUCER/DIRECTOR: David Anspaugh (director), Carter DeHaven (producer), Angelo Pizzo (producer)

WRITER(S): Angelo Pizzo

CAST: Gene Hackman (Coach Norman Dale), Barbara Hershey (Myra Fleener), Dennis Hopper (Shooter), Sheb Wooley (Cletus), Fern Persons (Opal Fleener), Chelcie Ross (George), Robert Swan (Rollin), Michael O'Guinne (Rooster), Wil Dewitt (Reverend Doty), John Robert Thompson (Sheriff Finley)

CINEMATOGRAPHY: Fred Murphy

MUSIC: Jerry Goldsmith

LENGTH AND RATING: 114 min; PG

A number of inspirational sports movies have touched the hearts of American movie audiences, including *For the Love of the Game* (1999), starring Kevin Costner, *Rudy* (1993), and more recently, *Friday Night Lights* (2004), *We Are Marshall* (2006), and *The Express* (2008), based on the life of Ernie Davis, the first African-American to win the Heisman trophy. *Hoosiers* is not just about high school basketball; it also captures the essence of small-town America, with its values, suspicions, and prejudices, and it confronts the themes of loss and redemption.

The opening scene is a loving portrait of the rural farmland of Indiana as coach Norman Dale (Gene Hackman) drives his vintage 1950s car to the small town of Hickory to assume the coaching position of the high school basketball team, the Huskers. He is immediately greeted with suspicion by the local townspeople, who have nothing but disdain for his coaching ability. Hired by his friend Cletus (Sheb Wooley), the superintendent/principal whom he hasn't seen in years, Norman spent a decade in the navy after working as a college coach in New York, where he was banned after striking a player. He has been hiding from his past, and for him this small town can be his redemption, not only returning him to the game he loves but also kindling his heart toward romance with fellow teacher and assistant principal Myra Fleener (Barbara Hershey). She has also returned to Hickory, after college and graduate school, ostensibly to help her mother operate the family farm after the death of her father, but she is using the community to shield herself from the hurt of failed relationships. And there is Shooter (Dennis Hopper), the town drunk and a talking basketball encyclopedia who embarrases his son, who is on the team and who Norman enlists as an assistant coach, casting him as an agent for Shooter's redemption.

Hickory has its own characters who passionately believe in their basketball team and jealously guard it from the influence of outsiders. They are perplexed when their star player, Jimmy (Maris Valainis), leaves the team and Myra warns Norman against recruiting him. Instead, she believes he can earn an academic scholarship to college, which would give him an opportunity to leave Hickory and the refuge of a lifetime of memories basking in the glory days of being a high school hero.

As Norman uses unorthodox methods to build his team the townspeople gather in the local church to vote on his dismissal. Prior to revealing the vote count, Jimmy takes the pulpit and announces that he's returning to the team but only if Coach Dale stays.

Although the theme may be familiar, the actors provide a rich portrayal of small-town life, its routines and lack of pretension. Their demeanor and charm are reminiscent of towns like Mayberry, whose residents may be somewhat eccentric but nonetheless express true, homespun values. It's a film that provides faith in redemption and the hopeful romantic notions of love. The 2004 film, *Friday Night Lights*, has a similar theme but it is about a high school football team in Texas and was adapted to network television.

RACE, RECONCILIATION, REDEMPTION

Mississippi Burning (1988)
Do the Right Thing (1989)
Driving Miss Daisy (1989)
Glory (1989)

These films are grouped together because they were produced during the same decade, were released and distributed close together (except for *Mississippi Burning*), and they deal with the issue of race in very different ways. Two of the films, *Glory* and *Mississippi Burning*, are referenced to historical events, while *Driving Miss Daisy* is based on a Broadway play about a white southern Jewish matron and her African-American chauffer, and *Do the Right Thing* is Spike Lee's compelling contemporary drama about race relations in America as told from a single block in New York's Brooklyn neighborhood of Bedford Stuyvesant. The singular themes these films have in common are intolerance, suspicion, victimization, and the brutal reality of racial hatred.

🎥 *MISSISSIPPI BURNING* (1988)

PRODUCER/DIRECTOR: Alan Parker (director), Robert F. Colesberry (producer), Frederick Zollo (producer)
WRITER(S): Chris Gerolmo
CAST: Gene Hackman (Agent Rupert Anderson), Willem Dafoe (Agent Alan Ward), Frances McDormand (Mrs. Pell), Brad Dourif (Deputy Clinton Pell), R. Lee Ermey (Mayor

Gene Hackman (as Agent Anderson) and Willem Dafoe (as Agent Ward). [Orion Pictures Corpo-ration/Photofest]

Tilman), Gailard Sartain (Sheriff Ray Stuckey), Stephen Tobolowsky (Clayton Town-
ley), Michael Rooker (Frank Bailey), Pruitt Taylor Vince (Lester Cowans), Badja Djola
(Agent Monk)

CINEMATOGRAPHY: Peter Biziou

MUSIC: Trevor Jones

LENGTH AND RATING: 128 min; R

In *Mississippi Burning*, the narrative is based on the 1964 disappearance of three civil
rights workers in Neshoba County, Mississippi: two white Jewish college students from
New York, Andrew Goodman and Michael Schwerner, and James Chaney, a young
southern black man from Meridian, Mississippi. The film, directed by Alan Parker,
became the subject of controversy because of its gross distortion of the subsequent FBI
investigation. The film was praised by *New York Times* reviewer Vincent Canby, who
noted that, "*Mississippi Burning* is so full of conviction in other ways, however, that its
drama cannot be ignored." Canby also wrote that the film was relentless in its focus
and that every image harkens back to the way things were in the South in 1964. But
other reviewers were less sanguine about the film and its gratuitous use of violence
and portrayal of the FBI as heroic vigilantes (http://query.nytimes.com/gst/fullpage.
html?res=940DE4D6113BF93AA35751C1A96E94).

Critic Pauline Kael criticized the film's "garish forms of violence" and described it
as "morally repugnant." In his scathing review of *Mississippi Burning* in *Time* magazine
entitled, "Just Another Mississippi Whitewash," Jack E. White writes that portraying
the FBI as heroes in this case is laughable because two weeks prior to the murder of
Goodman, Schwerner, and Chaney, a delegation from Mississippi went to Washington
to plead for protection of the civil rights workers streaming into Mississippi for
"Freedom Summer" and its voter registration drive, with FBI agents arriving in Philadelphia, Mississippi, only after the three young men had disappeared. He also referred
to the movie as a "cinematic lynching of the truth" and wrote:

> It is bad enough that most Americans know next to nothing about the true story of
> the civil rights movement. It would be even worse for them to embrace the fabrica-
> tions in *Mississippi Burning*. (http://www.time.com/time/magazine/article/0,9171,
> 956694-2,00.html) (http://www.geocities.com/paulinekaelreviews/m6)

But one statement in White's essay is a compelling reason to embrace *Mississippi
Burning* as a great film of cultural significance and stature. Not so much for its historical
accuracy, but for showing American audiences the bone-rattling, visceral hatred and
violence perpetrated by white southern Americans against black Americans:

> From its opening sequence, *Burning* convincingly recaptures the racial dread of
> 1964 Mississippi.

The story focuses around two FBI agents, Anderson (Gene Hackman), a former
Mississippi county sheriff who understands the culture of the South, its inbred bigotry
and its institutionalized corruption, and Ward (Willem Dafoe), who is young, by-the-
book college-educated, and the leading agent in charge of the investigation. While
Ward serves as the moral conscience and adheres to the limits of the law, Anderson
uses tactics like intimidation, entrapment, and violence to find the slain workers.

Early on the film establishes the stark differences between these two men, as when they enter a restaurant at lunchtime and Ward sits in the black section of the segregated counter. Of course, Anderson understands the folly of such heroic gestures, and rather than posture toward equality he confronts the evil with his own brand of terror, which includes shaving and cutting the face of complicit Deputy Clinton Pell (Brad Dourif) in a barber's chair, and squeezing the testicles of a redneck who threatens him in a "social club." While Ward, frustrated by the FBI's inability to find the evidence to identify the murder suspects, reluctantly agrees to Anderson's tactics, he morally abhors them with the condemnation that they as law enforcment officers are committing the same injustices as the criminals.

Finally, Ward in his zealousness to get Deputy Pell's wife, Mrs. Pell (Frances McDormand), to reverse her alibi supporting her husband on the evening of the murders, advocates Anderson's seduction of her, which later results in a brutal beating by her husband.

The argument of historical accuracy is moot when issues of cultural imperatives are concerned. In this case, *Mississippi Burning* provides an indelible portrait of a time when hatred consumed parts of the American South and blacks were lynched, their churches fire-bombed, and their lives made miserable by violence. In works of narrative cinematic fiction it's not necessarily the facts that must be scrutinized but the tenor of the moment and the mise-en-scène that provide a distinctive voice for a place, time, and events that provide its audience with a rich palette that captures a vivid portrayal of the fervor andemotion. That is why *Mississippi Burning*, with its resonance and compelling drama, is culturally significant.

🎥 *DO THE RIGHT THING* (1989)

PRODUCER/DIRECTOR: Spike Lee
WRITER(S): Spike Lee
CAST: Danny Aiello (Sal), Ossie Davis (Da Mayor), Ruby Dee (Mother Sister), Richard Edson (Vito), Giancarlo Esposito (Buggin Out), Spike Lee (Mookie), Bill Nunn (Radio Raheem), John Turturro (Pino), Paul Benjamin (ML), Frankie Faison (Coconut Sid)
CINEMATOGRAPHY: Ernest R. Dickerson
MUSIC: Bill Lee
LENGTH AND RATING: 120 min; PG

A radical tension fills the screen in Spike Lee's first studio movie, *Do the Right Thing*, and it is colored by voices that rebel against the status quo and those that confirm the sterotypes and traditions that personify their culture. It's filled with characters that resonate on the screen as they relate to the boiling temperatures of a hot summer day and deal with their daily routine. The neighborhood is Brooklyn's Bedford Stuyvesant and the action takes place on a single block, with themes and allusions of another time and another movie, *West Side Story*. In Lee's film, however, no one is dancing in the street but there is an underlying racial tension that eventually explodes on the screen. Like in *West Side Story*, the characters in *Do the Right Thing* are very territorial, protecting their neighborhood from intruders they perceive are invading their turf and changing the "color" of the community.

The film is thick with racial and political overtones that provide a steady chorus of epithets and deep-rooted conflict. But the characters have a depth of purpose imbued with the syntax of their culture that drives them toward the fiery conclusion. The tension simmers as Radio Raheem (Bill Nunn) carries his rap-music-blasting boom box through the block, confronting the Hispanics in a musical contretemps as they raise the volume of their Latin beat and he bests them with more decibels. When Radio enters the Korean store to buy twenty Energizer D batteries, he curses them for their broken English, but when the husband curses him back he accepts it with good humor. However, the loud music from the boom box annoys Sal (Danny Aiello), who for twenty-five years has owned Sal's Famous Pizzeria, which he operates with his two sons, Pino (John Tuturro), a rabid racist, and Vito (Richard Edson), who is friendly with their delivery man, Mookie (Spike Lee). It's Sal's shop and on his "Wall of Fame" hang pictures of Frank Sinatra, Al Pacino, Joe DiMaggio, Dean Martin, Robert De Niro, and other notable Italian Americans. When Buggin Out (Giancarlo Esposito) asks Sal why there are no brothers on the wall of fame, he answers that it's his shop and when Buggin gets his own store he can do what he wants. But there is breeding resentment by Buggin, who confronts a white man (John Savage) walking his bicycle who accidently bumps him and scuffs his new white Air Jordans. In a harbinger to the final scene of the movie, a crowd led by Buggin gathers by the stoop of the brownstone, and a confrontation ensues when they learn that the man has bought the building. It includes Buggin's rant about why a white man would want to live in a black neighborhood, and on the same block, on the same side of the street as him. When the man is told to go back to Massachusetts, he turns and tells the gathered group that he was born in Brooklyn, and that remark is greeted by a chorus of moans.

The fractious relationship between blacks and whites is articulated by individual commentaries on race: Mookie on Italian Americans, Pino on blacks, a Puerto Rican on Koreans, and Sonny (Steve Park), the Korean shop owner, on then-Mayor Ed Koch, who is Jewish. However, there is equality in the racial slurs as they are articulated under democratic equal-time provisions. The sheer bravado and rhythmic nature of the insults becomes a choir of hate that resonates in the meaningless futility of such language and demonstrates how benign its effect is when it becomes the pitter-patter of senseless rhetoric.

The end of the movie is cathartic for the block, which has been tense with racial jealousy and suspicion. Interestingly, it's the small injustices that build into the more substantive problems faced by the community, and Radio Raheem's loud rap music and the Wall of Fame serve as instigators for the movie's finale. After Sal tells Radio to lower the music and he doesn't, he smashes the boom box to pieces with a baseball bat, which results in a fight that spills into the street. The police arrive and Radio is killed when they use excessive force in a chokehold. Responding to his death, Mookie throws a garbage can through the window of Sal's Famous Pizzeria and the crowd enters, wrecking the business and setting it on fire. Threatened, the Korean shop keeper uses a broom to defend himself, his family, and his business, shouting to the crowd that he is black like them, and they disperse without harming him.

Standing in front of the smoldering wreckage of his store, Mookie tells Sal that he is there for his pay, $250 a week. They argue about what happened and Mookie responds that Radio is dead and Sal will collect insurance money to cover his loss. This scene reveals the essence of the differences between these two men. They worked together but never understood each other's cultural dialectic. For Mookie and the community, the tragic loss of Radio is another instance of unjustified police brutality, and Radio's murder means more to them than the white man's pizza business. But for Sal it's not about money or insurance but the self-made success of building a business and a store with his own hands, laying the tile and installing the electrical sockets. The store is his legacy, something he can pass along to his sons. But Mookie and the community can't relate to this because they have been unable to achieve that kind of financial independence, and they are bitter toward those "just off the boat Koreans," who have bought a building and started a business.

Reviews for the film were mixed, with Stanley Crouch of the *Village Voice* writing that Spike Lee

> either lacks the intelligence, maturity, and sensitivity necessary for drama, or hasn't the courage to give racial confrontation true dramatic complexity. At heart, he is for now a propagandist. (http://www.encyclopedia.com/doc/1G1-7813823.html)

Joe Klein of *New York* magazine described Lee as, "a classic art-school dilletante when it comes to politics. His film…is more trendoid than tragic." Vincent Canby, writing in the *New York Times*, described the movie as "…anything but minimalist. It is bursting with character, color, incident, and music, including a militant rap number performed by Public Enemy" (http://www.encyclopedia.com/doc/1G1-7813823.html) (http://movies.nytimes.com/movie).

🎥 *DRIVING MISS DAISY* (1989)

PRODUCER/DIRECTOR: Bruce Beresford (director), Lili Fini Zanuck (producer), Richard D. Zanuck (producer)

WRITER(S): Alfred Uhry (play), Alfred Uhry (screenplay)

CAST: Morgan Freeman (Hoke Colburn), Jessica Tandy (Daisy Werthan), Dan Aykroyd (Boolie Werthan), Patti LuPone (Florine Werthan), Esther Rolle (Idella), Joann Havrilla (Miss McClatchey), William Hall, Jr. (Oscar), Alvin M. Sugarman (Dr. Weil/Rabbi), Clarice F. Geigerman (Nonie), Muriel Moore (Miriam)

CINEMATOGRAPHY: Peter James

MUSIC: Hans Zimmer

LENGTH AND RATING: 99 min; PG

One may think that Spike Lee's confrontational film *Do the Right Thing* has very little in common with Bruce Bereford's *Driving Miss Daisy*, but both directors and the writers employ plot devices with similar thematic sensibilities. In *Do the Right Thing*, the black residents on the neighborhood block of Brooklyn's Bedford Stuyvesant resent the encroachment of whites and Korean immigrant shopkeepers, and in *Driving Miss Daisy*, Ms. Daisy Werthan decries the presence of servants in her home as an intrusion to her privacy. Both movies express a sentiment for the respect of territoriality, the former for a neighborhood enclave, the latter for the privacy of her home. But where *Do the Right Thing* is obvious in its manifestation of political, economic, and institutional racism,

Driving Miss Daisy is far more subtle and nuanced, with minimilast understated gestures that are more revealing than the most violent outbursts.

Driving Miss Daisy is a study of character, time, and place within the context of a changing South that has been ripped apart by hate and violence. The city is Atlanta where, after many years, the Werthan family has built a successful business that is now led by Miss Daisy's (Jessica Tandy) only child, her son Boolie (Dan Aykroyd). It's 1948 and Miss Daisy is seventy-two years old when she backs her car out of the garage and, mistaking the gas pedal for the brake, wrecks the Chrysler. Her son decides that her driving days are over and hires a black chauffer in his sixties, Hoke Colburn (Morgan Freeman). Strong-willed and determined to keep her independence, she rejects his presence and ruefully complains about having servants in the household who behave like children. She makes an exception for Idella (Esther Rolle), her long-term cook and housekeeper. Eventually she accepts a ride with Hoke to the Piggly Wiggly supermarket but complains when he picks her up in front of the market, because her neighbors will think she's putting on airs of being rich; she reacts the same way when Hoke picks her up in front of the synagogue after Saturday services. When Hoke echos the sentiment that she is rich, Miss Daisy is insulted by his remark and reminds him of her humble youthful years on Forsyth Street, where her family struggled and her sister saved so that she could attend college and become a teacher.

Conniving to dismiss him, she summons Boolie and accuses Hoke of stealing a can of salmon. As he arrives for work that morning, Hoke delivers a can of salmon he bought at the Piggly Willy, telling Miss Daisy that the pork chops she left for lunch the day before were spoiled, so he ate the salmon instead.

Over twenty-five years, their relationship slowly grows as Miss Daisy grudgingly accepts Hoke into her life as much more than a chauffer, but as a loyal and devoted companion. Although they have much in common Miss Daisy maintains a "separate but equal" mentality. He is her rock, always patiently administering to her needs, agreeable to her idiosyncracies with unlimited fortitude. Although Hoke can't read and eventually is taught by Miss Daisy, he is very wise in his assessment of people and events as they relate to the culture and racism of the South. On the way to Sabbath services, they get stuck in traffic, and Hoke returns to the car to report that the Jewish temple has been bombed. She doesn't believe him, telling him that he always mixes things up, but Hoke assures her it's true. When she asks who would do such a thing, Hoke gently berates her naïveté by saying that she knows who because it's always the same people. As he drives, he tells her a story from his youth about the father of a friend whom he saw hanging from a tree after being lynched, and she cries as she listens. For the first time, they have shared a communal sense of the South's bigotry and violence.

Although she professes not to be prejudiced and probably isn't, Miss Daisy sustains a legacy of seeing blacks as invisible, part of the household fixtures, like furniture. That's how Idella is perceived, but Hoke helps to change her impressions. He assists with her gardening, visits the grave of her husband to maintain the shrubs, and drives her to Mobile, Alabama, to celebrate the 90th birthday of her brother. On the way he must stop to "make water," and she chastises Hoke for not using the gas station facilities. He reminds her that "coloreds" are not allowed to, and when she demands that he drive, he tells her he's not a child and will not ask her permission to "make water." It is dark, and he leaves her alone in the car and she becomes frightened, calling out his name, but when he returns, asking if she's all right, she dismisses his concern.

One day, while working in Miss Daisy's kitchen, Idella dies, and now Hoke and she are alone together in the house. She is making fried chicken in a frying pan, and he warns that the flame is too high. She ignores him, but when he leaves she quickly lowers the flame. They have a bond, but after he places her plate of fried chicken on the long dining room table he retreats to the kitchen, each of them eating alone. During an ice storm with no power, Hoke arrives for work bringing hot coffee for her because he knows how she must have her coffee in the morning.

When Miss Daisy has an ischemic episode and thinks she is a school teacher rushing to find the graded papers of her students, Hoke calms her down and she holds his hand, telling him that he is her best friend. She is placed in a nursing home and her treasured house is sold. Hoke and Boolie visit her, and she shoos her son away to be with Hoke. They are an elderly couple with time and circumstance bringing them close together. As she struggles to eat her Thanksgiving pie, he begins to feed it to her, further sustaining their bond of friendship.

In his *New York Times* review, Vincent Canby praises the acting, writing, and directing, calling Miss Tandy's performance "selective understatement." About her performance, he notes, that there is "a fierce intelligence that comes through, no more movingly than in the film's final sequence." Writing about Morgan Freeman, who originated the role onstage, he notes that although he never appears to be tough, "it's a tough performance." And that his character Hoke "knows far more of the real world than Miss Daisy and remains steadfastly unsurprised by it" (http://movies.nytimes.com/movie).

Indeed, this film provides an intelligent yet subtle portrait of bigotry, friendship, and old age, bringing to mind Shakespeare's *The Seven Ages of Man* with a "shrunk shank, and his big manly voice,/Turning again towards childish treble, pipes/And whistles in his sound" (http://quotations.about.com/cs/poemlyrics/a/Seven_Ages_Of_M).

𝄞 *GLORY* (1989)

Producer/Director: Edward Zwick (director), Freddie Fields (producer)

Writer(s): Robert Gould Shaw (letters), Lincoln Kirstein (book "Lay This Laurel"), Peter Burchard (book "One Gallant Rush"), Kevin Jarre (screenplay)

Cast: Matthew Broderick (Col. Robert Gould Shaw), Denzel Washington (Pvt. Trip), Cary Elwes (Maj. Cabot Forbes), Morgan Freeman (Sgt. Maj. John Rawlins), Jihmi Kennedy (Pvt. Jupiter Sharts), Andre Braugher (Cpl. Thomas Searles), John Finn (Sgt. Maj. Mulcahy), Donovan Leitch (Capt. Charles Fessenden Morse), JD Cullum (Henry Sturgis Russell), Alan North (Gov. John Albion Andrew)

Cinematography: Freddie Francis

Music: James Horner

Length and Rating: 122 min; R

There is a Civil War monument located at the top of Boston Common, across from the State House, that is a bronze relief depicting Colonel Robert Gould Shaw riding his horse in command of his African-American regiment, the Massachusetts 54th. The movie *Glory*, starring Matthew Broderick as Colonel Robert Shaw, presents a compelling portrait of battle, heroism, and loyalty demonstrated by the first all-black regiment to be inducted into service and fight for the Union. Using the letters Shaw wrote to his mother, the film documents the challenges the regiment faced, not only among bigoted white officers and troops, but within the government hierarchy of institutionalized racism that demanded equal work and sacrifice by the black troops for less pay than the whites. The black troops received ten dollars a month, with three dollars deducted for a monthly clothing allowance, while white soldiers earned thirteen dollars a month with an additional three dollars for their clothing allotment. Protesting this injustice and led by Trip (Denzel Washington), the escaped slave and regiment rabble-rouser, the officers joined their men in refusing to accept pay, creating a unity and bond among the troops and the officers of the regiment.

The opening scene of the film shows Shaw as a Union captain with his sword drawn, leading a charge of his men (white troops) in the Battle of Antietam (also known as the Battle of Sharpsburg) in Maryland which, with its 23,000 casualties, was the bloodiest single-day battle in American history. It is a harrowing sight, with cannons and rifles blowing up the bodies of the charging troops. Wounded and dazed on the now-silent battlefield, Shaw is roused by a black gravedigger, Rawlins (Morgan Freeman), who later joins the Massachusetts 54th and becomes its trusted sergeant major. After recovering from his wounds and at the age of twenty-five, Shaw is given the rank of colonel and assigned to command the first black regiment. His two friends join him in this effort, Major Cabot Forbes (Cary Elwes), who first appears as a wayward officer with little direction, and his boyhood friend, a black, educated freeman named Thomas Searles (Andre Braugher).

The black recruits are personified by the four men assigned to bunk together in a tent: the tough, confrontational escaped slave Trip (Denzel Washington), Rawlins (Morgan Freeman), the oldest of the group who exudes a wise philosophical air, Sharts (Jihmi Kennedy), the innocent, stuttering country boy who has to learn his left foot from his right, and of course Searles (Andre Braugher), who because of his bookish and timid nature is nicknamed "snowflake" by Trip.

Understanding the need to create a disciplined military regiment, Shaw brings in Sergeant Major Mulcahy (John Finn), a tough Irish trooper to shape the men up. As the colonel of the regiment, Shaw's leadership adheres to the military code of non-fraternization between officers and enlisted men and he scolds Major Forbes for talking with Searles. But, after witnessing Mulcahy's browbeating of Searles, who has collapsed from exhaustion on the ground, Shaw calls the sergeant over, asking if his treatment may be too harsh. After confirming their friendship, Mulcahy advises the colonel to allow his friend to grow up. Understanding the need to maintain the order of command and give the men a sense of the reality of battle, Shaw presents a disciplined demeanor. Once again, during training with a bayonet, when Mulcahy taunts Searle, knocking him down and embrassing him to the point of tears, he demands to talk to his friend Robert, but Colonel Robert Shaw reminds his boyhood friend that he must go through channels requesting to see him. In another telling moment, Shaw has a flashback to a deadly battle as he watches the men play-act at being shot after new rifles are distributed. Shaw confronts Sharts on the firing practice range, where he has demonstrated that he's a "crack shot," and fires a revolver over his head, pressuring him to reload faster and giving him a sense of how it is to quickly reload his weapon under fire.

There are many emotional scenes in the film but one that speaks to the bravery of the men is the morning after Colonel Shaw, by order of President Lincoln, has gathered the men on a rainy night to read a proclamation by the Confederate Congress that has condemned to death any black man captured in a Union (Federal uniform) and any Union officer commanding black troops. After he dismisses the men he tells Major Forbes that he will understand if he departs the regiment. Anticipating a mass exodus of his troops the next morning, Shaw is grateful and relieved when the men assemble and none have deserted, reaffirming his faith in their courage.

One of the most visibly moving scenes is one that is not on the field of battle but occurs when Trip is escorted back to camp as a deserter. As his shirt is torn from him for his punishment, under Mulcahy's lash the scars from prior whippings vividly appear. Later that evening, a troubled Shaw walks up to Rawlins on guard duty and asks him if he can talk with him about the men from time to time. As Shaw leaves, Rawlins utters a line about shoes, and how the men's bare feet are scabbed and bloody and that Trip didn't desert but left the camp to find a pair of shoes. With more confidence, Shaw leads his men to the racist quartermaster, and to their delight they seize the shoes.

The instances of brutal prejudice are manifested by many white northern officers who have little faith in the fighting ability or bravery of colored troops. This becomes very evident when Shaw joins with battalion commander and leader of the Jayhawker Commandoes Colonel James Montgomery (Cliff de Young) as they descend on the town of Darien, Georgia, and he commands the troops to burn it to the ground even though there are only civilians present. Montgomery berates the black soldiers as little monkeys and undisciplined children who will never be given an opportunity to see combat. When Shaw refuses the order to command his troops to torch the town, Montgomery threatens court martial and Shaw yields to his superior officer.

Frusrated, Shaw writes a letter to his father pleading for help in moving his troops to the battlefront and away from the manual labor forced upon them. He confronts his superior officer with information about false quartermaster reports, confiscation of captured contraband for his personal use, and other crimes which results in the regiment's immediate transfer to a battle on James Island, South Carolina, where they successfully repulse the rebel troops. After the fight, Shaw meets with Trip to commend him on his fighting and tells him that Sergeant Major Rawlins has recommended him to carry the regimental colors. Attempting to explain why he has declined the honor, Trip tells the colonel that he is not fighting for anyone but himself, as he doesn't see how victory by either side will benefit him.

In the film's finale, Colonel Shaw volunteers the 54th for the charge on Fort Wagner on the end of Morris Island near Charleston, South Carolina. As the men march toward the heavily fortified fort, which had been under naval bombardment, they are cheered by the white troops and take heavy casualties as they charge. Pauisng for the cover of night, Shaw leads his troops and is shot but his men rally and continue the assault but are killed as they are confronted by the rebels. In a poignant finale Colonel Shaw joins his black troops in a mass grave, for in death there is no barrier toward color.

In his December 14, 1989, *New York Times* review Vincent Canby writes that "*Glory* is the first serious American movie about the Civil War to be made in years." He also discusses the compelling drama and the "pageantlike" narrative:

Very quickly, however, the strength of the idealism that fired these men becomes apparent and dramatically urgent. Though pageantlike, "Glory" has mind as well as soul. The movie unfolds in a succession of often brilliantly realized vignettes tracing the 54th's organization, training and first experiences below the Mason-Dixon line. The characters' idiosyncracies emerge. (http://movies.nytimes.com/movie/review)

And film critic Roger Ebert, in the *Chicago Sun-Times*, writes that "*Glory* is a strong and valuable film no matter whose eyes it is seen through" (http://rogerebert.suntimes.com/apps/pbcs.dll/article?AID=/19900112/REVIEWS/1120302/1023).

Although films that reconstruct history can have their message and value compromised by the overwhelming events they attempt to capture, this is not the case for *Glory*. It is a film that speaks to the very root of racism in America with so many of the prejudicial sentiments that continue to prevail. While the film doesn't preach, it does give the audience a context for understanding the challenge it was to emancipate the black slaves and integrate them into the Union army. Indeed, this was a slow process because blacks were segregated in the army during World War II and racial integration in the United States armed forces did not occur until the early 1950s, when black soldiers fought alongside white troops in Korea. In this film, the voice of discontent is loud and clear about injustice, but it also addresses bias within the black troops as exemplified by the slap in the face Trip receives from Rawlins when he calls Searles a nigger. It may be set during the Civil War but the issues of racism are just as contemporary as those presented in Spike Lee's *Do the Right Thing*.

8 GenX, Reality TV, Terror, Impeachment, Seinfeld, Beavis and Butthead, 1990–1999

Many cultural, political, technological, and economic milestones occurred in the 1990s that had a profound influence on American culture. A president was impeached by the House of Representatives for lying about his relationship with a White House intern, and the United States of America was shaken by two terrorist bombings: in Oklahoma City (1995), which killed 168 people, and the first World Trade Center attack (1993). With *Seinfeld* (NBC 1989–1998), America was captivated with a situation comedy "about nothing" except the minutiae of life's routines. And teen-adult animated cartoons (*Beavis and Butt-head, South Park, The Simpsons*), featuring ill-adjusted youths, dysfunctional families, and satirical parodies became part of the lexicon of American culture, while at the end of the decade America couldn't get enough of the head of a New Jersey Mafia family in therapy (*The Sopranos*, 1999-2007).

In economics, Alan Greenspan, former chairman of the Federal Reserve, uttered the now-famous phrase "irrational exuberance" and presided over the dot-com bubble as it burst. Science gave us Dolly, the cloned sheep, which raised religious, moral, and ethical questions, and the mapping of the human genome began. Pagers were discarded for cell phones and the Internet brought America into the age of e-mail, instant messaging, Web browsers, and buddy lists. Urban icons "rhapsodized" about ghetto life and Latin music was popularized by the artists Ricky Martin, Jennifer Lopez, and Selena, and a dance called the Macarena became popular. *The Real World* made its mark on reality television as it studied the psychological dynamics of youth culture.

Video games, led by "Super Mario Brothers," "Mortal Kombat," and "Doom" were supported by popular hardware that included the Sony PlayStation and Nintendo 64, which has created an online global universe of dedicated game players. NASCAR racing was popularized on television as a competitive sport, with drivers Dale Earnhardt (deceased), Rusty Wallace, and Jeff Gordon becoming celebrities, and American cyclist Lance Armstrong won his first Tour de France in 1999.

Unfortunately, violence was a recurring theme in the 1990s, when federal agents from the Bureau of Alcohol, Tobacco, and Firearms attempted to serve a search warrant on the Branch Davidian Ranch in Mount Carmel, Texas, near Waco, and its sect leader David Koresh, which resulted in the death of four agents and six sect members. After a 51-day siege by the FBI, a fire engulfed the compound and seventy-six people, including children, were killed. In Los Angeles (1992) black residents rioted after learning about the police officers who had been acquitted of the Rodney King beating. Between fifty and sixty people were killed, with damages from fire and looting estimated to be in the range of several hundred million dollars. A white truck driver, Reginald Denny, stopped at a light, was forcibly removed from his vehicle and beaten by angry rioters and was rescued by unarmed black residents who were watching the assault on television. And at Columbine High School in Littleton, Colorado, in 1999, two armed students killed twelve of their fellow students and a teacher before committing suicide.

The "trial of the century" took place in 1995, when O. J. Simpson was acquitted of murdering his wife Nicole Brown Simpson and her companion Ronald Goldman, with defense attorney Johnnie Cochran coining the famous phrase, "If it doesn't fit, you must acquit."

The films of the 1990s were notable for realistic period crime/gangster dramas, film noir (*Goodfellas, L.A. Confidential*), sylish and non-linear narrative (*Reservoir Dogs, Pulp Fiction*), westerns with compelling themes related to Native Americans and revenge (*Dances with Wolves, Unforgiven*), the tragedy of the Holocaust (*Schindler's List*), the tragedy and heroism of war (*Saving Private Ryan*), events that shaped history (*Titanic*), a psychological thriller (*Silence of the Lambs*), innovative comedy (*Groundhog Day*), black urban youths (*Boyz n the Hood*), and blockbuster sequels.

PERIOD CRIME DRAMAS

Goodfellas (1990)
L.A. Confidential (1997)

Although different in their thematic structure, style, and composition, *Goodfellas* and *L.A. Confidential* share the distinction of being period crime dramas with ensemble casts made up of compelling characters and events. Both films are set in the 1950s and each evokes a rich portrait of time and place. In *Goodfellas*, it's a New York City Mafia gang and the boy (Henry Hill) who becomes a man in its midst. *L.A. Confidential* is a smart film noir that vividly portrays the sounds and colors of 1950s Los Angeles.

Both films quickly establish a story line and cast of characters, helped by the use of dramatic action, period music, and voice-over.

GOODFELLAS (1990)

PRODUCER/DIRECTOR: Martin Scorsese (director), Irwin Winkler (producer)
WRITER(S): Nicholas Pileggi (book, screenplay), Martin Scorsese (screenplay)
CAST: Robert De Niro (James "Jimmy" Conway), Ray Liotta (Henry Hill), Joe Pesci (Tommy DeVito), Lorraine Bracco (Karen Hill), Paul Sorvino (Paul Cicero), Frank Sivero (Frankie Carbone), Tony Darrow (Sonny Bunz), Mike Starr (Frenchy), Frank Vincent (Billy Batts), Chuck Low (Morris "Morrie" Kessler)
CINEMATOGRAPHY: Michael Ballhaus
MUSIC: Christopher Brooks (music editor)
LENGTH AND RATING: 146 min; R

In *Goodfellas*, the audience sees the adult Henry Hill (Ray Liotta) driving a car in 1970 with his passengers and the two other leading characters in the film, fellow mobsters

Joe Pesci (as Tommy DeVito), Robert De Niro (as Jimmy Conway), Ray Liotta (as Henry Hill), and Paul Sorvino (as Paul Cicero). [Warner Brothers/Photofest]

Jimmy Conway (Robert De Niro) and Tommy DeVito (Joe Pesci), when a thumping sound is heard coming from the trunk. Pulling over, the trunk is opened to reveal a bloodied victim of a mob hit and Tommy, annoyed that the man is not dead, stabs him with a huge butcher knife as Jimmy fires several shots to seal his fate. Then the scene shifts (with period music, "Rags to Riches," written by Jerry Ross and Richard Adler and performed by Tony Bennett) to 1955 Brooklyn and a teenage Henry Hill (Christopher Serrone), who is the designated gopher for the local mob, operating out of a cab stand and led by Paul "Paulie" Cicero (Paul Sorvino), a very cautious man who shields himself from potential legal difficulties by never talking on a telephone (messages are relayed through a public pay telephone by his brother Tootie and other operatives) and only conducting business face-to-face. His family of seven lives in a cramped house across the street, led by his Irish father and Sicilian mother. For Henry, the world he sees is a dream come true as he parks the Cadillacs owned by the mobsters and scores money on his errands. When Henry is beaten by his father for cutting school, his wiseguy friends kidnap the mailman and, after putting his head in a pizza oven, convince him not to deliver truancy notices from the school to Henry's home.

After being introduced to Jimmy Conway, a master thief and hijacker, Henry and Tommy work for him but Henry is arrested for selling stolen cigarettes. In court he's represented by a mob attorney and is released and celebrated by the wiseguys because he "broke his cherry." He is told by Jimmy that "...you did it right you told them nothing and they got nothing...never rat on your friends and always keep your mouth shut." The scene changes to Idlewild Airport 1963 (now Kennedy), and Henry and Tommy are young adults working for Jimmy and hijacking freight carried by truck to and from the airport, which provides them with a steady stream of income. In a subsequent club scene, Tommy's psychotic personality is revealed when he tells a funny story that makes everyone laugh and then he baits Henry by asking him what makes him funny, the way he talks or his clown-like behavior. The tension cools when Tommy laughs and admits that he was baiting Henry but when Sonny (Tony Darrow), the owner of the Bamboo Lounge, brings him an accumulated bar tab of seven thousand dollars, Tommy breaks a bottle over his head. This behavior continues when he beats up and murders Billy Batts (Frank Vincent), a made man recently paroled from prison because Batts insults him by referring to Tommy's days as a shoeshine boy. In another scene, the wiseguys are playing cards and Tommy is annoyed that he is being ignored by Spider (Michael Imperoli), who is serving drinks, so he shoots him in the foot. On another visit, a limping Spider is shot to death by Tommy after he curses him. He's out of control and is set up by the senior mobsters on the pretense of attending a ceremony where he will become a made man but instead is killed because he murdered a made man without sanction.

The special treatment afforded the mobsters in prison via bribes is particularly amusing as they set up house in segregated confinement with fine food, liquor, and wine. After his release, Henry began selling heroin and cocaine and as his business grew he involved Jimmy and Tommy. Although he had pledged to crime boss Paulie that he was not involved in the drug trade, he carelessly pursued it while involved in other criminal activities. At that time the heads of the New York organized crime families discouraged drug dealing because the long sentences levied by convictions often resulted in cooperation with the authorities by those incarcerated.

The turning point in the film is the spectacular Lufthansa robbery at Kennedy Airport in 1978, which netted Jimmy Conway between five to six million dollars in cash. Warning crew members not to conspicuously spend money, suspicious of their loyalty and driven by greed, Conway had many of his co-conspirators murdered. He also suspected Henry as a possible informant and conspired to have his wife Karen (Lorraine Bracco) killed. Federal agents raided Hill's home as Karen feverishly flushed bags of heroin down the toilet and eventually he served as a government witness, testifying against his friends. Eventually, he and his family were relocated in the Federal Witness Protection Program.

L.A. CONFIDENTIAL (1997)

PRODUCER/DIRECTOR: Curtis Hanson (director, producer)

WRITER(S): James Ellroy (novel), Brian Helgeland (screenplay), Curtis Hanson (screenplay)

CAST: Kevin Spacey (Det. Sgt. Jack Vincennes), Russell Crowe (Officer Wendell "Bud" White), Guy Pearce (Det. Lt. Edmund Jennings "Ed" Exley), James Cromwell (Capt. Dudley Liam Smith), Kim Basinger (Lynn Margaret Bracken), David Strathairn (Pierce Morehouse Patchett), Danny DeVito (Sid Hudgens), Graham Beckel (Det. Sgt. Richard Alex "Dick" Stensland), Paul Guilfoyle (Meyer Harris "Mickey" Cohen), Ron Rifkin (Dist. Atty. Ellis Loew)

Cinematography: Dante Spinotti
Music: Jerry Goldsmith
Length and Rating: 138 min; R

"Off the record, on the Q.T., and very hush-hush." The opening scene of *L.A. Confidential* features a voice-over by the character Sid Hudgens (Danny DeVito), who is the editor of the Los Angles tabloid magazine *Hush-Hush*, based on the real tabloid *Confidential*. With the music and lyrics of Johnny Mercer's "Accentuate the Positive" under the voice-over, Hudgens provides the necessary exposition with the appropriate vintage images by portraying life in 1950s Los Angeles as the place where "the sun shines bright, the beaches are inviting, and the orange groves stretch as far as the eye can see... Every working man can have his own house, and inside every house is a happy all American family. Life is good in Los Angeles, it's paradise on earth... But there's trouble in paradise and his name is Meyer Harris Cohen, Mickey C. to his fans."

The plot weaves around Mickey C. (the real-life gangster and associate of Meyer Lansky and Bugsy Siegel), who, as the head of organized crime in 1950s Los Angeles, was sent to prison on tax evasion. Subsequent to his incarceration, as portrayed in the film, there is a war over control of his interests in dope, rackets, and prostitution. Like *Goodfellas*, there is an ensemble cast of characters that includes Officer Wendell "Bud" White (Russell Crowe), a feared cop who sometimes uses brawn instead of brains and can be counted on to rough up suspects on command. In the first scene, which introduces his character, he and his partner, Detective Sergeant Richard Alex "Dick" Stensland (Graham Beckel), are parked in front of a home on Christmas Eve, watching a recently released felon beat up his wife. Anxious to pick up the rest of the liquor for the station and drinking in the backseat, Stensland suggests leaving it for later. But White has a penchant for men who beat up women and so he administers a beating to the husband and handcuffs him to a railing. In a pivotal subsequent scene, White meets the beautiful hooker Lynn Bracken (Kim Basinger) while in the liquor store and, carrying the box outside to his car, he notices a vehicle idling nearby. In the backseat is an attractive woman, Susan Lefferts (Amber Smith), with a bandage on her nose sitting next to a moustached, dapper gentleman, Pierce Morehouse Patchett (David Strathaim), and their driver, former cop Leland "Buzz" Meeks (Darrell Sandeen). Suspecting some form of brutality, White rousts Meeks and after determining that Susan is all right, which is confirmed by Lynn, he allows them to drive off.

Three other prominent characters are introduced and they include the suave Detective Sergeant Jack Vincennes (Kevin Spacey), who is a consultant to the television police show *Badge of Honor*, modeled after the popular 1950s *Dragnet* starring Jack Webb. He is a "source" for the sleazy journalist Sid Hudgens, collecting money for arresting celebrities on camera in compromising positions, and is a "slick operator." As the officer in charge and on duty Christmas Eve, Detective Sergeant Edmund Exley (Guy Pearce) is being interviewed by the local newspaper because his father was a hero cop shot in the line of duty. He is told by his commanding officer Captain Dudley Smith (James Cromwell) that he ranked first on the lieutenant exam and when asked which area of law enforcment he wants to pursue Exley's choice is the detective bureau. Noting that Exley is an ambitious political animal, Smith mentions that the detective bureau might require him to plant evidence and break the law. An honest cop,

Exley rejects those compromised principles, revealing his sound moral and ethical judgment, and is told to "lose his glasses" if he wants to be a detective.

Three seemingly unrelated events are catalysts in the story. A brutal Christmas Eve beating of Mexican suspects arrested for assaulting two police officers is captured on camera by the reporters doing the feature story on Exley. As Exley attempts to stop the gang of cops, he is locked in a closet and while trying to restrain his partner Stensland, White returns a punch to a Mexican prisoner. An investigation follows and Exley is the star witness "ratting" on his fellow cops and is promoted to detective lieutenant, and Vincennes who was also implicated, is given a slap on the wrist for being a corroborating witness. When White is asked to testify against Stensland he refuses and is suspended but is later reinstated by Captain Smith, who needs him for various nefarious activities.

A massacre at the Nite Owl Coffee Shop has resulted in the murder of six victims. One is Dick Stensland and the other is Susan Lefferts, whom Bud White recognizes during the next-of-kin I.D. in the morgue as the girl in the car with the bandaged nose. Treated by police brass as a high-profile event, unlimited manpower is sent to the streets and the detectives are under pressure to find leads and make arrests. Leading the investigation is Captain Smith, with Exley his second in command. This leads them to three black suspects, who are mistakenly accused of the massacre but are implicated in the kidnapping of a young woman. This information is revealed through interrogations by Exley, with White leading the assault on the house where the woman is being held. After killing the unarmed suspect and planting a gun to make it appear that he fired a shot, the woman is rescued. After the rescue, a call over the police radio indicates that the three black suspects have escaped. Reviewing the interrogation notes, Exley follows up a lead with another detective and finds the three escaped suspects, who open fire, killing his associate, and he in turn kills them.

The newspaper headline screams the details of the shootout and Exley earns the nickname "Shotgun Ed" along with the police department's highest award, the medal of valor. Several subplots move through the undercurrent of the narrative, including the call girls who are "cut" to look like famous movie stars such as Lana Turner, and who are in Pierce Patchett's stable. Attracted to Lynn Bracken, Bud and she begin an affair.

Another sleazy subplot occurs when Hudgens and Vincennes set D. A. Ellis Loew (Ron Rifkin) up with the handsome aspiring actor Matt Reynolds (Simon Baker), and when Vincennes arrives at the motel room of their rendezvous he finds Reynolds dead. Soon, White and Exley both independently pursue their suspicions about the Nite Owl murders, the black suspects who were killed, and their doubts about the validity of their guilt. Teaming up with Vincennes, Exley and he visit Patchett and, after futile questioning, they each go to follow up on separate leads: Exley visits Lynn to learn about her relationship with White, and Vincennes checks the record of the currupt former police officer Leland "Buzz" Meeks. These parallel scenes both have closure, with Vincennes visiting Captain Smith at his home to talk about Meeks and, coming too close to the truth, he is murdered by a single shot from Smith's gun. In Lynn Bracken's apartment, Exley is seduced by her and photographed by Hudgens for attempted blackmail.

It's an elaborate ruse by Smith to instigate the killing of Exley using White as his executioner by setting him up to provide his brute force at the Victory Motel, where

Hudgens is the supposed victim. With revealing pictures of Lynn deliberately "stashed" in the trunk of Hudgens car, White sees them and races to the station to confront his nemesis. A brutal fight ensues until Exley has the opportunity to explain Smith's corrupt and murderous assumption of Mickey Cohen's rackets. The movie ends with a final shoot-out after Exley and White are lured to the Victory Motel. Outnumbered by Smith and his henchman, White is severely wounded by Smith but he manages to stab him as he is about to kill Exley. As the sound of police sirens come closer, Smith walks out with his hands up, ready to finesse the events, and is shot in the back by Exley.

After providing the police brass with his testimony about the corruption and murders by Captain Smith, a decision is made to "whitewash" the entire affair, proclaiming Smith a hero and awarding another medal of valor to Exley. And Lynn takes her wounded boyfriend, Bud White, back to her home in Arizona.

In her September 19, 1997, *New York Times* review, Janet Maslin compares *L.A. Confidential* to *Chinatown*, writing that it draws "...an entire socioeconomic cross-section and elaborate web of corruption out of an investigation that starts small." She also describes the film as "tough, gorgeous, and vastly entertaining" (http://movies.nytimes.com/movie).

Both *Goodfellas* and *L.A. Confidential* are rich in the character and imagery of portraying real events on-screen in a compelling and entertaining pastiche of story and action. They both represent a genre of film that gives the audience an almost tactile sensibility of the time and place of the narrative because of the living portraits presented to the audience. These two films are classics that added to the cultural mileu of the decade, with *L.A. Confidential* profiling the sleaze of tabloid journalism and corruption (a relevant theme for the 1990s and beyond) and *Goodfellas* adding to the mythology of the Mafia by humanizing gangsters and making them men earning a living to support their families. Indeed, this portrayal was adapted for the popular Home Box Office (HBO) television series *The Sopranos*.

HOODS AND CRIME CAPERS

Reservoir Dogs **(1992)**
Pulp Fiction **(1994)**

With the release of these two films, director Quentin Tarantino established himself as an auteur with a distinctive voice and a passion for film. In *Reservoir Dogs* and *Pulp Fiction*, he moved the caper crime drama and episodic storytelling to a level of "kitsch" artistry, demonstrating a creative sensibility toward a nonlinear chronology of events (in other words, telling a story out of chronological sequence).

In literature and film, nonlinearity is an element of design and technique that allows authors and filmmakers the creativity of defining a narrative structure not constrained by linear chapters or acts. The novelists James Joyce (*Ulysses, Finnegans Wake*), William S. Burroughs (*Naked Lunch*), Joseph Heller (*Catch-22*) and Irvine Welsh (*Trainspotting*) embraced this literary genre. In film, the tradition of flashbacks and flash-forwards can be considered nonlinear, as in the films *Citizen Kane* (1941) and *Rashomon* (1950).

During the silent film era, a number of directors experimented with nonlinear narratives, including D. W. Griffith (*Intolerance*, 1916) and Abel Gance (*Napoleon*, 1927). Though Quentin Tarantino rocked his audience with the nonlinear story structure in the 1990s, he wasn't the first modern American filmmaker to use this technique. Those before him included directors Robert Altman: *McCabe & Mrs. Miller* (1971), *Nashville* (1975), *The Player* (1992), *Short Cuts* (1993), *Gosford Park* (2001), and Woody Allen: *Annie Hall* (1997), *Interiors* (1978), and *Stardust Memories* (1980).

RESERVOIR DOGS (1992)

PRODUCER/DIRECTOR: Quentin Tarantino (director), Lawrence Bender (producer)

WRITER(S): Quentin Tarantino (written by, background radio dialog), Roger Avary (background radio dialog)

CAST: Harvey Keitel (Mr. White - Larry Dimmick), Tim Roth (Mr. Orange - Freddy Newandyke), Michael Madsen (Mr. Blonde - Vic Vega), Chris Penn (Nice Guy Eddie Cabot), Steve Buscemi (Mr. Pink), Lawrence Tierney (Joe Cabot), Randy Brooks (Holdaway), Kirk Baltz (Ofcr. Marvin Nash), Edward Bunker (Mr. Blue), Quentin Tarantino (Mr. Brown)

CINEMATOGRAPHY: Andrzej Sekula

MUSIC: Kathy Nelson (music supervisor MCA), Karyn Rachtman (music supervisor)

LENGTH AND RATING: 99 min; R

In *Reservoir Dogs,* Tarantino's debut film, the director pays homage to the B-caper movies of the 1950s with reference to Stanley Kubrick's *The Killing* (1956), starring Sterling Hayden, about the robbery of a racetrack and its aftermath. Indeed, another film that influenced Tarantino was *City on Fire* (1987), produced and directed by Ringo Lam and starring Chow Yun-Fat and Danny Lee. In *Reservoir Dogs*, as in *City on Fire*, there is a jewelry robbery and in both films the criminals wear black suits and dark glasses. The audience never sees the actual robbery in *Reservoir Dogs*, only events leading up to the heist and the aborted aftermath punctuated by a shoot-out. In *City on Fire* the robbery is seen, and after it is interrupted by an elderly woman who flees and summons the police, there is a bloody street confrontation. Both films have the plot device of an undercover police officer who has infiltrated the gang. However, *Reservoir Dogs* adds a stylistic and distinctive voice as the members of the gang, all strangers, are brought together by mastermind Joe Cabot (Lawrence Tierny) and never use their real names, instead using pseudonyms like Mister White and Mister Pink. In *The Thomas Crown Affair* (1968), starring Steve McQueen as the mastermind of a bank robbery, the gang members are also strangers and recognize each other dressed in suits, brimmed business hats, and dark glasses.

The opening breakfast scene of the film in a restaurant provides the audience with an introduction to the characters as they meet each other, using color referenced names: Mr. White (Harvey Keitel), a professional criminal, Mr. Orange (Tim Roth), an undercover police officer, Mr. Blonde (Michael Masden), a sadistic, psychotic criminal, Eddie Cabot, son of mastermind Joe (Chris Penn), Mr. Pink (Steve Buscemi), Mr. Brown (Quentin Tarantino), and Mr. Blue (Edward Bunker). Their conversation is somewhat bizarre as Mr. Brown provides them with a treatise of Madonna's song "Like a Virgin," which he construes as a reference to a male penis. Mr. Pink refuses to contribute to the tip and shares his philosophy on tipping with the group. And, Joe Cabot, who is looking at an old telephone diary, is obsessing on the whereabouts of a particular Asian woman. Annoyed by Joe's harangue, Mr. White seizes the diary and refuses to return it.

The action moves back and forth in time as the audience views the aftermath of the robbery and Mr. White driving a car with Mr. Orange, who has been shot in the abdomen by a woman who struggled with them after they hijacked her car. In another flashback, the audience learns how Mr. Orange infiltrated the gang and his rehearsal of a "commode" story with his police handler to convince Joe Cabot and the others that he is a drug dealer and a thief. The most abhorrently bloody and sadistic scene in the film is when Mr. Blonde draws a switchblade from his boot, mutilating a captured cop tied to a chair, cutting off his ear and drenching him with gasoline, readying to ignite him in the empy warehouse the gang uses as their rendezvous point. Music is important to the film and adds to the chilling effect in the scene as Mr. Blonde gleefully attacks the cop while dancing in rhythm to the tune of "Stuck in the Middle With You" playing on the radio.

The film ends with a Mexican standoff in the warehouse as "Nice Guy" Eddie Cabot finds Mr. Blonde dead, shot by Mr. Orange, who recovered consciousness just in time to kill him before he burned the cop. But Eddie knows that the gang was set up and is suspicious of the story that Mr. Orange has concocted about Mr. Blonde's purported disloyalty. He's perplexed that Mr. Blonde would double-cross him and his father after doing a prison stretch that would have earned him a ligher sentence if he had "snitched." Enraged, Eddie shoots the mutilated cop, Joe walks in, and they all draw their guns, ready to shoot Mr. Orange but Mr. White comes to his defense, threatening to kill Joe and Eddie if they shoot. They fire at each other and a wounded Mr. White crawls to Mr. Orange, cradling his head, who then confesses that he is an undercover cop. As the audience hears the police commands to drop his gun off camera, Mr. White shoots Mr. Orange and is in turn shot.

In his October 23, 1992, *New York Times* review of *Reservoir Dogs*, Vincent Canby notes the "dazzling cinematic pyrotechnics and over-the-top dramatic energy." He also writes that although the film has a complicated structure it, "…works with breathtaking effect" (http://movies.nytimes.com/movie/review?res=9E0CE6DD113EF930A15753C1A964958260).

Although the film's narrative was familiar as a B-movie crime caper story, its structure, dialogue, and ensemble cast was innovative and departed from the bound traditions of Hollywood movies. In his next movie, *Pulp Fiction* (1994), Tarantino captures the grit and fabric of story and action with a structure that once again defies tradition and is amazingly prescient in connecting with a generation of youths who abandoned routines and embraced innovation.

🎥 *PULP FICTION* (1994)

Producer/Director: Quentin Tarantino (director), Lawrence Bender (producer)

Writer(s): Quentin Tarantino (stories, written by), Roger Avary (stories)

Cast: John Travolta (Vincent Vega), Samuel L. Jackson (Jules Winnfield), Tim Roth (Pumpkin - Ringo), Amanda Plummer (Honey Bunny - Yolanda), Eric Stoltz (Lance), Bruce Willis (Butch Coolidge), Ving Rhames (Marsellus Wallace), Phil LaMarr (Marvin), Maria de Medeiros (Fabienne), Rosanna Arquette (Jody)

Cinematography: Andrzej Sekula

Music: Rolf Johnson (music editor), Karyn Rachtman (music supervisor)

Length and Rating: 154 min; R

John Travolta (as Vincent Vega) and Samuel L. Jackson (as Jules Winnfield). [Miramax Films/ Photofest]

Pulp Fiction represented a generational shift in movie-making that embraced pop culture with a language and style that proved to be derivative but unique in its voice. It is a visual comic book in which the audience can imagine the dialogue balloons over the heads of the characters. It opens and closes with a diner breakfast scene in which Pumpkin (Tim Roth) and Honey Bunny (Amanda Plummer), both petty criminals, decide to hold up the place.

Once again, Quentin Tarantino uses nonlinear structure to tell a story steeped in the mileu of the street culture of any city, and this one happens to be Los Angeles. He breathes a keen sense of intellectualism into his characters, who may not know Nietzsche and his brand of existentialism and post-modernism but can articulate constructs in the lingua franca of the gutter. As hit men working for Marsellus Wallace (Ving Rhames), Vincent Vega (John Travolta) and Jules Winnfield (Samuel L. Jackson) are professionals whose banter is engaged on a higher plain of thought and provocation, humanizing them as more than ordinary hoodlums. Driving together on their way to wreak Marsellus Wallaces' revenge on some young men who have double-crossed him, and dressed in business attire, Vincent, who has just returned from Europe, discusses his experiences and how in France they call the McDonald's Quarter Pounder with Cheese a "Royale with Cheese." He also regales Jules with stories about the hash bars in Amsterdam and how the police cannot search an individual stopped by them. Then he mentions the small differences between America and Europe, such as buying a glass of beer in an Amsterdam movie theater and being able to purchase beer in a Paris McDonald's. Ironically, even with his profanity-laced speech, Vincent sounds like a sophisticate, a man who has traveled Europe and is able to savor its culture and appreciate its distinctive flavor.

Arriving at Brett's (Frank Whaley) apartment, Vincent retrieves the attaché case they came for while Jules engages Brett in what appears to be friendly banter. There is a transition from the discussion about French hamburgers in the car to the Kahuna burger Brett is eating for breakfast, and Jules asks for a bite and then slurps down his Sprite soda. Commenting about the burger, Jules mentions how his girlfriend is a vegetarian and that practically makes him one. The conversation is very disarming and the expectation of the violence to come gradually builds as Jules reaches a crescendo of anger, shooting one of the men lying on a couch, apologizing for breaking Brett's concentration, using the phrase, "allow me to retort," inquiring about Wallace's appearance and whether he looks like a bitch, and, finally quoting Ezekiel 25/17:

And I will strike down upon thee with great vengeance and furious anger those who attempt to poison and destroy my brothers and you will know my name is the Lord when I lay my vengeance upon thee.

After blasting away, the scene breaks and later returns to Brett's apartment as Vincent and Jules are ambushed by another man hidden in the bathroom. Amazingly, the bullets go through them without any harm and Jules defines the event as divine intervention and a sign that he must retire as a hit man, while Vincent dismisses it as chance.

The narrative weaves through different story arcs that include: the opening diner scene, Mia Wallace and Vincent Vega, the gold watch past and present, the Bonnie situation, and the closing diner scene. Nervous about being assigned as Mia Wallace's chaperone while her husband Marcellus is out of town, Vincent makes the best of it and panics when she overdoses by sniffing his stash of heroin, which she mistakes for cocaine. He rushes her to the reluctant drug dealers Lance (Eric Stolz) and Jody (Rosanna Arquette) who, in a tense but funny scene, search for the adrenaline and attempt to figure out how to administer the shot.

In the gold watch scene, the prizefighter Butch Coolidge (Bruce Willis) has double-crossed Marcellus Wallace by not taking a "dive" and winning the bout. He and his girlfriend Fabienne (Maria de Mederios) have left their apartment and are hiding in a motel when Butch discovers that she has left his cherished watch behind. As a young boy, it was given to him as a memento of his father, a Vietnam veteran, by Captain Koons (Christopher Walken), who told him about the history of the watch worn by his father and passed down through generations of other family members. Returning to the apartment to retrieve the watch, he finds an automatic weapon on the kitchen counter, which he grabs, and as Vincent Vega comes out of the bathroom he fires, killing him. As he speeds away he sees Marsellus crossing the street and after they make eye contact Butch slams the car into him. Amidst the confusion and after a chase that brings them to a pawnshop, they are apprehended by the proprietor Maynard (Duane Whitaker), who is joined by Zed (Peter Greene), a local police officer, in the sadistic rape of Marsellus. Held prisoner during the rape, Butch frees himself and is about to leave when he decides to rescue Marsellus. He kills Maynard with a saber, and Marsellus shoots Zed in the groin while Butch agrees to Marsellus' terms, settling the boxing dispute in return for leaving Los Angeles forever and never revealing the rape in the pawnshop. The rape sequence is similar in tone and content to the one depicted in *Deliverance*, where the avenger, Burt Reynolds, uses another unconventional weapon, a bow and arrow.

In the Bonnie situation, Jules and Vincent are driving with Marvin (Phil LaMarr), the only survivor of Brett's crew, in the backseat discussing "divine intervention" when Vincent's gun accidently fires, shooting Marvin in the face and spraying blood all over the car. Faced with the need to get the car off the road, they drive to Jimmie's (Quentin Tarantino) house, where they have just over an hour before his wife comes home to get things cleaned up. With the aid of the Wolf, Winston Wolf (Harvey Keitel), they manage to hide the blood in the car, put the body in the trunk, follow Winston to a junkyard, get rid of the car and the evidence, and walk to a diner for breakfast.

The robbery in the diner continues. Pumpkin collects the wallets from the customers and wants to steal the attaché case that Jules has retrieved from Brett. Unwilling to give up the case belonging to Marsellus, Jules draws his gun, aiming at Pumpkin as Honey Bunny aims her gun at Jules. At that moment, Vincent draws his gun and aims it at Honey Bunny for a "Mexican standoff." Determined to repent and end his career as a hit man, Jules talks Pumpkin into leaving the diner with the cash and his girl-friend, Honey Bunny.

In her September 23, 1994, *New York Times* review of *Pulp Fiction*, Janet Maslin writes that the film is a work of "...depth, wit and blazing originality." She also notes that "*Pulp Fiction* leaves its viewers with a stunning vision of destiny, choice and spiritual possibility" (http://movies.nytimes.com/movie).

For audiences, *Pulp Fiction* is a visual poem with a symphnonic rhythm of sight, sound, and action that pulsates with a resounding beat and builds into a lustrous cacophony of confrontation and resolution. The stories separate, intersect, and converge with acute accuracy in a timely juxtaposition of character and setting nuanced by actors who don't merely play but meld into the sinew of their roles. Critic Roger Ebert noted the unique nonlinear stucture of the film and how with each viewing it appears fresh because the viewer is unable to remember what comes next:

> Like *Citizen Kane*, *Pulp Fiction* is constructed in such a nonlinear way that you could see it a dozen times and not be able to remember what comes next. It doubles back on itself, telling several interlocking stories about characters who inhabit a world of crime and intrigue, triple-crosses and loud desperation. (http://rogerebert. suntimes.com)

CODES OF THE OLD WEST

Dances With Wolves (1990)
Unforgiven (1992)

The western movie has an iconic legacy in American film nurtured by brilliant directors such as John Ford, who helped define the codes that were the essence of the western. At times these two films were defined as revisionist because they changed the long-held traditions of heroism, bravery, and the portrait of Native Americans. However, some critics have argued that *Dances With Wolves* reinforces the genre by portraying the Pawnees as "Indians" as they were depicted in movies of the 1950s and 1960s while treating the Sioux in a kinder, gentler way. Similarly, *Unforgiven* also embraces the traditions of the western but turns them around by making its hero a vengeful seeker of retribution. In *Dances With Wolves*, heroism is a virtue of both cultures, Native American and Caucasian, and Lieutenant John Dunbar (Kevin Costner) is rewarded for his bravery by being able to choose his next post, which is at the edge of the South Dakota frontier in an abandoned military outpost called Fort Sedgewick. However, in *Dances with Wolves* bravery is a recognized attribute inherent to both Native Americans and Caucasians. And *Unforgiven* gives a different connotation to bravery, convoluting its western ethos and steeping it in cowardice. The wizened gunslinger Will Munny (Clint Eastwood) ambushes a cowboy from afar, shooting him in the gut, and his young partner, the Schofield Kid (Jaimz Woolvett), guns down a man as he relieves himself in an outhouse.

🎥 *DANCES WITH WOLVES* (1990)

Producer/Director: Kevin Costner (director), Kevin Costner (producer), Jim Wilson (producer)

Writer(s): Michael Blake

Cast: Kevin Costner (Lt. John J. Dunbar), Mary McDonnell (Stands With A Fist), Graham Greene (Kicking Bird), Rodney A. Grant (Wind In His Hair), Floyd "Red Crow" Westerman (Ten Bears), Tantoo Cardinal (Black Shawl), Robert Pastorelli (Timmons), Charles Rocket (Lieutenant Elgin), Maury Chaykin (Major Fambrough), Jimmy Herman (Stone Calf)

Cinematography: Dean Semler

Music: John Barry

Length and Rating: 180 min; PG-13

Reporting to a delusional Major Fambrough (Maury Chaykin) for orders to his next command, the mad major provides some prescience to the narrative by behaving like a medieval king and dispatching Dunbar as his knight to conquer the frontier. It's a suitable allegory as Dunbar may be viewed as the conquering knight gaining the "keys" to a hostile kingdom. As Dunbar departs the military base, the major asks for his crown and then blows his brains out.

Dunbar is left with supplies at the abandoned outpost and his only companionship is the wolf he befriends and names "Two Socks." Expecting other soldiers to join him, Dunbar establishes a routine and order to his base. However, after the major commits suicide and the wagon driver who accompanied him and delivered supplies is murdered and scalped by the Pawnee, no one else knows of his whereabouts.

Slowly, curious members of the Sioux watch the lone soldier as he plays with Two Socks, and invites them to his outpost. While out riding, Dunbar meets Stands With a Fist (Mary McDonnell), a white woman captured as a young girl by the Sioux who has attempted suicide, mourning the death of her husband. He picks her up and returns her to the Sioux camp and a mutual bond develops between Dunbar and Kicking Bear (Graham Greene), a leader of the tribe. As they bond and their friendship develops, another brave, Wind in His Hair (Rodney A. Grant), harbors jealous resentment against Dunbar for the relationship he has with Kicking Bear.

As a man rather than as a soldier, Dunbar gains the trust of Kicking Bear and other members of the Sioux, including Chief Ten Bears (Floyd "Red Crow" Westerman), when he assists in the buffalo hunt and rescues a young brave who is knocked off his horse by a charging, wounded buffalo, which is poised to gore him when Dunbar aims his rifle, killing the renegade male. He measures up once again when he provides them with rifles from Fort Sedgewick to repel an attack by the Pawnee. Soon, he abandons his post and the trappings of a military uniform to become part of the Sioux, earning the name Dances With Wolves and marrying Stands With a Fist.

Having kept a detailed journal with copious notes and drawings, Dunbar returns to Fort Sedgewick to retrieve it, realizing that the pages served as a map for the soldiers to hunt down the Sioux. Out of uniform, he is arrested for desertion and put in chains. Offering his journal as proof of his accomplishments in befriending the Sioux and learning their customs, his evidence is deliberately hidden by a vengeful, lying soldier. Wind in His Hair leads a raiding party that rescues Dunbar who is being escorted by army troops to Fort Hayes for hanging. Later, a Sioux brave finds the journal floating in a stream.

The film concludes with Dunbar (Dances with Wolves) leaving the winter camp with Stands With a Fist because, as a deserter and a wanted man, he's a threat to the tribe's safety. Once a part of the establishment, he is now an outsider, and, like the Sioux, is a stranger in his own land.

With its breathtaking portrait and vast vistas of South Dakota, Costner emulated the work of John Ford, who used Monument Valley on the Utah/Arizona border like a character in many of his brilliant western films. *Dances with Wolves* was not the first modern Hollywood film to treat Native Americans in a sympathetic way; *Little Big Man* (1970), starring Dustin Hoffman, had a similar point of view. Criticism of the film was noted by Vincent Canby in his November 9, 1990, *New York Times* review. He questioned the film's authenticity and superficiality:

> Once Dunbar has taken up with the Sioux and starts strutting around with a feather stuck in his hair, the movie teeters on the edge of Boy's Life literature, that is, on the brink of earnest silliness.
>
> This Sioux camp not only looks as neat as a hausfrau's pin, but also unlived-in. It's a theme-park evocation, without rude odors to offend the sensitive nostril. (http://movies.nytimes.com/movie/review)

In his November 9, 1990, *Chicago Sun-Times* review of *Dances with Wolves*, Roger Ebert describes the film as a story magnificently told with epic sweep and clarity with vision and ambition:

> *Dances With Wolves* has the kind of vision and ambition that is rare in movies today. It is not a formula movie, but a thoughtful, carefully observed story. It is a Western at a time when the Western is said to be dead. It asks for our imagination and sympathy. (http://rogerebert.suntimes.com)

UNFORGIVEN (1992)

PRODUCER/DIRECTOR: Clint Eastwood

WRITER(S): David Webb Peoples

CAST: Clint Eastwood (William "Bill" Munny), Gene Hackman (Little Bill Daggett), Morgan Freeman (Ned Logan), Richard Harris (English Bob), Jaimz Woolvett (The Schofield Kid), Saul Rubinek (W. W. Beauchamp), Frances Fisher (Strawberry Alice), Anna Levine (Delilah Fitzgerald), David Mucci (Quick Mike), Rob Campbell (Davey Bunting)

CINEMATOGRAPHY: Jack N. Green
MUSIC: Lennie Niehaus
LENGTH AND RATING: 131 min; R

In the narrative history of the American western movie, the gunfigher became a casu-alty of his own celebrity, making him a victim of the hunt even in attempted retire-ment. In *Shane* (1953), Alan Ladd as the gunfighter Shane recognized that the days of the gunfighter were numbered and that his attempt to disappear into the domesticated lives of the Starrett family was only a temporary respite from his notoriety. Similarly, John Wayne, portraying the aging, sickly gunfighter J. B. Books in *The Shootist* (1976), cannot hide from his reputation when he returns to Carson City and learns of his diag-nosis of terminal prostate cancer. Hoping to reside peacefully, spending his final days in a rooming house, word of his arrival spreads quickly and he becomes a hunted man.

As Munny in *Unforgiven*, Clint Eastwood is a struggling pig farmer in western Kan-sas who is a widower with two young children. His dead wife changed him from being a drunken, murderous gunfighter to a domesticated and weathered family man, a shadow of his former gunfighting persona. His fate changes when a prostitute's face is cut by a drunken cowboy in the town of Big Whiskey, Wyoming, and the whores, led by Strawberry Alice (Frances Fisher), raise enough money to offer a bounty of one thousand dollars for the murder of the cowboys. They take matters into their own hands after Little Bill Doggett (Gene Hackman), the vicious town sheriff, refuses to whip the men and instead extracts a deal from the cowboys with a promise to deliver horses to Skinny (Anthony James), who owned the saloon and claims that his disfig-ured woman has lost her earning potential.

Women in westerns were not usually defined as characters with empowerment but these prostitiutes confronted Little Bill, and their action served as a catalyst for the story. In another western, *Destry Rides Again* (1939), Marlene Dietrich portrayed the saloon singer Frenchy, who was a match to any man when it came to drinking and fighting. She defined women of the West with a tough exterior and a resolute character.

At first, Munny declines to join the nearly blind Schofield Kid on the bounty hunt but then changes his mind, enlisting his former partner Ned Logan (Morgan Freeman) for the enterprise. Expecting gunmen to enter Big Whiskey to collect the bounty, Little Bill has invoked a law requiring that all weapons be surrendered. When the pompous British dandy, English Bob (Richard Harris), enters town with his own biographer, W. W. Beauchamp (Saul Rubinek), and refuses to surrender his weapon, he is merci-lessly beaten by Little Bill. A similar beating is administered in the saloon to Munny by Little Bill after he lies about having a gun.

Nursed back to health by Ned and the whores, the three men ambush one of the cow-boys and after Ned refuses to fire his rifle at the man, Munny shoots, hitting him in the ab-domen. Later, Ned leaves, saying that he no longer has the stomach for killing and the two men ambush the second cowboy in the outhouse, with the Schofield kid shooting him to death. Waiting for the bounty to be delivered, the Schofield Kid admits that the cowboy was his first victim and he has serious regrets about what they have done. Munny expressed his philosophy about killing, summing it up in a simple yet profound way:

> It's a hellava thing killin' a man. You take away all he's got and all he's ever gonna have.

297

When he learns that his friend Ned has been whipped and beaten to death by Little Bill, Munny exacts his revenge by returning to the saloon on a dark and rainy night. Outside, Ned's body is propped up for display and inside Little Bill and the men are celebrating. After he enters the first man to be shot by Munny is Skinny, the owner, and then after his rifle jams he uses his pistol to kill Little Bill and the others, five men in all. Leaving, he calls out to the others that they had better not shoot otherwise he'll return and kill them, their wives, and their friends. He also warns them to give Ned a proper burial and to not harm the whores.

Traditions of the Western film are reversed and nuanced in this film with humor and pathos. After his years raising pigs, Munny can barely ride a horse or hit a target with a gun. And the odd pairing of the nearly blind Schofield Kid with Munny and Ned is a contradiction in the ideology of the keen instincts of the western gunfighter. The comic-like affectations of English Bob traveling with his biographer W. W. Beauchamp and the repeated mispronunciation by Little Bill of the title of English Bob's biography "The Duke of Death" as "The Duck of Death" adds to compromising the traditions of the Western.

The reviews for *Unforgiven* were very favorable, and Vincent Canby in the August 7, 1992, *New York Times* writes that "the film looks great, full of broad chilly landscapes and skies." Writing in the August 10, 1992, issue of *Time* magazine, Richard Corliss notes that the film is "a dark, passionate drama with good guys so twisted and bad guys so persuasive that virtue and villainy become two views of the same soul" (http://www.time.com/time/magazine/article/0,9171,976223-1,00.html).

Both *Dances with Wolves* and *Unforgiven* won Academy Awards for Best Picture and Best Director in their respective years, marking the return of the American Western as a legitimate film genre.

🎥 *BOYZ N THE HOOD* (1991)

PRODUCER/DIRECTOR: John Singleton (director), Steve Nicolaides (producer)
WRITER(S): John Singleton
CAST: Laurence Fishburne (Jason "Furious" Styles), Cuba Gooding, Jr. (Tré Styles), Ice Cube (Darin "Doughboy" Baker), Morris Chestnut (Ricky Baker), Nia Long (Brandi), Angela Bassett (Reva Devereaux), Tyra Ferrell (Brenda Baker), Lexie Bigham (Mad Dog), Hudhail Al-Amir (S. A. T. Man), Lloyd Avery II (Knucklehead #2)
CINEMATOGRAPHY: Charles Mills
MUSIC: Stanley Clarke, Roger Troutman
LENGTH AND RATING: 107 min; R

For John Singleton, then a twenty-three-year-old African American director of *Boyz N the Hood*, who was raised in South Central Los Angeles, which is the setting of the movie, the story is a powerful statement about the black community, poverty, shattered dreams, and the importance of positive role models in the lives of young people. Like Spike Lee, Singleton's grasp of the sounds, sights, and language of the inner city provides a startling portrait of its daily rhythm, which is nuanced by the lingua franca of the street and the threats that lurk in the shadows.

The story is a compelling drama about Tre Styles (Desi Arnez Hines II, Cuba Gooding Jr.), a bright ten-year-old living with his mother, Reva Devereaux (Angela Bassett), who is studying for a master's degree. Realizing that her son must have a male role model, she decides to have him live with his father, Jason "Furious" Styles (Laurence Fishburne), a Vietnam veteran who works as a mortgage broker and is a loving father and a stern disciplinarian. He is also an outspoken advocate for empowerment of the black community and its need to protect its values against the encroachment of whites buying up depressed real estate and gentrifying the community while dispossessing the blacks.

As Tre grows up, his father's influence keeps him away from drugs and violent crime. However, the film articulates the peer pressure on black youths to conform to the violent nature of street culture. For Tre, his best friends are half brothers, Darin "Dough Boy" Baker (Ice Cube), recently released from prison, and Ricky Baker (Morris Chestnut), an aspiring athlete, and his girlfriend Brandi (Nia Long). A virgin, Tre feels the pressure from his friends to have sex with Brandi, but her reluctance as a Catholic and her desire to go to college without the burden of raising a child is the rationale for her denial.

The film brilliantly documents the community as an area under siege, with the sound of automatic weapons being discharged, police sirens, and hovering, whirring police helicopters spot-lighting their targets. It is portrayed as a war zone and the searing battle scars are evidence of the terror that reigns every day and night. After Ricky is murdered over a trivial "pushing" incident, Tre joins Dough Boy and the others in the hunt for the killers. His father sternly asks him not to go, but Tre's grief and anger drive him to join in the hunt. Before they locate Ricky's killers, Tre leaves the group and the others continue the hunt and find and kill the three young men.

At the end of the film Dough Boy utters some of the most profound and moving dialogue in the film when he tells Tre that he turned on the television and saw a report about living in a violent world that showed the violence in foreign countries. Then he reflects on what he saw and says:

> Either they don't know, don't show, or don't care 'bout what's goin' on in the hood.

The ending of the film is bittersweet, with a textual image noting that two weeks after burying his brother Ricky, Dough Boy was murdered. But there is also a thread of hope for Tre and Brandi, who attend the neighboring colleges of Morehouse and Spellman.

In Janet Maslin's July 12, 1991, *New York Times* review of *Boyz N the Hood*, she compares John Singleton to Spike Lee and mentions the dramatic force of the film and its gut-wrenching finale:

> Mr. Singleton may not be saying anything new about the combined effects of poverty, drugs and aimlessness on black teen-agers. But he is saying something familiar with new dramatic force, and in ways that a wide and varied audience will understand. His film proceeds almost casually until it reaches a gut-wrenching finale, one that is all the more disturbing for the ease with which it envelops the film's principals. (http://movies.nytimes.com/movie)

🎥 GROUNDHOG DAY (1993)

PRODUCER/DIRECTOR: Harold Ramis (director, producer), Trevor Albert (producer)
WRITER(S): Danny Rubin (story, screenplay), Harold Ramis (screenplay)
CAST: Bill Murray (Phil Connors), Andie MacDowell (Rita), Chris Elliott (Larry), Stephen Tobolowsky (Ned Ryerson), Brian Doyle-Murray (Buster Green), Marita Geraghty (Nancy Taylor), Angela Paton (Mrs. Lancaster), Rick Ducommun (Gus), Rick Overton (Ralph), Robin Duke (Doris, the Waitress)
CINEMATOGRAPHY: John Bailey
MUSIC: George Fenton
LENGTH AND RATING: 101 min; PG

One of the most interesting aspects of this satirical comedy, starring Bill Murray as Phil Connors, the pompous, arrogant weatherman who is condemned to relive February 2, Groundhog Day, over and over again, is how the religious community—Jews, Christians, and Buddhists—have embraced the allegorical religious faith that is intrinsic to its message.

Sent by a Pittsburgh television station to cover Groundhog Day, meteorologist Connors and his crew, consisting of his producer Rita (Andi MacDowell) and cameraman Larry (Chris Elliott), arrive in Punxsutawney, Pennsylvania, and Phil expresses contempt for the event and the townspeople. Although he predicted that a blizzard would miss the area, it arrives, preventing them from leaving. As a result, Phil is caught in a bizarre time warp where he is destined to relive February 2, Groundhog Day, every day. At first, when Phil realizes that he is destined to relive the same day in perpetuity he panics and acts out his frustration with hostile confrontations. Becoming frustrated with his plight, he attempts some very creative means of committing suicide, including kidnapping Punxsutawney Phil (the goundhog) and, after a police chase, driving his truck over a cliff, falling to a blazing explosion. No matter how many attempts at successful suicide he makes, he wakes up at 6:00 A.M. the next morning to his clock radio playing Sonny & Cher's "I Got You Babe," and he can quote what the disc jockeys are about to say.

Realizing that he can turn his misfortune into opportunity, Phil uses his ability to use information he learns about people the next day to seduce Nancy Taylor (Marita Geraghty). His next seductive challenge is Rita, who loathes him and whom he pursues with particular zest and delight. Offering to buy Rita a drink, he cultivates the accumulated encyclopedic knowledge about her to impress her with his knowledge, talent, and compassion. He learns that her favorite drink is sweet vermouth on the rocks and he toasts to world peace, a wish close to her. Although at first he laughs and condemns as a waste of time Rita's undergraduate major of nineteenth-century French poetry, in a subsequent meeting he is prepared to recite a poem to her in French. Building a snowman, they get into a snowball fight with some kids and he talks about his love for children and how he wants a brood of his own.

He takes piano lessons and shows off his talents, playing keyboard at a dance and impressing Rita with his talent. In his quest to have a meaningful relationship with Rita, Phil turns into a person who wants to help others and he becomes a town celebrity who is respected and loved. He has changed from a cynic to someone who can see the good side of people, hoping to earn the respect and love of Rita. Finally, Phil attempts to convince Rita of what has been happening to him and he does it by revealing intimate details about her life and others in the restaurant while predicting incidents that are about to happen. She is finally convinced and stays with him the entire day and night and proves to be the palliative he needs to break out of his frozen time zone, for he has been redeemed by love and faith.

For some religious leaders, *Groundhog Day* reflects the spirituality of their faith and dogma. Some Christians see the groundhog as the resurrection of Christ, while Jewish leaders note that Phil Connors is returned to Earth each day to perform mitzvahs, or good deeds (http://www.schindler.org/psacot/20010813_ghd_nyt.shtml).

In her February 12, 1993, *New York Times* review of *Groundhog Day*, Janet Maslin writes that it is a witty and resonant comedy:

> That glimmer of recognition is what makes "Groundhog Day" a particularly witty and resonant comedy, even when its jokes are more apt to prompt gentle giggles than rolling in the aisles. The story's premise, conceived as a sitcom-style visit to the Twilight Zone, starts out lightweight but becomes strangely affecting. Phil Connors, Mr. Murray's amusingly rude Pittsburgh television personality, surely deserves to be punished for his arrogance. But who in the audience hasn't ever wished time would stand still and offer a second, third or even a 20th chance? (http://movies.nytimes.com/movie)

In his updated review of the film, Rogert Ebert admits that he underrated *Groundhog Day* in his original review:

> *Groundhog Day* is a film that finds its note and purpose so precisely that its genius may not be immediately noticeable. It unfolds so inevitably, is so entertaining, so apparently effortless, that you have to stand back and slap yourself before you see how good it really is. (http://rogerebert.suntimes.com)

THE HOLOCAUST, PERSECUTION, ANNIHILATION

Schindler's List (1993)
The Pianist (2002)

Both of these films have a profound resonance in articulating the horror and tragedy of the Holocaust. Perhaps, one could ask, is there any beauty to be envisioned from the recounting of these heartrending stories? Visually, both films have striking, compelling images that sustain the scenes of human destruction, and the warped, gleeful psychology that some harbored as its facilitators. But there is beauty in both films that is demonstrated by people and their actions. The overwhelming cruelty was executed by characters like SS Commandant Amon Goeth (Ralph Fiennes), commander of the Plaszow camp in *Schindler's List* and the notorious Nazi who hunted Jewish men, women, and children hiding in the ghetto after the evacuation.

SCHINDLER'S LIST (1993)

PRODUCER/DIRECTOR: Steven Spielberg (director, producer), Branko Lustig (producer),
    Gerald R. Molen (producer)
WRITER(S): Thomas Keneally (book), Steven Zaillian (screenplay)
CAST: Liam Neeson (Oskar Schindler), Ben Kingsley (Itzhak Stern), Ralph Fiennes (Amon
    Goeth), Caroline Goodall (Emilie Schindler), Jonathan Sagall (Poldek Pfefferberg),

Embeth Davidtz (Helen Hirsch), Malgoscha Gebel (Wiktoria Klonowska), Shmuel Levy (Wilek Chilowicz), Mark Ivanir (Marcel Goldberg), Béatrice Macola (Ingrid)
CINEMATOGRAPHY: Janusz Kaminski
MUSIC: John Williams
LENGTH AND RATING: 195 min; R

Although the harsh reality of human extermination is articulated in the image of ash that falls like snow from the smoke stacks of the concentration camp crematoria, Oskar Schindler (Liam Neeson) is a muse who hoses down a train crammed with Jews in the stifling heat, and when offered three hundred units of new, fresh Jews by the Auschwitz Commandant whom he has bribed with diamonds, his simple response is, "I want these." Then he scolds an Auschwitz guard who is herding away the children of his workers, telling him that these belong to him and should be on his train and that they are skilled and essential munition workers. Holding up the right arm and hand of a young girl, he tells the guard that "their fingers polish the insides of shell metal casings. How else am I to polish the inside of a forty-five-millimeter shell casing?" His compassion is associated with the people who worked in his plant, D.E.F. DEUTSCHE EMAIL-WARENFABRIK, making enamel pots and pans. His Jewish accountant, Itzhak Stern (Ben Kingsley), compiled a list of those who worked in the factory. It's not just any Jews he wants to save, it's his Jews. Confronting inhumanity and the utmost lack of morality and compassion, Oskar Schindler became a caring man for the faces attached to the names.

Perhaps the most memorable image in the starkly black-and-white *Schindler's List* is that of the forced evacuation of Krakow Ghetto B, when the Jews are rounded up,

Liam Neeson (in hat, as Oskar Schindler). [Miramax Films/Photofest]

many of them indiscriminantly slaughtered, and the children flee into hiding. Gazing at the horror on horseback from a hilltop, Schindler and his mistress Ingrid (Beatrice Macola) watch the slaughter and the fate of a frightened little girl in a red dress running to hide. This is one of the color images in the film; another occurs at the beginning of the film when a hand lights the Friday night Shabbat (Sabbath) candles. They watch as she is led hand in hand by a German soldier amidst the point-blank murder of Jews shot against a wall. She sidesteps the carnage and is alone as she enters a building, goes upstairs, hides under a bed, and pushes her hair back from her face to reveal wide eyes of fear as the cadenced sound of the soldiers' boots hits the streets and fills the night air. This horror is accompanied by the innocent music of a well-known Yiddish ballad, "Oyfn Pripetchik" ("At the Fireplace"). It's a child's song that begins, in English translation:

> At the fireplace a little fire burns. And in the room it's warm. And the Rabbi teaches little children the aleph-bet (Hebrew alphabet). See you children-dear, remember dear, what you're learning here. Say once again, and then once again, "Komets-alef: o!" Children, learn with happiness, learn the aleph-bet. Lucky is the Jew who knows the Torah and the aleph-bet. (http://www.leechvideo.com/video/view3745176)

Apparently, when *Schindler's List* was in development, director Martin Scorsese was being considered to direct. He declined, offering it to Steven Spielberg, who eventually made the film. Spielberg did ask Roman Polanski, the Polish/American director and Holocaust survivor, if he wanted to make the film but Polanski respectfully declined because it was too close to his own experience. As a child, Polanski escaped from the Polish ghetto in Krakow and lived with a number of Catholic families. He was twelve years old when the war ended. In *The Pianist*, Polanski chose the autobiography of Wladyslaw Szpilman (Adrien Brody), the noted Polish pianist, to recount the terror and fears of Polish Jews during World War II. Like Polanski, Szpilman had escaped from the ghetto and relied upon the kindness of strangers for his survival. The story is about loneliness, as the Szpilmans, an affluent family, lose everything, including their dignity after they are forced to abandon their home and possessions. The parents, a brother, and two sisters manage to stay together and in one telling scene, as the refugees sit in the stifling heat waiting for transport, the family's patriarch (Frank Finlay) buys a caramel candy from a vendor and with a small pocket knife cuts it into six pieces. Just before they board a train to the Treblinka concentration camp, a Jewish ghetto police guard pulls Szpilman off the line and he escapes, avoiding certain death. Aided by an actress and her husband, former acquaintances, he is led to a safe apartment and begins a life of lonely exile in his own city. After looking for food, he drops a shelf of dishes and the noise attracts an upstairs neighbor, who threatens to call the police. Turning to an emergency address hidden in his shoe, he meets a woman whom he knew before, now married and pregnant, who can find him another safe apartment. After the Warsaw Ghetto uprising, the Germans level his bulding and he flees. The city's devastation is grotesque, a cityscape of abandoned, bombed-out shells of buildings that appear surreal, as though on a distant planet.

Alone, starving and hunting for food, Szpilman attempts to open a large can of pickles and is confronted by a German officer later identified as Captain Wilm

Hosenfeld (Thomas Kretschmann), who after learning that he is a pianist, leads Szpilman to a piano, where he plays Chopin's Ballade in G minor. Touched by the beauty of the music, Hosenfeld secretly brings food to Szpilman, helping him to survive until the Russian troops invade Warsaw. On his last visit before evacuating, Hosenfeld gives Szpilman his army overcoat and when he goes to greet the incoming Russians they shoot him, thinking he is a German soldier. He explains who he is and at the end of the film he is once again playing piano on Polish radio.

Each of these films confronts the Holocaust through the eyes of survivors nuanced by the pain of their horror. For *Schindler's List*, it was an epic story of survival in a smoldering of ashes and the unlikely humanity of a conniving ne'er-do-well named Oskar Schindler, who found his humanity in his Jews, the people he saved. It is a compelling visual narrative that is an emotionally draining experience. Perhaps its horror is only matched by the vivid scenes from Alain Resnais' *Nuit Et Brouillard* (*Night and Fog*) and the remains of concentration camp victims, their bones heaped high like mountains and bodies lying grotesquely without heads, which lie in a separate pail. Or in Art Spiegelman's graphic satiric novel *Maus: a Survivor's Tale*, in which the characters are personified as anthropomorphized animals.

The portrait of horror is more intimate in Polanski's *The Pianist* because the focus is on one man and his struggle to survive. For Wladyslaw Szpilman, life is privileged because of his stature as a well-known pianist but his celebrity is worthless in the face of the destruction of the Jews. His dignity is peeled away amidst the pain and horror of annihilation, and all that is left is a memory of who he was as his worn fingers sadly finger the notes on a piano.

In her December 13, 1993, review of *Schindler's List*, Janet Maslin writes about the film's "indelible images."

> *Schindler's List* brings a pre-eminent pop mastermind together with a story that demands the deepest reserves of courage and passion. Rising brilliantly to the challenge of this material and displaying an electrifying creative intelligence, Mr. Spielberg has made sure that neither he nor the Holocaust will ever be thought of in the same way again. With every frame, he demonstrates the power of the film maker to distill complex events into fiercely indelible images. (http://movies.nytimes.com/movie)

THE PIANIST (2002)

PRODUCER/DIRECTOR: Roman Polanski (director, producer), Robert Benmussa (producer), Alain Sarde (producer)

WRITER(S): Wladyslaw Szpilman (book), Ronald Harwood (screenplay)

CAST: Adrien Brody (Wladyslaw Szpilman), Thomas Kretschmann (Captain Wilm Hosenfeld), Frank Finlay (Father), Maureen Lipman (Mother), Emilia Fox (Dorota), Ed Stoppard (Henryk), Julia Rayner (Regina), Jessica Kate Meyer (Halina), Michal Zebrowski (Jurek), Wanja Mues (SS Slapping Father)

CINEMATOGRAPHY: Pawel Edelman

MUSIC: Wojciech Kilar

LENGTH AND RATING: 150 min; R

In a January 26, 2003, *New York Times* essay by Terrence Rafferty entitled "Polanski and the Landscape of Aloneness," he writes about "the hero's loneliness and dread."

In *The Pianist*, however, no otherworldly power is needed to explain the hero's overwhelming loneliness and dread, and if, at the end of his years of running and hiding, Wladyslaw Szpilman (played exquisitely by Adrien Brody) seems half-mad, it's an insanity fully justified by his circumstances: Nazi-occupied Poland is a paranoid fantasy grotesquely come to life. Although Roman Polanski did not invent Wladyslaw Szpilman, and the screenplay, by Ronald Harwood, is extraordinarily faithful to the pianist's memoirs, the movie's Szpilman is, in a way, the ultimate Polanski hero. He is solitude incarnate. (http://query.nytimes.com/gst/fullpage)

In A. O. Scott's December 27 *New York Times* review of *The Pianist*, he writes about Polanski's partial slice of history that made the film resonant:

The ambition to produce a comprehensive vision—a single spectacle adequate to the Holocaust—ultimately defeated Steven Spielberg's admirable and serious *Schindler's List*. Mr. Polanski, in staging a narrow, partial slice of history, has made a film that is both drier and more resonant than Mr. Spielberg's. (http://movies.nytimes.com/movie)

🎥 *HOOP DREAMS* (1994)

PRODUCER/DIRECTOR: Steve James (director, producer), Peter Gilbert (producer), Frederick Marx (producer)
WRITER(S): Steve James, Frederick Marx
CAST: William Gates (Himself), Arthur Agee (Himself), Emma Gates (Herself), Curtis Gates (Himself), Sheila Agee (Herself), Arthur "Bo" Agee (Himself), Earl Smith (Himself), Gene Pingatore (Himself), Isiah Thomas (Himself), Sister Marlyn Hopewell (Herself)
CINEMATOGRAPHY: Peter Gilbert
MUSIC: Ben Sidran
LENGTH AND RATING: 170 min; PG-13

In his essay entitled "Hoop Dreams Hollywood Dreams," Murray Sperber discusses the merits of the film as it relates to the traditions of documentary filmmaking and the exploitation of its subjects. He cites Robert Flaherty and his landmark documentary film, *Nanook of the North*, and compares Flaherty's concerns about filmmakers armed with their cameras as being "aliens" which alter their subjects responses, and that in today's "wall-to-wall media age," cinema verite is impossible to achieve.

It is an ambitious film that began as a thirty-minute project and blossomed into a four-and-a-half-year production that required two hundred and fifty hours of film. It provides a portrait of two African American boys, Arthur Agee and William Gates, from the inner city of Chicago who are scouted and then recruited to play basketball at St. Joseph High School, a predominantly white school with an ambitious basketball program. But the movie is much more than a "rags to riches" story as it portrays the struggles faced by the boys and their families as they make the transition from living and attending schools in the ghetto to St. Josephs, which is tutition-based and located in a white suburb.

The movie clearly articulates the influence of sports culture on American society as Arthur, William, and their families all succumb to the mythology of the message as they watch NBA basketball games on television, which nurture and manifest the merchandising of professional sports, selling its sizzle and dreams. The reality is that very few young basketball players, black, white, Asian, or other, make it to the NBA and the challenge is especially difficult for inner-city boys or girls, who are not performing at their academic grade level.

As Sperber points out in his essay, perhaps the real story is not about the achievements and failures of Arthur and William but more about the sacrifice of their mothers:

> The strength and power of *Hoop Dreams* is not its sports story—that becomes too predictable and genre driven—but its representation of the players' families, particularly their mothers, Emma Gates and Sheila Agee. Their lives are much more typical than those of their talented sons. Thus the revelation of their struggles makes a more powerful statement than do the stories of their kids' basketball careers. These two African-American women, who never dunked a basketball, are the true heroes of *Hoop Dreams*, and the reality of their lives is what rivets many viewers. Their strength is what we should admire, and their moments of despair and joy provide the best instances of documentary authenticity in the film. (http://www.ejumpcut. org/archive/onlinessays/JC40folder/HoopDreamsSperber)

There are also questions raised about the recruiting process, questions that still resound in 2009, from its dollars-and-cents, balance-sheet approach to the selection and retention of high school players. After his first year at St. Josephs and his poor academic work and lackluster peformance on the basketball court, Arthur must leave the school, although William is more fortunate, having a sponsor to pay his tuition and support the tutoring for his remedial course work. After William injures his knee, the surgery and rehabilitation are also covered.

But for Arthur, it's back to Marshall High, his inner-city high school, where he does well on the basketball team, receives a scholarship to a community college, and transfers to Arkansas State, while William is recruited by Marquette University. Neither of them ever made it to the NBA.

The filmmakers, Frederick Marx, Steve James, and Peter Gilbert did have the pioneering efforts of cinema verite, long-form documentary producers like Albert and David Maysles, Alan and Susan Raymond, and Michael Apted to serve as a paradigm for their work.

In her October 7, 1994, *New York Times* review of *Hoop Dreams,* Caryn James writes that the film is "a brilliantly revealing documentary." She also comments about "finding the complex people behind the stereotypes."

> Though it tries, "Hoop Dreams" doesn't find the complex people behind the stereotypes often enough; as viewers, we remain sympathetic voyeurs rather than intimates. The film's great achievement is to reveal the relentless way in which coaches and recruiters refuse to see Arthur and William as anything other than social clichés. (http://movies.nytimes.com/movie)

🎥 *FARGO* (1996)

PRODUCER/DIRECTOR: Joel Coen (director, producer), Ethan Coen (producer)

WRITER(S): Joel Coen, Ethan Coen

CAST: William H. Macy (Jerome "Jerry" Lundegaard), Frances McDormand (Marge Gunderson), Steve Buscemi (Carl Showalter), Peter Stormare (Gaear Grimsrud), Kristin Rudrüd (Jean Lundegaard), Harve Presnell (Wade Gustafson), Tony Denman (Scotty Lundegaard), Gary Houston (Irate Customer), Sally Wingert (Irate Customer's Wife), Kurt Schweickhardt (Car Salesman), Larissa Kokernot (Hooker #1)

CINEMATOGRAPHY: Roger Deakins

MUSIC: Carter Burwell

LENGTH AND RATING: 98 min; R

As producers and directors, Joel and Ethan Coen have demonstrated a knack for telling stories with relatively simple plots that evolve into complicated narratives that consume their characters with the consequences of their decisions and their actions. They have also redefined the role of the hero, and in *Fargo*, it's a pregnant, seemingly simple Brainerd, Minnesota, police chief named Marge Gunderson (Frances McDormand). Although her accent and speech pattern and those of the people she associates with make them seem like country bumpkins, Gunderson is a shrewd, smart, and formidable investigator.

Small-time criminals and businessmen with criminal minds populate *Fargo*. The character who sets the narrative in motion is Jerry Lundegaard (William H. Macy), the hapless, helpless husband of Jean Lundegaard, the daughter of a wealthy local businessman, Wade Gustafson (Harve Presnell) who owns the Oldsmobile dealership where Jerry works. Obsessed with the grandiose idea of acquiring land for a parking lot and needing money to finance it, he hatches a kidnapping scheme involving his wife to defraud his father-in-law of the one-million-dollar ransom. He connects with Carl Showalter (Steve Buscemi) and his psychopathic partner Gaear Grimsrud (Peter Stormare) and hires them to kidnap his wife.

When Wade and his accountant invite Jerry to discuss the parking lot deal, he tries to stop the kidnapping but has no way to reach Carl and Gaear. They kidnap his wife, Jean, who is wrapped in a blanket and lying in the backseat of the new Cutlass Ciera that Jerry has given them as part of their payment. While driving they are stopped by a state trooper, who notices that the car has no tags. Approaching the car, the trooper asks for Carl's license and he leaves an exposed fifty dollar bill in his wallet, prompting the officer to ask him to get out of the vehicle just as Jean squirms and makes a noise in the backseat. Acting swiftly, Grimsrud grabs the trooper's hair and shoots him in the head. As Carl attempts to move the body off the road, a vehicle passes by, slows down, and then speeds off. In hot pursuit, Grimsrud follows and finds the vehicle turned over in a snowy field, the driver running from the car. He shoots the fleeing driver and then bends down and shoots the female occupant stuck in the damaged car.

Arriving at the scene, Marge deduces the circumstances and that the occupants in the car were innocent victims who had seen the murderers. She also concludes from the different footprints at the accident and murder scenes that the perpetrators were two men, one large, the other small. When her dim deputy informs her that the trooper called in the vehicle plate as beginning with "DLR" she gently lets him know that it probably stands for "Dealer."

Both Marge and Carl travel to Minneapolis for different reasons: Marge to follow up on her leads and Carl to pick up the ransom money from Jerry. After Jerry meets with Marge at the car dealership, he "flees" her interview, and her suspicions about his involvement in the kidnapping are confirmed. Carl is surprised by Wade's presence at the ransom rendezvous site. After a shootout, Wade is killed and Carl suffers a bloody face wound. Grabbing the money, Carl learns there is considerably more than the $80,000 in the case and he schemes to split that amount with Grimsrud at the Lakehouse cabin. When he arrives he sees that Jean is dead, killed by Grimsrud for shrieking and making noise. He announces that he's taking the car, but Grimsrud insists that they split its value and that he be paid for his share. Driven by greed, Carl curses and leaves and as he walks away Grimsrud attacks him from behind with an ax.

While driving, Marge spots the Cutlass Ciera parked near the remote lake house and sees Grimsrud feeding a body into a woodchipper. She announces who she is, then shoots him in the leg as he tries to flee. In her squad car, she lectures Grimsrud on the futility of the crime and the needless violence.

And for what? For a little bit of money.

After fleeing to a motel just outside Bismarck, North Dakota, Jerry is apprehended by local police officers.

One of the most distinctive features of *Fargo* is the language used in the dialogue. The Swedish-American accented repetition of the word "yeah" by the locals makes them appear like hicks, but their lives seem rich in their frozen world. The relationship between Marge and her husband Norm (John Carroll Lynch) is loving and ordinary; they don't talk much, but they have deep feelings for each other. She encourages his painting of ducks, and he leaves the police work to her. In an essay by Paul Caughlin entitled, "Language Aesthetics in Three Films by Joel and Ethan Coen," the author writes about the Coen brothers and their challenge to Hollywood convention and their irregular dialogue forms:

> The Coen brothers are renowned for challenging Hollywood convention, typically employing irony to construct subversive applications. Their application of original and irregular dialogue forms extends and supports the seditious elements of their film making agenda. (http://www.thefilmjournal.com/issue12/coens)

In her March 8, 1996, *New York Times* review of *Fargo*, Janet Maslin calls it "a crazily mundane crime story."

> The Coens are at their clever best with this snowbound film noir, a crazily mundane crime story set in their native Midwest. Purportedly based on real events, it brings them as close as they may ever come—not very—to everyday life and ordinary people. Perversely, the frozen north even brings out some uncharacteristic warmth in these coolly cerebral film makers, although anyone seeking the milk of human kindness would be well advised to look elsewhere. (http://movies.nytimes.com/movie)

🎥 *TITANIC* (1997)

PRODUCER/DIRECTOR: James Cameron (director, producer), Jon Landau (producer)
WRITER(S): James Cameron
CAST: Leonardo DiCaprio (Jack Dawson), Kate Winslet (Rose DeWitt Bukater), Billy Zane (Caledon "Cal" Hockley), Kathy Bates (Molly Brown), Frances Fisher (Ruth DeWitt Bukater), Gloria Stuart (Old Rose), Bill Paxton (Brock Lovett), Bernard Hill (Captain Smith), David Warner (Spicer Lovejoy), Victor Garber (Thomas Andrews)
CINEMATOGRAPHY: Russell Carpenter
MUSIC: James Horner
LENGTH AND RATING: 194 min; PG-13

In his recreation of the disaster of the White Star shipping line's unsinkable cruise ship *Titanic*, James Cameron created an epic film with meticulous reproductions based on exhaustive research and an enduring love story. He also referenced the 1958 movie *A Night to Remember*, produced by the J. Arthur Rank organization, which rigorously held to the facts based on the recollections of survivors. Indeed, there are several scenes in the Cameron film that are almost identical to those in *A Night to Remember*, including steerage passengers attempting to escape the flooding and coming against a closed gate monitored by a steward who threatens them with paying for the damage they cause when they break through. Another scene in both movies is the meeting between Thomas Andrews, Jr., chief designer for Belfast-based Harland and Wolff, builders of the RMS *Olympic* and its sistership, RMS *Titanic*, and Edward J. Smith, the *Titanic's* captain, reviewing the plans and coming to the grim conclusion that the ship would sink within two hours after hitting an iceberg. Similar scenes in both movies involved Margaret (Molly) Brown, the American women's rights advocate and wife of a wealthy silver mining executive who exhorted her fellow women in the lifeboat to row and assist passengers floating in the ice-cold Atlantic ocean. In *A Night to Remember*, her exhortations succeed while in Cameron's *Titanic* she fails, as the others fear having their lifeboat "swamped" by desperate survivors. In both movies, the string quartet continues to play on the deck amid the chaos of the evacuation as the realization takes hold that there are insufficient lifeboats to accommodate all of the passengers. However, the distinctive dfference between *A Night to Remember* and *Titanic* is the passionate fictional love story between Jack Dawson (Leonardo DiCaprio), a poor, wandering American artist who is lucky at poker and wins a ticket on the *Titanic*, and Rose DeWitt Bukater (Kate Winslet), who is engaged to Cal Hockley (Billy Zane), the arrogant, pompous heir to a steel fortune.

Using the discovery of the lost ship in present-day by a crew of researchers led by Brock Lovett (Bill Paxton), who are searching for the fictional mammoth blue diamond, "Heart of the Ocean," thought to be on the ship, Cameron weaves a compelling story about greed, love, heroism, and jealousy, with the two lovers as witnesses and victims of the disaster. After discovering a drawing of a young nude Rose, as seen on television by the now one-hundred-year-old Rose (Gloria Stuart), she joins the research crew with her granddaughter and begins her narrative of the story. The end of the movie reveals that the elderly Rose is still in possession of the "Heart of the Ocean" and in a poignant moment of emotion she drops the diamond into the ocean to join the remnants of the ill-fated *Titanic*.

In her December 19, 1997, *New York Times* review of *Titanic*, Janet Maslin writes that the film "unerringly lures viewers into the beauty and heartbreak of its lost world." She compares its epic design to *Gone with the Wind*, saying that "*Titanic* is the first spectacle in decades that honestly invites comparison to *Gone with the Wind*." She also writes that the film has "tremendous momentum right from its deceptive, crass-looking start" (http://movies.nytimes.com/movie).

In another review, Roger Ebert writes:

James Cameron's 194-minute, $200 million film of the tragic voyage is in the tradition of the great Hollywood epics. It is flawlessly crafted, intelligently constructed, strongly acted and spellbinding. If its story stays well within the traditional formulas for such pictures, well, you don't choose the most expensive film ever made as your opportunity to reinvent the wheel. (http://rogerebert.suntimes.com)

9 The New Millennium, 2000–2008

This decade has been defined thus far by upheavals in culture, politics, economy, and technology in the United States and the global community. The presidential election of 2000 perhaps was a harbinger of the turbulent times to come. Election recounts in the state of Florida would decide who the new president would be, Vice President Al Gore, or Texas Governor Geroge W. Bush. While Gore won the popular vote, Bush claimed victory over the electoral votes and the United States Supreme Court ruled to end the Florida recount and certify the vote. In November 2008, Barack Obama was elected as America's first African American president.

On September 11, 2001, the United States suffered its worst terrorist attack when two hijacked passenger jets flew into the Twin Towers of the World Trade Center in New York City, causing them to collapse as many occupants jumped to their deaths. A third passenger jet crashed into the Pentagon in Washington, DC, while a fourth plane was deterred from its target by a group of passengers who challenged the hijackers, which caused the plane to crash in rural Shankesville, Pennsylvania. As a result of these attacks by the terrorist group Al-Qaeda, the United States invaded Afghanistan and, after a supposed threat of weapons of mass destruction, the U.S. entered Iraq.

The decade also experienced some of the largest meltdowns in corporate America, with the bankruptcy of the energy trading company Enron, the securitization of sub-prime loans, which created a huge strain on financial instruments, and a threat to the global economy, which forced Congress to approve a $700 billion bail-out package. The global economy teetered on the brink of collapse as the banks Washington Mutual and Wachovia failed and venerable financial firms like Lehman Brothers, founded in 1850, declared bankruptcy. Companies like the insurance giant AIG received massive infusions of capital, and Bear Stearns was bought by JP Morgan Chase, for as low as $10 a share, despite trading at a 52-week high of $133.20 per share.

In sports, baseball was subject to congressional scrutiny because of steroids while almost every sport was tarnished by doping. One of the most celebrated athletes of the decade was Marion Jones, the American track and field star who won five medals at the 2000 summer Olympic Games in Sydney, Australia. In 2007, Jones admitted to taking steroids before the Sydney games and was subsequently stripped of all her medals dating to September 2000. She received a six-month jail term for lying to federal agents.

Another champion was born when American swimmer Michael Phelps won eight gold medals at the Beijing, China, 2008 Summer Olympic games, breaking the previous record of Mark Spitz, and winning a total of fourteen career Olympic gold medals.

Video gaming became a major form of entertainment with the introduction of the Nintendo GameCube (2001) and Microsoft's Xbox (2001), which joined the Sony PlayStation, introduced in 1994. The Internet made global interactive gaming a reality, allowing for greater competition. One of the most popular games was the Grand Theft Auto series, and on April 29, 2008, Grand Theft Auto IV was released by Rockstar North for PlayStation 3 and Xbox 360. It sold 3.6 million units on its first day and grossed in excess of $500 million in its first week.

Another technological phenomenon was the iPhone by Apple, which was initially released in the United States on June 29, 2007; on July 11, 2008, a new, less expensive and faster 3G iPhone hit the market.

There were a number of films that were starkly innovative and creative in their narrative structure. Writer/director Christopher Nolan's film *Memento* (2001) was a tour de force in episodic nonlinear narrative structure, while Baz Luhrmann's *Moulin Rouge* (2001) deconstructed the format of the Hollywood musical, using well-known pop songs for its libretto. An unexpected blockbuster was the film *My Big Fat Greek Wedding* (2002), with an unknown cast and simple story line. The word-of-mouth hit cost $5 million to produce and earned $240 million at the box office.

Documentaries returned reflecting the mood of America's concern with safety, the environment, health care, and the intrusion of government. Three films by Michael Moore—*Bowling for Columbine* (2002), *Fahrenheit 9/11* (2004), and *Sicko* (2007)—revealed investigations into some very contemporary themes. The environment and global warming was addressed in the film *An Inconvenient Truth* (2006) presented by former Vice President Al Gore and directed by Davis Guggenheim.

PSYCHOLOGICAL DISSONANCE

American Psycho (2000)
Memento (2000)

These two films, although distinctive in their structure and narrative, do have a similar tone, sharing the psychological dynamic of detachment that is articulated by the lead characters, Patrick Bateman (Christian Bale) and Leonard Shelby (Guy Pearce). They are both conflicted human beings out of touch with reality and cavorting in a dream-like bubble of time and space. In each film, the audience faces the challenge of distinguishing the real from the fantasy, although that process may not be readily at hand. In *American Psycho*, Patrick is part of the 1980s consumer culture, portraying a young Wall Street executive with a Harvard MBA who outwardly sustains the narcissistic, self-indulging, competitive lifestyle of a hotshot deal maker in "murders and executions" while inwardly loathing the emptiness of his existence. Unlike Gordon Gekko (*Wall Street*, 1987) Patrick has a self-loathing that manifests itself in a murderous sexuality that may be real or simply a figment of his disturbed imagination. He is obsessed by his appearance and is just as competitive as his colleagues. That field of competition includes the best business card, reservations at celebrity restaurants, and important client accounts. Although he at times expresses social and environmental concerns, taking offense at anti-Semitic remarks, he is just as dismissive, obsessed, and inhuman as his counterparts.

So, he goes on a bloody killing spree that satisfies his jealous rage and soothes his self-betrayal. However, there are several scenes that portray his murderous escapade as a fantasy that by the end of the film he must reconcile with his own interpretation of reality. These scenes resonate with a comic book air of expectation and fulfillment.

AMERICAN PSYCHO (2000)

PRODUCER/DIRECTOR: Mary Harron (director), Christian Halsey Solomon (producer), Chris Hanley (producer)

WRITER(S): Bret Easton Ellis (novel), Mary Harron (screenplay), Guinevere Turner (screenplay)

CAST: Christian Bale (Patrick Bateman), Justin Theroux (Timothy Bryce), Josh Lucas (Craig McDermott), Bill Sage (David Van Patten), Chloë Sevigny (Jean), Reese Witherspoon (Evelyn Williams), Samantha Mathis (Courtney Rawlinson), Matt Ross (Luis Carruthers), Jared Leto (Paul Allen), Willem Dafoe (Det. Donald Kimball)

CINEMATOGRAPHY: Andrzej Sekula

MUSIC: John Cale, Eve Egoyan

LENGTH AND RATING: 101 min; R

Patrick finds a stray kitten near an ATM machine and, after inserting his card and watching as the screen reads, "feed me a stray cat," he aims a gun at the kitten but when a woman bystander screams in protest he shoots her instead. This results in a confrontation with the police, whom he blows away with his gun, causing a massive explosion. After his ménage a trois, where he videotapes the action and watches himself in a mirror as he has sex with the women, he chases one of his partners in the nude with a whirring chainsaw in hand down a hallway as she screams, shrieks, and bangs on all the closed doors. But all remains eerily quiet in that chaotic time continuum as Patrick hurls the chainsaw, killing her. At the end of the movie, Patrick returns to Paul Allen's apartment, his first murder victim where he has stored subsequent dead bodies. It's spotless and being shown by a real estate agent to a prospective buyer. At the end of the movie Patrick sits alone as his peers mingle and his narrative voice-over speaks to the utter mayhem he has caused and his utter indiffernce toward it. His pain is constant and sharp and he wants his pain to be inflicted on others and hopes no one will escape. But he does not experience catharsis, his punishment eludes him, and he does not gain a deeper knowledge of himself. After the camera zooms in on a close-up of Patrick's eyes, he says that this confession has meant nothing.

In his April 14, 2000, *New York Times* review of *American Psycho*, Stephen Holden writes, "the movie plays adroitly with the notion that his violent spasms are merely the revenge fantasies of a repressed corporate toady" and called it "a dazzling period satire" (http://movies.nytimes.com/movie).

MEMENTO (2000)

PRODUCER/DIRECTOR: Christopher Nolan (director), Jennifer Todd (producer), Suzanne Todd (producer),

WRITER(S): Jonathan Nolan (short story "Memento Mori"), Christopher Nolan (screenplay)

CAST: Guy Pearce (Leonard), Carrie-Anne Moss (Natalie), Joe Pantoliano (Teddy Gammell), Mark Boone Junior (Burt), Russ Fega (Waiter), Jorja Fox (Leonard's Wife), Stephen

Tobolowsky (Sammy), Harriet Sansom Harris (Mrs. Jankis), Thomas Lennon (Doctor), Callum Keith Rennie (Dodd), Kimberly Campbell (Blonde)

CINEMATOGRAPHY: Wally Pfister
MUSIC: David Julyan
LENGTH AND RATING: 113 min; R

Just as in *American Psycho,* the audience watching Leonard Shelby (Guy Pearce) in *Memento* as he searches for the man who raped and killed his wife, is somewhat unnerved by the nonlinear narrative that unfolds (as in *Pulp Fiction*) in reverse chronological order, with the end of the story at the beginning of the film. In a stark, strange opening scene, a hand waves an instant Polaroid picture in the air and instead of the image slowly appearing its process is reversed and the image fades away. This image is a harbinger of the reverse chronology of the narrative as Leonard struggles with his debilitating condition of anterograde amnesia, which means he has no short-term memory or new memories in the search for his wife's murderer. This makes Leonard an unusual diarist as he takes Polaroids of people and things, making notes on the photos' borders. He also tattoos important findings in text on his body; he becomes a walking *Wikipedia.*

The movie provides the audience with a number of clues that may or may not be accurate because there are several notations that Leonard has made about distrusting various characters. The director (Christopher Nolan) uses color and black-and-white as a narrative tool. Color sequences move in reverse chronological time while the other in black-and-white is told in linear order. A piece of the jigsaw puzzle is the anecdotal information about Sammy Jankis (Stephen Tobolowsky), in black-and-white, whose insurance claim for short-term memory loss Leonard, as a fraud investigator, is pursuing. He concludes that the problem is psychological and not physical, thus denying the claim. Upset by his denial, Jankis' wife confronts him but Leonard is convinced of his finding. To prove her contention that Sammy's condition is physical and real, she has her husband administer repeated doses of her insulin every fifteen minutes. He obliges, unaware that he gave her a shot just a few minutes before. As a result, she dies and Sammy is placed in a mental institution.

Now, because of a head injury suffered when he interrupted the murder of his wife and killed one of her assailants, ironically Leonard experiences the same condition as Sammy. He lives in a fleabag motel and is talking to an anonymous person on the telephone explaining his quest and telling the story about Sammy Jankis. In his search, Leonard meets two people, Natalie (Carrie-Anne Moss) and Teddy (Joe Pantoliano), both of whom manipulate him.

The film, because of its reverse chronological progression, provides its audience with the visualization of the effect and then the cause. When the movie opens, Leonard is driving a Jaguar and wearing a silk suit that belonged to a drug dealer named Jimmy Grantz, Natalie's boyfriend, and Teddy tricked Leonard into killing Grantz for the $200,000 in the trunk of his car, making him think that the drug dealer murdered his wife. At one point Teddy, who was posing as a cop, tells Leonard that he doesn't even remember how he got the suit or the Jaguar, which of course is a fact.

Everyone sees an opportuniy to manipulate Leonard, and even the manager of the motel has charged him for two rooms, admitting that he took advantage of Leonard's lack of short-term memory. There is a point, as in *American Psycho,* when the audience has difficulty distinguishing between reality and fantasy. Suspicions are raised when

Teddy tells Leonard that his wife survived the attack but died from an insulin overdose administered by Leonard, and that Sammy Jankis was a fraud who wasn't even married. He also tells Leonard that he is a police officer who took pity on him and that he helped Leonard track down John G., his wife's murderer, whom Leonard killed, but that he forgot and started his search over again. After Natalie traces the license plate of John G., the photo I.D. matches Teddy and Leonard concludes that he is his wife's murderer and kills him.

Like *American Psycho*, in the final scene of the film there is a voice-over narrative of Leonard thinking while driving in the Jaguar. In a metaphysical way, he is wondering about reality and the world around him, challenging his own sensibilities and the very existence of his being:

> I have to believe in a world outside my own mind. I have to believe that my actions still have meaning even if I can't remember them. I have to believe that when my eyes are closed the world is still here. Do I believe the world is still here? Is it still out there? Yeah, we all need Marys to remind ourselves who we are, I'm no different.

At the end of this monologue the car screeches to a halt in front of Emma's Tattoo Parlor, and Leonard glances down at a card with a familiar license plate number, "tattoo fact 6." His last line in the film is: "Now, where was I."

In his March 16, 2001, *New York Times* review of *Memento*, A. O. Scott explains that the film is "boilerplate noir" and that the reason to watch the film "is for the disorienting pleasure of its unusual narrative technique. The audience is plunged into a condition analogous to Leonard's, but also, logically speaking, the opposite." He notes that the director (Christopher Nolan) "is excited by the way the medium can manipulate time and information," and that the film is a "brilliant feat of rug-pulling." However, he also notes that while the director's accomplishments are impressive, "it doesn't in the end leave much of an impression."

COURAGE AND CONVICTION

Erin Brockovich (2000)
Traffic (2000)

While both of these films were directed by Steven Soderbergh, they are very distinct in their style and voice. Each showcases Soderbergh's talents as a versatile director with an ability to produce a blockbuster Hollywood film with an A-list actress (Julia Roberts portraying Erin Brockovich) or an esemble film where the actors are not the story but part of it. Although each film has a different narrative arc, there are some similarities in their themes.

ERIN BROCKOVICH (2000)

PRODUCER/DIRECTOR: Steven Soderbergh (director), Danny DeVito (producer)
WRITER(S): Susannah Grant
CAST: Julia Roberts (Erin Brockovich), David Brisbin (Dr. Jaffe), Dawn Didawick (Rosalind), Albert Finney (Ed Masry), Valente Rodriguez (Donald), Conchata Ferrell (Brenda),

George Rocky Sullivan (Los Angeles Judge), Pat Skipper (Defending Lawyer), Jack Gill (Defendant), Irene Olga López (Mrs. Morales), Scotty Leavenworth (Matthew Brockovich), Gemmenne de la Peña (Katie Brockovich (as Gemmenne De la Peña)), Erin Brockovich-Ellis (Julia)
CINEMATOGRAPHY: Edward Lachman
MUSIC: Thomas Newman
LENGTH AND RATING: 130 min; R

In *Erin Brockovich*, an attractive single mother of three with few employment prospects joins a law firm and uses her initiative to research claims of cancer and other illnesses from local homeowners concerned that contaminated water has been released by the Pacific Gas and Electric Company. The film portrays Brockovich as a struggling single parent who confronts the prejudice and bias of others who hold her lack of education, fashion choices, and single-parent status in disdain. While some film critics expressed their displeasure with what they describe as Julia Roberts' exaggerated performance portraying the real Erin Brockovich and referred to the movie as a "standard issue do-gooder melodrama," the fact is that the efforts of Brockovich and the law firm of Masry & Vititoe resulted in a settlement of $333 million.

The film was also about a woman who for much of her life was defined more by the men she was with rather than by her own achievements and character. Her role was that of mother and homemaker. Once she assumed her position as an investigator, interviewing residents, gathering evidence, and doggedly becoming an advocate, Brockovich could not abandon her new persona. Challenging her newfound identity, George (Aaron Eckhart), her boyfriend who had been caring for her three children, feels neglected and asks her to quit her job. This is the kind of selfishness that she experienced from other men and Erin tells him how important her work is and how it has affected her confidence and self-esteem.

While *Erin Brockovich* has been compared to other films involving crusading lawyers and advocates like *Silkwood* (1983), *Norma Rae* (1979), and *A Civil Action* (1998), each of the stories is unique because of the people involved, and those people are always different and so is Erin Brockovich. In the mold of Julia Roberts she may provoke jealously and disdain for her low-cut, cleavage-revealing tops, short skirts that show off sculpted legs, and her in-your-face language, but like other women, whether professional or not, sexuality is no strange accessory to the job market. A. O. Scott notes in his March 17, 2000, *New York Times* review that, "As the movie drags on, her performance swells to bursting with moral vanity and phony populism." But then he describes the film as "the feel-good movie of the year." Sometimes, we just don't know how our heroes or heroines should be portrayed.

TRAFFIC (2000)

PRODUCER/DIRECTOR: Steven Soderbergh (director), Richard Solomon (producer), Mike Newell (producer), Cameron Jones (producer)
WRITER(S): Simon Moore (miniseries Traffik), Stephen Gaghan (screenplay)
CAST: Michael Douglas (Robert Wakefield), Don Cheadle (Montel Gordon), Benicio Del Toro (Javier Rodriguez), Catherine Zeta-Jones (Helena Ayala), Albert Finney (Chief of Staff),

Amy Irving (Barbara Wakefield), Erika Christensen (Caroline Wakefield), James Brolin (General Ralph Landry), Dennis Quaid (Arnie Metzger), Benjamin Bratt (Juan Obregon), Jacob Vargas (Manolo Sanchez)
CINEMATOGRAPHY: Steven Soderbergh
MUSIC: Cliff Martinez
LENGTH AND RATING: 147 min; R

This film provides a riveting treatment of the drug trade and how it corrupts every segment of society, providing the tragic nirvana of temptation as it weaves a fabric that ensnarls its victims in a spiraling fate of dependance and desire. As in Robert Altman's film, *Nashville*, *Traffic* is a movie with several parallel stories that intersect with characters that are prominent and have compelling motivations that drive them. This type of cinematic narrative structure has been described by Alissa Quart as "hyperlink" which refers to interwoven story lines that follow the characters as they weave in and out of the narrative progression (http://www.alissaquart.com/articles/2005/08/networked_don_roos_and_happy_e.html).

In *Traffic*, mutiple layers of story yield compelling actions associated with the war on drugs. There's an honest Mexican cop, Javier Rodriguez (Benicio del Toro), who, after interdicting a large amount of drugs that are quickly confiscated by the corrupt General Salazar (Tomas Milian), enters his employ, thinking the general's intent to eliminate the Tijuana cartel is true. He, of course, is unaware that the general is affiliated with the Juarez Cartel, which is a rival of the Obregon Cartel. After Javier's partner is killed and he realizes that Salazar is a corrupt pawn of the drug lords, he becomes an FBI informant.

In another story line that corresponds to the previous action in Mexico, Robert Wakefield (Michael Douglas), a judge from Ohio, is selected as the president's new head of the Office of National Drug Control, known in the vernacular as the Drug Czar. On a trip to Washington, he is briefed by the White House Chief of Staff (Albert Finney), who instructs him about the do's and don't's. At Washington social gatherings, Wakefield is lectured by various constituents, including the "real" Senators Harry Reid, Barbara Boxer, Orrin Hatch, and Charles Grassley. However, as a metaphor for the US war on drugs, Wakefield must face the addiction of his sixteen-year-old honor student daughter Caroline (Erika Christensen), who runs away from her first treatment center and prostitutes herself to earn momey for her habit. He hunts for her in the inner city of Cincinnati and finds her in a seedy hotel. On the day scheduled for Wakefield to meet the press and make his first speech, he abruptly leaves the podium and returns home to be with his family.

Another weave in the story is the work of undercover drug enforcement officers (DEA) Montel Gordon (Don Cheadle) and Ray Castro (Luis Guzman), who are guarding Eduardo Ruiz (Miguel Ferrrer), a key witness against Carlos Ayala (Steven Bauer), the Obregon Drug Cartel's largest distributor in the United States. After he is arrested his unsuspecting wife Helena (Catherine Zeta-Jones), who thought her husband was a legitimate businessman, takes matters into her own hands and hires a hit man to kill Ruiz. The attempt fails but a bomb planted in the agent's car kills Montel Gordon's partner Ray. Undeterred, Helena visits Juan Obregon (Benjamin Bratt) in Mexico. He is the leader of the Obregon Drug Cartel and she convinces him, after demonstrating a doll made of cocaine for smuggling drugs, to kill Ruiz and the assassination succeeds when a poisoned breakfast is smuggled in. With the key witness murdered, Ayala is released. But Montel Gordon feigns a bout of rage and enters Ayala's home during a party, confronting the drug dealer and is thrown to the floor, which allows him to plant a hidden microphone under a coffee-table. The implication is that he will be vindicated for the death of his partner.

The end of the movie shows Javier watching a night youth baseball game in Mexico; the funding for the stadium and the lighting was the only request he made for his cooperation with the federal authorities. And Wakefield, along with his wife (Amy Irving) and daughter, attend a Narcotics Anonymous meeting.

The film is an outstanding example of technical achievement and acting talent. It has a gritty realism that demonstrates the compelling emotions that are evoked. The camera provides an intimacy with the characters that uses the stylistic virtues of cinema verite to outstanding effect.

In his December 27, 2000, *New York Times* review, Stephen Holden describes *Traffic* as a "sprawling multicultural jazz symphony."

"Traffic" is a sprawling multicultural jazz symphony of clashing voices sounding variations of the same nagging discontent. The performances (in English and Spanish), by an ensemble from which not a false note issues, have the clarity and force of pithy instrumental solos insistently piercing through a dense cacophony. (http://movies.nytimes.com/movie/review)

AN AMERICAN ORIGINAL

Fantasia (1940)
Fantasia 2000 (1999)

In the introduction to this chapter, various technological innovations are cited, such as Nintendo Gamecube, the Microsoft Xbox, and the Sony PlayStation, all of which created an industry of digital gaming. However, the design and functionality of these games wouldn't have been possible without the creative genius of Walt Disney. He pushed the envelope of technical innovation adding new dimensions to his animated characters and themes—like combining live action with animation in the feature film *The Three Caballeros* (1945), and in the short *Blame It on the Samba* (1948) from "Melody Time." His brilliance and artistry was captured in the two versions of *Fantasia* that are discussed in this section. His legacy is part of the dynamic for the creative media industry today and is the rationale for discussing *Fantasia* under the heading of this chapter.

FANTASIA (1940)

PRODUCER/DIRECTOR: James Algar (director), Samuel Armstrong (director), Ford Beebe (director), Norman Ferguson (director), Jim Handley (director), T. Hee (director), Wilfred Jackson (director), Hamilton Luske (director), Bill Roberts (director), Paul Satterfield (director), Walt Disney (producer), Ben Sharpsteen (producer)
WRITER(S): Lee Blair, Elmer Plummer, Phil Dike, Sylvia Moberly-Holland, Norman Wright, Albert Heath, Bianca Majolie, Graham Heid, Perce Pearce, Carl Fallberg, William Martin, Leo Thiele, Robert Sterner, John McLeish, Otto Englander, Webb Smith, Erdman Penner, Joseph Sabo, Bill Peet, Vernon Stallings, Campbell Grant, Arthur Heinemann, Phil Dike

"Sorceror's Apprentice" segment. [Walt Disney Pictures/Photofest]

CAST: Leopold Stokowski (Himself—Conductor, The Philadelphia Orchestra), Deems Taylor
    (Narrator—1940 original), Julietta Novis (Soloist—segment "Ave Maria"—voice)
CINEMATOGRAPHY: James Wong Howe, Max Morgan
MUSIC: Leopold Stokowski (orchestra)
LENGTH AND RATING: 120 min; G

A feature-length musical cartoon produced by Walt Disney and interpreting Bach's "Toccata and Fugue in D Minor," Tchaikovsky's "The Nutcracker Suite," Dukas's "The Sorcerer's Apprentice," Stravinsky's "The Rite of Spring," Beethoven's "Sixth (Pastoral) Symphony," Ponchielli's "Dance of the Hours," Mussorgsky's "Night On Bald Mountain" and Schubert's "Ave Maria"; score conducted by Leopold Stokowski and recorded by the Philadelphia Symphony Orchestra; narrative introductions by Deems Taylor; recorded by the new RCA Fantasound System under the supervision of William E. Garity, C. O. Slyfield and J. N. A. Hawkins; story direction by Joe Grant and Dick Huemer; production supervision, Ben Sharpsteen; animation directors. Samuel Armstrong, James Algar, Bill Roberts, Paul Satterfield, Hamilton Luske, Jim Handley, Ford Beebe, T. Hee, Norm Ferguson, Wilfred Jackson; photographed in Multiplane Technicolor; distributed by Walt Disney, Inc.

Since its premiere in 1940, Walt Disney's classic feature *Fantasia* has had a rich history in various forms of release. When first released by Disney the film's length was 124 minutes and it was a disappointment at the box office. In 1941, RKO Radio Pictures acquired *Fantasia* for distribution and it was re-released in an eighty-one minute version in 1942. Susequent release for *Fantasia* included five interations from 1946 to 1977 with the 1946 re-edited film restoring much of the original image and sound and running only nine minutes shorter than the original 1940 release. In 1982 *Fantasia* was released with a new digitally rcorded sound track with orchestrations conducted by Irwin Kostal but this version of the film was removed from distribution in 1990.

Faced with the waning populartity of Mickey Mouse, the Disney studio's singular franchise animated character, Walt Disney decided to make a short film entitled *The Sorcerer's Apperentice* featuring Mickey Mouse. However, in a striking departure from the studio's legacy in animation and sound Disney decided against dialogue. Instead, the short which was based upon a poem/ballad by the German writer Johann Wolfgang von Goethe, "der Zauberlehring" would include music, entitled "L' aprenti sorcier," by composer Paul Dukas and would be conducted by Leopold Stowkoski featuring an orchestra of over one hundred musicians. In addition, Mickey's features were redesigned by animator Fred Moore; he was given more weight and volume, and more expression by providing pupils for his eyes.

As production costs soared in excess of $100,000 for a nine-minute animated short film it was decided to add other animated segments set to classical musical works making the film feature length and presenting it in a reserved seating concert venue. There were eight classical musical pieces, with some of the original lengths modified for the production, and each was introduced by the film's host Deems Taylor. The compositions included, "Toccata and Fugue in D Minor" by Johann Sebastian Bach, "Nutcracker Suite" by Pyotr Llyich Tchaikovsky, "The Sorcerer's Apprentice" by Paul Dukas, "The Rite of Spring" by Igor Stravinsky, "The Pastoral Symphony" by Ludwig van Beethoven, "Dance of the Hours" by Amilcare Ponchielli, "Night on Bald Mountain," "Ave Maria" by Modest Mussrogsky and Franz Schubert respectively. The sound was recorded using a process called "Fantasound" which was an early use of stereophonic sound making this the first film to use the process. However, because of the expense for refitting a theater for the "Fantasound" process the film was screened in only twelve theaters and sixteen "Fantasound" prints were made. In 1942, the eighty-one minute RKO version of the film was released with a monophonic sound track.

The most popular animated segment of *Fantasia* was the "Sorcerer's Apprentice" featuring Mickey Mouse as the magician's helper. Laden down carrying buckets of water to fill his master's cauldron he watches as the sorcerer completes his magic and retires for the night leaving his magic hat behind. Unable to resist the temptation, he puts on the hat and, seeing a straw broom in the corner, casts a magic spell that allows him to teach the broom how to carry water. Soon the broom is ably doing Mickey's water chores, and so he takes a nap in the sorcerer's chair. He dreams of being in the heavens controlling the stars and the comets, ordering the oceans to do his bidding. He suddenly awakes floating in a sea of water because the broom continues to carry water to the cauldron even when it's full. Unable to stop it from its chores, Mickey finds an ax and spinters the wooden broom stick, but this action allows the broom to clone itself into an army of water carriers. As the volume of water increases, with Mickey caught up in its spiraling current, he desperately consults a magic book for the appropriate spell to end the invasion. However, the sorcerer returns and seeing the mayhem he raises his arms apart stopping the onslaught. Remorseful, Mickey returns the hat and broom to the sorcerer and picks up the buckets and then receives a powerful tap on the rear with the broom that catapults him away. Then Mickey approaches the composer Leopold Stokowski, standing on a podium and congratulates him.

In 2000, *Fantasia* was restored and reconstructed to its original 124-minute roadshow version for the the film's 60th anniversary DVD release which accompanied the DVD, VHS release of *Fantasia 2000*.

Writing in the November 14, 1940, *New York Times* critic Bosley Crowther raved about *Fantasia* calling it "terrific."

> Let us agree, as did almost every one present on the occasion, that the sly and whimsical papa of Mickey Mouse, Snow White, Pinocchio and a host of other cartoon darlings has this time come forth with something which really dumps conventional formulas overboard and boldly reveals the scope of films for imaginative excursion. Let us temperately admit that *Fantasia* is simply terrific—as terrific as anything that has ever happened on a screen. And then let's get on from there. (http://movies.nytimes.com/movie)

FANTASIA 2000 (1999)

PRODUCER/DIRECTOR: James Algar (director), Gaëtan Brizzi (director), Paul Brizzi (director), Hendel Butoy (director), Francis Glebas (director), Eric Goldberg (director), Don Hahn (director), Pixote Hunt (director), Donald W. Ernst (producer)

WRITER(S): Oliver Thomas, Joe Ranft, Elena Driskill, Hans Christian Andersen, Brenda Chapman, Carl Fallberg, Joe Grant, Irene Mecchi, Perce Pearce, David Reynolds, Tom Sito

CAST: Leopold Stokowski (Himself - Conductor), Ralph Grierson (Pianist), Kathleen Battle (Featured Soprano), Steve Martin (Himself - Introductory Host), Itzhak Perlman (Himself - Host), Quincy Jones (Himself - Host), Bette Midler (Herself - Hostess), James Earl Jones

(Himself - Host), Penn Jillette (Himself), Raymond Joseph Teller (Himself - Host), James Levine (Himself - Host), Angela Lansbury (Herself - Hostess), Wayne Allwine (Mickey Mouse), Tony Anselmo (Donald Duck), Russi Taylor (Daisy Duck)

CINEMATOGRAPHY: Tim Suhrstedt

MUSIC: "Symphony No. 5," directed by Pixote Hunt, composed by Beethoven; "Pines of Rome," directed by Hendel Butoy, composed by Respighi; "Rhapsody in Blue," directed by Eric Goldberg, composed by Gershwin; "Piano Concerto No. 2, Allegro, Opus 102," directed by Mr. Butoy, composed by Shostakovich; "Carnival of the Animals," directed by Mr. Goldberg, composed by Saint-Saens; "The Sorcerer's Apprentice," directed by James Algar, composed by Paul Dukas; "Pomp and Circumstance, Marches 1, 2, 3, and 4," directed by Francis Glebas, composed by Edward Elgar; "Firebird Suite, 1919 Version," directed by Gaetan Brizzi and Paul Brizzi, composed by Stravinsky; host sequences directed by Don Hahn. Music conducted by James Levine, performed by the Chicago Symphony Orchestra.

LENGTH AND RATING: 75 min; G

The film's United States premiere was on December 17, 1999, and was released to IMAX theaters on January 1, 2000 with a nationwide release to standard equipped theaters on June 16, 2000. Most of the music was conducted by James Levine and the Chicago Symphony Orchestra with the exception of "Rhapsody in Blue" and "The Sorcerer's Apprentice." For this production, "The Sorcerer's Apprentice" was the only sequence used from the 1940 version. Like the original, the film featured works by classical composers; Beethoven, Shostakovich, Stravinsky, and the more modern Gershwin.

Indeed, the most popular segment from *Fantasia 2000* was the animated sequence for *Rhapsody in Blue*. Featuring the music of George Gershwin, the segment opens with Duke, an African-American construction worker asleep in bed. He looks at his alarm clock and he realizes he's late for work. Grabbing his drumsticks, he darts down the stairs, knocks over a cat gleefully slurping from bottles of just-delivered milk, grabs a donut from a woman sitting by an open ground-floor window about to bite into it, and hitches a ride on the back of a newspaper delivery truck, which dumps a bundle of newspapers with a headline that reads, "Jobs Scarce," setting the narrative for New York City during the Depression. The next scene shows Joe sitting at a diner counter having time to drink numerous refills of coffee while the city rushes to work outside the large window. Reaching into his pockets for money to pay for the coffee he turns the empty lining inside out, but as the man sitting next to him puts on his coat a coin drops from his sleeve on to the counter and Joe leaves it there, exiting the diner. Other segments include the more affluent rushing out en masse from their luxury building, running over the doorman, and traveling like a herd in the subway to work.

In a tribute to the way parents overschedule their childen for extracurricular activities today, there's a scene of a governess dragging her charge, Rachel, from ballet lessons to vocal class, swimming lessons, painting, gymnastics, tennis, and piano.

Another beautifully metaphorical scene accompanied by the Gerhwin score depicts Rachel the overscheduled little girl, Joe the down-and-out coffee drinker, Duke the African-American construction worker, and John a henpecked wealthy husband waiting for his wife to buy items for her little dog in a fancy pet store; all are dreaming about ice-skating. Rachel happily dreams of skating, with her parents holding her hands; Joe dreams of gleefully spinning on the ice dressed in a shirt and tie, punching a time-clock, and scraping a dollar sign onto the ice; Duke conjures images of performing on his drums while ice skating; and John envisions himself skating joyously into the clouds dressed in a tuxedo, in a graceful acrobatic performance—until he is presented with a bill from the pet shop. This is followed by a serendipitous confluence of events, taking us back to reality; Duke, at work on a building site, looks at his drumsticks and jackhammer and discards the latter, which flies through the air and lands in Joe's arms; Joe is subsequently pulled in by the construction foreman to work the night shift. As he ascends on the up elevator, Duke descends on the down elevator, rushing away with his drumsticks. Then the little girl Rachel struggles with her governess, by an open hi-rise window, and drops her ball. She races down to retrieve it on the busy street and is rescued from the traffic by her parents. Now on the job site, Joe lowers a crane hook that accidently ensnares John's wife, lifting her away as he is laden with boxes from the pet shop. Peeking from behind the boxes and noticing that his wife is gone, he sees a flyer taped to a lightpost saying ""Harlem Jazz Talent Night Every Friday." The two men, Duke and John, both perform at the club; Duke plays drums, while John performs with the chorus girls; Rachel is happily reunited with her parents, and Joe is working in construction.

Commenting about the animation for *Rhapsody in Blue,* Eric Goldberg, the director spoke about how New York embraces all types of people.

> New York embraces all types of people, and they're all walking the streets at the same time, explains Eric. "How people of such diverse backgrounds affect one another when they live so closely together really interested me. We devised a story where they all help each other achieve their goals—without ever realizing that they're helping one another. *Rhapsody* has always been one of my favorite pieces of classical music; and the combination of Hirschfeld and Gershwin to evoke 1930's New York seemed like a real winner. (http://www.awn.com/mag/issue4.09/ 4.09pages/solomonrhapsody.php3)

In his December 31, 1999, *New York Times* review of *Fantasia 2000* Stephen Holden criticized the film writing that it had, "the feel of a giant corporate promotion."

> From the movie's wraparound Imax images to its hosts (Steve Martin, Itzhak Perlman, Quincy Jones, Bette Midler, James Earl Jones, Penn and Teller, Angela Lansbury and James Levine) who introduce the segments, "Fantasia/2000" often has the feel of a giant corporate promotion whose stars are there simply to hawk the company's wares. As smooth as these introductions are, they give the film a choppy momentum and only underscore the grandiosity of the idea of "improving" mass culture by wedding classical music and animation. (http://movies.nytimes.com/movie)

CHOCOLAT (2000)

PRODUCER/DIRECTOR: Lasse Hallström (director), Kit Golden (producer), Leslie Holleran (producer)

WRITER(S): Joanne Harris (novel) ,Robert Nelson Jacobs (screenplay)

CAST: Juliette Binoche (Vianne Rocher), Johnny Depp (Roux), Lena Olin (Josephine Muscat), Judi Dench (Armande Voizin), Alfred Molina (Comte De Reynaud), Carrie-Anne Moss (Caroline Clairmont), Aurelien Parent Koenig (Luc Clairmont), Antonio Gil-Martinez

(Jean-Marc Drou), Helene Cardona (Francoise Drou), Harrison Pratt (Dedou Drou), Gaelan Connell (Didi Drou)
CINEMATOGRAPHY: Roger Pratt
MUSIC: Rachel Portman
LENGTH AND RATING: 121 min; PG-13

This film begins like a fairy tale with a voice-over that describes the French village that provides the setting. "Once upon a time there was a quiet little village in the French countryside whose people believed in tranquility." As the camera slowly zooms in on the tops of the roofs of the village homes, it visually gives the impression of a Hansel and Gretel fantasy. The voice-over and the first scene of the villagers attending church services in preparation for Lent provide the exposition. The narrator entones, "…you knew your place in the scheme of things and if you happened to forget someone would help remind you."

As the Catholic priest preaches about the meaning of Lent and the abstinence required, the sound of wind increases, the flame on the church candles flicker, and two people, a mother and child dressed in red cloaks (Little Red Riding Hood), are trudging on a wintry path toward the village. Then the camera quickly zooms in from an aerial view, the sound of the wind eerily increasing and the flames on the candles dancing, the exterior image of the village swirling in circles and the wind blowing the large double doors of the church open. The sound and the imagery add to the sense of a fable that is about to unfold.

The north wind blows in a beautiful creature, Vianne (Juliette Binoche) and her young daughter Anouk (Victoire Thivisol). She rents a former patisserie from the gruff old woman Armande Voizin (Judi Dench) and opens a very special chocolate shop. However, her chocolate is laced with a mild dose of chili pepper, a secret ingredient that has an amorous and beguiling effect on the repressed townspeople of the village, who fear their autocratic mayor Comte De Reynaud (Alfred Molina), who writes the sermons for their priest, Pere Henri (Hugh O'Conor) and tells them how to behave. He is also battling with the reality that his wife has left him, although he attempts to cover it up by telling everyone of her sojourn in Venice, Italy.

The combination of chocolate and Vianne's free-wheeling determination to be independent and reach out to the people of the community is a challenge to De Reynaud's autocratic leadership. Her honesty and unabashed emotions bring people in the village together, like the elderly widow Mme. Audel (Leslie Caron), who is mourning her husband's death in World War I (the movie is set in the 1950s), and Guillaume Blerot (John Wood), who has for years admired her from afar. With a little coaxing from Vianne and a gift of her chocolate the two become a couple. In another instance, a woman buys some chocolate-covered nuts but, thinking they would have no amorous effect on her negligent husband, she tosses them into the garbage, missing the opening. Her husband finds the nuts, eats them, and is consumed with passion. Concerned about a wife's loveless marriage, Vianne becomes the protector of Josephine Muscat (Lena Olin), who leaves her abusive, drunken husband, Serge (Peter Stormare). And, her good nature and understanding melts the heart of Armande, and Vianne arranges for her to see her estranged grandson Luc Clairmont (Aurelien Parent Koenig).

The film clearly articulates the forces of good and evil and the efforts by De Reynaud to put Vianne out of business. When a group of gypsies led by Roux (Johnny Depp) docks their houseboat on the village shore, De Reynaud begins a morality campaign. In his effort, the misguided Serge sets the gypsy boats on fire after a birthday party celebration for Armande, nearly killing Anouk and Josephine. After Roux leaves, Vianne once again packs her bags but Anouk protests and the urn possessing her mother's ashes smashes to the ground. At that moment she realizes that she must stay in the village and resist De Reynaud. When she enters the kitchen she sees a number of townspeople whom she has helped, preparing chocolate for the festival. That night De Reynaud sneaks into the shop with a large knife and smashes the chocolate displays in the window. After tasting the chocolate he becomes "drunk" with "positive energy" and the next morning apologizes to Vianne, allows Pere Henri to preach his own sermon, and joins in the celebration at the chocolate festival. At the end of the movie Roux returns to be with Juliette and Anouk.

This film is a charming adult fairy tale about people's longings, fufillment, independence, and humanity. It evokes lessons as in an Aesop's fables, which are enduring and timeless. In setting the film in a small French village in the 1950s, director Lasse Hallstrom enables the audience to view the story in the simplistic venue of a small town that is a microcosm of society. The film's virtue is that unlike De Reynaud it doesn't preach but uses the beauty and heart of Vianne and her chocolate to release the passion and joie de vivre that the villagers harbor in their souls. *Chocolat* is a film that resonates with a fourth-dimension sensibility that offers an ode to the Greek gods of happiness and joy.

In his December 15, 2000, *New York Times* review of *Chocolat*, Elvis Mitchell writes that the movie is a "crowd-pleaser."

> If "Chocolat" sounds like a dangerous combination of stories—"Like Water for Footloose"—there's nothing dangerous about it. The director, Lasse Hallstrom, has an almost supernatural faith in his ability to pull the movie off, and darned if he doesn't. This crowd-pleaser is the feature-film version of milk chocolate: an art house movie for people who don't like art house movies. That's hardly a compliment (http://movies.nytimes.com/movie).

In his review of *Chcolat*, Roger Ebert writes, "The movie is charming and whimsical, and Binoche reigns as a serene and wise goddess." (http://rogerebert.suntimes.com)

MOULIN ROUGE (2001)

PRODUCER/DIRECTOR: Baz Luhrmann (director), Baz Luhrmann (producer), Fred Baron (producer), Martin Brown (producer)

WRITER(S): Baz Luhrmann, Craig Pearce

CAST: Nicole Kidman (Satine), Ewan McGregor (Christian), John Leguizamo (Henri de Toulouse-Lautrec), Jim Broadbent (Zidler), Richard Roxburgh (Duke of Worcester), Garry McDonald (The Doctor), Jacek Koman (The Unconscious Argentinean), Matthew Whittet (Satie), Kerry Walker (Marie), Caroline O'Connor (Nini Legs in the Air), David Wenham (Audrey), Christine Anu (Arabia), Natalie Mendoza (China Doll)

CINEMATOGRAPHY: Donald McAlpine

MUSIC: Craig Armstrong

LENGTH AND RATING: 127 min; PG-13

There is a sense of déjà vu when watching director Baz Luhrmann's period musical *Moulin Rouge*. It's a familiar love story that is part of the cultural mythology of Paris and its attraction to young creative artists. In *Moulin Rouge*, Christian (Ewan McGregor) is a British writer who in 1899 settles in Montmarte, Paris, wanting to write about love, something he knows nothing about. He meets a group of eccentric bohemians and becomes a writer for their show called "Spectacular, Spectacular." He of course falls in love with Satine (Nicole Kidman), one of the dancers, and a courtesan in the Moulin Rouge who will also have the lead in the show. However, the love story is complicated by characters and events that determine the conflict in the plot.

Moulin Rouge begins as a flashback to 1900, a year after Christian arrives in Montmarte as he struggles to write his tragic love story. As the curtain rises the audience is introduced to a bevy of eccentric, bohemian characters that Christian befriends, including Toulouse-Lautrec (John Leguizamo). As Christian impresses them with his songwriting talent (the movie uses traditional and pop songs, including The Beatles, Billy Joel, and others) he is hired, with the approval of Harold Zidler (Jim Broadbent), owner of the Moulin Rouge, to write the "Spectacular, Spectacular" show which will star Satine (Nicole Kidman). Needing the support of a wealthy benefactor, Zidler uses Satine as bait to attract the wealthy and lascivious Duke of Worcester (Richard Roxburgh) as an investor. Through a confluence of circumstances, Satine mistakes Christian for the Duke and they fall in love with each other. However, the jealous Duke, who has been unable to seduce Satine, threatens to withdraw his financial support and have Christian killed unless she has a private dinner with him. Enraged, Zidler forbids her to see Christian again. In the interim, Zidler, who has seen Satine coughing up blood, learns that she has tuberculosis. Finally, Satine has the private dinner with the Duke but rejects the wealth and comfort he offers her for Christian's love. After Zidler tells her of her terminal condition, Satine confronts Christian, telling him that she lied about loving him in an effort to have him leave Paris and save him from being killed by the Duke. Instead, Christian confronts Satine on stage as she performs in "Spectacular, Spectacular," taking the place of the hero, and they reconcile, declaring their love. The Duke tries to kill Christian but is thwarted by Zidler and, backstage, Satine dies in Christian's arms. This is the story that Christian is typing as the movie opens with a shot of a proscenium arch with a curtain that opens, reminding the audience that they are back in the theater.

As envisioned by director Baz Luhrmann, his *Moulin Rouge* is like an atom-smasher shooting particles into the air or a high-speed centrifuge spinning into a blur. The resounding energy in the film is unstoppable, with characters and camera in a perpetual state of motion. Everything moves and the close-ups of actors are grotesque or beautiful in a comical Monty Python tribute. The film seems to take on a life of its own as it rushes from scene to scene, using the quick-cutting stylistic virtues of a music video. The color is rich and vibrant, weaving its energy and adding to the visual rhythm of the film. Perhaps it is more performance than story, as Roger Ebert noted in his June 1, 2001, *Chicago Sun-Times* review when he wrote that:

> …while it might be most convenient to see it from the beginning, it hardly makes any difference; walk in at any moment and you'll quickly know who is good and bad, who is in love and why—and then all the rest is song, dance, spectacular production numbers, protestations of love, exhalations of regret, vows of revenge and grand destructive gestures. It's like being trapped on an elevator with the circus. (http://rogerebert.suntimes.com)

In his June 1, 2001, *New York Times* review, Elvis Mitchell describes the film as having "a frenetic influence that seems almost asexual," and calls the directing style obsessive-compulsive:

Mr. Luhrmann's directing style is almost a brand of obsessive-compulsive disorder. He has too much to say and grows faint over the prospect of getting all of the thoughts and ideas and words and production numbers out of his head. (http://www. nytimes.com/2001/05/18/arts/18ROUG.html?ex=1212811200&en=7a915c814ba9)

LORD OF THE RINGS: THE FELLOWSHIP OF THE RING (2001)

PRODUCER/DIRECTOR: Peter Jackson (director), Barrie M. Osborne (producer), Peter Jackson (producer), Fran Walsh (producer), Tim Sanders (producer)

WRITER(S): J. R. R. Tolkien (novel *The Fellowship of the Ring*) Fran Walsh (screenplay), Philippa Boyens screenplay), Peter Jackson (screenplay)

CAST: Elijah Wood (Frodo Baggins), Ian McKellen (Gandalf), Sala Baker (Sauron), Liv Tyler (Arwen), Viggo Mortensen (Aragorn), Sean Astin (Sam), Cate Blanchett (Galadriel), John Rhys Davies (Gimli), Billy Boyd (Peregrin "Pippin" Took), Dominic Monaghan (Meriadock "Merry" Brandybuck), Orlando Bloom (Legolas), Christopher Lee (Saruman), Hugo Weaving (Elrond), Sean Bean (Boromir), Ian Holm (Bilbo Baggins)

CINEMATOGRAPHY: Andrew Lesnie

MUSIC: Howard Shore

LENGTH AND RATING: 178 min; PG-13

This film was the first installment of director Peter Jackson's epic *Lord of the Ring* trilogy based on three novels by J. R. R. Tolkien. Two sequels came later: *Two Towers* (2002) and *Return of the King* (2003). They were filmed simultaneously over the course of 274 days at various locations in New Zealand, including conservation areas and national parks. The film is a technical tour de force, combining live action with computer generated imagery (CGI). Like many action adventure fantasy films, and the theme of the Tolkien books, it is a story about good versus evil and the search for a powerful ring whose owner can destroy the world.

By chance the ring is bequeathed to a young Hobbit, a resident of Middle Earth, named Frodo Baggins (Elijah Wood). He is told of the evil powers bestowed upon the ring by the benevolent wizard Gandalf (Ian McKellan), who ordered that the ring be destroyed. And, as is often the case in so many fantasy action adventure films, the ring must be returned to Mount Doom, in the fire pits of Mordor, for its destruction. However Saruman (Christopher Lee), who covets the ring for his evil purpose, rallies an army of spirits, creatures, and the undead to use every means to get the ring. During his trek to Mordor, Frodo is joined by fellow Hobbits Sam (Sean Astin), Merry (Dominic Monaghan), and Pippin (Billy Boyd). As they are dimunitive in size they are joined by the human warriors, Aragorn (Viggo Mortenson) and Borimor (Sean Bean), along with the Elf archer Legolas (Orlando Bloom) and the dwarf soldier Gimli (John Rhys-Davies), aligned to fight the evil Sauron (Sala Baker).

The battles they endure are monumental, with serpents, a giant ape, and battalions of upright, monster-looking warriors. Those in the audience old enough may remember *The 7th Voyage of Sinbad* (1958), another action adventure film trilogy that includes *The Golden Voyage of Sinbad* (1974) and *Sinbad and the Eye of the Tiger* (1977), which for its time had amazing special effects created by the technical wizard of stop-motion photography, Harry Harryhausen. In *The Seventh Voyage of Sinbad* there is an amazing scene as Sinbad fights a sword-wielding skeleton and then fends off the one-eyed Cyclops. In the film *Jason and the Argonauts* (1963), Harryhausen once again created a masterpiece in the scene known as "The Children of Hydra," a battle between Jason and a legion of armed skeletons.

There was a great deal of anticipation surrounding the release of *Lord of the Ring* because of the enthusiastic fans of the novels. Because it was designed as a blockbuster film series with a global reach, there was a great deal of buzz about the film on the Internet. The expectation was so high that when the first trailer for the film was released online, not in movie theaters, it garnered 1.6 million hits the first day.

Writing about *Lord of the Rings* in the *New York Times* on December 19, 2001, Elvis Mitchell praises the way director Peter Jackson addresses the complex exposition of the story and he noted the film's similarity to other action adventure fantasies:

> Rather than emphasize the similarities to George Lucas's mythology, Mr. Jackson gallops straight through them, trimming away as many of the complications as possible. "Fellowship" may still feel like "Star Wars" and just about every other otherworldly battle epic of the last 30 years—a whopping composite of Christian allegory, Norse mythology and a boys' book of adventure. (http://movies.nytimes.com/movie)

In his review in the *Chicago Sun-Times* on December 19, 2001, Roger Ebert writes about the film's innocence, which belongs to an earlier, gentler time:

> The Ring Trilogy embodies the kind of innocence that belongs to an earlier, gentler time. The Hollywood that made "The Wizard of Oz" might have been equal to it. But "Fellowship" is a film that comes after "Gladiator" and "Matrix," and it instinctively ramps up to the genre of the overwrought special-effects action picture. That it transcends this genre—that it is a well-crafted and sometimes stirring adventure—is to its credit. But a true visualization of Tolkien's Middle-earth it is not. (http://rogerebert.suntimes.com)

No doubt that *Lord of the Rings* has its share of special effects but the story is not driven by them. It is an episodic adventure, not unlike Homer's *Iliad* and *Odyssey* with mystery, magic, and the supernatural that make up the story dynamic. It is stirring and compelling with its own lessons of bravery and heroism.

THE CULTURE OF GANGS

City of God (Cidade de Deus) **(2002)**
Gangs of New York **(2002)**

Although these two films may be distinctive in the treatment of their subject matter, each of the directors, Fernando Meirelles and Martin Scorsese, had a grand vision for the design of his story. Of course, they both address the culture of gangs, corruption, poverty, greed, and government malaise. Thematically, they evoke a time and place that is foreign, both literally and figuratively, to the audience. It is a measure of each director's talent that the authenticity of their films provides a sensuality for their subject matter that lends to each film's realism. In *City of God*, the dusty slum with its unpaved streets is a metaphor for the frustrated lives that are claimed by abject poverty. Poverty is also a theme for *Gangs of New York*, which also addresses religious and ethnic discrimination. Both films deal with gang leadership and the rivalry that it sustains. Each film richly portrays the setting of the action that is like another character in the film. The richness of their production design and the strength of the acting make both films very compelling.

🎥 GANGS OF NEW YORK (2002)

PRODUCER/DIRECTOR: Martin Scorsese (director), Alberto Grimaldi (producer), Harvey
  Weinstein (producer)
WRITER(S): Jay Cocks (story), Jay Cocks (screenplay), Steven Zaillian (screenplay), Kenneth
  Lonergan (screenplay)
CAST: Leonardo DiCaprio (Amsterdam Vallon), Cameron Diaz (Jenny Everdeane), Daniel
  Day-Lewis (William Cutting/"Bill the Butcher"), Jim Broadbent (William "Boss" Tweed),
  John C. Reilly (Happy Jack), Henry Thomas (Johnny Sirocco), Brendan Gleeson (Walter
  "Monk" McGinn), Gary Lewis (McGloin), Stephen Graham (Shang), Eddie Marsan (Kill-
  oran), Alec McCowen (Reverend Raleigh), David Hemmings (Mr. Schermerhorn), Larry
  Gilliard, Jr. (Jimmy Spoils), Cara Seymour (Hell-Cat Maggie), Roger Ashton-Griffiths
  (P. T. Barnum), Liam Neeson (Priest Vallon)
CINEMATOGRAPHY: Michael Ballhaus
MUSIC: Howard Shore
LENGTH AND RATING: 167 min; R

There's a poignant scene in *Gangs of New York* when William (Bill) "the Butcher" Cutting (Daniel Day-Lewis), who is the crime boss of Five Points, an area in nineteenth-
century New York City, enters the bedroom of Amsterdam Vallon (Leonardo DiCaprio)
while he sleeps and sits by his side. After he wakes up, Bill who sustained a shoulder
wound in the process of Amsterdam's thwarting an assassination attempt, speaks about
how he has managed to live to the age of forty-seven and maintain his leadership as a
crime boss. He talks about instilling fear, "a spectacle of fearsome acts," in those who
threaten him; cutting off their hands if they steal from him, cutting out a tongue if
someone offends him, and if someone rises against him he cuts off his head and sticks
it on a pike.

Then he tells Amsterdam about Priest Vallon (Liam Neeson) and how he was the
last honorable man he killed fifteen years ago and the only man worth remembering.
He of course does not know that Amsterdam is Vallon's son, a young boy in 1846 who
witnessed his father's killing. He has returned from an orphanage to avenge his father's
death. However, now Bill and the young man have become close and at the end of the
scene he tells Amsterdam that he never had a son and says, "God bless you," kissing
his hand and placing it on Amsterdam's head.

A leader of the Catholic faith and the "Dead Rabbits," which were the Irish immigrants, Priest Vallon, Amsterdam's father, had battled with Bill, who led the anti-Catholic,
anti-immigrant Nativists over leadership of Five Points and whom Vallon had allowed to
live in shame after brutally beating Bill. But in their final battle Vallon succumbed to Bill
and died from his wounds.

The film also weaves history into the narrative as it portrays the Irish immigrants
landing in New York City, hated by Bill and others who deplored their presence, working for lower wages and "acting" like Americans. The corrupt local government was led
by Boss Tweed (Jim Broadbent) of Tammany Hall, who was aligned with Bill in all

manner of crime and corruption. As the Irish immigrants disembarked from the ships, Tweed's agents signed them into the Democratic party and they could also be conscripted into the Union Army (during the Civil War) if they didn't have three hundred dollars to buy their way out.

Using his friend Johnny Sirocco (Henry Thomas), who has joined with Bill's band of thieves and pickpockets, Amsterdam is introduced to Bill and gains his confidence. He is also attracted to the radiant beauty of Jenny Everdeane (Cameron Diaz), a pickpocket and petty thief who also enjoys the affections of Bill. Planning his assassination of Bill, Amsterdam chooses the holiday Bill created for the death of his father, Priest Vallon, when he appears before the community of Five Point for his traditional toast. But he is betrayed by his friend Johnny, who jealously harbors affection for Jenny, causing him to divulge Amsterdam's true identitiy to Bill and forewarning him of Amsterdam's plot.

On the day of the celebration, after goading Amsterdam by using Jenny as his model in a deadly knife-throwing act that superficially injures her throat, he throws a knife at Bill and misses. Bill retaliates by throwing a knife at Amsterdam that lands in his abdomen, and then Bill beats him mercilessly. Bill allows Amsterdam to live because now he is shamed, returning the gesture that Priest Vallon allowed Bill after beating him. In hiding, Jenny nurses Amsterdam back to health and after three months he has gained the loyalty of the Irish who rally around him and confront Bill, in a redux of the opening scene of the movie. However, on the day of the battle the New York draft riots of 1863 (July 11–16) break out. A large group of people rally against conscription but soon the demonstration degrades into destruction of homes and property and racial hatred against blacks. A large number of black people are murdered during the riot.

As their gangs faced off in Paradise Square, Bill and Amsterdam confronted each other just as the military enforced order by firing into crowds and bombarding the city with artillery from naval vessels offshore. Chaos soon ensued and in the lingering dust and smoke the two men fought alone when Bill realized that he had sustained a life-threatening wound from a piece of shrapnel and doesn't resist the final thrust of Amsterdam's knife.

In *Gangs of New York*, the audience bears witness to a New York City that is riddled with crime, corruption, and lawlessness. The streets are not paved with gold, but instead offer its struggling denizens survival by obeying the rule of law as imposed by Bill "the Butcher" and Boss Tweed. The plotting and deal-making offer a stark realism amidst the chaotic culture of the city. It's a place that reeks with the stench of human detritus as the poor endure the competition of "survival of the fittest." History engulfs the players, Bill and Amsterdam, as they move through its streets and catacombs in a pas de deux toward death.

In A. O. Scott's December 20, 2001, *New York Times* review of *Gangs of New York*, he writes that "...Mr. Scorsese has made a near great movie."

> And in recreating it, Mr. Scorsese has made a near-great movie. His interest in violence, both random and organized, is matched by his love of street-level spectacle. (http://movies.nytimes.com/movie)

In his January 5, 2003, *New York Observer* review, Andrew Sarris describes the deadly force and fury of the film:

The result reverberates on the screen with a deadly force and fury more intense than anything Mr. Scorsese has yet achieved on the meanest and most beloved streets he could imagine or recall. (http://www.observer.com/node/46937)

🎥 *CITY OF GOD* (2002)

PRODUCER/DIRECTOR: Fernando Meirelles (co-director), Kátia Lund (director), Mauricio Andrade Ramos (producer), Andrea Barata Ribeiro (producer)

WRITER(S): Paulo Lins (novel), Bráulio Mantovani (screenplay)

CAST: Alexandre Rodrigues (Buscapé—Rocket), Leandro Firmino (Zé Pequeno—Li'l Zé as Leandro Firmino da Hora), Phellipe Haagensen (Bené—Benny), Douglas Silva (Dadinho—Li'l Dice), Jonathan Haagensen (Cabeleira—Shaggy), Matheus Nachtergaele (Sandro Cenoura—Carrot), Seu Jorge (Mané Galinha—Knockout Ned), Jefechander Suplino (Alicate—Clipper)

CINEMATOGRAPHY: César Charlone

MUSIC: Ed Cortês , Antonio Pinto

LENGTH AND RATING: 130 min; R

In *City of God* Fernando Meirelles presents a disturbing portrait of crime, poverty, gang rivalry, and corruption in Brazil. The area known in Portugese as "Cidade de Deus" is west of Rio de Janeiro and its upscale hotels and beaches. It's a harsh story about

Douglas Silva (as Little Dice). [Miramax Films/Photofest]

young people, from grade school to teenagers, caught in a spiral of never-ending poverty in a dusty, dirty slum. The film portrays the environment as an "open city" with children carrying weapons and commiting crimes. Their aspirations are defined by the macho image of a gun-toting gangster determined to make their reputation on murder and theft.

It begins with one of the last scenes in the movie when Ze Pequeno, known as Li'l Ze (Leandro da Hora), a reigning gang leader in the "City of God," is butchering chickens and a lone bird manages to escape, which results in a funny chase as he orders his minions to get the chicken that eludes them as they fire their weapons at it. They suddenly come face to face with Buscape (Alexandre Rodrigues), whose nickname is Rocket. Their guns are drawn and Rocket stops and freezes, exchanging gazes with the gang.

Then the movie flashes back ten years to a trio of friends, "The Tender Trio," thus providing the exposition of the story. The group, which includes Rocket's brother Goose, commits crimes, sometimes sharing the loot with the community, for example, distributing canisters of propane gas after hijacking the delivery truck. They are convinced by the young hanger-on Li'l Dice (Douglas Silva) and Rocket's friend to hold up a local motel that serves as a brothel and he is relegated to act as lookout and shoot a window as a warning to the trio when the police arrive. Consumed with a passion to prove his manhood, and unbeknownst to the trio, after Li'l Dice shoots the window as a warning he goes on a murderous killing spree, executing several patrons of the brothel. Hunted by the police, the Trio splits up and Li'l Dice flees the community and with his friend Benny (Phellipe Haagensen) becomes a thief. Confronted by Goose for his share of the brothel loot, Li'l Dice kills him, providing further evidence of his psychopathic cold-blooded nature.

The film moves ahead ten years to when the drug culture of marijuana, cocaine, and heroin has invaded the streets of the slum and rival gangs fight for supremacy of the trade. In a bid toward gang supremacy, Li'l Ze (Leandro Firmino da Hora) kills the current drug lord and assumes leadership of the trade. His only rival is Carrot (Matheus Nachtergaele), whom he wants to kill, but his friend Benny, a popular figure bcause of his friendly nature and benevolence, deters him.

Using a hand-held camera and mostly non-professional actors, the gritty realism evokes a physicality that nurtures the sensory experience of the film. When the gangs battle each other the brutality is magnified by intimate cinema verite style of filming. The harsh life and instinct for survival penetrates even those who attempt to live above the violence and crime. When Li'l Ze notices a pretty girl dancing with her boyfriend, Mane Galinha, "Knockout Ned" (Seu George) at a party, he forces him to dance with his buttocks exposed and then rapes his girlfriend. Later in the evening he visits Ned's home and kills his brother and other relatives. Consumed with rage and revenge, Ned, who was never a criminal, joins Carrot's gang, robbing gun stores and banks to fund their battle with Li'l Ze. This creates an all-out battle between Ned supported by Carrot's gang and Li'l Ze.

As an aspiring photographer, Rocket has taken a job helping to deliver newspapers and by chance is designated the official photographer of Li'l Ze's gang. His photographs of the street fighting in the City of God slum are eventually published in the newspaper. In the chicken scene, reprised toward the end of the film, Rocket freezes, not knowing how Li'l Ze will react to the published picures. However, the gang leader is pleased and asks that he photograph him and his troops. As they pose, Ned, along with

Carrot's gang, appears and a fight starts, which is broken up by the police. Running for cover, Rocket photographs the action and then follows the police van, which is holding Li'l Ze. In a deserted area, Rocket hides and photographs Li'l Ze's pay off to the police and his release. He also captures the murder of Li'l Ze by the "Runts," a group of young children who want to take over the drug trade. They are a pathetic group as they query each other about needed skills, like reading and math, to run their business.

At the newspaper Rocket reviews his images and realizes that the photographs of the police would make him famous but would also pose a threat to his safety. Instead, he chooses to publish the images of Li'l Ze, which he knows will get him a job at the newspaper.

City of God received unanimous reviews for its realism, acting, cinematography, and narrative sructure. Writing in the *New York Times* on January 17, 2003, Stephen Holden notes that it's a "powerful movie" reminding "… us that the civilized society we take for granted is actually a luxury" (http://movies.nytimes.com/movie).

And Roger Ebert in his January 24, 2003, *Chicago Sun Times* review wrote, "Breathtaking and terrifying, urgently involved with its characters, it announces a new director of great gifts and passions" (http://rogerebert.suntimes.com/apps/pbcs.dll/article?AID=/20030124/REVIEWS/301240301/1023).

MILLION DOLLAR BABY (2004)

PRODUCER/DIRECTOR: Clint Eastwood (director, producer), Paul Haggis (producer), Tom Rosenberg (producer), Albert S. Ruddy (producer)

WRITER(S): F. X. Toole (stories), Paul Haggis (screenplay)

CAST: Clint Eastwood (Frankie Dunn), Hilary Swank (Maggie Fitzgerald), Morgan Freeman (Eddie Scrap-Iron Dupris), Jay Baruchel (Danger Barch), Mike Colter (Big Willie Little), Lucia Rijker (Billie "The Blue Bear"), Brian F. O'Byrne (Father Horvak), Anthony Mackie (Shawrelle Berry), Margo Martindale (Earline Fitzgerald), Riki Lindhome (Mardell Fitzgerald)

CINEMATOGRAPHY: Tom Stern

MUSIC: Clint Eastwood

LENGTH AND RATING: 132 min; PG-13

In his pitch to Warner Brother executives, Clint Eastwood gave an accurate description of his film, *Million Dollar Baby*, when he described it as a father-daughter love story. In the film Frankie Dunn (Clint Eastwood), the owner of a grimy, rundown boxing gym named the "Hit Pit" in Los Angeles, is lost to his own daughter, who returns his letters unopened. He finds a young female boxer, Maggie Fitzgerald (Hilary Swank), whom he first declines to train and then, because of her perseverance and grit, decides to manage her, and she becomes his surrogate daughter.

Both Frankie and Eddie "Scrap Iron" Dupris (Morgan Freeman) are relics from the past. Eddie is a former fighter with one eye who Frankie once managed and who now acts as his conscious, cleans up the gym, and acts as the film's narrator. Set in his ways, Frankie is a cautious man who has slowly been nurturing the career of Big Willie Little (Mike Colter), a heavyweight boxer concerned about bringing him up too fast. The fear of failure and Frank's own insecurity causes Willie to get another manager who arranges a title bout for him which he wins earning him the championship.

Clint Eastwood (as Frankie Dunn), Morgan Freeman (as Eddie Scrap-Iron Dupris), and Hilary Swank (as Maggie Fitzgerald). [Warner Bros./Photofest]

Although he steadfastly refused to train Maggie, she and Scrap prevail upon him and he teaches her the foundations and rhythm of boxing technique, which she learns and puts to use on her opponents in the ring. The two become closer and after a bitter disappointment with her mother and family Maggie realizes that Frankie is the only one who cares about her. He not only teaches her technique but also provides a paternal, loving relationship.

It's not the boxing scenes that make this movie so compelling, but the raw emotional bond that evolves between Frankie and Maggie as they reach the pinnacle of success after touring Europe and returning to the United States. Fighting in England, Frankie gives Maggie a green robe with the Gaelic text "Mo Cuishle" (correct Gaelic spelling Chuisle), which he declines to translate. Soon, the fans chant the motto and it stays with Maggie for the rest of her fights.

When Maggie finally gets a title match against Billie the Blue Bear (Lucia Rijker, a woman boxer), she performs admirably but after the bell rings Billie assaults her and Maggie loses her balance, hitting her head on the corner stool as she falls to the ground. The result is a massive spinal cord injury that turns her into a "frozen" quad. Distraught, Frankie tries to find doctors who can treat her but all have the same dismal diagnosis. He visits her and reads from a poem by Yeats, "The Lake Isle of Innisfree." He vents his grief on Scrap by faulting him for urging that he take Maggie on as a fighter. He is overcome with the request she makes that he end her life, which for Frankie means the loss of someone else that he loves. She pleads with him not to let her lie in bed until she can't hear the fans chanting her name anymore. Deciding to grant Maggie's wish he visits her bedside and in a poignant scene tells her that "Mo Cuishle" means, "my darling, my blood." He disconnects Maggie from the ventilator, injects her with adrenalin, and walks out of the nursing facility and never returns to the "Hit Pit."

In his December 15, 2004, *New York Times* review of *Million Dollar Baby*, A. O. Scott refers to the film's "unassuming naturalism and emotional directness."

> With its careful, unassuming naturalism, its visual thrift and its emotional direct-ness, "Million Dollar Baby" feels at once contemporary and classical, a work of utter mastery that at the same time has nothing in particular to prove. (http://movies.nytimes.com)

While *Million Dollar Baby* uses a boxing theme to address the overwhelming odds of achieving fame and fortune for someone like Maggie Fitzgerald, it is nevertheless a profoundly meaningful film about relationships, isolation, and loneliness. In today's high-tech marketplace of Internet and speed-dating, emphasis on youth and celebrity culture, it measures the worth of people, stripping them down to the bare essentials and revealing the essence of who they are.

DECEPTION AND OBSESSION

Bad Education (La mala educacion) (2004)
Volver (2006)

In the world of the Spanish film director Pedro Almodovar, there are references both subtly nuanced and strategically placed that reflect on his past working with women at the Telofonica telephone company in Madrid, Spain, and his education at a strict Cath-olic school. With no formal training in film but a keen sense for sound and image, he has the uncanny ability to express the rhythm and imagery of his characters on the screen. He is also a product of both nontraditional filmmakers like John Waters and those who embraced the Hollywood culture such as Alfred Hitchcock. Indeed, *Bad Edu-cation*, a film noir, has roots in Hitchcock's *Vertigo*. There is even a similarity in the opening credits of both films, with the camera in *Vertigo* zooming in on a woman's lips, then moving to her eyes with a close-up of her right eye bathed in a red hue. This is followed by a spiraling phantasm that begins in the pupil of her eye and moves to the screen, gradually transforming it into different geometric patterns, shapes, and colors. The haunting score by Bernard Herrmann featuring violins also lends to the anticipa-tion of what is to follow. In Almodovar's *Bad Education*, red, black, gray, and white geo-metric patterns glide from different directions on and off the screen, floating on a bold canvas that gradually reveals a variety of images, including a crucifix, a partial shot of a face from the nose to the eyes bathed in a red hue, strips of celluloid, and the out-lines of different characters, with all of the images pigmented with rich colors. The accompanying music by Alberto Iglesias features a powerful beat that portends evil.

BAD EDUCATION (LA MALA EDUCACION) (2004)

PRODUCER/DIRECTOR: Pedro Almodóvar (director), Agustín Almodóvar Pedro Almodóvar (producer)

WRITER(S): Pedro Almodóvar

CAST: Gael Garcia Bernal (Angel/Juan/Zahara), Fele Martinez (Enrique Goded), Javier Camara (Paquito), Daniel Gimenez Cacho (II) (Father Manolo), Lluis Homar

(Mr. Berenguer), Francisco Boira (Ignacio), Francisco Maestre (Father Jose), Juan Fernandez (Martin), Nacho Perez (Ignacio Kid), Raul Garcia Forneiro (Enrique Kid), Alberto Ferreiro (Enrique Serrano), Petra Martinez (Ignacio's Mother)
CINEMATOGRAPHY: José Luis Alcaine
MUSIC: Alberto Iglesias
LENGTH AND RATING: 106 min; R

Just as in *Vertigo*, the characters in *Bad Education* are not always who they appear to be as the film explores the themes of deception, obsession, transexuality, homosexuality, and drug use. Two young boys, Ignacio (Nacho Perez) and Enrique (Raul Garcia Forneiro), attend a strict Catholic boarding school during the time that dictator Generalissimo Francisco Franco ruled Spain and are attracted to each other as their sexuality begins to flourish. However, Father Manolo (Daniel Gimenez Cacho), a Catholic priest and the principal of the school, also desires Ignacaio and eventually expels Enrique, ridding himself of the competition. Time advances to the eighties, and Enrique (Fele Martinez) is now a successful film director struggling to find a subject for his next movie and he is visited by someone claiming to be Ignacio (Gael Garcia Bernal), an actor who has written a story entitled "The Visit," which he hopes will be adapted into a screenplay. It's about Igancio's experiences in Catholic school being abused by Father Manolo and his relationship with Enrique. However, Ignacio demands to play the part of Zahara, a transsexual prostitute who poses as Ignacio's sister to blackmail Father Manolo.

Seeing Ignacio after so many years Enrique is troubled by his appearance as it does not coincide with his recollection. Also, Ignacio insists on being called Angel, and even when he shaves off his beard he still doesn't resemble the Ignacio that Enrique went to school with. But Enrique is intrigued with the story and, as the plot visually unfolds, the audience sees scenes from the movie as Enrique envisions them with Angel (Ignacio) playing the role of Zahara.

Soon Enrique and Angel are involved in a passionate affair, but Enrique suspects that Angel is not Ignacio. In a visit to Ignacio's mother, he learns that his friend from school died several years before and that Juan, his younger brother, is impersonating him. He continues the ruse by allowing Juan to portray Ignacio in the film. After a particularly emotional scene is shot where Father Manolo's fellow priest murders Ignacio to stop the blackmailing, Angel who is really Juan, breaks down.

In a surprising twist the set is visited by Manuel Berenguer (Lluis Homar), the real Father Manolo, who has since left the priesthood. He tells Enrique that he paid blackmail to the real Ignacio, and soon he and Juan had an affair. Both realized that each would gain from Igancio's death; Manuel would end the blackmailing and Juan would be rid of his selfish brother, a heroin addict who refused to pay his school tuition. He is murdered when Juan provides Ignacio with a particularly pure form of heroin.

Following the traditions of classic film noir Pedro Almodovar's *Bad Education* sustains the virtues of this classic form by capturing the suspicions, intrigue, plot twists, passion, and obsession that are fundamental to this genre. The story is a puzzle that the viewer must help to unravel by paying close attention to the nuance of dialogue and character behavior. It effectively draws the audience into a complex narrative that twists and turns evoking surprise and confusion. It is a reinterpretation of a classic cinematic tradition that reflects modern morality and questions long held cultural mores. Writing in the *New York Times* on November 19, 2004, Stephen Holden wrote about Almodovar's understanding of film noir, "Mr. Almodóvar, unlike other filmmakers who lose their bearings, fully understands the degree to which film noir is synonymous with fantasy and a primal longing for the forbidden."

He also wrote about Almodovar's delirious reinvention of the style: "*Bad Education* is a delirious, headlong immersion and reinvention of a style that has lured countless filmmakers onto its treacherous shoals" (http://movies.nytimes.com).

VOLVER (2006)

PRODUCER/DIRECTOR: Pedro Almodóvar (director), Agustin Almodóvar (producer)
WRITER(S): Pedro Almodóvar
CAST: Penélope Cruz (Raimunda), Carmen Maura (Irene), Lola Duénas (Sole), Blanca Portillo (Augustina), Yohana Cobo (Paula), Chus Lampreave (Tia Paula), Antonio de la Torre (Paco), Carlos Blanco (Emilio)
CINEMATOGRAPHY: José Luis Alcaine
MUSIC: Alberto Iglesias
LENGTH AND RATING: 121 min; R

In the film *Volver* director Pedro Almodovar once again flouts convention by telling a woman-centered story about love, death, guilt, infidelity, betrayal, and murder conceptualized within a culture of the spritual world. In this film Almodovar embraces some of the stylistic and narrative foundations of Federico Fellini.

The story is about two sisters, Raimunda (Penelope Cruz) and Sole (Lola Duenas), who lost their mother and father in a tragic fire, or at least they think they did. In the opening scene, the two sisters along with Raimunda's daughter Paula (Yohana Cobo) are at a cemetery cleaning and polishing the headstone of their parents. While there they meet their friend Augustina (Blanca Portillo) who is visiting her future gravesite. She lives next door to their elderly aunt Tia Paula and helps to care for her and is searching for her mother who disappeared on the same day that Raimunda's parents were killed.

After visiting their aunt, Tia Paula (Chus Lampreave), who is living in their mother Irene's home, the audience is given a hint of what is to develop when Sole goes upstairs and smells the handlebars of an exercise bike. Soon their elderly aunt dies, and Sole attends the funeral on her own because Raimunda is handling a major crisis, the murder of her husband Paco (Antonio de la Torre) by her daughter Paula. He was stabbed with a long kitchen knife when he attempted to rape his daughter. Soon, however the audience learns that Paula is not his daughter. The two women clean the blood and move the body to a restaurant, where it's dumped into a freezer. A neighbor Emilio (Carlos Blanco), attracted to Raimunda, has entrusted her with the keys to his restaurant while he's on business in Madrid so that she can show it to prospective renters.

Attending the funeral, Sole learns from Augustina of the rumors about Irene (Carmen Maura), her dead mother's appearance as a spirit, and that she heard her aunt talking with her. Driving home alone after the funeral there is a knocking sound coming from the car; when Sole opens the trunk, she finds her mother Irene inside. Her mother, who is obviously not dead, reassures the frightened Sole that she means no harm. So, Irene stays with Sole posing as a Russian helping her with her illegal home hair-dressing business. They, of course, try to hide her presence from Raimunda, Every time she visits, Sole announces her presence by shouting out Raimunda's name. It gives the story a more light-hearted touch. So, the two sisters are hiding something from each other—the disappearance of Raimunda's husband Paco and the appearance of their mother Irene.

In the interim, a film producer has hired Raimunda to feed his crew, and she must hustle to buy everything she needs to serve them although she's short on cash. Banding together with her fellow women who have shopped and who contribute pork, dessert, and other food-stuffs on credit, Raimunda promises to pay them the next day. In another funny scene, Raimunda and her prostitute friend rent a van and haul the freezer containing Paco's body to a dump, dig a large grave, drop it in, and cover it up.

On another visit to Sole to pick up Paula who has discovered the secret of her grandmother, Raimunda sniffs the air and smells the familiar odor of her mother's farts and soon discovers her hiding under a bed. Eventually, the secret of Raimunda is told of how she was raped by her father (who is Paula's father) and then sent to live with her aunt. Her mother expresses her sorrow for Raimunda's ordeal and tells her how much she loves her. It was not Irene who died in the blaze, but Augustina's mother, who was having an affair with Irene's husband.

In *Volver*, men have no significant presence, they are tolerated but are usually a hindrance. All of the female characters are alone or had men that were insignificant. The women are comrades forming a sisterhood that help each other. The film articulates the empowerment of women as more than equal to men. In his November 3, 2006, review of *Volver* in the *New York Times*, Stephen Holden wrote about the "breathtaking ease and self-confidence" of the director. He also noted how Almodovar drew on classic Hollywood films:

> Drawing on influences ranging from Latin American telenovelas to classic Hollywood weepies and on an iconography of female endurance that includes Anna Magnani and Joan Crawford, Mr. Almodóvar has made yet another picture that moves beyond camp into a realm of wise, luxuriant humanism.

LOST IN TRANSLATION (2003)

PRODUCER/DIRECTOR: Sofia Coppola (director), Sofia Coppola (producer), Ross Katz (producer)
WRITER(S): Sofia Coppola
CAST: Scarlett Johansson (Charlotte), Bill Murray (Bob Harris), Giovanni Ribisi (John), Anna Faris (Kelly), Akiko Takeshita (Ms Kawasaki), Kazuyoshi Minamimagoe (Press Agent), Kazuko Shibata (Press Agent), Take (Press Agent), Ryuichiro Baba (Concierge), Akira Yamaguchi (Bellboy), Catherine Lambert (Jazz Singer)
CINEMATOGRAPHY: Lance Acord
MUSIC: Kevin Shields
LENGTH AND RATING: 102 min; R

Lost in Translation is a beautiful film with stunning cinematography, music, and sound that enhances every scene and charming performances by Bill Murray and Scarlett

Johansson. Although it may appear as a simple story of a young married woman who strikes up a relationship with an older American married movie star in Tokyo, there is a great deal of depth, passion, and longing to the story.

In Japan to do a Santory whiskey commercial, Bob Harris (Bill Murray) is a movie star whose career is in decline and who is remorseful about earning two million dollars for doing the commercial … he'd rather be in a play. He meets Charlotte (Scarlett Johansson), first exchanging looks in an elevator where he is the tallest passenger and then in the hotel bar. She has accompanied her husband John (Giovanni Ribisi), a celebrity photographer who rushes in and out of her life… scarcely noticing her.

The two are lost in Tokyo, emotionally and culturally, trying to get their bearings in a foreign city and their lives. For Bob it is a "fight or flight" reaction to his marriage, and he chose to run. He has left his wife and children, ostensibly to make a buck, but really to get his bearings. However, Japan's culture and the language barrier are equally unsettling. Everyone bows politely and he's treated with great respect, but just like his marriage, his interactions with the Japanese are not grounded. He appears to float in a dreamscape of innocuous experiences in a surreal landscape designed by Ridley Scott.

On the set filming the commercial, the director provides long discursive Japanese instructions that are translated to a few brief words by the interpreter that confounds Bob. As a gesture of polite gratitude his host sends a prostitute to Bob's room and she comes to his bed, shows her leg, and says "lick my stocking." He finally figures out that she means "rip my stocking" and, in a very funny scene as he resists her entreaties, they roll around on the floor. He is also being pursued by his wife who is redecorating their home and sends him faxes and swatches of fabric to choose from. He can't seem to sleep and spends a great deal of time sipping whiskey in the hotel bar.

Like Bob, Charlotte also seems lost with no professional goals and a marriage that is floundering because of neglect. She like Bob is also searching for someone or something to help ground her. The two finally meet in the hotel bar and immediately sense each other's needs, beginning a sincere friendship. Together, they explore Tokyo, which becomes an adventure as they party with young Japanese, joining them in using drugs and performing Karaoke. They watch old movies together sharing a bed and discuss life, marriage, children, and careers. Although there is a physical attraction between Bob and Charlotte, they never consummate the relationship in that way. There is sexual tension, however, which becomes evident when Bob wakes up in the morning and hears a woman singing in the bathroom. The lounge singer in the bar has spent the night with him; when Charlotte knocks on his door, she also hears the woman and is annoyed and leaves.

They reconcile when the fire alarm in the hotel rings and they meet outside as guests evacuate. Leaving Tokyo in a taxi, Bob suddenly notices Charlotte walking in a crowd. He asks the driver to stop and runs to her calling her name. They kiss and in a long embrace Bob whispers in her ear and then leaves.

In a very expressive way Sofia Coppola, the director of *Lost in Translation* uses the vibrancy of Tokyo, with its cacophony of sound, lighted buildings and facades, and the dizzying effervescence of video and Pachinko parlors to contrast the bland lives of Bob and Charlotte. But along with the personal chemistry nurtured between them they become a couple, away from their respective spouses, finding each other in a strange city.

In his September 12, 2003, *New York Times* review, Elvis Mitchell writes how Sofia Coppola, "thoroughly and touchingly connects the dots between three standards of yearning in movies." He also mentions that the film is "hilarious."

Ms. Coppola's movie also happens to be hilarious—a paean to dislocated people discovering how alive they are when they can barely keep their eyes open. The sexiness comes from the busy, desperate need-to-impress heat of a flirtation, an unrequited love communicated through a filter of sleep deprivation. (http://movies.nytimes.com/movie)

In Roger Ebert's November 12, 2003, *Chicago Sun Times* review, he writes that he loved the movie for several reasons.

I loved the way Coppola and her actors negotiated the hazards of romance and comedy, taking what little they needed and depending for the rest on the truth of the characters. I loved the way Bob and Charlotte didn't solve their problems, but felt a little better anyway. I loved the moment near the end when Bob runs after Charlotte and says something in her ear, and we're not allowed to hear it. (http://rogerebert.suntimes.com)

ETERNAL SUNSHINE OF THE SPOTLESS MIND (2004)

PRODUCER/DIRECTOR: Michel Gondry (director), Anthony Bregman (producer), Steve Golin (producer)

WRITER(S): Charlie Kaufman (story), Michel Gondry (story), Pierre Bismuth (story), Charlie Kaufman (screenplay)

CAST: Jim Carrey (Joel Barish), Kate Winslet (Clementine Kruczynski), Gerry Robert Byrne (Train Conductor), Elijah Wood (Patrick), Thomas Jay Ryan (Frank), Mark Ruffalo (Stan), Jane Adams (Carrie), David Cross (Rob), Kirsten Dunst (Mary), Tom Wilkinson (Dr. Howard Mierzwiak)

CINEMATOGRAPHY: Ellen Kuras

MUSIC: Jon Brion

LENGTH AND RATING: 108 min; R

Like *Lost in Translation, Eternal Sunshine of the Spotless Mind* is also a film about loneliness, longing, and frustrated love. It is also, as Roger Ebert noted a "maze" film, a term that alludes to the nonlinear story arc that at times moves frantically from present, to past, to past imperfect with the added twist of science fiction. Watching the movie is like playing a picture puzzle game matching two identical pictures while trying to find the minutest differences between them. And that's how the first scene in this movie begins as lonely and nerdy Joel Barish (Jim Carrey) blows off work on a winter's day. Instead of taking the Long Island Railroad train to his office, he runs to the opposite platform and takes the train to Montauk, Long Island. Exploring the beach in winter, he meets Clementine Kruczynski (Kate Winslet), a young woman with a lively personality and an engaging presence who dyes her hair different colors and loves adventure.

However, the two have met before and had a relationship for two years that ended badly. Wanting to erase Joel's memory from her mind forever, Celementine visits Dr. Howard Mierzwiak (Tom Wilkinson) at his clinic "Lacuna," which specializes in obliterating memories. After the procedure, Joel tries to apologize to her and delivers a Valentine's Day present to the bookstore where she works but she doesn't recognize him and has a new boyfriend, Patrick (Elijah Wood). Checking his mail, Joel mistakenly gets a card from the clinic indicating that Clementine has erased her memory of him, so he decides to do the same to her. The procedure requires that he bring all objects containing any references to Clementine to the clinic, undergo a brain mapping procedure, and be visited by staff technicians Stan (Mark Rufallo) and Patrick (Elijah Wood) in his home that evening for the erasing of her memory.

As Joel undergoes the procedure, Stan and Patrick make themselves at home in his house. In a weird revelation Patrick tells Stan that when they worked on Clementine he stole a pair of panties from her home and is now having an affair with her. Soon, they are visited by Mary (Kirsten Dunst) the office assistant who is also Stan's girlfriend. Answering a call from Clementine, who is in a panic, Patrick must leave to help her. He is also using materials he has gathered from Joel, including a love letter that Clementine wrote to him in his effort to seduce her. After Patrick leaves, Stan and Mary have an orgy ignoring Joel.

Under sedation and in a REM state, Joel is visually reliving his memories of Clementine including the first day he met her on the beach while visiting friends. He also appears in these memories in his present state and revisits his childhood morphing as an adult into a child with Clementine in his mother's kitchen. The memories visually explode on the screen, taking the audience on a roller-coaster ride through Joel's relationship with Clementine. However, he decides that he cannot part with all of Clementine's memories and struggles to stop the procedure, resulting in a technical malfunction. Upset by this error and responding to Mary's urging, Stan calls Dr. Mierzwiak who arrives and sets things right. However, Mary is attracted to him and they kiss and are interrupted by Mierzwiak's wife who was summoned by Stan. Soon, Dr. Mierzwiak must tell Mary that they had an affair and her memory of it was erased because of his wife's overwrought reaction.

Annoyed, Mary returns to the office and steals the confidential files and sends them, along with the tapes to the clients. The opening scene of the film is reprised and driving with Joel Clementine pops the tape in the cassette player and listens to her complaints about Joel. Upset, he stops the car and she gets out. When Joel returns to his apartment he listens to his tape complaining about Clementine. She appears and listens to some of it and then leaves, saying that any relationship between them could not work. He runs after her and they agree to give it a try one more time.

This film is a surrealistic journey into the mind of Joel Barish as his brain is searched for his lifelong memories, especially those of Clementine. The screenwriter Charlie Kaufman and director Michel Gondry created a visual ballad about longing and desire and how memories play into those feelings. The memories are what trigger the emotional attachment to people, places, and things...a beach, a diary entry, or a photograph. Visually, the film is a stunning voyage that moves the audience through the labyrinths and synapses of Joel's mind. Through his eyes and his memory the film provides a provocative texture of sight and sound.

In his March 19, 2004, *New York Times* review of *Eternal Sunshine of the Spotless Mind* Elvis Mitchell notes the "awe-inspiring piece of visual magic," in some of the scenes.

Mr. Gondry and the superlative cinematographer Ellen Kuras mock the title by setting the film in a wintry suburban New York and using as many available light sources as possible. A shot of Joel and Clem flat on their backs on a frozen lake is an awe-inspiring piece of visual magic, both romantic and conceptual; they'd both like to freeze the moment. It also captures the differences between the two; Clem had to coerce Joel out of his shell, and he doesn't bother to cloak his resentment until he joins her. (http://movies.nytimes.com/movie)

In his review, which appeared on March 19, 2004, in the *Chicago Sun Times*, Roger Ebert wrote that the emotional center of the film makes it work: "Despite jumping through the deliberately disorienting hoops of its story, *Eternal Sunshine* has an emotional center, and that's what makes it work."

He also mentions that the film "is a radical example of Maze Cinema, that style in which the story coils back on itself, redefining everything and then throwing it up in the air and redefining it again" (http://rogerebert.suntimes.com).

FAHRENHEIT 9/11 (2004)

PRODUCER/DIRECTOR: Michael Moore (director), Michael Moore (producer), Jim Czarnecki (producer), Kathleen Glynn (producer)
WRITER(S): Michael Moore
CAST: Ben Affleck (Himself), Stevie Wonder (Himself), George W. Bush (Himself), James Baker III (Himself), Richard Gephardt (Himself), Tom Daschle (Himself), Jeffrey Toobin (Himself), Al Gore (Himself), Condoleezza Rice (Herself), Donald Rumsfeld (Himself), Osama Bin Laden, (Himself)
CINEMATOGRAPHY: Urban Hamid (additional footage)
MUSIC: Jeff Gibbs
LENGTH AND RATING: 122 min; R

Taking a cue from Ray Bradury's *Fahrenheit 451*, a dystopian novel about a totalitarian state that forbids thinking and reading books, Michael Moore uses the title as a metaphor for his profile of President George W. Bush, his administration, the war in Afghanistan and Iraq, and the Bush connection to the Saudis and to the bin Laden family. It's a highly critical essay of the president, and Vice President Cheney and their ties to defense contractors and Saudi money.

As an award-winning documentary filmmaker addressing contemporary issues of American culture and policy, Moore has become a vociferous critic of General Motors and its then CEO Roger Smith in *Roger and Me* (1989). In *Bowling for Columbine* (2002), which won an Academy Award, he investigated the Columbine High School massacre and the violence in American culture as a possible cause, and in *Sicko* (2007), he investigated the American health care system and compared it to others around the world. But his documentary on George W. Bush and 9/11 was especially caustic.

In an opening scene, as a joint session of Congress attempts to certify the contentious 2000 presidential election results making George W. Bush the president-elect, a number of African-American congressmen and women rise to protest the vote count. However, the rules of the joint body do not permit such debate if a senator has not cosigned the document of the congressperson. The tone of the comments by the congressional representatives and the disappointment and frustration they express provides the opening scene with tension and emotion.

After 9/11, when the FAA grounded all planes, relatives of bin Laden and other Saudis related to the royal family were allowed to fly out of the country. Raising this issue, Moore interviews a retired FBI counterterrorism expert who questions the propriety of the action, noting that they should have been detained for questioning.

Alluding to George W. Bush as the tough cowboy sheriff who invades Afghanistan, Moore cleverly takes the opening scene from the *Bonanza* television series and superimposes the faces of Bush, Cheney, Rumsfeld, and Tony Blair in cowboy regalia riding horses. Then he cuts together segments of Bush repeating the phrase "smoke 'em out" and intercuts a scene from an old "B" western with the same dialogue.

Moore is also a shrewd manipulator of emotion, as in the scene where President Bush is being primped for his address to the nation about the military action and bombing of Iraq, which is intercut with scenes of daily life in the country; people shopping, children playing, followed by images of civilian Iraqi casualties. In another emotional scene, Lila Lipscomb, the mother of a daughter who had served in "Operation Desert Storm" and at the time of the interview, had a son serving in Iraq, expresses her patriotic pride for her children and the soldiers. After she is informed that her son has been killed, she tearfully reads his last letter home. It is an absorbing, sobering scene that wrenches the emotions and represents the heartache that so many families face after losing a loved one in battle.

There are instances in the film where Moore's interview subjects offer facts that are a matter of debate or hearsay, and yet they are deemed correct. In one case, his subject mentions that he's heard that total Saudi investment in the American economy may be as high as $860 billion, and Moore responds that the figure represents seven percent of the total US economy. However, a more accurate estimate would be $500–700 billion.

In his June 23, 2004, *New York Times* review of *Fahrenheit 9/11*, A. O. Scott writes: "Mixing sober outrage with mischievous humor and blithely trampling the boundary between documentary and demagoguery, Mr. Moore takes wholesale aim at the Bush administration, whose tenure has been distinguished, in his view, by unparalleled and unmitigated arrogance, mendacity and incompetence." He also writes that the film is "an authentic and indispensable document of its time."

In his June 24, 2004, *Chicago Sun Times* review of *Fahrenheit 9/11*, Roger Ebert wrote that "*Fahrenheit 9/11* is a compelling, persuasive film, at odds with the White House effort to present Bush as a strong leader. He comes across as a shallow, inarticulate man, simplistic in speech and inauthentic in manner (http://rogerebert.suntimes.com/apps/pbcs.dll/article?AID=/20040624/REVIEWS/406240301/1023).

MASSACRE, RETRIBUTION, AND FAITH

The Passion of the Christ (2004)
Hotel Rwanda (2004)
Munich (2005)

These three films address traumatic historical events that unsettled the world of politics and religious faith, and remain subjects of controversy. The films *Munich* and *Hotel Rwanda* address events that shocked the world community. The respective film directors Steven Spielberg and Terry George put faces to the narrative that humanized these stories of hostile conflict. For *Munich* Spielberg and screenwriters Tony Kushner and Eric Roth use the 1972 Munich Olympic massacre of the Israeli Olympic team by Palestinian terrorists to tell a story of revenge that Israel embarks upon to track down and kill those responsible. For *Hotel Rwanda* director Terry George and screenwriters Keir Pearson and Terry George utilize the heroic efforts of Paul Rusesabagina (Don Cheadle), the manager of the Sabena Hotel des Mille Collines to shelter and protect one thousand refugees from the genocide perpetrated by Hutu militias against the Tutsis.

In attempting to tell the story of Jesus Christ, actor/director Mel Gibson created controversy and devotion among movie audiences in his portrayal of the circumstances surrounding Chirst's crucifixion. The film presents very graphic scenes of Jesus being mercilessly tortured and beaten by the Romans and its portrayal of the Jewish priests and other visual representations were said by some critics to be referenced to the classical visual history of anti-Semitism.

🎥 *THE PASSION OF THE CHRIST* (2004)

PRODUCER/DIRECTOR: Mel Gibson (director), Bruce Davey (producer), Mel Gibson and Stephen McEveety (producers)
WRITER(S): Benedict Fitzgerald (screenplay), Mel Gibson (screenplay)
CAST: James Caviezel (Jesus), Maia Morgenstern (Mary), Christo Jivkov (John), Francesco De Vito (Peter), Monica Bellucci (Magdalen), Mattia Sbragia (Caiphas Caiphas), Toni Bertorelli (Annas), Luca Lionello (Judas), Hristo Shopov (Pontius Pilate), Claudia Gerini (Claudia Procles)
CINEMATOGRAPHY: Caleb Deschanel
MUSIC: John Debney
LENGTH AND RATING: 127 min; R

Prior to the release of the film, there was great controversy because of Mel Gibson's interpretation of the Gospels, his depiction and implication of Jewish priests, the graphic, bloody portrayal of Chirst's beatings by the Romans, and his anguish and suffering hanging on the cross of his crucifixion. Even the title, which was changed several times but included the word "passion," had anti-Semitic implications based on the passion plays of the Middle Ages, such as the Oberammergau Passion Play.

Organizations like the Anti-Defamation League claimed that the depiction of the Jewish High Priest Calaphas as the bullying Pontias Pilate who hesitates in harming Jesus and the blood-thirsty Jewish mob chanting for Jesus' death are indications that Gibson rejected the 1965 Second Vatican Council document *Nostra Aetate*, which rejected the concept that the Jewish people collectively were responsible for the death of Christ and condemned all forms of discrimination. Indeed Katha Pollitt, in her article, "The Protocols of Mel Gibson," which appeared on March 11, 2004, in *The Nation*, wrote that the United States Conference of Catholic Bishops endorsed the film even though the film violated the Council's 1988 criteria for how Jews are to be portrayed in dramatic adaptations of the Passion. She also wrote that Gibson's interpretation of the Jewish priests showed them as "bad Jews," as anti-Semitic cartoons; rich, arrogant, and gaudy, while the "good Jews"

> look like Italian movie stars (Magdalene actually *is* an Italian movie star, the lovely Monica Bellucci); Mary, who would have been around 50 and appeared 70, could pass for a ripe 35.

The film also takes creative and literary license with the beatings sustained by Jesus, which received a one-sentence reference in three Gospels but are depicted in the film as, "a ten-minute homoerotic sadistic extravaganza that no human being could have survived, as if the point of the Passion was to show how tough Christ was."

In addition to the writings of the Synoptic Gospels, and the first three Gospels of Matthew, Mark, and Luke as source material, other extra-biblical material is used including the writing of two nuns recognized for their anti-Semitic fervor: Mary of Agreda, from 17th-century Spain and a 19th-century nun, Catherine Emmereich, who wrote about Jews strangling Christian children for their blood (http://www.thenation.com/doc/ 20040329/pollitt).

In his March 1, 2004, *New Yorker* review of *The Passion of the Christ* entitled "Nailed," David Denby writes that Gibson ignores Jesus' eloquence, his ethical radicalism, and his personal radiance. He also criticizes Gibson for taking Jesus' message of love and turning it into one of hate. "As a viewer, I am equally free to say that the movie Gibson has made from his personal obsessions is a sickening death trip, a grimly unilluminating procession of treachery, beatings, blood, and agony—and to say so without indulging in 'anti-Christian sentiment' (Gibson's term for what his critics are spreading)" (http://www.newyorker.com/archive/2004/03/01/040301crci_ cinema).

"I want to kill him. I want his intestines on a stick. I want to kill his dog." This is the statement that director Mel Gibson made in the *New Yorker* magazine about *New York Times* columnist Frank Rich, who wrote crtitically about Gibson's traditionalist Catholic faith, which rejects the teachings of Vatican II, and his film *The Passion of the Christ*. In his writing, Rich exposed the hypocrisy of Gibson in his selected prescreening events for the film, which for the most part, excluded Jewish critics and journalists. In his columns, Rich also noted how Gibson used classic Jew-baiting language that referenced the classic anti-Semitic text "The Protocols of the Elders of Zion." Rich also stated that the film does not focus on Jesus' godly teachings.

> And that is indeed the message of his film. *The Passion* is far more in love with putting Jesus' intestines on a stick than with dramatizing his godly teachings, which are relegated to a few brief, cryptic flashbacks. (http://query.nytimes.com/gst/fullpage) (http://www.nytimes.com/2004/03/07/arts/07RICH)

There were many favorable reviews of the film, including Roger Ebert's. which appeared on February 24, 2004, in the *Chicago Sun-Times*. He felt that the film was not anti-Semitic:

> My own feeling is that Gibson's film is not anti-Semitic, but reflects a range of behavior on the part of its Jewish characters, on balance favorably. The Jews who seem to desire Jesus' death are in the priesthood, and have political as well as theological reasons for acting; like today's Catholic bishops who were slow to condemn abusive priests, Protestant TV preachers who confuse religion with politics, or Muslim clerics who are silent on terrorism, they have an investment in their positions and authority. (http://rogerebert.suntimes.com)

It is indeed an irony that, while Gibson and his supporters denied that he is anti-Semitic, when he was arrested for drunk driving in July 2006, he was relentless in spewing forth a tirade of anti-Semitic ramblings to the arresting officer.

HOTEL RWANDA (2004)

PRODUCER/DIRECTOR: Terry George (director and producer), A. Kitman Ho (producer)

WRITER(S): Keir Pearson, Terry George

CAST: Xolani Mali (Claudia Procles), Don Cheadle (Paul Rusesabagnia), Desmond Dube (Dube), Hakeem Kae-Kazim (George Rutaganda), Tony Kgoroge (Gregoire), Rosie Motene (Receptionist), Neil McCarthy (Jean Jacques), Mabutho "Kid" Sithole (Head Chef, as Kid Sithole), Nick Nolte (Colonel Oliver), Fana Mokoena (General Bizimungus)

CINEMATOGRAPHY: Robert Fraisse

MUSIC: Afro Celt Sound System, Rupert Gregson-Williams, Andrea Guerra

LENGTH AND RATING: 121 min; PG-13

An ordinary man in extraordinary circumstances: The film tells the true story of Paul Rusesbagnia, played by actor Don Cheadle, the manager of the Sabena Hotel des Mille Collines who, during the 1994 Rwandan genocide when 800,000 people, mostly Tutsis were killed, transformed his hotel into a safe haven for refugees. A Hutu married to a Tutsi, his wife Tatiana (Sophie Okonedo), Paul is in the precarious position of saving his family and being threatened for not joining his Hutu tribe in the mass murder. He mistakenly believes that his position and the contacts he has nurtured will protect him from harm along with the United Nations forces led by Colonel Oliver (Nick Nolte). In a harsh scene when Nolte strides into the hotel bar and Paul prepares two glasses of Scotch whiskey to offer the Colonel a toast and his thanks for the protection, Oliver scoffs that the forces can't protect them and the Western world doesn't care about the genocide in Rwanda. He bitterly tells Paul that he could probably own the hotel he manages except for the fact that he is black and African.

As the hotel fills with refugees, Paul visits his "friend" George Rutaganda (Hakeem Kae-Kazim) for rice and other supplies to feed the refugees. He is a vendor for the hotel and now doubles his prices and discusses the massacre of the Tutsis, using the derogatory term "cockroaches." When Paul asks incredulously whether he thinks they can kill them all, George brushes it off as something easily attained because they have already killed at leat half of the Tutsis. Returning with supplies on the river road,, the van thuds over bumpy terrain and Paul orders his driver to stop the van thinking they may mistakenly drive into the river. When he gets out to check, he sees that the road is strewn with dead bodies and he is overcome with grief.

However, Paul is the consummate dealmaker, and his bribes to the Hutu leaders keep the hotel safe for a time. After narrowly escaping death, Paul is reunited with his family as they and other refugees are moved to safety.

It's a tragic story of tribal hatred, geopolitical indifference, and mass genocide in the modern era. However, it also addresses the heroism of a single person who faced the murder and mayhem in his homeland with the dignity and perseverance to prevail.

There have also been accusations made by some workers and survivors from the hotel that events in the movie weren't accurately portrayed. Indeed, one of the hotel's workers told the press that Rusesabagnia kicked out refugees who could not pay their bills. There has also been some bad press from Rwanda about how Rusesabagnia is making money from the Hotel Rwanda Rusesabagnia Foundation charity. However, other witnesses do not dispute his story of heroism.

In his December 22, 2004, *New York Times* review, Stephen Holden writes that the film is a "political thriller based on fact that hammers every button on the emotional console."

> At the very least, this wrenching film performs the valuable service of lending a human face to an upheaval so savage it seemed beyond the realm of imagination when news of it filtered into the West. (http://movies.nytimes.com)

In the *New Yorker*, David Denby wrote about the unassuming nature of Rusesabagnia as portrayed by Don Cheadle:

> *Hotel Rwanda*, which was written by Keir Pearson and Terry George, who also directed, is the true story of a brave and wily man who never made a speech or indulged an instant of stiff-backed righteousness. The fascination of the movie lies in watching this unspectacular, mild-tempered fellow outwit some of the worst thugs and profiteers who ever managed to deliver their own country into disaster. (http://www.newyorker.com/archive)

MUNICH (2005)

PRODUCER/DIRECTOR: Steven Spielberg (director and producer), Kathleen Kennedy (producer), Barry Mendel (producer)

WRITER(S): Tony Kushner (screenplay), Eric Roth (screenplay), George Jonas (book *Vengeance: The True Story of an Israeli Counter-Terrorist Team*)

CAST: Eric Bana (Avner), Daniel Craig (Steve), Ciarán Hinds (Carl), Mathieu Kassovitz (Robert), Hanns Zischler (Hans), Ayelet Zurer (Daphna), Geoffrey Rush (Ephraim), Gila Almagor (Avner's Mother), Michael Lonsdale (Papa), Mathieu Amalric (Louis)

CINEMATOGRAPHY: Janusz Kaminski

MUSIC: John Williams

LENGTH AND RATING: 164 min; R

This film interweaves the kidnapping and killing of eleven Israeli Olympic athletes into the story of Avner (Eric Bana), a young Mossad agent, formerly on Prime Minister Golda Meir's security detail, whose father was a hero, selected because he is an unknown entity, having never served as a field agent. Anonymity is critical to the mission, and Avner must resign his position in the Mossad and leave his pregnant wife Daphna (Ayelet Zurer) so that he ceases to exist. He heads a team of four men, each with a special skill; a South African driver, shooter Steve (Daniel Craig), a German document forger Hans (Hanns Zischler), Robert (Mathieu Kassovitz) a Belgian toy-maker trained in explosives, and Carl (Ciaran Hinds) a methodical ex-soldier who lost a son in the 1967 Arab-Israeli War who "cleans up" after the assassinations.

As "deadly" spies they hardly fit the iconic cinematic image, but they manage to confront their victims and kill them. However, their inexperience is revealed by the encounter with their first victim in Rome, Abdel Wael Zwaiter. After following their victim, Robert and Avner confront him holding a bag of groceries while waiting for the elevator in his apartment building. They confirm his identity by asking his name. When he responds affirmatively, they nervously shoot him as his trembling hand tries to stop them. Confronting their victims as assassins is difficult as it humanizes their prey, so they use bombs in subsequent operations.

As the "eliminations" proceed, Avner, while a good soldier and a loyal Israeli, becomes more disillusioned with the killings. He meets a French information broker Louis (Mathieu Amalric) who works for his father Papa (Michael Lonsdale), and he sells Avner information on the location of their victims. Their singular philosophy is that they don't work for governments, and when Louis suspects that Avner is Israeli, Papa summons him for a meeting. During the trip he's blind-folded, and when he arrives at the compound in the French countryside, it is filled with Papa's extended family of children and grandchildren. He is taken in by the nurturing that family and a home offer and by the paternal expressions of Papa who, when he leaves, tells Avner that he could have been his son but he's not, so he had better be careful.

After some confusion in an Athens safe house that Louis has double-booked with a group of militant Palestinians, Avner with the help of Robert poses as a German radical and begins a conversation with Ali, their militant leader. This dialogue clearly articulates the dilemma between Palestinians and Israelis as each side pursues their dream of a secure homeland and Ali speaks of waiting and fighting for as long as it takes.

Although the team is successful, they must also suffer the consequences of their notoriety, and by the end of the movie only Steve and Avner are alive. The mission concluded, Avner returns to his wife and daughter whom he has sent to live in Brooklyn, New York. There he must confront the horror of Munich and the consequences of his actions. While walking with his daughter on the street, he notices a car following him. He calls Papa in France from a public telephone and is assured that no harm would ever come to his family from them. He is also met in Brooklyn by his handler Ephraim (Geoffrey Rush) who urges him to return to Israel with his family, but Avner is reluctant and when he extends an invitation for Ephraim to "break bread" with him, his handler refuses.

Although for the most part the film received excellent reviews as a thrilling story of retribution and revenge, it also was perceived by some to be hostile to the Palestinians and far too balanced. There were also some critics who noted that, in his portrayal of the PLO and the Israelis, Spielberg equated the Israeli actions as equal to the terrorists. He was also criticized by many as not taking sides, especially as a Jew, for not strongly endorsing Israel's actions.

However, Spielberg's perception as potrayed by Avner clearly articulates the frustration of the "eye for an eye" philosophy; after they confront and eliminate terrorists, they are quickly replaced by others.

In his December 23, 2005, *Chicago-Sun Times* review of *Munich*, Roger Ebert wrote that, "Munich is an act of courage and conscience." He also noted that the film was efficient, absorbing and haunting.

> As a thriller, "Munich" is efficient, absorbing, effective. As an ethical argument, it is haunting. And its questions are not only for Israel but for any nation that believes it must compromise its values to defend them. (http://rogerebert.suntimes. com)

In a December 23, 2005, *New York Times* review, Manohla Dargis writes that *Munich* is a nail-biter action movie, describing it as a meditation on ethics as well as a political action thriller:

> *Munich* is as much a meditation on ethics as a political thriller, but it takes nothing away from the film to say that the most adrenaline-spiked part of this genre hybrid involves getaway cars, false papers and the sight of the future Israeli Prime Minister Ehud Barak, who pops up during a mission in Lebanon, mowing down terrorists while dressed in a woman's wig and high heels. (http://movies.nytimes.com)

PAN'S LABYRINTH (2004)

PRODUCER/DIRECTOR: Guillermo del Toro (director and producer), Alfonso Cuarón (producer), Bertha Navarro (producer), Frida Torresblanco (producer), Alvaro Augustin (producer)
WRITER(S): Guillermo del Toro
CAST: Ivana Baquero (Ofelia), Sergi López (Captain Vidal), Maribel Verdú (Mercedes), Doug Jones (Fauno/Pale Man), Ariadna Gil (Carmen Vidal), Álex Angulo (Doctor), Manolo Solo (Garcés), César Vea (Serrano), Roger Casamajor (Pedro), Ivan Massagué (El Tarta)
CINEMATOGRAPHY: Guillermo Navarro
MUSIC: Javier Navarrete
LENGTH AND RATING: 119 min; R

This movie provides a visual and auditory feast for the viewer's senses as director Guillermo del Toro creates a fantasy world in the midst of a bloody 1944 resistance battle against the fascists of Franco's Spain. It begins by reciting the legend of the young Princess Moanna who lives in the Underground Realm and, curious about Earth, escapes and is blinded by the sun, forgetting her past, and dies. Her father hopes that one day her spirit will return. The story utilizes the rich, provocative images of fairy tales as its narrative about a young girl, Ofelia (Ivana Baquero) and her preganant mother Carmen (Ariadna Gil) travel to the forest to live with her stepfather Captain Vidal (Sergi Lopez), a cruel soldier in Franco's army.

As they travel with a military escort, her mother Carmen asks the driver to stop so that she can rest and deal with her nausea. During the drive Ofelia had immersed herself in reading a fairy tale, but instead her tale becomes a tragic one. During their rest stop Ofelia encounters a crumbling stone pagan gargoyle and stoops down to the ground to pick up a remnant that is the missing eye and returns it to its socket. That gesture appears to be a key for allowing Ofelia into the nether world of the Labyrinth, near the old mill that serves as Captain Vidal's headquarters and Ofelia's new home. After replacing the eye, she is visited by a praying mantis who swarms around her and follows her to the Captain's headquarters. Eventually the bug, a River Styx version of Tinker Bell, turns out to be one of the fairies.

The literary and cinematic references to fairy tales are prominent in the forest that Ofelia discovers along with the creatures that inhabit the labyrinth. It is a grim world, dark and dank, with terror lurking behind every bush. She encounters a faun (Doug

Jones) who gives her three tasks to complete. The faun is a gnarly creature who outwardly appears to be virtuous and kind but through speech and gestures allows evil to prowl in the shadows.

To complete one task, Ofelia must visit a Cyclops-like creature, the Pale Man, who has an eye in the palm of each hand, and she must use a key to retrieve a dagger. Before she leaves, the faun cautions that there will be a table set with sumptuous food and treats, but she must not be tempted to eat anything. This is a direct reference to the Grimm fairy tale of Hansel and Gretel, where a brother and sister are cast out of their home by an evil stepmother. In the forest they encounter a cottage made of candy, and inside the table is set with breathtaking food. The witch who lives there tempts them so that she can fatten them up and eat them.

Ignoring the entreaties of the fairies, Ofelia eats some grapes, which brings the Pale Man to life. In a corner is a pile of small shoes from his previous victims. He gives chase after Ofelia uses a magic piece of chalk to draw an escape hatch in the ceiling. After she returns, Ofelia is scolded by the faun for not obeying his order and he tells her that she will not continue to the third task that could prove that she is the Princess Moanna.

As Ofelia navigates her complex world, she also cares for her mother who is very sick, and she experiences the brutality of her stepfather. When a father and son are caught as suspected rebels and plead that they were merely hunting rabbits, Captain Vidal kills them. After searching the bag, he finds a dead rabbit proving their innocence. Feeling no remorse, he orders Mercedes (Maribel Verdie), his chief housekeeper to make a stew. She is aligned with the rebels and becomes like a mother to Ofelia after her own mother dies in childbirth.

Upon learning that Doctor Ferreiro (Alex Angulo), who had been caring for his wife Carmen, is a rebel sympathizer and has been aiding them with medical supplies, Vidal kills him. While attempting to flee with Ofelia, Mercedes is captured by the Captain's troops; during interrogation, she uses a concealed knife to stab the Captain, cutting his cheek, and then she is rescued by the rebels.

Once again Ofelia is visited by the faun who offers her the third task but only if she obeys all of his instructions. She agrees to take her baby brother to the Labyrinth and will receive futher instructions to complete her last task. However, to sneak the baby away she spikes Captain Vidal's drink with a sleeping drug and he staggers after her. Meeting Ofelia the faun tells her that to open the portal to the underworld he needs one drop of blood from an innocent, and he disappears when she refuses. Soon, the Captain appears and takes the baby from Ofelia, shooting her. He leaves the Labyrinth, and when he exits he is met by Mercedes and the rebels, who take the baby and kill him.

Entering the Labyrinth, Mercedes is tearfully reunited with Ofelia who is on the ground bleeding. However, she has learned that she passed the final test by sacrificing herself proving that she is Princess Moanna and is reunited with her resurrected father and mother as her earthly spirit dies.

Fairy tales have witches, demons, angels, and devils that conspire to capture a child's imagination. For Ofelia, to her mother's regret, these tales take her away from a reality she wants to escape from. After her father, a tailor, died her mother married the Captain that he made uniforms for. He is a murderous brute that is using her mother as a mere receptacle to carry his child.

Her fantasy world is also dangerous because fairy tales engage the reader with characters that can be beguiling and treacherous. She is given hazardous tasks to complete which parallel the risks to her life in the real world. In the end her spirit is saved for eternity because she has met the test of humanity and sacrifice.

In his December 29, 2006, review of *Pan's Labyrinth* in "Christianity Today" Jeffrey Overstreet writes that fairy tales can provide perspective on troubling realities:

> By contrasting the conflict of good and evil in the *real* world with the dramas that take place in fantasy land, Del Toro reminds us that children's stories—especially those dark and twisted fables from the Grimm Brothers and Hans Christian Andersen—can give us rewarding perspectives on troubling realities. (http://www. christianitytoday.com/movies/reviews/2006/panslabyrinth.html)

In A. O. Scott's December 29, 2006, *New York Times* review of *Pan's Labyrinth* he writes that, "the imaginative energy runs both ways," and calls the director Guillermo del Toro, "a real magician."

> The brilliance of *Pan's Labyrinth* is that its current of imaginative energy runs both ways. If this is magic realism, it is also the work of a real magician. The director, Guillermo Del Toro, unapologetically and unpretentiously swears allegiance to a pop-fantasy tradition that encompasses comic books, science fiction and horror movies, but fan-boy pastiche is the last thing on his mind. He is also a thorough-going cinephile, steeped in classical technique and film history. (http://movies.nytimes.com)

A HISTORY OF VIOLENCE (2005)

PRODUCER/DIRECTOR: David Cronenberg (director), Chris Bender (producer), J. C. Spink (producer)

WRITER(S): John Wagner (graphic novel), Vince Locke (graphic novel), Josh Olson (screenplay)

CAST: Viggo Mortensen (Tom Stall), Maria Bello (Edie Stall), Ed Harris (Carl Fogarty), William Hurt (Richie Cusack), Ashton Holmes (Jack Stall), Peter MacNeill (Sheriff Sam Carney), Stephen McHattie (Leland), Greg Bryk (Billy), Kyle Schmid (Bobby), Sumela Kay (Judy Danvers), Gerry Quigley (Mick)

CINEMATOGRAPHY: Peter Suschitzky (director of photography)

MUSIC: Howard Shore

LENGTH AND RATING: 96 min; R

Violence as a theme in film has evolved over the years from suggestion to graphic exploitation. The evolution can be attributed to codes, censorship, and changing cultural values. Crime, war, and terrorism punctuate the landscape of all Americans and while the routines of life intrude on overindulging in these horrors, they are a shocking part of everyday existence. Is small town America a fiction that exists only in film, or is it a memory that sustains its virtues over generations? Many of us long for the friendship and caring that such towns like the fictional Milbrook, Indiana, offer and Tom Stall (Viggo Mortenson) has satisfied that yearning by becoming part of the essence of that culture. He's living the American dream, a beautiful wife and lawyer Edie (Maria Bello), great children teenager Jack (Ashton Holmes) and little Sarah (Heidi Hayes), and he owns and operates a successful diner in town. The townsfolk congregate in the diner and Tom has their respect as an upstanding family man, a good Christian, "see ya in church," and a loyal American. After all, in Millbrook, "we take care of our own." But the dynamics of this staid life are about to unravel. In school Jack is harassed by a bully and rather than confront his threats he emulates his father's credo by backing down and swallowing his pride.

For Tom, his life and his family are shattered when two cold-blooded murderers, (Greg Bryk, Stephen McHattie) enter his diner at closing time for coffee and pie. The audience knows them from the opening scene of the film when they check out of a motel and leave dead bodies in their wake, including one of a whimpering little girl. Now they've descended on Tom's diner and their intent is not to make idle chitchat. The older man demands coffee, and the younger one wants a piece of pie. Although Tom has said that they are closing he accommodates their request and tells Charlotte (Deborah Drake-ford) the waitress that she can go home. However, the younger man grabs her, and his accomplice orders him to "do her." He is about to kill her when Tom springs into action—throws hot coffee on the older man's face, grabs his gun, and shoots the younger man, is stabbed in the foot by the older man, and then blows him away. The stealth of his actions and his cool demeanor suggest that he has done this before. In Jack's case, when he has finally reached a plateau of harassment, he takes out the bully with such professionalim and abandon that one must assume that he's had lessons in self-defense.

All of the media attention surrounding Tom's heroic actions bring his former adversary Carl Fogarty (Ed Harris) to town. He is accompanied by two enforcers, Charlie Roarke (Aiden Devine) and Frank Mulligan (Bill McDonald). Although Tom denies Fogarty's claim that he is really the former Philadelphia killer and hoodlum Joey Cusack, who mangled Fogarty's eye, the circumstancial evidence is convincing and proves to be true.

As Fogarty sets out to intimidate Tom and his wife Edie, she becomes more suspicious of her husband's true identity. After Edie has been followed and harassed, she contacts Sam Carney (Peter MacNeill), the local sheriff, who pulls Fogarty's car over, confronts him, and asks him to leave town. This scene is reminiscent of the classic cowboy Westerns as the local sheriff or marshal confronts the bad guy, running him out of town. Subsequent to this confrontation Sam asks Tom if he's in a witness protection program and if Fogarty was right about his real identity as Joey Cusak. Again, Tom denies that assertion confirming that he is whom he says.

In a deadly confrontation in front of their home, Fogarty arrives with his henchmen, holding Tom's son Jack as hostage, and confronts Tom. Fogarty offers to trade Jack if Tom enters the car to take a ride. Putting down his rifle, Tom negotiates Jack's release, and when one of the armed henchman attempts to escort him into the car, he attacks using the gunman's weapon to kill Fogarty's accomplices. Wounded, Fogarty stands over Tom ready to shoot, when Jack opens fire with the shotgun mortally wounding Fogarty. As a result of this carnage, the family realizes Tom's true identity, and he admits that he is Joey Cusack. Feeling betrayed, Edie is outraged and Jack is resentful. Understanding that he must confront his brother Richie (William Hurt), whom he used to work for, Tom drives to Philadelphia and meets one of his brother's associates, who takes him to Richie's estate. His brother greets him warmly, but as Tom sits with his back toward

Richie's henchman, the man attempts to garrot him. Once again Tom/Joey prevails, killing several of Richie's bodyguards, then shooting his brother in the forehead. When he returns home, the family is having dinner, and he sits down in his chair at the head of the table opposite Edie, whose head is bowed and hands are clasped in prayer. At the table, his young daughter Sarah retrieves a place setting, putting it on the table with the knife and fork facing in the wrong direction. His son Jack looks at his mother, whose head is still bowed, then takes the plate of meat loaf and sets it down by his father. Finally Edie raises her head and the couple gaze at each other—the pain showing in their eyes and faces, a haunting melody punctuating their anguish in the background. Then, without a word, the screen cuts to black.

This film harkens back to the traditions of American writers like Zane Grey and directors like John Ford who idolized the American West and its classic way of life frought with hard-won virtue achieved by violence and fortitude which brought recognition and honor. As in the film *Shane,* the title character, portrayed by actor Alan Ladd, joins a family farm providing relief from his violent occupation, but he must again strap on his gun to help his adopted family defend themselves from a brutal rancher. In *A History of Violence,* Tom defends his family against the "outlaws" but at the end of the film the audience does not know if, like Shane, he will ride off into the sunset.

In a September 23, 2005, *New York Times* review Manhola Dargis calls the film, "a sensational moviegoing experience," and noted how it, "explores the myth and meaning of America (or at least a representative facsimile) through its dreams, nightmares, and compulsive frenzies" (http://movies.nytimes.com/2005/09/23/movies/23viol. html?_r=1&oref=slogin).

In his December 23, 2005, *Chicago-Sun Times* review of *A History of Violence* Roger Ebert writes:

> *A History of Violence* seems deceptively straightforward, coming from a director with Cronenberg's quirky complexity. But think again. This is not a movie about plot, but about character. It is about how people turn out the way they do, and about whether the world sometimes functions like a fool's paradise. (http://rogerebert. suntimes.com)

CHILDREN OF MEN (2006)

PRODUCER/DIRECTOR: Alfonso Cuarón (director), Marc Abraham (producer), Eric Newman (producer), Iain Smith (producer), Hilary Shor (producer), Tony Smith (producer), Thomas A. Bliss (producer), Armyan Bernstein (producer)

WRITER(S): Alfonso Cuarón (screenplay), Timothy J. Sexton (screenplay), David Arata (screenplay), Mark Fergus (screenplay); Hawk Ostby (screenplay), P. D. James (novel *The Children of Men*)

CAST: Clive Owen (Theo), Julianne Moore (Julian), Chiwetel Ejiofor (Luke), Charlie Hunnam (Patric), Clare-Hope Ashitey (Kee), Pam Ferris (Miriam), Danny Huston (Nigel), Peter Mullan (Syd), Michael Caine (Jaspar).

CINEMATOGRAPHY: Emmanuel Lubezki

MUSIC: John Tavener

LENGTH AND RATING: 109 min; R

It's 2027, and the world has disintegrated into a dystopian society consumed by human misery, chaos, poverty, oppression, violence, disease, and infertility. The major nations of the world have broken down into anarchy, and only Britian still maintains the rule of law with armed troops patrolling its cities. In London, hordes of immigrants have sought refuge and are routinely rounded up and placed in cages. The streets are littered, violence and death lurk everywhere. The world has become sterile and no woman has been able to give birth in eighteen years.

In this seeming caldron of dysfunction Theo Falon (Clive Owen) a government bureaucrat and former activist numbs the horror and his frustration by drinking. He has retreated into a robotic state shutting the chaotic world out. Buying his morning coffee at a Fleet Street café Theo is walking on the sidewalk and nearly blown up by a bomb that is attributed to the Fishes, a rebel underground group advocating rights for all immigrants. From a television news report he learned that the youngest person in the world, eighteen-year-old "Baby Diego" has been murdered for not signing an autograph. He seeks solace by visiting his friend Jasper Palmer (Michael Caine) an editorial cartoonist and an old hippie who lives in a remote area, grows and smokes marijuana, listens to Beatles music and cares for his catatonic wife who was tortured by the government.

There is some resemblance in *Children of Men* to the dystopian universe in *Blade Runner* although the latter is contextualized driven by a science fiction narrative. However, both films present a pessimistic view of Earth being a sustainable planet for humans as global warming and toxic wastes pollute the planet. The issue of immigration is another element in these films that is raised as a dynamic that contributes to the unrest in society. In *Children of Men* illegal immigrants are penned up and live in shantytowns and in *Blade Runner* they congregate in the inner cities servicing a population that must endure the hardships of their fate. Ironically, a similar situation impacted Japanese nationals and American citizens after Imperial Japan's attack on Pearl Harbor. In the aftermath 110,000 Japanese, mostly on the West Coast, were interned in war relocation camps.

In London Theo is kidnapped by the Fishes which are led by his his former companion Julian Taylor (Julianne Moore). They had been separated since their young son Dylan died during a flu pandemic. She offers Theo 5,000 British pounds sterling to obtain travel permits to escort Kee (Clare Hope-Ashitey) a young, pregnant fugee (refugee) to the safety of the Human Project, a group that will shelter Kee and her baby. At first Theo is reluctant and then agrees and travels with the group along with Miriam (Pam Ferris) a midwife. During the road trip their car is ambushed by another rebel group and Julian is killed. After arriving at a safe house Theo learns that Luke (Chiwetel Ejofor), who had been second in command and is now leader of the Fishes plotted the ambush to assassinate Julian. He, Kee, and Miriam flee to Jasper's home and there arrangements are made for them to meet Syd (Peter Mullan) one of Jasper's weed customers and a guard at Bexhill, a shantytown. This is where Miriam said that a boat from the Human Project will rendezvous offshore at a buoy to pick Kee up. After meeting with them Syd arranges their entry as his "prisoners" but in an effort to distract a guard who is curious about Kee's condition Miriam feigns religious zealotry and is taken away.

They are led by a gypsy to a room, and inside Kee gives birth to a girl. This scene is a metaphor and symbolic to the birth of Jesus and the beginning of new life. After the baby is born, Syd attempts to kidnap Kee and the baby, holding them for ransom.

Fighting him off, Theo escapes with Kee but she is captured by the Fishes who have instigated an uprising in the Bexhill camp. During the confusion Theo manages to find her and the baby in an apartment building and as he escorts her outside he is shot by Luke who is killed by British soldiers called in to quell the insurgency. As the baby cries the soldiers and insurgents cease fire and incredulously listen to the baby allowing Kee and Theo safe passage. With the aid of the Gypsy woman Theo finds a small boat and rows out to the designated buoy and seeing the blood Kee tells Theo that she will name her child Dylan after his dead son. With the ship in sight Theo slumps over and dies from his wound.

The squalor and harsh conditions of the refugee camps are used as a metaphor for the coalition detention camps in Iraq and Guantanamo Bay, Cuba. Indeed, the visual imagery of armed troops, random bombings, and a country and city under siege are indicative of America's occupation of Iraq. Technically, the film is visually compelling as director Alfonso Cuaron uses long takes to portray the harsh, threatening landscape and the brutal conflicts that ensue.

In a December 25, 2006, *New York Times* review Manohla Dargis writes that the film looks like our own world, only darker and more grim:

Children of Men pictures a world that looks a lot like our own, but darker, grimmer and more frighteningly, violently precarious. It imagines a world drained of hope and defined by terror in which bombs regularly explode in cafés crowded with men and women on their way to work. It imagines the unthinkable: What if instead of containing Iraq, the world has become Iraq, a universal battleground of military control, security zones, refugee camps and warring tribal identities? (http://movies.nytimes.com)

In his October 5, 2007, review in the *Chicago Sun-Times*, Roger Ebert uses Alfred Hitchcock's term "MacGuffin" to describe the elements of plot structure in *Children of Men*.

I have been using Hitchcock's term "MacGuffin" too much lately, but there are times when only it will do. The lack of children and the possibility of children are the MacGuffins in *Children of Men*, inspiring all the action, but the movie significantly never tells us why children stopped being born, or how they might become possible again. The children-as-MacGuffin is simply a dramatic device to avoid actual politics while showing how the world is slipping away from civility and co-existence. The film is not really about children; it is about men and women, and civilization, and the way that fear can be used to justify a police state. (http://rogerebert.suntimes.com)

UNITED 93 (2006)

PRODUCER/DIRECTOR: Paul Greengrass (director), Debra Hayward (producer), Liza Chasin (producer), Tim Bevan (producer)
WRITER(S): Paul Greengrass
CAST: J. J. Johnson (Captain Jason Dahl), Gary Commock (First Officer LeRoy Homer), Polly Adams (Deborah Welsh), Opal Alladin (CeeCee Lyles), Starla Benford (Wanda Anita Green), Trish Gates (Sandra Bradshaw), Nancy McDoniel (Lorraine G. Bay), David Alan Basche (Todd Beamer), Richard Bekins (William Joseph Cashman), Susan Blommaert

(Jane Folger), Ray Charleson (Joseph DeLuca), Christian Clemenson (Thomas E. Burnett, Jr.), Liza Colón-Zayas (Waleska Martinez), Lorna Dallas (Linda Gronlund)
CINEMATOGRAPHY: Barry Ackroyd
MUSIC: John Powell
LENGTH AND RATING: 111 min; R

The normalcy that routines provide is what makes *United 93* so compelling, and the audience is shocked out of its complacency when that routine is broken, as when an Arabic prayer chant is heard. As Paul Greengrass, the director of the film, allows the story to unfold, it begins with the familiar cadence of boarding a plane at an airport. The flight attendants checking the passenger manifest and requesting more pillows, the copilot stepping out of the aircraft to observe the fueling of the aircraft, passengers settling in to their seats, an announcement by the pilot welcoming everyone on board, communicating the flying time from Newark Airport to the plane's San Francisco destination and providing an update on when they will be next to depart.

It's a typical airport scene, with planes lined up readying to take off, the jargon-filled radio talk between the pilot and air traffic control and bits of idle conversation in the cockpit, among the air hostesses, the passengers, and the air traffic controllers in the tower.

The cinema verite imagery and overlapping sound in *United 93* provide a realistic documentary tone to the film. As the events unfold the horror, confusion, and shock are brutally mesmerizing as air traffic controllers slowly come to realize the brazen scope of the terror. But the passengers on *United 93* are unaware of the planes crashing into the World Trade Center and the panic that they are about to face from the four hijackers who boarded their plane. That horror is quickly realized when one of the hijackers runs down the aisle, shouting in Arabic and tearing his shirt open revealing a bomb strapped to his chest. The hijackers breach the cockpit door by forcing a flight attendant to use her door signal to open it, then murder her, the pilot, and the copilot.

The film cuts back and forth between the drama on the plane, the chaos of the passengers, the controlled mayhem of the FAA command center, the military liaisons, and the futile attempts to respond. Unarmed jets are scrambled; others set off in the wrong direction heading east over the water, and pleading military requests for rules of engagement go unanswered. It is, in its most tragic sense, a comedy of errors.

As the camaraderie of the passengers grows and information from cell phone calls they make informs them of other hijackings and of the planes hitting the World Trade Center, they plan their assault in hushed conversation. They rush forward, attacking the hijacker carrying the bomb, then use a serving cart to ram the locked cockpit door, crashing through. But the plane has perilously lost altitude as the scholary looking hijacker at the controls with a picture of the Capitol building in Washington, DC, taped on the console continues to descend. It is a hectic, tension-filled scene, as hands grab for the controls, and the passengers make heroic efforts to wrestle the plane away from the hijckers, but they fail and it crashes into a field.

The ending of *United 93* is laden with emotion as the charred remains of the plane are smoldering on a barren field and loved ones learn of the crash. It's a poignant finale to the terror and bravery of *United 93,* and the audience is reminded that it was the only plane of the four hijacked on September 11 to miss its target.

It's a difficult film to watch because of the wanton murder of so many people on that day. The film is also a harsh reminder that the United States is vulnerable to terrorist attacks and, although every effort is made to thwart them, they can succeed. In its reportorial approach to the events that day, *United 93* serves as a visual document of fear, terror, outrage, and heroism.

In her April 28, 2006, *New York Times* review, Manohla Dargis writes that the film is "a persuasively narrated, scrupulously tasteful recreation of the downing of the fourth and final plane hijacked by Islamist terrorists on Sept. 11. *United 93* is the first Hollywood feature film to take on that dreadful day" (http://movies.nytimes.com/2006/04/28/movies/28unit.html).

In his review of *United 93* in the May 1, 2006, *New Yorker*, David Denby notes that:

> Greengrass's movie is tightly wrapped, minutely drawn, and, no matter how frightening, superbly precise. In comparison with past Hollywood treatments of Everyman heroism in time of war, such as Hitchcock's hammy *Lifeboat*, or more recent spectacles, like *War of the Worlds*, there's no visual or verbal rhetoric, no swelling awareness of the Menace We All Face. Those movies were guaranteed to raise a lump in our throats. In this retelling of actual events, most of our emotion is centered in the pit of the stomach. The accumulated dread and grief get released when some of the male passengers, shortly after those few words are spoken, rush the hijackers stationed at the front of the plane with the engorged fury of water breaking through a dam. (http://www.newyorker.com/archive/2006/05/01/060501crci_cinema)

THE QUEEN (2006)

PRODUCER/DIRECTOR: Stephen Frears (director and producer) Tracey Seaward (producer), Andy Harries (producer), Christine Langan (producer)

WRITER(S): Peter Morgan

CAST: Helen Mirren (The Queen), Michael Sheen (Tony Blair), James Cromwell (Prince Phillip), Sylvia Syms (Queen Mother), Helen McCrory (Cherie Blair), Alex Jennings (Prince Charles), Roger Allam (Sir Robin Janvrin), Mark Bazeley (Alastair Campbell), Earl Cameron (Portrait artist), Tim McMullan (Stephen Lamport), Robin Soans (Equerry)

CINEMATOGRAPHY: Affonso Beato (director of photography)

MUSIC: Alexandre Desplat

LENGTH AND RATING: 97 min; PG-13

Americans have a lasting relationship with the people of Great Britian that has endured world wars and profound hardship. When American journalist Edward R. Murrow broadcast from London during the German bombings of the city on shortwave radio, American listeners were compassionate and responsive to their plight. The two countries have been inseperable allies and each administration, whether Republican or Democrat, has confirmed that close relationship. Under the administrations of President George W. Bush and Prime Minister Tony Blair, Great Britian was one of the nations that supported the United States by sending a large number of British troops to Iraq.

In *The Queen*, actress Helen Mirren portrays Queen Elizabeth II during one of the greatest challenges to the monarchy. Ironically, it was not the bombings in London by the Irish Republican Army (IRA) or more recent terrorist attacks. Instead, it was the Queen's resistance to join the public sentiment of mourning after the tragic death of Princess Diana in a 1997 Paris car crash.

There was no other reigning princess in the British monarchy who captured world wide attention as did Princess Diana. She was beautiful, poised, and broke the rigid façade of the royal family. To the people of Great Britian, she was known as, "the people's princess." The film is about Elizabeth's stoic determination to keep Diana's death a private matter and Prime Minister Tony Blair's (Michael Sheen) advice that she, as the representative of the royal family, make a statement about her death.

The film provides an intimate look at the life of the royals and their world filled with servants and decorum. The Queen refuses to return to London while staying in her Scottish castle, Balmoral, or to lower the flag to half-mast over Buckingham Palace in London. She is resolute in maintaining the aloofness of the royal family and orders that no royals talk to the press about Diana's death.

However, the vast outpouring of grief by the British people as they left thousands of floral bouquets outside Buckingham Palace is an event that cannot be ignored. In his role as Prime Minister, Tony Blair once again calls on the Queen at Balmoral and tells her that a poll about to be released by a newspaper indicates that the British public is outraged by her behavior and are overwhelmingly supportive for ending the constitutional monarchy.

Dealing with this crisis and her own grief, the Queen drives a jeep into the countryside, enjoying the solitude; she sees a buck with his superb antlers and is moved by the magnificence of his appearance. At Balmoral, after speaking to the Prime Minister, she agrees to return to London and make a televised statement about the tragedy of Diana's death. She also appears, with Prince Philip (James Cromwell) and her two grandsons Princes William (Jake Taylor Shantos) and Harry (Dash Barber) among the crowds of people who congregate outside Buckingham Palace at the floral monument to Diana.

The film's theme presents the opposition of two leadership styles that collide in the midst of tragedy and the media's contextualization of the event. Throughout her life, Queen Elizabeth has maintained a public demeanor of royal stature defining her role as queen as befits a reigning monarch. However, Prime Minister Tony Blair is younger and understands the pulse of the public and identifies with their collective grief. The Queen resists displays of public emotion, while the Prime Minister understands how best to use them. It is a battle between perceptions and tradition along with the intransigence of power which finally yields to the public's mood.

In her September 29, 2006, *New York Times* review of *The Queen*, Manohla Dargis writes that actress Helen Mirren, "delivers a performance remarkable in its art and lack of sentimentalism" (http://movies.nytimes.com/2006/09/29/movies/29quee.html).

And Roger Ebert, in his October 16, 2006, *Chicago Sun-Times* review, called the movie, "a spellbinding story."

> Told in quiet scenes of proper behavior and guarded speech, *The Queen* is a spellbinding story of opposed passions—of Elizabeth's icy resolve to keep the royal family separate and aloof from the death of the divorced Diana, who was legally no longer a royal, and of Blair's correct reading of the public mood, which demanded some sort of public expression of sympathy from the crown for "The People's Princess." (http://rogerebert.suntimes.com)

🎥 *LETTERS FROM IWO JIMA* (2006)

PRODUCER/DIRECTOR: Clint Eastwood (director and producer), Steven Spielberg (producer), Robert Lorenz (producer)

WRITER(S): Iris Yamashita (screenplay and story), Paul Haggis (story), Tadamichi Kuribayashi (book *Picture Letters from Commander in Chief*), Tsuyoko Yoshido (book editor *Picture Letters from Commander in Chief*)

CAST: Ken Watanabe (General Kuribayashi), Kazunari Ninomiya (Saigo), Tsuyoshi Ihara (Baron Nishi), Ryo Kase (Shimizu), Shido Nakamura (Lieutenant Ito, as Shidou Nakamura)), Hiroshi Watanabe (Lieutenant Fujita), Takumi Bando (Captain Tanida), Yuki Matsuzaki (Nozaki), Takashi Yamaguchi (Kashiwara), Eijiro Ozaki (Lieutenant Okubo), Nae (Hanako), Nobumasa Sakagam (Admiral Ohsugi), Luke Eberl (Sam, as Lucas Elliot))

CINEMATOGRAPHY: Tom Stern (director of photography)

MUSIC: Kyle Eastwood, Michael Stevens

LENGTH AND RATING: 141 min; R

In *Letters from Iwo Jima*, director Clint Eastwood created a film that looks at one of America's most famous battles from the enemy's point of view. It is an uncompromising portrait of soldiers who discover that they are not that different from the enemy they are trying to kill.

As tools for propaganda and military recruitment, war movies have a singular purpose in helping Americans define the culture of war. They have been used to stir patriotic fervor emphasizing the virtues of heroic idealism in serving one's country and dying for a cause. In *Flags of Our Fathers* (2006), director Clint Eastwood used the battle of Iwo Jima and the famous flag-raising by American marines as a theme about how war, heroism, and sacrifice can be used as propaganda, compromising the values that are revered. Indeed, as history notes, there were actually two flag raisings on Mount Surabachi on the island of Iwo Jima. The first was raised on the morning of February 23, 1945, but the flag was small and could not be seen from the beach. The second flag raising, which occurred later in the day, was made famous by photographer Joe Rosenthal.

In the 1949 movie *Sands of Iwo Jima*, John Wayne is Sergeant John Stryker, a tough, no nonsense hardened marine who uses harsh methods to train his men to survive battle. The movie glorifies the virtues and sacrifice of war. In *Letters from Iwo Jima*, the perspective is very different, as it humanizes the enemy, giving him a face that audiences can identify with.

The conflict in *Letters from Iwo Jima* involves not only two nations at war but the soldiers of the Japanese Imperial army, sent to defend Iwo Jima and die in the process. For the Japanese infantryman, the only response to failure is suicide. However, some soldiers do question their responsibility to give their lives to a cause and a country on the brink of defeat, that cannot supply ammunition, food, water, or additional troops to defend the island. One of those is Saigo (Kazunari Ninomiya), a baker who left his pregnant wife and his business to serve. One night, elderly women and a soldier appeared at his door conscripting him and telling his crying wife what an honor it was for her husband to be chosen to die for his country. He is a shrewd survivor using his guile to avoid being killed by his comrades and the Americans.

359

Ken Kensei, Masashi Nagadoi, Hiroshi Watanabe, and Ken Watanabe. [Warner Bros./Dreamworks/Photofest]

For General Tadamichi Kuribayashi (Ken Watanabe), the task of defending the island with 20,000 troops against an invasion force of 100,000 Americans is hopeless; however, he is a professional soldier and will do his duty. Instead of wasting time building fortifications on the beach, General Kuribayashi orders the soldiers to dig tunnels in the mountains of Surabachi enabling their artillery to reign down on invading forces. He is also a family man, regretting that he was unable to finish the family's kitchen floor before he left. As a soldier, he has compassion for his men and stops his subordinates from mistreating them. Before the war Kuribayashi traveled to America as a military attaché, and in the movie, he is presented with a pearl-handled Colt revolver by admiring American military officers. At a dinner, the wife of an American officer asks if he would fire at her husband if Japan and America ever went to war, and he provides a philosophical answer about duty to one's country.

Another enlightened officer serving under General Kuribayashi is Baron Takeichi Nishi (Tsuyoshi Ihara), a lieutenant colonel who won a gold medal as an Olympic equestrian in the 1932 Los Angeles Olympics and who socialized with celebrities like actors Mary Pickford and Douglas Fairbanks. The movie portrays him as a compassionate man offering comfort (in English), aid, and scarce medication to a mortally wounded marine. After the marine dies, Nishi finds a letter from the soldier's mother and translates it into Japanese, reading it aloud for his troops. After hearing it, the soldiers realize the humanity of their enemy, and one remarks that what he heard is exactly what his own mother would say.

Overwhelmed by the Americans, some of the officers and men hold grenades to their bodies killing themselves. In one battle, Nishi is blinded and urges his men to fight on, killing himself after they leave the cave. At the end of the movie, General Kuribayashi is shot and dragged by Saigo to the beach. He asks if he is still on Japanese soil and when Saigo replies "yes," he removes his pearl-handled Colt and shoots himself. When he is captured, Saigo sees the Colt revolver in the waistband of a Marine and angrily shouts at him, wielding his shovel at the American in a threatening manner. He is taken prisoner and placed on a cot with wounded Americans on a troop ship.

In *Letters from Iwo Jima*, Clint Eastwood defies the conventions of war movies, which have become clichés for preserving the myths associated with nurturing the morality of war. Those who may doubt the horror of war need only watch the first twenty minutes of Steven Spielberg's *Saving Private Ryan* (1998), which graphically depicts the invasion of Omaha Beach in Normandy on D-day June 6, 1944.

In his December 20, 2006, review of *Letters from Iwo Jima* A. O. Scott writes of the film:

Letters, which observes the lives and deaths of Japanese soldiers in the battle for Iwo Jima, similarly adheres to some of the conventions of the genre even as it quietly dismantles them. It is, unapologetically and even humbly, true to the durable tenets of the war movie tradition, but it is also utterly original, even radical, in its methods and insights. (http://movies.nytimes.com/2006/12/20/movies/20lett.html)

In the December 20, 2006, *Los Angeles Times* Kenneth Turan wrote

Clint Eastwood's latest film, *Letters from Iwo Jima*, takes audiences to a place that would seem unimaginable for an American director. Daring and significant, it presents a picture from life's other side, not only showing what wartime was like for our Japanese adversaries on that island in the Pacific but also actually telling the story in their language. Which turns out to be no small thing. (http://www.calendarlive.com/printedition/calendar/cl-et-letters20dec20,0,1839926.story)

THE LIVES OF OTHERS (2006)

PRODUCER/DIRECTOR: Florian Henckel von Donnersmarck (director and producer)

WRITER(S): Florian Henckel von Donnersmarck

CAST: Martina Gedeck (Christa-Maria Sieland), Ulrich Mühe (Hauptmann Gerd Wiesler), Sebastian Koch (Georg Dreyman), Ulrich Tukur (Oberstleutnant Anton Grubitz), Thomas Thieme (Minister Bruno Hempf), Hans-Uwe Bauer (Paul Hauser), Volkmar Kleinert (Albert Jerska), Matthias Brenner (Karl Wallner), Charly Hübner (Udo), Herbert Knaup (Gregor Hessenstein), Bastian Trost (Häftling 227), Marie Gruber (Frau Meineke)

CINEMATOGRAPHY: Hagen Bogdanski

MUSIC: Stéphane Moucha, Gabriel Yared

LENGTH AND RATING: 137 min; R

This film, written and directed by Florian Henckel von Donnersmarck, presents a chilling portrait of life in East Germany, the German Democratic Republic G.D.R., under the brutal surveillance of the Stasi, the state police.

The principal characters are Georg Dreyman (Sebastian Koch) of East Berlin, a popular playwright who manages to tread a fine line between articulating his artisitic vision without violating state propaganda. His girlfriend, actress Christa-Maria Sieland (Martina Gedeck), is addicted to medication and is pursued by Minister Hempf (Thomas Thieme), a former Stasi official. Suspecting that Georg could be pro-Western and a potential dissident, Captain Gerd Wiesler (Ulrich Muhe) a Stasi agent is ordered by Colonel Grubitz (Ulrich Tukur), his superior officer and former classmate, to spy on him. This results in an elaborate operation involving twenty-four hour audio and video surveillance.

When Captain Wiesler (code named HGW XX/7) first appears on screen, he is lecturing to a class of Stasi students about interrogation techniques and using an example of the recent case of a suspect whom he questioned for assisting a friend escape to West Berlin. He explains the harsh techniques, including sleep deprivation, and is asked by a student if such a technique is inhuman. He replies that it is necessary and makes a notation in his book next to the student's name.

In a conversation with Grubitz, he learns about Minister Hempf's interest in Christa-Maria and the potential effect it could have on their careers if they could eliminate Georg. Listening and watching, Wiesler is consumed with their lives as his own life is sterile and routine. The only person whom he considers a friend is Grubitz, and he is using him. To satisfy his sexual needs, he hires a prostitute and when he asks her to stay, she is busy and admonishes him to schedule her for more time on her next visit. His existence is a metaphor for the sterility of life in the G.D.R.

At his fortieth birthday party, Jerska (Volkmar Kelinert), a black-listed writer, gives Georg a piece of sheet music entitled, "Sonata for A Good Man," and shortly after commits suicide. Frustrated by being used as an agent to arrest Georg so that Minister Hempf can have Christa-Maria to himself, Wiesler intrudes into the surveillance. After Christa-Maria has been picked up in Hempf's car and fondled by him, Wiesler remotely rings Georg's doorbell so that he walks downstairs and sees her leaving the car on the other side of the street.

Circumstances become tense, however, when an article about the high rate of suicide in the G.D.R. is anonymously published in *Der Spiegel,* a notable West German weekly magazine. Now Georg beomes a likely suspect, and his home is searched but nothing is found. As pressure builds to find evidence, Christa-Maria is picked up and interrogated by Wiesler under the watchful eye of Grubitz. Afraid and vulnerable, she reveals a secret compartment hidden under the floor where Georg hid the typewriter that he used to write the article. After hearing this, Christa-Maria is released and Wiesler rushes to the apartment to remove the damaging evidence before the Stasi raid. Distraught, Christa-Maria returns home, showers, and is in her bathrobe when Grubitz and the other agents arrive. She rushes into the street, stands in front of a truck, is hit, and killed. The Stasi agents leave, and Grubitz admonishes Wiesler, knowing that he removed the incriminating evidence, and assigns him to the tedious task of steaming open letters for censorship for the rest of his career. After the fall of the Berlin Wall, the end of the G.D.R., and the unification of Germany, Georg visits the Stasi archives and reads the voluminous file compiled by Wiesler. He confirms that his apartment was bugged and learns that Wiesler protected him by not documenting conversations with his friends and that it was Wiesler, not Christa-Maria, who removed the typewriter.

At the end of the movie, Wiesler's new job is delivering newspapers. As he passes a bookstore, he sees a new book published by Georg entitled *Symphony for A Good Man*. He buys the book, and when he opens it he sees that it dedicated to him, "HGWXX/7," with gratitude.

The film addresses contemporary themes about the curtailment of individual freedom, and the legality of eavesdropping and surveillance in a world concerned about terrorism. In the film *The Conversation* (1974), Gene Hackman plays Harry Caul, a paranoid surveillance expert who like Wiesler leads a nondescript life with no friends. Even the woman he's dating knows nothing about him. At the end of the movie, learning that he is now a victim, he tears apart his bugged aparment. Unable to locate the devices, he sits in the center of the room amongst the rubble and plays his saxaphone. The message in both films is that the right to privacy and the intrusion of government into the lives of its citizens cannot be compromised in the name of justice.

In his February 9, 2007, *New York Times* review of *The Lives of Others,* A. O. Scott wrote:

> There is a bracing, old-fashioned quality to Mr. von Donnersmarck's film, which supplies us with good guys to root for and villains to despise. But it also shows, with excruciating precision, the cruelty with which a totalitarian state can exploit the weakness and confusion of its citizens. And even as they are, to some extent, enacting a morality play, the actors also seem like real, vulnerable people forced into impossible choices. (http://movies.nytimes.com)

In his February 12, 2007, *New Yorker* review of *The Lives of Others* entitled, "Guilty Parties," Anthony Lane wrote, "It is a tribute to the richness of the film that one cannot say for sure who the hero is." He also cites *The Conversation* in his review:

> We are reminded of *The Conversation*, which kept Gene Hackman, king of the listening device, locked in a Wiesler-like solitude. Dazzling though Coppola's film was, it was at some level a fantasy, dreaming of dark conspiracies with which to spice our lives. That is a luxury von Donnersmarck cannot afford, and the paranoia shown within his movie is not a nightmare. It's government policy. (http://www.newyorker.com/arts/critics/cinema/2007/02/12/070212crci_cinema_lane?current Page=2)

AWAY FROM HER (2006)

PRODUCER/DIRECTOR: Sarah Polley (director), Daniel Iron (producer), Simone Urdl (producer), Jennifer Weiss (producer)

WRITER(S): Sarah Polley, Alice Munro (short story "The Bear Came Over the Mountain")

CAST: Gordon Pinsent (Grant Anderson), Stacey LaBerge (Young Fiona), Julie Christie (Fiona Anderson), Olympia Dukakis (Marian), Deanna Dezmari (Veronica), Clare Coulter (Phoebe Hart), Thomas Hauff (William Hart), Alberta Watson (Dr. Fischer), Grace Lynn Kung (Nurse Betty), Lili Francks (Theresa), Andrew Moodie (Liam)

CINEMATOGRAPHY: Luc Montpellier (director of photography)

MUSIC: Jonathan Goldsmith

LENGTH AND RATING: 110 min; PG-13

Perhaps the most touching and truthful observation about growing old is "The Seven Ages of Man" written by William Shakespeare and part of his play, *As You Like It*. Part of the text dealing with the end of life is excerpted below.

> The sixth age shifts
> Into the lean and slipper'd pantaloon,
> With spectacles on nose and pouch on side,
> His youthful hose, well sav'd a world too wide
> For his shrunk shank; and his big manly voice,
> Turning again toward childish treble, pipes
> And whistles in his sound. Last scene of all,
> That ends this strange eventful history,
> Is second childishness and mere oblivion;
> Sans teeth, sans eyes, sans taste, sans every thing. (II.vii)
>
> From: (http://shakespeare.about.com/od/faqshakespearesworks/
> f/sevenages.htm)

In the sixth stage of life, that manly voice and physical stature have shrunk into a shadow of what they were, and then the strange history ends as the elderly person faces oblivion with no teeth, eyes, taste…, with nothing.

In *Away from Her*, Grant (Gordon Pinsent) and Fiona Anderson (Julie Christie), a married couple together for forty-four years, live in quiet seclusion by a lake in the cold, snowy, climate of Ontario, Canada. Their life is punctuated by the comfort of two people who are very comfortable with each other, without the postured antics of besting one and other.

Their loving relationship is shattered when they both realize that Fiona is losing her memory to progressive Alzheimer's disease. A beautiful, strong, independent woman, she insists that she be placed in an assisted living facility hoping to protect her husband from the care she will need as a result of the degenerative disease. In an interesting narrative technique, the director Sarah Polley uses nonlinear editing as a metaphor for the mind bending experience that Fiona's memory is subjected to as a result of Alzheimer's.

Although Grant has witnessed Fiona's lapses—like losing her way while cross-country skiing in the snowy woods—he is reluctant to separate from her. He visits Meadowlake, the nursing facility, and is upset when he is shown the second floor for advanced Alzheimer's patients and cannot accept their policy that new clients cannot have any visitors for the first thirty days. He returns home with the admitting papers unsigned, but once again Fiona insists on going.

On the day she is admitted, Grant and Fiona make love in her new room and then he leaves the facility. When he returns after a month, he finds that Fiona doesn't recognize him as her husband and instead is quite reserved and aloof in her attitude toward him. Even more upsetting is that Fiona has become a principal caregiver to wheel-chair bound Aubrey (Michael Murphy), and they appear to be romantically involved. Resenting his wife's interest in another man, Grant wonders if she is putting on a charade to punish him for past infidelities with his female college students many years ago.

When Aubrey's wife Marian (Olympia Dukakis) decides to remove him from Meadowlake for financial reasons, Fiona falls into a deep depression and must be moved to the second floor. Seeing his wife deteriorate into a shadow of herself, Grant visits Marian inquiring about the possibility of returning Aubrey to the facility. A romantic friendship develops between these two, and eventually Marian trusts Grant to take Aubrey on a visit to see Fiona. On that day, after arriving at the facility, Grant sees Fiona alone prior to Aubrey's visit, and she demonstrates the rare spark of her former self, recognizing him and thanking Grant for not leaving her. They embrace and the movie fades out.

With the aging of the "baby boomers," there has been greater attention paid to the needs of the elderly concerning prescription drugs, health and nursing care, residential treatment, and funding of Medicare. One of the most tragic events for the family of an Alzheimer's patient is that the afflicted individual may not recognize their loved ones.

Without a nod to sentimentality, *Away from Her* tells a poignant story of Alzheimer's from a number of perspectives including the difficulty for a healthy spouse to accept the circumstances and the financial repercussions of residential treatment. It also addresses the courage of the afflicted person in the character of Fiona, who understands the need to leave her loving husband Grant and accept her fate.

In his May 4, 2007, *New York Times* review, A. O. Scott wrote of *Away From Her* that the film considered two great human mysteries, love and the workings of the brain.

> In a refreshingly direct, unassuming manner, *Away From Her* considers two great human mysteries: the persistence of love and the workings of the brain. It takes the twilight of a long, mostly happy marriage as a vantage point from which to look back at youth and forward into the waiting darkness. (http://movies.nytimes.com)

In the *New Yorker* magazine May 14, 2007, review of *Away from Her*, film critic David Denby praised actress Sarah Polley for her feature film debut and called the movie, "a small-scale triumph."

> The fading of memory, the anguish of losing the contours and the colors of the physical world, the mixture of loyalty and selfishness in the elderly—these are not subjects you would expect a young filmmaker to understand or even to take much interest in. Yet *Away from Her*, based on the Alice Munro story "The Bear Came Over the Mountain" (first published in this magazine in 1999), was written and directed by Sarah Polley, a Canadian actress who is still in her twenties. The movie, Polley's feature début, is a small-scale triumph that could herald a great career. (http://www.newyorker.com/arts/critics/cinema/2007/05/14/070514crci_cinema_denby?currentPage)

THE DEPARTED (2007)

PRODUCER/DIRECTOR: Martin Scorsese (director), Brad Grey (producer), Graham King (producer), Roy Lee (producer), Brad Pitt (producer)

WRITER(S): William Monahan (screenplay), Siu Fai Mak (2002 screenplay Mou gaan dou, as Alan Mak), Felix Chong (2002 screenplay Mou gaan dou)

CAST: Leonardo DiCaprio (Billy Costigan), Matt Damon (Colin), Jack Nicholson (Costello), Mark Wahlberg (Dignam), Martin Sheen (Queenan), Ray Winstone (Mr. French), Vera Farmiga (Madolyn), Anthony Anderson (Brown), Alec Baldwin (Ellerby), Kevin Corrigan (Cousin Sean), James Badge Dale (Barrigan), David O'Hara (Fitzy, as David Patrick

O'Hara), Mark Rolston (Delahunt), Robert Wahlberg (Lazio—FBI), Kristen Dalton (Gwen)

CINEMATOGRAPHY: Michael Ballhaus (director of photography)

MUSIC: Howard Shore

LENGTH AND RATING: 151 min; R

The genre of gangster films has reflected the struggle of various ethnic groups to legitimize themselves as upwardly mobile in American society. Historically, Italian Americans and the Mafia have been a group that became frequent subjects of these films. Indeed, the Italian American community expressed its outrage over the portryal of Italian Americans on the ABC television series *The Untouchables* (1959–1963) to Leonard Goldenson then president of the American Broadcasting Company. In 1987 *The Untouchables* was adapted into a successful theatrical feature film.

Of course, *The Godfather* trilogy created an epic that established the historical narrative structure that has had a lasting influence on the genre. Other gangster films associated with ethnic Italians include *Scarface* (1932), *Mean Streets* (1973), *Goodfellas* (1990), and *Donnie Brasco* (1997). Other ethnic groups including Jews, Irish, Hispanics, and Asians, have had their influence on organized crime and corruption documented on film. One film that was very ambitious in profiling Jewish gang activity was Sergio Leone's flawed masterpiece *Once Upon a Time in America* (1984). Other films that addressed the cooperation of Jews and Italians in organized crime and were based on real characters included *Casino* (1995) and *Bugsy* (1991).

The Irish and their involvement in criminal activity has also been the subject of numerous films. In *Miller's Crossing* (1990) Albert Finney, who portrays political boss Liam "Leo" O'Bannon, listens to a record of "Danny Boy" the signature Irish ballad in his bedroom. He narrowly escapes an assassination attempt and retrieves a machine gun killing the assassins while the music plays in the background. Other films featuring Irish underworld characters are *Road to Perdition* (2002) and *The Departed*.

There's a line in the film *Millers Crossing* when a character tells another, "Up is down, black is white," which is applicable to *The Departed*. It is a remake of the Hong Kong film *Infernal Affairs* (2002) directed by Andrew Lau and Alan Mak, with a screenplay adapted by William Monahan, set in Boston in the Irish community. The plot becomes intricate as there are bad guys masquerading as good guys and good guys masquerading as bad guys, and there is Francis "Frank" Costello (Jack Nicholson) the local Irish crime kingpin in the city of Boston. He leads his crew with the wisdom of an Eastern philosopher, "I don't want to be a product of my environment, I want my environment to be a product of me." He also advises that, "No one gives it to you, you have to take it." He's a tough and at times a cruel leader who understands human psychology and desire. His character is loosely based on James Joseph "Whitey" Bulger, Jr., who rose to prominence in Boston's Winter Hill Gang, was an FBI informant, and is on the FBI's ten most wanted list.

Clever and diabolically shrewd, Costello recruits Colin Sullivan (Matt Damon) as a young boy, nurturing him, which eventually results in him graduating from the Massachusetts State Police Academy. Although they don't know each other William "Billy" Costigan (Leonardo DiCaprio) is also a member of the same graduating class. Ironically, they are interviewed back to back by Captain Queenan (Martin Sheen) of the Special Investigations Unit (SIU) and Sergeant Dingham (Mark Wahlberg). Fortuitously,

Sullivan is assigned to the Organized Crime Unit of SIU, a task force commanded by Captain Ellerby (Alex Baldwin) and their only target of investigation is Frank Costello. Smart and ingratiating Sullivan rises quickly and is Costello's mole tipping him off by cell phone and text messaging about impending police raids and tails.

However, Queenan and Dingham have other plans for Costigan because of his family's previous involvement with Costello. He agrees to go undercover to infiltrate Costello's gang and serves a short jail sentence that includes probation and mandatory visits to the police psychiatrist, Dr. Madolyn Madden (Vera Farmiga). Although Madolyn has a relationship with Sullivan and moves into his apartment, she is attracted to Costigan and has sex with him. Eventually, the two form a trusting bond, and when Costigan's charade begins to crumble he entrusts Madolyn with evidence implicating Sullivan. In deep cover, Costigan's identity is known only to Queenan and Dingham.

Acting tough and beating up a couple of Italian American hoods infringing on Costello's protection racket brings him to the crime boss's attention. He becomes a member of the crew and is teamed up with Mr. French (Ray Winstone) Costello's second in command collecting debts owed to the boss. In one such visit he learns that Costello is an FBI informant.

Soon both Costello and Queenan learn that there are moles or "rats" in their respective organizations. For Sullivan and Costigan, concealing their identities and sustaining dual personalities takes its emotional and physical toll. Searching for the mole in the state police, Ellerby places Sullivan in command, checking out every member in the unit. Concerned about his rat, Costello orders every man in his crew to write his social security number down, and the information is placed in an envelope marked "citizen," and is given to Sullivan. The envelope has a distinctive marking because one crew member misspelled the word and it was crossed out and spelled correctly by Costigan.

When Sullivan learns that Queenan is meeting the mole (Costigan) in an abandoned building, he puts a police tail on him and informs Costello. The police are there when Costello's men arrive but are told not to engage them. Telling Costigan to flee, Queenan confronts Costello's men and is thrown off the roof. There's a shootout and Timothy Delahunt (Mark Rolston), a Costello crew member is severely wounded. In hiding, Delahunt who had called Costigan with the address for the rendezvous, admits that he mistakenly gave him the wrong address, but Costigan arrived at the correct building implying that he is the mole. However, he informs Costigan that he didn't tell anyone and is later revealed by the press to be an undercover police officer.

Subsequent to Queenan's death, Ellerby orders Dingham to reveal the file on Costello's mole, but he refuses threatening to resign and is given a two-week paid leave of absence. In the interim, Sullivan alerts Costello of a police tail on his way to pick up a shipment of cocaine and then calls the tail off lying that he knows where they are going because he is in contact with the mole. Suspecting trouble Costigan leaves the rendezvous, and the police attack the gang. Mortally wounded, Costello asks Sullivan for help but is shot and killed by him when he confronts him about being an FBI informant and asks if Costello informed on him.

Greeted as a hero, Sullivan basks in the glory of his "victory." Fumbling with Queenan's cell phone, he calls Costigan and convinces him to "come out of the cold." When Costigan arrives he sees the envelope with the word "citizen" on it and realizes that Sullivan is Costello's mole. He flees and his personnel file is erased by Sullivan. Later, the two men agree to meet at the same building where Queenan was killed. On the roof, Costigan takes Sullivan prisoner and is met by Trooper Brown (Anthony Anderson), a classmate from the police academy whom he called to witness the event. They confront each other with weapons drawn, and he takes Sullivan on the elevator heading to the first floor. Brown uses the stairs. As the elevator opens on the first floor, Trooper Barrigan (James Badge Dale), who went to the academy with Sullivan, shoots Costigan in the head and then kills Brown when he arrives. Telling Sullivan that he was also working for Costello, he says that they must stick together, but he is killed by Sullivan who wants to protect his secret.

In the aftermath, Sullivan tells his superiors that he is recommending Costigan for the department's highest honor, the Medal of Merit. When he arrives home, he finds that Madolyn was leaving him. She had opened the envelope left in her safe-keeping by Costigan, listened to tapes of conversations between Sullivan and Costello, and learned that he is the dirty cop. After Costigan's department funeral, Madolyn, who is pregnant, ignores Sullivan. Sullivan returns home with a bag of groceries, when he is confronted by Dingham as he enters his apartment. Dingham, dressed in an inert fiber suit, wearing gloves, and with his shoes covered, shoots Sullivan in the head.

Themes that are integrated in *The Departed* include loyalty, morality, religious faith, and respect for authority. For Sullivan and Costigan, crime boss Frank Costello is a paternalistic figure who represents the fathers they never had. In Costigan's case, his other father figure is Captain Queenan whom he meets surreptitiously at his home late one night and is asked to share in the captain's meal. When the two men face Costello's crew at the abandoned building, Queenan orders Costigan to flee, protecting him and sacrificing himself for the younger man. There is also a religious motif in the film as Costello rebels against the Catholic faith in a diner insulting two priests and a nun with crude pornographic drawings.

In her October 6, 2006, *New York Times* review, Manohla Dargis compared *The Departed* with the original *Infernal Affairs*, writing that the actors who played the same roles in the original seemed to have greater "adult assurance."

> Fine as Mr. DiCaprio and Mr. Damon are, neither is strong enough to usurp memories of the actors who played the same roles in the original—Tony Leung as the good guy, Andy Lau as the bad—both of whom register with more adult assurance. That's an observation, not an indictment. Comparisons between *Infernal Affairs* and its redo are unavoidable given how closely the screenwriter William Monahan follows the first film's beats and scenes. But as fans of *Infernal Affairs* (and its two sequels) know well, the Hong Kong film owes an enormous debt to Mr. Scorsese, whose imprint, along with that of Michael Mann, is all over the trilogy. (http://movies.nytimes.com)

Writing in the *Chicago Sun-Times*, on July 6, 2007, Roger Ebert said the Scorsese film is not merely a retread of *Infernal Affairs*:

> What makes this a Scorsese film, and not merely a retread, is the director's use of actors, locations and energy, and its buried theme. I am fond of saying that a movie is not about what it's about; it's about how it's about it. That's always true of a Scorsese film. (http://rogerebert.suntimes.com/apps/pbcs.dll/article?AID=/20070705/REVIEWS/70705002/1023)

🎥 *MICHAEL CLAYTON* (2007)

PRODUCER/DIRECTOR: Tony Gilroy (director), (producer)

WRITER(S): Tony Gilroy

CAST: Tom Wilkinson (Arthur Edens), Micheal O'Keefe (Barry Grissom), Sydney Pollack (Marty Bach), Danielle Skraastad (Bridget Klein, voice), Tilda Swinton (Karen Crowder), George Clooney (Michael Clayton)

CINEMATOGRAPHY: Robert Elswit

MUSIC: James Newton Howard

LENGTH AND RATING: 119 min; R

Corruption, greed, and mendacity have consumed corporate America for decades, and film has embraced these themes, sometimes making heroes of those who succeed in taming the titans of industry. Lawyers are particularly vulnerable to temptation but may rise to heights of morality and ethics. In *The Verdict* (1982), Paul Newman, an alcoholic ambulance chasing lawyer, takes on a hospital operated by the archdiocese of Boston and goes to trial instead of negotiating an out-of-court settlement for the negligent death of his client. Another crusading attorney, portrayed by John Travolta in *A Civil Action* (1993), represented a number of clients who suffered serious injuries from contaminated drinking water in Woburn, Massachusetts.

People who are not lawyers may also become crusaders based upon their circumstances. Women have made their mark on social justice, sometimes based upon real characters, in films that have chronicled their courage and sacrifice. These movies include *Norma Rae* (1979), starring Sally Field as a labor organizer at a southern textile factory, *Silkwood* (1983) starring Meryl Streep as Karen Silkwood, who died in a car crash while investigating the Kerr-McGee plutonium plant she worked in, and *Erin Brockovich* (2000) starring Julia Roberts Erin Brovkovich who joined a law firm (not as a lawyer but a clerk) and became the lead investigator in a class action suit investigating chemical groundwater contamination by the Pacific Gas and Electric Company.

In the movie *Michael Clayton,* George Clooney plays the title character, who has been at a prestigious New York law firm run by Marty Bach (Sydney Pollack) for fifteen years, but never making partner. Instead, his skills are put to better use as a fixer or janitor, cleaning up the messes of his partner colleagues. His private life impinges upon his professional life as he struggles to repay a $75,000 debt owed to underworld figures to finance a restaurant that he started with his alcoholic younger brother Timmy (David Lansbury) and dealing with his penchant for gambling. Divorced, he also tries to make regular contact with his son Henry (Austin Williams), whom he picks up and drives to school in the morning.

There are several story arcs at play including the impending merger of Bach's law firm with one from London and the settlement of a class action lawsuit that has been lingering for years. The suit brought against United Northfield or U-North claimed millions of dollars for the plaintiffs who were injured by the company's manufacture of a cancer-causing herbicide. The law firm's chief litigator Arthur Edens (Tom Wilkinson), has gone off his meds and during a crucial deposition, strips naked and is eventually arrested. The audience learns later that Edens has found evidence in a document prepared by U-North admitting that the herbicide (weed killer) caused cancer and was working against the firm's client conspiring with the claimants. Dispatched to handle Edens, Clayton fails to ameliorate the situation.

At the beginning of the movie, Clayton is in a poker game and when he leaves, a partner calls him on his cell phone asking for his help in representing a major client who was involved in a hit and run. Driving to Westchester, he meets the client who is hostile to Clayton when he is told about the reality of his situation. After leaving Westchester, Clayton drives on a country road, stops, and leaves his car to admire three horses grazing in a pasture. There is a sudden explosion, and his car is consumed by fire.

The narrative is told in flashback as the audience learns about what led up to the explosion. After meeting Clayton, Karen Crowder (Tilda Swinton), the corporate general counsel for U-North has deep reservations about Edens and the jeopardy that he has placed her firm in. She is a vicious, confident competitor who glories in her power and rehearses her presentations before making them. Deciding that Edens is irretrievably compromised by his mental instability she contacts a team of "plumbers" who tap his phone and terminate him, making it look like a suicide. Distraught over his friend's death and troubled by the police finding of suicide, Clayton asks his brother, (Sean Cullen), a New York police detective, to get him access to Edens' apartment which has been sealed by the police. Searching the apartment, Clayton comes across a note that falls out of a book but is arrested by two police officers for violating the seal on the apartment. The police were called by the same team who killed Edens and are now tailing Clayton. After being released by the police, Clayton goes to a copy center as indicated by the notepaper he found and retrieves the copy order placed by Edens which was for thousands of copies of the U-North report admitting complicity in releasing the cancerous herbicide. Taking a copy of the report, he is followed by the team of plumbers who obtain their own copy and inform Crowder, who authorizes Clayton's termination.

In the flashback, the team of "plumbers" is wiring Clayton's car with an explosive device, but he unexpectedly leaves the card game early, preventing them from wiring their remote tracking device. They follow Clayton to Westchester, and when he leaves they continue pursuit on the country road and activate the bomb, assuming they have killed him. Thinking fast, Clayton throws his wallet, watch, and cell phone into the burning car and later is reported dead.

At the U-North board of directors meeting, Crowder proposes that the company accept the settlement, which can be engineered as a huge tax write-off. Asked to leave the meeting so that the directors can confer, she is confronted by Clayton, whom she is shocked to see alive. He chastises her for trying to kill him because he's a fixer and then demands ten million dollars in hush money to remain quiet about his knowledge about her involvement in Edens' murder and the attempt on his life. She reluctantly agrees. Clayton reveals a telephone that recorded his conversation, which was monitored by his brother the police detective, and she is arrested. Leaving the scene, Clayton gets into a New York taxi and tells the driver to give him fifty dollars worth, referring to the length of the ride.

As a lawyer, Michael Clayton is not a heroic figure. He's a bagman for the firm insuring that none of its partners or clients is contaminated by any messy business. His job is to get Edens to take his medication so that he can continue to pursue the U-North case on behalf of the firm. But after Edens is murdered and his life is threatened, Clayton becomes a revenging angel, refusing the bribe and vindicating his worth as a lawyer, a person, and a friend.

Interestingly, Sydney Pollack (Marty Bach), the producer of *Michael Clayton,* directed *The Firm* (1993) about a law firm in Memphis that murdered its uncooperative associates.

In her October 5, 2007, *New York Times* review of *Michael Clayton*, Manohla Dargis writes that the movie, is absorbing and entertains without shame:

> It's a modest reappraisal, adult, sincere, intelligent, absorbing; it entertains without shame. Mr. Gilroy directs with a steady hand and a steady eye, too, with none of the visual frenzy that characterizes the "Bourne" thrillers. His movie moves rather than races. There's a little narrative tricky business (a sizable portion of the story occurs in extended flashback) and an unexpectedly tender moment when Michael stares into a new morning in a country field without uttering a single word. (http://movies.nytimes.com)

In his *New Yorker* review of *Michael Clayton* on October 8, 2007, David Denby wrote "Cutting from one place to another and jumping around in time, Gilroy keeps the tension level high. He's aided by Robert Elswit's gleaming cinematography, which turns the enormous law offices into a field of moral ambiguity—the shadows recede into the distance like little pockets of dread" (http://www.newyorker.com/arts/critics/cinema/2007/10/08/071008crci_cinema_denby).

DRAMAS OF PAUL HAGGIS

Crash **(2004)**
In the Valley of Elah **(2007)**

These two films were directed by screenwriter Paul Haggis who wrote the screenplay for Clint Eastwood's *Million Dollar Baby*. Although *Crash* received an Academy Award for best picture in 2005, some critics found it contrived and shallow in its treatment of bigotry and racism. As for the *Valley of Elah,* a film about a father searching for his son, an Iraq war veteran gone AWOL after returning to the States and found brutally murdered, the plot according to some critics was a pedestrian crime drama in the fashion of the *Law and Order* television franchise.

🎥 *CRASH* (2004)

PRODUCER/DIRECTOR: Paul Haggis (director and producer), Don Cheadle, (producer), Bobby Moresco (producer)

WRITER(S): Paul Haggis (story and screenplay), Robert Moresco (screenplay, as Bobby Moresco)

CAST: Karina Arroyave (Elizabeth), Dato Bakhtadze (Lucien), Sandra Bullock (Jean Cabot), Don Cheadle (Det. Graham Waters), Art Chudabala (Ken Ho), Sean Cory (Motorcycle Cop), Tony Danza (Fred), Keith David (Lt. Dixon), Loretta Devine (Shaniqua Johnson), Matt Dillon (Officer John Ryan), Jennifer Esposito (Ria), Ime Etuk (Georgie, as Ime N. Etuk), Eddie J. Fernandez (Officer Gomez, as Eddie Fernandez), William Fichtner (Flanagan), Howard Fong (Store Owner), Brendan Fraser (Rick)

CINEMATOGRAPHY: J. Michael Muro (director of photography)

MUSIC: Mark Isham

LENGTH AND RATING: 112 min; R

Poverty, crime, and unemployment can boil over into violent confrontations in the crowded big cities of America. The movie *Crash* weaves a complex narrative providing a racially charged canvas for people to ease their frustrations by hurting each other, emotionally and physically. Perhaps one of the most provocative films to study the alienation that is generated by the complexities of modern society was *Falling Down* (1993) starring Michael Douglas as William "Bill" Foster (aka "D-FENS" on his vanity license plate). Recently divorced and laid off from his job in the defense industry, Bill is driving to his daughter's birthday party on the hottest day of the year. He is estranged from his ex-wife who has an order of protection pending against him. After his car air conditioner breaks down in the bumper-to-bumper Los Angeles freeway traffic, he abandons the car and sets off on foot. During his trek, he has a number of violent confrontations displacing his anger on a Korean merchant who insults him with broken English and an exorbitant price for a can of Coke, a couple of Hispanic gang members who try to rob him, and an obnoxiously nice clerk and store manager of a Whammy Burger franchise restaurant who refuse to serve him breakfast as that menu ends at 11:30 and Bill's watch reads 11:35. Angry, he pulls an automatic weapon from a carry bag taken from the Hispanic gang members who had tried to kill him in a drive-by shooting, creating a panic in the Whammy Burger restaurant. As he tries to calm the patrons, he accidentally pulls the trigger, fires several rounds into the ceiling, and must then quell the panic again. Changing his mind, Bill orders a Whammy Burger from the lunch menu. Opening the package, he expresses his annoyance that the shrunken burger bears no resemblance to the picture of the plump, juicy burger on display.

In *Crash*, the characters are woven into the fabric of a culture that condones the manipulation of contrived displays of egalitarianism which are corrupt manifestations of unbiased equal opportunity. When Los Angeles District Attorney Rick Cabot's (Brendan Fraser) car is hijacked, he ruefully laments the fact that the hijackers were two black men attempting to assess the potential political damage to his career. Preoccupied with his own concerns about his political future, he offers condescending assurances to his wife Jean (Sandra Bullock), who is outraged by his nonchalant attitude toward her fear. She demands that the locks, which are being changed in her home, be changed again in the morning because the locksmith, a Mexican American named Daniel Ruiz (Michael Pena), could be a "gangbanger" who will sell copies of the keys on the street.

In another incident, a black married couple, Cameron (Terrence Howard) and Christine (Thandie Newton) Thayer, both educated professionals driving in an SUV, are pulled over by two police officers—John Ryan (Matt Dillon), a racist cop, and Tommy Hanson (Ryan Phillipe), a novice policeman—when Ryan notices that Christine had just performed fellatio on her husband while he was driving. A little tipsy, Christine objects to the police harassment, and both she and Cameron are asked to exit the vehicle to be searched for weapons. Wearing a sleek cocktail dress, Christine is subjected to a body search, with Ryan running his hands down and in between her legs. Ryan offers Cameron an opportunity to apologize, and the couple is allowed to leave. However, Christine is outraged that Cameron allowed Ryan to feel her up during the "search" and berates him for being a coward and an "Uncle Tom."

Her displeasure leads to two separate confrontations with the police—in one, Cameron's SUV is involved in an attempted hijack by Anthony (Chris "Ludacris"

Bridges). Fighting him off, Cameron continues to drive erratically through the streets and is chased by a number of police cars. When they finally stop, Anthony cowers in the passenger seat, and Cameron confronts the police refusing to heed their commands, reacting to Christine's criticism of him. Recognizing Cameron, Officer Tommy Hanson, who requested a transfer from being partnered with Ryan, whom he viewed as racist, intervenes and prevents his fellow officers from killing Cameron.

In another iteration of the Thayer story, Christine is involved in an automobile accident, her vehicle is upside down, and she is trapped inside. The first officer on the scene is John Ryan, and when Christine recognizes him, she refuses his assistance until he assures her that he will not harm her. Realizing the threat to her life, she cooperates with Ryan and he risks his life pulling her to safety just before the car catches fire and explodes.

Stealing cars and bemoaning the black man's fate in a bigoted white society, Anthony clings to the rituals of racism as he hypothesizes about the treatment of blacks by whites. He doesn't use the public buses because their large glass windows are tools for white people to subjugate blacks by putting them on display as downtrodden masses.

His friend and partner in crime is Peter Waters (Larenz Tate) who is the younger brother of Graham Waters (Don Cheadle) a detective in the Los Angeles police department. Their mother is a drug addict, and Graham has promised her that he will find Peter, who has not been in touch with them. But Graham is busy working a case involving a white policeman who shoots a black police officer. The white officer has a history of racism, and Graham gets caught in the middle when the assistant district attorney acknowledges Graham's findings that the black officer was corrupt but that the city needs an African American hero cop and asks him to suppress evidence in return for squashing a third felony arrest for his brother Peter. He's having an affair with Ria (Jennifer Esposito), his Latina detective partner, who derides him for being uncaring about his mother and prejudiced toward Hispanics. She is also insensitive when their unit is involved in an accident with a woman of Chinese descent and Jennifer mocks her accent. He finally finds his brother Peter shot dead at the side of a road, killed by Officer Tommy Hanson who gave him a lift in his car. Hanson saw Peter reach into his pocket, perceived it as a threat, and shot him.

Although the movie consists of subplots pertaining to the characters and their lives, their actions intersect, creating a compelling narrative. All of them face internal and external hostilities, perceived and real. Whether it's an Iranian immigrant who blames an innocent locksmith for the destruction of his business and attempts to shoot him, not knowing that his daughter loaded the weapon with blanks, or a truck stolen by Anthony loaded with illegal Chinese immigrants who can be sold on the black market, but instead he sets them free in Chinatown, there are lessons to be learned about people needing people. And perhaps that is the moral of the movie...hatred and bigotry have no value except to destroy the essence of humanity.

In his *New York Times* review of May 6, 2005, A. O. Scott wrote the *Crash* belongs to a genre of films that brings people of radical backgrounds together by grim serendipity.

> It belongs to a genre that has been flourishing in recent years—at least in the esteem of critics—but that still lacks a name. A provisional list of examples might include *Monster's Ball, House of Sand and Fog* and *21 Grams*. In each of these films, as in *Crash*, Americans from radically different backgrounds are brought together by a

grim serendipity that forces them, or at least the audience, to acknowledge their essential connectedness.

He also described *Crash* as a frustrating movie. "So what kind of a movie is *Crash*? A frustrating movie: full of heart and devoid of life; crudely manipulative when it tries hardest to be subtle; and profoundly complacent in spite of its intention to unsettle and disturb" (http://movies.nytimes.com).

In his January 8, 2006 *Chicago Sun Times* review of *Crash*, Roger Ebert wrote that the film's box office slowly increased due to word-of-mouth:

> The success of the film suggests it struck a lot of people the same way; opening last spring as a low-profile release, it held its box office and slowly built through word-of-mouth, as people told each other about it. It opened in May with a $9 million weekend, and by September had grossed $55 million. *Crash* and *March of the Penguins* were the two most successful "word-of-mouth" pictures of the year.
>
> In my original review, I wrote: "If there is hope in the story, it comes because as the characters crash into one another, they learn things, mostly about themselves. Almost all of them are still alive at the end and are better people because of what has happened to them. Not happier, not calmer, not even wiser, but better." (http://rogerebert.suntimes.com)

IN THE VALLEY OF ELAH (2007)

PRODUCER/DIRECTOR: Paul Haggis (director), Emilio Diez Barroso (producer), Erik Feig (producer), Stanley J. Wlodkowski (producer)
WRITER(s): Paul Haggis (screenplay and story), Mark Boal (story)
CAST: Tommy Lee Jones (Hank Deerfield), Charlize Theron (Det. Emily Sanders), Jason Patric (Lt. Kirklander), Susan Sarandon (Joan Deerfield), James Franco (Sgt. Dan Carnelli), Barry Corbin (Arnold Bickman), Josh Brolin (Chief Buchwald), Frances Fisher (Evie), Wes Chatham (Corporal Steve Penning), Jake McLaughlin (Spc. Gordon Bonner)
CINEMATOGRAPHY: Roger Deakins
MUSIC: Mark Isham
LENGTH AND RATING: 121 min; R

Movies about America's involvement in unpopular wars can be a tough sell at the box office, especially if the war is still in progress. This has been the case for films about the Iraq war, which have had a tepid reception by movie audiences. Some of the films are based on authentic events like Brian DePalma's *Redacted* (2007), about the rape and murder of a fourteen-year-old Iraqi girl by four American soldiers who killed the girl's family, then burned their home and their bodies. Another gruesome crime was the basis for *In the Valley of Elah,* based on Mark Boal's May 2004 investigative *Playboy* article "Death and Dishonor," about the murder and dismemberment of Richard Thomas Ong Davis, a Filipino American soldier who returned from Iraq. He came from a military family, his mother served as an Army medic, and his father was a twenty-year veteran serving as a military policeman in Korea and Vietnam.

There is a great deal of depth and substance to *In the Valley of Elah*. It addresses the pride and virtue of serving one's country and the respect that should be earned as a soldier. When his son Mike (Jonathan Tucker) returns to the United States from Iraq and is reported AWOL, his father and veteran military policeman Hank Deerfield (Tommy Lee Jones) kisses his wife Joan (Susan Sarandon) and takes the long drive to the Fort Rudd Army base in New Mexico to find his son. As he drives off, he stops at a local school where a Salvadoran custodian has displayed the American flag upside down; Hank assists, telling him that when an American flag is upside down it's a sign of great distress. He helps the custodian raise the flag the correct way and advises that it should never touch the ground and that it must be lowered at night. That scene reveals the character and disciplined military background of Hank Deerfield.

Arriving at the Army base, Hank is shown his son's quarters and, although nothing can be removed, he manages to take Mike's cell phone, which is "fried" from the heat in Iraq. He brings the phone to a techie and pays to have the images his son recorded assembled and sent to him by e-mail. When Hank visits the local police for their assistance in finding his son, he is rebuffed by Detective Emily Sanders (Charlize Theron), who tells him that as a former military man he should know that's it's a military matter.

A short time later, the local police including Detective Sanders, respond to a report of a burnt, dismembered body in a field near the army base. Sanders is a single mother who suffers the sexist ridicule of her colleagues who feel that she "fucked" her way to her job when she had an affair with the chief. However, she appears to be the police officer on the scene with the most savvy and is annoyed when the Army military police take over the investigation because of jurisdictional purview. The body parts are revealed to be Mike's from partial fingerprints, and Hank insists on seeing his son's remains. In a moving and emotionally wrenching scene, Hank calls his wife Joan to tell her the bad news, and as he tries to use his military discipline for self-control, Joan breaks down sobbing, pleading to understand why both her sons are dead. The audience learns that Hank and Joan had another son David, also in the military, who had been killed in a helicopter accident ten years earlier.

Returning to the police station, Emily drives Hank to the crime scene where he criticizes the local authorities for trampling evidence and concludes that Mike was dragged through the brush and killed in another part of the field, moving the crime scene into the jurisdiction of the local police. Wanting to continue the investigation, Emily pleads with her chief to allow her to proceed, and he agrees. She also works with Hank in establishing leads and investigating them. She learns that Private Robert Ortiez (Victor Wolf) is AWOL, and she and other officers hunt him down. Although he's ordered not to follow, Hank drives his truck and captures Ortiez, beating him up until he's subdued by the police. However, further investigation reveals that Ortiez had no involvement in Mike's death.

In a touching scene after dinner at Emily's home, Hank attempts to read her son David (Devon Brochu) a bed time story. However, the storybook is unfamiliar to him, and so he asks the boy if he knows whom he was named after. Not knowing, Hank relates the biblical story of David and Goliath and how the young diminutive Israelite confronted the giant Philistine with a mere slingshot and felled him in the Valley of Elah. He probably told the very same story about bravery to his sons Mike and David. After he leaves David's bedroom, Hank closes the door and when Emily mentions that he prefers the door open he replies that David will be fine. A few seconds later David calls out "door" and Emily opens it but he allows his mother to close it further than he has ever consented to before.

Although none of Mike's fellow soldiers, who were out with him on the night he disappeared, can provide information about the murder, there are lingering suspicions about their honesty. After a long evening, Emily takes a second look at copies of Mike's bank statements and notices a discrepancy in the signature used to charge three chicken dinners on the night of his disappearance. She visits Hank at his motel and they proceed to the military base where they learn that three soldiers, one of whom has committed suicide, have confessed to the killing. She demands to have Hank hear the confession, and the soldier who stabbed Mike over forty times tells what happened with emotionless detachment.

Returning home, Hank finds a package addressed to him from Mike while he was still in Iraq. Opening it he finds a tattered American flag and takes it to the local school, raises it in an upside down position and tapes it to the flag pole telling the custodian never to take it down.

The film is a realistically harsh portrayal of what happens to young soldiers placed in life-threatening danger and the post-traumatic stress they experience. Thinking that he knew his son, Hank is disturbed to learn that he earned the nickname "Doc" because of his sadistic pleasure in putting his hand in the wound of an Iraqi and asking if it hurt and, after hearing the cry of pain, would repeat the action asking the same question. He also recalls a telephone conversation with Mike when he called his father to ask his help in getting him out of Iraq. From his son's cell phone he witnesses an event where the Humvee he was driving, under orders never to stop, runs over a child. In retrospect, Hank now knows why Mike was so upset when he called.

This is not a movie of political protest like *Born on the Fourth of July* (1989), although both address the trauma and emotional injuries of war. Portraying Hank Deerfield as a loving husband and father, Tommy Lee Jones also shows a man wedded to the routine of military life and the discipline that it creates. Visiting topless bars and honky-tonks near the base, he confronts a familiar milieu but the young soldiers are very different from the men he served with decades earlier. He is troubled by their cold aloofness and compromised integrity. When he raises the flag in an upside down position he is crying out to help them because he fears they could be lost forever in "the fog of war."

In his September 24, 2007, *New Yorker* review of *In the Valley of Elah*, David Denby wrote that *"In the Valley of Elah* moves steadily and strongly forward on two tracks. Part of the movie is a complex and suspenseful police procedural, culminating in a set of unnerving interrogations. The picture is also a technological and metaphysical lunge at the truth" (http://www.newyorker.com/arts/critics/cinema/2007/09/24/070924crci_cinema_denby?curren).

In another review, Roger Ebert wrote in the *Chicago Sun Times* on September 14, 2007, that the movie succeeds so well because of the persona of Tommy Lee Jones.

> Paul Haggis' *In the Valley of Elah* is built on Tommy Lee Jones' persona, and that is why it works so well. The same material could have been banal or routine with an actor trying to be "earnest" and "sincere." Jones isn't trying to be anything at all. His character is simply compelled to do what he does, and has a lot of experience doing it. (http://rogerebert.suntimes.com)

In his *New York Times* review of *In the Valley of Elah* A. O. Scott called Tommy Lee Jones' performance, "irreducibly honest and right."

However you judge the movie's politics, and whatever its flaws, there is something inarguable, something irreducibly honest and right, about Mr. Jones's performance. Hank exists on a continuum with the other lawmen he has recently played, in particular the Texas sheriffs in *The Three Burials of Melquiades Estrada*, which he directed, and Joel and Ethan Coen's *No Country for Old Men*, which will be released later this fall. Like them, Hank carries around an innate sense of right and wrong, and Mr. Jones's creased face, at once kindly and severe, is a manifest sign of his old-school temperament. Hank is the kind of man who shines his shoes every night, says grace before each meal, and makes his motel room bed according to military standards. (http://movies.nytimes.com)

NO COUNTRY FOR OLD MEN (2007)

PRODUCER/DIRECTOR: Joel Coen (director), Ethan Coen (director), Robert Graf II (producer), Mark Roybal (producer), Scott Rudin (producer)

WRITER(S): Joel Coen (screenplay), Ethan Coen (screenplay), Cormac McCarthy (novel)

CAST: Tommy Lee Jones (Sheriff Ed Tom Bell), Javier Bardem (Anton Chigurh), Josh Brolin (Llewelyn Moss), Woody Harrelson (Carson Wells), Kelly Macdonald (Carla Jean Moss), Garret Dillahunt (Deputy Wendell), Tess Harper (Loretta Bell), Barry Corbin (Ellis), Stephen Root (Man who hires Wells), Rodger Boyce (Sheriff Roscoe Giddens), Beth Grant (Carla Jean's Mother), Ana Reeder (Poolside Woman), Kit Gwin (Sheriff Bell's Secretary), Zach Hopkins (Strangled Deputy)

CINEMATOGRAPHY: Roger Deakins

MUSIC: Carter Burwell

LENGTH AND RATING: 122 min; R

"I will not allow violence against this house," was a line uttered by David Sumner (Dustin Hoffman) in Sam Peckinpah's *Straw Dogs* (1971). The irony is that he's a mild-mannered American college mathematics professor who, with his attractive young British wife Amy (Susan George), escapes to her hometown in the English village of Cornwall. He has spent his entire life avoiding confrontation by running away, and after village locals gang-rape his wife, he becomes a virtual killing machine, transforming himself from being the hunted to the hunter. As a director Sam Peckinpah's oeuvre was creating rhapsodies of violence in his movies that reached a bloody crescendo in his film *The Wild Bunch* (1969). His influence is seen in the work of the brothers Joel and Ethan Coen, who wrote and directed *No Country for Old Men*.

Violence in film has been a part of the American movie experience for decades and could be measured in degrees by genre. In western movies by John Ford like *The Searchers* (1956), heroes of the American West slaughtered the Indians, who raped and killed the pioneers and settlers. Gangsters portrayed by James Cagney, James Mitchum, Hunphrey Bogart, and Edward G. Robinson killed indiscriminately, murdering those who stood in the way. Their modern incarnations in *Bonnie and Clyde* (1967), *The Untouchables* (1987), *Goodfellas* (1990), and *The Godfather* (1972) raised the ante on the sometimes poetic, graphic depiction of violence. In war movies, theater audiences celebrated when American soldiers killed, burned, and gassed their German and Japanese enemies and cheered John Wayne in the movie *The Green Berets* (1968) as he killed as

Tommy Lee Jones, Garret Dillahunt. [Miramax Films/Photofest]

many Viet Cong enemy soldiers as he could get in his sights. In Steven Spielberg's *Saving Private Ryan* (1998), the gruesome, bloody violence of American troops being cut down on D-day as they invaded the beaches of Normandy raised the graphic level of military carnage to new heights.

Comic book characters, cartoons, and video games have also been criticized for their violent content. Adapting popular cartoon characters like the *Simpsons* to a video game entitled *The Simpsons: Hit and Run*, rated for age seven and up, was criticized as being too violent for that age group. And of course the comic book franchises of Superman, Batman, and other characters have at times morphed from their status as heroes to something more villainous and gloomy. Indeed, the most recent Batman movie, *The Dark Knight* (2008), was described by Manohla Dargis in her July 18, 2008, *New York Times* review as going, "...darker and deeper than any Hollywood movie of its comic-book kind—including Batman Begins." She also wrote that Batman, "looks more like a gargoyle than a savior."

> When he perches over Gotham on the edge of a skyscraper roof, he looks more like a gargoyle than a savior. There's a touch of demon in his stealthy menace. During a crucial scene, one of the film's saner characters asserts that this isn't a time for heroes, the implication being that the moment belongs to villains and madmen. (http://movies.nytimes.com)

Having the moment belong to the villains and the madmen is an apt description of *No Country for Old Men*. It's theme of found treasure and the greed it provokes has been the foundation for many films including John Huston's 1948 classic *The Treasure of the Sierra Madre* (1948). The setting has been changed from Mexico to the plains of West Texas and its border towns, but the essence of the story is very familiar.

Surveying the scene of a drug deal gone wrong on a dry, sunbaked West Texas desert Sheriff Ed Tom Bell (Tommy Lee Jones) is a veteran lawman with a sardonic and dry view of the world; he feels somewhat helpless trying to control the rampant decline of law and order. As they gather spent cartridges and view the bloated bodies of dead Mexican drug dealers at the crime scene, his deputy remarks, "It's a mess, ain't it sheriff," and Bell replies, "If it ain't, it'll do till the mess gets here."

Out hunting and coming upon the scene of carnage, Llewellyn Moss (Josh Brolin) finds a satchel with two million dollars of uncollected drug money and takes it to his trailer, where he lives with his wife Carla Jean (Kelly Macdonald). During his survey of the scene, Llewellyn encounters a wounded Mexican sitting behind the wheel of a truck gasping for "agua" (water) and he replies that he doesn't have any. However, later that night his conscience forces him to return to the murder scene, and he is nearly killed when he confronts a gang of drug dealers and Anton Chigurh (Javier Bardam), an other-worldly assassin; Moss barely escapes, abandoning his truck in the process. His identity is traced from the vehicle registration, and he is separately pursued by the Mexicans and by Chigurh. Sending Carla Jean to her mother, Llewellyn begins his desperate escape from the maniacal and diabolical pursuit of Chigurh.

As a monster, Anton Chigurh is reminiscent of other cold, calculating murderers including Dracula and Hannibal Lector. Each of them demonstrates a different orientation on evil rising to a grotesque manifestation that in some ways could be interpreted as god-like. Like the Terminator, Chigurh appears to be even more invincible after each gruesome killing. He paints death on a canvas of sight and sound using as his "paint brush," a captive bolt pistol that operates with compressed air and is the preferred tool to stun animals before slaughter. It is indeed apropos that this is Chigurh's weapon of choice as he does slaughter his victims—up close and impersonal.

As he continues his pursuit of Llewellyn, Chigurh litters roads, plains, motels, hotels, and offices with dead bodies. He never raises his voice and makes his requests in a matter of fact manner as if his victims should understand that they need not hesitate to comply. When his car dies on the road and a farmer pulls up in his truck loaded with chicken crates and gets cables to help him jump-start his car, he simply asks the farmer how long it will take to remove the crates from the bed of the truck. At a remote Texaco rest stop, he pulls in for gas and the proprietor (Gene Jones) innocently asks, "Y'all are getting any rain up your way?" and Chigurh asks, "What way would that be?" to which the man responds, "I seen you was from Dallas." In a menacing tone of voice Chigurh asks, "What business is it of yours where I'm from, friendo?" This leads to a strange conversation between the proprietor and Chigurh about the time he closes the store, the time he goes to bed, and the way he married into the businesses. The scene finally ends with a quarter coin toss that the man reluctantly agrees to and calls heads. Little does he know that he has correctly answered Chigurh's earlier question about the most he ever lost in a contest, which could have been his life.

This scene evokes an eerie portrayal of innocence confronting evil with the subtle images richly nuanced by sound. As the scene opens in a long shot, the screen is filled with the remote location of the rest stop with the sound of the Texaco sign mildly squeaking in a light breeze. The sound and image of a crinkled candy wrapper tossed on the counter adds to the tension as the paper twists and turns. The intimacy and potential horror that it suggests is never elevated to a level of kitschy drama as the tension rises from the mere sense of quiet and doom that prevails.

On the run and wounded, Llewellyn narrowly escapes across the border into Mexico and while recovering in a hospital is visited by Carson Wells (Woody Harrelson), a bounty hunter whose help Llewellyn rejects. Wells is later killed by Chigurh.

Hoping to save herself and her husband, Carla Jean calls Sheriff Bell telling him about the location of her rendezvous with Llewellyn in El Paso Texas. By the time he arrives, Llewellyn has been killed in an intense firefight with Chigurh and the Mexicans. Locating Carla Jean, Chigurh waits for her to return from her mother's funeral, then offers to gamble her life on a coin toss. She refuses. As he drives away, Chigurh is injured in a terrible car crash. He walks away with a bone protruding from his arm and buys a shirt, to act as a sling, from two young boys riding their bicycles. He pays them to tell the police that they did not see him.

At home with his wife (Tess Harper), Bell, now retired, is thinking about what he will do and suggests riding his horse, asking his wife what she thinks. She responds that she can't plan his day. He asks his wife to join him, but she says that she's not retired. When Bell says that he'll help out at home she responds "better not." Answering her question about how he slept, Bell tells her that he had a dream about his father that appeared to symbolize a time past and the longing for safety and security. In one dream he and his father are on horseback riding through the mountains on a cold dark night, and his father passes his son without acknowledging him. But in the dream he knows that his father, even though he was ahead of Bell, would be there when he arrived.

In his November 9, 2007, *New York Times* review, A. O. Scott called the film, "pure heaven." *No Country for Old Men* is purgatory for the squeamish and the easily spooked. For formalists—those moviegoers sent into raptures by tight editing, nimble camera work, and faultless sound design—it's pure heaven.

In his February 28, 2008, *New Yorker* review of *No Country for Old Men*, David Denby wrote about the film's physical and psychological realization of dread:

> So powerful are the first twenty minutes or so of *No Country*—so concentrated in their physical and psychological realization of dread—that we are unlikely to ask why Chigurh kills with a captive-bolt gun (the kind used in killing cattle) rather than a revolver, or if it makes any sense for Llewellyn, a likable welder and roughneck, to return to the scene with water for a wounded man after he's made off with two million dollars in drug money. *No Country* is based on Cormac McCarthy's 2005 novel, and the bleak view of life that has always existed in the Coen's work merges with McCarthy's lethal cool. (http://www.newyorker.com/arts/critics/atlarge/2008/02/25/080225crat_atlarge_denby) (http://movies.nytimes.com)

Appendix 1

Alphabetical Listing of Films

THE AFRICAN QUEEN (1951)
ALIEN (1979)
ALL QUIET ON THE WESTERN FRONT (1930)
AMERICAN GRAFFITI (1973)
AN AMERICAN IN PARIS (1951)
AMERICAN PSYCHO (2000)
ANNIE HALL (1977)
APOCALYPSE NOW (1979)
AWAY FROM HER (2006)
BACK TO THE FUTURE (1985)
BAD EDUCATION (LA MALA EDUCACION) (2004)
THE BEST YEARS OF OUR LIVES (1946)
THE BIRTH OF A NATION (1915)
BLADE RUNNER (1982)
BLAZING SADDLES (1974)
BONNIE AND CLYDE (1967)
BOYZ N THE HOOD (1991)
BREATHLESS (1960)
THE BRIDGE ON THE RIVER KWAI (1957)
BUTCH CASSIDY AND THE SUNDANCE KID (1969)
CASABLANCA (1942)
CHOCOLAT (2000)
CHILDREN OF MEN (2006)
CHINATOWN (1974)
CITIZEN KANE (1941)
CITY OF GOD (CIDADE DE DEUS) (2002)
A CLOCKWORK ORANGE (1971)
CLOSE ENCOUNTERS OF THE THIRD KIND (1977)
THE CONVERSATION (1974)
CRASH (2004)
CROSSFIRE (1947)
DANCES WITH WOLVES (1990)
DEATH WISH (1974)

THE DEER HUNTER (1978)
DELIVERANCE (1972)
THE DEPARTED (2007)
DO THE RIGHT THING (1989)
DR. STRANGELOVE OR: HOW I LEARNED TO STOP WORRYING AND LOVE THE BOMB (1964)
DRACULA (1931)
DRIVING MISS DAISY (1989)
E.T. (1982)
EASY RIDER (1969)
EL NORTE (1983)
ERIN BROCKOVICH (2000)
ETERNAL SUNSHINE OF THE SPOTLESS MIND (2004)
THE EXORCIST (1973)
FAHRENHEIT 911 (2004)
FANTASIA (1940)
FANTASIA 2000 (1999)
FARGO (1996)
THE 400 BLOWS (1959)
FRANKENSTEIN (1931)
THE FRENCH CONNECTION (1971)
FROM HERE TO ETERNITY (1953)
GANGS OF NEW YORK (2002)
THE GENERAL (1927)
GENTLEMEN'S AGREEMENT (1947)
GLORY (1989)
THE GODFATHER (1972)
THE GODFATHER PART II (1974)
GONE WITH THE WIND (1939)
GOODFELLAS (1990)
THE GRADUATE (1967)
THE GRAPES OF WRATH (1940)
GROUNDHOG DAY (1993)
HIGH NOON (1952)
A HISTORY OF VIOLENCE (2005)

HOOP DREAMS (1994)
HOOSIERS (1986)
HOTEL RWANDA (2004)
THE HUSTLER (1961)
I AM A FUGITIVE FROM A CHAIN GANG (1932)
IN THE HEAT OF THE NIGHT (1967)
IN THE VALLEY OF ELAH (2007)
INTOLERANCE (1916)
INVASION OF THE BODY SNATCHERS (1956)
IT HAPPENED ONE NIGHT (1934)
IT'S A WONDERFUL LIFE (1946)
JAWS (1975)
THE JAZZ SINGER (1927)
JULES AND JIM (1962)
KING KONG (1933)
L.A. CONFIDENTIAL (1997)
LA DOLCE VITA (1960)
LA STRADA (The Road) (1954)
LAWRENCE OF ARABIA (1962)
LETTERS FROM IWO JIMA (2006)
LITTLE CAESAR (1930)
THE LIVES OF OTHERS (2006)
LORD OF THE RINGS: THE FELLOWSHIP OF THE RING (2001)
LOST IN TRANSLATION (2003)
M*A*S*H (1970)
MEDIUM COOL (1969)
MEMENTO (2000)
METROPOLIS (1927)
MICHAEL CLAYTON (2007)
MIDNIGHT COWBOY (1969)
MILLION DOLLAR BABY (2004)
MISSISSIPPI BURNING (1988)
MODERN TIMES (1936)
MOULIN ROUGE (2001)
MUNICH (2005)
MY DARLING CLEMENTINE (1946)
MY FAIR LADY (1964)
NANOOK OF THE NORTH (1922)
NASHVILLE (1975)
NO COUNTRY FOR OLD MEN (2007)
NORTH BY NORTHWEST (1959)
ON THE WATERFRONT (1954)
ONE FLEW OVER THE CUCKOO'S NEST (1975)
OTTO E MEZZO (8 1/2) (1963)
THE OUTLAW JOSEY WALES (1976)

PAN'S LABYRINTH (2004)
THE PASSION OF THE CHRIST (2004)
PATTON (1970)
THE PIANIST (2002)
PLANET OF THE APES (1968)
PLATOON (1986)
PSYCHO (1960)
THE PUBLIC ENEMY (1931)
PULP FICTION (1994)
THE QUEEN (2006)
RAGING BULL (1980)
RAIDERS OF THE LOST ARK (1981)
REAR WINDOW (1954)
REBEL WITHOUT A CAUSE (1955)
RESERVOIR DOGS (1992)
RETURN OF THE SECAUCUS SEVEN (1980)
RIDE THE HIGH COUNTRY (1962)
ROCKY (1976)
SATURDAY NIGHT FEVER (1977)
SCHINDLER'S LIST (1993)
THE SEARCHERS (1956)
SEVEN SAMURAI (1954)
SEX, LIES, AND VIDEOTAPE (1989)
SHAFT (1971)
SHANE (1953)
SINGIN' IN THE RAIN (1952)
SNOW WHITE AND THE SEVEN DWARFS (1937)
THE SOUND OF MUSIC (1965)
STAGECOACH (1939)
STAR WARS (1977)
TAXI DRIVER (1976)
THE TEN COMMANDMENTS (1956)
THE TERMINATOR (1984)
THIS IS SPINAL TAP (1984)
TITANIC (1997)
TO KILL A MOCKINGBIRD (1962)
TOOTSIE (1982)
TRAFFIC (2000)
2001: A SPACE ODYSSEY (1968)
UNFORGIVEN (1992)
UNITED 93 (2006)
THE VERDICT (1982)
VERTIGO (1958)
VOLVER (2006)
WEST SIDE STORY (1960)
THE WILD BUNCH (1969)
THE WIZARD OF OZ (1939)
YOUNG FRANKENSTEIN (1974)

Appendix 2

Chronological Listing of Films

THE BIRTH OF A NATION (1915)
INTOLERANCE (1916)
NANOOK OF THE NORTH (1922)
METROPOLIS (1927)
THE GENERAL (1927)
THE JAZZ SINGER (1927)
ALL QUIET ON THE WESTERN FRONT (1930)
LITTLE CAESAR (1930)
THE PUBLIC ENEMY (1931)
DRACULA (1931)
FRANKENSTEIN (1931)
I AM A FUGITIVE FROM A CHAIN GANG (1932)
KING KONG (1933)
IT HAPPENED ONE NIGHT (1934)
MODERN TIMES (1936)
SNOW WHITE AND THE SEVEN DWARFS (1937)
GONE WITH THE WIND (1939)
STAGECOACH (1939)
THE WIZARD OF OZ (1939)
FANTASIA (1940)
THE GRAPES OF WRATH (1940)
CITIZEN KANE (1941)
CASABLANCA (1942)
THE BEST YEARS OF OUR LIVES (1946)
IT'S A WONDERFUL LIFE (1946)
MY DARLING CLEMENTINE (1946)
CROSSFIRE (1947)
GENTLEMEN'S AGREEMENT (1947)
THE AFRICAN QUEEN (1951)
AN AMERICAN IN PARIS (1951)
SINGIN' IN THE RAIN (1952)
HIGH NOON (1952)
SHANE (1953)
FROM HERE TO ETERNITY (1953)

REAR WINDOW (1954)
ON THE WATERFRONT (1954)
LA STRADA (The Road) (1954)
SEVEN SAMURAI (1954)
REBEL WITHOUT A CAUSE (1955)
THE SEARCHERS (1956)
INVASION OF THE BODY SNATCHERS (1956)
THE TEN COMMANDMENTS (1956)
THE BRIDGE ON THE RIVER KWAI (1957)
VERTIGO (1958)
NORTH BY NORTHWEST (1959)
THE 400 BLOWS (1959)
BREATHLESS (1960)
LA DOLCE VITA (1960)
WEST SIDE STORY (1960)
PSYCHO (1960)
THE HUSTLER (1961)
LAWRENCE OF ARABIA (1962)
TO KILL A MOCKINGBIRD (1962)
RIDE THE HIGH COUNTRY (1962)
JULES AND JIM (1962)
OTTO E MEZZO (8 1/2) (1963)
DR. STRANGELOVE OR: HOW I LEARNED TO STOP WORRYING AND LOVE THE BOMB (1964)
MY FAIR LADY (1964)
THE SOUND OF MUSIC (1965)
IN THE HEAT OF THE NIGHT (1967)
BONNIE AND CLYDE (1967)
THE GRADUATE (1967)
2001: A SPACE ODYSSEY (1968)
PLANET OF THE APES (1968)
EASY RIDER (1969)
BUTCH CASSIDY AND THE SUNDANCE KID (1969)
THE WILD BUNCH (1969)

MEDIUM COOL (1969)
MIDNIGHT COWBOY (1969)
PATTON (1970)
M*A*S*H (1970)
A CLOCKWORK ORANGE (1971)
THE FRENCH CONNECTION (1971)
SHAFT (1971)
DELIVERANCE (1972)
THE GODFATHER (1972)
AMERICAN GRAFFITI (1973)
THE EXORCIST (1973)
CHINATOWN (1974)
BLAZING SADDLES (1974)
YOUNG FRANKENSTEIN (1974)
THE CONVERSATION (1974)
THE GODFATHER PART II (1974)
DEATH WISH (1974)
NASHVILLE (1975)
JAWS (1975)
ONE FLEW OVER THE CUCKOO'S NEST (1975)
ROCKY (1976)
THE OUTLAW JOSEY WALES (1976)
TAXI DRIVER (1976)
STAR WARS (1977)
CLOSE ENCOUNTERS OF THE THIRD KIND (1977)
THE DEER HUNTER (1978)
APOCALYPSE NOW (1979)
SATURDAY NIGHT FEVER (1977)
ANNIE HALL (1977)
ALIEN (1979)
RETURN OF THE SECAUCUS SEVEN (1980)
RAGING BULL (1980)
RAIDERS OF THE LOST ARK (1981)
BLADE RUNNER (1982)
TOOTSIE (1982)
THE VERDICT (1982)
E.T. (1982)
EL NORTE (1983)
THIS IS SPINAL TAP (1984)
THE TERMINATOR (1984)
BACK TO THE FUTURE (1985)
PLATOON (1986)
HOOSIERS (1986)
MISSISSIPPI BURNING (1988)
DO THE RIGHT THING (1989)
DRIVING MISS DAISY (1989)
SEX, LIES, AND VIDEOTAPE (1989)

GLORY (1989)
GOODFELLAS (1990)
DANCES WITH WOLVES (1990)
BOYZ N THE HOOD (1991)
RESERVOIR DOGS (1992)
UNFORGIVEN (1992)
GROUNDHOG DAY (1993)
SCHINDLER'S LIST (1993)
HOOP DREAMS (1994)
PULP FICTION (1994)
FARGO (1996)
TITANIC (1997)
L.A. CONFIDENTIAL (1997)
FANTASIA 2000 (1999)
AMERICAN PSYCHO (2000)
MEMENTO (2000)
ERIN BROCKOVICH (2000)
TRAFFIC (2000)
CHOCOLAT (2000)
MOULIN ROUGE (2001)
LORD OF THE RINGS: THE FELLOWSHIP OF THE RING (2001)
CITY OF GOD (CIDADE DE DEUS) (2002)
GANGS OF NEW YORK (2002)
THE PIANIST (2002)
LOST IN TRANSLATION (2003)
MILLION DOLLAR BABY (2004)
BAD EDUCATION (LA MALA EDUCACION) (2004)
ETERNAL SUNSHINE OF THE SPOTLESS MIND (2004)
FAHRENHEIT 911 (2004)
THE PASSION OF THE CHRIST (2004)
HOTEL RWANDA (2004)
PAN'S LABYRINTH (2004)
CRASH (2004)
MUNICH (2005)
A HISTORY OF VIOLENCE (2005)
VOLVER (2006)
CHILDREN OF MEN (2006)
UNITED 93 (2006)
THE QUEEN (2006)
LETTERS FROM IWO JIMA (2006)
THE LIVES OF OTHERS (2006)
AWAY FROM HER (2006)
THE DEPARTED (2007)
MICHAEL CLAYTON (2007)
IN THE VALLEY OF ELAH (2007)
NO COUNTRY FOR OLD MEN (2007)

Bibliography

Abele, Elizabeth. "30 Great Westerns: *Ride the High Country*." *Images*, no. 10.

Adherents.com. "The Religious Affiliation of Director Federico Fellini." http://www.adherents. com/people/pf/Federico_Fellini.html.

Adler, Renata. Review of *2001: A Space Odyssey* (1968), NYT Critics' Pick: The Screen: "*2001 Is Up, Up, and Away: Kubrick's Odyssey in Space Begins Run.*" *New York Times*, http:// movies.nytimes.com/movies/critics/critics-picks.

Alemdar, Melis. "*Breathless*: The Use of Parody and Subversive Devices in a Bout De Souffle." http://www.geocities.com/melisalemdar/breathless.html.

Bible. *Pew Bible: King James Version*. Philadelphia: National Publishing Company, 2000.

Billen, Andrew. "The Birds Attacked Me but Hitch Was Scarier." *Times Online*. http://www. entertainment.timesonline.co.uk/article.

Block, Tom. *Ride the High Country*. http://www.thehighhat.com/Nitrate/002/ride_the_high_ country.html.

Bogle, Donald. *Blacks in American Films and Television: An Encyclopedia*. New York: Simon & Schuster, 1989.

Brady, Frank. *Citizen Welles: A Biography of Orson Welles*. New York: Charles Scribner's Sons, 1989.

Brosnan, John. 1978. *Future Tense: The Cinema of Science Fiction*. New York: St. Martin's Press.

Bukatman, Scott. *Blade Runner*. BFI Modern Classics Series. New York: Macmillan, 1997.

Canby Vincent. *New York Times* on the web, "*Rear Window*—Still a Joy." Oct. 9, 1983, www. newyorktimes.com/library/film/100983hitch-window-reflect.html.

Canby, Vincent. Review of *Butch Cassidy and the Sundance Kid* (1969), NYT Critics' Pick: *Butch Cassidy*. *New York Times*, http://movies.nytimes.com/movies/critics/critics-picks.

———. Review of *The Wild Bunch* (1969), NYT Critics' Pick: *The Wild Bunch*. *New York Times*, http://movies.nytimes.com/movies/critics/critics-picks.

———. Review of *Midnight Cowboy* (1969), NYT Critics' Pick: *Midnight Cowboy*. *New York Times*, http://movies.nytimes.com/movies/critics/critics-picks.

———. Review of *Midnight Cowboy*. *New York Times*, http://movies.nytimes.com/movies/critics/ critics-picks.

———. Review of *A Clockwork Orange* (1971), NYT Critics' Pick: "*A Clockwork Orange* Dazzles the Senses and Mind." *New York Times*, http://movies.nytimes.com/movies/critics/critics-picks.

———. "*Shaft*—At Last, a Good Saturday Night Movie." *New York Times*, http://movies. nytimes.com/movies/critics/critics-picks.

———. Review of *The Godfather*. *New York Times*, http://movies.nytimes.com/movies/critics/ critics-picks.

———. Review of *Blazing Saddles*. *New York Times*, http://movies.nytimes.com/movies/critics/ critics-picks.

———. Review of *Young Frankenstein*, A Monster Riot. *New York Times*, http://movies. nytimes.com/movies/critics/critics-picks.

———. Review of *The Conversation* (1974), NYT Critics' Pick: A Haunting Conversation. *New York Times*, http://movies.nytimes.com/movies/critics/critics-picks.

———. Review of *Death Wish* (1974), Screen: *Death Wish* Hunts Muggers: The Cast Story of Gunman Takes Dim View of City. *New York Times*, http://movies.nytimes.com/movies/critics/critics-picks.

———. Review of *Nashville*. *New York Times*, http://movies.nytimes.com/movies/critics/critics-picks.

———. "Jack Nicholson, the Free Spirit of *One Flew over the Cuckoo's Nest*." *New York Times*, http://movies.nytimes.com/movies/critics/critics-picks.

———. Review of *Rocky* (1976), Film: *Rocky*, Pure 30's Make-Believe. *New York Times*, http://movies.nytimes.com/movies/critics/critics-picks.

———. Review of *Taxi Driver* (1976), NYT Critics' Pick: *Taxi Driver*. *New York Times*, http://movies.nytimes.com/movies/critics/critics-picks.

———. Review of *Annie Hall* (1977), NYT Critics' Pick: *Annie Hall*. *New York Times*, http://movies.nytimes.com/movies/critics/critics-picks.

———. Review of *The Deer Hunter* (1978), NYT Critics' Pick: Screen: *The Deer Hunter*. *New York Times*, http://movies.nytimes.com/movies/critics/critics-picks.

———. Review of *Apocalypse Now*. *New York Times*, http://movies.nytimes.com/movies/critics/critics-picks.

———. Review of *Raiders of the Lost Ark*. *New York Times*, http://movies.nytimes.com/movies/critics/critics-picks.

———. Review of *E.T. The Extra-Terrestrial*. *New York Times*, http://movies.nytimes.com/movies/critics/critics-picks.

———. Review of *Rear Window*—Still a Joy. *New York Times*, http://movies.nytimes.com/movies/critics/critics-picks.

———. Review of *Platoon* (1986), NYT Critics' Pick: Film: The Vietnam War in Stone's *Platoon*. *New York Times*, http://movies.nytimes.com/movies/critics/critics-picks.

———. Review of *Mississippi Burning*: Generating Heat or Light? Taking Risks to Illuminate a Painful Time in America. *New York Times*, http://movies.nytimes.com/movies/critics/critics-picks.

———. Review of *Do the Right Thing* (1989), Critic's Notebook; Spike Lee Stirs Things up at Cannes. *New York Times*, http://movies.nytimes.com/movies/critics/critics-picks.

———. Review of *Driving Miss Daisy* (1989), Review/Film; *Miss Daisy*, Chamber Piece from the Stage. *New York Times*, http://movies.nytimes.com/movies/critics/critics-picks.

———. Review of *Glory* (1989), Review/Film; Black Combat Bravery in the Civil War. *New York Times*, http://movies.nytimes.com/movies/critics/critics-picks.

———. Review of *Dances with Wolves* (1990), http://movies.nytimes.com/movies/critics/critics-picks.

———. "NYT Critics' Pick: Review/Film; a Soldier at One with the Sioux." *New York Times*, November 9, 1990. http://movies.nytimes.com/movies/critics/critics-picks.

———. Review of *Reservoir Dogs* (1992), Review/Film; A Caper Goes Wrong, Resoundingly. *New York Times*, http://movies.nytimes.com/movies/critics/critics-picks.

———. Review of *Unforgiven* (1992), Review/Film: *Unforgiven*; A Western without Good Guys. *New York Times*, http://movies.nytimes.com/movies/critics/critics-picks.

Carpenter, Lynette. "There's No Place Like Home. *The Wizard of Oz* and American Isolationism." *Film and History* 15 (May, 1985).

Chandler, Charlotte, ed. 1995. "Fellini." In *I, Fellini*. New York: Random House.

Collins, Felicity. Review of *Lawrence of Arabia*, by Steven C. Caton. *A Film's Anthropology*. Berkeley: University of California Press, 1999.

Connell, Richard. *The Most Dangerous Game*. Filiquarian Publishing, LLC, 1924.

Corliss, Richard. "The Last Roundup." *Time*. http://www.time.com/time/magazine/article/0,9171,976223-1,00.html.

Cowie, Peter. *The Apocalypse Now Book*. Cambridge: Da Capo Press, 2001.

Crist, Judith. "Stanley Kubrick, Please Come Down." *New York Magazine* 1962; http://www. encyclopedia.com/doc/1G2-3406800916.html.

Crouch, Stanley. "Do the Race Thing: Spike Lee's Afro-Fascist Chic." *The Village Voice*, June 20, 1989.

Crowdus, Gary and Dan Georgakas. "Sidebar from Encarta: Interview with Akira Kurosawa." Cineaste Publishing, Inc., http://encarta.msn.com/sidebar_762510083/interview_with_akira_kurosawa.html.

Crowther, Bosley. "Sordid View of French Life: *Breathless* in Debut at the Fine Arts, Jean-Paul Belmondo, Jean Seberg Starred," *New York Times*, Screen: Feb. 8, 1961.

Crowther, Bosley. "The Screen; Delinquency: *Rebel Without A Cause* Has Debut at Astor" *New York Times*, October 27, 1955.

Crowther, Bosley. Review of *The Best Years of Our Lives* (1946), NYT Critics' Pick: The Screen in Review; at the Laffmovie. *New York Times*, http://movies.nytimes.com/movies/critics/critics-picks.

———. Review of *It's a Wonderful Life* (1946), NYT Critics' Pick: The Screen in Review: At Three Theatres; *It's a Wonderful Life*, with James Stewart, at Globe—'Abie's Irish Rose' and 'the Wicked Lady' Also Seen Here at the Gotham. *New York Times*, http://movies.nytimes.com/movies/critics/critics-picks.

———. Review of *My Darling Clementine* (1946), NYT Critics' Pick: The Screen; *Darling Clementine*, with Henry Fonda as Marshal of Tombstone, a Stirring Film of West. *New York Times*, http://movies.nytimes.com/movies/critics/critics-picks.

———. Review of *Gentleman's Agreement* (1947) NYT Critics' Pick: *Gentleman's Agreement*, Study of Anti-Semitism, Is Feature at Mayfair—Gregory Peck Plays Writer Acting as Jew. *New York Times*, http://movies.nytimes.com/movies/critics/critics-picks.

———. Review of *An American in Paris* (1951), NYT Critics' Pick: The Screen: Four New Movies Open; *An American in Paris*, Arrival of Music Hall, Has Gene Kelly and Leslie Caron in Leads. *New York Times*, http://movies.nytimes.com/movies/critics/critics-picks.

———. Review of *Seven Samurai* (1954), *New York Times*, http://movies.nytimes.com/movies/critics/critics-picks.

———. Review of NYT Critics' Pick: Screen: Japanese Import. *New York Times*, http://movies.nytimes.com/movies/critics/critics-picks.

———. "Movie Review Screen: *The Ten Commandments*; De Mille's Production Opens at Criterion the Cast." *New York Times*, http://movies.nytimes.com/movies/critics/critics-picks.

———. "Screen: Fellini's Contemplation of a Director's Life." *New York Times*, http://movies.nytimes.com/movies/critics/critics-picks.

———. Review of *The Sound of Music* (1965), NYT Critics' Pick: *The Sound of Music* Opens at Rivoli. *New York Times*, http://movies.nytimes.com/movies/critics/critics-picks.

———. Review of *Bonnie and Clyde*. *New York Times*, http://movies.nytimes.com/movies/critics/critics-picks.

———. Review of *The Graduate*. *New York Times*, http://movies.nytimes.com/movies/critics/critics-picks.

Denby, David. "Nailed. Mel Gibson's *The Passion of the Christ*." *New Yorker*, March 1, 2004.

———. "High Rollers *The Aviator, Million Dollar Baby, Hotel Rwanda*." *New Yorker*, December 20, 2004.

Dickey, Christopher. "*War and Deliverance*: A New DVD of an Old Movie May Offer Perspective on American Attitudes Behind the Invasion of Iraq." *Newsweek*, October 17, 2007 2007.

Ebert, Roger. Review of *Blazing Saddles*. *Chicago-Sun Times*. http://rogerebert.suntimes.com/apps/pbcs.dll/frontpage.

———. Review of *Young Frankenstein*. *Chicago-Sun Times*. http://rogerebert.suntimes.com/apps/pbcs.dll/frontpage.

———. Review of *Rocky*. *Chicago-Sun Times*. http://rogerebert.suntimes.com/apps/pbcs.dll/frontpage.

———. Review of *Apocalypse Now*. *Chicago-Sun Times*. http://rogerebert.suntimes.com/apps/pbcs.dll/frontpage.

———. Review of *Platoon*. *Chicago-Sun Times*. http://rogerebert.suntimes.com/apps/pbcs.dll/frontpage.

———. Review of *Glory*. *Chicago-Sun Times*. http://rogerebert.suntimes.com/apps/pbcs.dll/frontpage.

———. Review of *Dances with Wolves*. *Chicago-Sun Times*. http://rogerebert.suntimes.com/apps/pbcs.dll/frontpage.

———. Review of *Pulp Fiction*. *Chicago-Sun Times*. http://rogerebert.suntimes.com/apps/pbcs.dll/frontpage.

———. Review of *La Dolce Vita* (1960). *Chicago-Sun Times*. http://rogerebert.suntimes.com/apps/pbcs.dll/frontpage.

———. Review of *Titanic*. *Chicago-Sun Times*. http://rogerebert.suntimes.com/apps/pbcs.dll/frontpage.

———. Review of *The 400 Blows*. *Chicago-Sun Times*. http://rogerebert.suntimes.com/apps/pbcs.dll/frontpage.

———. Review of *The Conversation* (1974). *Chicago-Sun Times*. http://rogerebert.suntimes.com/apps/pbcs.dll/frontpage.

———. Review of *Moulin Rouge*. *Chicago-Sun Times*. http://rogerebert.suntimes.com/apps/pbcs.dll/frontpage.

———. Review of *Lord of the Rings: The Fellowship of the Ring*. *Chicago-Sun Times*. http://rogerebert.suntimes.com/apps/pbcs.dll/frontpage.

———. Review of *City of God*. *Chicago-Sun Times*. http://rogerebert.suntimes.com/apps/pbcs.dll/frontpage.

———. Review of *Lost in Translation*. *Chicago-Sun Times*. http://rogerebert.suntimes.com/apps/pbcs.dll/frontpage.

———. Review of *Eternal Sunshine of the Spotless Mind*. *Chicago-Sun Times*. http://rogerebert.suntimes.com/apps/pbcs.dll/frontpage.

———. Review of *Fahrenheit 9/11*. *Chicago-Sun Times*. http://rogerebert.suntimes.com/apps/pbcs.dll/frontpage.

———. Review of *The Passion of the Christ*. *Chicago-Sun Times*. http://rogerebert.suntimes.com/apps/pbcs.dll/frontpage.

———. Review of *Groundhog Day*. *Chicago-Sun Times*. http://rogerebert.suntimes.com/apps/pbcs.dll/frontpage.

Eder, Richard. "The Outlaw Josy Wales." *New York Times*, http://movies.nytimes.com/movies/critics/critics-picks.

Erickson, Hal. "Review of *Dracula*." http://www.allmovie.com/cg/avg.dll?p=avg&sql=1:14637.

Fawell, John. "Fashion Dreams: Hitchcock, Women, and Lisa Fremont." *Literature Film Quarterly* (2000): 4-6.

Fellini, Federico, and Charlotte Chandler. *Fellini in I, Fellini*. Lanham, MD: Cooper Square Press, 1995.

Fellini, Federico. "Classics of 20th Century Film." *New York Times,*. http://movies.nytimes.com/movies/critics/critics-picks.

Film Features: Moments. *Guardian*. http://film.guardian.co.uk/features/apicturestory/0,,132242,00.html.

FilmReference.com. Review of *The Wild Bunch*." http://www.filmreference.com/Films-Vi-Wi/The-Wild-Bunch.html.

Frascella, Lawrence and Al Weisel. *Live Fast, Die Young*. New York: Simon & Shuster, 2005.

Garrett, Greg. 1999. "Hitchcock's Women on Hitchcock: A Panel Discussion with Janet Leigh, Tippi Hedren, Karen Black, Suzanne Pleshette, and Eva Marie Saint." *Literature Film Quarterly*.

Goode, Erica. "A Conversation With: Glen Gabbard; A Rare Day: The Movies Get Mental Illness Right." *New York Times*, http://movies.nytimes.com/movies/critics/critics-picks.

Greenspun, Roger. *The French Connection*. *New York Times*, http://movies.nytimes.com/movies/critics/critics-picks.

———. Review of *American Graffiti* (1973), NYT Critics' Pick: *American Graffiti*. *New York Times*, http://movies.nytimes.com/movies/critics/critics-picks.

Hall, Mordaunt. Review of *The General* (1927), NYT Critics' Pick: The Screen; A Civil War Farce. *New York Times*, http://movies.nytimes.com/movies/critics/critics-picks.

———. Review of *All Quiet on the Western Front* (1930), NYT Critics' Pick: The Screen; Young Germany in the War. *New York Times*, http://movies.nytimes.com/movies/critics/critics-picks.

———. Review of *Little Caesar*. *New York Times*, http://movies.nytimes.com/movies/critics/critics-picks.

———. Review of *Dracula* (1931), NYT Critics' Pick: The Screen; Bram Stoker's Human Vampire. *New York Times*,. http://movies.nytimes.com/movies/critics/critics-picks.

———. Review of *King Kong* (1933), NYT Critics' Pick: A Fantastic Film in Which a Monstrous Ape Uses Automobiles for Missiles and Climbs a Skyscraper. *New York Times*, http://movies.nytimes.com/movies/critics/critics-picks.

Hanley, Robert. "Undeterred by Pleas, the Faithful Again Seek out a Vision of the Virgin." *New York Times*, http://movies.nytimes.com/movies/critics/critics-picks.

Herrmann, Bernard. "Sound in *Psycho*." *Learning Space Dedicated to the Art and Analyses of Film Sound Design*. FilmSound.org.

Hibberd, Laurie. "Anniversary of Film Classic Video." In *The Early Show*. CBS News, 2005. http://www.cbsnews.com/video/watch/?id=671721n%3fsource=search_video.

Hoberman, J. "Before Bourne … There Was Popeye Doyle." *The Village Voice*, August 21, 2007.

———. "Film Noir with Fantasy and a Transsexual Femme Fatale. *New York Times*, http://movies.nytimes.com/movies/critics/critics-picks.

———. "Holding a Moral Center as Civilization Fell." *New York Times*, http://movies.nytimes.com/movies/critics/critics-picks.

———. Review of *City of God* (2002) Film Review; Boys Soldiering in an Army of Crime. *New York Times*, http://movies.nytimes.com/movies/critics/critics-picks.

———. Review of *Volver*. *New York Times*, http://movies.nytimes.com/movies/critics/critics-picks.

Holden, Stephen. "American *Psycho* (2000), NYT Critics' Pick: Film Review; Murderer! Fiend! (But Well Dressed)." *New York Times*, http://movies.nytimes.com/movies/critics/critics-picks.

Hughes, Howard. *Crime Wave: The Filmgoers' Guide to the Great Crime Movies*. New York: I.B. Tauris, 2006.

Insdorf, Annette. Review of *El Norte*: On Screen and in Reality, a Story of Struggle." *New York Times*, http://movies.nytimes.com/movies/critics/critics-picks.

The Internet Movie Database. "Nicholas Ray." http://www.imdb.com.

James, Caryn. Review of *Hoop Dreams* (1994), NYT Critics' Pick: Film Festival Review: *Hoop Dreams*; Dreaming the Dreams, Realizing the Realities. *New York Times*, http://movies.nytimes.com/movies/critics/critics-picks.

James, Caryn. Review of *Sex, Lies, and Videotape* (1989), Review/Film; A Dance of Sex and Love, through a Lens Darkly. *New York Times*, http://movies.nytimes.com/movies/critics/critics-picks.

Kael, Pauline. "The Current Cinema: Apes Must Be Remembered, Charlie." *The New Yorker*, February 17, 1968.

Kael, Pauline. *The Sound of Music*, http://www.geocities.com/paulinekaelreviews/s6.html.

———. Review of *The Wild Bunch*. http://www.geocities.com/paulinekaelreviews/s6.html.

———. Review of *The Godfather*. http://www.geocities.com/paulinekaelreviews/g3.html.

————. Review of *Blazing Saddles*. http://www.geocities.com/paulinekaelreviews/b6.html.

————. Review of *Young Frankenstein*. http://www.geocities.com/paulinekaelreviews/xy. html.

————. Review of *Saturday Night Fever*. http://www.geocities.com/paulinekaelreviews/s1. html.

————. Review of *E.T. The Extra-Terrestrial*. http://www.geocities.com/paulinekaelreviews/ e1.html.

————. Review of *Mississippi Burning*. http://www.geocities.com/paulinekaelreviews/m6. html.

————. Review of *The Godfather Part II*. http://www.geocities.com/paulinekaelreviews/g3. html.

————. "Strangely Stangelove." *The New Yorker Magazine*, January 1972.

Kakutani, Michiko. "What Is Hollywood Saying about the Teen-Age World Today?" http:// select.nytimes.com/gst/abstract.html?res=F00A17FE3E5C0C718EDDAD0894DC484D81.

Kaplan, Fred. "Truth Stranger Than 'Strangelove'." *New York Times*, http://movies.nytimes. com/movies/critics/critics-picks.

Kauffmann, Stanley. "Lost in the Stars." *The New Republic*. http://www.krusch.com/kubrick/ Q16.html.

Kemp, Peter. "Love Me Tonight" *Senses of Cinema* 2008, no. September 1 (2004, 1997). http://www.sensesofcinema.com/contents/cteq/04/32/love_me_tonight.html.

Kemp, Phillip. *Ride the High Country*. http://www.filmreference.com/Films-Ra-Ro/Ride-the-High-Country.html.

Khurana, Simran. "The Seven Ages of Man." http://quotations.about.com/cs/poemlyrics/a/ Seven_Ages_Of_M.htm.

Kingsbury, Nancy and Robert B Minda. "An Analysis of Three Expected Intimate Relationship States: Commitment, Maintenance, and Termination." *Journal of Social and Personal Relationships* 5 (1988): 405–22.

Klein, Joe. "Spiked?" *New York Magazine*, June 26, 1989, 14–15.

Kriedl, John Francis. "*Breathless*: Out of Breath: Two Negatives Make a Positive." In *Jean-Luc Godard*. Boston: Twayne, 1980.

LaValley, Al, editor. 2000. *Invasion of the Body Snatchers: A Tribute*. Berkeley: Berkeley Boulevard Books.

LoBianco, Lorraine. "Starring Eva Marie Saint." *TCM This Month*. http://www.tcm.com/this month/article?cid=135982.

LoBianco, Lorraine. "Starring Eva Marie Saint." Turner Classic Movie: This Month. www.tcm.com.

Look Magazine, Unsigned. "Hitchcock's New Grace Kelly." *Look Magazine*, December 4, 1962.

Lyman, Rick. "Robert Altman, Iconoclastic Director, Dies at 81." *New York Times*, http:// movies.nytimes.com/movies/critics/critics-picks.

MacDonnell, Francis. "The Emerald City Was the New Deal." *Journal of American Culture* 13, no. Winter (1990): 71–75.

Macklin, Tony. "Plant Your Feet and Tell the Truth: An Interview with Clint Eastwood." *Bright Lights Film Journal*, February, no. 47 (2005).

Margaret Mitchell House Museum. "Margaret Munnerlyn Mitchell, 1900–1949." http:// www.gwtw.org/margaretmitchell.html.

Martinetti, Ron. "American Legends, James Dean." http://www.americanlegends.com.

Maslin, Janet. Review of *This Is Spinal Tap* (1984), Film: *This Is Spinal Tap*, A Mock Documentary. *New York Times*, http://movies.nytimes.com/movies/critics/critics-picks.

————. Review of *Boyz 'N the Hood* (1991), NYT Critics' Pick, Review/Film; A Chance to Confound Fat. *New York Times*, http://movies.nytimes.com/movies/critics/critics-picks.

———. Review of *Groundhog Day* (1993), NYT Critics' Pick: Review/Film; Bill Murray Battles Pittsburgh Time Warp. *New York Times*, http://movies.nytimes.com/movies/critics/critics-picks.

———. Review of *Schindler's List* (1993), NYT Critics' Pick: Review/Film: *Schindler's List*; Imagining the Holocaust to Remember It. *New York Times*, http://movies.nytimes.com/movies/critics/critics-picks.

———. Review of *Pulp Fiction* (1994), NYT Critics' Pick: Film Festival Review: *Pulp Fiction*; Quentin Tarantino's Wild Ride on Life's Dangerous Road. *New York Times*, http://movies.nytimes.com/movies/critics/critics-picks.

———. Review of *L.A. Confidential* (1997), NYT Critics' Pick Film Review; the Dark Underbelly of a Sunny Town. *New York Times*, http://movies.nytimes.com/movies/critics/critics-picks.

———. Review of *Titanic* (1997), NYT Critics' Pick Film Review; A Spectacle as Sweeping as the Sea. *New York Times*, http://movies.nytimes.com/movies/critics/critics-picks.

Matthews, Melvin E., Jr. 2007. *Hostile Aliens, Hollywood and Today's News: 1950s Science Fiction Films and 9/11.* New York: Algora Publishing.

McElhaney, Joe. *The Death of Classical Cinema: Hitchcock, Lang, Minnelli.* Albany, NY: State University of New York Press, 2006.

Menand, Louis. "Finding It at the Movies." *The New York Review of Books* 42, no. 5 (1995).

Mitchell, Elvis. Review of *Chocolat* (2000), Film Review; Candy Power Comes to Town. *New York Times*, http://movies.nytimes.com/movies/critics/critics-picks.

———. Review of *Moulin Rouge*: An Eyeful, an Earful, Anachronism. *New York Times*, http://movies.nytimes.com/movies/critics/critics-picks.

———. Review of *The Lord of the Rings: The Fellowship of the Ring* (2001), NYT Critics' Pick: Film Review; Hit the Road, Middle-Earth Gang. *New York Times*, http://movies.nytimes.com/movies/critics/critics-picks.

———. Review of *Lost in Translation* (2003), NYT Critics' Pick: Film Review; An American in Japan, Making a Connection. *New York Times*, http://movies.nytimes.com/movies/critics/critics-picks.

———. Review of *Eternal Sunshine of the Spotless Mind* (2004) NYT Critics' Pick: Film Review; Washing That Girl out of His Head. *New York Times*, http://movies.nytimes.com/movies/critics/critics-picks.

Mueller, John. "Fred Astaire and the Integrated Musical." *Cinema* 24, no. 1 (1984): 28–40.

Muir, John Kenneth. "The Best Science Fiction Movie Ever Made: *Planet of the Apes*." http://reflectionsonfilmandtelevision.blogspot.com/2006/10/best-science-fiction-movie-ever-made.html.

New York Times. "Patton's Career a Brilliant One." *New York Times*, http://movies.nytimes.com/movies/critics/critics-picks.

———. "The Screen: *Nanook of the North*." *New York Times*, http://movies.nytimes.com/movies/critics/critics-picks.

———. "Radio Listeners in Panic, Taking War Drama as Fact: Many Flee Homes to Escape 'Gas Raid from Mars'—Phone Calls Swamp Police at Broadcast of Welles Fantasy." *New York Times*, http://movies.nytimes.com/movies/critics/critics-picks.

———. Unsigned review of *Birth of a Nation. New York Times*, http://movies.nytimes.com/movies/critics/critics-picks.

Nickens, Christopher, and Janet Leigh. *Psycho: Behind the Scenes of the Classic Thriller.* New York: Random House, 1995.

Norton, Chris. "Shut Yo' Mouf' the Blaxploitation Film Era." http://www.blackfilm.com/0107/features/may1_Blaxsp_1.shtml.

Nugent, Frank. *"Gone with the Wind* (1939), NYT Critics' Pick: The Screen in Review; David Selznick's *Gone with the Wind* Has Its Long-Awaited Premiere at Astor and Capitol, Recalling Civil War and Plantation Days of South—Seen as Treating Book with Great Fidelity." *New York Times*, http://movies.nytimes.com/movies/critics/critics-picks.

————. Review of *In Name Only* (1939), the Screen in Review; *The Wizard of Oz*, Produced by the Wizards of Hollywood, Works Its Magic on the Capitol's Screen—March of Time Features New York at the Music Hall at the Palace. *New York Times*, http://movies. nytimes.com/movies/critics/critics-picks.

————. Review of *The Adventures of Huckleberry Finn* (1939), the Screen; a Ford-Powered 'Stagecoach' Opens at Music Hall; Mickey Rooney Plays Huck Finn at the Capitol. *New York Times*, http://movies.nytimes.com/movies/critics/critics-picks.

————. Review of *The Grapes of Wrath* (1940), NYT Critics' Pick: The Screen in Review; Twentieth Century-Fox Shows a Flawless Film Edition of John Steinbeck's *The Grapes of Wrath*, with Henry Fonds and Jane Darwell, at the Rivoli. *New York Times*, http:// movies.nytimes.com/movies/critics/critics-picks.

Oates, Joyce Carol. *On Boxing*. Garden City; NY: Dolphin/Doubleday, 1987.

Ofarim, Esther and Mark Warshawsky. "Oyfn Prpetchik (at the Fireplace) Yiddush Ballad." http://www.leechvideo.com/video/view3745176.html.

The Paris Review. *Writers and Work: The Paris Review Interviews 1959*, 1st edition. Writers at Work: Picador, 2007.

Peary, Danny. 1981. *CultMovies*. New York: Delta Books.

Peary, Gerald. "*The Conversation*." American Movie Classics 2000.

Pollitt, Katha. "The Protocols of Mel Gibson: Subject to Debate." *The Nation*, March 29, 2004. http://www.thenation.com/doc/20040329/pollitt.

Quart, Alissa. "Networked: Don Roos and 'Happy Endings'." *Film Comment*, August (2005).

Rafferty, Terrence. "Film, Polanski, and the Landscape of Aloneness." *New York Times*, http://movies.nytimes.com/movies/critics/critics-picks.

Rebello, Stephen. *Alfred Hitchcock and the Making of Psycho*. New York: St. Martin's Press, 1998.

Rich, Frank. "Mel Gibson's Martyrdom Complex." *New York Times*, http://movies.nytimes. com/movies/critics/critics-picks.

Rosenbaum, Jonathan. "Senses of Cinema: Nicholas Ray." http://www.sensesofcinema.com.

Rothstein, Edward. "Connections: Hitchcock, Thrilling the Ears as Well as the Eyes." *New York Times*, http://movies.nytimes.com/movies/critics/critics-picks.

Russell, Lawrence. "*La Dolce Vita* the Sweet Life." Film Court, http://www.culturecourt.com/ F/Fellini/LaDV.htm.

Sarris, Andrew. "*2001: A Space Odyssey*." In *The Village Voice Film Guide: 50 Years of Movies from Classics to Cult Hits*, edited by Dennis Lim, 336: Wiley, 2006.

Sarris, Andrew. "Gruesome, Never Gratuitous, *Gangs of New York* Rings True." *New York Observer*, January 5, 2003.

Savard, Catherine. "Midnight Oil: Movies and More, *Rebel Without A Cause* (1955), and *September 30, 1955* (1977). http://www.midnightoil.squarespace.com.

Savard, Catherine. "*September 30, 1955*." http://www.midnightoil.squarespace.com.

Savard, Catherine. Review of *Rebel without a Cause* (1955). http://midnightoil.squarespace. com/rebel-without-a-cause-james-de.

Scott, A. O. Review of *Erin Brockovich* (2000), Film Review; High Ideals, Higher Heels. *New York Times*, http://movies.nytimes.com/movies/critics/critics-picks.

————. "3 People Seduced by the Bloody Allure of the Ring." *New York Times*, http:// movies.nytimes.com/movies/critics/critics-picks.

————. Review of *Gangs of New York* (2002), NYT Critics' Pick: Film Review; To Feel a City Seethe. *New York Times*, http://movies.nytimes.com/movies/critics/critics-picks.

————. Review of *Memento* (2000), NYT Critics' Pick: Film Review; Backward Reel the Grisly Memories. *New York Times*, http://movies.nytimes.com/movies/critics/critics-picks.

————. Review of Moore's *Fahrenheit 9/11* Wins Top Honors at Cannes *New York Times*, http://movies.nytimes.com/movies/critics/critics-picks.

————. Review of *The Pianist* (2002), NYT Critics' Pick: Film Review; Surviving the Warsaw Ghetto against Steep Odds. *New York Times*, http://movies.nytimes.com/movies/critics/critics-picks.

Sherwood, Robert E. *The Best Moving Pictures of 1922–23: Nanook of the North*, Boston: Small, Maynard, 1923.

Sickels, Robert C. "A Politically Correct Ethan Edwards: Clint Eastwood's *The Outlaw Josey Wales*." *Journal of Popular Film and Television*, no. January 1 (2003).

Simon, John. *Movies into Film: Film Criticism 1967–1970*. New York: The Dial Press, 1968.

Stone, Alan A. "*8 1/2*: Fellini's Moment of Truth." *Boston Review*, Summer (1995).

Taubin, Amy. *Taxi Driver*. London: BFI Publishing, 2000.

ThinkExist.com. "Quotations Online: Akira Kurosawa Quotes." http://thinkexist.com/quotes/Akira_Kurosawa.

Thompson, Kristen and David Bordwell. *Film History and Introduction*, 2 edition. New York: McGraw-Hill, 2003.

Walsh, David. "American Madness: *Apocalypse Now Redux*." http://www.wsws.org/articles/2001/aug2001/apoc-a25.shtml.

Wander, Brandon. "Black Dreams: The Fantasy and Ritual of Black Films." *Film Quarterly* 29, no. 1 (1975): 2–11.

Warner, Jack L. *My First Hundred Years in Hollywood*. New York: Random House, 1965.

Weaver, Tom. "Janet Leigh, the Star of *Psycho* Relives Her Finest Shower." bmonster.com. http://www.bmonster.com/horror19.html.

Weidhorn, Manfred. "*High Noon*—Liberal Classic? Conservative Screed?" *Bright Lights Film Journal*, no. 47 (2005).

Weiler, A. H. Review of *North by Northwest* (1959), NYT Critics' Pick: Hitchcock Takes Suspenseful Cook's Tour; *North by Northwest* Opens at Music Hall. *New York Times*, http://movies.nytimes.com/movies/critics/critics-picks.

Wexman, Virginia Wright. *A History of Film*, 6th edition. New York: Allyn & Bacon, 2005.

White, Jack E. "Just Another Mississippi Whitewash." *Time*. http://www.time.com/time/magazine/article/0,9171,956694-2,00.html.

Index

About the Author

JAMES ROMAN is Professor of Film and Media Studies at Hunter College, City University of New York. He is the author of *Love, Light, and a Dream* (Praeger, 1996) and *From Daytime to Primetime* (Greenwood, 2005).